Biblical Aramaic and Related Dialects

Biblical Aramaic and Related Dialects is a comprehensive, introductory-level textbook for the acquisition of the language of the Old Testament and related dialects that were in use from the last few centuries BCE. Based on the latest research, it uses a method that guides students into knowledge of the language inductively, with selections taken from the Bible, the Dead Sea Scrolls, and papyrus discoveries from ancient Egypt. The volume offers a comprehensive view of ancient Aramaic that enables students to progress to advanced levels with a solid grounding in historical grammar.

- Provides the most up-to-date description of Aramaic in light of modern discoveries and methods
- Provides more detail than previous textbooks
- Includes comprehensive description of the Biblical dialect, along with Aramaic of the Persian period and of the Dead Sea Scrolls
- Guided readings begin with primary sources, enabling students to learn the language by reading historical texts

Edward Cook is Ordinary Professor of Semitic Languages at the Catholic University of America in Washington, DC. He is the author of several books, including *The Dead Sea Scrolls: A New Translation* (2005, with Martin Abegg and Michael Wise) and *Dictionary of Qumran Aramaic* (2015).

Biblical Aramaic and Related Dialects
An Introduction

EDWARD COOK
Catholic University of America

CAMBRIDGE
UNIVERSITY PRESS

University Printing House, Cambridge CB2 8BS, United Kingdom

One Liberty Plaza, 20th Floor, New York, NY 10006, USA

477 Williamstown Road, Port Melbourne, VIC 3207, Australia

314–321, 3rd Floor, Plot 3, Splendor Forum, Jasola District Centre, New Delhi – 110025, India

103 Penang Road, #05–06/07, Visioncrest Commercial, Singapore 238467

Cambridge University Press is part of the University of Cambridge.

It furthers the University's mission by disseminating knowledge in the pursuit
of education, learning, and research at the highest international levels of excellence.

www.cambridge.org
Information on this title: www.cambridge.org/9781108494366
DOI: 10.1017/9781108637596

© Cambridge University Press 2022

This publication is in copyright. Subject to statutory exception
and to the provisions of relevant collective licensing agreements,
no reproduction of any part may take place without the written
permission of Cambridge University Press.

First published 2022

Printed in the United Kingdom by TJ Books Ltd, Padstow Cornwall

A catalogue record for this publication is available from the British Library.

Library of Congress Cataloging-in-Publication Data
Names: Cook, Edward, 1952– author.
Title: Biblical Aramaic and related dialects : an introduction / Edward Cook.
Description: Cambridge, UK ; New York : Cambridge University Press, 2022. | Includes bibliographical references and index.
Identifiers: LCCN 2021037825 (print) | LCCN 2021037826 (ebook) | ISBN 9781108494366 (hardback) | ISBN 9781108714488
   (paperback) | ISBN 9781108637596 (epub)
Subjects: LCSH: Aramaic language–Grammar. | Bible. Old Testament–Language, style. | BISAC: RELIGION / Biblical Studies /
   Old Testament / General
Classification: LCC PJ5213 .C66 2022 (print) | LCC PJ5213 (ebook) | DDC 492/.2–dc23
LC record available at https://lccn.loc.gov/2021037825
LC ebook record available at https://lccn.loc.gov/2021037826

ISBN 978-1-108-49436-6 Hardback
ISBN 978-1-108-71448-8 Paperback

Cambridge University Press has no responsibility for the persistence or accuracy
of URLs for external or third-party internet websites referred to in this publication
and does not guarantee that any content on such websites is, or will remain,
accurate or appropriate.

CONTENTS

Preface *page* ix
Acknowledgments xi
Abbreviations and Note xiii

CHAPTER 1
Introduction: Aramaic and Its Dialects 1
  Beginnings of Aramaic 1
  Aramaic and Empire 2
  Imperial Aramaic 3
  Aramaic in the Jewish Community after the Exile 7
  After Imperial Aramaic 8
  Biblical and Qumran Aramaic 9
  Tools for Research 16

CHAPTER 2
Orthography 19
  Consonantal Alphabet 20
  Vowel Points 20
  Matres Lectionis (Consonants as Vowel Indicators) 22
  Other Graphic Signs 24
  Ketiv-Qere 25

CHAPTER 3
Phonology 27
  Consonantal Inventory 27
  Historical Changes to the Consonantal Inventory 29
  Phonetic Processes Affecting Consonants 31
  Historical Changes Affecting Vowels 36
  Vowel Inventory of Biblical Aramaic 40
  Phonological Rules Summary 48

v

CHAPTER 4

Nouns and Adjectives: Inflection and Derivation 52

Inflectional System of Nouns and Adjectives 52

Declensions 52

Declensional Suffixes 54

Derivation of Nouns and Adjectives 59

CHAPTER 5

Pronouns 74

Independent Personal Pronouns 74

Pronominal Suffixes 75

The Particle דִּי 84

Demonstrative Pronouns 84

Interrogatives/Indefinite Nouns 85

CHAPTER 6

Noun Phrases 87

Simple Noun Phrases 87

Headed Noun Phrases 90

CHAPTER 7

Numerals and Other Quantifiers 105

Numerals: Form 105

Syntax of Numerals 107

Noun + כל 109

Distributive and Reciprocal Phrases 112

מה as Quantifier 113

CHAPTER 8

Adjective Phrases 114

Adjectives without Nouns 114

Comparative Grade 115

CHAPTER 9

Prepositions: Form and Function 116

Prepositional Phrases 116

Prepositional Survey 117

CHAPTER 10

Verbs: Derivation and Inflection 139

Finite Verb Conjugations and Non-Finite Forms 140

Strong and Weak Roots 140

Suffix Conjugation Inflectional Suffixes 141

Prefix Conjugation Inflectional Prefixes and Suffixes 142

Verbs with Weak Roots 158

Verbs with Borrowed Base Forms 178

CHAPTER 11

Tense, Aspect, and Mood in the Verbal System 180

TAM Features of the Suffix Conjugation 180

TAM Features of the Prefix Conjugation (Indicative) 183

TAM Features of the Active Participle 187

Use of the Passive Participles 193

Volitive Forms: Jussive and Imperative 194

Infinitives 196

CHAPTER 12

Verb Types: Valence, Voice, and *Aktionsart* 199

Valence 199

Voice 199

Aktionsart 201

Verb Types: Intransitive 201

Transitive 207

Semi-Transitive Verbs 211

CHAPTER 13

Adverbs and Adverbial Phrases 213

Adverbial Form 213

Adverbial Function 214

CHAPTER 14

Clauses 219

Verbal Clauses 219

Copular Clauses 228

Existential Clauses 233

vii

Presentative Constructions   236
Negation   237
Interrogative Sentences   239

CHAPTER 15
Clause Combining: Coordination   243
Simple Coordination with ן   243
Other Coordinating Conjunctions   245

CHAPTER 16
Clause Combining: Subordination   247
Purpose Clauses   247
Causal Clauses   250
Manner Clauses   253
Temporal Clauses   254
Conditional Clauses   256
Clauses as Embedded Constituents   258

CHAPTER 17
Discourse Markers (Half-Conjunctions)   261

CHAPTER 18
Reading Guide for Biblical Aramaic and Related Dialects   264
Reading 1: Daniel 3   264
Reading 2: Daniel 6   286
Reading 3: Daniel 3:31–4:34   297
Reading 4: Daniel 7   310
Reading 5: Ezra 4:24–5:17   319
Reading 6: Petition to Rebuild the Temple in Elephantine (TAD A4.7)   325
Reading 7: Seventeen Proverbs of Ahiqar   338
Reading 8: Genesis Apocryphon cols. 21:23–22:26   343
Reading 9: Targum Job from Qumran, cols. 37–38   351

Appendices   355
Aramaic Glossary   367
Bibliography   389
Index of Citations   397
Subject Index   413

PREFACE

This grammar consists of two parts: the grammar and the readings. The descriptive grammar is based on Biblical Aramaic and the elements it shares with the older Imperial Aramaic and the (almost) contemporary Qumran Aramaic. The readings – from all three dialects – are intended to be studied in the order given, using the lessons, which make constant reference to the grammar; in this way, students will acquire an inductive control over the grammatical phenomena by constant engagement with primary texts.

Each of the corpora has its own set of problematic details and textual uncertainties; for these, one must consult the specialist literature when necessary. However, this introductory grammar will bring students to a reading knowledge of these important texts, as well as others written in the same dialects, and enable them to move forward, well equipped, to more advanced study.

ACKNOWLEDGMENTS

I would like to express my thanks to the kind people of Cambridge University Press, especially Beatrice Rehl, for their patience in seeing this book through its various stages, especially as the coronavirus pandemic made research, writing, and meeting deadlines more challenging. I also acknowledge, with gratitude, the help and insights of Makenzi Crouch, Dhanuja Ragunathan, and others not known to me, who have helped make this a better book.

In addition, I am indebted to the faculty of the Department of Semitic and Egyptian Languages and Literatures, who have endured many discussions of particular issues arising from the teaching of Aramaic and the Semitic languages. In particular, I am grateful to Aaron Butts, who suggested both the topic of this book and the publisher. I also greatly appeciate the assistance of my student Paul Major, for invaluable help with the proofing and indexing.

I have gained many insights on particular details from conversations with other Aramaists, particularly Stephen A. Kaufman abd Steven Fassberg. Of those who have passed on, I want to mention in particular the names of William Sanford LaSor and F. W. Bush of Fuller Seminary, under whose tutelage I first encountered Aramaic via the inductive method.

None of the people named above may be held responsible for any errors, which are mine alone.

Finally, and most of all, I am thankful for the gift of loving parents, Charles Galloway Cook and Miriam Morgan Cook, who believed that a proper home should be full of books of all kinds. They would have been happy to see this one, I think, even if they read no further than this page. This book is dedicated, with love, to their memory.

Edward Cook

Easter Week 2022

ABBREVIATIONS AND NOTES

*	original form, hypothetical form
^^	supralinear correction
1 Chr	1 Chronicles
1 Cor	1 Corinthians
1cp	first person common gender plural
1cs	first person common gender singular
2fp	second person feminine plural
2fs	second person feminine singular
2mp	second person masculine plural
2ms	second person masculine singular
3fs	third person feminine singular
3mp	third person masculine plural
3ms	third person masculine singular
abs.	absolute
adj.	adjective
adv.	adverb, adverbial
Akk.	Akkadian
art.	article
BA	Biblical Aramaic
BH	Biblical Hebrew
BHS	Biblia Hebraica Stuttgartensia
C	C stem
CAL	Comprehensive Aramaic Lexicon
cf.	see, refer to
conj.	conjunction
Cp	causative passive stem
cp.	compare
cstr.	construct
D	D stem
Dan	Daniel
decl.	declension
def.	definite
demon.	demonstrative

det.	determined state
Deut	Deuteronomy
dir.	direct
DJD	Discoveries in the Judean Desert
DNWSI	*Dictionary of North-West Semitic Inscriptions* (Hoftijzer and Jongeling 1995)
Dp	D passive stem
DQA	*Dictionary of Qumran Aramaic* (Cook 2015)
du.	dual
Ez	Ezra
Ezek	Ezekiel
f.	feminine
fem.	feminine
fp	feminine plural
fs	feminine singular
G	G stem
GEA	*A Grammar of Egyptian Aramaic* (Muraoka and Porten 2003)
Gen	Genesis
gen.	genitive
gent.	gentilic
GKC	Gesenius-Kautzsch-Cowley (*Gesenius' Hebrew Grammar*, 1910)
GN	geographical name
HALOT	*Hebrew and Aramaic Lexicon of the Old Testament* (see §19)
Heb.	Hebrew
IA	Imperial Aramaic
impv.	imperative
indef.	indefinite
inf.	infinitive
IPA	International Phonetic Alphabet

intrans.	intransitive		prep.	preposition
Jer	Jeremiah		pron.	pronoun, pronominal
JLA	Jewish Literary Aramaic		Ps	Psalms
juss.	jussive		ptcp.	participle
K	Ketiv		Q	Qere
KAI	*Kanaanäische und aramäische*		QA	Qumran Aramaic
	Inschriften (Donner and		Qoh	Qoheleth (Ecclesiastes)
	Röllig 2002)		Quad.	Quadriliteral
LBA	*Lexicon of Biblical Aramaic* (Vogt		rel.	relative
	and Fitzmyer 2011)		RSV	Revised Standard Version
lit.	literally		s.v.	sub verbum, indicates head word
m.	masculine			in a dictionary entry
masc.	masculine		SC	suffix conjugation
MH	Middle Hebrew		sg.	singular
mp	masculine plural		suff.	suffix
ms	masculine singular		TAD	*Textbook of Aramaic Documents*
MSS	manuscripts			(Porten & Yardeni)
MT	Masoretic text		tD	tD stem
n.	noun		Tg	Targum
Neh	Nehemiah		tG	tG stem
num.	numeral		TO	Targum Onqelos
OA	Old Aramaic		trans.	transitive
obj.	object		V	vowel
part.	particle		vb.	verb
PC	prefix conjugation		w.	with
pl.	plural			
PN	proper name			

A note on citation form: The Elephantine papyri are cited by volume letter of the set by Porten and Yardeni, i.e., A, B, C, D, followed by the subcorpus number, text number, and line number, e.g., A4 7:1 means Volume A (Letters), Archive 4 (Jedoniah archive), text 7 (Temple Petition), line 1.

The Qumran texts are cited by cave number (e.g., 4Q = Cave 4), text number, fragment number, column number (if any) in lowercase Roman numerals, and line number. Thus, 4Q246 1 ii 1 = text 246 from Qumran Cave 4, fragment 1, column 2, line 1.

CHAPTER 1

Introduction

Aramaic and Its Dialects

Aramaic is a language of central importance for the study of the ancient world, beginning from the early first millennium BCE up to the Islamic period and beyond. Aramaic stories are found in the Hebrew Bible (Christian Old Testament), and Aramaic influence is felt in the Greek text of the New Testament. It was the language of Eastern Christianity for centuries, as well as a major language of Jewish literature (along with Hebrew) through most of the first millennium CE. It still survives as a spoken language in a few communities (and their diasporas) in parts of the Middle East.

This grammar focuses on the Aramaic of the second half of the first millennium BCE and the 1st century CE, a crucial era which saw the rise and fall of the Persian and Hellenistic empires and the rise of early Judaism and the birth of Christianity. It also saw the ascent of Aramaic to the status of a major language. From this period, we have Aramaic writings that are relevant for the history of law, religion, language, and literature, including many that shed light on the most pivotal events and ideas of the time. Knowledge of Aramaic and its literature is a key that opens many doors.

The basis of the grammatical description in this book is Biblical Aramaic, the language of the Aramaic sections of the canonical books of Ezra and Daniel (as well as one verse, Jeremiah 10:11, and a phrase in Genesis 31:47). They are the only Aramaic writings accepted as Scripture by both Jews and Christians, and therefore claim the attention of anyone interested in the Bible. Biblical Aramaic is also fully provided with signs that indicate the vowels, so that the pronunciation of it is not left to guesswork, unlike the primarily consonantal writing of other early dialects. However, Biblical Aramaic only comprises 1 percent of the biblical text, and a deeper knowledge of Aramaic requires a larger corpus. Fortunately, Biblical Aramaic reaches a hand backwards to its predecessor, Imperial Aramaic – the official Aramaic of the Persian empire – and another to its successor, the Aramaic of the Dead Sea Scrolls, almost contemporaneous with the Aramaic of Daniel. These three forms of the language – Biblical, Imperial, and Qumran Aramaic – share many similarities, both in grammar and subject matter, so that they can be conveniently learned together.

BEGINNINGS OF ARAMAIC

§1. Aramaic is a member of the Semitic language group. It is part of the North-West branch of the family, along with Hebrew, Phoenician, Ugaritic, and other lesser-known ancient dialects such as Moabite, Ammonite, and Edomite. North-West Semitic in turn is part of the Central Semitic family (which includes Arabic), itself part of the West Semitic group, which includes, among others, the Ethiopian languages. The East Semitic division, now extinct, encompassed Akkadian (Babylonian and Assyrian) and Eblaite, ancient languages written in cuneiform. (See Huehnergard 2005; Huehnergard & Rubin 2011, for a survey.)

In the late second millennium and early first millennium BCE, Aramaic emerged as the language of various small kingdoms located in what is today northern Syria, northern Iraq, and southern Turkey, primarily west of the Euphrates. They adopted the twenty-two-letter alphabet of the Phoenicians and left behind inscriptions, primarily incised in stone monuments, in "Old Aramaic," the first written witness to the Aramaic language. The language of these inscriptions is not uniform, and they bear witness to the variety of dialects of Aramaic in the 10th–8th centuries BCE. Although the evidence is sparse, there seems to already be a rough dialect division between dialects west of the Euphrates and those east of it.

In addition to KAI, see Fales and Grassi (2016); Gibson (1975); Bekins (2020).

ARAMAIC AND EMPIRE

§2. The rise to power of imperial Assyria in the 8th century BCE, followed by the Neo-Babylonian empire in the 6th century BCE, put an end to the independent Aramean kingdoms. However, submission to imperial power did not suppress or limit the use of Aramaic; if anything, it enhanced it. We find ample testimony to the continued and expanded use of Aramaic in the Assyro-Babylonian cultural sphere, side by side with Akkadian. Loan contracts in Aramaic and dockets, endorsements, and other "minor" genres are extant, as well as an Aramaic letter written by one Assyrian official to another (KAI 233); or, from the 6th century BCE, an Aramaic letter on papyrus from Adon, the king of Philistine Ekron, to the Pharoah of Egypt (TAD A1.1). Aramaic had become a "link language," used cross-culturally throughout the ancient Near East.

For the Neo-Assyrian period, see Fales (1986); for the Neo-Babylonian period, see the bibliography in Fitzmyer and Kaufman (1992: 44–51). For the grammar of this largely pre-Persian period, see Hug (1993).

A vivid illustration of the spread of Aramaic beyond its original homeland is found in the Hebrew Bible. When the officials in charge of the invading Assyrian army come to Jerusalem, they speak to the leaders and people of Judah in "Judean" (Hebrew), but the Judean leaders plead, "Pray, speak to your servants in the Aramaic language, for we understand it; do not speak to us in the language of Judah within the hearing of the people who are on the wall" (2 Kings 18:26, RSV). Aramaic was apparently known as a diplomatic language even in a small kingdom like Judah, but not yet as a common second tongue.

IMPERIAL ARAMAIC

§3. The regional power that succeeded the Neo-Babylonian empire was the Persian empire under the Achaemenid dynasty (538–331 BCE). The documentation of the use of Aramaic increases dramatically in this period, since it became the official language of the Persian chancelleries and was widely employed for both official and informal purposes. The languages of the ancient Near East – Persian, Elamite, Akkadian, Phoenician, Hebrew, Egyptian, Arabic, and others – all maintained their position in their native habitats, but Aramaic became the default second language of wider communication. (For a recent survey of research, see Dušek 2013.)

Aramaic continued to be the mother tongue for many, as well, but the form of it acquired by other groups as a necessary second language, referred to in this grammar as Imperial Aramaic (IA),[1] was actually a somewhat simplified compromise between dialects, that is, a *koine*, although the Eastern dialects had the most influence on its formation.

§4. The most important changes that took place in IA during this period are the following:

1. The phonemic inventory was reduced and simplified by the merger of the interdental stops with their dental counterparts (§36), and the merger of the reflex of the phoneme *$\acute{s}$, written with ק in Old Aramaic, with ʿ*ayin* (written ע, §37). Although the prevailing historical spelling was often maintained, there are enough telltale phonetic spellings to betray the true phonetic situation.
2. Nasalization of doubled consonants (§54b) was common, which also blocked the assimilation of *n* to contiguous consonants (§42), a feature of the Western dialects.
3. The feminine plural inflections and pronouns were dropped in favor of a generic use of the masculine plural (§212f).

---

[1] Other names: Official Aramaic, *Reichsaramäisch*. Because many of the surviving texts come from Egypt, some scholars speak of "Egyptian Aramaic."

4. The demonstrative pronoun אלֵה *these*, found in the Eastern dialects, was generalized in preference to the Western form אלֵן (§136), as was the 3mp[2] independent pronoun הִמּוֹ for הֵם (§125).

5. The preposition אית, marking the definite direct object in Western dialects, was dropped in favor of using the preposition לְ, as in the Eastern dialects (§359).

6. Various forms of the prefix conjugation (PC) were simplified: the preterite (short PC), used in some OA texts, no longer appears in IA; the jussive with *l*- preformative for third-person forms, used primarily in Eastern dialects, was replaced by the jussive with *y*- prefix prevalent in the West.

7. The G stem infinitive with *m*- prefix was generalized and the Western form without *m*- disappeared (§225).

8. The preformative *h* of the C stem (§232c) was frequently elided in the prefix conjugation, but it is uncertain whether this change was complete in every register in the spoken language.

9. The periphrastic genitive, that is, the use of the particle דִי (spelled זִי in IA) as a genitive particle, was adopted from the Eastern dialects alongside the typical Semitic construct genitive (§160).

10. The active participle became fully integrated into the verbal system as a relative present tense, and the verb הוי was sometimes used as an auxiliary with the participle to indicate past or future progressive action (§313).

11. The flexible word order of the Eastern dialects, especially allowing the verb to come after the subject and object, reflecting Akkadian or Persian influence, became common in IA (§363).

Some of these developments became standard throughout all of Aramaic and were inherited by the later dialects, namely 1, 7, 8, 9, and 10. Features 3 and 4 are peculiar to IA. Features 2 and 5 are limited in later times to Eastern varieties of Aramaic. The use of the *y*- prefix (6) remained general in the West, although the jussive form was lost in the later dialects; the *l*- prefix resurfaced in the later Eastern dialects on the indicative form.

§5. Imperial Aramaic, besides being a *koine*, also became a supra-regional standard; in sociolinguistic terms, it became a prestige language. It was used in the highest echelons of government, diplomacy, and commerce, and a control of it became the mark of a cultivated, powerful person.

> For the term *koine* (a simplified compromise among dialects), see Tuten (2007); for standard (a dialect considered prestigious), see Milroy (2007); for *lingua franca* (language used for communication among groups with different mother tongues), see Wardhaugh (2011).

---

[2] For abbreviations, see pp. xiii–xiv.

As such, it influenced the vernacular forms of Aramaic that continued in use alongside it; and it even left its mark on other languages. The Jewish politician Nehemiah (mid-5th century BCE), for instance, in his memoirs had a liking for Hebrew expressions modeled on IA, such as אִם־עַל־הַמֶּלֶךְ טוֹב "if it pleases the king" (Neh 2:5, cp. Ez 5:17 הֵן עַל־מַלְכָּא טָב and the Elephantine temple petition [TAD A4.7:23] הן על מראן טב, "if it pleases our lord"), and many Aramaic words and expressions entered the Hebrew lexicon at this time. Akkadian also borrowed many words from Aramaic, and the impact of Aramaic on Iranian languages was significant and long-lasting. By the same token, IA absorbed words and grammatical features from other languages, especially Akkadian and Persian, and in turn became the conduit through which these words were passed to other languages.

> For Aramaisms in Hebrew, see Kautzsch (1902), Wagner (1966), Hurvitz (1968); in Akkadian, see von Soden (1966, 1968, 1977), Abraham and Sokoloff (2011). For Aramaic as influenced by Akkadian, see Kaufman (1974); for Persian loanwords, Hinz (1975).

The Elephantine Papyri: Publication and Contents

§6. As noted, the documentation of IA is significantly greater than that of Old Aramaic; the hot and dry climate of Egypt has been particularly favorable to the preservation of antiquities, including Aramaic texts written on soft media such as papyrus or leather. The primary, although not exclusive, source of our knowledge of Persian-period Aramaic is a large number of papyri discovered on the island of Elephantine, located in the south of Egypt near the city of Aswan (ancient Syene).

Like the Dead Sea Scrolls, the Elephantine papyri first appeared on the antiquities market, in this case brought by Egyptian peasants who came across them while digging up ancient garbage to use as fertilizer; many of the papyri were first published in Sayce and Cowley (1906). More were discovered by German archaeologists working at Elephantine and appeared in a sumptuous volume edited by Eduard Sachau (1911). The photographs in Sayce and Cowley, and Sachau, made soon after discovery, are still of great use today. In 1923, A. E. Cowley collected all the texts known at that time (including those published before 1906), with commentary but no photographs or drawings (Cowley 1923). Cowley's text was for decades the comprehensive resource, and some publications still refer to the texts by their "Cowley numbers" (e.g., "Cowley 1" or "C 1").

Decades later, further documents appeared. An additional seventeen papyri had been discovered in 1893 but were not studied until they turned up as part of a bequest to the Brooklyn Museum; they were published by Emil Kraeling (1953). These are sometimes referred to by their "Kraeling numbers" (e.g., "K 1").

All of the Egyptian Aramaic texts (including the Driver letters and Hermopolis papyri; see §7 below) have been collected and reedited in the *Textbook of Aramaic Documents from Ancient Egypt*, by Bezalel Porten and Ada Yardeni, in four volumes (A: *Letters*, 1986; B: *Contracts*, 1989; C: *Literature, Accounts, Lists*, 1993; D: *Ostraca and Inscriptions*, 1999), cited as *TAD*. Individual texts are cited by volume (A–D) and number. This is now the standard text edition.

Some of the most important Egyptian texts are grouped together in archives. The *Jedoniah* archive (TAD A4.1–10) consists of letters written on papyrus by the Jewish community at Elephantine in the late 5th century BCE (419–post-407 BCE), including a petition for the rebuilding of the temple of the god Yaho (or Yahu) sent to the governor of Judah in 407 BCE (TAD A4.7 and a second copy, TAD A4.8) (see Reading 6). The *Mibtahiah* archive preserves legal texts belong to the Judean woman Mibtahiah (TAD B2.1–11), and the *Anani* archive is likewise a collection of legal texts of the Judean man Anani (B3.1–13; these are the texts originally published by Kraeling 1953). Many unarchived texts, both letters and legal documents, have also been found, including ostraca (singular *ostracon*, potsherd) bearing short notes or letters.

Also at Elephantine, an ancient copy in Aramaic of the *Words of Ahiqar* (TAD C1.1) was found, a literary text telling the story of the Aramean sage Ahiqar; an official in the Assyrian court, he was falsely accused by his traitorous nephew Nadan and deposed but later regained his position. Embedded in the story is a collection of the *Proverbs of Ahiqar*, short sayings in the wisdom tradition familiar from the biblical books of Proverbs, Qoheleth (Ecclesiastes), and Job, as well as other Near Eastern literatures. (See Reading 7.)

Other Imperial Aramaic Texts

§7. *Arshama letters*. Outside of Elephantine, a cache of letters from Egypt was acquired by the Bodleian Library at Oxford University in 1944 from the estate of the German archaeologist Ludwig Borchardt; the ultimate provenance is unknown. They are from the office of the Persian satrap Arshama (or Arsames) to his Egyptian estates and date from the reign of Darius II (423–405 BCE). They were originally published by G. R. Driver (1954, 1957) and are still sometimes cited as the "Driver letters" (TAD A6.3–16; two previous letters relating to Arshama were discovered at Elephantine [A6.1–2]).

Hermopolis papyri. Also separate from the Elephantine material are the *Hermopolis* papyri, a cache of private letters of an Aramean family discovered in the temple of Thoth in Hermopolis and published in full in 1966 (Bresciani & Kamil 1966; see TAD A2.1–7). Although undated, they are assigned paleographically to the late 6th or early 5th century BCE and are therefore earlier than most of the Elephantine papyri.

Bactrian documents and other texts. Outside of Egypt, Aramaic texts written primarily on hard media such as stone or pottery have been discovered, including texts from Palestine, Arabia, Asia Minor, Iraq (Babylon), and Iran (Persepolis). A recent discovery, of uncertain provenance, is a relatively large collection of documents, now in a private collection, consisting mainly of the correspondence of the official Akhvamazda of Bactria dating from 354 to 324 BCE (Naveh & Shaked 2012). They are similar in some ways to the Arshama archive published by Driver; the find-spot was no doubt Afghanistan.

Aramaic texts in non-alphabetic script. Two texts written in non-alphabetic scripts should be mentioned: *Papyrus Amherst 63*, of unknown provenance but certainly from Egypt, is a long papyrus document containing Aramaic literary texts recorded in the Demotic Egyptian writing system. Its decipherment has been a challenge to scholars, but recent advances have done much to elucidate it. An *editio princeps* is still lacking, but a preliminary translation is available (Steiner 1997 and literature cited there; see also Van der Toorn 2018; and Holm forthcoming). The *Uruk incantation* is a magical text in Aramaic written in syllabic cuneiform, discovered in the excavations of ancient Uruk in southern Iraq. It dates from the Hellenistic period; the writing system preserves the Aramaic vocalization and thus provides a unique aid to the reconstruction of the ancient Aramaic pronunciation (see, most recently, Geller 2006).

§8. Although IA became a widely used standard language, it was not completely homogeneous, and it is still possible to detect dialectal differences in the texts. The Arshama correspondence (§7) is written in a conservative "proper" IA, as expected from a Persian official (Whitehead 1978), while the Hermopolis papyri (§7) give us a glimpse at a Western version of Persian-period Aramaic with its own peculiarities (see Greenfield 1978). For a comprehensive survey of variation in the Imperial Aramaic texts, see Folmer (1995).

ARAMAIC IN THE JEWISH COMMUNITY AFTER THE EXILE

§9. As we saw above, Aramaic was known to some in the kingdom of Judah in the 8th century BCE; whether it became more widely known there between that time and the Babylonian conquest of Judah in 586 BCE is unclear. However, the Jewish exiles in the Babylonian empire and afterwards in the Persian period obviously came into contact with Aramaic, and when many of them returned to Judea under the Achaemenids, beginning in 538 BCE, they brought Aramaic with them as a second language.

Possibly the earliest Aramaic text in the Bible is the solitary verse Jeremiah 10:11, which was probably added to the prophecy in the Persian period. It uses the final *m* form of the 3mp pron.

suff. (לְהֹום, cf. §128g), an archaic spelling of the word for "earth" (אַרְקָא), and the demonstrative pronoun אֵלֶּה "these," typical of IA (§136b).

Many Aramaic words and expressions entered Hebrew at this time, showing that both languages enjoyed a healthy symbiosis within the community. "Late Biblical Hebrew" is typified by borrowings from Aramaic, and Aramaic was also the medium through which Akkadian and Persian words (like פִּתְגָם "word, decree"; דָּת "law," later "religion") enriched the Hebrew vocabulary. However, there is no evidence that Aramaic completely replaced Hebrew in the Judean homeland as a mother tongue.[3]

§10. The canonical book of Ezra, set in the Persian period, contains long sections in Aramaic (ch. 4:8–6:18 and 7:12–26), much of which plausibly originated in the Achaemenid period, although the orthography and morphology have been updated to reflect the norms of a later time. In particular, the excerpts of correspondence with the Persian monarchs (4:11–16, Rehum and Shimshai to Artaxerxes; 4:17–22, Artaxerxes' reply; 5:8–17, Tattenai and Shethar-Boznai to Darius; 6:3–12, Darius' reply, quoting a memorandum of Cyrus [6:3–5]; 7:12–26, Artaxerxes to Ezra) are probably based on actual documents from that time (Williamson 2008), although they contain a mixture of both earlier and later forms, e.g., both the older and later spellings of the 3mp suffix, הם- and הון-, respectively. (See Reading 5.)

AFTER IMPERIAL ARAMAIC

§11. The conquests of Alexander the Great in 334–323 BCE put an end to Persian hegemony in the Near East and ushered in a new era of Hellenization. They also dethroned Aramaic from its position as the official language of empire, although the change in the linguistic situation was not instantaneous. Aramaic continued to be a link language in the East for many centuries after the advent of Hellenism. However, its prestige was affected by the entrance of Greek as the preferred

---

[3] The anxiety of Nehemiah about the language situation of postexilic Judea – "half of the children [of intermarried couples] spoke the language of Ashdod, and they did not know how to speak the language of Judah, but [spoke] according to the language of each people" (Neh 13:24) – has been interpreted with unwarranted specificity to refer to the "death" of Hebrew at the hands of Aramaic, which Nehemiah supposedly deplored. In fact, Nehemiah's own style flaunts a knowledge of Aramaic as a prestige language, which he apparently had no qualms about. The "language of Ashdod" (אשדודית) more likely refers to what he regarded as substandard pronunciation or usage in the local Hebrew or Canaanite dialect, which fell short of his prescriptive requirements (which themselves were noticeably different from the literary Hebrew of the preexilic period).

language of the conquerors, and all the more so as the appeal of Greek culture increasingly made itself felt among the indigenous populations.

Nevertheless, Aramaic lived on in both speech and writing, and indeed the erstwhile Imperial dialect was still valued as a literary standard. At the same time, literary texts began increasingly to display vernacular forms in regions where the local Aramaic varieties were still vital. This ill-defined period of transition to the eventual emergence of regional dialects as literary standards in their own right is called "Middle Aramaic" (Fitzmyer 1979), although it should be stressed that Middle Aramaic is the name of a period, not the name of a dialect. Others prefer to speak of "post-Achaemenid Imperial Aramaic" (e.g., Beyer 1984), although this overstresses the dominance of Imperial Aramaic.

The language situation of Judea during the Hellenistic and early Roman period (323 BCE–70 CE) exemplifies much of the linguistic complexity and fluidity that characterizes Middle Aramaic. Judea had a local ethnic language, Hebrew, known to some degree in Jewish communities outside Judea, but still spoken natively only in the small Judean homeland. In addition, Aramaic was used throughout the region, and most Judeans spoke both Aramaic and Hebrew; Jews outside Judea used primarily Aramaic and Greek.

Within Judea, Greek was no doubt generally known, but was disfavored by traditionalists and nationalists, while being adopted by those friendly to Hellenistic culture. Immigrants and colonists primarily spoke Greek, and probably also acquired Aramaic as a general means of communication. During the Hasmonean period (165–37 BCE), Judea grew into an independent regional power, and Hebrew acquired more prestige. The resulting acquisition of Hebrew by Aramaic-speaking populations left its mark, leading to the formation of Middle Hebrew (the language of the Mishnah and later rabbinic Judaism) as an alternative to the classical Biblical dialect (Cook 2017).

For a survey of the period, see Barr (1989).

BIBLICAL AND QUMRAN ARAMAIC

§12. The best-known Aramaic text from the Jewish biblical canon comes from the Hellenistic period, namely the Aramaic portions of the Book of Daniel (Dan 2:4b–7:28). The Aramaic portions of Ezra (see §10) and Daniel, as part of the traditional Masoretic text, were provided with vowel points, cantillation marks, and Masoretic notes (§17) in the Middle Ages, but the consonantal text of Daniel is a product of the 2nd century BCE. The Aramaic texts among the Dead Sea Scrolls also were likely composed in the Hellenistic period, although the documents themselves are mainly products of the 1st century BCE and CE.

Chapters 2–6 of Daniel relate the stories of Daniel and his friends, exiles from Judah, who are portrayed as officials in the court of Babylon during the 6th century BCE. They all hold fast to the covenant faith of Israel in their pagan environment, and Daniel wins favor from the foreign kings as a seer and interpreter of dreams and visions. Chapter 7 presents a personal vision of Daniel, symbolically foretelling the crisis of persecution in Judea under Antiochus Epiphanes. Despite the setting in the Neo-Babylonian and Persian period, it is clear from internal evidence (particularly the prophetic visions of chapters 2 and 7, and the Hebrew chapters 8–12) that the real time of composition was the 2nd century BCE against the backdrop of the Antiochene crisis (166–164 BCE).

The Aramaic of Daniel

§13. The Aramaic of Daniel is still under the spell of IA's prestige and often follows in its linguistic footsteps. The following points, applicable to the consonantal text, are noteworthy.

Some of the traits of the Aramaic of Daniel are very much *like Imperial Aramaic*: (1) The preposition ל is still the primary marker of the definite direct object, but ית occurs one time (Dan 3:12). (2) The periphrastic genitive and verbal use of the predicative participle are fully integrated into the grammar. (3) The word order allows the subject and object to appear before the verb, as in many IA texts. (4) The fp forms have an inconsistent pattern. The 3/2 fp pronominal suffixes are lacking in the consonantal text (*Ketiv*) but are present in the *Qere* reading tradition (§33). The 3fp inflection of the PC is sometimes found in the *Ketiv*, sometimes in the *Qere*. The 3fp SC inflection does not appear in the consonantal text, but only in the *Qere*. Overall, the IA pattern of avoiding fp suffixes and verbal forms is maintained. (5) The replacement of preformative *h* by *'aleph* in the suffix conjugation, imperative, and infinitive of the C stem (§4[8]) is very rare, as in IA. (6) Persian loanwords are common.

Differences from Imperial Aramaic. In other ways, the Aramaic of Daniel (and Ezra) is different from IA:

1. The mergers described in §§36–37 are fully reflected in the orthography without exception. In IA, historical spellings, particularly ז for ד, are common.
2. Nasalization (§54b) is frequently found, but so is assimilation of *n*, and it is likely that the nasalized spellings are historical remnants only of IA.
3. The mp/fp pronominal suffixes have completely replaced the IA forms ending in *-m* with forms ending in *-n*. This change was already starting to happen in some IA texts (see Folmer 1995: 139ff.).
4. The demonstrative plural אלה *these* has been replaced by the Western form אלן (§136).
5. Two forms of the 3mp independent personal pronoun are found, המון and אינון, while IA (and Ezra) uses המו (§124). The 3ms and 3fs personal pronouns are spelled הוא and היא respectively (instead of הו and הי, as in IA) (§§124–125).

6. The G stem of the verb הוי *to be* uses the prefix *l-* in the prefix conjugation instead of *y-*, to avoid the forms *יהוה or *יהוא, too similar to the divine name יהוה in Hebrew (§268a).

7. The preformative element of the T-stem verbs in the SC is sometimes spelled הת־ *ht-*, possibly under Hebrew influence, instead of את־ *ʾt-*, as in IA (§50b).

8. Long vowels in any position are usually signaled by *matres lectionis* (§25). This is not the case in IA, which leaves many long vowels unmarked.

9. The particle איתי is sometimes used as a copula (not attested in IA) (§315, §376d).

10. The prefix conjugation is sometimes used to describe events in past time, a function that does not appear in IA (§§303–304).

The Aramaic of Daniel, then, is not the same as Imperial Aramaic but is indebted to it, and the author of the stories considers a form of it the proper medium for a literary account of Jewish heroes in the Eastern courts.

Qumran Aramaic Texts

§14. The discovery of the Dead Sea Scrolls from 1948 to 1956 revolutionized the study of ancient Judaism in many areas, not least in the realm of language. Although most of the 800 or so scrolls are written in Hebrew, over 100 of them were written in Aramaic. They are not explicitly dated, but based on paleographic and archaeological evidence, we know that most were copied in the 1st century BCE and 1st century CE, and a few stem from the 2nd century BCE. From a literary standpoint, some texts contained in the MSS were composed earlier than their paleographic date.

The most important Aramaic documents found in the Qumran area (the 11 caves in the vicinity of the Wadi Qumran) are described below. A conventional title is given, followed by the standard scholarly abbreviation by cave number (e.g., 1Q = Qumran Cave 1); some MSS are named by number without a standard abbreviation.

The *Genesis Apocryphon* (1QapGen) contains a number of extra-canonical stories about the patriarchs from the book of Genesis, including Lamech, Noah, and Abraham. The latter columns (19–22), with the Abraham narrative, are better preserved than the rest of the document and constitute the longest consecutive readable Aramaic text from Qumran. (See Reading 8.) The text is paleographically dated to the 1st century BCE.

The *Targum of Job* (11QtgJob) is an Aramaic translation of the canonical book of Job, surviving fragmentarily from chapters 17 to 42, with the latter chapters in a better state of preservation. The paleographic date of the MS is the 1st century CE, but the text of the translation is no doubt older. (See Reading 9.)

The original Aramaic version of the *Book* (or books) of *I Enoch*, known previously only in Ethiopic or Greek translation, survives in a number of fragmentary manuscripts (4Q201–202, 4Q204–207, 4Q212), the earliest of which (4Q201) is paleographically dated to the 2nd century BCE; the rest are from the 1st centuries BCE and CE. A separate part of the Enoch material, called *Astronomical Enoch*, is contained in four MSS (4Q208–211).

An Aramaic version of the deuterocanonical *Book of Tobit* was also discovered in several fragmentary MSS (4Q196–199). Fragments of a Hebrew version were also found (4Q200). *Tobit* was probably originally written in Hebrew in the Persian period, but the Aramaic translation dates from Hellenistic times. The entire book survives only in Greek translation.

An Aramaic precursor to the *Testament of Levi* (known from the pseudepigraphic *Testaments of the Twelve Patriarchs*, extant in Greek) was found at Qumran. This is referred to as the *Aramaic Levi Document* (1Q21, 4Q213, 4Q213a–b, 4Q214, 4Q214a–b), a partial copy of which had previously been discovered among the medieval manuscripts of the Cairo Geniza. The MSS date from the 1st century BCE. Other testamentary literature in Aramaic, previously unknown, was also uncovered among the finds: the *Testament of Kohath* (4Q542), the *Visions of Amram* (4Q543–549), the *Testament of Jacob* (4Q537), the *Testament of Judah* (4Q538).

In addition, apocalyptic works were found: a visionary *Description of the New Jerusalem* (1Q32, 2Q24, 4Q554, 4Q554a, 4Q555, 5Q15, 11Q18); a fragment describing "the son of God" (4Q246), a prophecy possibly describing Noah or a future savior (4Q534–536), a work connected to traditions about Levi, with eschatological predictions (4Q540–541); and others of smaller compass and damaged context. All of these fall within the 1st century BCE–CE.

> The literature on the Qumran texts is vast; a good introduction for the uninitiated is VanderKam (2010); for bibliography, a useful handbook is Fitzmyer (2008).

Qumran Aramaic: The Language

§15. Since the Qumran Aramaic texts mostly stem from the century after the writing of Daniel, it is not surprising that in most details Qumran Aramaic is very similar to Biblical Aramaic. The following characteristics are worthy of mention.

Orthography

1. Nasalization (§54b) appears much less often compared to BA, and the few occurrences are historical remnants of IA norms.
2. The use of ס for etymological *$\acute{s}$ (earlier written with שׁ) is more widespread, showing that *$\acute{s}$ had merged with s (§40).

3. Long vowels are routinely signaled by the presence of *matres lectionis*, and the short vowel $*u$ is sometimes marked by the *mater* ו (§26b).

4. The 2ms pron. suff. is sometimes spelled ־כה (instead of ־ך as in IA and BA), and the 3fs suffix is sometimes spelled ־הא (instead of ־ה). These are probably not innovative pronunciations but innovative spellings of the traditional pronunciation (Cook 1990).

5. The elision of preformative *h* (§50a) in the C stem is reflected in the orthography in the majority of cases, with preformative *'aleph* in the SC. Some texts have a more conservative orthography in this respect, such as 11QtgJob.

6. Although the spelling די is prevalent, there are many instances where the particle is written as ד־ attached directly to a host word, as will be the norm in subsequent dialects (§135c).

Morphology

1. The demonstrative ms pronoun דנה is still sometimes used, but the shortened form דן is prevalent (like דֵּין of JLA) (§136).

2. The 3mp independent pronoun אנון is dominant, with המון limited to four occurrences in the Prayer of Nabonidus (4QPrNab) and 11QtgJob.

3. The occurrence of ית to introduce the definite direct object is attested a few times, but the use of ל still prevails (§359).

4. The 3fp form for the SC, as well as for the rest of the verbal and pronominal systems, is fully reflected in the consonantal text.

5. The *l*- prefix in the PC of the root הוי *to be* is still used, as in BA (§268a).

6. The passive C stem ("Hophʕal") is still sometimes used, as in BA (§235); it would disappear in later dialects.

7. The forms of the infinitive largely align with those of IA and BA, although there are a few attestations of D stem infinitives with *m*- preformative (§230c).

Syntax

1. The word order in which the object precedes the verb is much less common than in BA, and QA's word order patterns are much more "traditional" than those of Daniel.

2. With a few exceptions, the PC is not used to describe past time (§§303–304). This aligns QA more with IA than with BA (Daniel).

Lexicon

1. The particles בדיל, בדי, and ארו in the meaning *because* appear in QA and are likely absent from BA purely by chance (cf. §§411–413).

2. Hebraisms are more frequent in QA than in BA (Stadel 2008), and Greek loanwords are completely absent.

Qumran Aramaic as a literary dialect is, like BA, indebted to Imperial Aramaic, but has drifted further away from it, with more forms from the local vernacular entering (or reentering) the literary dialect. The orthography has fewer historical spellings, showing that the spell of IA was weakening.

The Uniformity of the Dialects

§16. Despite the differences among the dialects treated in this grammar (IA, BA, QA), there is still a large degree of uniformity among them. Most of the texts were written within a few centuries of each other (5th–1st centuries BCE). The verbal and nominal inflection is largely the same throughout the corpora. Noun phrases are built the same way, and the system of verbal stems and complements is similar throughout. The potentially confusing variety of word orders is offset by identical rules of agreement. Clauses are linked together in the same way, although there is some diversity in the subordinating particles.

The most striking difference for the learner is in the orthography, with IA standing apart due to a large number of historic spellings, as well as frequent defective writing of long vowels. Allowing for this difference, the overall likeness among these language varieties, as well as their historical connectedness, allows them to be treated together in a single grammar.

The Vowel Points of the Masoretic Text

§17. The scholarly guild of the Masoretes added vowel points to the consonantal text of the Hebrew Bible, including the Aramaic portions, in the early Middle Ages to preserve the pronunciation of the traditional oral recitation (Khan 2020). The pronunciation of Aramaic thus preserved postdates the composition of the texts by almost a millennium, although aspects of the reading tradition may go back considerably further.

In some cases, the text presupposed by oral tradition is at variance with the consonantal text, and these variations are preserved in Masoretic notes referring to the *Ketiv* ("written") and the *Qere* ("read") (see §33). These notes are evidence of some dialectal change and variation, and they also simply correct errors that have crept into the consonantal text. The vowel points themselves betray occasional competing dialectal pronunciations.

The vocalization of the text preserves certain phonological regularities that may go back to the period of composition. (1) The reduction of short vowels $*a$, $*u$, $*i$ to shewa ($ə$) in unstressed open syllables (§61c) may have begun in the Hellenistic period (therefore affecting BA and QA, but not IA). (2) The spirantization of the consonants $b\,g\,d\,k\,p\,t$ /ת כ פ ד ג ב (§55) may have begun earlier still, but since variants of this kind are not registered in consonantal orthography, it is hard to tell (§55c). (3) Change in vowel quality according to stress and syllable type (§78, Rule 7) is also hard to measure for the pre-Masoretic period, although there is some evidence that short $*i > e$ in stressed closed syllables.[4] In general, though, we have to assume that most of the vocalic rules that obtain in Masoretic Aramaic are anachronistic.

That does not mean that they are without use. Despite some inconsistencies, the Tiberian vocalization of Aramaic is a system that is useful for learners. There is no tradition of pronunciation for the unpointed epigraphic texts of IA and QA, but inserting the Tiberian vowels in these texts is no more of an anachronism than the Masoretic text itself, with its later reading tradition mapped onto texts from a thousand years earlier. However, it must always be borne in mind that the further back the texts go, the less likely it is that their phonology would bear close resemblance to the Tiberian vocalization of Biblical Aramaic. A complete scientific reconstruction of the vocalization of ancient Aramaic may be beyond our power, but it should always be a goal, however convenient the later Tiberian system may be for pedagogical purposes.

Jewish Literary Aramaic

§18. The 1st and 2nd centuries CE saw the end of the Jewish commonwealth and a drastic reduction in the Jewish population of Judea and Jerusalem. But literary activity in Hebrew and Aramaic continued in other centers. Among the most noteworthy literary projects in Aramaic in the centuries following the Second Temple period (post-70 CE) is the production of the *targums*, Aramaic translations of Hebrew scripture for use in synagogue worship. The most widely used were *Targum Onqelos*, a translation of the Torah, or Pentateuch, and *Targum Jonathan*, a translation of the Former Prophets (Joshua, Judges, 1–2 Samuel, 1–2 Kings) and the Latter Prophets (Isaiah, Jeremiah, Ezekiel, the Twelve Minor Prophets).

They are written in an Aramaic dialect descended from the same kind of literary tongue we see at Qumran, and which was understandable in the synagogues of the East as well as in those of Palestine. This supra-regional standard, *Jewish Literary Aramaic* (JLA), varies too much from its predecessors to be included in this grammar; but Targums Onqelos and Jonathan, like the Hebrew Bible, have been supplied with full vocalization through vowel points. Hence, JLA gives valuable knowledge about the pronunciation of ancient Aramaic, and sometimes JLA forms will be cited in this grammar for that purpose.

---

[4] The Uruk incantation (§7) has forms such as *le-e* "to him" = לֵהּ (*leh* < *lih*). The tablet dates from the 3rd century BCE; see Geller (2006).

TOOLS FOR RESEARCH

§19. For full bibliographic details, see the Bibliography (pp. 389ff.).

Bibliography

For an overview of Aramaic language studies as a whole, see Koller (2017). Writings on OA, IA, and BA are covered in Fitzmyer and Kaufman (1992), with updates available on the *Comprehensive Aramaic Lexicon* website (see next §). Up-to-date bibliography for all the Qumran material, including the Aramaic texts, is available at the website of the Orion Center for the Study of the Dead Sea Scrolls (http://orion.mscc.huji.ac.il/); see also Fitzmyer (2008).

Text Editions

All texts in BA, IA, and QA are available online at the *Comprehensive Aramaic Lexicon* website (http://cal.huc.edu/). [CAL]

The standard text for scholarly work on Biblical Aramaic is the *Biblia Hebraica Stuttgartensia* (Deutsche Bibelgesellschaft, 1990), with the text based on the magisterial Masoretic codex Leningrad 19B, dated to 1008 or 1009 CE. [BHS] The critical apparatus of Ezra was prepared by W. Rudolph and that of Daniel by W. Baumgartner.

The successor to BHS, the *Biblia Hebraica Quinta* (Deutsche Bibelgesellschaft), is not yet complete. A fascicle containing Ezra and Nehemiah, prepared by David Marcus, appeared in 2006. It is also based on Codex Leningrad and has a new apparatus, with textual commentary. Other text editions of interest are those of Strack (1921) and Ginsberg (1967).

As noted in §6, the standard edition of the documents in Imperial Aramaic from Egypt is the *Textbook of Aramaic Documents* by B. Porten and A. Yardeni. The older text editions by Sayce and Cowley (1906), Sachau (1911), Cowley (1923), Kraeling (1953), Driver (1954, 1957), and Bresciani and Kamil (1966) are still worth consulting. The newly discovered Bactrian material is available in the edition of Naveh and Shaked (2012), with commentary and glossary, and on the CAL website.

Many of the letters have been collected and translated in Lindenberger (2003); the Hermopolis papyri are also available with translation and commentary in Gibson (1975).

The relevant volumes of *Discoveries in the Judean Desert* are still the starting point for most scholarly work on the Dead Sea Scrolls. [DJD] The Qumran Aramaic texts have not been collected as a group in a single authoritative volume. Beyer (1984, 1994, 2004) contains most of the material, although not all of his readings have been accepted, and his editions for some documents are eclectic (combinations of readings from several documents), rather than diplomatic (based on individual MSS). Fitzmyer and Harrington (1978) cover the larger texts, but the new material published since 1991 is lacking. Outside of DJD, most of the Qumran corpus, both Hebrew and Aramaic, is available in García Martínez and Tigchelaar (2000) and Parry and Tov (2004).

Dictionaries and Other Lexical Resources

The online *Comprehensive Aramaic Lexicon* (http://cal.huc.edu/), an ongoing project, includes lexical and textual databases for research in the Aramaic dialects from the beginnings to the 1st millennium CE, including all of the material included in this grammar. It is indispensable for the study of Aramaic. [CAL]

Of dictionaries devoted to Biblical Aramaic, the Aramaic section of *The Hebrew and Aramaic Lexicon of the Old Testament*, by L. Koehler, W. Baumgartner, and J. J. Stamm (2000), a translation of *Hebräisches und Aramäisches Lexikon zum Alten Testament* (1967), is the standard reference. [HALOT] A shorter edition, with revised etymologies, is *Konzise und aktualisierte Ausgabe des Hebräischen und Aramäischen Lexikons zum Alten Testament* (ed. W. Dietrich and S. Arnet; Leiden: Brill, 2013).

The most useful lexicon for comparative study is Vogt and Fitzmyer, *Lexicon of Biblical Aramaic* (2011), an updated edition and translation of Vogt (1971). The exemplification in the entries includes texts from both IA and QA. [LBA]

Another valuable tool is the *Theological Dictionary of the Old Testament, Vol. 16: Aramaic Dictionary* (Gzella 2018), a rich survey of BA vocabulary with many references to IA and QA.

For Imperial Aramaic, as well as Old Aramaic, one should consult Hoftijzer and Jongeling (1995), which contains entries for all the IA material known up to the date of publication. For more recently published material, consult CAL. [DNWSI]

For the most recent lexicon of Qumran Aramaic, see Cook (2015). [DQA] Another resource for QA, including much BA and IA material as well as later texts, is the glossaries in Beyer (1984, 2004).

Grammars

The most detailed reference grammar of Biblical Aramaic is still Bauer and Leander (1981; orig. pub. 1927), although it is outdated in many respects.

Still worth consulting, despite their age, are the grammars of K. Marti (1896), E. Kautzsch (1884), and Strack (1921). That of Strack also gives the texts with a critical apparatus listing variants which are sometimes cited in BHS as "V^S." The selection of texts includes some with supralinear vocalization.

The standard grammar in English has been Rosenthal (7th rev. ed. 2006). The reference grammar of Qimron (1993) is worthwhile for those who can read Modern Hebrew. Teaching grammars in English include those of Alger Johns (1972), T. Muraoka (2015), M. van Pelt (2011), and A. Schuele (2012).

For Imperial Aramaic, the reference grammar of Muraoka and Porten (2003) is thorough and comprehensive, although it does not cover IA texts found outside Egypt. For a briefer coverage of the material, see Muraoka (2012). Still useful despite its age is Segert (1975), which treats OA, IA, and BA together, with a glossary and selection of readings.

For Qumran Aramaic, the most complete grammar is Muraoka (2011). See also Schattner-Rieser (2004); Beyer (1984, 2004); Cook (1998).

Concordances

Electronic concordances for most of the relevant texts are available at the CAL website. For printed concordances, one may consult Porten and Lund (2002) for the Egyptian Aramaic documents; for the Qumran texts, Abegg, Bowley, and Cook (2003). Concordances for the entire Hebrew Bible include Biblical Aramaic; especially noteworthy are Mandelkern (1896) and Even-Shoshan (1990).

CHAPTER 2
Orthography

§20. Biblical Aramaic, as part of the Masoretic text of the Hebrew Bible, is written with the same consonantal signs, vowel points, and cantillation marks as the Hebrew portions (§17), as well as having the same types of scribal annotation and marking (the *Ketiv-Qere* [§33] and other notes). Although the languages are different, there is no graphic differentiation between Hebrew and Aramaic in the Masoretic text.

The primary task of the Masoretes, who flourished toward the end of the first millennium CE, was to faithfully transmit the traditional fixed consonantal text of the Jewish Bible canon and to provide it with (1) vowel signs (*nequdot* "points"), based on the reading tradition of the synagogue and rabbinic academies, as well as (2) marks to guide the cantillation of the text. Hence, the Masoretic text represents an interweaving of written and oral tradition.

The consonants of the text were considered unchangeable and, in intent, do not vary across Masoretic manuscripts, despite minor scribal differences. There was more than one system of vowel points, however, varying by both the number of vowels and the shape and position of the points. The system that became standard, and the one used today in Hebrew Bible editions such as the *Biblia Hebraica*, was the Tiberian system. Its vowel points (with the exception of *holem*) are sublinear, that is, the points are placed below the consonant that they follow in pronunciation. (There are supralinear systems that will not be considered in this grammar.) Other points that govern the articulation of certain consonants are also used in the Tiberian system.

Those who are used to reading Hebrew with the Tiberian vowel points will have little difficulty with the Aramaic portions of the Bible. For those who are coming to the system for the first time, the following paragraphs will introduce the consonantal orthography, the vowel points, and the other relevant pronunciation signs.

The standard edition of the Masoretic text for scholars, the *Biblia Hebraica*, presents the text of the oldest complete Masoretic manuscript, the Leningrad Codex, dated to 1008 or 1009 CE (Khan 2020: 27–28). Citations from Biblical Aramaic in this grammar generally follow the fourth edition of the Biblia Hebraica, *Biblia Hebraica Stuttgartensia* (BHS).

CONSONANTAL ALPHABET

§21. The consonantal alphabet of Aramaic (and Hebrew) from antiquity consisted of twenty-two letters; since Masoretic times, the list has been given as twenty-three, with the original שׁ sign differentiated by supralinear dots into שׁ and שׂ, representing two different phonemic values. Some of the other letters, even in pre-Masoretic antiquity, had more than one phonemic or phonetic value as well, as will be indicated below.

Table 1 gives the letter in the "square script," its name, its phonemic transcription, the phonological description of its ancient articulation, and the conventional modern pronunciation. The order given is the conventional order of the Hebrew/Aramaic alphabet. Some letters have two values, differentiated by the inner *dagesh* dot (§28). Others have two shapes, final and non-final, which are not relevant to the pronunciation (§22).

Final Letters

§22. Some letters (namely *k m n p ṣ* / כ מ נ פ צ) have different forms when appearing at the end of a word (ץ ף ן ם ך respectively). These are graphic variations only and do not affect the pronunciation. (Historically, the longer forms with descending strokes are more original; the descenders were shortened within a word by the exigencies of right-to-left cursive writing.)

VOWEL POINTS

§23. In Table 2, note that the vowel usually is placed below the consonant it follows in pronunciation (with *ḥolem*, by the upper left part of the letter).

The terms *front/back* refer to articulation in the front or back of the mouth; *high/mid/low* refers to jaw/tongue position.

Ḥaṭeph vowels

§24. In addition, there are three signs that are combinations of vowel signs with shewa. As a group they are called compound *shewas*, or *ḥaṭeph* vowels (Table 3). In transcription, they are marked with a breve (˘).

Table 1: *Consonantal alphabet*

Letter	Name	Transcription	Description	Conventional pronunciation
א	aleph	ʾ	glottal stop	zero or interruption of sound
בּ	bet	b	voiced bilabial stop	b
ב		b̲	bilabial spirant	v
ג	gimel	g	voiced velar stop	g
ג		ḡ	voiced velar spirant	
ד	dalet	d	voiced dental stop	d
ד		d̲	voiced interdental spirant	th as in *the*
ה	heh	h	laryngeal fricative	h
ו	waw	w	bilabial glide	w
ז	zayin	z	voiced alveolar sibilant	z
ח	ḥet	ḥ	voiceless pharyngeal spirant	ch as in *loch*
ט	ṭet	ṭ	voiceless dental emphatic	t
י	yod	y	palatal glide	y
כ	kaph	k	voiceless velar stop	k
ך כ		k̲	voiceless velar spirant	ch as in *loch*
ל	lamed	l	voiced alveolar lateral	l
ם מ	mem	m	bilabial nasal	m
ן נ	nun	n	voiced alveolar nasal	n
ס	samekh	s	voiceless alveolar sibilant	s
ע	ayin	ʿ	voiceless pharyngeal stop	like *aleph* or as a "gulping" interruption
פ	peh	p	voiceless bilabial stop	p
ף פ		p̲	voiceless bilabial spirant	f
ץ צ	ṣadeh	ṣ	voiceless dental emphatic sibilant	ts as in *Tsar*
ק	qoph	q	voiceless uvular stop	k
ר	resh	r	uvular continuant/alveolar flap	r
שׁ	shin	š	voiceless palatal sibilant	sh
שׂ	sin	ś	voiceless lateral sibilant	s
ת	taw	t	voiceless alveolar stop	t
ת		t̲	voiceless interdental spirant	th as in *thing*

Table 2: *Masoretic vowel points*

Vowel point	Name	Transcription	Description	Conventional pronunciation
◌	qameṣ	ɔ̄	back, low-mid	*aw* as in "ought"
	qameṣ ḥaṭuph	ɔ		*o* as in "boat"
◌	pataḥ	a	front, low	*ah* as in "father"
				or *a* as in "back"
◌	segol	ɛ	front, low-mid	*e* as in "egg"
◌	ṣereh	e	front, mid	*a* as in "late"
◌	ḥireq	i	front, high	*i* as in "bit"
◌	ḥolem	o	back, mid	*o* as in "boat"
◌	qibbuṣ	u	back, high	*oo* as in "loot"
◌	shewa	ə or zero	central, mid	murmured vowel or no vowel

Table 3: Ḥaṭeph *vowel signs*

Vowel point	Name	Transcription	Description	Conventional pronunciation
◌	ḥaṭeph qameṣ	ɔ̆	back, low-mid	*o* as in "boat"
◌	ḥaṭeph pataḥ	ă	front, low	*ah* as in "father"
				or *a* as in "back"
◌	ḥaṭeph segol	ɛ̆	front, low-mid	*e* as in "egg"

The *ḥaṭeph* vowels are used mainly with gutturals (§34c) under certain conditions (§§75c, 76a).

MATRES LECTIONIS (CONSONANTS AS VOWEL INDICATORS)

§25. In pre-Masoretic times, before the advent of vowel points, the letters *ʾaleph, w, h, y* / אהוי were used at the end of words to indicate the presence of long vowels (§66); in addition, י and ו, and sometimes א, were used within words to indicate long vowels as well. When used for that purpose, the letters are called *matres lectionis* (Latin, "mothers of reading"; singular *mater lectionis* or just *mater*). In the Tiberian text, they are accompanied by vowel points.

Table 4 gives the letters plus their accompanying Tiberian vowels.

Matres lectionis originated in Old Aramaic to indicate the presence of long vowels, generally at the end of words. They were not used consistently, and when the final long vowel was unstressed

Table 4: *Long vowels with* matres lectionis

Letter	Name	Transcription	Description	Conventional Pronunciation
אָ (final only)	qameṣ ʾaleph	ɔ̄	long, back, low-mid	*aw* as in "ought" or *ah* as in "father"
הָ (final only)	qameṣ heh			
הֵ (final only)	ṣereh heh	ē	long, front, mid	*a* as in "late"
אֵ (final only)	ṣereh ʾaleph			
ֵי	ṣereh yod	ē	long, front, mid	*a* as in "late"
ֶי	segol yod			
ִי	ḥireq yod	ī	long, front, high	*ee* as in "beet"
ֹו	ḥolem waw	ō	long, back, mid	*o* as in "boat"
ו	shureq	ū	long, back, high	*oo* as in "loot"

(§56), they were often omitted (Cook 1990). In IA texts, there is still much inconsistency, and many long vowels, both within and at the end of words, are not indicated by the presence of *matres*. By the later first millennium BCE, however, in the unpointed consonantal texts of BA and QA, long vowels were generally indicated by *matres*, and even the short vowel *u* was occasionally indicated by ו in QA.

§26. The orthography of Qumran Aramaic has some uses of *matres lectionis* not shared by the other dialects.

a. *Medial* א. In QA, medial ʾaleph can occur, usually after consonantal *w* or *y*, to indicate long vowel *ā* (BA ɔ̄). Examples: כואתך (= כְּוָתָךְ) "like you" (1QapGen 11:15); יואן (= יָוָן) "Greece" (1QapGen 12:12); משריאתי (= מַשְׁרִיָתִי) "my encampments" (1QapGen 21:1); יאתה (= יָתֵהּ) "him" (4Q196 2 13); כלאן (= כַּלָּן) "brides" (1QapGen 20:6).

b. *Medial* ו *for short* *u. In addition, medial ו can be used to indicate original short *u. Examples: קודש *qudš "holiness" (4Q213a 3 18); עולימי *ʿulēmay "my lads" (1QapGen 22:23); ישכונן *yiškunān "they will dwell" (4Q542 1 ii 3); קושטא *qušṭā "truth" (4Q204 1 v 4).

c. *Graphic final* א. Rarely a non-etymological א will occur in word-final position after a י or ו *mater*. This purely graphic letter was not pronounced. (For a similar phenomenon in Qumran Hebrew, see Qimron 1986: 21–23.) Examples: הווא (= הֲווֹ) "they were" (1QapGen 21:26); תבוא (= תָּבוּ) "they returned" (11QtgJob 32:3); שויא (= שַׁוִּי) "he made" (11QtgJob 29:6); ביא (= בַּי) "house" (4Q204 1 vi 23); and note also לְגוֹא "into" (Dan 3:6 etc.).

Defective and *Plene* Spelling

§27. In the Masoretic text, most Aramaic long vowels (except for *qameṣ* / ָ) are written with *matres*, but when long vowels are indicated by vowel points only, unaccompanied by a *mater*, they are said to be written "defectively" (from the old grammatical term *scriptio defectiva* "defective writing"). By the same token, spelling that employs *matres lectionis* for a vowel, whether long or (exceptionally) short, is called *plene* spelling (from *scriptio plena* "full writing").

The historical arc of orthographical development is toward the increase of *plene* spelling, from fewer to more *matres lectionis*. In the unpointed texts of IA and QA, they provide valuable hints on the pronunciation of words.

Dagesh

§28. a. *Dagesh* is a dot inside a consonant indicating that it is either (1) geminated (§54) and, in the case of the consonants בגדכפת, also a stop; or (2) in בגדכפת, a stop without gemination. The first kind (stop + gemination) is called *dagesh forte* ("strong dagesh") and the second kind (stop only) is *dagesh lene* ("weak dagesh"). They are distinguished as follows:

b. *Dagesh forte* only appears after a vowel, principally after the short vowels ◌ (*pataḥ*), ◌ (*hireq*), ◌ (*qibbuṣ*), sometimes ◌ (*holem*) and short ◌ (*qameṣ ḥaṭuph*). Since it indicates gemination (doubling) of a consonant, it necessarily also marks the boundary between the end of a closed syllable and the beginning of another (§57), e.g., מִלְּה *mil | lɔ̄*, קַטֵּל *qaṭ | ṭil*, גֻּבָּא *gub | bɔ̄*, גֹּדּוּ *gód | dū*, כָּלְהֵין *kɔl | lɔ | hen* (Dan 7:19 Qere).

c. Rarely, *dagesh forte* appears on a word's first consonant, when it is preceded by a word ending in an unstressed vowel: שָׂמְתָּ טְּעֵם *śɔ́mtɔ ṭṭəˤem* (Dan 3:10); כֹּלָּא מְטָא *kóllɔ mmɔṭɔ̄* (Dan 4:25); דִּי־מְּרִיטוּ *dī mmərīṭū* (Dan 7:4); etc. In such a case, it is called "conjunctive dagesh" (Yeivin 1980: 289ff.).

d. *Dagesh lene* occurs only in the consonants *b g d k p t* / בגדכפת at the onset of a syllable, e.g., the כ in מִשְׁכְּבֵה *miškəḇeh*; the ב in בִּשְׁנַת *bišnaṯ*; etc. Within a word, then, it is always preceded by silent shewa (§74b).

OTHER GRAPHIC SIGNS

§29. The *dagesh* should not be confused with two other internal points:

a. The point in *šureq* וּ indicating the long vowel *ū* is not a *dagesh*, although *dagesh forte* may appear in a consonantal ו (e.g., נְחַוֵּא *nəhawwē* Dan 2:4). If ו does not have a vowel point, it is *šureq*.

b. A point in word-final ה, called *mappiq*, indicates that the letter is a consonantal ה and not a silent *mater lectionis* (e.g., אֱלָהּ *ʾɛlɔh* Dan 2:45, not * *ʾɛlɔ̄*).

§30. *Maqqeph* is a line ⁻ connecting two or more words, making them a single stress unit. Often, it connects a preposition to the word or phrase it governs, e.g., מִן־כָּל־חַיָּא֨ *min kɔl ḥayyayyɔ* "more than all living things" (Dan 2:30).

§31. Additional signs, either above or below the line, indicate (1) how the word is to be cantillated, i.e., sung, (2) which syllable bears the stress, and (3) the internal sense divisions of the verse.

The names and particular functions of the cantillation marks form their own specialized subject of study and will not be covered in detail here. It is helpful to note which marks are disjunctive (marking a pause or end of a sense division) and which are conjunctive (joining the words of a sense division). For a detailed survey, see Yeivin (1980); GKC §15e–i.

They should also be noticed because they mark word stress, and because the accents indicating the end of a major sense division (disjunctive) sometimes affect the vocalization of a word. This is particularly true of the pausal accents (§32).

§32. Words occurring at the principal divisions of a verse are said to be "in pause." These divisions are commonly signaled by the cantillation mark ◌̤ (*atnaḥ*) within a verse and ◌̤ (*silluq*) on the last word of a verse. Occasionally pause affects the vocalization of words:

short *a* becomes long *ɔ*, as in בְחָ֑יִל *bəhɔ̄yil* for בְחַיִל (Dan 3:4), יְדָ֑י *yədɔ̄y* for יְדַי (Dan 3:15); short *a* becomes *ε*: הוֹדַעְתֶּ֑נָא *hōdaʕtέnɔ* for הוֹדַעְתַּנָא (Dan 2:23); original short *i* in verbal forms is often retained instead of lowering (§63c): נֶחֵ֑ת *nɔ̄hit* for נֶחֵת (Dan 4:10); מַשְׁפִּ֑יל *mašpil* for מַשְׁפֵּל (Dan 5:19); יִתְעֲבֵ֑ד *yitʕắbid* (Ez 6:12), cp. יִתְעֲבֵד (Ez 7:23); etc.

In general, the effect of pause in Biblical Aramaic is less marked than in Biblical Hebrew.

KETIV-QERE

§33. An important feature of the Masoretic text is the notation of *Ketiv-Qere* variants. The word *ketiv* כְּתִיב is an Aramaic passive participle (§224a) meaning "written" and refers to the traditional consonantal text of the Bible. *Qere* קְרֵי is also an Aramaic passive participle and means "read," referring to the Tiberian reading tradition. As noted above, one of the principal tasks of the Masoretes was to map the oral reading tradition onto the separately transmitted consonantal text.

In the large majority of cases, the text presupposed by the reading tradition is the same as the consonantal text; but occasionally there were discrepancies. In such cases, the Masoretes recorded in the margin the consonantal reading presupposed by the Qere; the traditional Ketiv was unchanged, though supplied with the discrepant vowels of the Qere.

In most cases, the differences between Ketiv and Qere amount to a single letter, e.g., in Dan 2:4 the Leningrad Codex reads לְעַבְדָיִךְ. The *circellus* above the word alerts the reader to look in the margin, where the consonants לעבדך are given, accompanied by the abbreviation ק for Qere. This means "the vowels given in the text belong to the form לעבדך." In other words, the reading tradition pronounced the word לְעַבְדָּךְ, without the *yod* found in the Ketiv.

Note that the apparatus in BHS (provided by the editors) also calls the reader's attention to the Ketiv-Qere variant, and gives a hypothetical vocalization of the Ketiv. Some online editions of the Masoretic text[1] give the Ketiv unvocalized, and the Qere vocalized, while others give the Ketiv with hypothetical vocalization alongside the vocalized Qere.

It must be emphasized that the variants given in the Ketiv-Qere notes are not the invention of the Masoretic editors, nor are they the product of ancient collation of texts; they are careful notations of differences between the two traditional strands of the biblical text, written and oral. They are in effect warnings to copyists to preserve the text as given, and not to change the Ketiv to match the Qere or vice versa.

In Biblical Aramaic, the differences between Ketiv and Qere reflect in some cases ancient dialectal differences. For instance, the 2ms independent pronoun (§124) always has the Ketiv אַנְתָּה and the Qere אנת, that is, the dialect of the Ketiv probably pronounced the pronoun as אַנְתָּה *ʾantā*, that of the Qere as אַנְתְּ *ʾant*. One Qumran text of Daniel (4Q112) has the reading אנת at Dan 2:31 (like the Tiberian Qere), while another (4Q113) has אנתה at Dan 6:17 (like the Tiberian Ketiv), confirming that both traditions are ancient.

In other instances, the Ketiv preserves ancient scribal errors, as in Ez 4:12, where the Ketiv has וְשׁוּרֵיַ אֲשַׂכְלֽלוּ, with a mistaken word division; the Qere has the correct ושוריא שכללו, "and the walls they have finished."

In this grammar, when Ketiv-Qere variants occur in quoted verses, the Ketiv will be given as it appears in the Leningrad Codex, with the unpointed Qere following in square brackets.

---

[1] Such as http://tanach.us or www.sefaria.org.

CHAPTER 3
Phonology

3

CONSONANTAL INVENTORY

§34. The phonemic inventory of Biblical Aramaic consonants is given in Table 5.

Other than the alphabetic grouping given in Table 1 and the phonemic chart in Table 5, the consonants can be listed under certain common characteristics.

a. *Non-emphatic stops.* The pronunciation of the non-emphatic stops, namely בגדכפת, varies with the presence of the *dagesh* inner dot (§28). The variations are alternate realizations of the same phoneme (allophones) and not additions to the overall consonantal inventory. Without the *dagesh*, these consonants are realized as spirants (fricatives), usually after a vowel (§55). This post-vocalic change in בגדכפת is here called spirantization.

b. *Emphatics.* The "emphatics," that is ק צ ט, were anciently distinguished by some articulatory feature that is now unclear, although many believe that the emphatics were originally glottalic ejectives (Moscati 1980: 23). For occasional dissimilation of ק in a word with other emphatics, see §45.

c. *Gutturals.* The glottals ה א and the pharyngeals ע ח are jointly known as *gutturals* and have similar effects on the quality of neighboring vowels (§§75–77). Occasionally ר has the same effects.

d. *Sibilants.* The consonants שׂ שׁ צ ס ז are jointly known as *sibilants* and are all involved in consonantal metathesis (§53) in the tG and tD verbal stems (§§237ff.).

Note that the supralinear dots distinguishing שׁ and שׂ are innovations of the Masoretes; ancient texts (including those in IA and QA) have שׁ alone, without dots, which stands for two separate phonemes.

The fricativized (spirantized) variants of בגדכפת are not phonemic and are not included in Table 5.

Table 5: *Consonantal Phonemes of Aramaic*

Manner of articulation	Place of articulation								
	Bilabial	Interdental	Dental/Alveolar	Palato-alveolar	Palatal	Velar	Uvular	Pharyngeal	Laryngeal (glottal)
Stop									ʔ א
Voiceless	p פ		t ת			k כ			
Voiced	b ב		d ד			g ג			
Emphatic			ṭ ט			q (k) ק			
Fricative									
Voiceless		*θ ס/שׁ	s ס	š שׁ		*ḫ ח		ḥ ח	h ה
Voiced		*ð ז	z ז			*ġ ע		ʕ ע	
Emphatic		*θ̣ צ	ṣ צ						
Trill							r ר		
Lateral									
Voiceless			ś שׁ						
Voiced			l ל						
Emphatic			*ṣ́ (ḍ) ק						
Nasal	m מ		n נ						
Glide	w ו				y י				

Phonemes found in Old Aramaic but which merged in later dialects with other phonemes are marked with *.

Several of the Old Aramaic letters, namely ח ק ס צ ז שׁ, have more than one value. The phonemic mergers that took place in IA are inconsistently reflected in the consonantal orthography (see §38).

HISTORICAL CHANGES TO THE CONSONANTAL INVENTORY

§35. It is often helpful to look at Biblical Aramaic and related dialects diachronically, that is, in terms of how they developed from earlier dialects. The ancestor dialect of Aramaic, called *Proto-Aramaic*, passed on its phonemes to the daughter dialects, sometimes with changes.

The descendant versions of the original phonemes are called *reflexes*. Both consonantal and vocalic phonemes display *mergers*, when one phoneme becomes pronounced exactly like another. In such a case, a single phoneme in the daughter language may be the reflex of two historically separate phonemes. Other phonemes develop *allophones* – alternate pronunciations – in certain phonetic environments. These allophones are not additions to the phonemic inventory but are considered as the same phoneme (contrastive sound) with a different realization.

Old Aramaic had more consonantal phonemes than later dialects of Aramaic (such as Biblical and Qumran Aramaic), although the same twenty-two-letter alphabet was used to write them. The following changes are relevant for understanding (1) the orthographical differences between Imperial Aramaic and the later dialects and (2) the historical relationships of cognate words in other Semitic languages, especially Hebrew.

Phonemic Mergers

As a language changes over time, some phonemes may merge with others, i.e., come to be pronounced the same way in all environments.

§36. *Interdentals*. Old Aramaic (as well as the ancestral language of Hebrew) had an interdental triad consisting of δ (voiced interdental fricative), θ (voiceless interdental fricative), and θ (voiceless interdental emphatic). The twenty-two-letter alphabet inherited from the Phoenicians had no signs for these consonants, and so in Old Aramaic they were conventionally indicated by the letters ז for δ, שׁ (or ס) for θ, and צ for θ. In the Imperial Aramaic period, these three merged with their dental counterparts d, t, and t, and began to be written with the conventional signs for those phonemes (ד for d, ת for t, ט for t).

a. In IA, the letter ז was still used to express etymological *δ, even after it merged with d, especially in word-initial position; in word-medial and word-final position, the spelling most often changed to ד (Folmer 1995: 60–61). In BA and QA, the spelling is always with ד in all positions.

b. In IA, the letter ת was almost always used for etymological *θ, reflecting its merger with *t*. The same is true of BA and QA (Folmer 1995: 70–74).

c. In IA, the letter ט was almost always used for etymological *θ, reflecting its merger with *ṭ*. The same is true of BA and QA (Muraoka & Porten 2003: 9).

§37. *Emphatic lateral fricative.* In addition, an original emphatic lateral fricative (IPA ɬ ["belted L dot"]), now often transcribed by Semitists as *ṣ́*, merged in Old Aramaic with a (uvular or pharyngeal?) phoneme signified by ק. Beginning in Imperial Aramaic, this phoneme merged with *ʿayin* and began to be written with ע, although exceptions are frequent.

In IA, original *ṣ́* is sometimes represented by ק, sometimes by ע, although it seems likely that the merger of *ṣ́* with *ʿayin* was complete. In BA and QA, ע is always used, with one exception – אַרְקָא "earth" in Jer 10:11 – although the spelling אַרְעָא also appears in the same verse (Folmer 1995: 63–70).

§38. *Hebrew cognates.* In Canaanite (Phoenician and Hebrew), the same interdental triad *ð θ $\thetạ$* merged with the sibilants *z š ṣ*, written ז ש צ. Therefore, cognate words in Hebrew and Aramaic will have different reflexes of the ancient interdentals. The emphatic lateral fricative *ṣ́* merged with *ṣ* in Hebrew, written צ.

Ancestor phoneme	Old Aramaic orthography	Merger	Later Aramaic orthography	Hebrew equivalent
ð	ז	*ð > d*	ד	*ð > z*, ז
θ	(ס) ש	*θ > t*	ת	*θ > š*, ש
$\thetạ$	צ	*$\thetạ$ > ṭ*	ט	*$\thetạ$ > ṣ*, צ
ṣ́	ק	*ṣ́ > ʿ*	ע	*ṣ́ > ṣ*, צ

Examples: *ðahab* "gold" > OA זהב, BA דְּהַב, BH זָהָב; *θawr* "ox" > OA שור, BA תּוֹר, BH שׁוֹר; *nθr* "to guard" > OA נצר, BA נְטַר, BH נָצַר; *ʾarṣ́* "earth" > OA ארק, BA אֲרַע, BH אֶרֶץ.

(A note on transcription. Semitists of the past and present have used a variety of transcriptions for the ancestor phonemes. Some of the most common are *ḏ* for *ð*, *ṯ* for *θ*, *ẓ* or *ṱ* for *$\thetạ$*, *ḍ* for *ṣ́*.)

§39. *Velar fricatives.* The original velar fricatives *$ḫ$* (voiceless, IPA [x]) and *$ġ$* (voiced, IPA [ɣ]) existed in Old and Imperial Aramaic and were written with ח and ע respectively, i.e., with the same signs used for the pharyngeals *ḥ* and *ʿayin*. Later, probably by the time of Biblical and Qumran Aramaic, the velars merged with the pharyngeals: *$ḫ$ > ḥ, ġ > ʿ* (Steiner 2005).

§40. *Voiceless lateral fricative.* The voiceless lateral fricative *ś* was written with ‏שׁ‎, the same letter used for *š*. Towards the end of the first millennium BCE, *ś* merged with *s* (written with ‏ס‎), leading to spelling variations in which ‏ס‎ appeared in place of etymological ‏שׂ‎. In Biblical Aramaic, this appears, e.g., in ‏שַׂבְּכָא‎ *śabbəkā* (Dan 3:7, 10, 15), in ‏סַבְּכָא‎ *sabbəkā* (Dan 3:5), and in the gentilic ‏כַשְׂדָּאֵה‎ *kaśdāʾē* (Dan 5:30 Qere), ‏כַּסְדָּאֵה‎ *kasdāʾē* (Ez 5:12 Qere).

In QA, examples of ‏ס‎ for etymological *ś* are more frequent, e.g., ‏סימו‎ for ‏שׂימו‎ "put" (11QtgJob 4:4), ‏עסר‎ for ‏עשׂר‎ "ten" (4Q201 1 ii 5). This occasionally led to hypercorrections, e.g., ‏שכירו‎ "they were closed up" (4Q206 4 ii 2) for ‏סכירו‎.

PHONETIC PROCESSES AFFECTING CONSONANTS

Some processes, both diachronic and synchronic, add, delete, or change consonants based on their local environment, that is, their position in the word (initial, medial, or final) as well as their proximity to other consonants.

Word-Initial *w > y*

§41. Common to all North-West Semitic dialects (Phoenician, Hebrew, Aramaic, etc.) is the change of word-initial **w* to *y*. This affected all initial-*w* words except for the frequently occurring conjunction **wa-* "and." When not word-initial, the original *w* remained. For example, the verbal root ‏ידע‎ *ydʿ* appears in its etymologically original form ‏ודע‎ *wdʿ* in the C-stem (§251).

Assimilation and Dissimilation

In assimilation, consonants take on some or all of the articulation of other nearby consonants. In dissimilation, consonants reduce their similarity to nearby consonants.

§42. *Assimilation of* n. Sometimes the nasal *n* totally assimilates to the following consonant when no vowel separates them, resulting in gemination, e.g., ‏יִפֵּל‎ *yippel* < **yinpel* (Dan 3:6), from the root ‏נפל‎ *npl.* [§78, Rule 11a]

However, non-assimilation of *n* is more common, e.g., ‏יִנְתֵּן‎ *yinten* (Dan 2:16) from the root ‏נתן‎ *ntn.* It is likely that such apparent non-assimilation is in fact due to nasalization substituting for gemination (§54b) rather than the absence of assimilation.

§43. *Assimilation of* l. In the verbal root ‏סלק‎ *slq* "to go up" (G stem), ‏ל‎ assimilates to ‏ס‎ when inflection makes the two consonants contiguous, e.g., C stem ‏הַסִּקוּ‎ *hassíqū* < **hasliqū* (Dan 3:22). (Note an example in Biblical Hebrew as well: ‏אֶסַּק‎ *ʾessaq* [Ps 139:8].) The resulting gemination is also subject to nasalization, e.g., ‏לְהַנְסָקָה‎ *ləhansāqā* < **ləhassāqā* < **ləhaslāqā* (Dan 6:24, §54).

§44. *Assimilation in the tG and tD stems.* In Biblical Aramaic, the preformative ת *t* of the tG and tD stems (§§237ff.) partially assimilates when contiguous to the first root letter after metathesis (§53) in the following cases:

a. When the first root letter is צ *ṣ*, then ת > ט *ṭ*, that is, it becomes emphatic, e.g., יִצְטַבַּע *yiṣṭabbaʿ* < *yiṣṭabbaʿ < *yitṣabbaʿ from the root צבע "to drench" (tD).

b. When the first root letter is ז, ת > ד *d*, that is, it becomes voiced, e.g., הִזְדְּמִנְתּוּן *hizdəmintūn* < *hiztəmintūn < *hitzəmintūn "you have conspired" (Dan 2:9 Qere; the Ketiv reading הזמנתון may evince total assimilation of the ת or it may simply be an ancient scribal error), from the root זמן; also in IA and QA, e.g., אזדהרו *ʾizdəhárū* "take care," tG stem from the root זהר (4Q542 1 i 4); אזדמנו "they met together" (1QapGen 21:25), tD stem from זמן.

c. In Qumran Aramaic, when the first root letter is ט, ת > ט (total assimilation), e.g., הטמרו *hiṭṭəmárū* "was hidden" < *hiṭṭəmárū (11QtgJob 14:4), tG from the root טמר.

§45. *Dissimilation of *q to k.* In some IA texts, the emphatic phoneme *q dissimilates to *k* before the emphatics *ṣ or *ṭ in the same word, that is, it becomes non-emphatic (§34b), e.g., כצפה (C1 1:85, Ahiqar) for קצפה* "his anger"; כשיטא (C1 1:158) for קשיטא* "true"; כרצי D20 5:2 (Carpentras Stele) for קרצי* "slander." Such a change is sporadically found both in earlier dialects and in later ones.

See Folmer (1995: 94–101) and Kaufman (1974: 121–122).

§46. *Dissimilation of *ʿayin to ʾaleph.* In one lexeme, etymological *ʿayin dissimilates to ʾaleph in the presence of another ʿayin: in the word אָע *ʾ5ʿ* "wood" < עע (as in 4Q214b 2–6 i 3) < Imperial Aramaic עק (as in A4 7:11). The ancestor form was *ʿiś (cp. Hebrew cognate עֵץ). Note also that the initial ʿayin of the compound preposition לעורע (§199), IA לערק, becomes ʾaleph in later Aramaic (e.g., Syriac ܠܐܘܪܥܐ). In both cases, the second ʿayin is a reflex of original *ś (§37).

Changes Involving ʾAleph

ʾAleph is a "weak" consonant, prone to elision in a number of environments; it may also be inserted in certain environments.

§47. *Syllable-final elision.* Original glottal stop א ʾaleph elides (is not pronounced) when it closes a syllable, e.g., שַׂגִּיא *śaggī* < *śaggīʾ, but is retained within a word when it begins a syllable, e.g., שַׂגִּיאָן *śaggīʾ5n* "many" (Dan 2:48).

If the original vowel preceding elided א ʾaleph was short, it becomes a long vowel, e.g., רֵאשׁ rēš < *riʾš "head"; מָאן mɔ̄n < *maʾn "vessel"; מָרֵא mɔ̄rē < *mɔ̄riʾ "lord." Word-finally, this elision is to be distinguished from purely orthographic word-final use of א as a *mater lectionis* for a final long vowel (§25).

In Biblical Aramaic, the elided א usually remains written word-finally as a historical spelling, but occasionally is omitted within a word (§246a); see also Imperial Aramaic forms such as לממר (A4 9:2) < *למאמר* "to say"; יתה (B3 4:22) < *יאתה* "he shall come." In Qumran Aramaic, elided א may be omitted in writing at the end of words, e.g., שגי for שַׂגִּיא (1QapGen 19:27).

§48. *Elision after a reduced vowel.* Occasionally א elides within a word after zero or reduced vowel, e.g., בְּאִישְׁתָּא bīštɔ̄ < *bəʾištɔ̄ (Ez 4:12); often with lengthening of the resulting vowel בֵּאדַיִן bēdáyin < *bə+ʾɛdáyin, בָּאתַר bɔ̄tar < *bə+ʾătar; but this is not regular, cp. וֶאֱנָשׁ wɛʾɛ̆nɔ̄š < *wə + ʾɛ̆nɔ̄š (Dan 6:13) and וֶאֱלָהָא wēlɔ̄hɔ̄ < *wə+ʾɛ̆lɔ̄hɔ̄ (Ez 6:12).

The א that elides in this environment is sometimes also omitted in the orthography, e.g., מָרִי mɔ̄rī (Dan 4:16 Qere; Ketiv מראי "my lord") < *mɔ̄rəʾī < *māriʾī; אתחדו "were seized" (A4 4:6) for אתאחדו < *ʾitʾaḥídū; בישתא (1QapGen 1:13) for באישתא (see above, Ez 4:12).

§49. ʾAleph can also be inserted secondarily (non-etymologically):

a. To separate contiguous vowels, in the G-stem participle of Hollow roots, e.g., קָאֵם qɔ̄ʾem, from the root קום qwm "stand" (see further §273a).

b. To replace intervocalic *yod* when the determining suffixes -ɔ̄ or -ē are added to adjectives ending in -ɔ̄y (§97), e.g., מָדָאָה mɔ̄dɔ̄ʾɔ̄ "the Mede" (Dan 6:1 Qere) for מדיא mɔ̄dɔ̄yɔ̄ (Ketiv); רְבִיעָאָה rəbīʾɔ̄ʾɔ̄ "fourth" (Dan 2:40 Qere) for רביעיה rəbīʾɔ̄yɔ̄ (Ketiv); כַּשְׂדָּאֵי kaśdɔ̄ʾē "Chaldeans" (Dan 2:5 Qere) for כשדיא kaśdɔ̄yē (Ketiv). This is a feature mainly of the BA Qere and occasionally occurs in QA, e.g., אמוראא "Amorites" (= אֱמֹרָאֵי; 1QapGen 21:21).

c. To separate contiguous vowels produced by verbal inflection (rare, QA only), e.g., אתבניאת ʾitbəníʾat < *ʾitbənī + at "it was built" (1QapGen 19:9; tG 3fs from the root בני bny), cp. אֶתְכְּרִיַּת (Dan 7:15).

d. The spelling of the word מֹאזַנְיָא mōzanyɔ̄ < *mōznayyɔ̄ "scales" (Dan 5:27) is derived from a folk etymology of Hebrew מֹאזְנַיִם mōznayim (connected with BH אֹזֶן "ear"); the ʾaleph is not etymological, cp. IA מוזנא mawznā (B3 8:26).

e. A non-etymological word-initial ʾaleph + vowel (prothetic ʾaleph) is added to a few words to resolve a consonant cluster, e.g., אִשְׁתִּיו ʾištīw < *štīw < *šatīw "they drank" (Dan 5:3–4); אֶדְרָע ʾɛdrɔ̄ʿ < drɔ̄ʿ "arm" (Ez 4:23), cp. דְּרָעֹוהִי dərɔ̄ʿōhī "its arms" (Dan 2:32). This is not a productive or common process.

Changes Involving *h*

§50. In general, *h* was not prone to elide in any position in Biblical Aramaic and related dialects.

a. The one exception is in the C-stem, where the derivational preformative ה *h* often elides after inflectional prefixes in the prefix conjugations and the participle (§232): *yəhaqṭil > yaqṭil*. By analogy, the *h* also is omitted in some suffix conjugation forms, being replaced by א *ʾaleph*.

b. Similarly, the usual *h* of the derivational preformative הת *hit-* of the T-stems (§§237ff.) is occasionally replaced by את *ʾit-* or *ʾet-* in the suffix conjugation. Etymologically, the form with א is diachronically prior to the form with ה, which originated from analogy to the preformative *ha-* of the C stem, with perhaps added influence from the Hebrew Hithpaʿel, corresponding to the Aramaic tD stem. In the prefix conjugation and participial forms, the *h* was never present, and its absence is therefore not due to elision.

Change of Word-Final **m* to *n*

§51. In the 3mp/2mp pronominal suffixes in BA (§128g), earlier ם *m* in word-final position is replaced by ן *n*, e.g., לְכֹם *ləkom* "to you" (Ez 5:3), cp. לְכוֹן *ləkon* "to you" (Dan 3:4); לְהֹום *ləhom* "to them" (Jer 10:11), cp. לְהֹון *ləhon* "to them" (Dan 2:35). This is not the result of a phonetic process, but is rather due to analogy, as the final plural *n* of the absolute plural nouns ־ִין/־ִֹין *-īn/-ɔ̄n* (§§89–90) and the prefix conjugation plural verbs ־וּן/־ֹון *-ūn/-ɔ̄n* (§220) spread to all the plural forms.

Note that in the Qumran texts of Daniel, the older ם is sometimes preserved, e.g., מנהם (4Q112 3 ii–6:11), MT מִנְּהֹון "of them" (Dan 2:42).

Changes Involving *w* and *y*

§52. The glides *w* and *y* are sometimes called "semivowels," and resemble vowels in their articulation. In some environments they become vowels, or vowels articulated in the same part of the mouth become consonantal *w* ו or *y* י.

a. **uw > ū*. Consonantal *w* when preceded by *u* becomes vocalic *ū*, as in הוּסְפַת *hūsəpat < *huwsəpat* "was added" (Dan 4:33).

b. **ī + ū > īw*. Final long *ū* added to a verbal base ending in *ī* in III-*y* verbs (§§257b, 263b, 265, 266, etc.) becomes consonantal *waw*, e.g., שַׁנִּיו *šannīw < *šannī + ū* (Dan 3:28).

c. **wə > ū*. The proclitic conjunction ו *wə*, when joined to a host word (1) beginning with any bilabial consonant ב מ פ, becomes וּ *ū*, e.g., וּבַדַּרוּ *ūbaddarū < wə + baddarū* (Dan 4:11); וּמִן *ūmin < wə + min*; וּפַרְסִין *ūparsīn < wə + parsīn* (Dan 5:25); and so on; (2) beginning with a consonant vocalized with *shewa* becomes וּ *ū*, e.g., וּרְבוּתָא *ūrḇūṯā* < *wə + *rəḇūṯā*; וּקְצַף *ūqṣap* < *wə* + *qəṣap*; etc. The *shewa* of the host word reduces to zero (medium *shewa*, §74c).

d. *yə* > *ī*. Word-initial יְ *yə* becomes vocalic *ī* when וְ or a proclitic preposition בְּ כְּ לְ (§176c) is added, e.g., בִּידֵהּ *bīḏeh* < *bə* + *yəḏeh*; וְיִקָּר *wīqār* < *wə* + *yəqār*; לִיהוּד *līhūḏ* < *lə* + *yəhūḏ*; and the like.

Metathesis

§53. In the tG and tD stems, the *t* of the derivational prefix undergoes metathesis (switches places) with a first root letter that is a sibilant (§34d). Under certain conditions the *t* may undergo partial assimilation as well (§44b). [§78, Rule 10]

Gemination and Nasalization

§54. *Gemination* is the doubling or prolonged articulation of a consonant. It cannot occur word-initially (except in special circumstances, §28c) or word-finally. It is indicated in transcription by writing the consonant twice.

a. Gemination may be *primary* (part of the inherent structure of the word form) or *secondary* (due to assimilation [§42] or other phonetic processes). In the Tiberian Masoretic text, gemination is indicated by *dagesh forte* (§28).

b. Occasionally, instead of secondary gemination occurs *nasalization*; graphically this is the writing of נ *n* before a consonant instead of the gemination of that consonant, e.g., מַנְדַּע *mandaʿ* "knowledge" (Dan 5:12) instead of *maddaʿ. It is first found in IA and continues to appear in BA and QA. It is disputed whether in the post-IA dialects it is anything more than a historical spelling, since it is not consistently written.

Spirantization (Fricativization)

§55. The non-emphatic stops ת פ כ ד ג ב / *b g d k p t* undergo spirantization (become fricatives in manner of articulation) after vowels, including reduced vowels (*shewa* and the *ḥateph* vowels, §74 and §24) and medium *shewa* (a reduced vowel that has become zero, §74c). This is a species of partial assimilation, since a spirant, like a vowel, is articulated with a continuation of the airstream, instead of stopping it altogether.

a. Spirantization also can occur across word boundaries, when the words in question are joined by conjunctive Masoretic accents (§31) or by *maqqeph* (§30), e.g., compare חַכִּימֵי בָבֶל *ḥakkīmē ḇāḇel* (Dan 2:12, with conjunctive accent on the first word) and חַכִּימֵי בָּבֶל *ḥakkīmē bāḇel* (Dan 2:14, with disjunctive accent on the first word).

b. Two exceptions to the rule of spirantization occur: in the final letter *t* of הִשְׁתְּכַחַתְּ *hištəkáhat* "you have been found" (Dan 5:27; §239d) and in the *t* of בָּתֵּיכוֹן *bōtēkōn*, "your houses" (Dan 2:5), the plural of the word בַּי "house." In these cases, the *dagesh* does not indicate gemination.

c. The dating of the process of spirantization is unclear, since the purely consonantal texts of the ancient period (IA and QA) do not register pronunciation variants of this type (see §17). Since spirantization is a feature of all the later Aramaic dialects for which we have evidence of pronunciation, it may have begun early, when the dialects were more unified; or it may have spread throughout all the dialects through a dialect continuum at a later time.

> See Muchiki (1994) (no spirantization in IA); Beyer (1984: 126–128) (spirantization began in the 1st century BCE); Steiner (2007) (spirantization began with different phonemes in different places and spread at a variable rate).

HISTORICAL CHANGES AFFECTING VOWELS
Stress

§56. Each word has one stressed syllable, that is, one given greater vocal prominence relative to the others. Stress or its absence has effects on vowel quality and quantity.

a. In the ancestor dialect of Aramaic, stress was automatic and placed on the *last pre-consonantal vowel*. If a word ended in a consonant, then the stress was on the last syllable; if it ended in a vowel, then the stress was penultimate (on the next-to-last syllable).

b. After the complete loss of final short vowels (§59), words originally ending in a short vowel with penultimate stress ended in a consonant, with final stress, e.g., *$^{\varsigma}$álamu > $^{\varsigma}$alám* "eternity, long time." In general, this final stress remains as the most common stress pattern.

c. Words originally ending in a single consonant, with final stress, continued to have final stress, e.g., *qaṭalát* (3fs suffix conjugation); *millát* (fs construct), etc.

d. Words originally ending in a long vowel, with penultimate stress, continued to have penultimate stress, e.g.:

Suffix conjugation verbal forms (§217): 2ms, e.g., חֲזַיְתָה *ḥăzáytɔ* "you saw" (Dan 2:41); 3mp, e.g., סְלִקוּ *səlíqū* "they went up" (Dan 2:29); 3fp, e.g., נְפָקָה *nəpáqɔ* "they came out" (Dan 5:5 Qere); 1cp, e.g., שְׁלַחְנָא *šəláḥnɔ* "we sent" (Ez 4:14).

Jussive verbal forms (§222): 3mp, e.g., יֵאבַדוּ *yēbádū* "let them perish" (Jer 10:11).

Imperative verbal forms (§222): fs, e.g., אֲכֻלִי *ʾăkúlī* "eat!" (Dan 7:5); mp, e.g., שְׁבֻקוּ *šəbúqū* "leave!" (Dan 4:12).

Certain pronominal suffixes (§127ff.), e.g., 3ms on 1st decl. plural noun עַבְדוֹהִי *$^{\varsigma}$abdóhī* "his servants" (Dan 2:7); 1cs, e.g., הוֹדַעְתַּנִי *hōda$^{\varsigma}$táni* "you told me" (Dan 2:23); 1cp, e.g., אֱלָהַנָא *ʾɛ̄lɔhánɔ* "our god" (Dan 3:17); and 1cp pronoun: אֲנַחְנָא.

The adverbial ending -ɔ (§344), e.g., כֹּלָּא *kóllɔ*; עֵלָּא *$^{\varsigma}$éllɔ* "above" (Dan 6:3).

Final unstressed long vowels in IA are sometimes *not* indicated in the orthography, e.g., אנחן (= אַנַֿחְנָא), עבדוה (= עָבְדֹֿהִי), אספרן (= אָסְפַּֿרְנָא).

e. Many words not originally ending in a long vowel, but which added final long vowels in a later period, default to the common final syllable stress pattern; therefore the marker of the determined state *-ꜣ (default spelling אָ◌, §85) is always stressed, as is the final 2nd decl. singular absolute marker *-ꜣ (default spelling, ◌ָה, §90), which evolved from original *-*át*.

A number of words ending in long vowels originating in contracted triphthongs also have final stress (§58).

f. Words ending in a consonant cluster (two consonants together) after the loss of final short vowels eventually generated a new (anaptyctic) vowel separating the two final consonants (§60). In Biblical Aramaic, in such cases, the stress sometimes remained on the penultimate, original, short vowel (e.g., אֶבֶן *ʾében* < **ʾabn* < **ʾábnu* "stone") but more commonly shifted to the separating vowel, e.g., כְּסַף *kəsáp* < **kásap* < **kásp* < **káspu* "silver") in the final syllable (§101).

For more on stress shift, see §60b below.

Syllables

§57. Syllable type plays an important role in determining whether and how vowels change. Biblical Aramaic syllables are, as a rule, of two types: Consonant–Vowel (CV), called *open*, or Consonant–Vowel–Consonant (CVC), called *closed*.

a. There are a few cases in which two final consonants (CVCC) are allowed in word-final position: the 2ms suffix conjugation (§212) inflectional suffix, e.g., עֲבַדְתְּ *ʿábadt* "you have done" (Dan 4:32); the 2ms pronoun (§124) אַנְתְּ *ʾant* (Qere); the Persian personal name אַרְתַּחְשַׁשְׂתְּא *ʾartaḥšaśt*, "Artaxerxes."

b. In this grammar, a consonant followed by vocal *shewa* (§74a) is considered an open syllable by itself, although there is evidence that the Masoretes considered such a consonant to be part of the following syllable (Yeivin 1980: 275–276).

c. When combined with stress, four syllable types emerge: CV (unstressed open), CV́ (stressed open), CVC (unstressed closed), and CV́C (stressed closed).

d. Short vowels in unstressed open syllables reduce to vocal *shewa* (§78, Rule 1, e.g., **qatál* > *qətal* קְטַל "he killed."

If the syllable begins with a guttural, the vowel reduces to compound *shewa* [§75c; §78, Rule 4b], e.g., **ʾamar* > *ʾămar* אֲמַר "he said."

e. Consecutive unstressed open syllables with short vowels do not reduce as in §57d. Instead, the second short vowel reduces to zero (the medium *shewa*, §74c) and the vowel in the first syllable is not reduced, although it may change quality, e.g., *malakín > malkín* מַלְכִין "kings," *baśaró > biśró* בִּשְׂרָא "flesh." In other words, the sequence CV_1CV_2 simplifies to CV_1C (§78, Rule 2). This process is sometimes called syncopation.

This rule is modified when the second consonant is a guttural; the second vowel reduces to compound *shewa*, not zero, e.g., *dahabó > dahăbó* דַּהֲבָא "gold."

f. There is a tendency for the vowel in CVC syllables (unstressed closed) to be short, although there are exceptions, e.g., the second syllable in מְדִינְתָּא *mədīntó* "the province" (Ez 5:8).

g. Except for the conjunction וְ, no syllables begin with a vowel (§52c).

Simplification of Triphthongs

§58. A *triphthong* denotes the occurrence of intervocalic *y* in the formation of words or their inflection. Word-final and some word-internal triphthongs simplified (contracted) to monophthongs (single sounds) or diphthongs (double sounds) early on in the development of Aramaic. These changes affect mainly the weak roots of the III-*y* class (§§255ff.) and a few nominal forms.

a. **aya > ā*, as in **banáya > baná* "he built" (3ms suffix conjugation; BA בְּנָא); **banayát > banát* "she built" (3fs suffix conjugation; BA בְּנָת).

b. **ayū > aw* (final), as in **banáyū > banáw* "they built" (3mp suffix conjugation; BA בְּנוֹ), followed by contraction of *aw* to *ō* (§72);

c. **iyu > ē* (final), as in **yibníyu > yibné* "he will build" (3ms prefix conjugation; BA יִבְנֵא); **bāníyu > bāné*, "(one who) builds" (ms participle; BA בָּנֵה); **θamāníyu > tamāné*, "eight" (1st decl.; cf. Syriac ܬܡܢܐ).

d. **iyī > ayi*, as in **bāniyín > bānáyin* "(ones who) build" (mp participle, BA בָּנַיִן); **tibniyín > tibnáyin* "you will build" (2fs prefix conjugation); **tibníyī > tibnáy* "you must build" (2fs jussive).

e. **iyū > aw*, as in **yibniyúna > yibnáwn* "they should build" (3mp prefix conjugation; BA יִבְנוֹן, with contraction *aw* to *ō*). This change was probably not phonological but rather a product of analogy to §58b above, resulting in the uniform endings *-aw(n) > -ō(n)* for the mp endings of the III-*y* finite verbs (§256c).

f. **iya* did not contract, but, when final, underwent the loss of final short vowels (see below, §59) to be realized as *ī*, as in **šatíya > šatí* "he drank" (3ms suffix conjugation, BA אִשְׁתִּי); also the 1cs pronominal suffix, e.g., **baytíya > baytí* "my house" (BA בֵּיתִי). The stress remained on the reflex of the original vowel.

g. Simplification of triphthongs is a feature of North-West Semitic in general, although the outcomes are different in the various dialects.

Loss of Final Short Vowels

§59. Also quite early, although later than triphthong simplification, was the loss of final short vowels. This had far-reaching effects on the phonological development of Aramaic, leading to a change in the overall default placement of word stress (§56), the generating of separating vowels for words ending in a consonant cluster (§60), the disappearance of the morphological case system on nouns, and a partial merger of indicative and jussive forms in the prefix conjugation (§§220, 222).

The loss of final short vowels is a feature of all Aramaic dialects and, indeed, of all North-West Semitic in the first millennium BCE.

Separating Vowels in a Consonant Cluster

§60. A consonant cluster is a sequence of two consonants not separated by a vowel. In final position they must ordinarily be eliminated as follows:

a. Words that ended in a consonant cluster after the loss of final short vowels (§59) added a short separating (anaptyctic) vowel to break up the cluster (§56f). The outcome of this process was not uniform, however, since some words retained stress on the original vowel and others shifted the stress to the added anaptyctic vowel. (See also §§101ff.)

b. The same lack of uniformity is visible in the anaptyctic vowels in verbal forms:

   Stress shift. Addition of a separating vowel with stress-shift, e.g., 1cs suffix conjugation אֲמְרֵת *ʾamrét* < **ʾamárit* < **ʾamárt* "I said" (Dan 4:5).

   No stress shift. Addition of a separating vowel without stress-shift, e.g., 1cs suffix conjugation הֲקֵימֶת *hăqémɛt* < **haqímt* "I raised up" (Dan 3:14); 2ms suffix conjugation הִשְׁתְּכַחַתְּ *hištəkáḥat* < **hištakáḥt* < **hištakáḥtā* "you were found" (Dan 5:27).

   No separating vowel. No addition of separating vowel, with consonant cluster left in place, e.g., 2ms suffix conjugation יְהַבְתְּ *yəhábt* < **yahábtā* "you gave" (Dan 2:23) (§57a).

c. It is probable that anaptyxis (addition of the separating vowel) was not fully operative in IA, based on transcriptions of Aramaic names into Akkadian and Greek. Nevertheless, such forms as 1cs suffix conjugation מיתת *mítit* "(if) I die" (B3 1:14) or 1cs suffix conjugation עשתת *ʿašátit* "I thought" (B3 6:3) suggest that it had taken place in the 1cs inflectional suffix (§217b). It appears to be at least partially operational by the time of the BA and QA consonantal texts, e.g., QA attests forms such as קשוט < **qušṭ* "truth," with the separating vowel indicated by the *mater* ו (Tiberian pointing קְשֹׁט *qəšóṭ* (§26 and §101)).

3

VOWEL INVENTORY OF BIBLICAL ARAMAIC

Vowels in BA can be either long (marked with a macron, e.g., *ā*) or short (unmarked). These include the original six vowels (*a i u ā ī ū*) of the ancestor language, as well as other vowels that developed from them. The descendant vowels are called *reflexes* of the original six.

Short Vowels

§61. a. Short vowels belong to one of three classes: the *a*-class (reflexes of original short *a), *i*-class (reflexes of *i), and *u*-class (reflexes of *u).

b. In BA, short vowels are normally written with vowel points only, although sometimes they will be written *plene* (§27).

c. They can occur in any syllable type (§57) except for open unstressed syllables. If a short vowel is placed by inflection or word formation in an open unstressed syllable, it reduces to vocal *shewa ə* (§78, Rule 1).

d. Short vowels are not found in word-final position (§59).

§62. a. Short *a* is indicated by the vowel sign ◌ַ(*pataḥ*). It can occur unchanged in open stressed syllables, e.g., עֲבַדוּ *ʿăbádū* "they made" (Jer 10:11); closed stressed syllables, e.g., כְּתַב *kətáb* "he wrote" (Dan 6:26); closed unstressed syllables, e.g., מַלְכָּא *malkɔ́* "king" (Dan 2:4).

b. Short *a* reduces to vocal *shewa* ◌ְ *ə* in open unstressed syllables, e.g., עָלְמָא *ʿɔləmɔ́* < **ʿɔ-la-mɔ́* (§78, Rule 1).

c. If the open unstressed syllable begins with a guttural (§34c), the short *a* reduces to compound *shewa* (§24 and §78, Rule 4b) ◌ֲ *ă*, *ḥateph pataḥ*, as in עֲבַדוּ *ʿăbádū* < *ʿabádū.

d. The vowel ◌ַ *a* can occur in an apparently open unstressed syllable before a "virtually doubled" guttural consonant, which does not graphically mark doubling (see §77b).

e. There is a tendency for short *a to become short *i* or sometimes *ε* in unstressed closed syllables when followed by a stressed syllable, usually when the first syllable is closed due to syncopation (§57e and §78, Rule 2) and not if it is etymologically closed; for example, בִּשְׂרָא *biśrɔ́* < **baśarɔ́* "flesh"; נִטְלֵת *niṭlét* < *naṭalít "I lifted" (Dan 4:31); צִדְקָה *ṣidqɔ́* < *ṣadaqā "righteousness" (Dan 4:24); נֶפְקַת *nεpqát* < *napaqát "it went forth" (Dan 2:13); etc. (In one instance, *a becomes short *u*, i.e., *gabarīn > *gubrīn* "men," e.g., גֻּבְרִין [Dan 3:8], due to the influence of the bilabial *b*; non-Tiberian texts have *gabrīn*.)[1]

f. The change in §62e is blocked when a guttural is in the first syllable, e.g., עַבְדֵת *ʿabdét* < *ʿabadít "I made" (Dan 3:15).

---

[1] This phenomenon is not to be confused with the so-called *qitqat* dissimilation in Tiberian Hebrew (Blake 1950), which is not generally operative in Aramaic. Such forms as מִשְׁכַּן <*maškan "tent"; מִשְׁכַּב < *maškab "bed," may be influenced by Hebrew pronunciation.

§63. a. Short *i* is indicated by ◌ִ *ḥireq*. It can occur in open stressed syllables, e.g., קְרִבוּ *qəríḇū* "they approached" (Dan 3:8); closed stressed syllables, e.g., דָּלִק *dɔ́líq* "burning" (Dan 7:9); closed unstressed syllables, e.g., מִלְכִּי *milkí* "my counsel" (Dan 4:24).

b. Short *i* reduces to vocal *shewa* ◌ְ *ə* in open unstressed syllables, e.g., זְבְנִין *zɔ̄ḇənín* < *zɔ̄binín* "buying" (Dan 2:8); מְאָה *məʾɔ̄́* < *miʾɔ̄́* "hundred" (Dan 6:2; §78, Rule 1).

c. Routinely, but not invariably, short *i* lowers to *e*, indicated by ◌ֵ *ṣereh*, in *closed stressed syllables*, e.g., יְהֵב *yɔ̄héḇ* < *yɔ̄híb* "gives" (Dan 2:21); שְׁאֵלְנָא *šəʾélnɔ̄* < *šaʾílnā* "we asked" (Ez 5:9), or in *open stressed syllables*, e.g., הַדֵּקֶת *haddéqet* < *haddiqat* "it smashed" (Dan 2:34; §78, Rule 7).

When this closed stressed syllable is followed by *maqqeph* (§30), the stress is lost and the vowel can further lower to ◌ֶ *seghol*: יִפֶּל־לָךְ *yippel-lɔ́k* "it falls to you" (Ez 7:20) < *yippél* < *yippil*; מִתְעֲבֶד־בַּהּ *mitʿăḇed-báh* "built in it" (Ez 4:19) < *mitʿăḇéd* < *mitʿabid*.

d. If *e* ◌ֵ appears in an *open unstressed syllable*, it may be a loanword (§122), e.g., לְחֵנָתֵהּ "his concubines" (Dan 5:2) < Akk. *laḥḥinu*; גְּזֵרַת *gəzerat* "decree" < Hebrew (Dan 4:14); or it may be a defectively (§27) written long *ē*: compare מֵמַר *mēmar* "saying" (Ez 5:11) and מֵאמַר (Dan 2:9). However, בְּטֵלַת "ceased" (Ez 4:24) is a true anomaly, not a loanword, and is not compliant with Rule 1 (§78).

Note that among defective writings are those in which etymologically original א is no longer written (§§47–48), such as גֵּוָה *gēwɔ̄* (Dan 4:34) < גֵּאוָה < *gaʾwā* "pride" and probably רֵו *rēw* < רֵאו < *riʾw* "appearance" (Dan 3:25).

e. In a *closed unstressed syllable*, *i* sometimes lowers to ◌ֶ *ε* *seghol*, especially (but not exclusively) in the vicinity of gutturals (§34c): אֶשְׁתּוֹמַם *ʾeštōmam* < *ʾištōmam* "was dismayed" (Dan 4:16); חֶלְמָא *ḥelmɔ̄* < *ḥilmɔ̄* "the dream" (Dan 2:4); יַבֶּשְׁתָּא *yabbeštɔ̄* < *yabbištɔ̄* "earth" (Dan 2:10); הֲקֵימֶת *hăqémet* < *haqēmit* "I raised" (Dan 3:14); etc.

f. If short *i* occurs on a guttural beginning an *open unstressed syllable*, it reduces to ◌ֱ *ɛ̆* *ḥateph seghol*, e.g., אֱלָהּ *ʾɛ̆lɔ̄h* < *ʾilāh* "god" (§24, §78, Rule 4b). Short *i* can also reduce to ◌ֲ *ă* *ḥateph patah*: e.g., כַּהֲנָא *kɔhănɔ̄* < *kɔ̄hinɔ̄* "priest" (Ez 7:12).

g. Rarely, short *i* reduces to *ɛ̆* (*ḥateph segol*) with a non-guttural letter: מְמַלֱּלָה *məmallɛ̆lɔ̄* < *məmallilɔ̄* "speaking" (Dan 7:11).

§64. a. Short *u* is indicated by ◌ֻ *qibbus*, which can occur in open stressed syllables, e.g., שְׁבֻקוּ *šəḇúqū* "leave" (Dan 4:12); closed stressed syllables, e.g., יִסְגֻּד *yisgúd* "shall bow down" (Dan 3:6); closed unstressed syllables, e.g., כֻּתְלַיָּא *kutlayyɔ̄* "walls" (Ez 5:8), etc.

b. It reduces to vocal *shewa* in open unstressed syllables, e.g., שְׁמֵהּ *šəméh* < *šumeh* "his name" (Dan 2:20). [§78, Rule 1]

c. Often short *u* lowers to ◌ָ *ɔ* (without macron) *qames hatuph* (§67a) in closed unstressed syllables only: חָכְמָה *ḥɔkmɔ̄* < *ḥukmɔ̄* "wisdom"; כָּרְסֵא *kɔrsē* < *kursē* "throne."

Table 6: *Short vowel chart*

	Position in oral cavity		
Jaw/tongue position	Front	Central	Back
High	i		u
Middle high	e		o
Middle		ə	
Middle low	ɛ ɛ̃		ɔ ɔ̃
Low		a ã	

d. Sometimes short *u* lowers to ◌ֹ *o*, ḥolem in *closed stressed syllables*, e.g., גֻּדּוּ *góddū* < **guddū* "cut down" (Dan 4:11); כֹּלָּא *kóllɔ* < **kullɔ* "all" [§78, Rule 7]; or rarely in closed unstressed syllables, e.g., אׇרְחָתֵהּ *ʾorḥɔ̱téh* < **ʾurḥɔ̱téh* "his ways" (Dan 4:34).

e. If *o / ḥolem* appears in an open unstressed syllable, it is in fact a defectively written (§27) long *ō* וֹ (§71), e.g., רַעְיֹנֹהִי "his thoughts" (Dan 4:16) for רַעְיוֹנֹהִי *raʿyōnóhī*.

f. If short *u* occurs on a guttural at the onset of an open unstressed syllable, instead of reducing to vocal *shewa*, it lowers and reduces to ◌ֳ *ɔ̆* (with breve), ḥateph qameṣ (§24), e.g., הׇקִימַת *hŏqīmát* < *huqīmat* "was raised up" (Dan 7:4); קֳדָם *qɔ̆dɔ́m* < **qudɔ́m* "before" [§78, Rule 4b]

g. Uniquely, ק *qoph* sometimes preserves unreduced short *ɔ* in open unstressed syllables: קֳדָמַי *qɔ̆dɔ̄máy* "before me" (Dan 5:15). Note also the *mater lectionis* in QA קודם (1QapGen 21:3), קושט (1QapGen 2:7), and the like, which may indicate an unreduced short **u* (§26b).

h. In the derivation (§98) of nouns and pronouns, patterns with consecutive **u*-class vowels (including long *ū* and *ō*) tend to change to *i-u(ū/ō)* patterns by dissimilation; e.g., the IA 3mp pronoun המו *hummú* (§125) becomes הִמּוֹ(ן) *himmō(n)* in BA (§124); note also the **quṭlōn* < **quṭlān* noun pattern changing to *qiṭlōn* (see examples in §115; Fassberg 2009: 332).

§65. Short vowels, as can be seen (Table 6), change quality mainly by lowering within the same general position, i.e., **i* > *e* > *ɛ* or **u* > *o* > *ɔ*.

Long Vowels

§66. Long vowels are unchangeable, that is, they do not change their quality or quantity (i.e., their length) based on stress placement or syllable type. They are conventionally indicated in transcription by a macron. There are five long vowels in Biblical Aramaic: *ɔ̄, ē, ī, ō, ū*.

Long vowels are normally associated in the orthography with *matres lectionis*, an unpronounced consonant, either ׳ *yod* for *ī ē*, ו *waw* for *ō ū*, א *ʾaleph* or ה *heh* for *ɔ̄ ē* in word-final position (see on *matres lectionis*, §25).

§67. a. The vowel ◌ֳ *ɔ̄*, *qameṣ*, is the reflex of original long **ā* in the parent dialect of Biblical Aramaic. Within a word it is usually unaccompanied by a *mater*, while at the end of words it usually has ה or א as a *mater*.

The Tiberian *qameṣ* reflects a change in quality from the original long *ā* of which it is a reflex. It signifies a mid-back vowel with rounding, somewhat raised from the original *ā*, a low vowel (front and back). In this grammar the transcription *ɔ̄* will be used only with BA transcriptions; reconstructions of IA or QA vocalizations will use *ā* for the same phoneme.

The short *qameṣ ḥatuph*, which uses the same vowel sign, was qualitatively the same vowel (same articulation), but short (less prolonged) and a reflex of short **u*, not long **ā* (§64c). Conventionally, the long *qameṣ* is pronounced by moderns as "ah" or "aw" (like *ought*), while the short *qameṣ ḥatuph* is pronounced like the "o" of *boat*. In the original Tiberian pronunciation, they evidently sounded alike except for length.

b. Long *ɔ̄* occurs in any syllable type: open stressed (word-final): אַרְעָא *ʾarʿɔ̄* "earth"; open unstressed: רָזָה *rɔ̄zɔ̄* "secret"; עָלְמָא *ʿɔ̄ləmɔ̄* "eternity, long time"; closed stressed: אִילָן *ʾīlɔ̄n* "tree"; closed unstressed (rare): מָרָדְתָּא *mɔ̄rɔ̄dtɔ̄* "rebellious" (Ez 4:12, second syllable).

c. Occasionally the 2ms suffix conjugation inflectional suffix -*tɔ̄* is written without a *mater* in final position, e.g., רְשַׁמְתָּ *rəšámtɔ̄* "you signed" (Dan 6:13).

d. In the word מָאן *mɔ̄n* "vessel," *ɔ̄* is written with an internal א (probably a historical remnant of original form **maʾn*); for other instances of non-etymological internal א, see §26a.

e. Note that the "Canaanite shift," that is, the merger of **ā* with long *ō* typical of the Canaanite languages, did not take place in Aramaic (although see §71b).

§68. a. The vowel ◌ִי *ī*, *ḥireq + yod*, the unchanged reflex of ancestral *ī*, can occur in any syllable type: open stressed: גְּלִי *gălī* "was revealed" (Dan 2:19); מְרִיטוּ *mərī́ṭū* "were plucked off" (Dan 7:4); open unstressed: אִילָן *ʾīlɔ̄n* "tree"; closed stressed: עִירִין *ʿīrín* "watchers"; closed unstressed (rare): מְדִינְתָּא *mədīntɔ̄* "province" (Ez 5:8).

b. Occasionally the long vowel will be written without its unpronounced consonantal *mater* (defectively, §27), e.g., שַׁלִּטִן *šallīṭín* "rules" (Dan 4:23), compare שַׁלִּיטִין (Ez 4:20).

§69. a. Long *ū* ו is indicated by *šureq*, a *waw* with a point inside it. It is the unchanged reflex of original **ū* and can appear in all syllable types: open stressed: וְזָכוּ *zɔ̄kǘ* "innocence" (Dan 6:23); אֲבוּהִי *ʾăbǘhī* "his father"; open unstressed: שְׁבֻקוּ *šəbúqū* "leave" (Dan 4:12); גָּלוּתָא *gɔ̄lūtɔ̄* "the exile" (Dan 2:25); closed stressed: תֵּאמְרוּן *tēmərǘn* "you shall say" (Jer 10:11); אֲבוּךְ *ʾăbúk* "your father" (Dan 5:11); closed unstressed (rare): גְּבוּרְתָּא *gəbūrtɔ̄* "power" (Dan 2:20, variant; note also the frequent word initial ו conjunction, §52c).

b. Sometimes $\bar{u}$ is written defectively (§27) within a word with ◌ֻ *qibbuṣ* instead of ו *šureq*, e.g., לְבֻשֵׁיהוֹן *ləbūšēhōn* "their clothes" (Dan 3:21) for לְבוּשֵׁיהוֹן, and the like.

§70. a. Long $\bar{e}$ is indicated by ◌ֵי, *ṣere* + *yod* as *mater*. Historically, $\bar{e}$ is usually the reflex of original diphthong (§73) **ay*, which has contracted in many positions. This reflex can occur in the following syllabic types: open stressed (often word-final): מָאנֵי *mōnḗ* "vessels" (Dan 5:2); open unstressed: חֵיוָה *ḥēwȯ́* < **haywā* "beasts" (Dan 4:13); closed stressed: הֲוֵית *hăwḗt* < **hawayt* "I was" (Dan 4:1); closed unstressed, before *maqqeph* (§30), e.g., בֵּית־אֱלָהָא *bēt-ʾĕlȯhȯ́* "the house of God" (Ez 4:24).

b. Long $\bar{e}$ may also be the reflex of original **aʾ* or **iʾ* (short a/i followed by syllable-closing *ʾaleph*, §47). In such cases, the original *ʾaleph* may remain as a historical remnant, as in, e.g., רֵאשׁ *rēš* < **riʾš* or **raʾš* "head"; יֵאמַר *yēmar* < **yiʾmar* "he will say"; מָרֵא *mȯrḗ* < **māriʾ* "lord," etc.

c. But often the elided *ʾaleph* is no longer written: מֵמַר *mēmar* "saying" (Ez 5:11), cp. מֵאמַר (Dan 2:9) < **miʾmar*; יבדון *yēbədūn* "they will perish" (4Q202 1 iv 10), cp. יאבדון (4Q204 1 v 2); גֵּוֶה *gēwā* "pride" (Dan 4:34), < גֵּאוָה < **gaʾwā*; etc. (§47).

d. In Qumran Aramaic, a regular *mater* may be used in place of or in addition to the historical *ʾaleph*, e.g., ראיש "head" (1QapGen 14:9) for רֵאשׁ, מרה "lord" (1QapGen 20:13) for מָרֵא.

e. In final position, long $\bar{e}$ can be the reflex of an original triphthong that has contracted (§58c). In such cases, the *mater* is ה or א: יִמְטֵא *yimṭē* "it reached" (Dan 4:8); תִּתְבְּנֵא *titbənē* "it will be rebuilt" (Ez 4:21); שְׁלֵה *šəlē* "tranquil" (Dan 4:1); לֶהֱוֵה *lehĕwē* "he/it will be"; כָּרְסֵא *kᵊrsē* "throne"; and so on. (For the special case of יִתְקְרֵי *yitqərē* [Dan 5:12], see §259b.)

§71. a. Long $\bar{o}$ is indicated typically by וֹ, *ḥolem-waw*. This is most often the reflex of the historical diphthong **aw*, which has contracted to $\bar{o}$ in all syllabic positions (§72): open stressed: עֲלוֹהִי *ʿălȯ́hī* < **ʿaláwhī* "upon him"; open unstressed: הוֹדַע *hōdáʿ* < **hawdiʿ* "he told"; closed stressed: יוֹם *yȯm* < **yawm* "day" (Ez 6:9); closed unstressed: מוזניא *mȯznayyā* < **mawznayyā* "scales" (4Q318 7:2, cf. §49d).

b. Long $\bar{o}$ in some cases is found in loanwords from Hebrew or other dialects wherein original long **ā* become long $\bar{o}$, e.g., עֶלְיוֹנִין *ʿelyōnín* "Most High" (Dan 7:18); נִיחוֹחִין *nīḥōḥín* (Ez 6:10); מְדוֹרֵה *mədȯrḗh* (Dan 5:21); אנושא *ʾĕnȯšȯ́* (Dan 4:13, Ketiv). For the use of the derivational suffix וֹן־, see §115.

c. Long $\bar{o}$ also in some cases appears to be (1) the reflex of original short **u*, e.g., in the 3mp suffix הוֹן־ *-hōn* < **hum*; 2mp suffix כוֹן־ *-kōn* < **kum*; also חֲזֵיתוֹן "you saw" (Dan 2:8) < **hazaytun* (a product of analogy); or (2) the lengthening of a short **u* anaptyctic vowel (§60): נְהוֹרָא *nəhȯrȯ́* < **nuhrā* "light" (Dan 2:22 Qere); חֲשׁוֹכָא *ḥăšȯkȯ́* < **huškā* "darkness" (Dan 2:22).

d. Sometimes וֹ appears as a *plene* spelling (§27) for simple (short) *ḥolem*, e.g., גּוֹב "pit" (Dan 6:13), cp. גֹּב (Dan 6:8) < **gub(b)*; the contrary case, simple *ḥolem* defectively for long $\bar{o}$, also appears: מְדֹרָךְ *mədȯrȯ́k* "your dwelling" (Dan 4:22); שִׁלְטֹנֵי *šilṭōnē* "rulers" (Dan 3:3); נִיחֹחִין "fragrance" (Dan 2:46), cp. נִיחוֹחִין *nīḥōḥín* (Ez 6:10); רַעְיֹנֹהִי *raʿyōnȯ́hī* "his thoughts" (Dan 4:16) (§64e).

Diphthongs

The original diphthongs *aw and *ay – that is, short *a followed by a bilabial or palatal glide – have various reflexes in Biblical Aramaic.

§72. *aw. Original *aw has contracted to long ō in all positions. The sequence aw does remain, however, when the glide w is geminated, e.g., כַּוִּין kawwín "windows" (Dan 6:11); צַוְּארֵהּ ṣawwəréh "his neck" (Dan 5:7). When w is degeminated (undoubled), contraction does occur; cp. בְּגַוַּהּ bəgawwáh "within it" (Ez 4:15) and בְּגוֹא bəgṓ "within" (Dan 7:15) < *bəgaw < *bəgaww (§104).

§73. *ay. Original *ay has reflexes in ay (unchanged) and long ē (contracted) and sometimes in short or long a (in the Qere).

a. It remains uncontracted in the following cases:

When the glide y is geminated, as in the 1st decl. pl. det. ending ־ַיָּא -ayyā́; חַיִּין ḥayyín "life"; and even when it has been degeminated, e.g., חַי ḥay(y) "living" (Dan 4:31), and in the 1cs suffix on 1st decl. pl. endings, e.g., לֵאלָהָי lēlāhay(y) "to my gods" (Dan 3:14).

When stressed and followed by the anaptyctic vowel short i (§103), e.g., אֱדַיִן ʾĕdáyin < *ʾidayn "then"; קַיִט qáyiṭ < *qayṭ "summer" (Dan 2:35), and in the dual ending -ayin < *-ayn (§95), e.g., בִּידַיִן "by hands" (Dan 2:34).

Sometimes when the original *ay formed the last part of a closed syllable: בַּיְתֵהּ baytéh "his house" (Dan 2:17); הֲוַיְתָ hăwáytā "you were" (Dan 2:31).

In the existential particle אִיתַי ʾītáy (§380) without suffixes.

b. It contracts to long ē in the following cases:

When followed by an unvocalized consonant, e.g., בֵּית bēt < *bayt "house" (in construct; Dan 4:27); הֲוֵית hăwḗt < *hawayt "I was" (Dan 4:1); etc.

As the 1st decl. pl. cstr. ending (§89), e.g., חַכִּימֵי ḥakkīmḗ < *ḥakkīmay "wise men" (Dan 2:12).

Often as the last part of a closed syllable, e.g., חֵיוָה ḥēwṓ < *ḥaywā "beasts" (Dan 4:13); בֵּיתִי bētī < *baytī "my house" (Dan 4:1); חֲזֵיתוֹן ḥăzētṓn < *ḥazaytun "you saw" (Dan 2:8); זְעֵירָה zəˤērṓ < *zuˤayrā "little" (Dan 7:8); and so on.

c. Original *ay contracts to long ṓ or short a in certain cases, all of them found only in the Qere (§33):

*ay > ṓ before the 2ms pronominal suffix (§129f): Ketiv עליך *ˤaláyk(ā), Qere עֲלָךְ ˤălṓk "unto you" (Dan 3:12); Ketiv עבדיך *ˤabdáyk(ā), Qere עֲבְדָךְ ˤabdṓk "your servants" (Dan 2:4); Ketiv איתיך ʾītáyk(ā), Qere אִיתָךְ ʾītṓk "you are" (Dan 2:26), etc.

*ay > a before the 3fs pron. suffix (§129e): Ketiv עליה *ˤaláyh(ā), Qere עֲלַהּ ˤaláh "over it" (Dan 4:14); Ketiv גפיה *gappáyh(ā), Qere גַּפַּהּ gappáh "its wings" (Dan 7:4); Ketiv רגליה *ragláyh(ā), Qere רַגְלַהּ ragláh "its feet" (Dan 7:7); before the 1cp pron. suffix: Ketiv איתינא ʾītáynā, Qere אִיתַנָא ʾītánṓ "we are" (Dan 3:18); but also cp. עֲלַיְנָא ˤălḗnṓ "unto us" (Ez 4:12, 18) < *ˤaláynā.

Shewa

§74. The vowel sign *shewa* ֶ may indicate either a reduced, murmured vowel ə (vocal *shewa*) or the absence of a vowel (silent *shewa*). Generally, vocal *shewa* is the reflex of an original short vowel that has reduced.

a. *Vocal shewa. Shewa* is vocal when it occurs:

On the first letter of a word, e.g., בְּשַׂר *bəśar* "flesh."

On a geminated letter (i.e., with *dagesh forte*), e.g., שַׁבְּחֵת *šabbəḥet* "I praised" (Dan 4:31).

As the second of two consecutive *shewas* within a word, e.g., אַרְבְּעָה *ʾarbəʕɔ* "four."

(Usually) when preceded by a long vowel (§66), e.g., עָלְמָא *ʕɔləmɔ* "eternity, long time."

When written on the first of two consecutive selfsame consonants, e.g., עַמְמַיָּא *ʕaməmayyɔ* "peoples."

b. *Silent shewa.* In most cases, silent *shewa* marks the boundary of an unstressed closed syllable. *Shewa* is silent when:

The conditions for vocal *shewa* are not present.

It occurs on a non-geminate consonant preceded by an unstressed vowel (usually short) as in מַלְכָּא *malkɔ*; גֻּבְרַיָּא *gubrayyɔ*; שִׁבְעָה *šibʕɔ*; כָּרְסֵא *kɔrsē*; etc.

c. *Medium shewa.* In some cases, silent *shewa* is the reflex of an original short vowel that has reduced to zero instead of to vocal *shewa*. This "medium" *shewa* occurs when short vowel reduction (§78, Rule 1) would result in two consecutive vocal *shewas*, in which case the first vowel does not reduce and the second reduces to zero (silent *shewa*) (§57e; §78, Rule 2, syncopation). The presence of this medium *shewa* can sometimes be detected when a silent *shewa* is followed by spirantized בגדכפת (§55): מַלְכִין *malkīn* < *malakīn*; עַבְדֹוהִי *ʕabdṓhī* < *ʕabadṓhī*; etc.

Gutturals and Their Effect on Vowels

The pharyngeals ע and ח, the glottals א and ה, and sometimes the uvulars ר and ק are together known as the gutturals (§34c). They induce some phonological changes in vowels as follows:

§75. Gutturals may change the quality of a vowel:

a. *The change *i to a in stressed syllables.* Due to their rearward place of articulation, they can change the high vowel short *i* in a stressed syllable to the low vowel short *a*, especially when the guttural closes the syllable, regardless of etymology, e.g., הַצְלַח *haṣláḥ* < *haṣliḥ (Dan 6:29); אֲמַר *ʾəmár* < *ʾəmir (Dan 2:5); מְשַׁבַּח *məšabbaḥ* < *məšabbiḥ (Dan 4:34); יָדַע *yɔdaʕ* < *yɔdiʕ (Ez 7:25); הִשְׁתְּכַחַת *hištəkáḥat* < *hištakiḥat (Dan 6:5); etc. [§78, Rule 4a]

b. *The change* *i or *a *to* ε. Gutturals can change the high vowel short *i* in a closed syllable to the mid vowel ε, e.g., תֶּעְדֵּא *tɛʕdḗ* < **tiʕdē* "pass away" (Dan 6:9), לֶהֱוֵא *lɛhɛ̆wḗ* < *lihwē* "will be"; לְמֶעְבַּד *mɛʕbád* < **miʕbad* "to do" (Ez 4:22). Occasionally short *a* is also changed to ε, e.g., הֶחֱסִנוּ *hɛhɛ̆sínū* < *hahsínū* (Dan 7:22). [§78, Rule 4a]

c. Following a guttural, short vowels do not fully reduce in open unstressed syllables but are lowered and partially reduced to vowels indicated by *hateph* (compound) *shewas* (§24). [§78, Rule 4b]

d. The rule described in §75c also occurs twice following the velar ג: גְּלִי *gắlī* (Dan 2:19) and גֱּלִי *gḗlī* (Dan 2:30); and once preceding it: וּסֲגַר *ūsăḡár* (Dan 6:23).

e. Rarely, the unreduced vowel ◌ֶ *e* will occur instead of a *hateph* vowel, e.g., אֵזֵה *ʾezē* "heated" (Dan 3:22) instead of אֱזֵה* or אֲזֵה*. This may be due to the influence of Eastern dialects, where *hateph* vowels are not used (a Babylonian MS in Strack [1921: 32*] vocalizes as *ʾizē*).

§76. Gutturals may generate new vowels:

a. *Secondary opening.* When the gutturals ע ח ה close a syllable within a word, they often generate "echo" *hateph* vowels after them, without changing the quantity (length) of the vowel being echoed, although they may change its quality (timbre). This process is called *secondary opening*. [§78, Rule 5]

   With *a*-class (quality unchanged): אַחֲרִית *ʾahărīṯ* < **ʾahrīṯ* "end" (Dan 2:28); אֱלָהֲכוֹן *ʾɛ̆lɔhăkōn* <**ʾɛ̆lɔhkōn* "your god" (Dan 2:47); מַעֲבָדוֹהִי *maʕăḇɔdṓhī* < **maʕbɔdṓhī* "his deeds" (Dan 4:34); הֶחֱסִנוּ *hɛhɛ̆sínū* < **hɛhsínū* "they took possession" (Dan 7:22); etc.

   With *i*-class (opening with quality change, §75b): מֶחֱזֵא *mɛhɛ̆zḗ* < **mihzē* "to see" (Ez 4:14); תֶּהֱוֵה *tɛhɛ̆wḗ* < **tihwē* "shall be" (Dan 2:42); etc.

   With *u*-class (opening with quality change): אָחֳרָן *ʾɔhŏrɔ́n* < **ʾuhrɔn* "another", אָחֳרִי *ʾɔhŏrî* < **ʾuhrī* "another"; etc.

   The syllables thus affected are still considered closed for purposes of vowel assignment.

   Note that secondary opening does not always occur, e.g., רַעְנַן *raʕnɔ́n* (not רֲעֲנַן) "flourishing" (Dan 4:1); יַחְלְפוּן *yahləp̄ūn* "they will pass" (Dan 4:13); מְהַעְדֵּה *məhaʕdē* "removes" (Dan 2:21); מַהְלְכִין *mahləḵīn* "walking" (Dan 3:25); etc.

b. *Vowel assimilation.* When the proclitic particles וְ כְּ לְ בְּ (§176, §393) are added to words beginning with gutturals vocalized with *hateph shewas*, the particles are vocalized with the corresponding full short vowel ("vowel harmony"), e.g., אֲנָשׁ + וְ > וֶאֱנָשׁ (Dan 6:8); לְ + אֱלָהּ > לֶאֱלָהּ (Dan 2:19); כְּ + עֲמַר > כַּעֲמַר (Dan 7:9); וְ + אֲמַר > וַאֲמַר (Dan 6:25); בְּ + עֲשַׂב > בַּעֲשַׂב (Dan 4:12); לְ + הֲדָה > לַהֲדָה (Dan 3:2); לְ + חֲנֻכַּת > לַחֲנֻכַּת (Dan 3:2); בְּ + חֲשׁוֹכָא > בַּחֲשׁוֹכָא (Dan 2:22); לְ + קֱבֵל > לָקֳבֵל (Dan 3:3).

Here the "echo" operates regressively, as it were, affecting the vowel preceding the guttural instead of generating one after it.

When כְּ is added to לְקֳבֵל, the short ◌ֳ *o* moves to כָּ and the ל has zero *shewa*: כָּל־קֳבֵל *kɔl-qɔ̆bel* (e.g., Dan 3:7). The graphic separation of the proclitic elements is perhaps due to a scribal confusion with the word כֹּל *all*. In QA, these particles are not separated: כלקובל 4Q204 1 vi 13, 17.

c. *Pataḥ furtivum.* When the pharyngeals ע or ח occur in word-final position after the vowels *ū, ī, ē,* or *o,* a short *a* is added before the guttural (so-called *pataḥ furtivum*), e.g., רוּחַ *rūaḥ* < **rūḥ* (Dan 4:5); רֵיחַ *rēaḥ* < **rēḥ* (Dan 3:27); יֵשׁוּעַ *yēšūaʕ* < **yēšūʕ* (Ez 5:2); שְׁלִיחַ *šəlīaḥ* < **šəlīḥ* (Ez 7:14); יְדִיעַ *yədīaʕ* < **yədīʕ* (Ez 4:12); תְּרֹעַ *tēroaʕ* < **tēroʕ* < **tirruʕ* (Dan 2:40). Only in this case are two vowels allowed to occur contiguously.

§77. Gutturals deal with gemination in different ways.

a. The gutturals א ה ח ע ר do not indicate gemination (§54) by *dagesh*, and presumably were not in fact geminated, even when the word structure required it.

b. *Virtual doubling.* Nevertheless, the vowels preceding the simplified (degeminated) guttural often do not reduce, and act as if the consonant were still doubled, as in, e.g., יְבַהֲלוּךְ *yəbah(h)ălūk* "(let not) them terrify you" (Dan 5:10); יִמְחֵא *yəmaḥ(ḥ)ē* "one may strike" (Dan 4:32); יְבַעוֹן *yəbaʕ(ʔ)ōn* "they sought" (Dan 4:33); הֻעַל *huʕ(ʔ)al* "he was brought in" (Dan 5:13); etc. This is referred to as virtual doubling.

c. *Compensatory lengthening.* In some cases (and always with ר), the short vowel preceding the degeminated guttural may change both quality and quantity as a substitute for gemination, e.g., אִתְיָעַטוּ *ʔityɔ̄ʕátū* < **ityaʕʕátū* "they consulted together" (Dan 6:8); מִתְבָּהַל *mitbɔ̄hal* < **mitbahhal* "agitated" (Dan 5:9); מְשָׁרֵא *məšɔ̄rē* < **məšarrē* "solve" (Dan 5:12); בָּרָא *bɔ̄rɔ̄* < **barrɔ̄* "the field"; תְּרֹעַ *tēroaʕ* < **tirroaʕ* "it will smash" (Dan 2:40); etc. This is called compensatory lengthening.

d. Nasalization (§54b) may also substitute for gemination before a guttural, e.g., הַנְעֵל *hanʕel* < **haʕʕel* "he brought in" (Dan 2:25).

PHONOLOGICAL RULES SUMMARY

§78. The following list summarizes the most important phonological rules and processes necessary for understanding the structure and vocalization of Biblical Aramaic.

Rule 1: *Vowel Reduction.* Short vowels reduce in open unstressed syllables: CV > Cə. (§§57d, 61c. See also Rule 4b below.)

Rule 2: *Vowel Syncopation.*

    a. If two consecutive open unstressed syllables with short vowels would occur, the second vowel reduces to zero (medium *shewa*), and the first remains a full vowel: CVCV > CVC.

    b. If the second consonant is of the identical type as the preceding consonant, the reduction is to vocal *shewa*, not zero, e.g., עַמְמַיָּא *ʿaməmayyɔ̄* < **ʿamamayyā* "peoples" (Dan 3:4). [§§57e, 74c]

Rule 3: *Shewa.*

    a. Silent *shewa* cannot occur on the first syllable of a word.

    b. *Shewa* preceded by an unstressed short vowel is silent.

    c. The second of two consecutive *shewas* is always vocal. [§74]

Rule 4: *Gutturals.*

    a. The gutturals א ע ה ר change short $\circ$ *i* preceding them to $\circ$ *a* or $\circ$ *ɛ*.

    b. A short vowel in an unstressed open syllable beginning with a guttural will reduce to compound *shewa* (*ḥaṭeph shewa*) instead of vocal *shewa*. [§75]

Rule 5: *Secondary Opening.* Gutturals that would normally close a syllable with silent *shewa* often have compound *shewa* or a full vowel instead. [§76a]

Rule 6: *Spirantization.* The non-emphatic stops בגדכפת become spirantized after a vowel, vocal *shewa*, or medium *shewa*. [§55]

Rule 7: *Short Vowel Lowering.* Often (but not always) $\circ$ > $\circ$ (*i* > *e*) and $\circ$ > $\dot\circ$ (*u* > *o*) in stressed syllables (when not influenced by Rule 4a). Short *a* does not change in stressed syllables. [§§63c, 64d]

Rule 8: *Stress Assignment.*

    a. The default location of stress is on the final syllable.

    b. Penultimate stress is preserved in some forms with original final long vowels. [§56]

Rule 9: *Diphthong Contraction.*

    a. *aw* > *ō* (always).

    b. *ay* > *ē* (under certain conditions). [§§72–73]

Rule 10: *Metathesis.*

    a. In tG and tD verbs, the ת of the preformative metathesizes with initial root letters that are sibilants (ז ס צ שׁ).

    b. After the metathesis, the ת partially assimilates to ז and צ: תצ > צט and תז > זד. [§§44, 53]

Rule 11: *Assimilation* of *n* or *Nasalization.*

    a. *Nun* sometimes assimilates when no vowel separates it from a following consonant (unless the "no vowel" is the result of syncopation, Rule 2).

    b. Non-assimilation is more frequent, and there are many cases of nasalization of geminate consonants (generating non-etymological *n*). [§§42, 54b]

Rule 12: *Consonant Clusters*.

    a. Words originally ending in a consonant cluster normally add a separating (anaptyctic) vowel between the consonants (§60).

    b. If two clustered consonants are identical, they are simplified to a single consonant at the end of a word (degemination or undoubling, §104).

Vocalization and Transcription of Unpointed Texts

§79. Two approaches are possible when vocalizing the unpointed texts of IA and QA. One is to provide them with the vowels of Biblical Aramaic as we understand them from the Tiberian system. This approach is anachronistic, in that the Tiberian system postdated all of these dialects (including the original BA text) and was based on a pronunciation that in many details belonged to later forms of the language and not to the original dialect. Nevertheless, for heuristic purposes and for informal reading, adding Tiberian vowels is a valuable exercise for the student.

The second approach is to reconstruct the hypothetical pronunciation of the unpointed material based on our understanding of the original vocalic phonemes. In this case, too, certainty is not attainable, but it also has heuristic value for understanding the diachronic development of the language. This pays off in the comparative study of Aramaic and the Semitic languages in general. In the guided readings of this grammar (ch. 18), both approaches will be employed as appropriate.

The following observations address particular issues in the transcriptions of the unpointed texts, especially IA.

According to the limited data at our disposal, most of the phonological rules given in §78 were developments of later Aramaic.

Rule 1 (vowel reduction) was likely not operational in IA, and even in QA (and the "original" BA) was still in its beginning stages (Kaufman 1984). Therefore, reconstructed vocalization of IA will not show vowel reduction.

In QA, short *u* was resistant to reduction, although *i* and *a* may have commonly been reduced. Compare such forms as ישכונן *yiškunā́n* "they will dwell" (4Q542 1 ii 3), Tiberian rules יִשְׁכְּנֻן; יכולון *yikkulū́n* "they could" (1QapGen 20:19), Tiberian יְכֻלוּן; קודמיהון *qudā́mēhon* "before them" (1QapGen 19:25), Tiberian קֳדָמֵיהוֹן.

Rule 2 (syncopation) likewise cannot be assumed in our IA transcriptions.

Rule 3 (behavior of *shewa*) is not applicable in IA because of the likely absence of vowel reduction (Rule 1).

Rules 4 and 5 (gutturals) may have applied at the sub-phonemic level, but cannot be assumed in our IA transcriptions.

Rule 6 (spirantization), as noted (§55c), is impossible to detect in unpointed texts, although it is possible that the origins of the phenomenon were in the IA period. The IA transcriptions in this grammar will not indicate spirantization.

Rule 7 (short vowel change) is suggested by some ancient evidence (see §17); it is uncertain how widespread the phenomenon was. Except for the 3ms suffix -eh, short vowel change will not appear in our IA transcriptions.

Rule 8 (stress assignment) is applicable to the IA texts, where the stress generally falls on the same syllable types as in BA (§56). It is not clear whether some of the dialect-specific stress shifts (e.g., in the 1cs suffix conjugation, §56f) had taken place in IA.

Rule 9 (contraction of diphthongs) was probably not fully operative in IA; the only way to verify contraction would be to find cases of diphthongs spelled defectively (§27), that is, without *y* or *w*. These are sporadic (Muraoka & Porten 2003: 36–38) and uncommon. Such spellings are more common in QA, suggesting that diphthongs were contracted in that dialect.

Rules 10 and 11 are fully operational in IA and QA.

Rule 12 (anaptyxis), as noted (§60c), was certainly operative in some cases in IA but cannot be assumed to be universal.

It is almost certain that the consonantal mergers of the interdentals with the dentals (§36) were complete in the IA period, despite a lack of complete orthographic uniformity. Therefore, words containing etymological original *θ $\underline{\theta}$ $\eth$ will be transcribed with, respectively, *t* *ṭ* *d*, regardless of the consonantal orthography, which preserves some historical spellings.

CHAPTER 4

Nouns and Adjectives

Inflection and Derivation

§80. Word formation has two components: derivation and inflection. *Derivation* refers to the formation of the lexical base of nouns and verbs, and *inflection* refers to the addition of suffixes or prefixes to express gender, person, number and (in verbs) tense, aspect, and mood.

The relatively simpler system of nominal/adjectival inflections will be introduced, followed by a survey of the various and complex groups of nominal/adjectival derivations.

INFLECTIONAL SYSTEM OF NOUNS AND ADJECTIVES

§81. Nouns and adjectives have the same inflections for gender, number, and state and may be treated together. Although some derivational patterns tend to appear mainly with adjectives, there is no morphological difference in the inflection of nouns and adjectives. Adjectives have no inherent grammatical gender and assume the gender of the noun that they modify. For the syntax of the adjective, see §§145, 171ff.

The order of inflectional suffixes (endings) on the noun is (1) derivational, (2) inflectional, (3) pronominal. That is, any sufformatives that are part of the word base occur before any of the inflectional endings outlined below.

DECLENSIONS

§82. Noun inflection is organized into declensions. The term *declension* refers to a pattern of noun inflectional suffixes that go together in a systematic paradigm. In Aramaic, there are two declensions.

All nouns and adjectives are inflected, although sometimes the inflection will be a "significant zero," i.e., nothing will be added to the lexical base. The inflections simultaneously express the three categories of gender, number, and state by means of suffixes.

§83. *Gender.*

a. All nouns and adjectives are of either *masculine* or *feminine* gender. "Gender" as a morphological category marks sexual differentiation in the case of nouns referring to humans and animals, but is formally applied to all nominal forms both animate and inanimate. There is no neuter category.

b. Note that the declensions do not invariably align with gender, except in the case of adjectives (1st declension is masculine, 2nd declension is feminine) and cardinal numbers (1st declension is feminine, 2nd declension is masculine, §164d).

§84. *Number.* There are three possible numbers: *singular*, *plural*, and *dual*, although the dual is rarely used. Number refers in the first instance to real-world singularity and plurality, but nouns in the singular may also refer to abstractions (such as יְקָר "honor") or to plural (collective) entities (such as אֵב "fruit"), and nouns in the plural may likewise refer to abstractions (such as רַחֲמִין "mercy") or to single (if complex) entities (such as אַנְפִּין "face").

§85. There are three possible states: *determined*, *absolute*, or *construct*.

a. The *determined* state is indicated by the suffix אָ◌ or הָ◌, and expresses *definiteness*, like the English definite article, e.g., מַלְכָּא "the king"; אִגַּרְתָּא "the letter."

b. Definiteness is not solely expressed by the determined state; proper nouns (names) and nouns with pronominal suffixes are also definite. Nouns in construct (§87) with a definite noun are also definite.

c. In addition to referring to definite (unique or identifiable) entities, the determined state may refer to abstractions, e.g., עִדָּנָא "time" (Dan 2:8), בִּשְׂרָא "flesh" (Dan 2:11), חָכְמְתָא "wisdom" (Dan 2:20); or to generic types, e.g., פַּרְזְלָא "iron" (Dan 2:40), זְמָרָא "music" (Dan 3:5), etc.

d. Apparent exceptions to the equation of determination with definiteness are actually instances of generic usage, e.g., הוא כפנא בארעא דא כולא "there was *famine* [not: *a famine*] in all this land" (1QapGen 19:10).

e. The determined state suffix may also appear on nouns used as vocatives in direct address, e.g., מַלְכָּא לְעָלְמִין חֱיִי "*O king*, live forever" (Dan 2:4).

§86. a. The *absolute state* corresponds with *indefiniteness*, i.e., like English "a, an" with singular nouns or "some" with plural nouns, e.g., גְּבַר "a man" (Dan 2:25), אֱלָה "a god" (Dan 2:28), מַתְּנָן "(some) gifts" (Dan 2:48), גֻּבְרִין "(some) men" (Dan 3:8, etc.).

b. The absolute plural may also denote generic types, e.g., חֶלְמִין "dreams (in general)" (Dan 5:12), אָתִין וְתִמְהִין "signs and wonders" (Dan 6:28), or abstractions, e.g., חַיִּין "life" (Dan 7:12), רַחֲמִין "mercy" (cf. *tantum plurale*, §92).

c. Occasionally, the absolute singular is also used for the generic, e.g., מִדָּה בְלוֹ וַהֲלָךְ "tribute, tax, and toll" (Ez 4:20).

d. The absolute state of adjectives or nouns is used for predicates in copular clauses with definite subjects; see §§374ff.

e. Nouns or noun phrases used adverbially are usually in the absolute state (§352).

§87. *Construct state*. A noun is placed in the construct state, corresponding to the head of a genitive construction ("X of Y"), when bound to an immediately following dependent noun. For more on these notions, see §153.

DECLENSIONAL SUFFIXES

§88. a. Besides having different sets of inflections, the declensions differ on whether the absolute singular (the default or "dictionary" form) usually ends in a consonant (1st declension) or a long vowel (2nd declension).

b. The final consonant of the 1st declension abs. sing. belongs to the noun base and is not an inflectional suffix.

c. The final vowel of the 2nd declension abs. sing. is usually הָ◌ (or אָ◌) -ā, but can be ו -ū or יִ◌ -ī (§90d). The typical הָ◌ -ā historically derives from final *-at or *-t, which remains as the cstr. sing. ending ת, and ו ū and ◌ī from *ūt and *īt, respectively, which continue to be the cstr. forms. ◌.

d. Nouns therefore belong to a particular declension by virtue of their derivational base; adjectives, however, as noted, use the 1st declension endings if they modify a masculine noun, the 2nd declension endings if they modify a feminine noun. These adjectival endings are determined by noun gender and not by noun declension (e.g., a feminine noun of the 1st declension will still be modified by adjectives of the 2nd declension).

The declensional inflectional suffixes follow below.

First Declension

§89. a. In the *first declension*, nouns in the absolute and construct singular states have no suffixes; in the det. sg., and all plural forms, the inflectional suffixes are added to the derivational base (i.e., the combination of consonantal root and typical vowel pattern).

The addition of inflectional endings to the base can change the syllabic structure of the word and can create the environment for the operation of various phonological rules (§78).

Number	Absolute state	Construct state	Determined state
Singular	Ø (no suffix)		אָ◌ -ā
Plural	יִן◌ -īn (ין IA)	יֵ◌ -ē (< *ay)	אַיָּ◌ -ayyā
Dual	יִן◌ -áyin	same as plural	

b. The 1st decl. abs. pl. יִן֖ -*īn* is very rarely in BA and QA replaced by יִם֖ -*īm*, under the influence of Biblical Hebrew, e.g., מַלְכִים "kings" (Ez 4:13) for מַלְכִין; עלמים "ages" (1QapGen 21:10) for עלמין.

c. The det. state suffix, as noted, can be written הֵ֖ (sing.) or יָּהֵ֖ (pl.), e.g., פִּשְׁרָה "the interpretation" (Dan 2:7); רָזֵה "the secret" (Dan 2:19); יוֹמַיָּה "days" (Dan 4:31).

Second Declension

§90. a. In the *second declension*, singular absolute nouns usually end in הֵ֖ (rarely אֵ֖) -*ɔ̄*, construct in תֵ֖ -*at*, and determined in תָא or תָּא -*tɔ̄/tɔ̄*. In the plural, the endings are יֵ֖ -*ɔ̄n*, תֵ֖ -*ɔ̄t*, and תָא֖ -*ɔ̄tɔ̄*.

Number	Absolute state	Construct state	Determined state
Singular	הֵ֖ -*ɔ̄*	תֵ֖ -*at*	תָא֖, תָּא֖ -*ətɔ̄, -tɔ̄*
	אֵ֖		
Plural	יֵ֖ -*ɔ̄n*	תֵ֖ -*ɔ̄t*	תָא֖ -*ɔ̄tɔ̄*

b. The det. state suffix -*ɔ̄* is usually spelled אֵ֖, but may also be spelled הֵ֖ (§85); likewise, the 2nd decl. sing. abs. ending -*ɔ̄* is usually spelled הֵ֖, but may also be spelled אֵ֖, e.g., אנתא "woman" (instead of אנתה) (4Q197 4 i 13 [Tobit]).

c. The 2nd decl. sing. det. has two variants, one with vocal *shewa* preceding the characteristic ת *t*, the other, less common, with silent *shewa* preceding ת *t*. These are reflexes of two original endings **-at* and **-t* in the ancestor language. In the cstr. sg., the reflex of both endings is תֵ֖-*at*.

  Historically, the **-at* and **-t* endings were followed by short vowel case endings in the ancestor language. When the case endings were dropped (§59), final **-at/-t* in the absolute state evolved into final -*ā* (BA -*ɔ̄*) and -*at* remained as the construct state ending. Original **-at* and **-t* remained before suffixes (including the det. state suffix).

d. The 2nd declension has other forms used less frequently, with the derivational endings **-ū(t)* and **-ī(t)* with corresponding inflections. These are used only on nouns and not on adjectives. The final vowel of the absolute state becomes the corresponding consonant in the plural forms, as in the following table.

Number	Absolute state	Construct state	Determined state
Singular	וּ -*ū*	וּת -*ūt*	וּתָא -*ūtɔ̄*
	יִ -*ī*	יִת -*īt*	יִתָא -*ītɔ̄*
Plural	וָן -*wɔ̄n*	וָת -*wɔ̄t*	וָתָא -*wɔ̄tɔ̄*
	יָן -*yɔ̄n*	יָת -*yɔ̄t*	יָתָא -*yɔ̄tɔ̄*

e. The Akkadian loanwords כְּנָת "colleague" and פֶּחָה "governor" were Aramaized as 2nd decl. masc. nouns with plural endings of this subtype, e.g., פַּחֲוָתָא "the governors" (Dan 3:2); כְּנָוָתְהוֹן "their colleagues" (Ez 5:3).

Declensions and Gender

§91. a. As noted above (§83), the paradigms given do not infallibly indicate gender, but 1st declension nouns are usually masculine in gender, and 2nd declension nouns are usually feminine. (In most Aramaic grammars, the 1st declension is called "masculine" and the 2nd "feminine.")

b. However, some 1st declension nouns are feminine in gender, some 2nd declension nouns are masculine, and some nouns of either gender have singular endings in the 1st declension and plural endings in the 2nd, or vice versa. Therefore, it is better to keep the declensional inflections separate from gender. The inherent gender of a noun must be learned with the noun.

c. Note again, however, that adjectives (and participles) will have 1st declension endings when modifying masculine nouns and 2nd declension endings when modifying feminine nouns, regardless of the declension of the noun.

d. Cardinal numbers from 3–19 (§164d–e) have 1st declension endings when quantifying feminine nouns and 2nd declension endings when quantifying masculine nouns.

Tantum Plurale

§92. Some words occur only in the 1st declension plural. In traditional grammars these are called *tantum plurale* (Latin, "only plural"). These often have abstract meaning, such as רַחֲמִין "mercy"; דְּמִין (IA דמן) "price, value." Others may refer to complex body parts, e.g., מעין "stomach, belly"; אַנְפִּין "face" (see also §84).

Nouns of Mixed Declensions

§93. As noted (§91b), some nouns have inflections that are a mixture of 1st and 2nd declensions. The following are the most common:

Singular 1st Declension, Plural 2nd Declension

אַב "father" (abs. pl. אֲבָהָן; IA 1st decl.) (masc.)

אֹרַח "way" (אֹרְחָן) (fem.)

אֶצְבַּע "finger" (אֶצְבְּעָן) (fem.)

שֵׁם "name" (שְׁמָהָן) (masc.)

Singular 2nd Declension, Plural 1st Declension (All Feminine in Gender)

אַמָּה "cubit" (אַמִּין)

אֻמָּה "tribe" (אֻמַּיָּא)

אִנְתָּה "woman" (נְשִׁין)

מִלָּה "word" (מִלִּין)

כַּוָּה "window" (כַּוִּין)

שְׁנָה "year" (שְׁנִין)

Irregular Nouns

§94. Some common nouns have construct forms and plurals with unpredictable derivational bases. The most common such irregular forms are given below.

Absolute singular	Construct singular	Absolute plural	Declension	Gender	Gloss
אַב	אֲבוּ before suffixes	אֲבָהָן	mixed	masc.	father
אָח	אֲחוּ before suffixes	אַחִין	1st	masc.	brother
אִנְתָּה	אִנְתַּת	נְשִׁין	mixed	fem.	woman
בַּי	בֵּית	בָּתִּין	1st	masc.	house
בַּר	בַּר	בְּנִין	1st	masc.	son
בְּרָה	בְּרַת	בְּנָן	2nd	fem.	daughter
כְּנָת	כְּנָת	כְּנָוָן	2nd	masc.	colleague
רַב	רַב	רַבְרְבִין	varies (adj.)	varies (adj.)	great
		רַבְרְבָן			

The Dual

§95. a. The dual absolute ending ◌ַיִן -*áyin* is the only marked dual form; the construct and determined dual are formally the same as the 1st declension construct plural and determined state forms, although the gender of most nouns with dual endings is feminine.

b. The dual has almost vanished from regular use in Aramaic but is preserved in certain lexemes referring to paired anatomical features, e.g., יְדַיִן "hands" (Dan 2:45), רַגְלַיִן "feet" (Dan 7:4), קַרְנַיִן "horns" (Dan 7:7), שִׁנַּיִן "teeth" (Dan 7:7), or numbers, e.g., מָאתַיִן "two hundred" (Ez 6:17). In other instances, doubled or paired entities can be marked with the 1st decl. pl., e.g., עַיְנִין "eyes" (Dan 7:8), with feminine gender.

c. The words שְׁמַיִן "heaven" and מַיִן "water" (IA, QA) have dual endings without signifying dual number. Only the determined form שְׁמַיָּא appears in BA. Both are masculine in gender.

Final -ē Nouns

§96. A small number of nouns end in the long vowel -ē in the absolute and construct states (written אֶ◌, הֶ◌, or יֶ◌). In the plural, their inflections resemble the 2nd declension plurals with added -w. Originally, their final consonant was *y*, and their abs. and cstr. forms were affected by the contraction of triphthongs (§58).

Number	Absolute state	Construct state	Determined state
Singular	יֶ◌ / הֶ◌ /אֶ◌ -ē		יָא- -yɔ
Plural	יָן- -wɔn	יָת- -wɔt	יָתָא -wɔtɔ

Examples: אַרְיֵה "lion," det. sg. אריא (QA), det. pl. אַרְיָוָתָא (Dan 6:8); כָּרְסֵא "throne," det. sg. כורסיא (QA),[1] abs. pl. כָּרְסָוָן (Dan 7:9); לֵילֵה "night," det. sg. לֵילְיָא (Dan 7:13), pl. לֵילָוָן (JLA); סוּסֵה "horse," abs. pl. סוּסָוָן (JLA).

These are not to be confused with adjectives or passive participles from III-y roots ending in -ē (§106).

Adjectives Ending in -ay

§97. a. Adjectives referring to ethnic origin (gentilics) and ordinal numbers have a paradigm unique to themselves. The 1st decl. absolute singular form (the construct is not used) ends in *-ay (BA יֶ◌ -ɔy). In the BA Qere, the original *y* is replaced by *ʾaleph* before the det. state ending (Table 7).

Table 7: *Adjectives ending in -ay, 1st declension (masculine)*

Number	Absolute state	Determined state
Singular	יֶ◌ -ɔy	הֶ◌ -ɔyɔ (Q)
		יא -ɔyɔ (K)
Plural	יֶ◌ -ɔʾin (Dan 3:8)	יֶ◌ -ɔʾē (Q)
		יֶ◌ -ɔyē (K)

Note that the determined state (Qere) uses the *mater* ה, to avoid two consecutive *ʾaleph*s.

b. The det. pl. יֶ◌ -ɔyē has a Qere alternative in the noun כַּשְׂדָּי "Chaldean": כַּשְׂדָּיֵא (K), כשדאי (כַּשְׂדָּאֵי Q), Dan 2:5, 10, 4:4, 5:7; see also אמוראא "the Amorites" (= אֱמוֹרָאֵא, 1QapGen 21:21) (§49b). The substitution of *ʾaleph* for *y* in this form is regular in JLA (e.g., מִצְרָאֵי "the Egyptians," TO Gen 12:12).

---

[1] But see כרסאא in IA (C1 1:133, Ahiqar).

Examples: Gentilics abs. sg. כַּשְׂדָּי "Chaldean" (Dan 2:10); det. sg. מָדָיָא K, מדאה Q "the Mede" (Dan 6:1); abs. pl. כַּשְׂדָּאִין "Chaldeans" (Dan 3:8); det. pl. יְהוּדָיֵא "the Judeans/Jews" (Dan 3:8). Ordinal numbers: abs. sg. קדמי "first" (QA); det. sg. קדמיא "the first" (IA); abs. pl. not attested (cf. JLA רְבִיעָאִין, Tg II Kings 15:12); det. pl. קַדְמָיֵא "the first ones" (Dan 7:24).

 c. The IA orthography is similar to the BA Ketiv: abs. sg. יהודי "Jew/Judean", det. sg. יהודיא, abs. pl. יהודין (*yəhūdāyīn*), det. pl. יהודיא.

Table 8: *Adjectives ending in -āy, 2nd declension*

Number	Absolute state	Determined state
Singular	◌ָה -*ā* (Q), יה -*āy* (K)	◌ָיְתָא -*āyəṯā*
Plural	not attested	◌ָיְתָא -*āyāṯā*

Examples: Gentilics: abs. sg. ארמיה "Aramean" (D2 10:2); others not attested. Ordinals: abs. sg. תְּלִיתָיָא "third" (Dan 2:39 K), תְּלִיתָאָה (Dan 2:39 Q); det. sg. קַדְמָיְתָא "the first one" (Dan 7:4); det. pl. קַדְמָיָתָא "the first (horns)" (Dan 7:8).

 d. The adjective נכרי *nukrāy* "foreigner" belongs here as a kind of gentilic: masc. abs. sg. נכרי (QA), masc. abs. pl. נכראין (QA), masc. det. sg. or pl. נכריא (C1 1:139, Ahiqar); cf. JLA fem. abs. sg. נוּכְרָאָה (TO Exod 2:22).

 e. The adjectives עלי *ʿillāy* "high"; תחתי *taḥtāy* "low"; מציעי *maṣīʿāy* "middle" have the same ending, although only the first is attested with any frequency in our corpora: masc. det. sg. עֶלָּיָא Ketiv, עֶלָּאָה Qere "Most High" (Dan 3:26), fem. abs. sg. עליא "superior" (1QapGen 20:7). See also בי תחתי "lower house" (B3 5:8); JLA masc. det. sg. מְצִיעָאָה, תַּחְתָּאָה.

DERIVATION OF NOUNS AND ADJECTIVES

§98. Nominal and verbal derivation in Aramaic, as in the other Semitic languages, typically operates by the combination of a *root* of three consonants with a *pattern* that specifies where vowels and (sometimes) consonantal affixes are added to the root. This combination of consonantal root + vowel pattern forms the lexical *base*. This triliteral system is supplemented by words with two root consonants instead of three and by loanwords forming atypical bases.

For the description of triliteral and biliteral bases, the following conventions are observed:

The paradigm root *qtl will be used such that q = first root consonant, t = second root consonant, and l = third root consonant. If there are only two root consonants, the paradigm root is *ql. Any short vowel is indicated by V, any long vowel by V̄.

The derivations of Aramaic and other Semitic languages are commonly organized by base, as they are below. The vowels given are those found in Biblical Aramaic or that can be inferred from a comparison with other Aramaic dialects. Only examples are given from each category, not an exhaustive list. The "dictionary form" of example words is given, with the underlying original pattern if phonological changes have obscured it.

The suffix *-at* or sometimes *-t* is included here as a derivational ending, although it also plays a part in the inflectional system in the 2nd declension as the common (although not invariable) indicator of feminine gender (§90).

Biliteral bases

Some noun bases use a consonantal "skeleton" of only two consonants.

§99. *qVl*: two consonants, one short vowel.

These are the simplest forms; with the addition of inflections and other suffixes, they become subject to Rule 1 (§78).

Pattern	Base	Without suffixes	With suffixes	Gloss
qal	*ʾab	אב IA	אֲבִי Dan 5:13, 1cs suffix	father
	*yad	יַד Dan 5:5	יְדָה Dan 5:5, det. sg.	hand
	*bar	בַּר Dan 7:13	בְּרֵה Dan 5:22, 3ms suffix	son
qal-at	*barat	ברא QA	ברתה IA, QA, 3ms suffix	daughter
	*šanat < *šant	שְׁנַת Dan 7:1	שתא QA, det. sg.	year
qul	*šum	שֻׁם Dan 4:5	שְׁמֵה Dan 4:16, 3ms suffix	name
qil	*ǵiś > *ǵaʿ	עק IA		wood
	*ʾil	אל IA, QA		god, El
qil-at	*šinat < *šint		שְׁנָתֵּהּ Dan 6:19, 3ms suffix	sleep

When vocalic endings are added, the original short vowel is reduced by Rule 1 (§78), as can be seen in יְדָה, בְּרֵה, and שְׁמֵה above.

Some *qVl biliteral bases add a consonantal *h* before plural inflectional suffixes: 2nd decl. cstr. pl. שְׁמָהָת "names" (Ez 5:4); 2nd decl. pl. with 1cs suffix אֲבָהָתִי "my fathers" (Dan 2:23); IA 1st decl. (?) pl. עקהן *gaʿāhīn* "wood." Others have irregular plurals (§94).

§100. *q̄Vl*: two consonants, one long vowel.

a. Nouns of this pattern provide no environment for the operation of reduction (§78, Rule 1 or Rule 2), so the addition of inflectional endings does not affect the internal vocalization.

Pattern	Base	Without suffixes	With suffixes	Translation
qāl	*šōq		שָׁקוֹהִי Dan 2:33, pl. with 3ms suffix	thigh
	*qōl	קָל Dan 4:28	קלה QA, 3ms suffix	sound, voice
	*ʾōt	את QA	אָתִין Dan 6:28, abs. pl.	sign
qāl-at	*šōʿat	שָׁעָה Dan 4:16	שַׁעְתָּא Dan 4:30, det. sing.	hour, moment
qīl	*ṭīn		טִינָא Dan 2:43, det. sing.	clay
	*ʿīr	עִיר Dan 4:10	עִירִין Dan 4:14, abs. pl.	watcher
qīl-at	*bīnat	בִּינָה Dan 2:21		insight
qūl	*ʿūr	עוּר Dan 2:35		chaff
	*rūḥ	רוּחַ Dan 4:5	רוּחָא Dan 2:35, det. sing.	wind
qēl	rēš < *riʾš	רֵאשׁ	רֵאשָׁהּ Dan 2:38, det. sing.	head
	rēw < *riʾw		רֵוֵהּ Dan 2:31	appearance
	rēḥ	רֵיחַ Dan 3:27		odor
qōl	sōp < *sawp	סוֹף Dan 4:8	סוֹפָא Dan 6:27	end
	yōm < *yawm	יוֹם Ez 6:9	יוֹמָא Dan 6:11	day

b. Some nouns of the *qāl* pattern are in fact loanwords (§122) such as דָּת "decree"; רָז "secret," both from Persian.

c. The form שַׁעְתָּא we would expect to be שָׁעְתָּא, which in fact appears in some Masoretic manuscripts.

d. Note that some words in this category come from a triliteral root with elided *ʾaleph* (§47, רֵאשׁ, רֵו) or with contraction of *aw > ō* (§72, סוֹף, יוֹם).

Triliteral Bases

Most Aramaic words have a three-consonant root with a unique vocalic pattern.

§101. *qVṭl*: three consonants with one short vowel after the first consonant.

This complex group corresponds to the segholates in Biblical Hebrew, that is, nouns whose base ends in a cluster of two consonants.

a. Since Aramaic (like Hebrew) disfavors consonant clusters at the ends of words (Rule 12, §78; §60), secondary separating vowels are generated to eliminate the final consonant cluster: *qVṭl* > *qVṭVl*. However, in the determined state, or when pronominal suffixes are added, the cluster is not final, and the secondary separating vowel is not generated, e.g., in det. state *qVṭl* > *qVṭlā*.

Example: *málk* "king" > abs./cstr. sing. מֶ֫לֶךְ *mélɛk*, det. sing. מַלְכָּא "the king." Note that the original vowel in the abs./cstr. still has the stress, although it has changed quality (from **a* to **ɛ*). There is no vowel reduction (§78, Rule 1).

b. In most cases, the stress is moved to the secondary separating vowel (§60b), and, in the abs. and cstr. sing., an environment for Rule 1 is created:

Example: **sipr* "document," abs./cstr. sing. סְפַר *səpár* (< **sipár* < **sípar* < **sípr*), det. sing. סִפְרָא "the document." In this example, the original **i* vowel has lost the stress in the abs. state, which has shifted to the secondary vowel *a*, and the *i* is reduced to *shewa*. (Contrast BH סֵ֫פֶר.)

Example: **ʿabd* "slave," abs./cstr. sing. עֲבֵד *ʿăbéd* (< *ʿabéd* < *ʿabed* < **ʿábd*), det. sing. עַבְדָּא "the slave." In this example, Rule 1 is modified by the guttural ע, which makes **a* reduce to **ă* (with a *ḥaṭeph* vowel, Rule 4b, §78) instead of *shewa* *ə*. (Contrast BH עֶ֫בֶד.)

c. Hence, nouns with bases of this type, in the 1st decl. singular abs./cst., may look like Hebrew segholates (as with מֶ֫לֶךְ) with penultimate stress, or may be more typically Aramaic, with final stress (like סְפַר and עֲבֵד) and vowel reduction. Some nouns, like **ṣalm* "image," may show both patterns (abs. sing. צְלֵם, Dan 2:31 or cstr. sing. צְלֵם, Dan 3:18; det. sing. צַלְמָא).

d. Note that the quality of the separating vowel in the second type is not predictable; it may be *a*, as in כְּתַל "wall" < **kutl* (Dan 5:5); כְּסַף "silver" < **kasp* (Dan 2:32); *e*, as in עֲבֵד "slave" (Dan 6:21); בְּעֵל "master" < **baʿl* (Ez 4:8); ɛ, as in לְחֶם "feast" < **laḥm* (Dan 5:1); or *o*, as in קְשֹׁט "truth" < **qušṭ* (Dan 4:34).

e. In det. and suffixed sing. forms, nouns whose base has original **u* generally have short בֻּ in BA, e.g., תָּקְפָּא *toqpɔ* "strength" < **tuqp* (Dan 2:37), עָפְיֵהּ *ʿopyeh* "its foliage" < **ʿupy* (Dan 4:9).

f. In the unpointed texts of IA and QA, it is not possible to discern the vocalization of the forms, or whether the separating vowel had been added in these dialects. In QA, some forms have a ו *mater* after the first or second consonant or both, e.g., קושט "truth" (1QapGen 3:13), קושט (1QapGen 5:8), קושוט (4Q542 1 ii 1). Clearly the separating vowel was present in some words, but it is not clear where the stress was.

§102. *qVṭl plurals*: The plural nouns of this category have a different base, with *a* after the second syllable; that is, the plural base has two syllables, without a consonant cluster: *qVṭal-*.

Example: abs. pl. מַלְכִין "kings" < **malakín* (Dan 7:17). In this example, the abs. pl. base has two consecutive unstressed syllables with short vowels, which are thus subject to Rule 2 (syncopation, §78): *malakín* > *malkín*. The second of the two short vowels has syncopated, i.e., reduced to zero.

Note that the *k* of the base is spirantized (§78, Rule 6), being preceded by a vowel in the base form.

Example: pl. with 3ms suffix עַבְדֹוהִי "his servants" < *ʕabadṓhī (Dan 3:26). Here again, the plural form is subject to Rule 2 (§78); the second *a* has syncopated, leaving behind a spirantized *d*.

§103. When the *qVṭl* base pattern is *qayl*, that is, with original *a* and second consonant *y*, the abs. sing. has penultimate stress with an *i* separating vowel: קַיִט "summer" < *qayṭ (Dan 2:35). In the cstr. sing. the original diphthong *ay* contracts to *ē* (§73b), e.g., cstr. sing. חֵיל *ḥēl* "force" (Dan 4:32), abs. sing. חַיִל < *ḥáyl. The diphthong is not contracted when suffixes or inflectional endings are added, e.g., חַיְלֵה "his army" (Dan 3:20).

For the pattern *qayl-at*, the diphthong is found contracted in חֵיוָה "beasts" from *ḥaywat (e.g., Dan 4:13).

Pattern	Basic form	Written form, no suffixes	Written form, suffixed	Plural form	Gloss
qaṭl	*kasp	כְּסַף	כַּסְפָּא		**silver**
	*malk	מֶלֶךְ	מַלְכָּא	מַלְכִין Dan 2:21	king
	*taʕm	טְעֵם	טַעְמָא		decree
	*ʕabd	עֲבֵד	עַבְדָּא	עַבְדֹוהִי Dan 2:7	slave
qayl	*qayṭ	קַיִט			summer
	*ʕayn	עֵין cstr. Ez 5:5	עַיְנָא	עַיְנִין Dan 7:8	eye
	*ḥayl	חַיִל Dan 3:20	חַיְלֵה Dan 3:20		strength
qaṭl-at	*malkat	מַלְכָּה	מַלְכְּתָא Dan 5:10		queen
qiṭl	*ḥilm	חֵלֶם Dan 4:2	חֶלְמָא		dream
	*sipr	סְפַר Ez 4:15	סִפְרָא	סִפְרִין Dan 7:10	document
	*ḥizw		חֶזְוָא	חֶזְוֵי Dan 7:2, pl. cstr.	vision
	*milk		מִלְכִּי Dan 4:24		counsel
qiṭl-at	*biqʕat	בִּקְעַת Dan 3:1			valley
	*ʾintat	אנתה QA	אנתה QA, IA		woman
	*ḥidwat	חֶדְוָה Ez 6:16			joy
quṭl	*kutl	כְּתַל Dan 5:5	כותלא QA	כֻּתְלַיָּא Ez 5:8	wall
	*qušṭ	קְשֹׁט	קושטא QA		truth
		קשוט קושט, QA			
	*tuqp	תְּקַף Dan 4:27	תָקְפָּא Dan 2:37		strength
quṭl-at	*ḥukmat	חָכְמָה	חָכְמְתָא Dan 2:20		wisdom

§104. *qVṭl* forms in which the final cluster is a geminated consonant (*qVll*) simplify (undouble) the final consonant when no suffixes follow (*qVll > qVl*) (§78, Rule 12b).

Pattern	Basic form	Simplified form	Written form, no suffixes	Written form, suffixed	Gloss
qall > qal	*rabb	rab	רַב	רַבָּא	great
	*ʿamm	ʿam	עַם	עַמָּא	people
	*gaww	gaw > gō (§78, Rule 9)	גּוֹא	גַּוַּהּ Ez 4:15	interior
	*barr	bār	בַּר	בָּרָא Dan 2:38	field
	*yamm	yam	יַם	יַמָּא Dan 7:2	sea
qall-at	*kawwat			כַּוִּין Dan 6:11	window
qill > qel (§78, Rule 7)	*libb	leb	לֵב	לִבִּי Dan 7:28	heart
	*ʾimm	ʾem	אֵם	אמי QA	mother
qill-at	*millat		מִלָּה	מִלְּתָא	word
	*ʾiššat		אֶשָּׁא Dan 7:11		fire
qull > qul	*kull	kol (§78, Rule 7)	כֹּל, כָּל	כֹּלָּא	all
	*pumm	pum	פֻּם	פֻּמַּהּ Dan 7:5	mouth
	*gubb	gob (§78, Rule 7)	גֹּב	גֻּבָּא Dan 6:17	pit
qull-at	*ʾummat		אֻמָּה	אֻמַּיָּא Dan 3:4	tribe

The plural forms of this type sometimes preserve all three root letters in the plural, e.g., עַמְמַיָּא "the peoples" (Dan 3:4); others have unique or irregular forms, e.g., רַבְרְבִין "great" (Dan 3:33), with reduplication.

§105. *qVṭVl*: three consonants, two short vowels.

a. Nouns of *qVṭVl* form develop alternate surface forms due to the operation of Rules 1 and 2 (§78). As a result, they may at times resemble nouns with original *qVṭl* base.

In the 1st declension abs./cstr., the first vowel reduces to *shewa* (Rule 1): *qVṭVl > qəṭVl*. When inflectional endings are added, Rule 2 (syncopation) is applied, e.g., *qVṭVl-ɔ > qVṭlɔ*.

b. Note that when Rule 2 creates a closed syllable, the short vowel may change quality, e.g.:
*baśar > baśarɔ > (Rule 2) > biśrɔ (§62e).

Pattern	Base form	After reduction	Written form, no suffixes	With suffixes	Translation
qaṭal	*nahar	nəhar	נְהַר	נַהֲרָא, det. sg.	river
	*baśar	bəśar	בְּשַׂר	בִּשְׂרָא, det. sg.	flesh
	*dahab	dəhab	דְּהַב	דַּהֲבָא, det. sg.	gold
*qaṭal-at > qiṭlat	*našamat	nišmɔ̄	נִשְׁמָה	נִשְׁמְתָךְ, Dan 5:23	breath
	*barakat	birkɔ̄	ברכה QA	ברכתא QA	blessing
	*ṣadaqat	ṣidqɔ̄	צִדְקָה Dan 4:24		charity
qaṭal-at	*qaṣayat > qaṣāt	qəṣɔ̄t (§58a)	קְצָת Dan 4:26		portion, end
qaṭal-t	*ḥazawt	ḥazōt (§78, Rule 9)		חֲזוֹתֵהּ Dan 4:8	tree-top
qaṭil	*namir	nəmar (§78, Rule 4a)	נְמַר Dan 7:6		leopard
*qaṭil-at > qaṭlat	*ḥabirat	ḥabrɔ̄	חַבְרָה	חַבְרָתֵהּ, Dan 7:20, pl.	companion
qiṭal	*libab	ləbab	לְבַב	לִבְבֵהּ, Dan 4:13	heart

When the middle consonant is a guttural, as with דְּהַב or נְהַר, the operation of Rule 2 may be affected by Rule 4b (reduction to *ḥateph* vowel instead of to zero).

§106. When a *qVṭil* pattern is formed from a III-y root, the final segment is realized as -*ē* (cf. §58c). These are adjectives or passive participles.

Pattern	Base form	After reduction	Written form	Gloss
qaṭē (<*qaṭiy)	*šalē	šəlē	שְׁלֵה Dan 4:1	tranquil
	*naqē	nəqē	נְקֵא Dan 7:9	pure
	*šawē	šəwē	שוה IA	worth
	*šarē	šərē	שְׁרֵא Dan 2:22	dwell

§107. *qV̄ṭVl*: three consonants, long vowel after the first consonant.

In *qV̄ṭVl* forms, after the addition of suffixes, Rule 1 operates on the second syllable. The first syllable remains unaffected. The G stem participle (§223) belongs to this pattern.

Pattern	Base	Written form, no suffixes	Written form with suffixes	Gloss
qāṭal	*ʿālam	עָלַם	עָלְמָא	eternity, long time
qāṭil	*nāziq	נְזַק Dan 6:3		harm, G ptcp.
	*kātib	כָּתֵב	כָּתְבִין	write, G ptcp.
	*kāhin	כָּהֵן	כָּהֲנָא	priest
	*māriʾ	מָרֵא	מָרִי Qere, Dan 4:16	lord
qāṭil-at	*yāqidat	יָקְדָה	יָקֵדְתָּא Dan 3:6	burn, G ptcp.
qōṭal	*kōkab < *kawkab	כוכב	כוכבין QA	star

§108. *qVṭ Vl*: three consonants, long vowel in second syllable.

a. Rule 1 operates on the first syllable, with or without suffixes: *qVṭ Vl* > *qəṭ Vl*. If the first consonant is a guttural, then Rule 4b (§78, reduction to *ḥaṭeph* vowel) is applied. Note that the G stem passive participle (§224) belongs to this pattern.

Pattern	Base	Without suffixes	With suffixes	Gloss
qaṭāl	*zamār	זְמָר	זְמָרָא Dan 3:5	music
	*yaqār	יְקָר	יְקָרָא Dan 2:37	honor
	*šalām	שְׁלָם	שְׁלָמָא Ez 5:7	peace
qaṭāl-at	*ʿawāyat	עֲוָיָה	עֲוָיָתָךְ pl. w. suff., Dan 4:24	iniquity
qiṭāl	*ʾilāh	אֱלָה	אֱלָהָא	god
	*ʾināš	אֱנָשׁ	אֲנָשָׁא Dan 4:22	human
quṭāl	*nuḥāš	נְחָשׁ	נְחָשָׁא Dan 2:35	copper
	*qudām	קֳדָם	קָדָמַי Dan 2:6	before
		קודם QA		
qaṭīl	*ʿatīd	עֲתִיד	עֲתִידִין Dan 3:15	ready
	*nahīr	נְהִיר	נְהִירָא Dan 2:22 K	light
qaṭīl-at	*ʿabīdat	עֲבִידָה	עֲבִידְתָּא Dan 2:49	work
qaṭūl	*labūš	לְבוּשׁ	לְבוּשֵׁהּ Dan 7:9	clothing
qaṭūl-at	*nabūʾat	נְבוּאָה		prophecy
qiṭūl	*ʾisūr	אֱסוּר Dan 4:12		band
qaṭōl	*nahōr ?	נְהוֹר	נְהוֹרָא Dan 2:22 Q	light
qiṭōl	*ʾinōš ?	אנושׁ	אנושׁא Dan 4:13 K	human
qaṭēl-at	*šaʾēlat	שְׁאֵלָה	שְׁאֵלְתָּא Dan 4:14	question
	*gazērat	גְּזֵרָה		decree
	*yaqēdat	יְקֵדָה		burning

b. The *qaṭēl-at* forms are most likely loans from Hebrew (§63d).

§109. *qV̄ṭV̄l*: three consonants, long vowels in both syllables.

No environment for operation of Rule 1 or Rule 2 exists. This category is not common.

Pattern	Base	Without suffixes	With suffixes	Gloss
qāṭōl	*kārōz		כָּרוֹזָא Dan 3:4	herald
	*māzōn	מָזוֹן Dan 4:9		food
qīṭāl	*ʔīlān	אִילָן	אִילָנָא Dan 4:8	tree
qīṭōl	*nīḥōḥ	נִיחוֹחַ	נִיחֹחִין Dan 2:46	incense offering

§110. *qVṭṭV̄l*: three consonants, geminate middle consonant, long vowel in final syllable.

a. Due to the syllable structure, the *qVṭṭV̄l* pattern does not have vowel reduction after suffixation.
b. The *qaṭṭāl* pattern is used to denote permanent properties (e.g., קַיָּם "enduring") and especially professions. The *qaṭṭīl* pattern is a common adjectival pattern.

Pattern	Base	Without suffixes	With suffixes	Gloss
qaṭṭāl	*zammār	זַמָּר	זַמָּרַיָּא Ez 7:24	musician
	*dayyān	דַּיָּן	דַּיָּנִין Ez 7:25	judge
	*qayyām	קַיָּם	קַיָּמָה Dan 4:23	enduring
	*tarrāʕ	תָּרָע	תָּרָעַיָּא Ez 7:24	gatekeeper
	*paḥḥār	פֶּחָר Dan 2:41		potter
qaṭṭāl-at	*marrādat	מָרְדָה	מָרָדְתָּא Ez 4:12	rebellious
qiṭṭāl	*gibbār	גִּבָּר	גִּבָּרֵי Dan 3:20	mighty
	*ʕiqqār	עִקַּר Dan 4:12		stump
	*ʕiddān	עִדָּן	עִדָּנָא Dan 2:8	time
	*liššān	לִשָּׁן	לִשָּׁנַיָּא Dan 3:4	tongue
	*hiwwār	חִוָּר Dan 7:9		white
qaṭṭūl	*ʔattūn	אַתּוּן	אַתּוּנָא Dan 3:19	furnace
qaṭṭīl	*yaṣṣīb	יַצִּיב	יַצִּיבָא Dan 3:24	firm, true
	*šallīṭ	שַׁלִּיט	שַׁלִּיטָא Dan 2:15	ruler
	*qaddīš	קַדִּישׁ	קַדִּישִׁין Dan 4:5	holy
	*ʕattīq	עַתִּיק Dan 7:9		ancient

(cont.)

Pattern	Base	Without suffixes	With suffixes	Gloss
	*ḥakkīm	חַכִּים	חַכִּימַיָּא Dan 2:13	wise
quṭṭāl	*ḥullāq	חולק QA		portion
qiṭṭōl	*kittōn ?	כתן IA		tunic
		כתון QA		

§111. *qVṭṭVl*: geminate middle consonant, short vowels in both syllables.

The final syllable has vowel reduction (§78, Rule 1) when suffixes make it open.

Pattern	Base	Without suffixes	With suffixes	Gloss
qaṭṭal	*ṣawwar	צַוַּאר	צַוְּארָה Dan 5:7	neck
	*kakkar	כַּכַּר	כַּכְּרִין Ez 7:22	talent
		כנכר IA		
qiṭṭal	*ʾiddar	אִדַּר	אִדְרֵי Dan 2:35	threshing floor
	*ṣippar	צִפַּר	צִפְּרִין Dan 4:30	bird
		צנפר IA		
qiṭṭil	*ʾimmir	אִמַּר	אִמְּרִין Ez 6:9	lamb
qaṭṭil-t	*yabbišt > yabbišat	יַבֶּשָׁה	יַבֶּשְׁתָּא Dan 2:10	dry land

§112. *Quṭayl* diminutive pattern.

The diminutive pattern *quṭayl*, with a diphthong in the second syllable, appears rarely in the texts. The short *u* is subject to reduction, and the diphthong *ay* to contraction. Examples are זְעֵירָה "little" < *zuʿayr-at (Dan 7:8); עלים or עולים "boy" < *ʿulaym, IA or QA (JLA עוּלַיִם).

Patterns with Consonantal Afformatives

Some derivational patterns supplement a triliteral base with additional consonantal elements added before or after the base.

§113. With 2nd declension *-ū(t)*. This derivational ending occurs primarily with abstract nouns (§90d). The original final *-t* is preserved in the cstr. state and before suffixes.

Pattern	Base	Without suffixes	With suffixes	Gloss
qaṭal-ū(t)	*mal(a?)kū	מַלְכוּ	מַלְכוּתָא	kingdom
qaṭl-ū(t)	*ḥashū	חַשְׁחוּת Ez 7:20		need
qāl-ū(t)	*gālū	גְּלוּ	גָּלוּתָא Dan 2:25	exile
	*bāʿū	בָעוּ Dan 6:8	בָּעוּתֵהּ Dan 6:14	petition
	*zākū	זָכוּ Dan 6:23		innocence
qal-ū(t)	*rabū	רְבוּ Dan 4:33	רְבוּתָא Dan 5:18	greatness
	*raʿū	רְעוּת Ez 5:17	רעותה QA	will
qaṭṭīl-ū(t)	*nahhīrū	נַהִירוּ Dan 5:11		illumination
qaṭīl-ū(t)	*bahīlū	בְּהִילוּ Ez 4:23		haste

§114. With 2nd declension -ī(t). The original final -t is preserved in the cstr. state and before suffixes. For the plural forms, see §90d.

Pattern	Base	Without suffixes	With suffixes	Gloss
qaṭl-ī(t)	*ʾaḥrī	אַחֲרִית Dan 2:28	אחריתך QA	end
	*arʿī	אַרְעִית Dan 6:25		bottom
qill-ī(t)	*ʿillī		עִלִּיתֵהּ Dan 6:11	upper room

This suffomative element is probably an archaic feminine adjectival ending (as in BH), and the words in the table are nominalized adjectives; note also adjectival אָחֳרִי (§116) and אֵמְתָנִי (§119).

The words נְוָלִי "latrine" (Dan 2:5, 3:29) and שְׁרֹשִׁי "corporal punishment" (Ez 7:26 Qere) are loanwords (Akkadian and Persian, respectively) (§122).

§115. With sufformatives -ōn/-ɔ̄n (< *ān). These forms present no environment for the operation of vowel reduction or syncopation.

Pattern	Base	Without suffixes	With suffixes	Gloss
quṭl-ān	*šulṭān	שָׁלְטָן Dan 4:31	שָׁלְטָנֵהּ Dan 7:14	dominion
	*dukrān	זכרן IA	דָּכְרָנַיָּא Ez 4:15	record
qaṭl-ān	*ʿarbān	ערבן IA		pledge, guarantee
qiṭl-ān	*binyān	בנין, בניאן QA	בִּנְיָנָא Ez 5:4	building
	*tinyān	תנין QA	תִנְיָנָה abs. f., Dan 7:5	second
	*minyān	מִנְיָן Ez 6:17		number
qiṭl-ōn	*riʿyōn		רַעְיוֹנָךְ Dan 2:29, pl. w. suff.	thought

4

(cont.)

Pattern	Base	Without suffixes	With suffixes	Gloss
	šilṭōn		שָׁלְטֹנֵי Dan 3:2, pl.	ruler
	dikrōn	דכרון QA	דָּכְרֹונָה Ez 6:2	record
	ʿilyōn	עליון QA	עֶלְיֹונִין Dan 7:27	most high
qall-ān	*rabbān*	רבן QA		chief

The forms with final *-ōn* are likely influenced by Hebrew (in the case of עליון, a direct borrowing), while the more indigenous Aramaic form is *qutl-ān*. The *qitl-ān* forms were probably originally *qutl-ān*, with the third radical *y* inducing *u > i*. The form *ʿarbān* may originally have been *ʿurbān*, with the guttural inducing *u > a*.

§116. The adjective אָחֳרִי / אָחֳרָן.

a. In BA, only the sing. abs. forms of the adjective meaning "other, another" are attested: masc. אָחֳרָן, fem. אָחֳרִי. The masc. is formed like a *qutl-ān* noun (*ʾuḥrān*, §115), the fem. with final *-ī* (§114).

    In IA and QA, a wider range of inflections is attested. Plural determined forms are not attested in the corpora.

b. Note that in IA, the plural of this adjective does not always agree in state or number with the noun it modifies (§145), e.g., נכסיא אחרנן "the other possessions" (A6 10:8, pl. abs. with pl. det.); בר וברה אחרנן "any other son or daughter" (B2 3:10, pl. abs. with pl. det.); חילא אחרנן "other troops" (A4 7:8, Petition, pl. abs. with sg. det.).

c. A related adverbial form is אָחֳרֵין (עַד) "finally, last of all" (Dan 4:5). It has been proposed[2] to emend the vocalization to אַחֲרֵין, similar to קדמין "first of all" (§350d).

d. In IA, the expression ואחרן means "and so on, *et cetera*," e.g., נכסן וכסף עבור ואחרן "property, money, grain, and so on" (B2 9:12).

§117. With *mV*- preformative. These patterns are sometimes associated with location (*miqtal*, *maqtil*), and some are verbal nouns (G-stem infinitives or *nomina actionis*, §320). When the base ends with *-Vl* (short vowel plus consonant), it is subject to Rule 1 when suffixes are added.

---

[2] Cf. the references in HALOT s. v. אחרין.

Pattern	Base	Without suffixes	With suffixes	Gloss
ma-qtal	*manda⁽	מַנְדַּע Dan 5:12	מַנְדְּעָא Dan 2:21	knowledge
	*malʾak	מלאך QA	מַלְאֲכֵהּ Dan 6:23	angel
ma-qtal-at	*mantanat		מַתְּנָן Dan 2:6, pl.	gift
mi-qtal	*miškab		מִשְׁכְּבִי Dan 4:2	bed
	*miškan		מִשְׁכְּנֵהּ Ez 7:15	dwelling
ma-qtil	*madbiḥ	מדבח QA	מַדְבְּחָה Ez 7:17	altar
ma-qtāl	*maᶜbād		מַעֲבָדוֹהִי Dan 4:34, pl.	work
ma-qāl	*madār		מְדָרְהוֹן Dan 2:11	dwelling
ma-qōl	*madōr		מְדוֹרֵהּ Dan 5:21	dwelling
ma-qīl-at	*madīnat	מְדִינַת Dan 2:48	מְדִינְתָּא Ez 5:8	province
ma-qill-at	*magillat	מְגִלָּה Ez 6:2		scroll
ma-qqāl	*maᶜᶜāl		מֵעָלֵי Dan 6:15, cstr. pl.	entering
ma-qtōl-īt	*mašrōqī(t)		מַשְׁרוֹקִיתָא Dan 3:5	pipe
ma-qtul-at	*maḥluqat		מַחְלְקָתְהוֹן Ez 6:18, pl.	division

§118. With *ta-* preformative. The preformative, when open, has a reduced vowel (§78, Rule 1).

Pattern	Base	Written form	Root	Gloss
ta-qīl	*tadīr	תְּדִירָא Dan 6:17	דור	constancy
ta-qtīl	*tašnīq	תשניקין QA	שנק	torment
ta-qtāl	*tawtāb	תותב IA, QA	יתב	foreigner
ta-qtul-at	*tašbuḥat	תשבחא QA	שבח	praise
ta-qūl-at	*takūnat	תכונה IA, QA	כון	jewelry

Some such forms, like IA תרבצא "courtyard" (e.g., B3 10:4), are Akkadian loanwords.

§119. With *-ōn-V̄* sufformatives. These infrequent forms compound a series of sufformatives. Note two BA examples: אֵימְתָנִי "frightening" (Dan 7:7); שָׂכְלְתָנוּ "intelligence" (Dan 5:11).

§120. Bases formed from *reduplication*. Some bases are formed from syllabic reduplication (in the case of רַעֲנַן, consonantal reduplication).

Pattern	Base	Without suffixes	With suffixes	Gloss
qalqal	*galgal		גַּלְגִּלּוֹהִי Dan 7:9	wheel
	*rabrab	רַב	רַבְרְבִין Dan 3:33	great

(cont.)

Pattern	Base	Without suffixes	With suffixes	Gloss
qalqalān	*rabrabān	רַב	רַבְרְבָנ֫וֹהִי Dan 6:18	ruler
qalqul	*harhur		הַרְהֹרִין Dan 4:2	thought
qaṭalṭal	*šaparpar		שְׁפַרְפָּרָא Dan 6:20	dawn
qaṭlal	*raʿnan	רַעֲנַן Dan 4:1		flourishing (adj.)

Note that the singular of רַב (*rabb) is not reduplicated, in the adjectival (*great*) or nominal (*ruler*) meaning. The words *galgal, *harhur, *šaparpar display in the final syllable secondary gemination (גַּלְגִּלּ֫וֹהִי) or compensatory lengthening (שְׁפַרְפָּרָא, הַרְהֹרִין) to avoid short vowel reduction, which was evidently disfavored in this derivational category.

§121. Nouns with *more than three root letters*, without consonantal afformatives, tend to be borrowings from non-Semitic languages, such as פַּרְזֶל "iron" or חַרְטֹם "magician" (see §122), etc. However, there are some native Aramaic words with four or more root letters, e.g., ארמלה "widow" (e.g., 11QtgJob 14:8), ערטלי "naked" (JLA עַרְטִלַּאי, with final -āy, §97) (e.g., 1QapGen 22:33); כוכב "star" (e.g., C1 1:164; see §107).

Borrowed Nouns

§122. All languages "borrow" words from other languages, and Aramaic is no exception. In its long history, many words originating in other languages have become part of the standard vocabulary of Aramaic or one of its dialects. Etymologists sometimes make a rough distinction between two types of word borrowing, using the German terms *Lehnwort* (loanword) and *Fremdwort* (foreign word). The former is a borrowed word that has been "adopted" and given inflections like that of a native word, while a *Fremdwort* is still felt to be foreign, without, as it were, full inflectional or derivational privileges (see Durkin 2009: 139–140).

Many nouns borrowed from other Semitic languages (i.e., Hebrew and Akkadian) resemble indigenous Aramaic words in their formation and were absorbed, one may presume, without difficulty. Nominal forms ending in *-ōn* (§115) probably derived from Hebrew. Jewish religious terms such as the gentilic לֵוָיֵא "Levites" (Ez 6:18) or שָׁפְטִין "judges" (Ez 7:25) were part of the cultural heritage and flowed easily into the patterns of Jewish Aramaic.

Akkadian words could also be accommodated into the derivational-inflectional system. Many, like נִכְסִין "property" or אִגְּרָה "letter," could assume shapes that fit into known Aramaic types. (For borrowed Akkadian verbs, see §288; for Akkadian loanwords in general, see Kaufman 1974; Muraoka & Porten 2003: 375–377.)

Some Persian words could be borrowed as units and inflected according to Aramaic declensions: e.g., רָז "secret," abs. plural רָזִין (Dan 2:28); דָּת "decree," sg. det. דָּתָא (Dan 2:13); or the unwieldy pl. det. אֲחַשְׁדַּרְפְּנַיָּא "satraps" (Dan 3:2), but the internal form of many Persian words could not be adjusted to Aramaic derivational schemes and most of them remained, we may presume, *Fremdwörter*.

In the Persian period, we find Persian words in Aramaic texts without change (Muraoka & Porten 2003: 378–379) and virtually without inflection, e.g., הנגית והנבג ואדרנג "partner-in-chattel or partner-in-realty or guarantor" (B3 11:12), with Persian *hangaitha, hanbāga, ādranga* used as legalese in a contract; or in the Petition (Reading 6), וידרנג זי פרתרך תנה הוה "Waidranga who was the governor (*frataraka*) here" (A4 7:5).

Of course, a word that begins as a *Fremdwort* may end as a *Lehnwort*; e.g., the term המרכר, Persian *hmārakara* "accountant," is used in IA (with 1st decl. pl. inflection), mainly in the Arshama correspondence (§7), most likely as a technical Persian title; but it shows up centuries later in QA, supplied with an Aramaic abstract ending -*ū(t)*, המרכלות "accountancy" (4Q196 2 6 [Tobit]) and an un-Persian form (Old Persian has no *l* phoneme). (For the later history of the word, see Greenfield 1970.)

The Greek words for musical instruments – קַתְרֹס < κίθαρις "lyre"; סוּמְפֹּנְיָה < συμφωνία "bagpipe" (?), and פְּסַנְתֵּרִין < ψαλτήριον "harp" (e.g., Dan 3:5) – were written in the Aramaic alphabet but otherwise left uninflected, without so much as a determined state affix. These bits of foreign matter (possibly also שַׂבְּכָא σαμβύκη "trigon," although here the borrower was probably Greek) were not Aramaized at all and were used to signify the wide reach of the "tribes, peoples, and tongues" brought under the imperial aegis. It would be centuries before Greek words were made to feel welcome in Jewish Aramaic texts, in corpora beyond the scope of this grammar.

The Glossary (pp. 367–388) indicates which words in the readings are not of Aramaic origin. See also Rosenthal (2006: 61–63) and Muraoka and Porten (2003: 370–382).

CHAPTER 5

Pronouns

INDEPENDENT PERSONAL PRONOUNS

§123. Independent personal pronouns are differentiated by person, gender, and number. They serve primarily as the subjects of copular and verbal clauses (§353). The 3mp/3fp pronouns also serve as direct objects in lieu of a dedicated 3mp object suffix.

The pronouns of BA and QA are largely the same, while those of IA vary from them in orthography and structure.

§124. *Biblical Aramaic independent pronouns.*

Person	Gender	Number	
		Singular	Plural
3rd	masc.	הוּא	הִמּוֹ, הִמּוֹן, אִנּוּן
	fem.	הִיא	אִנִּין
2nd	masc.	אנתה (K), אַנְתְּ (Q)	אַנְתּוּן
	fem.	not attested	not attested
1st	common	אֲנָה	אֲנַחְנָא, אֲנַחְנָה

a. The 3mp form (הִמּוֹ(ן) *himmō(n)* derives from the IA form *hummū* via dissimilation of consecutive *u*-class vowels (§64h).
b. The 3mp form אִנּוּן is an innovation, perhaps due to the spread of the initial אִנ־ of other pronouns (אנחנה, אנה, אנתון, אנתה).

§125. *IA independent pronouns.*

Person	Gender	Number	
		Singular	Plural
3rd	masc.	הו *hū*	המו *hum(m)ū*
	fem.	הי *hī*	—

(cont.)

		Number	
Person	Gender	Singular	Plural
2nd	masc.	אנת *ʾántā*	אנתם *ʾantum*
	fem.	אנתי *ʾántī*	—
1st	common	אנה *ʾanā*	אנחנה, אנחן *ʾanáḥnā*

a. The 2ms pronoun does not indicate the final unstressed vowel. The same is sometimes true of the 1cp pronoun (אנחן).

b. IA does not have fp independent personal pronouns.

§126. *QA independent pronouns.*

		Number	
Person	Gender	Singular	Plural
3rd	masc.	הוא	המון, אנון
	fem.	היא	אנין
2nd	masc.	אנתה	אנתון
	fem.	את \ אתי	not attested
1st	common	אנה	אנחנה, אנחנא

The 2fs independent pronouns are not attested in QA proper, but are attested in post-Qumran documents from the Judean desert.

PRONOMINAL SUFFIXES

§127. Pronominal suffixes are attached to nouns, verbs, or prepositions, and take different forms according to their number, gender, and person. They represent *possessors* (on nouns), *objects*, or sometimes *subjects* (on verbs) or *complements* (on prepositions).

There are two series of pronominal suffixes on nouns.

Nouns: First Series

§128. a. The first series is attached to nouns (and some prepositions) ending in a consonant *in the construct state* (§87), although the pre-suffixal noun form may differ slightly from the construct state form.

b. If the suffix begins with a vowel (i.e., all the singular forms and the 1cp form), it is subjoined directly to the last consonant of the noun.

c. If the suffix begins with a consonant (3/2mp, 3/2fp), and the host word ends with -V̄C (long vowel + consonant) or with -CC (consonant cluster), a vocal *shewa* appears between the host word and the suffix, e.g., רֵאשְׁהוֹן *rēšəhōn* "their head" (Dan 3:27); גֶּשְׁמְהוֹן *gešməhōn* "their body" (Dan 3:27), etc. If the final consonant is a guttural, the inserted vowel is a *ḥateph* vowel, in accordance with Rule 4b (§78), as in אֱלָהֲכֹם *ʾĕlāhăḵōm* "your god" (Ez 7:18).

d. If the host word ends with -VC (short vowel + consonant), then the consonantal suffix is subjoined without vocal *shewa*, e.g., יְדְהֹם *yeḏhōm* "their hand" (Ez 5:8).

Person	Gender	Number			
		Singular	Example	Plural	Example
3rd	masc.	הֶ◌ *-eh*	רֵאשֵׁהּ	הוֹן *-hōn*	רֵאשְׁהוֹן
	fem.	הַ◌ *-ah*	רֵאשַׁהּ	הֵן *-hēn* (Q only)	מִנְּהֵן Dan 2:42
2nd	masc.	ֹךְ◌ *-ōḵ*	רֵאשָׁךְ	כוֹן *-ḵōn*	שְׁלָמְכוֹן Dan 3:31
				כֹם *-ḵōm* (Ez)	אֱלָהֲכֹם
	fem.	not attested		not attested	
1st	common	ִי◌ *-ī*	רֵאשִׁי	אֲנָא◌ *-ánā*	אֱלֹהֲנָא Dan 3:17

e. The 3ms and 3fs forms are descended from the forms *-íhi* and *-áhā*, respectively, as the original case vowels assimilated to the original suffixes *-hi* and *-hā*. With the loss of final short vowels (§59) the 3ms became *-eh* (< *-ih*). The 3fs *-ah* in BA remained after the loss of unaccented final *-ā*, a phenomenon of late dialects.

f. The 2ms form derives from an original *-ákā*. The penultimate vowel must have lengthened in order to share in the change *ā > ō (§67a). Although not attested in BA, the 2fs form was no doubt ־ךְ *-ik* or ־כִי *-íkī*, as in IA and QA; see also JLA ־יךְ *-iḵ*.

g. The 3/2mp forms with final *n* derived from original forms with final *m* (§51); the final *m* forms are normal in IA and OA (and attested in Ez and occasionally in QA). Some final *n* forms begin to show up earlier in some subcorpora (such as the Hermopolis papyri, §7).

The IA suffixes are somewhat different:

h. Since the *plene* orthography of QA occasionally shows a final long vowel in the 2ms, the unstressed final long vowel was likely still present in IA and written defectively (§27). The same is true of the 3fs form (Cook 1990).

Person	Gender	Number	
		Singular	Plural
3rd	masc.	ה -*eh*	הם -*hum*
			הום
			הן -*hun* (dialectal)
	fem.	ה -*áh(ā)*	not used
		הה / הא (rare)	
2nd	masc.	ך -*ák(ā)*	כם -*kum*
			כן -*kun* (dialectal)
	fem.	כי -*íkī*	כן -*ken*
1st	common	י -*ī*	ן -*ánā*
			נא

i. In general, standard IA did not use fp suffixes, having generalized the masculine forms for all genders. The feminine forms continued to be used in local dialects and re-emerged in texts in the Middle Aramaic period (§4(3)).

j. The 3fs final vowel is very rarely written with a *mater*, e.g., אחתהה *ʾaḥatáhā* "her sister" (A2 7:4, Hermopolis papyri).

The Qumran suffixes are very like those of BA.

Person	Gender	Number	
		Singular	Plural
3rd	masc.	ה -*eh*	הן, הון -*hon*
	fem.	ה, הא -*áh(ā)*	הן, הין -*hin*
2nd	masc.	ך, כה -*ák(ā)*	כן, כון -*kon*
	fem.	כי -*íkī*	not attested
1st	common	י -*ī*	נא, נה -*ánā*

k. The *plene* forms of the 3fs and 2ms in QA, as noted (§128e–f), suggest that the final long vowels of these suffixes were present in an earlier period (Cook 1990). Examples: 3fs כולהא *kulláhā* "all of it" (1QapGen 11:12); בעלהא *baʿláhā* "her husband" (1QapGen 20:23); 2ms דמכה *damákā* "your blood" (4Q541 4 ii 4); אלהכה *ʾilāhákā* "your god" (4Q243 1 2); etc.

Nouns: Second Series

5

§129. a. The pronominal suffixes of the second series are added to plural nouns of the 1st declension (§89), some prepositions, 1st decl. nouns whose construct form ends in a long vowel -$\bar{u}$, or the diphthong -ay (as in the existential particle אִיתַי).

b. Second declension nouns ending in -$\bar{u}$ in the absolute state end in -$\bar{u}t$ in the construct state (§90d), and the suffixes are added to the construct form (therefore they take suffixes of the first series).

c. Nouns ending in -$\bar{u}$ before suffixes are the biliteral forms אַב "father" (אֲבוּ before suffixes, §94), אָח "brother" (אֲחוּ before suffixes).

Person	Gender	Singular	Example	Plural	Example
				Number	
3rd	masc.	וֹהִי (on 1st decl. pl.)	עַבְדוֹהִי	הוֹן	בְּנֵיהוֹן
		הִי (after final -$\bar{u}$)	אֲבוּהִי	הֹם (Ezra)	רָאשֵׁיהֹם Ez 5:10
	fem.	יה (K)	שניה	הֵן Qere	בֵּינֵיהֶן Dan 7:8 Qere
		הֹ (Q, replaces final -$\bar{e}$)	שַׁנַּהּ		
2nd	masc.	יך (K)	אחיך	כוֹן	בָּתֵּיכוֹן
		ךֹ (Q, replaces final -$\bar{e}$)	אֲחָךְ		
	fem.	not attested		not attested	
1st	common	יֹ (replaces final -$\bar{e}$)	אֱלָהִי	ינא (K)	איתינא
				אֲנַ (Q, replaces final -$\bar{e}$)	אִיתַנָא Dan 3:18
				יֹנָא	עֲלֵיֹנָא Ez 4:12
				נָא	אבונא QA

d. The origin of the form וֹהִי is disputed. It may have originated from the secondary addition of the 3ms -$h\bar{\imath}$ suffix to an original segment *aw, which in turn derived from a pre-Aramaic contraction of *ay (plural construct) + the ancient suffix hu: *$ayhu$ > *aw > *$aw+h\bar{\imath}$.

e. As suggested by the Ketiv spelling ־יה, the original form of the 3fs suffix was *-$\acute{a}yh(\bar{a})$. In the Qere, the original *ay has contracted to short a (§73c). Reconstructions of the Ketiv such as שַׁנְיַהּ (BHS, Dan 7:5, note c, presumably *$\check{s}innayyah$) are without foundation.

f. As in the previous case, the Ketiv spelling supports an original form of the 2ms suffix as *-$ayk(\bar{a})$. In the Qere, it has merged wholly with the equivalent form in the first suffix series (§73c). The reconstruction of the Ketiv as ךָיֹ (as, e.g., in BHS, Dan 2:4, note c) is not historically supported.

g. The 3fp suffix הֵן -hen occurs in BA only in the Qere (e.g., Dan 7:8).

h. The 1cp suffix was originally *$\acute{a}yn\bar{a}$, replaced in the Qere of Dan 3:18 with נָאֹ. In Ez, the prepositional עֲלֵיֹנָא (Ez 4:12, 18, 5:17) preserves the suffix in a form closer to the etymological original.

Imperial Aramaic Pronominal Suffixes: Second Series

Person	Gender	Number	
		Singular	Plural
3rd	masc.	והי -*áwhī*	הם -*hum*
		וה -*áwhī*	הום
		הי -*hī*	
	fem.	ה, הא -*hā*	הין, הן -*hin, -hen*
2nd	masc.	ך -*kā*	כם -*kum*
	fem.	כי -*kī*	כן -*kin* (non-standard)
1st	common	י -*ay*	ן -*nā*

i. Except for the 3ms form, the IA second series is much like the first series, without the preceding remnant case vowel.

j. Spellings of 3fs with a *mater lectionis* are rare, e.g., אחוהא *ʾaḥúhā* "her brother" (D7 57:4).

QA Pronominal Suffixes: Second Series

Person	Gender	Number	
		Singular	Plural
3rd	masc.	והי -*óhī*	הן, הון -*hun, -hon*
		הי -*hī*	
	fem.	ה, הא -*hā*	הין, הן -*hin, -hen*
2nd	masc.	כה, ך -*kā*	כון -*kun, -kon*
	fem.	כי -*kī*	not attested
1st	common	י -*ay*	נא -*nā*

k. The QA second series is much like the IA second series, except for the $m > n$ change in the 3rd and 2nd plural forms.

l. The occasional *plene* orthography of the final -*ā* in QA of the 3fs and 2ms is best explained as an overt indication of unstressed vowels surviving from an earlier stage, instead of innovations due to Hebrew influence (Cook 1990). (In general at this period, the influence went from Aramaic to Hebrew, rather than the reverse.)

> Examples: 2ms אחיכה *ʾaḥḥáykā* "your brothers" (4Q541 24 ii 5), עליכה *ʿaláykā* "upon you" (4Q531 5 4); 3fs אבוהא *ʾabúhā* "her father" (4Q197 4 ii 2), עיניהא *ʿaynáyhā* "her eyes" (1QapGen 20:3), אנפיהא *ʾanpáyhā* "her face" (1QapGen 20:2); etc.

In the majority of cases, the orthography of these suffixes matches the defective spelling of IA and the BA Ketiv.

Pronominal Suffixes on Finite Verbs and Volitives

§130. The suffixes on finite verbs (including the jussives [§317]), indicating the direct object or rarely the indirect object, generally follow the pattern of the suffixes on nouns: verbs ending in consonants follow the first series, those ending in vowels the second series. Note the following details:

a. The suffixes on the prefix conjugation indicative (future-modal tense) are preceded by the empty (semantically meaningless) morpheme *-inn-* followed by the first series of pronouns. Traditionally, this is referred to as the "energic" *n* or *nun energicum*.[1] In the 3/2mp forms ending in *-ūn* the energic morpheme is simply *-n-*, yielding *-ūnn-*. With the consonant-initial 2mp suffixes, the energic morpheme is *-in-* or *-ɛn*.

Examples: תְּדוּשַׁנַּהּ "it will trample it" (Dan 7:23) < *tadūš - inn - ah* (3fs); יְשַׁמְּשׁוּנֵּהּ "they serve him" (Dan 7:10) < *yəšamməšūn - n - eh* (3ms); יִשְׁאֲלֶנְכוֹן "he will ask you" (Ez 7:21) < *yišʾal - ɛn - kōn*.

b. The energic morpheme is not used with volitives (jussive and imperative).
c. The 1cs suffix is נִי -*ánī* (after consonants) or נִי -*nī* (after vowels and final-consonant volitives).
d. There is no object suffix for the 3mp; the independent pronoun הִמּוֹן or אֶנּוּן (written as a separate word) is used instead.

BA Suffixes on Verbs Ending in Consonants

		Number	
Person	Gender	Singular	Plural
3rd	masc.	הֶ◌ -*eh*	(הִמּוֹן)
		הֶנֵּ◌ -*inneh* (PC)	
		הֶנֵּ -*(ūn)neh* (PC)	
	fem.	הַ◌ -*ah*	
		הַנֵּ◌ -*innah* (PC)	

[1] The traditional term *nun energicum* is a remnant of the influence of Arabic grammar, which has an "energic" (emphatic) mood particle *-anna* or *-an* appearing on the jussive. Although etymologically related to the Arabic energic, the Aramaic *-inn-* before suffixes does not have any modal significance.

(cont.)

		Number	
Person	Gender	Singular	Plural
2nd	masc.	דָ֫ךְ -ɔ́k	(כוֹן) -kɔ̄n
		דִּנָּ֫ךְ -innɔ́k (PC)	נְכוֹן -inkɔ̄n
	fem.	not attested	not attested
1st	comm.	נִי֫ -ání	נָא -nɔ̄
		נִּנָּ֫נִי -innáni (PC)	
		נֻּנָ֫נִי -(ūn)náni (PC)	

BA Suffixes on Verbs Ending in Vowels

		Number	
Person	Gender	Singular	Plural
3rd	masc.	הִי -hī	(הִמּוֹן)
	fem.	not attested	
2nd	masc.	ךְ -k	not attested
	fem.	not attested	not attested
1st	comm.	נִי -nī	נָא -nɔ̄

§131. IA pronominal suffixes on verbs

IA Suffixes on Verbs Ending in Consonants

		Number	
Person	Gender	Singular	Plural
3rd	masc.	ה -eh	(המו)
		נה -inneh ? (PC)	
		נהי -inníhī ? (PC)	
	fem.	ה, הא -ah(ā)	not used
		נה -innáh(ā) (PC)	
2nd	masc.	ך -ák(ā)	כם -kum
		נך -innák(ā) (PC)	נכם -inkum ? (PC)

(cont.)

		Number	
Person	Gender	Singular	Plural
	fem.	כי -*íkī*	not used
		נכי -*inníkī* (PC)	
1st	comm.	ני -*ánī*	ן -*ánā*

a. The vocalization of IA ־נהי on the PC indicative verbs is uncertain. It may derive from the energic particle *-*anna*- plus the 3ms -*hī*: *-*annáhī* > *-*inníhī* > BA -*inneh*. (For discussion, see Beyer 1984: 476–479; Muraoka & Porten 2003: 149–151.)

b. By chance, there are no attestations in IA of 1cs with the energic morpheme -*inn*-.

c. As in BA, there is no suffix object pronoun for the 3mp; instead, the independent pronoun המו is used, e.g., יתן המו "he will give them" (B3 8:10).

Imperial Aramaic: Suffixes on Verbs Ending in Vowels

		Number	
Gender	Person	Singular	Plural
3rd	masc.	הי -*hī*	(המו)
	fem.	הא, ה -*hā*	
2nd	masc.	ך -*kā*	כם -*kum*
	fem.	not attested	not attested
1st	comm.	ני -*nī*	נא, ן -*nā*

§132. In QA, the consonantal texts present generally the same picture as BA, although the precise vocalization is not known.

QA Suffixes on Verbs Ending in Consonants

		Number	
Person	Gender	Singular	Plural
3rd	masc.	ה -*eh*	(המון, אנון)
		נה -*inneh* (PC)	

(cont.)

		Number	
Person	Gender	Singular	Plural
	fem.	ה, הא *-áhā*	(אנין)
		נה *-innah* (PC)	
2nd	masc.	ך, כה *-ák(ā)*	כון *-kun*
		נך *-innák(ā)* (PC)	נכון *-(i)nkun* (PC)
	fem.	כי *-íkī*	not attested
		נכי *-inníkī* (PC)	
1st	comm.	י *-ánī*	נא, נה *-ánā*
		נני *-innánī* (PC)	

a. The 3ms suffix on jussives is attested as תמחולהי "(do not) neglect it" (4Q541 24 ii 4), probably *timḥúlhī, the same pattern (final consonant + *hī*) found on imperatives in BA and QA.

b. For the 3rd plural object, QA uses the independent personal pronouns אנון and המון.

QA Suffixes on Verbs Ending in Vowels

		Number	
Gender	Person	Singular	Plural
3rd	masc.	הי *-hī*	(אנון)
	fem.	הא *-hā*	(אנין)
2nd	masc.	ך *-kā*	not attested
	fem.	not attested	not attested
1st	comm.	ני *-nī*	נא *-nā*

Pronominal Suffixes on Infinitives and Participles

§133. a. Infinitives are regarded as nouns for the purpose of suffixation; hence the suffixes are the same as those appearing on nouns (first series). The only exception is 1cs נִי֫ (instead of י֫) as an object suffix on infinitives.

b. The infinitives of the derived stems (those that are not G stem) change the final הָ *-ā́* to וּת *-ū́t-* (sometimes spelled תְ) before adding suffixes, e.g., unsuffixed לְהֹודָעָה (Dan 5:8), with 1cs suffix לְהֹודָעֻתַנִי (Dan 5:15).

c. Likewise, participles are regarded as nouns for the purposes of suffixation, and the paradigms applying to nouns may be applied to them as well. The participle does not take pronominal object suffixes; suffixes that appear are only possessive, e.g., יָעֲטוֹהִי "his counselors" (Ez 7:15).

Pronominal Suffixes on Prepositions

§134. Some take the first series; others take the second; still others take no suffixes at all. For more details, see §§176ff.

THE PARTICLE דִי

§135. a. The particle דִי (spelled זי in IA) functions as an invariable relative pronoun. It also serves as a genitive exponent (§160), as a complementizer (§426b), and as a conjunction (§409). For its pronominal use in relative clauses, see §148.

b. Although in IA the particle is generally spelled זי, there are a few spelled די, and it is likely that the etymological *ð of the original form had merged with d in Imperial Aramaic (§36). The spelling זי is a historical spelling inherited from the OA period, when it represented *ðī.

c. In Qumran Aramaic, the majority form is די, but there are several dozen cases of proclitic ד־, like the later JLA form דְ־, usually when it is used in the periphrastic genitive (§160).

DEMONSTRATIVE PRONOUNS

§136. Demonstrative pronouns are deictic markers that modify nouns (§146) or substitute for nouns or noun phrases as clause subjects or (rarely) prepositional complements. They occur in two types, *proximal* (referring to a location near the speaker) and *distal* (not near the speaker). They are marked for gender and number in the singular, and for number only in the plural. There is also a common gender singular distal, דִּכֵּן.

a. *Biblical Aramaic demonstrative pronouns*

Gender/Number	Proximate	Distal
masc. sing.	דְּנָה "this"	דֵּךְ "that"
fem. sing.	דָּא "this"	דָּךְ "that"
common sing.		דִּכֵּן "that"
common pl.	אִלֵּן, אֵלֶּה "these"	אִלֵּךְ "those"
	אֵלֶּה (Jer 10:11, Ez 5:15 K)	
	אֵל (Ez 5:15 Q)	

b. *Imperial Aramaic demonstrative pronouns*

Gender/Number	Proximate	Distal
masc. sing.	דנה, זנה *dínā*	דך, זך *dik*
		זנך *dināk* ?
fem. sing.	דה, זא *dā*	זך *dāk*
common sing.		דכי, זכי *dikī* ?
common pl.	אלה *'illē*	אלך *'illik* ?
		אלכי *'illikī* ?

c. *Qumran Aramaic demonstrative pronouns*

Gender/Number	Proximate	Distal
masc. sing.	דן *den*	דך *dek* ?
	דנא, דנה *dénɔ*	
fem. sing.	דא *dā*	not attested
common pl.	אלין, אלן *'illen*	אלך *'illik*
	אלה (once)	

The Qumran paradigm is in most respects identical to that of BA. However, the ms proximate pronoun is commonly דן instead of דנה, anticipating JLA דֵּין.

Third Person Independent Pronouns as Demonstratives

§137. In BA, IA, and QA, the 3rd person pronouns are rarely used as distal markers, although they eventually would replace the other distal markers in later Aramaic. Only a few cases are attested in the corpora (e.g., הוּא צַלְמָא "that statue" [Dan 2:32]; מַלְכַיָּא אִנּוּן "those kings" [Dan 2:44]; יומא הו "that day" [C3 15:123], etc.).

INTERROGATIVES/INDEFINITE NOUNS

§138. Certain pronouns have no antecedent – refer to no specific entity in the discourse – and hence are used in questions and in indefinite noun phrases. By definition, they have no gender, person, or number.

מַן "who"? See §391a for its use as an interrogative; see §151 for indefinite usage, מַן (דִּי) "whoever."

מָה/מָא "what"? See §391b for its use as an interrogative; see §151 for indefinite usage, מָה (דִּי) "whatever"; as a quantifier, see §170.

Other interrogatives include אן "where"? (§391c); אֵיךְ "how"? (§391d); אמת "when"? (§391e).

§139. a. The noun מנדעם or מדעם (*manda$^\varsigma$am, madda$^\varsigma$am, perhaps from *man yāda$^\varsigma$ mā* "who knows what?") in the absolute state means *thing, something, anything*, and is used to talk about general, unspecified entities (not attested in BA):

מנדעם באיש לא עבדת	she did nothing bad (lit., "a bad thing she did not do") D20 5:2 (Carpentras stele)
לא שביק לי כל מנד[עם]	nothing was left to me 4Q196 2 2
אתה לכן מדעם	I will bring you something A2 1:10

b. The nouns איש "man" and אנש "human" in the absolute state can be used in similar fashion to refer to *someone, anyone*, with the negator לא "no one, nobody."

איש מנדעם באגורא זך לא חבל	no one damaged anything in that temple A4 7:14 (Petition)
מדבר די לא אנש בה	a wilderness with no one in it 11QtgJob 31:4
כָּל־אֱנָשׁ דִּי־יִקְרֵה כְּתָבָה דְנָה	anyone who can read this writing Dan 5:7

CHAPTER 6
Noun Phrases

6

Nouns and noun phrases are used in clause roles such as subject, object, prepositional complement, nominal predicate, or (sometimes) adverbials.

Noun phrases can be divided into two groups: *simple* noun phrases and *headed* noun phrases.

SIMPLE NOUN PHRASES

§140. Simple noun phrases have no internal structure, such that one part of the phrase is the head or nucleus and the other parts are dependent in some way upon the head, or are governed by it.

Simple noun phrases are further subdivided into the following groups: single nouns, compound noun phrases, and appositives.

§141. *Simple nouns* are single nouns (or pronouns), either in the absolute or determined state (§§85–86), including adjectives or participles used substantively. (Nouns with pronominal suffixes are included with genitive constructions [§158] below.)

Examples are plentiful; see, for instance, חֱמָא (Dan 3:19; complement to verb); חֵלֶם (Dan 4:2; direct object); כָּרוֹזָא (Dan 3:4; subject); אַתּוּנָא (Dan 3:22; subject); and so on.

§142. a. *Compound noun phrases* are chains of nouns or noun phrases with different referents that may or may not be joined by the conjunction וְ. They belong in the simple noun phrase category because there is no hierarchy or governing relation between the conjoined nouns. They are a list, short or long, that can be used as a unitary constituent in the sentence.

לַאֲחַשְׁדַּרְפְּנַיָּא סִגְנַיָּא וּפַחֲוָתָא אֲדַרְגָּזְרַיָּא גְדָבְרַיָּא דְּתָבְרַיָּא תִּפְתָּיֵא וְכֹל שִׁלְטֹנֵי מְדִינָתָא

the satraps, officials, and governors, counselors, treasurers, judges, magistrates, and all the rulers of the provinces
Dan 3:2 (direct object)

מִן־קֳדָם מַלְכָּא וְשִׁבְעַת יָעֲטֹהִי	from the king and his seven counselors Ez 7:14 (complement of preposition)
בית בתאל ובית מלכת שמין	the house of Bethel and the house of the queen of heaven A2 1:1 (addressee)
שלם נכי ועשה ותשי וענתי ואטי ורע	greetings, Nikki and Ashah and Tashi and Anathi and Itti and Rea A2 1:3 (addressee)
עלואן ומנחה	burnt offerings and a cereal offering 1QapGen 21:2 (direct object)

Note that headed phrases (see below) may be part of a simple compound noun phrase, as in Ez 7:14 above (וְשִׁבְעַת יָעֲטֹהִי, a construct phrase)

b. Compound phrases that are governed by a preposition may repeat the governing preposition before each conjunct.

ביב ובסון ובמדנתא	in Elephantine and in Syene and in the province B3 13:11
יְהוּדָיֵא דִּי בִיהוּד וּבִירוּשְׁלֶם	the Judeans who were in Judah and in Jerusalem Ez 5:1
קרית לממרה ולערנם ולאשכול	I summoned Mamre, and Arnem, and Eshkol 1QapGen 21:21

c. Compound phrases that serve as the subject may have a verb in the singular (see §355c for examples).

d. The conjunction אוֹ *or* may also link nouns in a compound phrase. (For its use in coordination of clauses, see §397.) Note that וְ may also be translated *or* if the context demands it.

גבר או אנתא	man or woman 4Q197 4 i 13
דרגמן או בר זילה	Dargaman or his son B2 3:26
מחר או יום אחרן	tomorrow or another day B2 1:6
כָּל־אֱלָהּ וֶאֱנָשׁ	any god or human Dan 6:8

§143. a. *Appositives* are adjacent nouns or noun phrases (two or more) that have the same referent. They are not related by syntactic structure or hierarchy; one of them could be deleted without changing the syntax or the meaning (truth-value) of the sentence.

In these examples, the apposition is marked with "=" in the translations:

נְבוּכַדְנֶצַּר מַלְכָּא   Nebuchadnezzar = the king
Dan 3:1 (subject; two simple nouns in apposition)

לַחֲנַנְיָה מִישָׁאֵל וַעֲזַרְיָה חַבְרוֹהִי   to Hananiah, Mishael and Azariah = his friends
Dan 2:17 (object of preposition; compound noun phrase in apposition to suffixed noun)

זְרֻבָּבֶל בַּר־שְׁאַלְתִּיאֵל   Zerubbabel = son of Shealtiel
Ez 5:2 (subject; simple noun with construct phrase in apposition)

אל מראן בגוהי פחת יהוד   to our lord = Bagavahya = governor of Judah
A4 7:1 (Petition) (prepositional complement; two nouns with construct phrase in apposition)

עבדיך ידניה וכנותה כהניא זי ביב בירתא   your servants = Jedoniah and his colleagues = the priests that are in (Yeb = the fortress)
A4 7:1 (simple noun with compound phrase with further embedded appositional phrases)

b. In IA, a person is introduced into the discourse by apposition as follows:

שֵׁשְׁבַּצַּר שְׁמֵהּ   "Sheshbazzar" his name (= one named Sheshbazzar)
Ez 5:14

מלי אחיקר שמה ספר חכים   the words of "Ahiqar"
his name, a wise scribe (= one named Ahiqar)
C1 1:1 (Ahiqar)

c. In some cases, appositional nouns or expressions are joined with the conjunction ְו, like compound phrases, but with the same referent. The second conjunct explains or clarifies the first one.[1]

---

[1] See Baker (1980). The instance he cites at Dan 6:29 (p. 134) is not a credible example.

עִיר וְקַדִּישׁ	a watcher and a holy one (= that is, a holy one) Dan 4:10
חֶלְמָה וְחֶזְוֵי רֵאשָׁהְ	your dream and the visions of your head (= that is, the visions of your head) Dan 2:28

d. The occurrence of nouns or pronouns after pronominal suffixes (postcedents) is not apposition (*contra* Muraoka & Porten 2003: 250ff.), but extraposition (§372).

HEADED NOUN PHRASES

§144. a. *Headed* noun phrases have an internal structure of *head* followed by *modifier*. The head nominal is the nucleus of the construction, i.e., what the noun phrase refers to, while the modifier is dependent on the noun and serves to modify or classify or limit the range of application of the head noun in some way.

  b. The modifier can sometimes occur without the head noun, but only the head noun, as subject (even if only implied) agrees in gender, number, and person with the verb of the sentence (or gender and number, if the predicate is an adjective in a copular clause) (§355).

The following are the main types of headed noun phrase constructions:

Noun + Adjective (Attributive Adjective)

§145. a. The most typical head-modifier phrase is a noun plus an adjective. The attributive adjective agrees with the head noun in gender, number, and definiteness.

דְּהַב טָב	*fine* gold Dan 2:32
אֱלָהּ רַב	a *great* god Dan 2:45
בָּבֶל רַבְּתָא	*great* Babylon Dan 4:27
מִלַּיָּא רַבְרְבָתָא	the *great* words Dan 7:11
אחוהי זעירא	his *young* brother 4Q545 1a i 5

b. There may be more than one attributive adjective, joined by וְ:

אָסְנַפַּר רַבָּא וְיַקִּירָא   the *great* and *noble* Osnappar
Ez 4:10, cf. 4:12

בלבב דכא וברוח קשיטה וטבה   with a *pure* heart and an *honest* and *good* spirit
4Q542 1 i 10

c. Adjectives can be used with an unexpressed but implicit head noun (see §172).

Noun + Demonstrative Pronoun

§146. a. A demonstrative pronoun (§136) modifying a definite head noun can occur after the noun or before it. It agrees in number and gender with the head:

כָּל־אִלֵּין מַלְכְוָתָא   all *these* kingdoms
Dan 2:44, cp. Dan 7:17

דְּנָה חֶלְמָא חֲזֵית   *this* dream I saw
Dan 4:15, cp. Ez 5:4, 15

שְׁמַיָּא אֵלֶּה   *these* heavens
Jer 10:11

גֻּבְרַיָּא אִלֵּךְ   *those* men
Dan 3:12

הוּא צַלְמָא   *that* image
Dan 2:32

ארעא דא   *this* land
1QapGen 21:10

זא באישתא   *this* evil thing
A4 7:17 (Petition)

זנה יומא   *this* day
A4 8:19 (Petition)

b. Both adjective (or numeral) and demonstrative pronoun can modify the same noun:

רוחא דא באישתא   *this* *evil* spirit
1QapGen 20:28

גבריא אלך תרין   *those two* men

C1 1:56 (Ahiqar)

ימא רבא דן   *this great* sea

1QapGen 21:16

Noun + Prepositional Phrase

§147. a. The head noun may be modified by an immediately following prepositional phrase:

עוּר מִן־אִדְּרֵי־קַיִט   chaff *from the summer threshing floors*

Dan 2:35

בֵּית־אֱלָהָא בִּירוּשְׁלֶם   the house of God *in Jerusalem*

Ez 6:3

When the modifying phrase begins with לְ, a species of genitive construction is formed (see §163 below).

b. Rarely, a prepositional modifier may function as a nominal without an overt head noun:

כְּבַר אֱנָשׁ אָתֵה הֲוָה   (one) *like a human being* was coming

Dan 7:13

וּמִן־נִצְבְּתָא דִּי פַרְזְלָא לֶהֱוָא־בַהּ   (some) *of the stock of iron* shall be in it

Dan 2:41

c. Ordinarily prepositional phrases do not modify nouns directly, but in a relative clause (§148).

Noun + Relative Clause

§148. a. A noun or noun phrase can be modified by a following verbal or copular clause (§§354, 373) introduced by דִּי as a relative pronoun. In this function, דִּי serves as pronominal substitute for the subject, object, or other grammatical role in its clause, like English *who, which,* or *that,* or like Hebrew אֲשֶׁר.

גֻּבְרַיָּא אִלֵּךְ דִּי הַסִּקוּ לְשַׁדְרַךְ מֵישַׁךְ וַעֲבֵד נְגוֹ   those men *who* brought up Shadrach, Meshach, and Abed-nego

Dan 3:22 (subject)

צַלְמָא דִּי הֲקֵים נְבוּכַדְנֶצַּר מַלְכָּא   the image *that* Nebuchadnezzar the king erected

Dan 3:2 (object)

בֵּית־אֱלָהָא דִּי בִּירוּשְׁלֶם	the house of God *that* is in Jerusalem Ez 4:24 (subject of copular clause)
כל נכסין זי קנה	all the possessions *that* he acquired A4 7:16 (Petition) (direct object)

b. *Resumptive pronoun.* When דִּי substitutes for a possessor or a prepositional complement (§175a), there has to be an additional pronoun within the clause filling that grammatical role, a *resumptive* pronoun or "shadow" pronoun:

דָּנִיֵּאל דִּי שְׁמֵהּ בֵּלְטְשַׁאצַּר	Daniel, whose name was Belteshazzar (= lit. "Daniel, who *his* name was B.") Dan 2:26, possessor
מדבר די לא אנש בה	a wilderness in which no one is (= lit. "a wilderness that no one is in *it*") 11QtgJob 31:4, prepositional complement
ירחא זי לא אנתן בה מרבית	the month in which I shall not pay interest (= lit. "the month that I do not pay in *it* interest") B4 2:4–5, prepositional complement

c. The object is given a resumptive pronoun only rarely:

גֻּבְרִין יְהוּדָאִין דִּי־מַנִּיתָ יָתְהוֹן	Jewish men whom you appointed (lit., "Jewish men that you appointed *them*") Dan 3:12
בָּבֶל רַבְּתָא דִּי־אֲנָה בֱנַיְתַהּ	great Babylon, which I have built (lit., "which I have built *it*") Dan 4:27
כעפר ארעא די לא ישכח כול בר אנוש לממניה	like the dust of the earth, which no one is able to count (lit., ". . .which no one is able to count *it*" 1QapGen 21:13

d. *Participle in a relative clause.* The active participle, which morphologically behaves like an adjective, can be used attributively (§145): אַתּוּן נוּרָא יָקִדְתָּא "the furnace of burning fire" (Dan 3:26); איש מצלח עקן בחשוכא "a man chopping wood in the dark" (C1 1:173; Ahiqar).

But it is more usual for a modifying participle to appear in a relative clause:

יְדָה דִּי כָתְבָה	the hand *that was writing* Dan 5:5
כְּנָוָתְהוֹן דִּי יָתְבִין בְּשָׁמְרָיִן	their colleagues *that reside* in Samaria Ez 4:17
גנב זי שתר בי	a thief *who breaks into* a house C1 1:173 (Ahiqar)
דרגא די סלק לידה	the stairway *that goes up* by it 5Q15 1 ii 5 (New Jerusalem)

§149. *Restrictive and non-restrictive.* The relative clause, as in English, may be *restrictive* or *non-restrictive*; that is, it may limit the referent of the noun to how it is described by the clause (*restrictive*) or it may just give added, non-defining information about the noun (*non-restrictive*).

שְׁמָהָת גֻּבְרַיָּא דִּי־דְנָה בִנְיָנָא בָּנַיִן	the names of the men *who are building this building* Ez 5:4 (restrictive)
וְלֵאלָהֵי כַסְפָּא־וְדַהֲבָא נְחָשָׁא פַרְזְלָא אָעָא וְאַבְנָא דִּי לָא־חָזַיִן וְלָא־שָׁמְעִין וְלָא יָדְעִין	the gods of silver and gold, bronze, iron, wood, and stone, *who do not see or hear or perceive* Dan 5:23 (non-restrictive)

There is no grammatical difference between restrictive and non-restrictive relative clauses; however, only non-restrictive clauses can appear at some distance from the head noun, and occasionally it can be difficult to tell if דִּי is the relative pronoun or a causal conjunction (§409):

לָךְ אֱלָהּ אֲבָהָתִי מְהוֹדֵא וּמְשַׁבַּח אֲנָה דִּי חָכְמְתָא
וּגְבוּרְתָא יְהַבְתְּ לִי
	you, god of my fathers, I thank and praise, *who* have
	     given me wisdom and power (or: . . . *for* you have
	     given me . . .)
	Dan 2:23

וּלְחַי עָלְמָא שַׁבְּחֵת וְהַדְּרֵת דִּי שָׁלְטָנֵהּ שָׁלְטָן עָלַם	the eternal living one I praised and glorified, *whose* rule is an eternal rule (or: . . . *for* his rule . . .) Dan 4:31

§150. *Independent relative clause.* Like other modifying elements, the relative clause can appear independently, with the head noun only implied (the free or "headless" relative).

דִּי מַהְלְכִין בְּגֵוָה	(the ones) *who* walk in pride Dan 4:34
דִּי־הֲוָה צָבֵא הֲוָא קָטֵל וְדִי־הֲוָה צָבֵא הֲוָה מַחֵא	*whomever* he wanted, he would kill; and *whomever* he wanted, he would keep alive Dan 5:19
הוֹדַעְתַּנִי דִּי־בְעֵינָא מִנָּךְ	you told me (that) *which* we requested from you Dan 2:23
וְדִי לָא יָדַע תְּהוֹדְעוּן	and (anyone) *who* does not know, you shall inform Ez 7:25
דזרע טב טב מעל	*whoever* sows good will harvest good 4Q213 1 i 8 (Aramaic Levi)

Headless relatives often appear as topical elements (§370):

וְדִי חֲזָה מַלְכָּא . . . דְּנָה פִּשְׁרָא	as for (that) *which* the king saw . . . this is the interpretation Dan 4:20–21

§151. *Light-headed relative clause.* Relative clauses may also appear with interrogative pronouns מַן or מָה used as indefinites (§138) (the "light-headed" relative).

וּמָה דִי עֲלָיִךְ [ועל] וְעַל־אֶחָיִךְ [אחך] יֵיטַב	*whatever* to you and to your brethren shall seem good Ez 7:18
וְגָלֵא רָזַיָּא הוֹדְעָךְ מָה־דִי לֶהֱוֵא	the revealer of secrets has told you *what* is to be Dan 2:29
מה די אנתה צ[ב]א פקדני	*whatever* you desire, command me 4Q550 5+5a 6
מה זי תעבדון לחור	*whatever* you shall do for Hor A4 3:8
למן זי רחמתי תנתננה	*to whomever* you wish you may give it B2 7:8
וּלְמַן־דִּי יִצְבֵּא יִתְּנִנַּהּ	*to whomever* he wishes he will give it Dan 4:29

The indefinite pronoun מָה is attested on its own as a relative pronoun:

[הת]נדע מא שויא אלהא עליהון	do you know *what* God has placed on them?
	11QtgJob 29:6

§152. *Absolute nouns with relative clause.* Absolute state אתר "place," יום "day," and עדן "time," when modified by relative clauses, can be used with definite meaning:

אֲתַר דִּי־דָבְחִין דִּבְחִין	*the place where* they make sacrifices
	Ez 6:3
ביתאל אתר די אנתה יתב	Bethel, *the place where* you dwell
	1QapGen 21:9
עד יום זי אשלמנהי לך	up to *the day when* I pay it to you
	B4 2:10
מן יום די נפקתה מן חרן	from *the day when* you left Haran
	1QapGen 22:28
עד עדן די [י]נדע תלתת ספריא	until *the time when* he knows the three books
	4Q534 1 i 4–5
בעדן זי זא באישתא עביד לן	at *the time when* this evil was done to us
	A4 7:17–18 (Petition)

Genitives: Construct Phrases

§153. The various genitive constructions are very common types of headed noun phrase.

a. When a noun is in the construct state (§87), it is bound to an immediately following noun to form a phrasal unit. The construct noun is the head of the phrase and the post-construct noun is dependent on it. In traditional grammars, the construct noun is called the *nomen regens* (governing noun) and the post-construct the *nomen rectum* (governed noun); in this grammar, the terms *head* and *dependent* will be used.

b. The relationship between the head noun in construct and its following dependent is in most respects the same as that expressed by the genitive case in Latin and Greek or by English "of" or possessive "'s." Although there is no genitive case in Aramaic, the term "genitive" can be used as a syntactic shorthand for this kind of construction.

c. The prototypical genitive relationship is possession (the dependent being the possessor), but many other kinds of semantic relationship can exist between the head and dependent in construct phrases. These semantic relationships – such as part/whole, specific/general, thing/

material, thing/location, and so on – are inferred from the meaning of the nouns in the phrase and not from the syntax alone. These are best met in context, rather than spelled out in a list.

d. The gender and number of the head noun determine the agreement properties (§§145, 355) of the construct phrase as a whole, but the dependent noun determines the definiteness of the phrase. A dependent noun that is definite (i.e., it is a proper noun, or one with a pronominal suffix, or one in the determined state; §85) makes the whole phrase definite.

§154. a. Typical construct phrases consist of two nouns:

מִלַּת מַלְכָּא	the business of the king Dan 2:10
חַכִּימֵי בָבֶל	the wise men of Babylon Dan 2:12
אֱלָהּ שְׁמַיָּא	the God of heaven Dan 2:18
אֶצְבְּעָת רַגְלַיָּא	the toes of the feet Dan 2:42
זְרַע אֲנָשָׁא	the seed of humankind Dan 2:43
אֱלָהּ אֱלָהִין וּמָרֵא מַלְכִין	god of gods and lord of kings Dan 2:47
רֵיחַ נוּר	a smell of fire Dan 3:27
עִקַּר שָׁרְשׁוֹהִי	the core of its roots Dan 4:20

b. Construct phrases may consist of more than two words when the dependent member is itself a noun phrase, including another construct phrase. The head noun can only be a single noun.

עֲבִידַת מְדִינַת בָּבֶל	the work of the province of Babylon Dan 3:12 (noun + cstr. phrase)
מִנְיָן שִׁבְטֵי יִשְׂרָאֵל	the number of the tribes of Israel Ez 6:17 (noun + cstr. phrase)
בית מלכת שמין	the house of the queen of heaven A2 1:1 (noun + cstr. phrase)

לִתְרַע אַתּוּן נוּרָא יָקִדְתָּא	to the gate of the furnace of burning fire Dan 3:26 (noun + cstr. phrase [noun + [noun + attrib. part.]])
שְׁאָר חַשְׁחוּת בֵּית אֱלָהָךְ	the rest of the needs of the house of your God Ez 7:20 (noun + cstr. phrase [noun + cstr. phrase [noun + cstr. phrase]])
דָּת־מָדַי וּפָרַס	the law of Media and Persia Dan 6:9 (noun + compound phrase)
מָאנֵי דַהֲבָא וְכַסְפָּא	vessels of gold and silver Dan 5:2 (noun + compound phrase)

In one instance, the place of the dependent nominal is taken by a prepositional phrase:

מַלְכְוָת תְּחוֹת כָּל־שְׁמַיָּא	the kingdoms under all the heaven Dan 7:27

c. Pronominal or adjectival modifiers modifying the head word occur after the entire phrase:

שָׂבֵי יְהוּדָיֵא אִלֵּךְ	those elders of the Judeans Ez 6:8 (head word modified)
עקי ארז חדתן	new beams of cedar A6 2:14 (head word modified)
טור תורא דן	this mount of the ox 1QapGen 17:10 (head word modified)

§155. Instead of nouns, other morphological types can be the head word of a construct phrase:

מְהַנְזְקַת מַלְכִין	(this city is) a harmer of kings (= one that harms kings) Ez 4:15, participle
עבדי חמסא ורשעא ושקרא	the doers of violence, wickedness, and deceit 1QapGen 11:14, participle
דרכי ארקא	the walkers of the earth (= those who walk the earth) C1 1:92 (Ahiqar), participle
אַחֲוָיַת אֲחִידָן	telling of riddles Dan 5:12, infinitive
שוית עננין [לבו]שה	the making of clouds into his garments 11QtgJob 30:7, infinitive

שְׁפַל אֲנָשִׁים	(a) low (one) of humans (= a lowly human being) Dan 4:14, adjective
עַתִּיק יוֹמִין	an old (one) of days Dan 7:9, adjective
חכים ממלל	wise of speech C1 1:114 (Ahiqar), adjective

Note that when the head word is a participle or infinitive, the dependent is equivalent to an object in a verbal clause.

§156. When the dependent word is an abstraction, the phrase can be taken as the equivalent of an attributive adjective phrase (the *attributive genitive*):

גִּבָּרֵי־חַיִל	mighty warriors (lit., "warriors of might") Dan 3:20
בִּתְקָף חִסְנִי וְלִיקָר הַדְרִי	in my mighty strength and for my glorious honor (lit., "in the strength of my might and for the honor of my glory") Dan 4:27
ארחת קשט[א]	righteous ways (lit., "ways of truth") 4Q212 1 ii 18
שהד חמס	a malicious witness (lit., "a witness of malice") C1 1:140 (Ahiqar)

This is particularly common with the word עָלַם "eternity, time without limit": מַלְכוּת עָלַם "kingdom of eternity (= eternal kingdom)" (Dan 3:33); מרה עלמיא "lord of ages (= eternal lord)" (1QapGen 21:2), etc.

§157. a. Cardinal numbers (§166) can appear as the head of construct phrases when the dependent word or phrase is definite:

שבעת ראשי נהרא דן	the seven heads (extremities) of this river 1QapGen 19:12
שִׁבְעַת יָעֲטֹהִי	his seven advisors Ez 7:14

b. Nouns indicating measurements of time are used in construct with cardinal numbers as equivalent to ordinals (§165). The cardinals agree with the head noun in gender.

שְׁנַת תַּרְתֵּין לְמַלְכוּת דָּרְיָוֶשׁ   the *second year* of the reign of Darius
Ez 4:24

יוֹם תְּלָתָה לִירַח אֲדָר דִּי־הִיא שְׁנַת־שֵׁת לְמַלְכוּת דָּרְיָוֶשׁ   the *third day* of the month Adar, which is the *sixth year* of the reign of Darius
Ez 6:15

שנת 3 דריהוש   the *third year* of Darius
B3 7:1

בלילא תשעה   on the *ninth night*
4Q209 1 i 7

Nouns with Pronominal Suffixes

§158. Nouns with pronominal suffixes (§§127ff.) form single units, but they are like construct phrases in having two components, head and dependent. The dependent noun is replaced by a pronominal suffix, which *ex officio* makes the noun definite.

a. Semantically, the relationship of head and dependent suffix is usually *possessed–possessor*: אֱלָהַנָא "our God" (Dan 3:17); יְדָךְ "your hand" (Dan 3:17); אַנְפּוֹהִי "his face" (Dan 3:19); לְבֻשֵׁיהוֹן "their garments" (Dan 3:21), etc.

b. Cardinal numbers (§§164ff.) can also take pronominal suffixes, with the quantification applying to the suffix, which controls agreement:

גֻּבְרַיָּא אִלֵּךְ תְּלָתֵּהוֹן שַׁדְרַךְ מֵישַׁךְ וַעֲבֵד נְגוֹ   those men, *the three of them*, Shadrach et al.
Dan 3:23

תרינא מן שרש [ח]ד צֹמ֯ח֯[נ]א   *the two of us* have sprouted from one root
1QapGen 19:16

§159. a. The pronominal possessive relation can also be expressed by the combination of דִּי and the preposition לְ with pronominal suffixes, written as one word or as two (דִּי ל־, דִּיל־ and the like).

בצדקת לוי ודילי   by the righteous acts of Levi *and of me*
4Q542 1 i 8

נשׁיא זילן	*our* wives	A4 7:20 (Petition)
עלים אחרן זילי	another servant *of mine*	A6 11:5
תאתא זי לך רבתא	*your* large ewe	D7 8:2–3
אישׁ זילכם	a man *of yours*	B2 9:14

As these examples show, the head noun may be indefinite (absolute state) in this construction.

b. The דִּיל־ possessive with its suffix can be used independently of a head noun:

אוספת לה על דילה שׂגי	I added to him much to *what was his*	1QapGen 21:6
חָכְמְתָא וּגְבוּרְתָא דִּי לֵהּ־הִיא	wisdom and power are *his*	Dan 2:20
דילכי הו	it is *yours*	B2 7:7

דִי Genitives (Periphrastic Genitives)

§160. a. In addition to the construct phrase, a *periphrastic* genitive phrase is frequently used, in which the head noun and dependent noun (or noun phrase) are linked by the particle דִי. In such constructions, דִי is equivalent to English *of* or Middle Hebrew שֶׁל.

b. In the דִי genitive, the head nominal must be in the absolute or determined state (not construct) and the dependent nominal will normally be in the same state as the head noun. The head noun may have a pronominal suffix in certain cases (§162).

c. The constituents of the דִי genitive, on either side of דִי, can be any type of noun or noun phrase, including a construct phrase, except that a quantifier (cardinal number or כֹּל) or a proper name generally cannot be the head.[2]

---

[2] A rare exception is אבוד זי מצרין "Abydos of Egypt" (D24 1:4).

בי זי לבנן	a house of bricks B3 1:9
דכר די ען	a ram of a flock 4Q197 4 iii 11
אֶצְבְּעָן דִּי יַד־אֱנָשׁ	fingers of a hand of a human Dan 5:5
שִׁלְטָא דִּי־מַלְכָּא	the official of the king Dan 2:15
עֲבִידְתָּא דִּי מְדִינַת בָּבֶל	the work of the province of Babylon Dan 2:49
הֵיכַל מַלְכוּתָא דִּי בָבֶל	the palace of the kingdom of Babylon Dan 4:26
גִּירָא דִּי־כְתַל הֵיכְלָא דִּי מַלְכָּא	the plaster of the wall of the palace of the king Dan 5:5
גַּפִּין אַרְבַּע דִּי־עוֹף	four wings of bird-kind Dan 7:6
בִּסְפַר־דָּכְרָנַיָּא דִּי אֲבָהָתָךְ	in the book of records of your fathers Ez 4:15
סָפַר דָּתָא דִּי־אֱלָהּ שְׁמַיָּא	the scribe of the law of the God of heaven Ez 7:12

As can be seen from the examples above, the periphrastic genitive allows longer combinations of nominal phrases that might become unwieldy or ambiguous in the construct phrase alone.

d. In IA, a head noun in the absolute state may sometimes have a determined or definite dependent, the latter usually a proper name.

ארמי זי סון	an Aramean of Syene B2 1:2
בר זי אפולי	a son of Apuli B3 4:21
קִרְיָה דִּי שָׁמְרָיִן	a city of Samaria Ez 4:10

e. Semantically, the periphrastic genitive is synonymous with the construct phrase, although there may be pragmatic reasons for the choice of one or the other (see Garr 1990).

גֹּב אַרְיָוָתָא   the den of lions
Dan 6:8

גֻּבָּא דִּי אַרְיָוָתָא   the den of lions
Dan 6:17

§161. The *genitive of material*, in which the dependent noun signifies the material from which the head noun is made, is particularly common with the periphrastic genitive, although it is also found with the construct state:

צְלֵם דִּי־דְהַב   an image of gold
Dan 3:1; cp. צְלֵם דַּהֲבָא
Dan 3:5

מזרקיא זי זהבא וכסף   the bowls of gold and silver
A4 7:12 (Petition)

חרבן די פרזל   swords of iron
4Q202 1 ii 26

רֵאשֵׁהּ דִּי דַהֲבָא   the head of gold
Dan 2:38

In the genitive of material, the dependent is not the possessor of the head but is a property of the head. The דִּי + material part of the phrase can be used alone as an adjective:

רֵאשֵׁהּ דִּי־דְהַב טָב חֲדוֹהִי וּדְרָעוֹהִי דִּי כְסַף מְעוֹהִי
וְיַרְכָתֵהּ דִּי נְחָשׁ   its head was *of fine gold*, its breast and arms were *of silver*, its belly and thighs were *of bronze*
Dan 2:32

§162. a. When the head noun of a דִּי genitive is a noun with pronominal suffix (§158), the pronoun refers forward to ("anticipates") the dependent nominal. In such cases, the semantic relationship of the two terms is *inalienable*, that is, the possessor and the possession are strongly or intrinsically joined. The dependent is necessarily definite (§85b) in this construction.

שְׁמֵהּ דִּי־אֱלָהָא   the name of God (lit., "his name of God")
Dan 2:20

וּבְיוֹמֵיהוֹן דִּי מַלְכַיָּא אִנּוּן	in the days of those kings Dan 2:44
עִקַּר שָׁרְשׁוֹהִי דִּי אִילָנָא	the core of the roots of the tree Dan 4:23
אֱלָהֵהּ דִּי־דָנִיֵּאל	the God of Daniel Dan 6:27
אבוהי זי אסרחאדן זנה מלכא	the father of this Esarhaddon, the king C1 1:47 (Ahiqar)
ברה די אל	the son of God 4Q246 1 ii 1

b. Note that a phrase like רַגְלוֹהִי דִּי פַרְזְלָא וְחַסְפָּא "its feet of iron and clay" (Dan 2:34) is not an example of this construction, since the suffix on "feet" does not refer forward to the dependent nouns. Here the genitive of material דִּי פַרְזְלָא וְחַסְפָּא is used in a quasi-adjectival manner (see §161 above).

Periphrastic Genitive with לְ

§163. Another kind of periphrastic genitive uses the preposition לְ instead of דִּי.

מֶלֶךְ לְיִשְׂרָאֵל רַב	a great king *of Israel* Ez 5:11
אנת ובר לך וברה לך אח ואחה לך	you or a son *of yours* or a daughter *of yours*, a brother or sister *of yours* B2 2:13
קוניה בר צדק ארמי זי סון לדגל וריזת	Koniah son of Zadok, an Aramean of Syene *of the troop of Varyazat* B2 1:2

The numerous combinatory possibilities of the noun phrase constructions can be seen in the last example in §163, which has an appositional phrase (קוניה בר צדק), of which the second constituent is a construct phrase (בר צדק), itself followed by a further apposition ארמי זי סון, which is a די genitive, followed by a לְ genitive, with a construct phrase דגל וריזת as the prepositional complement.

CHAPTER 7
Numerals and Other Quantifiers

7

Numerals and other words signify the quantity of an entity. The cardinal numbers are not adjectival in that they do not identify or describe a noun but rather indicate how many or how much of something there is. The ordinals, however, are adjectives both morphologically and syntactically.

NUMERALS: FORM

§164. The cardinal (counting) and ordinal (series order) numbers are given in Table 9.

a. In form, the numbers are, like nouns, part of the system of bases formed from triconsonantal roots and patterns.

b. The cardinal חד "one" and ordinal קַדְמָי "first" are etymologically separate from each other, as is common cross-linguistically.

c. The numerals תְּרֵין (masc.) and תַּרְתֵּין (fem.) "two" are derived from a primitive form *θṇayn (masc.), *θṇtayn (fem.). The "vocalic" n becomes -ar- in Aramaic. (Another example of this change is *bṇ, Aramaic בַּר "son"; Testen 1985). The ordinal תִּנְיָן "second" is from the same primitive root and preserves the original n unchanged.

d. The numerals 3–10 are inflected like the noun declensions. The numerals quantifying feminine nouns are in the 1st declension, and those quantifying masculine nouns are in the 2nd declension (§83b).

e. The numerals 11–19 are formed by placing the construct form of the cardinals 1–9 before forms of עֲשַׂר (masc.), עשׂרה (fem., *עֲשָׂרֵה), e.g., תְּרֵי־עֲשַׂר "twelve" (Ez 6:17, masc.), תרתי עשרה "twelve" (1QapGen 21:26, fem.); תלת עשרה "thirteen" (1QapGen 21:27, fem.); ארבעת עשר "fourteen" (2Q24 4 13, masc.); etc.

f. The decimals (20, 30, etc.) are formed with the 1st decl. mp ending ין -īn added to the unmarked (fem.) form, but are not otherwise declinable (do not change state or gender). עֶשְׂרִין "twenty" is formed from עֲשַׂר "ten" (fem.), תְּלָתִין "thirty" from תְּלָת "three" (fem.), and so on.

g. The higher numerals מְאָה "hundred," אֲלַף "thousand," רְבוֹ "ten thousand" are lexical nouns and can be quantified by the lower numerals, e.g., אַרְבַּע מְאָה "four hundred" (Ez 6:17).

Table 9: *Cardinal and ordinal numbers (includes reconstructed forms)*

Cardinals		Ordinals	Fractions	11–19		tens	hundreds
masculine	feminine	(§97)		masc.	fem.		
1 אֶחָד	אַחַת	רִאשׁוֹן		אַחַד עָשָׂר	אַחַת עֶשְׂרֵה	—	100 מֵאָה
2 שְׁנַיִם	שְׁתַּיִם	שֵׁנִי	1/2 חֵצִי	שְׁנֵים־עָשָׂר	שְׁתֵּים עֶשְׂרֵה	20 עֶשְׂרִים	200 מָאתַיִם
3 שְׁלֹשָׁה	שָׁלֹשׁ	שְׁלִישִׁי	1/3 שְׁלִישׁ	שְׁלֹשָׁה עָשָׂר	שְׁלֹשׁ עֶשְׂרֵה	30 שְׁלֹשִׁים	300 שְׁלֹשׁ מֵאוֹת
4 אַרְבָּעָה	אַרְבַּע	רְבִיעִי	1/4 רֹבַע	אַרְבָּעָה עָשָׂר	אַרְבַּע עֶשְׂרֵה	40 אַרְבָּעִים	400 אַרְבַּע מֵאוֹת
5 חֲמִשָּׁה	חָמֵשׁ	חֲמִישִׁי	1/5 חֹמֶשׁ	חֲמִשָּׁה עָשָׂר	חֲמֵשׁ עֶשְׂרֵה	50 חֲמִשִּׁים	etc.
6 שִׁשָּׁה	שֵׁשׁ	שִׁשִּׁי	1/6 שִׁשִּׁית	שִׁשָּׁה עָשָׂר	שֵׁשׁ עֶשְׂרֵה	60 שִׁשִּׁים	
7 שִׁבְעָה	שֶׁבַע	שְׁבִיעִי	1/7 שְׁבִיעִית	שִׁבְעָה עָשָׂר	שְׁבַע עֶשְׂרֵה	70 שִׁבְעִים	
8 שְׁמֹנָה	שְׁמֹנֶה	שְׁמִינִי	1/8 שְׁמִינִית	שְׁמֹנָה עָשָׂר	שְׁמֹנֶה עֶשְׂרֵה	80 שְׁמֹנִים	
9 תִּשְׁעָה	תֵּשַׁע	תְּשִׁיעִי	1/9 תְּשִׁיעִית	תִּשְׁעָה עָשָׂר	תְּשַׁע עֶשְׂרֵה	90 תִּשְׁעִים	
10 עֲשָׂרָה	עֶשֶׂר	עֲשִׂירִי	1/10 עֲשִׂירִית	—	—	—	

h. Combined forms have the structure: $(1–99) \times 1000 + (1–9) \times 100 + 10–90 + 1–19$, with the last number preceded by conjunctive וְ, e.g., תלתין ותרין אלפין ותשע מאה "32, 900" (11Q18 18:3); מאתין וחמשן "250" (A6 2:14); תלת מאא ותמניאת עשר "318" (1QapGen 22:6); מאתין שבען וחמשה "275" (A6 2:15); ארבע מאה עשרן וחמשה "425" (A6 2:16); שִׁתִּין וְתַרְתֵּין "62" (Dan 6:1), etc. Most of the numbers in the Egyptian papyri are written in ciphers.

i. The multiplicatives are חד + cardinal number: חַד־שִׁבְעָה "sevenfold" (Dan 3:19); חד תרין "twofold" (11QtgJob 38:4); חד אלף "thousandfold" (A4 7:3, Petition).

SYNTAX OF NUMERALS

Ordinal Numbers

§165. a. Ordinal numerals are a subset of attributive adjectives (§145):

<blockquote>
קַרְנַיָּא קַדְמָיָתָא   the *first* horns

Dan 7:8
</blockquote>

<blockquote>
וּמַלְכוּ רְבִיעָיָה [רביעאה]   a *fourth* kingdom

Dan 2:40
</blockquote>

b. Like attributive adjectives, they can be used without the head noun:

<blockquote>
קַדְמָיְתָא כְאַרְיֵה   the *first* (beast) was like a lion

Dan 7:4
</blockquote>

c. Beyond the number 10, the cardinal numbers are used for ordinals, e.g., שהריאל [ש]תֹת עסר לה "Sahariel, sixteenth to him; Tumiel, seventeenth to him" (4Q201 1 iii 11).

Cardinal Numbers

§166. a. *Word order*. The cardinal number may occur before or (more often) after the head noun or noun phrase, which, unless the number is חַד "one," is absolute plural.

b. *Agreement*. As noted (§164d), the cardinal numerals use the 2nd declension for masculine nouns and the 1st declension for feminine nouns.

<blockquote>
גֻּבְרִין אַרְבְּעָה   *four* men

Dan 3:25
</blockquote>

אַרְבַּע חֵיוָן רַבְרְבָן	*four* great beasts
	Dan 7:3
בנן נקבן חמש	*five* female children
	1QapGen 12:11
אַמִּין שִׁתִּין	*sixty* cubits
	Dan 3:1
שִׁבְעָה עִדָּנִין	*seven* times
	Dan 4:29

c. *Ciphers*. The epigraphic texts (IA and QA) sometimes use ciphers for numerals. These are represented by Arabic numerals in most publications:

14 אמין	14 cubits
	4Q554a 1 5
2 שקלן	2 shekels
	B2 6:6

d. The cardinal numeral חַד "one" is treated as an attributive adjective, with the adjectival norms of agreement (§145), and as a rule occurs after the head noun:

כְּשָׁעָה חֲדָה	about *one* moment
	Dan 4:16
לִשְׂטַר־חַד	to *one* side
	Dan 7:5

In some cases, it has become less of a quantifier and more of an indefinite article:

כְּתַבוּ אִגְּרָה חֲדָה	they wrote *a* letter
	Ez 4:8
רכב בסוסה חד קליל	he rode on *a* swift horse
	C1 1:38 (Ahiqar)

Like other adjectives, it can appear without a head noun:

חַד מִן־קָאֲמַיָּא   *one* of those standing there
Dan 7:16

חד מן בני ביתי   *one* of the members of my household
1QapGen 22:33

חד דרך קשתה   *one* strung his bow
C1 1:190 (Ahiqar)

For the use of cardinals in temporal construct phrases, see §157b.

e. When the quantified noun/noun phrase is definite, the cardinal is in the construct state (§157a).

NOUN + כל

§167. a. The universal quantifier כֹּל "all" is frequently the head of a construct phrase (§153).

b. When the dependent is a singular indefinite (absolute state) countable noun or nominal, it means *every* or *any*. When the dependent is a singular definite nominal, it means *all (the whole of)*; when the dependent is plural, or a singular noun of mass or material, it means *all (without exception)*.

כָּל־אַרְעָא   *all* the earth
Dan 2:35

כָּל־אֱנָשׁ   *every* man (or: *any* man)
Ez 6:11

כָּל־עַם אֻמָּה וְלִשָּׁן   *any* people, nation, or language
Dan 3:29

כָּל־חַכִּימֵי בָבֶל   *all* the wise men of Babylon
Dan 2:48

ריקן מן כל נהור   empty of *any* light
4Q209 6 9

נצלה עליך בכל עדן   we shall pray for you at *every* time
A4 7:26 (Petition)

c. When the verb or other sentence element is negated with לָא or אַל (§§386ff.), כֹּל means *none, not any* (that is, the negation of כֹל never means *some*).

וְכָל־אֲתַר לָא־הִשְׁתְּכַח לְהֹון   *no (not any)* place was found for them
Dan 2:35

לָא־יִפְלְחוּן וְלָא־יִסְגְּדוּן לְכָל־אֱלָהּ לָהֵן לֵאלָהֲהֹון   they would *not* worship or bow down to *any* god except their god
Dan 3:28

כל בתולן וכלאן די יעלן לגנון לא ישפרן מנהא   *no (not any) virgins or brides* who enter the canopy are more beautiful than she
1QapGen 20:6

כול דם לא תאכלון   *no blood* shall you eat
1QapGen 11:17

d. The quantified noun, although syntactically not the head, controls verbal agreement (§355).

נָפְלִין כָּל־עַמְמַיָּא אֻמַיָּא וְלִשָּׁנַיָּא   all of the peoples, tribes, and tongues *were* falling down
Dan 3:7 (pl. verb)

וכל בתולן וכלאן די יעלן לגנון   all the virgins and brides who *enter* the canopy
1QapGen 20:6 (fem. pl. verb)

§168. a. Besides appearing as head of a construct phrase (prepositive), כֹּל can appear appositionally, after the quantified noun or noun phrase (postpositive). Postpositive כֹּל is used only in the determined state (IA):[1]

יהודיא כלא   all the Judeans
A4 8:22 (Petition)

אלהיא כלא   all the gods
A3 9:1

שְׁלָמָא כֹלָּא   all peace
Ez 5:7

Note also prepositive determined כֹּל in כלא מליא "all the matters" (A4 7:29, Petition).

---

[1] Postpositive כֹּל apparently in the absolute state is most likely defective writing for penultimately accented כֹּלָּא (§§25, 344b).

b. Postpositive כֹל can also appear with resumptive pronominal suffixes referring to the quantified noun:

אתור כולה   all Assyria (lit., "Assyria, all of it")
C1 1:55 (Ahiqar)

ארעא כולהא   all of the land
1QapGen 11:12

Prepositive (construct) כֹל can occur together with postpositive suffixed כֹל (QA):

כול ארעא כולהא   all of the earth
1QapGen 10:13

כול אילניא כולהון   all of the trees
4Q204 1 i 28

c. The form כֹּלָּא "everything, all" (§344b) can appear independently, with the scope determined by context:

כֹּלָּא מְטָא עַל־נְבוּכַדְנֶצַּר מַלְכָּא   *all* (of the aforementioned) came upon king Nebuchadnezzar
Dan 4:25

כלא באשה שרפו   *everything* (in the temple) they burned with fire
A4 7:12 (Petition)

לה מחוין כולא   they tell him *everything*
1QapGen 2:21

אנתה מרה ושליט על כולא   you are lord and ruler over *all things*
1QapGen 20:13

d. In IA, כל is used in some contexts as a lexical noun, *total*, in construct with cardinal numbers.

חלכין תרין אמן חד כל תלתה   two Cilicians, one artisan, a *total* of three
A6 9:4

מחסיה בר נתן 1 ידניה בר נתן 1 כל 2   Mahseiah son of Nathan, 1, Jedoniah son of

Nathan, 1, a *total* of 2

B2 11:2

DISTRIBUTIVE AND RECIPROCAL PHRASES

§169. Distributivity is a type of quantification that views all the members of a quantified set as single individuals, like English *each* instead of *all*. Several strategies are used to express distributivity:

a. The number חד "one" (or the cipher 1) can denote the individual member of the quantified set, as in the following examples:

מסמרי נחש מאה וחמשן לחד פשכן תלתה   nails of bronze, one hundred and fifty,

each one three handbreadths

A6 2:15

חלרן 2 לתקל 1 לירח 1   (the interest shall be) 2 ḥallurin *per* shekel

per month

B3 1:5

אמין 4 לשוק חד   4 cubits to *each* street

4Q554 1 ii 20

b. The noun גבר "man" can also be used in the sense *each* (cp. BH אִישׁ), when the member set is human:

גבר חלקה נהחסן   we shall inherit *each* his share

B2 11:14

ויהבו לה גבר אמרה חדה   they gave him *each* one ewe-lamb

11QtgJob 38:7

c. *Reduplication.* The distributive expression may be reduplicated, sometimes with כל "all":

יהב כסף ליהו אלהא לגבר כסף ש 2   (the Judeans who) gave silver to the god Yaho,

each man 2 silver shekels

C3 15:1

איל ען חד לכול גבר וגבר	one ram of the flock for *each and every man* 2Q24 4 18
לכול חד וחד	to *every single one* 4Q204 1 vi 1
בין פרזא לפרזא שוק	between *each block* was a street 4Q554 1 ii 14–15
שָׁלְטָנֵהּ עִם־דָּר וְדָר	his dominion is with *each generation* Dan 3:33

d. *Reciprocal* phrases express identical relations between members of a distributed set:

שָׁנְיָן דָּא מִן־דָּא	(the beasts) differed from *each other* Dan 7:3
לָא־לֶהֱוֺן דְּבָקִין דְּנָה עִם־דְּנָה	they will not stick *with each other* Dan 2:43

The expression of reciprocal relations is not limited to pronouns, as in the following example.

אנתה לחברתה חענן	each enfolds the other [using אנתה "woman" and חברה "companion"] 11QtgJob 36:2–3 (MT Job 41:9)

מה AS QUANTIFIER

§170. In some contexts, the interrogative מָה (§138) can serve as a quantifier *any/whatever*:

מָה חַשְׁחָן	any needed things Ez 6:9
מה צבו ומלה	any desire or thing A4 3:6

CHAPTER 8

Adjective Phrases

§171. Adjectives, as noted (§81), are inflected in the same way as nouns, although there are some derivational patterns that are mainly used with adjectives (§§97, 110). They differ from nouns in having no intrinsic gender, agreeing with the gender of whatever noun they modify. This occurs when the adjective is used attributively (§145) or predicatively (§376).

ADJECTIVES WITHOUT NOUNS

§172. a. Adjectives can be used as nouns themselves when the head noun they modify is recoverable from context, often when the head is very general in meaning. Consider the following examples:

עַמִּיקָתָא וּמְסַתְּרָתָא *deep* (things) and *hidden* (things)
Dan 2:22

יִנְדְּעוּן חַיַּיָּא דִּי־שַׁלִּיט עִלָּיָא [עלאה] the *living* (ones) shall know that the *Most High* (God) rules
Dan 4:14

קדישא רבא the great *holy* (God)
1QapGen 2:14

ישימון טב בחנכה למאמר they will put a *good* (thing) in his palate to say
C1 1:163 (Ahiqar)

b. Some adjectives, if frequently used without their head nouns, become in effect nouns themselves, such as רַב "ruler, noble" (adj. "large"); חַכִּים "sage" (adj. "wise"); שַׁלִּיט "ruler" (adj. "having authority"), and so on. This is particularly true of participles, which are adjectives syntactically; see such examples as רָחֵם "friend" (רחם G stem, "love"); שָׂנֵא "enemy" (שׂני G stem, "hate"); יָעֵט "advisor" (יעט G stem, "advise"), רָעֵה "shepherd" (G stem, "graze"), and so on.

COMPARATIVE GRADE

§173. Aramaic has no inflection for the comparative grade, that is, no inflection such as *-er* on English *bigger*. However, the same meaning is accomplished syntactically with a prepositional phrase adjective complement headed by מִן "from"(§182ff.).

וְחֶזְוַהּ רַב מִן־חַבְרָתַהּ	its appearance was *greater than* its fellows Dan 7:20
תקיפין מני	(ones) *stronger* than me 4Q531 22 7
זערין מני ביומין	*smaller* than me in days (i.e., younger) 11QtgJob 15:4
לא איתי זי [מ]ריר מן ענוה	there is nothing *more bitter* than poverty C1 1:89 (Ahiqar)

In 1QapGen, the preposition ברא מן (§192) is used once for the same function: תקיף ברא מנך "(I will be your shield against) anyone *stronger* than you" (1QapGen 22:31). This is unusual, and possibly a scribal error.

CHAPTER 9

9

Prepositions

Form and Function

§174. Prepositions, by and large, stand outside of the three-consonant root system, although some triliteral nouns have developed into prepositions.

Prepositions, and especially the single-consonant proclitic ones (§176), tend to have only very general meanings and as a rule are best interpreted in context. The main functions of each are laid out below, but for a comprehensive description, the dictionaries should be consulted.

PREPOSITIONAL PHRASES

§175. a. The prepositional phrase is composed of *preposition* plus a *noun, noun phrase*, or *pronominal suffix*, which is the *object* or *complement* of the preposition.

b. The phrase has four functions: (1) to mark verbal complements (direct or indirect objects or other kinds of complements), (2) to express adverbial modification of a clause; (3) to modify nouns directly or in a relative clause (§148); (4) to serve as predicate of a copular clause (§377). These functions are distinguishable only in context and not morphologically.

c. Structurally, the preposition, whether proclitic or not, occurs immediately before the noun that is its complement. The complement may be the head of a further noun phrase or may be an entire noun phrase, as in the following examples:

> לַחֲנַנְיָה מִישָׁאֵל וַעֲזַרְיָה   to Hananiah, Mishael, and Azariah
> Dan 2:17

> בִּרְגַז וַחֲמָה   in anger and rage
> Dan 3:13

The preposition may also be repeated before each conjunct (§142b).

d. For emphasis, the preposition may have a pronominal suffix that refers forward to ("anticipates") a following noun:

> בַּהּ־זִמְנָא   at that very time
> Dan 3:8

בַּהּ־שַׁעֲתָא	at that very moment
	Dan 3:6

מִנַּהּ מַלְכוּתָה	from that very kingdom
	Dan 7:24

PREPOSITIONAL SURVEY

Simple Proclitic Prepositions: מִן־, כְּ, בְּ, ל

§176. These very common prepositions are directly attached to a host noun complement (or pronominal suffix). מִן־, although usually written separately, can be treated among these "primitive" prepositions.

a. *Vocalization of inseparable prepositions.* The inseparable prepositions בְּ, ל, כְּ are vocalized with *shewa* when added to a word whose first consonant is followed by a full vowel. If the first consonant is followed by a *shewa*, then the preposition is vocalized with *hireq*, e.g., ל + תְרַע > לִתְרַע (Dan 3:26).

b. If the word begins with a *hateph* vowel, it has the corresponding short vowel (§24).

c. If the word begins with יְ, the combination yields לִי/בִּי/כִּי (§52d).

d. When vocalic suffixes (beginning with a vowel) are added to בְּ and ל, the prepositions are attached directly to the suffix, e.g., ל + 3ms suffix > לֵהּ; when consonantal suffixes are added, the prepositions are vocalized with *shewa*, e.g., ל + 3mp suffix > לְהוֹן. The preposition כְּ does not take pronominal suffixes.

The Preposition ל

The proclitic preposition ל can have many meanings, but its main function is marking transitions. The functions below are organized by the role of the noun complement.

§177. a. The ל may mark complements of particular classes of verbs or clauses:

b. With verbs of giving or transferring (§339), ל marks the *recipient* of the giving (indirect object).

מַתְּנָן רַבְרְבָן שַׂגִּיאָן יְהַב־לֵהּ	many great gifts he gave *to him*
	Dan 2:48

רְבוּ יַתִּירָה הוּסְפַת לִי	exceeding greatness was added *to me*
	Dan 4:33

Related to *recipient,* the *addressee* is the indirect object of verbs of speaking or informing (339c).

כְּדְנָה תֵּאמְרוּן לְהוֹם thus you shall say *to them*
Jer. 10:11

מִלְתָא הוֹדַע אַרְיוֹךְ לְדָנִיֵּאל Arioch told the matter *to Daniel*
Dan 2:15

שְׁאֵלְנָא לְשָׂבַיָּא אִלֵּךְ we asked *those elders*
Ez 5:9

c. The *direct object* receives the action of a transitive verb (§337). The direct object is usually marked with לְ only if it is definite (§359a). The לְ is semantically empty in this function and is not represented in translation.

אֱדַיִן מַלְכָּא לְדָנִיֵּאל רַבִּי then the king magnified *Daniel*
Dan 2:48

לְמָאנַיָּא דִי־בַיְתֵהּ הַיְתִיו קָדָמָיךְ [קדמד] *the vessels of his house* they brought before you
Dan 5:23

שריו לקטלה לאנשא they began to kill *humanity*
4Q201 1 iii 19

חמרא רכב לאתנא the jack mounted *the jenny*
C1 1:186 (Ahiqar)

d. With verbs of motion (§331), לְ marks the *goal* or endpoint of the action.

דָּנִיֵּאל לְבַיְתֵהּ אֲזַל Daniel went *to his house*
Dan 2:17, also Dan 6:19

וְלִשְׂטַר־חַד הֳקִמַת it was raised up *to one side*
Dan 7:5

דבקת לפורת נהרא I reached *the Euphrates River*
1QapGen 21:17

e. With verbs denoting stance, לְ may mark *orientation* or direction.

יִפֵּל וְיִסְגֻּד לְצֶלֶם דַּהֲבָא

he must fall and bow down *to the image of gold*
Dan 3:10

כונה 1 פתיח לתרי רבתא

its one window is open *to the large room*
B3 12:21

f. In copular clauses (§377b) or existential clauses (§380d), לְ marks the *possessor* of a thing or trait. See those sections for exemplification.

g. With verbs of *becoming* or *making*, the לְ may indicate the *product* or final state.

הֲוָת לְטוּר רַב

(the stone) became *a great mountain*
Dan 2:35

אֲנָה בֱנֵיתַהּ לְבֵית מַלְכוּ

I have built it *into a royal house*
Dan 4:27

אהוא לעפר

I shall become *dust*
11QtgJob 37:8

h. The לְ may mark the pronominal subject of a verb; in such cases, the construction marks a heightened participation of the subject in the verbal action (the "ethical dative"). The prepositional phrase always occurs after the verb. For exemplification and further discussion, see §336.

§178. The לְ may also introduce prepositional phrases used *adverbially*, not as introducing objects or other verbal complements.

a. The לְ may mark one who receives *advantage* (or disadvantage) from an action or situation (*dativus commodi sive incommodi*), where the verbal meaning does not require such a complement.

בֵּלְשַׁאצַּר מַלְכָּא עֲבַד לְחֶם רַב לְרַבְרְבָנוֹהִי

Belshazzar the king made a great feast *for his nobles*
Dan 5:1

הֲווֹ בָעַיִן עִלָּה לְהַשְׁכָּחָה לְדָנִיֵּאל

they were seeking to find a pretext *against Daniel*
Dan 6:5

זבנת משח זית ליקה

I have bought olive oil *for YQH*
A2 2:11

b. The ל may mark a stretch of *time*, either with or without definite boundaries.

מַלְכָּא לְעָלְמִין חֱיִי   O king, live *for ages*
Dan 2:4

לִקְצָת יַרְחִין תְּרֵי־עֲשַׂר   *at the end of twelve months*
Dan 4:26

עד זי לעדן [א]חרן ליומן אחרנן   until *another time and other days*
C1 1:49 (Ahiqar)

c. The ל may mark the *intended purpose* of a thing or action.

לְפָלְחָן בֵּית אֱלָהָךְ   (vessels) *for the service* of the house of your god
Ez 7:19

יעית לקושט   I grew *for truth*
1QapGen 6:1

d. A *distribution* by quantity or by time (§169) can be marked with ל:

יהב כסף ליהו אלהא לגבר לגבר כסף ש [2]   (the garrison that) gave silver to YHW the god, *each man* 2 shekels of silver
C3 15:1

תְּרֵי־עֲשַׂר לְמִנְיָן שִׁבְטֵי יִשְׂרָאֵל   twelve (he-goats) *corresponding to the number* of the tribes of Israel
Ez 6:17

e. Phrases with ל may modify nouns or noun phrases (§147), by marking genitival dependents (see §163) or by *linking* nouns in compound phrases (§142b), as here:

פַּחַת יְהוּדָיֵא וּלְשָׂבֵי יְהוּדָיֵא   the governor of the Jews and *the elders of the Jews*
Ez 6:7

לְבַקָּרָא עַל־יְהוּד וְלִירוּשְׁלֵם   to investigate Judah *and Jerusalem*
Ez 7:14

ל appears in fixed combinations with other forms:

f. לְ plus *infinitive* marks either an infinitival complement (§428, with exemplification) or an adverbial clause (usually purpose clauses, §401, with exemplification).

g. לְ is joined to lexical words or other prepositions to make further prepositions. It is joined to the noun **gaw(w)* "interior," making לְגוֹא "into" (Dan 3:23, etc.); the noun **ṣad(d)* "side," making לְצַד "towards" (Dan 7:25); to the noun יַד "hand," meaning "alongside" (e.g., 1QapGen 21:15); to the (unattested) noun *qubl "front" (?) making לָקֳבֵל "facing opposite" (§200); with added כְּ, making כָּל־קֳבֵל (§200d); to the preposition קֳדָם (§203a).

The Preposition בְּ

§179. The proclitic בְּ denotes very generally the location of an entity in or near another entity. It may also be used to mark obliquely the complements of verbs, but the adverbial function is more common than the complement one.

The adverbial uses are as follows:

a. The preposition signifies location *in* or *near* a physical space:

שְׁלֵה הֲוֵית בְּבֵיתִי וְרַעְנַן בְּהֵיכְלִי
I was tranquil *in my house* and flourishing *in my palace*
Dan 4:1

יְבַקַּר בִּסְפַר־דָּכְרָנַיָּא
one should search *in the book of records*
Ez 4:15

b. Some usages may be more readily translated with *into, on, with* (accompaniment):

קַרְנַיָּא עֲשַׂר דִּי בְרֵאשַׁהּ
the ten horns that were *on* its head
Dan 7:20

יְהַב בִּידָךְ
he put (them) *into* your hand
Dan 2:38

אזלת אנה אברם בנכסין שגיאין לחדא
I, Abram, went *with* very many possessions
1QapGen 20:33

The preposition can be added to **gaw(w)*, interior, to yield בְּגוֹא "within" (§104; Dan 3:25, etc.).

c. It can signify position in *time*:

בַּהּ־שַׁעֲתָא   *in* that moment

Dan 4:30

וּבְיוֹמֵי אֲבוּךְ   *in* the days of your father

Dan 5:11

בִּשְׁנַת חֲדָה לְכוֹרֶשׁ מַלְכָּא   *in* the first year of Cyrus the king

Ez 5:13

d. It can indicate *figurative location* with nouns of subjective experience.

בְּחֶדְוָה   *in* joy (= joyfully)

Ez 6:16

בִּטְעֵם חַמְרָא   *in* the command of wine (= under the influence of wine)

Dan 5:2

בְּהִתְבְּהָלָה   *in* agitation

Dan 2:25, 3:24, 6:20

e. With concrete or abstract nouns, it can denote *instrument*, the means of carrying out an action.

וַחֲטָיָךְ [וחטאך] בְּצִדְקָה פְרֻק   remove your sins *by* almsgiving

Dan 4:24

קָרֵא בְחָיִל   calling *with* force

Dan 3:4

אִשְׁתִּיו בְּהוֹן   they drank *with* (by means of) them (the vessels from the Jerusalem temple)

Dan 5:3

f. It can indicate the *role* or *position* that something has:

גֻּבְרַיָּא דִּי בְרָאשֵׁיהֹם   the men who are *in the role of* their leaders

(= who are their leaders)

Ez 5:10

למה אלהיא יסגה בעדרה   lest God should come *as* his help

C1 1:126

g. Other less frequent adverbial functions of בְּ include marking reciprocal participants (פַּרְזְלָא מְעָרַב בַּחֲסַף טִינָא "iron mixed *in/with* clay," Dan 2:41, 43), temporal distribution (יוֹם בְּיוֹם "day by day," Ez 6:9), and general association (דִּי לָא־תִשְׁנֵא צְבוּ בְּדָנִיֵּאל "that nothing would change *with regard to* Daniel," Dan 6:18).

§180. The role of בְּ in marking verbal complements is as follows:

a. The preposition בְּ marks the complements of the G-stem verb שׁלט and its associated adjective שַׁלִּיט (§342a):

שְׁלִטוּ בְהוֹן אַרְיָוָתָא	the lions overpowered *them* Dan 6:25
שַׁלִּיט עִלָּיָא [עלאה] בְּמַלְכוּת אֲנָשָׁא [אנשא]	the Most High rules *over the realm of humankind* Dan 4:14

b. Other verbs also have complements marked with בְּ (see §342a for exemplification).

The Preposition כְּ

§181. Phrases with the preposition כְּ occur adverbially or as the predicate of a copular clause. It indicates resemblance or identity, therefore *like, according to* (with laws or instructions), *about = approximately* (with quantities):

לְבוּשֵׁהּ כִּתְלַג חִוָּר	his clothing was *like white snow* Dan 7:9
אסר נא כגבר חלציך	gird up your loins *like a man* 11QtgJob 34:2–3
נשיא זילן כארמלה עבידין	our wives are in the condition *of a widow* A4 7:20 (Petition)
כִּכְתָב סְפַר מֹשֶׁה	*according to* the writing of the book of Moses Ez 6:18
אלפונה כרעות אל	his teaching is *according to* the will of God 4Q541 9 i 3
כְּבַר שְׁנִין שִׁתִּין וְתַרְתֵּין	*about* sixty-two years old Dan 6:1

Pronominal suffixes are attached only to the longer form כְּוָת (cp. §197, לְוָת):

בניך די להון כואתך　　your sons who will be *like you*
　　　　　　　　　　　1QapGen 11:15

For the use of the preposition with the infinitive in a temporal clause, see §419.

Combinations: כָּל־קֳבֵל (§200d), כַּחֲדָה (§351d), כְּדִי (§§417–418), כְּמָה (§347d).

The Preposition מִן

§182. מִן expresses the notion of separation or movement away from a source. It marks verbal complements and adverbials.

a. מִן is usually written as a separate word, but in a few cases it merges with the host word, the final *n* assimilating (§42) to the first consonant, e.g., מִטּוּרָא "from the mountain" (Dan 2:45).
b. If the host word begins with a guttural, the *n* is dropped, and the short *i* becomes *e* in compensation (§77c), e.g., מֵאַרְעָא "from the earth" (Jer 10:11). מִן is always written separately in IA and QA.
c. Before suffixes, the *n* geminates: with 1cs מִנִּי *minnī* "from me" (Dan 3:29), מִנְּהוֹן *minnəhon* "from them" (Dan 6:3), and the like.

§183. מִן marks the complement of verbs that typically express separation, removal, absence, or other ablative movement (away from something).

a. The preposition marks the *point of origin*, especially with verbs signifying moving, removing, or separation:

מַלְכוּתָה עֲדָת מִנָּךְ　　the kingdom has passed away *from you*
　　　　　　　　　　　Dan 4:28

הַנְפֵּק מִן־הֵיכְלָא　　he took them *from the temple*
　　　　　　　　　　Ez 5:14

מַן־הוּא אֱלָהּ דִּי יְשֵׁיזְבִנְכוֹן מִן־יְדָי　　who is the god who can rescue you *out of my hands*?
　　　　　　　　　　　　　　　　　　　　　　Dan 3:15

b. The preposition may mark the *original state or location* of something undergoing change.

דִּי תִשְׁנֵא מִן־כָּל־מַלְכְוָתָא　　a kingdom that will be different *from all the (other)*
　　　　　　　　　　　　　　　　　　kingdoms
　　　　　　　　　　　　　　　　Dan 7:23

לְבָבֵהּ מִן־אֲנָשָׁא [אנשא] יְשַׁנּוֹן   his mind will be altered *from the human race*
Dan 4:13

יֵאבַדוּ מֵאַרְעָא   they will perish *from the earth*
Jer 10:11

c. With hiding verbs, the preposition may mark a *perceiver* of something hidden.

לא יתכסון מן ענני   they shall not be hidden *from Anani*
A4 3:11

הצפנתך מנה   I hid you *from him*
C1 1:49 (Ahiqar)

§184. The uses of מִן as a modifier, adverbial or nominal, are various:

a. The preposition can mark the *cause* of an action:

וּמִן־רְבוּתָא דִּי יְהַב־לֵהּ   *because* of the greatness that he gave him
Dan 5:19

מִן־טַעַם אֱלָהּ יִשְׂרָאֵל   *because* of the command of the God of Israel
Ez 6:14

מן עובד רעותנא   *because* of the action of our shepherds
1QapGen 21:5

b. The preposition can mark the *whole* from which a part or an amount is taken (*partitive* function):

רַגְלוֹהִי מִנְּהֵון [מנהין] דִּי פַרְזֶל וּמִנְּהֵון [ומנהין]   its feet, (part) *of them* of iron and (part) *of them* of
דִּי חֲסַף   clay
Dan 2:33

וּתְלָת מִן־קַרְנַיָּא קַדְמָיָתָא   three *of the first horns*
Dan 7:8

מעשר מן כול נכסיא   a tenth *of all the possessions*
1QapGen 22:17

חד מן רבי אבי   one of the nobles of my father
C1 1:33 (Ahiqar)

c. The preposition can mark the *starting point* of a range of time or space:

וּמִן־אֱדַיִן וְעַד־כְּעַן   *from* then until now
Ez 5:16

מן מדנחא למערב[א]   *from* east to west
4Q554 1 ii 16

מן ירח תמוז   *from* the month of Tammuz
A4 7:19 (Petition)

d. It can mark a comparison, *more than* (with adjective phrases, see §173).

מן כל מנטרה טר פמך   *more than* any watching, watch your mouth
C1 1:82 (Ahiqar)

רעיתך מן כל בשר[א]   I favor you *more than* all flesh
4Q213b 1 1

חָכְמָה דִּי־אִיתַי בִּי מִן־כָּל־חַיַּיָּא   wisdom that there is in me *more than* all the living
Dan 2:30

Biconsonantal Prepositions

These particles are not transparently derived from nouns or combinations of other particles.

§185. The preposition אל (cp. BH אֶל) is used only in the opening address of letters in IA, e.g., אל מראן בגוהי "to our lord Bagavahya" A4 7:1 (Petition). It is not found in later dialects.

§186. The preposition יָת has no semantic content and is used to indicate the definite direct object (§359b); it occurs but once in BA, with the 3mp suffix: יָתְהוֹן (Dan 3:12). It is not attested in IA and is infrequently used in QA, e.g., אולד ית עמ[ר]ם "(Kohath) begot Amram" (4Q559 3 3). In these corpora, ל is more commonly used as a direct object marker.

§187. Phrases with the preposition עַד mark a spatial or temporal limit to a state or process, or the time within which a condition holds. When combined with דִּי, it forms a temporal clause (§420). It is sometimes coordinated with מִן "from" (§184c) to mark an entire span of space or time. It does not take pronominal suffixes.

a. Spatial limit, *up to, as far as.*

מן ימא רבא עד חורן   from the Great Sea *as far as Hauran*
1QapGen 21:11

נדשוהי עד ארעא   they destroyed it *to the ground*
A4 7:9 (Petition)

עַד־עַתִּיק יוֹמַיָּא מְטָה   he came *up to* the one advanced in days
Dan 7:13

This includes figurative extensions:

עד כא סוף חלמא   *up to here* is the end of the dream (= this is the entire
dream)
4Q530 2 ii + 6-12(?):12

b. Temporal limit, *until, up to.*

וּמִן־אֱדַיִן וְעַד־כְּעַן   from then *until now*
Ez 5:16

עַד מֶעָלֵי שִׁמְשָׁא   *until* sunset
Dan 6:15

עַד שְׁנַת תַּרְתֵּין לְמַלְכוּת דָּרְיָוֶשׁ   *until* the second year of King Darius
Ez 4:24

מן ירח תמוז . . . ועד זנה יומא   from the month of Tammuz . . . *up to* this day
A4 7:19–20 (Petition)

c. Temporal extent, *for (amount of time), during.*

עַד־יוֹמִין תְּלָתִין   (whoever petitions any god or human) *for thirty days*
Dan 6:8

אַרְכָה בְחַיִּין יְהִיבַת לְהוֹן עַד־זְמַן וְעִדָּן   a prolongation in life was given to them *for a time
and a season*
Dan 7:12

e. Limit of amount:

עַד־חִנְטִין כֹּרִין מְאָה   *up to* one hundred kors of wheat
Ez 7:22

מן חוט עד ערקא דמסאן   from a thread *to* a shoelace
1QapGen 22:21

For conjunctive (דִּי) עַד, including the meaning "while," see §420. See also: עַד־דִּבְרַת (§404).

§188. The preposition עַל serves to mark prepositional complements, adverbials, and nominal modifiers. The basic meaning is "on, over," but it develops specialized nuances.

a. עַל takes the suffixes of a 1st decl. pl. noun.

b. Location, *on* or *upon*.

שִׂמַת עַל־פֻּם גֻּבָּא   (a stone) was placed *on the mouth of the pit*
Dan 6:18

אסמֹוך ידי עלוהי   I shall place my hands *upon him*
1QapGen 20:22

על מדבחא זי יהו אלהא   (they shall make offerings) *on the altar* of YHW the god
A4 7:26 (Petition)

This includes abstract (figurative) location:

מרביתה זי ישתאר עלי   (the money) and its interest that will remain *on me* (= *incumbent on me to pay*)
B4 2:9

הן אשבקן על לבבך   if I leave you *on your mind* (= *dependent on your own judgment*)
C1 1:177 (Ahiqar)

c. *Direction*, indicating the goal (usually human) of a verb of motion (§331):

אתה עלי חרקנוש   Horqanosh came *to me*
1QapGen 20:21

קִרְבֵת עַל־חַד מִן־קָאֲמַיָּא	I approached *one of those standing* Dan 7:16
פַּרְשֶׁגֶן אִגַּרְתָּא דִּי שְׁלַחוּ עֲלוֹהִי	the copy of the letter that they sent *to him* Ez 4:11

d. The agent's own *body part* may be the end point of a change of posture:

נְפַל עַל־אַנְפּוֹהִי	he fell *on his face* Dan 2: 46
הוּא בָּרֵךְ עַל־בִּרְכוֹהִי	he was kneeling *on his knees* Dan 6:11

e. *Area of control,* with verbs of rule or authority:

הוא מלך על כל רחש	he is king *over every crawling thing* 11QtgJob 37:2

f. *Experiencer,* with stative verbs (§330) or copula (§373a):

מִלְכִּי יִשְׁפַּר עֲלָיִךְ [עלך]	let my counsel be pleasing *to you* Dan 4:24
כְּדִי מִלְּתָא שְׁמַע שַׂגִּיא בְּאֵשׁ עֲלוֹהִי	when he heard the word, it was very displeasing *to him* Dan 6:15, cf. 6:24
הן על מראן טב	if it is pleasing *to our lord* A4 7:23 (Petition)

g. *Beneficiary/maleficiary,* marks someone advantaged or disadvantaged by an event:

זִיוֹהִי שָׁנַיִן עֲלוֹהִי	his countenance altered *against him* (= *for the worse*) Dan 5:9
שְׁנָתֵּהּ נַדַּת עֲלוֹהִי	his sleep wavered *to him* (= *to his discomfort*) Dan 6:19
יצלה עלוהי	he will pray *for him* 1QapGen 20:23

h. *Additive.* The object of the preposition signifies a measure that is surpassed, with verbs of increase.

לְמֵזֵא לְאַתּוּנָא חַד־שִׁבְעָה עַל דִּי
חֲזֵה לְמֵזְיֵהּ

to heat the furnace seven times *over what* was proper to heat it

Dan 3:19

אנה אוספת לה על דילה שגי

I added to him very much *over what* he had

1QapGen 21:6

i. Object of attention (*about, concerning*).

שְׁמְעֵת עֲלָיִךְ [עלך]

I have heard *about you*

Dan 5:14

רְעוּת מַלְכָּא עַל־דְּנָה

the will of the king *concerning this*

Ez 5:17

והוטבת לבבי על ארקא זך

you have satisfied my mind *concerning that land*

B2 2:11–12

אתעשת על אגורא זך

take thought *about that temple*

A4 7:23

אתמה על כול שפרהא

he was amazed *at all her beauty*

1QapGen 20:9

This may merge with the idea of cause:

בכא אברם על לוט

Abram wept *about Lot* (= *because of Lot*)

1QapGen 22:5

j. In IA, the combination עַל דבר, usually written as one word עלדבר, is used prepositionally in the meaning "concerning, because of" (דבר + עַל "reason"):

אסרני עלדבר אבנצרף 1

he arrested me *because of* a dyer's stone

A4 3:3

יקטל איש למ[רא]ה על דבר כספה

a man may kill his master *because* of his money

C1 2:23

For the related phrase עַל־דְּבְרַת דִּי, see purpose clauses (§404).

§189. The preposition עִם serves to mark prepositional complements, adverbials, and nominal modifiers.

a. It takes pronominal suffixes as a singular noun; before suffixes, the מ is geminated.

b. *Accompaniment* (comitative, sharing in the same action):

עִמְּהוֹן נְבִיַּאיָּא [נביייא] דִּי־אֱלָהָא *with them* were the prophets of God
Ez 5:2

עִם־עֲנָנֵי שְׁמַיָּא כְּבַר אֱנָשׁ אָתֵה *with the clouds of heaven* one like a human being
was coming
Dan 7:13

פתכר סוסה עם רכבה a sculpture of a horse *with its rider*
A6 12:2

אנחנה עם נשין ובנין we *with our wives and children*
A4 7:15 (Petition)

This can extend to benefactive action:

אָתַיָּא וְתִמְהַיָּא דִּי עֲבַד עִמִּי the signs and wonders that he has done *with me* (= *for me*)
Dan 3:32, cp. Ez 6:8

The comitative function can also have a temporal meaning:

שָׁלְטָנֵהּ עִם־דָּר וְדָר his dominion is *with every generation*
Dan 3:33

חֶזְוִי עִם־לֵילְיָא my vision *with the night* (= *at night*)
Dan 7:2

c. *Reciprocal* (subject and prepositional object perform the same action towards each other):

לָא־לֶהֱוֺן דָּבְקִין דְּנָה עִם־דְּנָה they do not adhere one *with the other* (lit., this with this)
Dan 2:43

לִבְבֵהּ עִם־חֵיוְתָא שַׁוִּי [שויו] his mind was made equal *with the beasts*
Dan 5:21

| דָּנִיֵּאל עִם־מַלְכָּא מַלִּל | Daniel spoke *with the king*
Dan 6:22 |

| [מ]ה ישפטון עקן עם אשה בשר עם סכין איש
עם מ]לך[| how can wood dispute *with fire*, meat *with a knife*, a man *with a king*?
C1 1:88 (Ahiqar) |

Derived Prepositions

Derived prepositions function exactly like the morphologically simpler ones, but etymologically derive from either nouns, which affects their morphology, especially with suffixes, or from combinations of other particles.

§190. The preposition אַחֲרֵי (< *ʾaḥar "back") has a purely temporal meaning, "after." As its form indicates, it takes suffixes as a 1st declension plural noun.

| אָחֳרָן יְקוּם אַחֲרֵיהוֹן | another will arise *after them*
Dan 7:24, cf. 2:29, 45 |

| לזרעך אנתננה אחריך | to your seed I will give it *after you*
1QapGen 21:14 |

§191. Not used in IA, the grammaticalized prepositional phrase בָּאתַר (בְּ + אֲתַר "place") or בָּתַר has a temporal meaning, "after," in BA. It takes suffixes as a 1st declension singular noun.

| בָתְרָךְ תְּקוּם מַלְכוּ אָחֳרִי | *after you* will arise another kingdom
Dan 2:39 |

| בָּאתַר דְּנָה | *after this*
Dan 7:6, 7 |

| בתר פתגמיא אלן | *after* these things
1QapGen 22:27 |

It is sometimes locative in QA:

| הוא רדף בתרהון | he was pursuing *after them*
1QapGen 22:7 |

It can also be used in combination with מֵן:

מן בתר מבולא

after the Deluge
1QapGen 12:9

מן בתרה יקום שבוע תמיני

after it will appear an eighth week
4Q212 1 iv 15

§192. The preposition ברא מן is composed of בַּר "outside" linked to מֵן "from" (§§182ff.) and means "aside from, except for." ברא has the adverbial ending -*ā* (unstressed) (§344). In IA it appears as בר *bárrā*, with the final vowel omitted in the orthography (§56d).

לא שליטה יהוֹ[ישמע ל]הבעלה בעל אחרן
בר[מן] ענני

Jehoishma does not have the right to marry another husband *aside from* Anani
B3 8:33

ברא מן די אכלו כבר עולימי

(I will not take anything from you) *except* that which my lads have already eaten
1QapGen 22:23

§193. The preposition בדיל "because of, on account of" (QA; cf. JLA בְּדִיל) is a combination of בְּ + דִּי + לְ: בדיל שרי "on account of Sarai" (1QapGen 20:25); תפלט נפשי בדיליכי "my life will be safe because of you" (1QapGen 19:20); etc. (For its use in causal clauses, see §411; see the related conjunction בדי, §413.)

§194. The preposition בֵּין "between, among" (< *bayn*, "interval"?) takes suffixes as a 1st declension plural noun.

תְּלָת עִלְעִין בְּפֻמַּהּ בֵּין שִׁנַּהּ [שׁנה]

three ribs in its mouth *between* its teeth
Dan 7:5

תנתנון לי ביניכון שם טב

you shall give me a good name *among* you
4Q542 1 i 10

It can be coordinated with לְ or another בין:

בין מדי לפרס

between Media and Persia
4Q583 1 4

בין תמת ובין ענני

between Tamut and Anani
B3 3:12–13

§195. The compound preposition בלחוד (בְ + לחוד "alone") "by . . . self," is suffixed as a 1st declension plural noun, e.g., בלחודיהה "by herself" (1QapGen 19:15), בלחודוהי "by himself" (11QtgJob 25:7).

§196. The preposition חלף (< *ḥulāp, "exchange"?) "in place of, in exchange for," is used with the suffixes of a 1st declension singular noun (§128):

אחיהון עללין חלפהון	their brothers enter *in place of them*
	11Q18 15 3
המו שליטן בה חלף עבידתא זי אנת עבדת	they have authority over it *in exchange for* the work that you did
	B2 4:10

§197. The preposition לְוָת (composed of לְ + the archaic object marker *wāt) is always directional, *to* a person:

אתין לות איוב כל רחמוהי	all his friends came to Job
	11QtgJob 38:4–5

When coupled with מִן (§§183ff.), it means directionally *from* a person:

יְהוּדָיֵא דִּי סְלִקוּ מִן־לְוָתָךְ עֲלֶינָא	the Jews who have come up *from you* to us
	Ez 4:12
פרש לוט מן לואתי	Lot departed *from me*
	1QapGen 21:5

§198. The noun טלל "shade, protection" has been used to form the preposition בטלל (or בטל) "with the help of, because of":

בטלל אלה שמיא	with the help of the God of heaven
	A4 3:5
שביק ארזא בטלל תמרתא	the cedar was spared because of the palm tree
	1QapGen 19:16
אחי בטליכי	I shall survive because of you
	1QapGen 19:20

§199. The preposition לְ combined with the noun עורע "meeting," yields a meaning "towards" (< "for meeting"). The IA form לערק displays the old orthography of the root (< *ʿrś̂, §37).

אזלו לערקה   they went *towards him*
C2 1:V.15

נפק מלך סודם לעורעהון   the king of Sodom came out *towards them*
1QapGen 21:31

§200. The compound preposition לָקֳבֵל (< lə + *qubl, "front"?) is used in adverbial phrases or as a nominal modifier, in the following meanings.

a. Its original concrete meaning is "facing opposite":

קָאֵם לְקָבְלָךְ   standing *opposite* you
Dan 2:31

תרע לקבל תרעא   a gate *opposite* the (other) gate
4Q554 1 iii 18; cf. 11Q18 19 1

See also Dan 3:3, 5:1, 5.

b. A figurative extension is "corresponding to, according to":

עמיר לקבל רכשה   (give) fodder *according* to (the number of) horses
A6 9:4

ספרא זך הנפקי ולקבלה דין עבדי עמה   produce this document and litigate with him
according to it
B2 3:27

לָקֳבֵל דִּי־שְׁלַח דָּרְיָוֶשׁ   *according* to that which Darius sent
Ez 6:13

c. A further extension of the sense yields "because."

לָקֳבֵל מִלֵּי מַלְכָּא   *because* of the words of the king
Dan. 5:10, cf. Ez 4:16

d. לָקֳבֵל also appears in BA with proclitic כְּ, as כָּל־קֳבֵל. (For the phonology of כָּל־קֳבֵל, see §76b.) As a preposition, in BA it is only found in the phrase כָּל־קֳבֵל דְּנָה "because of this" (Dan 2:12), "according to this" (Ez 7:17; see also Dan 2:24; 3:7, 8, 22; 6:10). When preposed to דִּי, לָקֳבֵל / כָּל־קֳבֵל serves as a subordinating conjunction with causal clauses (§408) or manner clauses (§415).

§201. The Hebraism נֶגֶד is used infrequently in the same sense as לָקֳבֵל (§200).

נֶגֶד יְרוּשְׁלֵם

facing Jerusalem
Dan 6:11

לא איתי [כ]ל מחיר נגדה

there is no price *corresponding to it*
4Q213 1 ii+2 4

§202. The preposition עלוי, probably vocalized like JLA עִלָּוֵי ʿillāwē, is infrequently used in the spatial meaning "above, on top of." It is not found in BA.

עלוי אגרא זך

on top of that wall
B2 1:6

עלוי ארעא

on the earth
4Q203 4 4

§203. a. The preposition קֳדָם (< *qudām, "forepart"?) has the basic meaning "before, in front of." It takes suffixes as a 1st declension plural noun.

רִבּוֹ רִבְוָן [רבבן] קָדָמוֹהִי יְקוּמוּן

ten thousand ten thousands were standing *before him*
Dan 7:10

קדם גבר או אנתא

in front of a man or a woman
4Q197 4 i 13

It also may have a temporal meaning:

כָּל־חֵיוָתָא דִּי קָדָמַיהּ [קדמה]

all the beasts that were *before it*
Dan 7:7

In QA, it can combine with לְ:

אקרבו פת[ו]רא לקודמי   they brought the table *before me*
4Q196 2 11

Its primary function, however, is to serve as an honorific preposition with nouns that signify gods, kings, or others of high rank (see Klein 1979). As such, it substitutes for other prepositions:

b. Substituting for לְ (§§177ff.):

לָא אִיתַי דִּי יְחַוִּנַּהּ קֳדָם מַלְכָּא   there is none who can tell it *before the king*
(= *to the king*)
Dan 2:11

אודית תמן קודם אלהא   I gave thanks there *before God* (= *to God*)
1QapGen 21:3

c. Substituting for עַל (§188):

הַנְעֵל לְדָנִיֵּאל קֳדָם מַלְכָּא   he brought Daniel *before the king* (= *unto the king*)
Dan 2:25

קרבתך קדם סנחאריב מלכא   I presented you *before Sennacherib the king* (= *unto S. the king*)
C1 1:50 (Ahiqar)

שְׁפַר קֳדָם דָּרְיָוֶשׁ   it was pleasing *before Darius* (= *to Darius*)
Dan 6:2

d. The combination מִן־קֳדָם substitutes for מִן (§§183ff.):

מַתְּנָן וּנְבִזְבָּה וִיקָר שַׂגִּיא תְּקַבְּלוּן מִן־קֳדָמָי   gifts and reward and much honor you will receive *from before me* (= *from me*)
Dan 2:6

וכולהון הווא ערקין מן קודמוהי   all of them were fleeing *from before him* (= *from him*)
1QapGen 22:9

מן קדם אוסרי מין קחי   *from before Osiris* (= *from Osiris*) take water
D20 5:3 (Carpentras Stele)

The preposition accordingly does not always need to be represented in translation.

§204. The noun קדמה* "first part" (?) has been wholly converted to a preposition "before" (spatial or temporal): קדמת יומיא אלן "before these days" (1QapGen 21:23); קדמתך מנדעם קשה "before you is something difficult" (C1 1:85, Ahiqar). See also §350e (adverbs).

§205. The preposition תְּחוֹת marks the location *under*. It takes suffixes as a 1st declension plural noun. The spelling תחת is used in IA.

> תְּחֹתוֹהִי תַּטְלֵל חֵיוַת בָּרָא   *under it* (the tree) the wild animals found shade
> Dan 4:9

> מַלְכְוָת תְּחוֹת כָּל־שְׁמַיָּא   the kingdoms *under* all the heavens
> Dan 7:27

The form תַּחְתּוֹהִי (Dan 4:11) for תְּחֹתוֹהִי is a Hebraism.

CHAPTER 10
Verbs
Derivation and Inflection

§206. Derivational verbal bases, like those of nouns and adjectives, are built by combining the *root* morpheme (usually of three consonants) with a *pattern* of vowels and other modifications. The root + pattern *base* in verbs is organized into a group of verbal *stems*, which form a syntactic–semantic system. Various default settings of valence (§323), voice (§325), and *Aktionsart* (§328) are assigned to particular stems, although these settings can be neutralized or set aside in particular cases.

§207. a. *Roots and root meaning.* When different stems use the same root morpheme, there is a semantic connection between them that is at least partially systematic but not completely predictable. Few roots, if any, appear in every stem.

b. When verbs are encountered, they must be learned as root-pattern wholes. Although one may loosely say that the root has a "meaning," strictly speaking the root exists only at the level of word formation and receives a meaning only when instantiated in a verbal stem (or nominal base).

§208. *Stem names.* The derivational stems in Biblical Aramaic are here indicated by alphabetic abbreviations. In many older grammars, the paradigm root פעל *pʿl* "to act" was used to create stem names from the root-pattern shape. The chart below gives the alphabetic abbreviations this grammar uses, along with the older traditional names. The alphabetic names are based on some identifying feature of the stem, while the traditional names give the phonological shape of the simplest (3ms) suffix conjugation of the stem.

Stem abbreviation	Traditional name
G (from German *Grundstamm*)	Pəʿal
Gp (*passive of G stem*)	Pəʿil
tG (prefix *(h)it* + G stem)	(H)ithpəʿel
D (the *doubled* stem, with doubled middle root letter)	Paʿel
tD (prefix *(h)it* + D stem)	(H)ithpaʿal
C (the *causative* stem)	Haphʿel (or Aphʿel)
Cp (*passive of C stem*)	Hophʿal
tC (prefix *(h)it* + C stem)	(H)ittaphʿal

From this point on, the alphabetic abbreviations will be primarily used.

There are other verbal stems that are not very productive (§§236, 276) as well as verbal bases that are borrowed from other languages (§288).

FINITE VERB CONJUGATIONS AND NON-FINITE FORMS

§209. a. The TAM (tense–aspect–mood) system of Biblical Aramaic will be described in Chapter 11, but for understanding the stem shapes, it is important to know that finite verbs (those inflected for both person and tense) have two conjugations, one inflected with suffixes only (mainly used for past tense, §292) and one inflected with both prefixes and suffixes (mainly used as the future-modal tense, §300). A variation of the prefix conjugation is used in the volitive mood (jussive, §317).

b. A note about terminology: in this grammar, the terms *sufformative* and *preformative* are used only in the context of derivation, that is, the formation of word bases and verbal stems. *Suffixes* can be *inflectional*, as in the noun declensions and the verbal conjugations, or *pronominal*. *Prefixes* are only inflectional, in the verbal conjugation described in §§300ff.

c. Only in the G stem do the two finite verb conjugations have different bases. In all the other stems the base remains the same in both conjugations.

d. In addition to the finite verb conjugations, there are non-finite (not inflected for both person and tense) verbal forms: the participle (used as a present tense, but originally a verbal adjective, §§305ff., and therefore having inflectional suffixes of the 1st or 2nd declension) and the infinitive (not inflected for person, gender, or tense). Each stem has its own base for these forms.

§210. The *theme vowel* of a verbal stem is the vowel occurring *before the last root consonant*. In non-G stems, the theme vowel is the same in both conjugations, but in G stem verbs the theme vowel usually varies by conjugation, and weakly aligns with certain kinds of valence (§323) or *Aktionsart* (§328).

STRONG AND WEAK ROOTS

§211. Roots that display all three root consonants throughout the entire paradigm are called "strong" roots. However, a large number of roots undergo loss or change of one or more root consonants during inflection due to diachronic and synchronic phonological processes. These are "weak" roots. The inflectional system will be laid out on the basis of strong roots, and then the specific changes induced by weak roots will be dealt with.

Note that some verbs are strong (with three stable consonants) in the suffix conjugation, but weak (unstable root) in the prefix conjugation; others are weak in the suffix conjugation, but strong in the prefix conjugation.

SUFFIX CONJUGATION INFLECTIONAL SUFFIXES

§212. Throughout all the stems, the suffix conjugation (SC) adds inflectional suffixes to a verbal base to express person, gender, and number. The traditional paradigmatic ordering of the suffixes begins with the 3ms inflection. The table below gives the inflectional suffixes only, not attached to bases.

Note that in weak verbs of the III-y class, the endings may be somewhat different due to the phonological changes described in §58; see §§256ff.

Inflectional suffixes of the BA suffix conjugation

Person, gender, number	Forms	Transcription
3ms	---	(no suffix)
3fs	ת‍ֲ---	. . . -a*ṯ*
	ת‍ֶ‍ֱ--	. -*έ.εṯ*
2ms	תָּ--- or תְּ---,	. . . -t, . . . -tā
	‍תָּה---, אתְ---	
2fs	תְּ---*	. . . -tī
1cs	ת‍ֲ---, ת‍ֵ---	. . . -e*ṯ*, . . . -ε*ṯ*
3mp	ו---	. . . -ū
3fp	ה‍ָ---	. . . -ā
2mp	תּוּן---	. . . -tūn
2fp	תֵּן---*	. . . -ten
1cp	נָא---	. . . -nā

a. The 3ms ending was originally short *a*, but it fell away with the loss of final short vowels (§59), leaving a "meaningful zero."

b. The 3fs ending normally is -*át*, with final stress, but a minority of forms have unstressed -*εt*, with accent on a penultimate vowel -*έ*.

c. The 2ms ending is originally -*tā* (BA -*tɔ*). The unstressed vowel is generally not indicated by a *mater* in IA (§25). In BA and QA, the final vowel sometimes falls away.

d. The 2fs form is not found in BA. In IA, the ending is written תי -*tī*. In later JLA, it is simply ת־ -*t* (no vowel).

e. The 1cs form is derived from an anaptyctic (separating) vowel added after the loss of short vowels (§60, see §217b).

f. The 3fp and 2fp forms are not used in IA, which uses the 3mp form for both genders.

g. The 2mp form תון־ -*tūn* is historically derived from תם -*tum*, which is still the predominant form in IA.

PREFIX CONJUGATION INFLECTIONAL PREFIXES AND SUFFIXES

§213. The attested prefixes of the PC, with their associated suffixes, are given below.

Person, gender, number	Forms	Transcription
3ms	י ---	*y-* . . .
3fs	ת ---	*t-* . . .
2ms	ת ---	*t-* . . .
2fs	*ת---ׂין	*t-*. . .*īn*
1cs	א ---	*ʾ* . . .
3mp	י --- ון	*y-* . . . *ūn*
3fp	י --- ָן	*y-* . . . *ān*
2mp	ת --- ון	*t-* . . . *ūn*
2fp	ת --- ָן	*t-* . . . *ān*
1cs	נ ---	*n-* . . .

a. The 2fs form is not attested in BA, but the form given occurs in IA and QA and is well established in the other dialects.

b. The jussive inflections of the 3ms, 3fs, and 2ms are the same as the indicative forms. In the 2fs, 3mp, and 2mp, the jussive forms are the same without the final *nun*, i.e., ־ׂי -*ī* (2fs), ו-*ū* (3mp, 2mp). The 3fp/2fp forms are not attested.

c. Note that suffixes in the prefix conjugation serve to differentiate forms with the same prefix: forms with the *y-* prefix are differentiated by zero (3ms), -*ūn* (3mp), -*ān* (3fp); with the *t-* prefix, by zero (3fs, 2ms), -*īn* (2fs), -*ūn* (2mp), -*ān* (2fp). Only the 3fs and 2ms have the same inflection in the paradigm.

G Stem, Strong Roots

§214. a. G stem (from German *Grundstamm*, "basic stem") is by far the most common stem. When it shares three-consonant roots with non-G stems, the G stem meaning is usually the simple "default" signification, while the non-G stems are variations or complications of this basic one.

b. However, as noted, not every root occurs in the G stem; that is, roots can be represented in non-G stems only (e.g., מלל, "speak," D stem).

§215. *Base of the G stem.* As noted (§209c), the G stem base varies with the conjugation. There are two principal bases for the suffix conjugation: one with a short *a*-theme vowel and one with a short *i*-theme vowel (§210).

a. Verbs with an *a*-theme in the suffix conjugation often have a short *u* theme in the prefix conjugation, while the *i*-theme suffix conjugation is often matched with an *a*-theme prefix conjugation.

b. The most common suffix conjugation bases are **qǝṭal* (*a*-theme) and **qǝṭil* (*i*-theme). The corresponding prefix conjugation bases are (with prefix attached) respectively **(yi)qṭul* and **(yi)qṭal*. Classes of G stem verbs can thus be characterized by their thematic vowels: *a/u* verbs (*a*-theme SC, *u* theme PC), *i/a* verbs, etc. There are less frequent types such as *i/u* (the root יכל), *a/i* (the root אזל), *i/i* (the root יתב), *a/a* (the root אבד), and others.

c. Roots with final guttural will normally have *a*-class themes in both conjugations for phonological reasons (§78, Rule 4a).

d. Although the theme vowels have no invariable relationship with voice or *Aktionsart*, there is a tendency, inherited from older dialects, to associate statives and intransitives (§§329ff.) with the *i/a*-theme vowel class.

For unpointed corpora like IA and QA, the vowels must be inferred from a comparison with pointed texts.

G Stem Suffix Conjugation, Strong Root

§216. The inflectional suffixes are added to the base form. In the paradigms below, the original inflections from the ancestor language of Aramaic are given along with their reflexes in Biblical Aramaic. The suffixes simultaneously are marked for gender (except in the first person), person, and number.

§217. Most G stem SC verbs have short *a*-theme vowel, as given in the chart below. The asterisk indicates either a hypothetical or reconstructed form.

Form	Biblical Aramaic	Transcription	Original form	Gloss
3ms	קְטַל	qǝṭál	*qaṭál(a)	he killed
3fs	קִטְלַת	qiṭláṯ	*qaṭalát	she killed
2ms	קְטַלְתְּ	qǝṭalt	*qaṭáltā	you (ms) killed
2ms (alt.)	קְטַלְתְּ	qǝṭáltɔ		
2fs	*קְטַלְתִּי	qǝṭáltī	*qaṭáltī	you (fs) killed
1cs	קִטְלֵת	qiṭléṯ	*qaṭalt(u)	I killed
3mp	קְטַלוּ	qǝṭálū	*qaṭálū	they (mp) killed
3fp	קְטַלָה	qǝṭálɔ	*qaṭálā	they (fp) killed
2mp	קְטַלְתּוּן	qǝṭaltū́n	*qaṭaltúm	you (mp) killed
2fp	*קְטַלְתֵּן	qǝṭaltḗn	*qaṭaltín	you (fp) killed
1cp	קְטַלְנָא	qǝṭálnɔ	*qaṭálnā	we killed

a. Note that the BA base is always ־קְטַל qǝṭal- except for the 3fs and 1cs, where it is ־קִטְל qiṭl- due to the operation of Rule 2 (§78, §62e).

b. In the 1cs, a separating vowel was generated after the loss of final short vowels (§59), and the stress has shifted to the separating vowel: *qaṭáltu > qaṭált (after loss of final short vowels) > qaṭálit (insertion of separating vowel) > qaṭalít (stress shift) > qiṭlét (§78, Rule 2, Rule 7). In some stem inflections in BA, the stress has not shifted (§60b). It is likely that in IA and QA the stress assignment was different in some respects.

c. In IA, the 3fp and 2fp are not used. In BA, the 3fp is attested only in the Qere, and the 2fp not at all. The reconstruction given is based on the vocalization of JLA.

§218. The *i*-theme suffix conjugation is not fully exemplified in all categories in BA. In general, the same paradigm as the one above may be applied to *i*-theme perfects, except the theme vowel is *i* (*ḥiriq*) or *e* (*ṣere*). The change of *i* to *e* is frequent in stressed closed syllables (§78, Rule 7).

3ms	קְטֵל, קְטִל	qǝṭíl, qǝṭél
2ms	קְטֵלְתְּ	qǝṭélt
3mp	קְטִלוּ	qǝṭílū
1cp	קְטֵלְנָא	qǝṭélnɔ

An anomalous *i*-theme verb is 3fs בְּטֵלַת Ez 4:24 (§63d), which has resisted syncopation (§78, Rule 2) even though the stress is final (that is, we expect *בְּטְלַת).

BA examples of the SC: 3ms יְהַב (Dan 2:37), שְׁלַח (Dan 3:2, final guttural), שְׁפַר (Dan 6:2, final guttural); שְׁאֵל (Dan 2:10), סְגִד (Dan 2:46), קְרֵב (Dan 3:26), שְׁלֵט (Dan 3:27); 3fs תִּקְפַת (Dan 5:20),

סְלֵקָת (Dan 7:20); 2ms יְהַבְתְּ (Dan 2:23), רְשַׁמְתָּ (Dan 6:13, 14) (a Qumran text has רשמתה), יְכֵלְתָּ (Dan 2:47), תְּקֵפְתְּ (Dan 4:19); 1cs נִטְלֵת (Dan 4:31), שִׁמְעֵת (Dan 5:14), עַבְדֵת (Dan 6:23); 3mp כְּתַבוּ (Ez 4:8), נְפַלוּ (Dan 3:23), נְפַקוּ (Dan 5:5 K), סְלִקוּ (Dan 2:29), קְרִבוּ (Dan 3:8), שְׁלֵטוּ (Dan 6:25); 3fp נְפַקָה (Dan 5:5 Q), נְפַלָה (Dan 7:20 Q); 2mp שְׁלַחְתּוּן (Ez 4:18); 1cp שְׁלַחְנָא (Ez 4:14), שְׁאֵלְנָא (Ez 5:9, 10).

> Exercise. Identify the root of the occurrences above. Where the form is singular, give the form of the plural; where plural, give the singular. (See the complete paradigm in the Appendix, p. 356.)

§219. a. Strong roots whose first root letter is a guttural (א ה ח ע) have *ḥaṭeph pataḥ* instead of *shewa* in the first syllable when it is open (§24), and *a* (*pataḥ*) when it is closed by Rule 2 (§78).

b. Some consonants, including *r* (ר) and *q* (ק), occasionally resist not only the reduction of short vowels preceding them (as Rule 2 may require) but also final stress following them. Thus אֲמֶרֶת (*ʾămέreṯ* < *ʾamarát*) instead of *אֲמַרֹת* "(the queen) said" (3fs; Dan 5:10). See §212b.

Examples: 3ms אֲמַר (Dan 2:24), עֲבַד (Dan 3:1); 3fs אֲמֶרֶת (Dan 5:10); 2ms עֲבַדְתְּ (Dan 4:32); 1cs אַמְרֵת (Dan 4:5), עַבְדֵת (Dan 3:15); 3mp אֲזַלוּ (Dan 3:8), עֲבַדוּ (Jer 10:11); 1cp אֲמַרְנָא (Ez 5:4).

G Stem Prefix Conjugation, Strong Root

§220. The prefix conjugation in the indicative mood is the future-modal form. For the volitive mood, see §317.

Form	Biblical Aramaic	Transcription	Original form	Gloss
3ms	יִקְטֻל	*yiqṭúl*	**yiqṭúlu*	he will kill
3fs	תִּקְטֻל	*tiqṭúl*	**tiqṭúlu*	she will kill
2ms	תִּקְטֻל	*tiqṭúl*	**tiqṭúlu*	you (ms) will kill
2fs	*תִּקְטְלִין	*tiqṭəlín*	**tiqṭulína*	you (fs) will kill
1cs	אֶקְטֻל	*ʾeqṭúl*	**ʾiqṭúlu*	I will kill
3mp	יִקְטְלוּן	*yiqṭəlún*	**yiqṭulúna*	they (mp) will kill
3fp	יִקְטְלָן	*yiqṭəlán*	**yiqṭulna (?)*	they (fp) will kill
2mp	תִּקְטְלוּן	*tiqṭəlún*	**tiqṭulúna*	you (mp) will kill
2fp	תִּקְטְלָן	*tiqṭəlán*	**tiqṭulna (?)*	you (fp) will kill
1cp	נִקְטֻל	*niqṭúl*	**niqṭúlu*	we will kill

10

a. The original vowel of the *yi-/ti-/ʾi-/ni-* prefixes was short *a* in the ancestor language but became *i* in the *yi-* prefixes by assimilation to the glide *y*, and then spread by analogy to the *ti-/ʾi-/ni-* prefixes. The *ʾi* commonly changes to *ʾɛ-* (with *seghol*) under the influence of *ʾaleph* (§75b).

b. The 3fp/2fp ending was originally *-nă* (Huehnergard 1987) in Old Aramaic, but was transformed by analogy to a form resembling the 3fp suffix conjugation ending *-ā + n* (BA *-ɔn*).

c. IA generalizes the mp forms for all plural forms, and no fp forms are attested.

d. Verbs with theme vowel other than *u* have the same paradigm given above except for the theme vowel *i* or *a* in the base (*yiqṭil*, *yiqṭal*) when the vowel does not reduce.

Examples: PC 3ms וְיִסְגֻּד (Dan 3:6), יִשְׁלַט (Dan 5:7); 3fs תִּשְׁלַט (Dan 2:39); 2ms וְתִרְשֵׁם (Dan 6:9), תְלַבַּשׁ (Dan 5:16); 3mp יִסְגְּדוּן (Dan 3:28), יִפְלְחוּן (Dan 3:28); 3fp יִשְׁכְּנָן (Dan 4:18); 2mp תִּשְׁמְעוּן (Dan 3:5), וְתִסְגְּדוּן (Dan 3:5); 1cp נִכְתֻּב (Ez 5:10), נִסְגֻּד (Dan 3:18).

> Exercise. Identify the root of the cited examples above. Where the form is singular, give the form of the plural; where plural, give the singular.

§221. Roots with guttural consonants have some noteworthy characteristics in the PC.

a. Roots with initial *ʾaleph* (I-*ʾaleph*) are weak (§§245ff.).

b. Roots with initial ה ח ע are strong, with the following characteristics:

   The prefix vowel is *a* or *ɛ* instead of *i*, due to Rule 4a (§78): *ya-/ta-/ʾa-/na-* or *yɛ-/tɛ-/ʾɛ-/nɛ-*; e.g., יַחְלְפוּן (Dan 4:13), יֶעְדֵּה (Dan 7:14).

   An "echo" vowel is often inserted after the guttural root letter, whether initial or medial, e.g., תַּעַבְדוּן (Ez 7:18) (secondary opening, §76a).

For הוי in the prefix conjugation, see §268.

G Stem Jussive and Imperative, Strong Root

§222. The volitive mood (§291a) is expressed in two ways, by the jussive prefix conjugation and by the imperative. These in effect form a single paradigm, with the imperative taking the place of the 2nd person jussive except when negated.

3ms jussive	יִקְטֵל	*yiqṭúl*
3fs jussive	תִּקְטֵל	*tiqṭúl*
2ms jussive	תִּקְטֵל	*tiqṭúl*
ms impv	קְטֵל	*qəṭúl*

2fs jussive	*תִּקְטְלִי	tiqtúlī
fs impv	קְטֻלִי	qətúlī
3mp jussive	יִקְטְלוּ	yiqtúlū
2mp jussive	תִּקְטְלוּ	tiqtúlū
mp impv	קְטֻלוּ	qətúlū

a. The jussive is a "short" PC, that is, in the ancestor language the 3ms *yiqtúl* and similar forms did not have a final short vowel like the "long" indicative PC *yiqtulu*, nor did the mp/fp and the 2fs end in -n(a).

b. After the loss of final short vowels in the indicative PC (§59), the jussive paradigm became very similar to the indicative (identical in the 3s/2ms/1cp), except for the 2fs and 3/2mp inflectional suffixes lacking the final -n.

  The original penultimate stress pattern (§78, Rule 8b) is retained for the jussives with final long vowel inflections, as well as for the imperatives, which, as can be seen from the paradigm, are abbreviated forms of the jussive 2nd person forms.

c. Jussives are thus morphologically distinct (in a consonantal text) only in the 2fs and 3/2mp forms. However, verbs negated with אַל (§388) are always jussive, regardless of their form.

d. In the dialects covered in this grammar, no fp jussive forms are certainly attested. In JLA, the (rare) fp impv is קְטֻלָא (Dalman 1960 [1905]: 278), suggesting that the jussive of the previous stage was *tiqtúlā. (For Old Aramaic, see Huehnergard 1987.)

e. The later Aramaic dialects (post-QA) do not use the jussive, the indicative having completely replaced it. Only the imperatives remain as a remnant of the full volitive paradigm.

f. In IA, there are a very few instances of an "energic" ending -n (see §130a) that may form a remnant of a first-person form with a subjunctive or modal nuance: אשלמן "I shall pay" (B4 6:5), perhaps *ašallim-ánna*; הן אשבקן "if I should leave (you)" (C1 1:177), perhaps *ašbuq-ánna* (for other examples, see Muraoka & Porten 2003: 106).

Examples of jussives, strong verbs, G stem: 3ms יִשְׁפַּר (Dan 4:24); 2ms תשבק (A3 8:11), תקרוב (4Q541 24 ii 5); 2fs תזבני (A2 3:10), תדחלי (4Q197 4 i 3); 3mp ינדשו (A4 7:8, Petition); 2mp תנתנו (A6 9:6), תמחלו (4Q213 1 i 13).

G Stem Participle, Strong Root

§223. The active participles have become part of the verbal system of tenses (§§305ff.), although their gender/number inflection is the same as that of the nominal-adjectival declensional endings. Because the participles are mainly used to indicate the relative present tense, they rarely appear in the cstr. or det. form, and only when they are used as nouns (§172b). The table below will give the cstr. and det. forms only when they are attested.

The base form of the G stem ptcp is *qə̄ṭil* or *qə̄ṭel*, קְטֵל / קְטַל. When the third root letter is ה, ע, or ר, the *i/e* vowel of the second syllable becomes short *a* (§78, Rule 4a).

Gender/Number	Paradigm form	Examples
ms	קְטַל / קְטֵל *qə̄ṭil, qə̄ṭel*	קָטֵל Dan 5:19, דָּלִק Dan 7:9, אָמַר Dan 4:4
fs	קָטְלָה *qə̄ṭəlā*	כָּתְבָה Dan 5:5
fs det.	קָטְלְתָא *qə̄ṭiltā*	יָקֶדְתָּא Dan 3:6
mp	קָטְלִין *qə̄ṭəlīn*	דָּבְקִין Dan 2:43
fp	קָטְלָן *qə̄ṭəlān*	נָקְשָׁן Dan 5:6

Exercise: For the BA examples given in the table, change them from singular to plural and vice versa.

G Stem Passive, Strong Root

§224. a. The passive participle of the G stem has the underlying base **qaṭīl > qəṭīl* with long *ī* as the theme vowel. In most cases, it expresses the passive state of an active G stem verb.

When the final root letter is ה or ע, a short *a* is inserted before that root letter in the ms form, e.g., שְׁלִיחַ *šəlīaḥ* (see §76c).

b. The passive participle also provided the basis of a separate stem, only used in the suffix conjugation, by the addition of the person/number/gender inflections. This stem may have originally been vocalized **quṭil* (cp. Arabic passive *quṭila*), but was refashioned to resemble the G passive participle.

ms	קְטִיל *qəṭīl*	בְּרִיךְ Dan 3:28, יְדִיעַ Ez 4:12, גניב A4 3:4, כתיש 4Q242 1+3 3
fs	קְטִילָה *qəṭīlā*	פְּלִיגָה Dan 2:41, שביקה B3 6:9, חליקא 4Q197 4 ii 17
mp	קְטִילִין *qəṭīlīn*	חֲשִׁיבִין Dan 4:32, אסירין 11QtgJob 27:2
mp cstr.	קְטִילֵי *qəṭīlē*	נגיעי 4Q197 4 i 13
fp	קְטִילָן *qəṭīlān*	פְּתִיחָן Dan 6:11, אטימן 5Q15 1 ii 11

Exercise: For the unpointed examples in the chart above, provide vocalization according to the Biblical Aramaic form.

c. The G passive suffix conjugation (only attested forms are shown):

3ms	קְטִיל *qəṭil*	שׁמיע A3 3:13, 1QapGen 12:10 יליד, Dan 4:30 טְרִיד
3fs	קְטִילַת *qəṭilat*	יהיבת B8 2:5, 1QapGen 20:11 דבירת, Dan 7:11 קְטִילַת
2ms	קְטִילְתָּה *qəṭiltɔ*	תְּקִילְתָּה Dan 5:27
1cs	קְטִילֵת* *qəṭilet*	שביקת 1QapGen 20:10
3mp	קְטִילוּ *qəṭilū*	קטילו A4 7:17 (Petition), 4Q206 4 ii 2 שכירו, Dan 7:10 פְּתִיחוּ
2mp	קְטִילְתֶּם* *qəṭiltum* (IA)	שאילתם B2 9:8

The 3ms finite form is distinguishable from the ms ptcp only in context.

G Stem Infinitive, Strong Root

§225. The G stem infinitive has a preformative *mi-*, added to a base *qtal*, yielding *miqtal* מִקְטַל. The theme vowel does not vary except with III-y weak roots (§261c). The preformative vowel may become ε if the first root consonant is a guttural (§75b).

Examples: מִכְנַשׁ (Dan 3:2), מִשְׁבַּק (Dan 4:23), מִפְשַׁר (Dan 5:16), מֶעְבַּד (Ez 4:22).

> Exercise: (1) Identify the roots of the examples given above. (2) Point the following examples from QA texts: מדרך, מדחל, מכחל, מסחר, מקרב, מעקר, מפלח.

D Stem

§226. A D stem verb may occur without a corresponding G stem, so synchronically it should be considered as another verbal pattern, with no obligatory systemic relationship to the other stems. The semantics of the D stem are discussed below (§231).

§227. a. *Base of the D stem.* The D stem has a triliteral base *qaṭṭil* (less often *qaṭṭel*) whose middle radical is doubled (hence "D"), that is, geminated (§54). Unlike the G stem, the same base is used for the suffix conjugation and prefix conjugation. The strong verb paradigm in the Appendix (pp. 356–357) can be consulted for a complete reconstruction.

    b. The original *i*-theme vowel does not generally lower to *e* in closed stressed syllables in the attested forms (see §78, Rule 7).

    c. The prefixes of the prefix conjugation, forming an open unstressed syllable, always have a *shewa* (§78, Rule 1), except in the 1cs (§78, Rule 4a), which has ֲ *ḥateph pataḥ*. The theme vowel *i/e* also reduces to *shewa* when vocalic endings are added, including the pre-suffixal "energic" morpheme *-inn-* (§130a) on the indicative PC.

d. When the middle root letter is a strong consonant other than a guttural, the gemination is indicated by *dagesh* (§28).

e. When the D stem has a final root letter of ע, ר, or ח, the characteristic *i*-theme vowel becomes *a* (§78, Rule 4a).

f. When the middle radical is ר, ע, ח, or ה, (1) *dagesh* is not used to indicate gemination; (2) the characteristic *a* of the base before the middle root consonant may or may not become long *ɔ̄* as compensation (§77c); (3) the reduced vowel with ח, ע, or ה is ◌ֲ *ḥaṭeph paṭaḥ* instead of simple *shewa* (§78, Rule 4b).

Examples: SC: 3ms קַטֵּל (Dan 3:22), שָׁכֵן (Ez 6:12), קַבֵּל (Dan 6:1); 2ms שַׁבַּחְתָּ (Dan 5:23, final guttural); 1cs שַׁבְּחֵת (Dan 4:31); 3mp בַּטִּלוּ (Ez 4:23); with suffixes: 3mp + 1cs חַבְּלוּנִי (Dan 6:23); PC: 3ms יְבַקַּר (Ez 4:15, final guttural); 2ms תְּקָרֵב (Ez 7:17, medial guttural); 3mp יְקַבְּלוּן (Dan 7:18), יְטַעֲמוּן (Dan 4:22); 2mp תְּקַבְּלוּן (Dan 2:6); with suffixes: 3mp + 1cs suff., יְבַהֲלֻנַּנִי (Dan 4:2) (root בהל).

> Exercise: Provide vocalization for the following D stem verbs from QA: SC 3mp שבחו; 1cs יכפר; 3ms יברכון 3mp; תפלט 3fs; תמללין 2fs; נקבל PC 1cp; פרש 3ms; פלטנא 1cp; כפרת.

g. *Imperative.* The D stem imperative consists of the *qaṭṭil/qaṭṭel* base with the same inflectional endings as the G stem imperative (§222): ms קַטֵּל, fs קַטִּלִי, mp קַטִּלוּ. Pronominal suffixes of the *second* series are added, even to the ms form.

Examples: ms אַלֵּף (4Q569 1–2 9), fs unattested, mp קַצִּצוּ (Dan 4:11), בַּדַּרוּ (Dan 4:11), fp unattested. Suffixed forms: ms + 1cs suff. פקדני (4Q550 5+5a 6) (פַּקֵּדְנִי), mp + 3ms suff. חַבִּלוּהִי (Dan 4:20).

§228. The D stem active participle attaches the preformative *m-* to the base *qaṭṭil*, yielding *məqaṭṭil* or *məqaṭṭel*, to which the nominal-adjectival declensional endings are added.

ms	מְקַטֵּל / מְקַטִּל	*məqaṭṭel, məqaṭṭil*
fs	מְקַטְּלָה	*məqaṭṭəlɔ̄*
mp	מְקַטְּלִין	*məqaṭṭəlīn*
fp	מְקַטְּלָן	*məqaṭṭəlɔ̄n*

BA examples: ms מְהַלֵּךְ (Dan 4:26), מְמַלִּל (Dan 7:8), מְשַׁבַּח (Dan 4:34, final guttural); fs מְמַלֲלָה (Dan 7:11), mp מְצַבְּעִין (Dan 4:22), מְסָעֲדִין (Ez 5:2, medial guttural with compensation).

§229. The passive form of the D stem survives only in participial forms, which function as adjectives. The D passive participle has the *m* preformative with *qaṭṭal* base (note the *a*-theme vowel characteristic of the passive).

a. When the middle radical is ר, ע, ח, or ה, it may not geminate and the preceding *a* vowel may become ɔ in compensation (as with §227f).

Examples: BA ms מְעָרַב (Dan 2:41, medial guttural); fs מְשַׁנְיָה (Dan 7:7); mp מְכַפְּתִין (Dan 3:23); fp det. מְסַתְּרָתָא (Dan 2:22).

b. Note that only in the ms is the D passive ptcp distinguishable in form from the active participle due to the operation of Rule 1 (§78).

§230. a. The D stem infinitive has the strong root pattern קַטָּלָה *qaṭṭɔlɔ*, with a characteristic *-ɔ-ɔ* vocalic pattern of all the infinitives not of the G stem.

   b. When pronominal suffixes are added to the D stem, the final *-ɔ* becomes *-ūṯ*: קַטָּלוּת־ *qaṭṭɔlūt-* (§133b).

Examples: לְקַטָּלָה (Dan 2:14); לְכַפָּתָה (Dan 3:20); with 3ms suffix לתרכותה (B2 6:30).

> Exercise: Provide vowels for the following participles and infinitives: mp מכפרין, ms מעשר, mp משמשין, ms מחבל, מפקד, fp מדחלן; inf לאלפה, למללה, לשבחא.

   c. In rare cases in QA and IA, the D stem infinitive has an *m* preformative before the base, like the G stem infinitive (§225): cp. לעמרה (4Q545 1a+b ii 13; = לְעַמָּרָה) and למעמרא (4Q544 1 1; = לִמְעַמָּרָא "to dwell"); משלמותה with suffix (C1 1:131; Ahiqar). Such forms also occur with the C stem (§251c). Infinitives with *m* are dialect forms that will become standard in some Late Aramaic dialects.

Semantics of the D Stem

§231. Many roots are used only or principally in the D stem and thus are unrelated semantically to any G stem verb.

a. The D stem can be intransitive (e.g., הַלֵּךְ "walk about"), but is more often transitive.

b. If the G stem denotes a stative property or intransitive action, the D stem can be used as a causative of the property (such causation is called factitive) or of the intransitive action (causative proper), e.g., בְּטֵל "cease" (G) ~ בַּטֵּל "make something cease" (D); דְּחֵל "be afraid" (G) ~ דַּחֵל "frighten" (D).

c. Sometimes the D stem is related as a factitive to an adjective or participle instead of directly to another verbal stem, e.g., בְּרִיךְ "blessed" ~ בָּרֵךְ "bless" (D); יַצִּיב "certain" ~ יַצֵּב "make certain" (D).

d. Rarely, the D stem is used as a causative of a transitive G stem, e.g., זְבַן "buy" (G) ~ זַבֵּן "sell" (D).

e. If the G stem denotes a simple transitive action, the D stem can be used to denote multiple iterations of that action, e.g., קְטַל "kill" (G) ~ קַטֵּל "kill many" (D).

f. The D stem can imply that the action results in a permanent change, while the G stem, if it exists, may not have such an implication, e.g., שְׁלַח "send" (G) ~ שַׁלַּח "let go, set free" (D).

C Stem

§232. The C stem is normally the causative (therefore "C") of G stem verbs (§324). However, C stem verbs exist when there is no corresponding G stem, e.g., הַשְׁכַּח "find, be able."

a. The characteristic feature of the C stem base is the segment הַ- *ha-* added to the segment *qtil*, yielding הַקְטִל *haqtil* or (more commonly) הַקְטֵל *haqtel* (also called the "Haphʿel," §208). As with the D stem, the same base is used for both suffix and prefix conjugations.

b. A less common form in our corpora in the suffix conjugation is the C stem with the preformative segment אַ- *ʾa-* instead of *ha-*, yielding *ʾaqtil*, *ʾaqtel* (the "Aphʿel," §208). In the prefix conjugation, this base is just *-aqtel-*, without *ʾaleph*.

c. The Haphʿel patterns outnumber the Aphʿels in our corpora, but they can co-occur in the same texts. It is possible that in the spoken language the speakers preferred the Aphʿel even at the time of IA, and the continuing preference for Haphʿel in writing preserves a "proper," historic spelling only. In post-QA dialects, the C stem is uniformly expressed by the Aphʿel.

d. The change of the prefix *ha-* to *ʾa-* is through the development of the prefix conjugation. The *h* of the base tended to elide after the vowelless inflectional prefix: **yəhaqtil > yaqtil*. By process of analogy, the suffix conjugation base became **aqtil-*, with *ʾaleph* added as a placeholder for the vocalic onset: *ʾaqtil*. This is borne out in IA by the higher frequency of Aphʿel prefix conjugation forms (i.e., those without ה) than Aphʿel suffix conjugation forms (Folmer 1995: 123–137).

e. In BA, the Haphʿel is still the dominant written form. It should be borne in mind that Haphʿel and Aphʿel are *not different verbal stems*, but are both expressions of the C stem.

C Stem Finite Verbs, Strong Root

§233. Most of the forms given in the strong verb paradigm (Appendix, pp. 356–357) are reconstructed through comparison with other dialects.

a. The original *i*-theme vowel commonly (but not invariably) lowers to *e* in the paradigm in closed stressed syllables (§78, Rule 7).

b. The prefixes of the prefix conjugation, being in an open unstressed syllable, always have a *shewa* when the *h* of the base is not elided. When the *h* is elided, the prefix vowel is *a*. The theme vowel *i/e* reduces to *shewa* when vocalic inflectional suffixes are added (§78, Rule 1).

c. When the C stem has a final root letter of ע or ח, the characteristic *i*-theme vowel becomes *a* (§78, Rule 4a).

d. When the first or second root letter is a guttural, an "echo vowel" (secondary opening) may be inserted after it (§78, Rule 5).

e. In the 1cs form הַשְׁכַּחַת (Dan 2:25), the final guttural ח has generated not only a vowel change (final *-et* > *-at*), but also preserved the penultimate stress: *haškíḥt > *haškáḥat* (instead of *haškəḥét) "I found."

f. If the first root letter is ח or ע, the preformative *ha-* in the SC may be changed to *hɛ-*, as in הֶחֱסִנוּ *hɛḥɛsínū* (Dan 7:22) (< *haḥsínū) (§75b).

Examples: BA SC 3ms הַצְלַח (Dan 3:30, final guttural), הַנְפֵּק (Dan 5:2); 2ms הַשְׁפֵּלְתְּ (Dan 5:22); 1cs הַשְׁכַּחַת (Dan 2:25, final guttural). PC 3ms יְהַשְׁפִּל (Dan 7:24); 3fs תְּהַנְזִק (Ez 4:13), תַּטְלֵל (Dan 4:9); 2ms תְּהַשְׁכַּח (Ez 4:15, final guttural); 3mp יַחְסְנוּן (Dan 7:18); 1cp נְהַשְׁכַּח (Dan 6:6, final guttural).

> Exercise: (1) Give the root of the examples cited above. (2) Provide vowel points for the following examples from QA and IA: SC 2ms השכחת; 3mp הנפקו; 3ms הרכב; 1cs אקטרת; 3fs אדבקת; PC 3mp יהרגשון; 2mp תשכחון; 3ms יקדש; 1cs אהקרב; 3ms יההסן.

C Stem Participles and Infinitives, Strong Root

§234. a. The C stem participle combines *m* preformative with the standard C *haqtil* base, yielding *məhaqtil/mehaqtel* or (in the Aphʿel) *maqtil/maqtel*.

    ms   מַקְטֵל or מְהַקְטֵל, מַקְטֵל, or מְהַקְטֵל

    fs   מְהַקְטְלָה (מַקְ׳)

    mp   מְהַקְטְלִין (מַקְ׳)

    fp   מְהַקְטְלָן (מַקְ׳)

b. The infinitive has the shape הַקְטָלָה *haqtɔlɔ* or אַקְטָלָה *ʾaqtɔlɔ*. When pronominal suffixes are added, the final *-ɔ* becomes *-ūt*: הַקְטָלוּת־ *haqtɔlūt-* (§133b).

BA examples: Participle: ms מַשְׁפִּיל (Dan 5:19), מַצְלַח (Ez 5:8, final guttural); mp מְהַקְרְבִין (Ez 6:10), מַצְלְחִין (Ez 6:14); מַהְלְכִין (Dan 4:34);[1] infinitive לְהַשְׁפָּלָה (Dan 4:34), לְהַשְׁכָּחָה (Dan 6:5), לְהַשְׁמָדָה (Dan 7:26); with 3ms suffix לְהַצָּלוּתֵהּ (Dan 6:15) (I-n root); see also לאפטרותני (4Q196 6 8).

> Exercise: (1) Give the roots of the examples listed above. (2) Point the following examples from QA and IA: participles ms מהחסן, משכח; fs מהשכחה; mp משלמין, מהשפלין; fp מקרבן; infinitive לאפטרה.

Cp Stem, Strong Root

§235. a. The passive of the C stem is the Cp stem (causative passive). Like the C stem, it has a consonantal *h* derivational preformative, but with a different vowel, *hu-*. This preformative attaches to a base *qtal* to produce *huqtal*. Unlike the C stem, the *h* of the stem does not elide or become *ʾaleph* in BA.[2] In QA, however, there are some instances where the Cp is written with initial *ʾaleph* (i.e., "Ophʿal" instead of "Hophʿal").

b. In BA, the *u* of the prefix is normally realized as short ◌ except preceding geminated consonants, where it remains short *u* ◌. In Cp participles and the root אתי (§283c), the prefix vowel is short *a* ◌.

The Cp is only attested in a limited number of forms of the suffix conjugation.

Examples: BA 3ms הָנְחַת (Dan 5:20); 3fs הָתְקְנַת (Dan 4:33); הָחָרְבַת (Ez 4:15, first guttural); IA: 3mp הפקדו (B2 9:7); QA 1cs אדבקת (4Q204 1 vi 23).

c. The C passive participle is rarely used. As with the C active participle, it has a prefix *m*, while the base differs from that of the finite verbs, with a derivational performative *ha-*, yielding *məhaqtal*.

ms	*məhaqtal, maqtal*	מְהַקְטַל (unattested)
fs	*məhaqtəlā, maqtəlā*	מְהַחְצְפָה Dan 2:15, מַחְצְפָה Dan 3:22, מהשלמא 4Q542 1 i 4[3]
mp	*məhaqtəlīn, maqtəlīn*	מְהַנְחֲתִין Ez 6:1[4] (*)

---

[1] The mp מַהְלְכִין should doubtless be emended to D stem מְהַלְכִין, the normal stem for the root.

[2] There is some evidence that the Cp stem base was actually **haqtal* instead of **huqtal* (Cook 2010).

[3] Note that in 4Q542 the ptcp was originally written without the *h* preformative, which was then added above the line.

[4] The form מְהַנְחֲתִין Ezra 6:1 is listed here for convenience. For the assimilation of the נ in the root נחת, see §254.

The L/tL Stem

§236. A stem attested but once in the corpora is the "Poʿel" stem, here called "L" because of the characteristic long *ō* occurring after the first root letter: the mp participle מְסוֹבְלִין "supporting" (Ez 6:3) from the strong root סבל. A similar verb with the same meaning is found in JLA סוֹבַר "bear, support."

A T stem passive (§237) of the L stem ("Ithpoʿal") is used with the root שׁמם (geminate [§§278ff.], but strong in this stem): אֶשְׁתּוֹמַם "he was astonished" (Dan 4:16). Compare the R/tR stems (§276).

T Stems

§237. a. T stems have a derivational preformative הִת־ *hit-* or אִת־ *ʾit-* attached to a triliteral base. They are systematically (but not invariably) associated with another stem, expressing the passive, reflexive, or middle voice of that stem (§327).

b. Historically, the *ʾit-* preformative is original, the *hit-* form developing by analogy to the *ha-* of the C stem (§50b), or perhaps under the influence of Hebrew.

c. Sometimes אֶת־ *ʾet-* will occur instead of אִת־ *ʾit-*. Since הֶת־* never occurs, the vocalization with ◌ְ *ɛ* must be due to the *ʾaleph* (§75b).

tG Stem, Strong Root

§238. The tG stem conveys normally the passive/reflexive/middle voice of the G stem (§326). Occasionally it can be the passive of a verb formed from another stem, e.g., הִשְׁתְּכַח "to be found," passive of the C stem הַשְׁכַּח "to find" (root שׁכח).

§239. a. The tG is formed by prefixing *hit-/ʾit-* to the segment **qaṭil*, yielding *(h/ʾ)itqaṭil*. With the operation of vowel reduction (§78, Rule 1) in BA, the default base without suffixes becomes *(h/ʾ)itqəṭil*, and with lowering of *i* may become *(h/ʾ)itqəṭel* ("Hithpeʿel" or "Ithpeʿel," §208). The same base is used in both suffix and prefix conjugations, although in the prefix conjugation the *(h/ʾ)it-* of the prefix is just *-it-*.

The strong verb paradigm (Appendix, pp. 356–357) gives a complete reconstruction.

b. As with the other strong verbs, a verb with a final guttural root consonant will have an *a-*theme vowel instead of the characteristic *i* (§78, Rule 4a).

c. Roots with a guttural root consonant will have *ă* ◌ֲ *ḥaṭeph pataḥ* instead of *shewa* in cases where vowel reduction (§78, Rule 1) or syncopation (§78, Rule 2) would normally apply (§78, Rule 4b).

d. Irregular stress and vocalization are found in some forms with final guttural root consonants: 3fs הִתְגְּזֶרֶת "it was cut out" (Dan 2:34), אִתְגְּזֶרֶת "it was cut out" (Dan

2:45), instead of *hitgazrát*; הִשְׁתְּכַחַת "was found" (Dan 5:11), instead of *hištakhat*. In both instances, instead of syncopation (§78, Rule 2), an unsystematic stressed separating vowel was generated between the second and third root letters, causing a change in phonological pattern.

In the case of 2ms הִשְׁתְּכַחַתְּ *hištakáhat* "you were found" (Dan 5:27, instead of *hištəkaht[ā]*), a separating vowel was generated between the final root letter and the vowelless 2ms inflection -*t* (in accordance with the consonant cluster rule (§78, Rule 12a). In this instance, the final *t* does not spirantize (contrary to the normal pattern, §78, Rule 6; cf. §55b).

e. If the initial root consonant is a sibilant (§34d), it metathesizes (§78, Rule 10a) with the *t* of the preformative. If the sibilant is *z* or *ṣ*, the *t* of the preformative partially assimilates to the sibilant after metathesis (§78, Rule 10b).

BA examples: SC 3ms הִשְׁתְּכַח (Ez 6:2, metathesis); 3mp הִתְרְחִצוּ (Dan 3:28); 3fp אֶתְעֲקַרָה (Dan 7:8 Q, final guttural); PC 3ms יִתְיְהִב (Dan 4:13), יִתְעֲבֵד (Dan 3:29, first guttural); 3fs תִּשְׁתְּבִק (Dan 2:44, metathesis); 3mp יִתְיַהֲבוּן (Dan 7:25, medial guttural); 2mp תִּתְעַבְדוּן (Dan 2:5).

> Exercise: (1) Give the root of the above examples. (2) Provide a possible pointing for the following forms from IA and QA: SC 3ms אתחלם, אתהפך, התהער, התגער; 3fs התנצבת; 1cs אתבהלת; תזדהרון 2mp; יתלקחון; 3mp jussive ישתבקו; 3mp יתקטל, ישתלח; PC 3ms אתכנשו, אשתכחו; 3mp אתכנשו, אשתכחו.

§240. a. The tG stem *participle* adds the preformative *mit-* to the tG base **qaṭil* to yield **mitqaṭil*, plus the standard nominal-adjectival declensional endings, modified by the phonological rules, e.g., ms מִתְיְהֵב (Ez 4:20), fs מִתְיַהֲבָא (Ez 6:8), mp מִתְיַהֲבִין (Ez 7:19).

b. The *infinitive* form is (*h/ʾ)itqəṭɔ̄lɔ̄*, as in לְהִתְקְטָלָה (Dan 2:13), הִתְבְּהָלָה (Dan 2:25).

tD Stem, Strong Root

§241. a. The tD stem is the default passive of the D stem, e.g., הִצְטַבַּע "be drenched," הִתְבַּקַּר "be searched," etc.

b. It can also be used independently of other stems, as in, e.g., הִתְנַדַּב "act generously," with no corresponding G or D stem. It can have a middle, reflexive, or reciprocal meaning (§327), e.g., הִשְׁתַּמַּע "become obedient," cf. G שְׁמַע "hear"; הִתְנַבִּי "prophesy, act like a prophet," cf. נְבִי "prophet" (reflexive); הִתְכַּנַּשׁ "assemble" (reciprocal), cf. D כַּנֵּשׁ "assemble" (transitive), etc.

c. As with the D stem, the characteristic is the doubled (geminated) middle radical, in a base *qaṭṭal* (with *a*-theme) and derivational preformative *hit-* or *ʾit-*: (*h/it)qaṭṭal* (traditionally, Hithpaʿal or Ithpaʿal, §208). The initial *h/ʾ-* is not present in the PC *yitqaṭṭal, titqaṭṭal*, etc.

The strong verb paradigm (Appendix, pp. 356–357) gives a complete reconstruction.

d. When the middle root letter is ר or sometimes ה, it does not geminate, but the preceding short *a* becomes long *ɔ* in compensation (§77c).

e. If the initial root consonant is a sibilant (§34d), it metathesizes (§78, Rule 10a) with the *t* of the preformative. If the sibilant is *z* or *ṣ*, the *t* of the preformative partially assimilates to the sibilant after metathesis (§78, Rule 10b).

f. The Ketiv form הזמנתון "you conspired" at Dan 2:9 is probably an ancient scribal error for tD הִזְדַּמִּנְתּוּן (despite the tG Qere הִזְדְּמִנְתּוּן). The D/tD stem is normal for this root in the other dialects.

BA and QA examples: SC 3ms הִתְחָרַךְ (Dan 3:27, medial guttural); 1cs השתלמת (11QtgJob 23:6); אתחננת (1QapGen 20:12); 3mp הִתְנַדַּבוּ (Ez 7:15); 1cp אתכנשנא (1QapGen 12:16); PC 3ms יִצְטַבַּע (Dan 4:12, metathesis), יִתְבְּקַּר (Ez 5:17); 3fs תִּתְחַבַּל (Dan 2:44); 1cs אתנסך (11QtgJob 37:8); 3mp יִשְׁתַּמְּעוּן (Dan 7:27, metathesis), יתכנשון (4Q243 24 2).

> Exercise: (1) Give the root of the cited examples. (2) Change the singular forms to plural, and the plural to singular; provide pointing for the unpointed forms.

§242. a. The tD participle is formed by adding *mit-* to the tD base *qaṭṭal*. The gender/number inflections of the participle are the same as those of the nouns and adjectives.

ms	מִתְקַטַּל	*miṭqaṭṭal*
fs	מִתְקַטְּלָה	*miṭqaṭṭalɔ*
mp	מִתְקַטְּלִין	*miṭqaṭṭalīn*
fp	מִתְקַטְּלָן	*miṭqaṭṭalɔn*

BA and IA examples: ms מִתְנַדַּב (Ez 7:13), מִתְבָּהַל (Dan 5:9, medial guttural); fs מִתְנַשְּׂאָה (Ez 4:19); mp מִתְקַטְּלִין (Dan 2:13), מתנצחן (A6 10:4), מִתְעָרְבִין (Dan 2:43, medial guttural), מִתְכַּנְּשִׁין (Dan 3:3).

b. The infinitive has the form הִתְקַטָּלָה (*h/ʾ*)*itqaṭṭɔlɔ*; only the nominalized form הִתְנַדָּבוּת "gift, offering" (Ez 7:16) is attested in BA.

> Exercise: Using the roots of the participial examples, write out the infinitives, with vowel points.

tC Stem

§243. A T-stem of the causative may be attested in IA (Muraoka & Porten 2003:117), but is distinctly rare. It is not found in BA or QA and only begins to occur with greater frequency in Late Aramaic. See below under I-w (initial *waw*) verbs, §251e.

VERBS WITH WEAK ROOTS

§244. Weak verbs are verbs with one or more unstable root consonants (such as *ʾaleph*, *y*, *w*, or *n*) that may change or disappear in the course of a paradigm. Within the three-consonant system, the roots may be weak in the initial consonant (initial weak, or I-weak), the middle consonant (middle weak, or II-weak), or the final consonant (final weak, or III-weak).

Verbs whose roots are not really triliteral, such as the "hollow" verbs (with a long vowel instead of a middle consonant, §271) or the "geminate" verbs (whose second and third root letters are the selfsame consonant, §278), are also considered weak.

Initial *ʾAleph* Roots (I-*ʾaleph*)

§245. Initial weak roots, like I-*ʾaleph* roots, typically show instability when derivational and/or inflectional prefixes are added, i.e., not in forms without prefixes such as the G, D, or C stem suffix conjugation or in the G stem participles.

§246. a. In the G stem prefix conjugation of I-*ʾaleph* roots, the initial *ʾaleph* elides (is no longer pronounced) when it closes a syllable after prefixation, accompanied by lengthening of the prefix vowel (§47), e.g., **yiʾkul > yēkul* (from the root אכל), **yiʾmar > yēmar* (from the root אמר). The same elision occurs in the G infinitive: **miʾmar > mēmar*.

b. The א usually continues to be written, but omission of it is not uncommon. In the 1st cs, the root letter א is omitted after inflectional prefix א, e.g., אמר *ʾēmar* "I will say" (B2 3:20), instead of **אאמר*.

c. Infinitive: לְמֵאכַל *(lə)mēkal.*

BA, IA, and QA examples (PC and infinitive only): 3ms יֵאמַר (Dan 2:7), ימר (4Q550 7+7a 2, root אמר); 3fs תֵאכֻל (Dan 7:23); 2ms תאכל (IA, C1 1:127, Ahiqar); 2fs תאמרן (IA, D7 16:12); 1cs אמר (IA, e.g., B2 1:12); 3mp jussive יֵאבְדוּ (Jer 10:11, root אבד); 3mp יאמרון (C1 2:25), יבדון (4Q202 1 iv 10, root אבד), ימרון (4Q551 1 4, root אמר); 2mp תֵאמְרוּן (Jer 10:11), תמרון (4Q214 3 2); 1cp נֵאמַר (Dan 2:36), נאכל (IA, D7 8:14). Infinitive: לְמֵאמַר (Dan 2:9), לְמֵמַר (Ez 5:11), לממר (A4 9:2), למחד (B3 13:10, root אחד), cp. למאחד (B4 4:17), למאכל (4Q197 4 iii 12).

Exercise: Provide vowel points for all the unpointed examples given above.

d. When the *ʾaleph* of the root begins an open unstressed syllable in the suffix conjugation or imperative, it takes a *ḥaṭeph* vowel instead of simple *shewa* (§78, Rule 4b), like the other gutturals: SC 3ms אֲזַל (Dan 2:17), imperative ms אֱמַר (Dan 4:15), imperative fs אֲכֻלִי (Dan 7:5).

e. The ms impv אֱזֶל "go!" (Ez 5:15; attached asyndetically via *maqqeph* [§30] to the following verb) has a stressed first syllable. This is anomalous, and perhaps due to the influence of JLA on the reading tradition (cp. JLA אִיזֵיל).

§247. In the tG stem, syllable-initial א is sometimes omitted (§48) after preformative (*h/ʾ)it-* (no BA attestations): SC 3ms איתחד (= אתאחד, 11QtgJob 11:10, root אחד); 3mp אתחדו (=אתאחדו, A4 4:6); PC 3ms יתחז (= יתאחז, 4Q541 9 i 4, root אזי).

§248. a. In the C stem, I-*ʾaleph* roots have merged with I-y/w (initial *y* or *w*) roots (§249), generating the initial segment *hō-* instead of the expected **haʾ* > *hā* or *hē*. In the corpora of this grammar, in this category only the roots אבד and אתי are commonly attested in the C stem. For the case of the frequent doubly weak root אתי, see §283.

BA examples: PC 2ms jussive: תְּהוֹבֵד (Dan 2:24); 3mp יְהֹבְדוּן (Dan 2:18, defectively written); infinitive לְהוֹבָדָה (Dan 2:24).

b. In the Cp stem, the initial segment is *hū-*: SC 3ms הוּבַד (Dan 7:11, root אבד).

Initial *Yod/Waw* Roots (I-y/w)

§249. The initial *y* (in many cases originally **w*, §41) of the I-y roots is strong when it begins a word, as in the suffix conjugations and G stem participles. When prefixes are added, it is unstable.

§250. a. In the G stem prefix conjugation, the initial *y* (originally *w*) may elide, followed by gemination of the second root letter: **yi(w)tib* > *yittib* (root יתב), **yi(w)kul* > *yikkul* (root יכל). The gemination is secondary and keeps the prefix vowel from reducing to *shewa* (but see *c* below). (Compare Hebrew יֵשֵׁב < **yišib*.)

Examples are given of the PC only: 3ms יִכֻּל (Dan 3:29), יִתֻּב (Dan 7:26); 3fs תלד (B2 6:33, root ילד); 2ms jussive תצף (A2 4:3, root יצף), תזף (C1 1:130, root יזף); 2fs jussive תצפי (4Q197 4 i 3, root יצף); 1cs אכל (B2 6:31, root יכל); 3mp יכולון (1QapGen 20:19, *yikkulūn*, root יכל); 3fp ילדן (11QtgJob 32:2, root ילד); 2mp תרתון (4Q213 1 ii+2 9, root ירת); 2mp jussive תצפו (A2 2:3, root יצף); 1cp נכל (B3 4:12, root יכל).

Exercise: For the unpointed examples given, provide a possible pointing on the basis of BA pointed occurrences.

b. In the infinitive, there are few attestations: למירת (=לְמֵירַת, 1QapGen 16:14); למנדע (=לְמִנְדַּע, 4Q197 3 5). In IA, the original *w* was retained: למובל (A3 10:4), למונק (C1 1:168, root ינק).

c. Note: in some later dialects, the initial *y* (**w*) elides without the following gemination of the second root letter, e.g., JLA תֵּזִיף "you will borrow" TO Deut 15:6 (root יזף), תְּלִידִין "you will give birth" TO Gen 3:16 (root ילד). The consonantal orthography of IA and QA allows a reconstruction with or without gemination.

d. In the PC of the root ידע, the gemination of the second root letter is often (but not always) replaced by nasalization (§54b), **yi(w)daʕ > yiddaʕ > yindaʕ*. See for example, 3ms ינדע (1QapGen 2:20), 2ms תִּנְדַּע (Dan 2:30), but 2mp תדעון (4Q212 1 ii 19). This was the case in the G stem infinitive as well, e.g., למנדע (1QapGen 2:22).

e. For the root יטב, the *y* (probably not originally **w*) is not elided and forms a vowel in the G stem PC, e.g., 3ms יֵיטַב (Ez 7:18).

f. The root יכל in the G stem PC "be able" has an alternate vocalization influenced by the Hebrew cognate: 3ms יוּכַל (Dan 2:10); 2ms תוכל (Dan 5:16, Ketiv and 4Q113); 1cp נוכ[ל] (4Q547 4 ii 1). This vocalization is not found in Aramaic outside of BA and QA.

g. In the G stem imperative, the initial root consonant *y* (< **w*) is dropped.

Examples: ms הַב "give!" (Dan 5:17, root יהב), דַּע "know!" (Dan 6:16, root ידע), זֻף "borrow!" (C1 1:129 [Ahiqar], root יזף); fs הבי (A3 4:4); mp הבו (A3 10:3); with suffixes: ms with 1cs pron. suff. בלני "carry me!" (C1 1:52, **búlnī*).

§251. a. In the C stem, initial *y/w* roots preserve etymological **w* after the preformative *ha-/ʔa-*, with subsequent contraction of the resulting diphthong: **haw-/*ʔaw- > hō-/ʔō-* (§78, Rule 9).

b. A minority of verbs have *hē-* (< **hay-*) instead of *hō-*.

Examples: SC 3ms הוֹדַע (Dan 2:15), הוֹתֵב (Ez 4:10, root יתב), הוסף (4Q198 1 1, root יסף); הֵיבֵל (Ez 6:5, root יבל), הֵילֵל (C1 1:41 [Ahiqar], root ילל); PC 3ms יְהוֹדַע (Dan 2:25); 3fs תושר (A2 2:7, root ישר); 3mp יְהוֹדְעוּן (Dan 2:30), יהוספון (A6 2:18). Participles mp מְהוֹדְעִין (Dan 4:4); inf. לְהוֹדָעָה (Dan 5:8), לְהֵיבָלָה (Ez 7:15); with suffix, לְהוֹדָעֻתַנִי (Dan 5:16).

c. למושרתהם "to send them" at Hermopolis (A2 2:13) is a non-standard infinitive from the root ישר (with pron. suff.) with preformative *m* by analogy to the G stem infinitive. This would later become standard in the Late Western dialects. (See also §230c.)

d. In the Cp stem, the I-y/w verbs have *hū-/ʾū-* (<*huw-*) as the preformative (§52a).

Examples: SC 3ms הובל (4Q530 7 ii 8, root יבל); 3fs הוּסְפַת (Dan 4:33, root יסף); 1cs אובלת "I was borne" (4Q204 1 xiii 25), הובלת "I was borne" (4Q206 1 xxvi 18 = הוּבְלַת).

e. The tC stem is attested in a couple of cases with the root יסף, "to add." Judging by the evidence of the later dialects, the derivational *h* of the base elided, and the *t* of the preformative was geminated, i.e., *ʾit-hō-* > *ʾittō-*.

    3ms SC   אתוסף (C3 11:8, *ʾittōsap*)
    3mp PC juss   יתוספו (C3 11:10, *yittōsápū*)

f. The root הלך "go, walk" appears as a I-y root in the C and tC stem in 4Q542: SC 3ms הילכתון (1 i 12, הֵילֶכְתּוּן) and inf with 2mp suffix באתהילכותהון (1 ii 13, אִתְהֵילָכוּתְהוֹן), in the meaning "pass on, transmit" (C) or "be passed on, transmitted" (tC). This root-stem combination is unique in Aramaic.

Initial Nun (I-*n*) Roots

§252. a. When the initial *n* of the root is contiguous to the second root consonant, it can either (1) assimilate to it, rendering it geminate (§78, Rule 11a); or (2) not assimilate, remaining stable. The second option may in fact be a case of nasalization of a geminate consonant (§78, Rule 11b), in effect "restoring" the etymological *n*. The relevant phonetic environments are the G stem prefix conjugation and infinitive and C and Cp stems (all forms).

b. The IA texts have more nasalization; the later QA texts have more assimilation. This progression is more likely a case of a local dialect trait reemerging in orthography (the Western OA texts have assimilation) rather than a phonetic change.

c. When *n* does not assimilate, the forms follow the strong verb paradigm.

§253. a. The prefix conjugation and infinitive provide the environment necessary for possible assimilation.

Examples: PC 3ms יִנְתֵּן (Dan 2:16), ינפק (4Q201 1 i 5, root נפק); יִפֵּל (Dan 3:6, root נפל), יפוק (1QapGen 22:34, root נפק); 2ms תִּנְתֵּן (Ez 7:20); תסב (4Q541 2 ii 3, root נסב); תשא (B1 1:13, root נשא); 3mp ינתנון (B3 4:18); יטלון (2Q24 4 5, root נטל); 3mp jussive ינדשו (A4 7:8, Petition); תִּפְּלוּן (Dan 3:15, root נפל); infinitive לְמִנְתַּן (Ez 7:20), מנשא (C1 1:171), למנפק (B3 11:3); למפק (4Q209 7 iii 2, root נפק), במטל (11QtgJob 35:3, root נטל).

| 10 | Exercise: Provide possible pointings for all of the unpointed examples in the above citations. |

b. In the G stem imperative, I-*n* roots drop the initial *n* and use only the final two root letters.

Examples: ms שֵׂא (Ez 5:15, root נשׂא), סב (4Q537 1+2+3 3, root נסב), טר (C1 1:82 [Ahiqar], root נטר); mp פֻּקוּ (Dan 3:26), טרו (A6 10:6).

§254. In the C/Cp stems, the *n* of the triliteral root will always be contiguous to the second root consonant throughout the paradigms. The result will be either assimilation (§78, Rule 11a) of the *n*, or (re)nasalization (Rule 11b) of the gemination resulting from assimilation.

The paradigm in the Appendix (p. 356) uses the root נפק (G stem, "go out"; C stem, "bring out, bring forth"). There is some variation in the sources between the presence or absence of *n* and, as usual in the C stem, of the preformative *h*.

Examples: SC 3ms הַנְפֵּק (Dan 5:2), אנפק (1QapGen 22:14); אצל (1QapGen 22:10, root נצל); 3fs אתרת (1QapGen 13:17, root נתר); 3mp הַנְפִּקוּ (Dan 5:3); אַתָּֽרוּ (Dan 4:11, root נתר); PC 3ms יהנפק (A6 13:3), ינפק (11QtgJob 29:1); יהפק (D7 14:3); 3fs תְּהַנְזִק (Ez 4:13); 2ms תַּחֵת (Ez 6:5, root נחת); 1cs אהנצל (B2 3:18); imperative ms אֲחֵת (Ez 5:15, root נחת); fs הנפקי (B2 3:27); infinitive להנפקה (11QtgJob 31:5); לְהַצָּלָה (Dan 3:29, root נצל); participle msc מְהַנְזְקַת (Ez 4:15); mp מחתין (4Q211 1 i 2, root נחת), מפקן (A2 5:3, root נפק).

| Exercise: Provide vowel points to all of the unpointed examples in the list of citations above. |

Final-Weak Roots: III-y (*III-ʾ*aleph*)

§255. a. Through the workings of analogy, III-ʾ*aleph* roots have generally merged with III-y roots in BA and QA and form in the large majority of cases a single group. This merger is obscured by the use of final א as a *mater* for roots with both etymologies (§25), and by the stubborn persistence of the lexica in listing some roots as III-ʾ*aleph* when these roots have merged with III-y (e.g., *HALOT* lists the root קרי "read, call" as קרא although its inflections in BA are wholly those of a III-y root).

b. In IA, many roots that are etymologically III-ʾ*aleph* retain א in parts of their paradigm, and in such cases it is hard to tell whether a complete merger with the III-y roots has taken place. Such a merger was virtually complete, however, in the BA and QA texts. Exceptions will be noted below.

§256. III-y roots present a complicated paradigm, since the early contraction of final triphthongs in these roots (§58) led to systematic variations in the derivational stem bases and vowel-initial inflectional suffixes. These will be treated by stem.

G stem, III-y roots. The paradigm given in the Appendix (pp. 358–359) uses the III-y root בני "build" as a paradigm root for *a*-theme forms.

The *a*-theme SC base with zero inflection (the 3ms) and with vocalic inflectional suffixes develops as follows (§58):

a. The 3ms has final -ɔ́ as a contraction of *-aya: bənɔ́ < *banaya, BA בְּנָא or בְּנָה.
b. The 3fs similarly ends in -ɔ́t as a contraction of *-ayat: bənɔ́t < *banayat, BA בְּנָת. In QA, the root הוי sometimes has a disambiguating א after ו, as in הואת (הֲוָת = הֲוָאת, 1QapGen 12:9). Note also the variant reading מלָאת for מְלָת at Dan 2:35.
c. The 3mp has final -ō as a contraction of *-aw < *-áyū (§58b); bənō < *banaw < *banáyū, BA בְּנוֹ. In QA, an unpronounced א is occasionally added to the 3mp: הווא "they were" (= הֲוֹו, 1QapGen 13:9), שבוא "they took captive" (= שְׁבוֹ, 1QapGen 22:10) (§26c).
d. The 3fp SC in its few occurrences in QA is strong, i.e., the etymological final *y* does not change: banáyā, e.g., הויה hawáyā "they were" (root הוי, 4Q201 1 iii 16). (In JLA, the intervocalic *y* is replaced by *ʾaleph*: הֲוָאָה TO Gen 27:23.)
e. When the inflectional suffix begins with a consonant, the resulting *ay* diphthong can contract or remain uncontracted: 2ms bənaytɔ́ BA בְּנַיְתָה; 1cs bənēt̠ < *banayt, BA בְּנֵית; 2mp bənēt̠ōn < *banaytun BA בְּנֵיתוֹן; 1cp bənēnɔ́ < *banaynā, BA בְּנֵינָא.
f. Note that the 2mp suffix is -tōn, not -tūn, due to analogy with the -ō suffix of the 3mp SC and -ōn of the 3mp/2mp PC.

§257. a. The III-y verbs with *i* as theme vowel in the G stem SC present a different picture than that of the *a*-themes given above. Instead of the disappearance of the original *y* third root letter, as in the 3ms, 3fs, and 3mp of the *a*-theme, the root letter *y* either remains or coalesces with the *i*-theme vowel to produce long *ī* in the second syllable. The inflectional suffixes are added to the base with minimal further change.

b. The attested inflectional endings are 3ms -ī, 3fs -īyat; 2ms -ít̠ɔ́ or -ít; 1cs -īt; 3mp -īw (< *iyū). Note that these endings are also applicable to non-G stems with *i*-theme vowels (that is, the D, C, tG stems).

The paradigm (Appendix, pp. 358–359) gives a complete reconstruction.

§258. The verbs with *a*-theme and *i*-theme in the SC have the same form in the G stem PC.

a. Forms without inflectional suffixes (3ms, 3fs, 2ms, 1cs, 1cp) end in -ē ($<$ *-iyu*, §58c) in the indicative PC and -ī ($<$ *-iy*) in the jussive PC. The final *mater* on the indicative in IA is ה, in BA and QA ה or א.

b. The 2fs PC indicative ends in -áyin ($<$ *-iyīn*). It is unattested in BA and QA, but examples are found in IA (e.g., תצבין *tiṣbáyin*, B2 7:16, root צבי) (§58d).

c. The 3mp and 2mp forms end in -ōn ($<$ *- iyūn*) (§58e).

d. The 3fp and 2fp forms end in -yᵊn, that is, the *y* is a strong consonant.

BA examples of SC and PC: SC 3ms הֲוָא (Dan 6:4), רְבָה (Dan 4:8); 3fs הֲוָת (Dan 2:35); 2ms חֲזַיְתָ (Dan 2:43), רְבַיְת (Dan 4:19); 1cs חֲזֵית (Dan 2:26), צְבֵית (Dan 7:19, *i*-theme); 3mp רְמוֹ (Dan 6:25), אֶשְׁתִּיו (Dan 5:4, *i*-theme), 2mp חֲזַיְתוֹן (Dan 2:8); 1cp בְעֵינָא (Dan 2:23); PC 3ms יִבְעֵה (Dan 6:8), יִשְׁנֵא (Dan 7:24); 3fs תֶעְדֵּא (Dan 6:9); 3mp יִשְׁתּוֹן (Dan 5:2), יִבְנוֹן (Ez 6:7).

> Exercise: (1) Give the root of the verbs cited above. (2) Give the root and provide vowel points for the following examples from IA and QA: SC 3ms הוה, קנה; 3fs צבית (i-theme); 2ms בנית; 2fs מלתי; 1cs קרית; 3mp שבו, שגיו (i-theme); 1cp רשׁינא; PC 3ms יחזא, ירבה; 2ms תשתה; 3mp ירשׁון; 2mp תבעון, 1cp נרשׁה.

§259. a. The G stem jussive forms of IA differ from those of the indicative prefix-conjugation. The jussive 2fs–3mp–2mp forms lack the final *n* on the inflectional endings, as in the strong verbs (§222): -*ay* (2fs), -*ō* (3mp, 2mp).

b. The theme vowel, reconstructed on basis of the imperative of pointed texts, is *ī*: *yíbnī, tíbnī* (with penultimate stress, §56d). This final *y* spelling survives occasionally in QA and possibly BA (cf. the tG יִתְקְרֵי "let him be called" [Dan 5:12], despite the vocalization).

c. In Ahiqar and elsewhere, the jussive sometimes ends in ה, especially after אַל (§388), e.g., אל יהוה (C1 1:81), אל תכסה (C1 1:84).

Examples of the jussive (G stem): 3ms יהוי (A4 4:9); 3fs תהוי (C1 1:84 [Ahiqar]); 2ms תהוי (A5 1:3); 2mp תשתו (A4 1:6).

§260. As with the strong verbs, the *G stem imperative* is a shortened form of the 2nd person jussive: ms בְּנִי, fs בְּנִי (unattested in BA), mp בְּנוֹ.

Examples: ms חֱיִי (Dan 2:4), חזי (1QapGen 21:9), הוי (A4 7:3, Petition); fs הוי (A2 2:14); mp אֱתוֹ (Dan 3:26), חזו (4Q201 1 ii 2), חזוא (4Q204 1 i 20, with silent א, §26c).

§261. a. The ms and mp declensional endings of the *G stem participle* of III-y roots have been affected by the contraction of triphthongs (§58). The ms ends in -ē אֵ◌/הֵ◌ (< *-iyu) and the mp in -áyin יִן◌ (< *-iyīn); the feminine endings (fs -yā, fp -yān) are strong, i.e., the etymological *y* is present.

Examples: ms עָנֵה (Dan 2:5), חזה (C1 1:173); fs שָׁנְיָה (Dan 7:19), אתיה (4Q583 1 1); mp חָזַיִן (Dan 3:27), שתין (A4 7:21, Petition); fp שָׁנְיָן (Dan 7:3).

b. In some IA forms, the ptcp fs termination is ת־, not ה־, e.g., חזית (*ḥāziyat; A2 7:3, Hermopolis).

c. The G infinitive, in line with the PC 3ms and like forms, ends in -ē אֵ◌/הֵ◌: לְמִבְנֵא (Ez 5:2), לְמִבְעֵא (Dan 2:18), לְמִשְׁרֵא (Dan 5:16), למשתה (4Q197 4 iii 12); etc.

The anomalous form לִבְנֵא (Ez 5:3, 13) should be emended to לְמִבְנֵא, and the anomalous form לְמִבְנְיָה (Ez 5:9) to the suffixed form לְמִבְנְיֵה.

d. When vowel-initial pronominal suffixes are added to the infinitive, the final root consonant *y* is strong, e.g., with 3ms suffix מִצְבְּיֵה (Dan 4:32), לממניה (1QapGen 21:13).

Exercise: Give the root and vocalization for the following participles and infinitives from IA and QA: inf למבנה ,למרשה ,למהוא; ptcp ms חזה ,פנה ,דמה; mp שבין ,מחין ,שרין ,בעין.

§262. a. *The G stem passive participles* of III-y roots have the same declensional endings as the G active participles; the short vowel in the first syllable reduces normally (§78, Rule 1).

Examples: ms בְּנֵה (Ez 5:11), חֲזֵה (Dan 3:19); fs שביא (שְׁבִיָא, 1QapGen 22:25); mp שְׁרַיִן (Dan 3:25, root שרי). The Masoretic term *Qere* קְרֵי is a ms example from the root קרי "read."

b. The G passive SC has the same inflectional endings as the *i*-theme G stem SC (§257b), e.g., 3ms גְּלִי (Dan 2:19, root גלי); 3mp רְמִיו (Dan 7:9, root רמי).

D Stem, III-y Roots

§263. a. The SC base of the III-y D stem (using the root *bny*) is בַּנִּי *bannī*, while the PC base is יְבַנֵּא *(yə)bannē*.

b. In the SC, the inflectional suffixes -*at* (3fs), -*tā* (2ms), -*t* (1cs), -*ū* (3mp), -*ā* (3fp), etc., are added directly to the base without further change, except in the 3mp the sequence *bannī*

+ *ū* becomes *bannīw*, according to the Tiberian pointing (§52b). For the similar treatment of G stem *i*-theme verbs, see §257.

c. In the PC, the inflectional suffixes are like those in the G stem: -*ē* (3ms, 3fs, 2ms, 1cp), -*ayin* (2fs), -*ōn* (3mp, 2mp), -*yān* (3fp, 2fp) (§258).

The paradigm (Appendix, pp. 358–359) gives a complete reconstruction.

BA examples: SC 3ms מַנִּי (Dan 2:24); 2ms מַנִּיתָ (Dan 3:12); 3mp שַׁנִּיו (Dan 3:28); PC 3ms יְבַלֵּא (Dan 7:25); 1cs אֲחַוֵּא (Dan 2:24); 3mp יְשַׁנּוֹן (Dan 4:13); 1cp נְחַוֵּא (Dan 2:4).

> Exercise: Give the root for the following D stem examples from IA and QA and provide a possible vocalization: SC 3ms שוי, כסי; 1cs רבית, צלית; 3mp שריו; 2mp שניתן; 1cp גרין; PC 3ms אמלא, אנקה; 1cs תכסה, תשוא; 2ms יצלה, ישוה; 3mp ישון.

d. The imperative/jussive forms have endings like the equivalent forms of the G stem. Most of the paradigm is unexampled in the corpora.

Examples: imperative ms מְנִי (Ez 7:25), צלי (1QapGen 20:28).

§264. a. The participle is based on the addition of preformative *m* to the base *bannē* (like that of the PC), with declensional endings like those of the G stem participles (§261).

BA examples: ms מְצַלֵּא (Dan 6:11, root צלי); mp מְצַלַּיִן (Ez 6:10, root צלי).

IA examples: mp מצלין (A4 7:15, Petition).

QA examples: ms מדמה (4Q197 4 ii 18, root דמי); mp מדמין (4Q580 4 4, root דמי); fp מגליאן (4Q541 24 ii 3, root גלי), with א *mater* for long -*ā* (§26).

b. The D passive participle is attested only once in BA: fs מְשַׁנְּיָה (Dan 7:7, root שני).

c. In the infinitive, the *y* root letter remains strong, although in the Qere, א is substituted for it (see §49): (לְ) בַּנָּאָה (לְ) בַּנָּיָה.

BA and QA examples: לחטיא (Ez 6:17 Ketiv), לְחַטָּאָה (Ez 6:17 Qere); לצליא (1QapGen 20:22), לגליה (4Q202 1 iii 5), with 3ms suffix לאסיותה "to heal him" (= לְאַסָּיוּתֵהּ 1QapGen 20:20).

d. The form למחזיא 4Q542 1 ii 6 is not a D stem infinitive with preformative *m*, but an anomalous spelling of the G stem with יא for final -*ē* (= לְמֶחֱזֵא) (§26c).

C and Cp Stem, III-y Roots

§265. a. The III-y verbs in the C stem suffix conjugation have an *i*-theme, and in the SC are inflected like G stem with an *i*-theme (§257). The SC base (using *bny* as paradigm root) is *habnī/ʾabnī*.

b. In the PC, the forms without inflectional suffix, as in the G and D stems, end in *-ē*, written אֶ◌ or הֶ◌, and the forms with inflectional suffixes are the same as those of the G stem and D stems (§258): 3ms *yəhabnē*, 3mp *yəhabnōn*, etc. Forms without *h* preformative are rare. The paradigm (Appendix, pp. 358–359) gives a complete reconstruction.

Examples: SC 3ms הַגְלִי (Ez 4:10); 3fs אכליאת (1QapGen 19:16, root כלי); 3mp הֶעְדִּיו (Dan 5:20, initial guttural); PC 3ms יְהַשְׁנֵא (Ez 6:11); 3mp יְהַעְדּוֹן (Dan 7:26); 2mp תְּהַחֲוֹן (Dan 2:6, initial guttural); 1cp נְהַחֲוֵה (Dan 2:7, initial guttural).

> Exercise: (1) Give the root for the cited examples above, and (2) give a possible vocalization for the following unpointed examples: SC 3ms החוי, אעדי; 3mp הסגיו; PC 3ms יהעדא; 1cs אשגה; 3mp יהחוון; 1cp נהשנה.

c. The C stem jussives have the same suffixes as those of the G stem (§259): 2ms *-ī*, 2fs *-ay*, 2mp *-ō*. Examples: ms תהעדי (C1 1:146 [Ahiqar]), יהעדו (A4 7:6, Petition).

d. The C stem participles have the same declensional endings as the G stem participles (§261), e.g., ms מְהַשְׁנֵא (Dan 2:21), מְהַעְדֵּה (Dan 2:21), mp משקין (4Q530 2 ii 7).

e. The imperative endings are like those of the G stem (§260), i.e., ms *-ī*, mp *-ō* (feminine forms are not attested). Known examples include ms החוי "tell!" (4Q242 1+2 5), העדי "remove!" (11QtgJob 34:6), אחזי "show!" (1QapGen 20:14); mp with 1cs suffix הַחֲוֹנִי "tell me!" (Dan 2:6); with 3ms suffix, החווהי (A6 11:5, *haḥwáwhī*).

f. The C stem infinitive is strong, i.e., the etymological final *y* is retained, e.g., לְהַשְׁנָיָה (Dan 6:9, root שני).

g. The Cp stem of III-y roots (other than אתי, §283c) occurs only in QA, e.g., אחזית SC 1cs "I was shown" (4Q206 1 xxvii 21, *ʾaḥzayit* ?), אחזיאת SC 1cs "I was shown" (4Q204 1 xii 27, *ʾaḥzayit* ?, with *ʾaleph* indicating consonantal *y*), אחוית SC 1cs "I was told" (4Q196 2 1, *ʾaḥwayit* ?).

tG Stem, III-y Roots

§266. a. The tG stem in III-y verbs in the SC displays the same inflectional suffixes as the G stem *i*-themes (§257), the D stem, and the tD stem, i.e., with the suffixes attached to final *-ī*. The SC base is **hitbənī/ʾitbənī*.

b. The PC base without suffixes, as with the PC G stem, D stem, and tD stem, ends in -*ē*, written אֶ֯ or הֶ֯. The inflectional suffixes are the same as in the G stem PC (§258). The paradigm (Appendix, pp. 358–359) gives a complete reconstruction.

BA examples: SC 3ms הִתְמְלִי (Dan 3:19); 3fs אֶתְכְּרִיַת (Dan 7:15); PC 3ms יִתְרְמֵא (Dan 3:6, 11, 6:8, 13); 3fs תִּתְבְּנֵא (Ez 4:13, 16, 21); 2mp תִּתְרְמוֹן (Dan 3:15).

> Exercise: (1) Give the root of the examples cited above. (2) Provide a possible vocalization of the following examples from QA: SC 3ms אתחזי; 3fs אתחזיאת; 1cs אתפנית; PC 3ms יתקרה; 2ms תתקרה; 3mp יתבנון; 3fp תתבנין; 1cp נתמחה; juss 3ms יתחזי.

c. Participles have the same declensional endings as the G stem participles (§261), e.g., ms מִתְבְּנֵא (Ez 5:8), מתחזה (C1 1:90 [Ahiqar]); fs מתבניה (4Q529 1:9).

d. In the infinitive, the root letter *y* remains strong: (לְ)הִתְבְּנָיָה *(lə)hitbənāyā*. Examples: לאתחזיא "to be seen" (4Q210 1 ii 18), לאתקריה "to be called" (4Q553 1 i 4).

tD Stem, III-y Roots

§267. Unlike the strong verbs of the tD stem, which have short *a*-theme vowel (§241c), the theme vowel of the III-y roots in this stem is *i*. Indeed, the inflection of the tD stem is identical to that of the D stem, except for the addition of the preformative *hit-/ʾit-* to the conjugational base throughout: SC *(h)(ʾ)itbannī-*, PC *-itbannē-* with the appropriate pre- and suffixes as in the D stem.

The forms given in §263 for the D stem can be applied to the tD stem, allowing for the addition of the *hit-/ʾit-* preformative.

BA examples: SC 3ms הִתְנַבִּי (Ez 5:1), אֶשְׁתַּנִּי (Dan 3:19 Qere); 3mp אֶשְׁתַּנּוּ (Dan 3:19 Ketiv); PC 3ms יִשְׁתַּנֵּא (Dan 2:9); 3ms יתכנה (4Q246 1 i:9); 2ms תשתנה (C 1 1:200); 3mp יִשְׁתַּנּוֹן (Dan 7:28); PC jussive 3mp יְשַׁתַּנּוּ (Dan 5:10).

> Exercise: Give the root of the above examples. Change all of the singular forms to plural, and vice versa.

The Root הוי *be*

§268. a. In the G stem, הוי "be, exist" is like other III-y roots, but in the PC it uses ל *l* instead of *y* as a prefix consonant in the 3ms, 3mp and 3fp forms, apparently to avoid having the PC 3ms resemble the letters of the Tetragrammaton: לֶהֱוֵה or לֶהֱוֵא instead of יהוה*. In non-Jewish texts, the euphemistic inflection does not occur. This innovation was not maintained in later dialects of Jewish Aramaic.

b. Note also change of vowel quality due to the first radical *h* (§75b), and the recurrent secondary opening (§76a) in the PC: 3ms *lihwē* > *lɛhwē* > *lɛhɛ̆wē*; 3mp *lihwōn* > *lɛhɛ̆wōn*; 3fp *lihwəyɔn* > *lɛhɛ̆wəyɔn* > *lɛhɛwyɔn* (§78, Rule 2).

IA PC 3ms יהוה (A3 6:3, *yihwē*); 3mp יהוון (A4 5:7, *yihwōn* or *yihwawn*).

BA/QA PC 3ms לֶהֱוֵא (Dan 2:20), להוא (4Q204 5 ii 25), לֶהֱוֵה (Dan 4:22); 3mp לֶהֱוֹן (Dan 2:43), להון (1QapGen 15:18), להוון (4Q537 12 3); 3fp לֶהֶוְיָן (Dan 5:17), להוין (4Q561 3 5).

The III-ʾaleph Roots

§269. As noted, the III-ʾaleph roots have generally merged with III-y verbs (§255a). Nevertheless, there are still some remnant examples where an original final ʾaleph root letter serves as a stable consonant or is consistently retained as a historical spelling. This is more common in IA than in BA or QA.

BA: tD ptcp fs מִתְנַשְׂאָה (Ez 4:19, root נשא); IA: G SC 1cs נשאית *naśaʾit* > *naśayit* (C1 1:159 [Ahiqar], root נשא); PC 2ms תתמלא (B3 1:17, root מלא); 1cs, with 2ms suffix אמחאנך *ʾɛmḥāʾinnákā* (C1 1:177 [Ahiqar], root מחא); G ptcp fs מטאה (A2 4:4, root מטא); G PC 3mp יקראון *yiqrāʾūn* (C1 1:165 [Ahiqar], root קרא; cp. יִקְרוֹן Dan 5:15); impv ms שֵׂא (Ez 5:15, III-y would be שִׂי*). (For further discussion, see Muraoka & Porten 2003: 127–129.)

III-y Verbs with Pronominal Suffixes

§270. Verbs with unstable final root letter affect the attachment of pronominal suffixes in the following ways:

a. *Final-vowel forms.* Verbs ending with a vowel in the SC or imperative add suffixes of the second series (§129): בְּנָהִי G SC 3ms + 3ms suff., "he built it" (Ez 5:11); חזהא G SC 3ms + 3fs suff., "he saw her" (1QapGen 20:9); שְׁנוֹהִי G SC 3mp + 3ms suff., "they changed (to) him" (Dan 5:6); אחזיוני C SC 3mp + 1cs suff., "they showed me" (4Q204 5 ii 26); פצהי G impv ms + 3ms suff., "deliver him" (= פְּצִיהִי, 11QtgJob 23:1); הַחֲוֹנִי C impv mp + 1cs suff., "tell me" (Dan 2:6).

Jussive forms in IA also add the pronominal suffixes of the second series: יחזני C juss 3ms + 1cs suff., "may he show me" (A2 2:2, *yaḥzínī),

b. *Final-consonant forms.* Verbs ending with a consonant in the SC take suffixes of the first series (§128), e.g., בֱנֵיתַהּ G SC 1cs + 3fs suff., "I built it" (Dan 4:27); החזיתה C SC 1cs + 3ms suff., "I showed him" (4Q529 1 5).

In QA, 3ms SC forms in the D and C stems retain consonantal *y* before suffixes, and therefore take the first series endings: חויה D SC 3ms + 3ms suff., "he told me" (1QapGen 22:3, *ḥawwiy + eh > חַוְיֵהּ); אחזיאני C SC 3ms + 1cs suff., "he showed me" (5Q15 1 ii 6, *ʾaḥziy + ání > אַחְזִיאָֽנִי, with *ʾaleph* replacing intervocalic *y*, §49c).

In IA, 3ms SC forms in the D and C stems are treated as vowel-final, e.g., גרך D SC 3ms + 2ms suff., "(if) he sues you" (B3 2:8, *garríkā); החוין C SC 3ms + 1cp suff., "he showed us" (A4 7:16, *haḥwínā); etc.

c. *Forms with energic morpheme.* In BA, the PC 3ms drops the final *-ē* and adds the energic morpheme (§130a) *-inn-* with suffixes of the first series: יְחַוִּנַּהּ D PC 3ms + 3fs suff., "he will tell it" (Dan 2:11, *yǝhaww(ē) + inn + ah > yǝhawwinnah); יְחַוִּנַּנִי D PC 3ms + 3fs suff., "he will tell me" (Dan 5:7). The vocalization of the unpointed IA and QA is uncertain: יגרנך D PC 3ms + 2ms suff., "he will sue you" (B2 2:14, *yǝgarrinnákā ?); ירשנכי G PC 3ms + 2fs suff., "he will sue you" (B2 3:12, *yiršinníkī ?); יחזנה G PC 3ms + 3fs suff., "he will see her" (1QapGen 19:23, יְחֶזְנַּהּ ?).

In BA, there is one example of the PC 2mp dropping final *-ōn* before suffixes and adding the unique energic *-unn-* before the suffix: תְּהַחֲוֻנַּנִי C PC 2mp + 1cs suff., "you will tell me" (Dan 2:9, *tǝhaḥǎwōn + n + ání > tǝhaḥǎwunnání). It is unclear whether IA and QA are similar; cf. יקרונה G PC 3mp + 3ms suff., "they will call him" (4Q246 1 ii 1, perhaps *יִקְרוֹנֵּהּ, like JLA יִשְׁתּוֹנֵיהּ "they will drink it" Targum Isa 62:9).

Hollow Verbs (Medial Long Vowel)

§271. The "hollow" verbs consist of a two-consonant root with a long vowel in place of the middle consonant. The lemma (dictionary form) of the root is indicated by ו or י as the middle component, depending on which consonant is used as a *mater* in the G stem PC.

§272. a. As with the strong roots, the G stem SC and PC have different bases. The *a*-theme (paradigm root קום) has a base with middle *-ō̄-* in the SC and middle *-ū-* or *-ī-* in the PC. The *i*-theme (paradigm root מות) has *-ī-* in the SC and *-ū-* in the PC. The prefix vowel of the PC is always *shewa*: יְקוּם יְשִׂים *yǝqūm, yǝśīm*.

A paradigm in the Appendix (pp. 360–361) gives a complete reconstruction.

BA examples: SC 3ms קָם (Dan 3:24); 3fs סָפַת (Dan 4:30); 2ms שָׂמְתָּ (Dan 3:10); 1cs שָׂמֶת (Ez 6:12); 3mp קָמוּ (Ez 5:2); PC: 3ms יְתוּב (Dan 4:31); 3fs תְּדוּר (Dan 4:18); 3mp יְקוּמוּן (Dan 7:10); 3fp יְדוּרָן (Dan 4:9 Qere).

Note that the 3fs and 1cs examples are stressed on the penultimate syllable.

> Exercise: (1) Give the root of the examples cited above, with the aid of a lexicon, if necessary. (2) Point the following examples: SC 3ms שם, תב; 3fs קמת; 2ms דרת; 3mp שמו; PC 3ms יקום, ישים; 3fs תמות; 1cs אשים; 3mp ימותון; 1cp נדור.

The *i*-theme SC is attested in BA only in רם (Dan 5:20, root רום), but QA has SC 3ms מית (4Q196 18 12; cp. JLA מִית).

b. The unique verb הוך "go, walk" appears only in the PC and infinitive and has the middle vowel -ֹ-: PC 3ms יְהָךְ, inf. לְמְהָךְ (Ez 7:13; also IA, QA, and JLA). In our corpora, this verb forms a suppletive paradigm with G stem אֲזַל "go, walk" – that is, הוך is used for the PC and infinitive, while אזל is used for the SC and participles.

c. *Jussives*, not attested in BA in this category, appear in IA, e.g., 2ms אל תשים (C1 1:130 [Ahiqar]); 2fs אל תקמי (A2 2:15, defectively written); 3mp ישמו (A6 6:1, root שים, defectively written).

Imperatives, as elsewhere, are based on the PC jussive base: fs קֻוּמִי (Dan 7:5, jussive *təqū́mī); mp שִׂימוּ (Ez 4:21, jussive təśī́mū), סימו (11QtgJob 4:4).

§273. a. *Participles*. Verbal patterns that require a consonantal middle radical are dealt with in various ways by hollow verbs. In the G stem participle, a consonantal *ʾaleph* is generated to enable the participial pattern, as seen in the example root קום "rise, stand":

ms   קָאֵם   *qāʾem*

In the absolute plural form, the Ketiv still has *ʾaleph*, but the Qere has consonantal *y* for the middle radical:

mp   קאמין Ketiv, קָיְמִין *qāyəmīn*

With these "substitute" middle root consonants, the inflection of the participle is regular. IA texts use the middle *y* throughout the paradigm, QA texts the middle *ʾaleph*.

Examples: ms קָאֵם (Dan 2:31), קאם (4Q550 5+5a 5); fs תאבה (4Q550 7+7a 6); mp דארין (Dan 2:38 K), דָּיְרִין (Q, root דור), זאעין (Dan 5:19 K), זָיְעִין (Q, root זוע), קימן (A4 7:10, Petition), קאמין (4Q206 4 i 19); mp det. קָאֲמַיָּא (Dan 7:16).

    b. *Infinitives* of hollow roots have preformative *mə-* on a base *qɔm*, (ל)מְקָם: לְמְהָךְ (Ez 7:13), למקם (1QapGen 20:20), למתב (4Q209 7 iii 2, root תוב), למדן (4Q542 1 ii 5, root דין).

    c. The only attested hollow verb in the *Gp stem* is שִׂים, as in the frequent expression שִׂים טְעֵם "an order is given/has been given." The irregular SC 3fs שֻׂמֵת "was put" (Dan 6:18, 4Q113 שימת) is without analogy in other dialects.

IA/QA examples: fs ptcp שימה (C1 1:79 [Ahiqar]), שימא (1QapGen 22:10).

§274. In the tG stem of hollow roots, preformative *(h/ʾ)it-* becomes *(h/ʾ)itt-*, with geminate *t*, generating a base form of **(h/ʾ)ittaqɔm* or **(h/ʾ)ittaqīm* (root קום). No SC forms occur in BA in the tG stem, but examples of PC forms are 3ms יִתְּזִין (Dan 4:9, root זון), יִתְּשָׂם (Ez 4:21); 3mp יִתְּשָׂמוּן (Dan 2:5); note also the ptcp ms מִתְּשָׂם (Ez 5:8).

Since the preformative *(h/ʾ)itt(a)-* is not contiguous to the first root consonant, sibilant-initial roots do not undergo metathesis in this category (§53).

Other examples: SC 1cs אתעירת "I awoke" (= אֶתְעִירֵת, 4Q213b 1 2); PC 3ms יתשים (C1 1:175 [Ahiqar]), יתשם (A6 7:8), יתרם (4Q547 9 6, root רום).

§275. As with G stem participles (§273), hollow verbs must generate a middle consonant to form a D stem base. This consonant is usually *y*, although a different strategy is taken with the R stem (§276).

    a. The D stem base with medial *y* is strong, and follows the strong root pattern (§§226ff.). The same is true of the tD stem.

    b. The infinitive of the D also follows the strong root pattern: D inf. לְקַיָּמָה (Dan 6:8) (§230).

Examples: חיבנא D SC 3ms + 1cp suff. (11QtgJob 21:5, *חַיְּבָנָא, root חוב); תחיבנני D PC 2ms + 1cs suff. (11QtgJob 34:4, *תְּחַיְּבְנַּנִי); תתקיאם tD PC 2ms (1QapGen 0:5), מתקימין tD ptcp mp 4Q201 1 ii 5).

§276. a. *The R stem.* Instead of generating a non-etymological middle radical *y* for the D stem, some hollow roots derive a stem with the same function by reduplication of the final root consonant. Traditionally called "Polel," this stem is here called the R (for reduplication) stem.

The invariant base of the R stem, using the example root רום "be high," is *-rōmem-*, with a long vowel *ō* after the first consonant and a reducible vowel between the reduplicated consonants: SC 3ms רוֹמֵם, PC 3ms יְרוֹמֵם, ptcp ms מְרוֹמֵם, etc.

b. *The tR stem*. The tR base is *-rōmam-*, with regular inflections: SC 3ms הִתְרוֹמַם, etc. The semantic functions of the R/tR stem are the same as those of the D/tD stem (§231).

Examples: R ptcp ms מְרוֹמֵם (Dan 4:34); tR SC 2ms הִתְרוֹמַמְתָּ (Dan 5:23); 3mp התרוממו (11QtgJob 27:3); PC tR 1cs אתבונן "I will consider" (4Q553 3+2 ii+4:3, root בין); ptcp ms מתבונן "considering" (1QapGen 13:14).[5]

§277. a. The base form of the hollow verbs in the C stem is a single syllable: *-qīm-* or *-qēm-*, preceded by the typical *ha-* (or *ʾa-*) causative preformative.

b. In the SC, the vowel of the preformative reduces to *ḥaṭeph pataḥ* (§78, Rule 4b): SC 3ms הֲקֵים, הֲקִים.

c. In the Haphʿel-type PC, the *a* vowel of preformative *ha-* sometimes lengthens to *-ō-*, instead of reducing, as in 3ms יְהָקֵים (Dan 5:21) and sometimes reduces, as in 3mp יַהֲתִיבוּן (Ez 6:5).

d. In the Aphʿel-type PC, the prefix vowel usually reduces to *shewa*, as in 3ms יְקִים (Dan 2:44), but sometimes lengthens, as in 3fs תָּסֵיף (Dan 2:44).

Examples: SC 3ms הֲקֵים (Dan 3:2), הֲתִיב (Dan 2:14); 2ms הֲקֵימְתָּ (Dan 3:12); 1cs הֲקֵימֶת (Dan 3:14), הקימת (C1 1:44 [Ahiqar]); 3mp הֲקִימוּ (Ez 6:18), אתבו (A4 4:8); PC 2ms תְּקִים (Dan 6:9); 3mp יְתִיבוּן (Ez 5:5, root תוב); 3ms with 3ms suff. יהתיבנהי (C1 1:126 [Ahiqar]).

A paradigm in the Appendix (pp. 360–361) gives a complete reconstruction.

e. The same irregular variation is found in the participle: compare ms מְהָקֵים (Dan 2:21) and ms מָרִים (Dan 5:19, root רום).

f. The infinitive has the pattern *hăqɔmɔ̄* (לַ)הֲקָמָה.

g. Participle: ms מהתיב (D2 29:6); fp מְגִיחָן (Dan 7:2, root גוח); inf.: לַהֲזָדָה "to act proudly" (Dan 5:20, root זיד); with 3ms suffix לַהֲקָמוּתֵהּ (Dan 6:4).

---

[5] Note: the form יתרום (C1 1:138 [Ahiqar]) is surely a scribal error for יתרומם (with Beyer 1984: 488, *contra* Kottsieper 1990: 154).

h. Imperatives are scantily attested: ms התב "return!" (A6 15:7); הצת "hear!" (11QtgJob 23:9, root צות); with 1cs pron. suff. הקימני "raise me!" (C1 1:109, Ahiqar); התיבני "answer me!" (11QtgJob 34:3, הֲתִיבְנִי*).

i. The only pointed examples of the Cp stem are the SC 3fs הֳקִימַת "was raised" (Dan 7:4), הֳקֵמַת (Dan 7:5). The medial vowel -ī- is unexpected for this stem; note the defective spelling in Dan 7:5 and the SC 3fs form אתבת (4Q196 2 10, root תוב).

The Geminate Verbs

§278. Geminate verbs are those in which the second and third root letters are the selfsame consonant (II = III). The term "geminate" here does not here mean doubled (§54), but reduplicated.

§279. The most common geminate root in BA is עלל "enter," which accounts for many of the occurrences. Since the first consonant is a guttural, the vocalization is affected by the changes associated with that group (§§75–76).

See the Synoptic Paradigm in the Appendix (pp. 361–363) for a reconstruction of the forms.

a. The G stem SC base is עַל *ʿal, to which the standard set of inflectional suffixes is added. When vowel-initial suffixes are added, the final root letter is doubled: SC 3ms עַל (Dan 2:16), 3fs עַלַּת (Dan 5:10 Qere); see also נַדַּת (Dan 6:19, root נדד) "wavered."

b. In the 3mp form דָּקוּ (Dan 2:35, root דקק), the vowel is long ō and the final root letter does not geminate, a pattern which is usual in JLA (cp. עָלוּ TO Gen 7:9). Some Masoretic MSS of Daniel have both lengthening and gemination (דָּקּוּ), and one has gemination without lengthening (דַּקּוּ) (see the apparatus in BHS).

c. In the Ketiv of Dan 5:10, the 3fs is עללת, i.e., the root is strong (both final consonants are represented). The root is also strong in the Ketiv active participles (mp עללין; see below §279f).

d. In the PC and infinitive, the first root letter is doubled after the addition of inflectional prefixes, or, if the first root letter is a guttural, the prefix vowel may change instead to ē. Nasalization instead of gemination (§54) is sometimes found.

There is one PC example in BA: תֵרֹעַ *tēroaʿ < *tirruʿ (Dan 2:40, root רעע). The later JLA is similar, e.g., יֵיעוֹל *yēʿol < *yiʿʿul (TO Ex 21:3).

Exercise: Give the root of the following examples from QA and IA and provide a possible vocalization: SC 3ms בז; 1cs עלת; 3mp בזו ,עלו; 1cp בזנא; PC 3ms יקל (root קלל); 2ms תנעל, יעלון 3mp; אעל 1cs (root מרר); תמר.

174

e. The imperative shows gemination before the inflectional suffix: גֻדּוּ (Dan 4:11, 20). A jussive example is 2mp תקוצו "(do not) cut down!" (1QapGen 19:16, possibly *tiqqússū*, root קצץ).

f. The ms ptcp is strong in QA (unattested in BA): עלל (1QapGen 14:17, JLA עָלִיל).

G plural participles are strong in the Ketiv of BA, with second and third root letters appearing, but weak in the Qere, with the standard כ ◌ in the first syllable (§223): mp עָלְלִין (Dan 4:4, 5:8 Qere; Ketiv עללין).

In QA, the plural participles can be strong or weak: mp עללין (11Q18 15:3); note על^ל^לין (4Q197 4 ii 8), with the second ל added as a correction above the line; בזין "plundering" (1QapGen 22:4, root בזז), also בזזין (4Q318 8 8); קצין "cutting down" (1QapGen 13:9, root קצץ).

g. The infinitive, like the PC, geminates the first root letter after the addition of preformative *mi*-: בְּמֵחַן (Dan 4:24, *miḥḥan*, root חנן); למנעל (A6 7:7, with nasalization instead of gemination), למעֹ]ל (= לְמֵעַל, 4Q204 5 ii 18).

§280. The D/tD stems are strong with geminate roots and present no special problems.

Examples: SC 3ms מַלֵּל (Dan 6:22); 1cs אתחננת (1QapGen 20:12); PC 3ms יְמַלֵּל (Dan 7:25); participle mp מתקצצין (4Q558 33 ii 4); impv mp קַצִּצוּ (Dan 4:11).

§281. a. In the C stem, the first root letter is geminated after the addition of the preformative *ha-/ʾa-*, yielding a pattern, with the root דקק, of *haddeq* (SC), *yəhaddeq* (PC); without preformative *h*, the forms are *ʾaddeq, yaddeq*. With the common root עלל, the forms are *haꜥꜥel* (SC), *yəhaꜥꜥel* (PC). Frequently nasalization will appear in place of gemination (§54): *hanꜥel, yəhanꜥel*.

See the Synoptic Paradigm in the Appendix (pp. 361–363) for a complete reconstruction.

Examples: BA SC 3ms הַנְעֵל (Dan 6:19, < *haꜥꜥel*); אעל (4Q197 4 iii 4); 3fs הַדֵּקֶת (Dan 2:34, root דקק); הנעלת (B2 6:6); 3mp הַדִּקוּ (Dan 6:25, root דקק); PC 3fs תַּדִּק (Dan 2:40); 2ms תעל (4Q550 5+5a 7); PC 3mp יהנעלן (A3 8:12); SC 3ms with 1cs suff. אעלני (= אַעֲלַנִי, 5Q15 1 ii 6); imperative mp הנעלו A6 10:7).

b. Note the 3fs הַדֵּקֶת (< *haddiqat*), with penultimate stress and change of vowel quality in the final syllable (-*at* > -*ɛt*). This may reflect the influence of JLA, which has penultimate stress in the 3fs SC.

c. The geminate root טלל is strong in the C stem in תַּטְלֵל (Dan 4:9). Since the root is weak elsewhere in the Aramaic C stem, this might originally have been a tD form misvocalized as C: *tittallal* תִּטַלַּל "be shaded, covered" (Tropper 1997: 112). However, the strong IA geminate C stem verb הגשש "he spied" (C1 1:139, root גשש) shows that some C stem geminates could be strong.

d. The participial prefix *m-* is added to the base, whether the *h* is retained or not: ms מְהַדֵּק (Dan 2:40); fs מַדְּקָה (Dan 7:19); QA ms מעל *maꜥꜥel* (4Q213 1 i 8).

e. Infinitives: BA לְהַנְעָלָה (Dan 4:3 < *ləhaꜥꜥ5l5), but also without nasalization לְהֶעָלָה (Dan 5:7, 4Q112 להנעלה).

Doubly Weak Verbs

Some verbs are weak in two root consonants and combine the features of both weak verb classes.

§282. The verb אתי (G stem, "come") is both I-*ʾaleph* and III-*y*. In the G stem, it combines the characteristics of both of these categories.

a. In the SC, the inflectional suffixes are those of the other III-y verbs, and the initial *ʾaleph* is strong.

Examples: אֲתָה (Dan 7:22), אֲתָא (Ez 5:3); 2ms אתית (D7 20:10); 1cs אתית (B3 3:3, 1QapGen 2:25); 3mp אֲתוֹ (Ez 4:12); 2mp אתיתון (4Q197 4 iii 4).

b. In the PC, the א is weak, eliding after the prefixes (§246) and often (especially in QA) omitted in the orthography, while the suffixes follow the III-y pattern.

Examples: 3ms יאתה (A6 13:5, יתה B3 4:22), יתה (1QapGen 15:11; cp. BH יֶאֱתֶה Job 37:22, JLA יֵיתֵי); 3fs תאתה (D7 6:8), תתא (4Q246 1 i 4); 2ms תאתה (A3 3:7, 4Q197 5 10); 1cs אתה (1QapGen 20:21, JLA אֵיתֵי); 3mp יאתו (A6 5:3, jussive), יתון (11QtgJob 16:2, JLA יֵיתוֹן); 2mp תאתון (A3 3:5).

c. The ms imperative irregularly has final -*ā* instead of -*ī* as in the other III-y verbs. Cp. Syriac ܐܬܐ, JLA אֵיתָא (sic). Note also μαράνα θά, "Our lord, come!" (1 Cor 16:22).

Examples: ms אתה (D7 8:6; *אֱתָה); fs אתי (C1 1:166 [Ahiqar]); mp אֱתוֹ (Dan 3:26).

d. The infinitive follows the I-*ʾaleph* pattern after the addition of preformative *m* (§246c), and the III-y pattern in the second syllable (§261c): לְמֵתָא (Dan 3:2), למאתה (D7 20:4), למתה (4Q209 7 iii 2).

e. The participles inflect like the other III-y verbs (§261a).

Examples: ms אָתֵה (Dan 7:13), אתה (A2 5:6, 4Q246 1 i 2); fs אתיה (4Q583 1 1); mp אתין (A4 3:5, 11QtgJob 38:4; *אָתַיִן).

§283. a. In the C stem, the base of אתי is formed as if the root were יתי, with strong initial *y*, and the usual III-*y* inflectional suffixes (§265): SC (h/ʾ)aytī, PC *yəhaytē* (*yaytē*). In some texts, as often in JLA, the diphthong *ay (§78, Rule 9) has contracted.

Examples: SC 3ms הַיְתִי (Dan 5:13), היתי (A6 12:1, 11QtgJob 38:7), איתי (11Q18 13 3); 2fs התתי (A2 1:6, *hētītī); 1cs איתית (A3 3:10); 3mp הַיְתִיו (Dan 5:23), היתיו (A6 15:4), איתיו (4Q530 2 ii 24); PC 3ms יהיתה (A6 2:13); 2mp (or 2fs) תהיתן (A2 5:5); 1cs אתה (A2 1:10, *ʾētē, JLA אַיְתֵי < *ʾahaytē); 3mp [י]היתון (A3 9:3), יהתו (A2 5:4, jussive), יתו (A2 1:7, jussive) (cp. JLA PC 3mp יַיְתוֹן).

b. In the infinitive, as in other III-*y* roots, the final *y* is strong: לְהַיְתָיָה (Dan 3:13); note the dialect form with *m* preformative למתיה (A2 4:11), cp. JLA לְאֵיתָאָה, Jewish Palestinian Aramaic למייתייה (Targum Neofiti Exodus 35:29).

c. The causative passive displays several irregularities in BA. The preformative segment is *hē-* (< **hay-*) instead of **hu-* (§251d), and the theme vowel is long *ō*.

3fs	הֵיתָיִת (Dan 6:18)
3mp	הֵיתָיִו (Dan 3:13)

There are no attestations of this stem and root combination in the other Aramaic corpora.

§284. In BA and QA, the roots אזי "heat" and אבי "be willing" in the G stem are vocalized like the equivalent forms of אתי: PC יבא (11QtgJob 32:8 < *יֵאבֵא, cp. JLA יֵיבֵי); infinitive לְמֵזָא (Dan 3:19); with 3ms suffix: לְמֵזְיֵה (Dan 3:19); note also tG PC 3ms: יתזה (4Q541 9 i 4, < *יתאזה; see §247 for the quiescence of *ʾaleph*).

As a transitive verb, the G stem of אזי may occur in the passive voice: G passive ptcp: אֵזֵה (Dan 3:22; for the vocalism of the first syllable, see §75e).

§285. a. In the G stem, the root ימי "swear an oath" is weak in the PC. In IA, it is always spelled with final *ʾaleph*, the original final root letter (§269)

G stem SC 2ms ימאת (B2 2:4); 2fs ימאתי (B2 8:5); 1cs ימאת (B2 3:24); 3mp ימו (4Q201 1 iii 5); PC 2ms תמא (B7 1:6); 1cp [א]נמ (4Q201 1 iii 1); 2mp juss ^ו^תמאו (B8 9:3); inf. למומא (B2 2:6).

b. In the C stem, the roots ידי "thank, praise" and ימי (both originally I-w, §249) are doubly weak.

SC 1cs אודית "I gave thanks" (1QapGen 21:3); with 2ms suff. אומיתכ [sic] "I adjure you" (4Q560 1 ii 6); ptcp ms מְהוֹדֵא "thanking" (Dan 2:23); מהודה (4Q196 17 ii 3), מוֹדֵא "thanking" (Dan 6:11), מומה (4Q560 1 ii 5); inf. להודיה (4Q196 18 15).

§286. The root חיי could potentially be taken as III-y (if the middle y is strong) or geminate. In fact, it shows traits of both patterns:

As III-y (strong middle y): G impv ms חֱיִי (Dan 6:7); PC 3ms יחיה (B4 1:3, *yiḥyē); infinitive למחיה (4Q553 2 i 6, *ləmiḥyē).

As geminate: SC 3ms חי (4Q196 18 14, cp. JLA חֲיָא); PC 3ms יחה (1QapGen 20:23, JLA יֵיחֵי); C stem ptcp ms מַחֵא (Dan 5:19, instead of *מַחְיֵה); suffixed C stem inf. לאחיתה (4Q210 1 ii 2, instead of *לאחיאותה).

A couple of occurrences are ambiguous: C stem SC 1cs + 2ms pron. suff. החיתך "I let you live" (C1 1:51, haḥyītákā or haḥḥītákā?); PC juss 3ms + 1cs pron. suff. יחיני "may he let me live" (C1 1:54, yəḥaḥyīnnī or yəḥaḥḥīnnī?).

The Root סלק

§287. The middle l of the root סלק assimilates to the first root consonant s when they are contiguous, in the G stem PC and infinitive, and throughout the C/Cp stems (§43). The resulting gemination may be replaced by nasalization (§54b).

G stem: there are no PC attestations in the corpora, but see 1cs אֶסַּק in BH (Ps 139:8); inf. למנסק (B3 7:10, *mislaq > missaq > minsaq).

C stem SC 2ms אסקת (1QapGen 21:20); 3mp הַסִּקוּ (Dan 3:22); ptcp mp מסקין (4Q537 12 2, massəqīn < *masləqīn); inf. לְהַנְסָקָה (Dan 6:24), [ל]אסקא (4Q214b 2–6 i 3); with pron. suff. אסקה C SC 3ms + 3fs suff., "he offered it" (11Q18 13 4).

Cp stem SC 3ms הֻסַּק (Dan 6:24, < *huslaq).

There is some evidence that this assimilation was not consistent; see G inf. למסלק (B3 10:15); G impv ms סלק (1QapGen 21:8, instead of סק as in JLA and other dialects).

VERBS WITH BORROWED BASE FORMS

§288. Some verbs are borrowed from other languages (§122) and cannot be treated as derived from triliteral roots. In BA, these are verbs with preformative שׁ, and the verb הימן.

a. Verbs with initial שׁ in the derivational base are importations from Akkadian, where *ša-* is the causative stem preformative: שֵׁיצִיא (Ez 6:15, from Akkadian *ušēṣī*), שֵׁיזִב (Dan 3:28 etc., from Akkadian *ušēzib*), שׁכלל (Ez 4:12, etc., from Akkadian *ušaklil*).

שׁיצי *finish* is inflected like an *i*-theme III-*y* verb (§257). Besides the one BA example from Ez, it is used in QA, e.g., ptcp mp משׁצין (= מְשֵׁצְיֵן*, 11Q18 15 2), and has a T stem passive form, e.g., SC 3mp אשׁתציו (= אִשְׁתְּצִיו*, 4Q545 1a i 7). It is often attested in JLA.

שֵׁיזִב "save, rescue" has the same base in SC, PC, and participle. BA examples include SC 3ms שֵׁיזִב (Dan 3:28, 1Q72 שׁזב), שֵׁיזִיב (Dan 6:28); 3ms with 2ms suffix שׁזבך (C1 1:46 [Ahiqar]); PC 3ms יְשֵׁיזִב (Dan 3:17); with 2mp pron. suff. יְשֵׁיזְבִנְכוֹן (Dan 3:15); ptcp ms מְשֵׁיזִב (Dan 6:28); infinitive with 2ms suffix לְשֵׁיזָבוּתָךְ (Dan 6:21).

שַׁכְלֵל "finish building" is inflected like a strong verb of the C stem (§§232ff.), with *ša-* substituted for stem prefix *ha-*. BA examples include SC 3mp שַׁכְלִילוּ (Ez 4:12 Qere), שַׁכְלִלוּ (Ez 6:14); inf. לְשַׁכְלָלָה (Ez 5:3, 9); and the T-stem passive, with metathesis (§53): PC 3mp יִשְׁתַּכְלְלוּן (Ez 4:13, 16).

b. הֵימִן "trust, rely on" is likely a loan from Hebrew (or Canaanite) הֶאֱמִין. It is inflected like a C stem verb with an initial *y* root consonant (§251). There is one finite form in BA: SC 3ms הֵימִן (Dan 6:24); the adjectival form (vocalized like a C passive participle) is מְהֵימַן "trustworthy" (Dan 2:45, 6:5, also found in IA and QA). An abstract noun הימנו *haymānū* (resembling an infinitive) is found in C1 1:132 הימנותה חן גבר, "a man's charm is his dependability."

All of these verbs were true *Lehnwörter* (§122), being wholly adapted to the Aramaic inflectional system.

CHAPTER 11

Tense, Aspect, and Mood in the Verbal System

Verbs in Aramaic can express different semantic features morphologically and syntactically. The inflectional system (the finite conjugations, and the non-finite forms) signifies the features of tense, aspect, and mood.

For the features expressed by the lexical-derivational system, namely, voice, valence, and *Aktionsart*, see Chapter 12.

§289. *Tense* refers to the way languages encode past, present, and future time. Usually, BA expresses past tense grammatically by the suffix conjugation, future tense by the indicative prefix conjugation, and present tense by the active participle. In addition, past tense and present tense are occasionally signified by the prefix conjugation.

§290. Verbal *aspect* refers to the way languages encode whether an action is viewed as a whole, from beginning to end (perfective aspect), or whether it is encoded as in process (imperfective aspect). In general, BA only explicitly expresses aspect (imperfective) in the active participle, especially when it occurs with the verb הוי "be" (periphrastic construction, §313). The suffix conjugation is usually perfective in aspect, although this can be neutralized in certain contexts. The prefix conjugation is not marked for aspect at all.

§291. a. *Mood* refers to the speaker's wish or command that an action be performed or not. The *volitive* mood is signified in BA by the imperative and by the jussive form of the PC (§§317–318); all other forms are in the *indicative* mood.

b. *Modality* in this grammar is taken to be a semantic feature of the indicative mood, referring either to *epistemic* modality (whether an action is possible or likely) or *deontic* modality (whether an action is obligatory, permissible, or desirable). Modality is naturally connected to the future tense and therefore is usually expressed by the indicative PC in BA, although in certain constructions the SC may express epistemic modality (see conditional clauses, §422b).

c. Deontic modality differs from the volitive mood in that it has truth-value (may be true or false), while volitives do not have truth-value.

TAM FEATURES OF THE SUFFIX CONJUGATION
For the inflection of the suffix conjugation, see §212.

Past Tense

§292. The SC is the default form for expressing past tense. Fine-grained distinctions such as perfect (past with present relevance), pluperfect (past action before another past action), and future perfect (past action before a future action) can only be inferred from context and are a matter of English translation choice. Past tense usages are perfective (§290) in aspect.

פִּתְגָמָא שְׁלַחוּ עֲלוֹהִי	they *sent* him a statement Ezra 5:7 (simple past)
מִלַּת מַלְכָּא הוֹדַעְתֶּנָא	the matter of the king you *have told* us (or "you *told* us") Dan 2:23 (perfect or simple past)
אִיתַי גֻּבְרִין יְהוּדָאיִן דִּי־מַנִּיתָ יָתְהוֹן	there are Judean men whom you *have appointed* (or "whom you *appointed*") (perfect or simple past) Dan 3:12
נשאית חלא וטענת מלח ולא איתי זי יקיר מן נכ[רי]	I *have lifted* sand and *loaded salt,* and nothing is more onerous than a foreigner C1 1:159 (Ahiqar) (perfect)
מִן־דִּי הַרְגִּזוּ אֲבָהֳתַנָא לֶאֱלָהּ שְׁמַיָּא	because our fathers *had angered* the God of heaven (or "our fathers angered") Ezra 5:12 (pluperfect or simple past)

§293. The SC is the default form in *narrative*, and usually the sequence of SC verbs indicates the sequence of events in the story. Sequence may additionally be signaled by the adverbs אדין or באדין (§431) "then" or, in IA, אחר "after that," קרבתא "immediately after that" (§435). (For temporal clauses, see §§418ff.)

אֱדַיִן דָּנִיֵּאל לְבַיְתֵהּ אֲזַל וְלַחֲנַנְיָה מִישָׁאֵל וַעֲזַרְיָה חַבְרוֹהִי מִלְּתָא הוֹדַע	then Daniel *went* to his house and *told* the matter to Hananiah, Mishael, and Azariah Dan 2:17
וחזהא ואתמה על כול שפרהא ונסבהא לה לאנתא ובעא למקטלני	he *saw her* and *was amazed* at all her beauty, and *he took her* as wife and *sought* to kill me 1QapGen 20:9

§294. Sometimes a sequence of SC verbs may not be sequential but *parallelistic*, especially in direct discourse (see also §393 under coordination):

הָנְחַת מִן־כָּרְסֵא מַלְכוּתֵהּ וִיקָרָה הֶעְדִּיו מִנֵּהּ	he *was brought down* from the throne of his kingdom and honor *they removed* from him Dan 5:20
צלית ובעית ואתחננת ואמרת באתעצבא	I *prayed* and *made petition* and *sought mercy* and I *said* in distress 1QapGen 20:12
גהנת וסגדת לם אחיקר קדם אסרח[אד]ן	I *prostrated* and *bowed* – said Ahiqar – before Esarhaddon C1 1:13 (Ahiqar)

§295. a. The formula introducing direct speech using the coordinated G stem verbs ענה "answer" and אמר "say" is expressed in the SC in IA; where the consonantal text shows a distinction between SC and participle, IA always shows SC (e.g., C1 1:45 ענית ואמרת "I answered and said"). In QA, there are no relevant examples that allow one to distinguish SC from participle.

b. In BA, the formula usually uses active G stem participles. In some cases, the first verb ענה is in the SC, and the second אמר is participial: עֲנוֹ וְאָמְרִין, "they answered and said" (see also Dan 2:7, 10; 3:9, 16; 6:14).

c. Note, however, Dan 3:24 עָנֵין וְאָמְרִין (both participial). Only in Dan 5:10 are both forms in the SC: עֲנָת מַלְכְּתָא וַאֲמֶרֶת "the queen answered and said." It has been suggested (as in the BHS apparatus) that the typical עָנֵה וְאָמַר formula of the MT should be vocalized as SC: עֲנָה וַאֲמַר. Examples such as Dan 3:24 (both unambiguously participles) show that this is not necessary.

Present Tense

§296. In the proverbs of Ahiqar, the SC can serve to indicate the gnomic (general) present: מאן טב כס[י] מלה בלבבה והו ז[י]תביר הנפקה ברא "a good vessel *hides* a thing in its interior, but one that is broken *lets it outside*" (C1 1:93). Alternatively, perhaps the past tense is used gnomically, as in English "Curiosity *killed* the cat."

§297. Occasionally the SC is used to express present tense with stative verbs (§328).

אֲנָה יִדְעֵת דִּי רוּחַ אֱלָהִין קַדִּישִׁין בָּךְ	I *know* that a spirit of holy gods is in you Dan 4:6
וכמא שלמא להן לה שקיהא	how *perfect are* her thighs! 1QapGen 20:6
למן זי רחמתי תנתננה	to whomever *you please* you may give it B2 7:8

§298. The SC is the default tense for *performative* utterances, that is, verbs that perform an act by their utterance (see also §316c for the performative use of the passive participle):

קבלתך מרי על פרעו צען

I hereby lodge a complaint with you, my lord, against Pharaoh Zoan
1QapGen 20:14

שנאת לאסחור בעלי

I hereby divorce Eshor my husband (lit., "I hate")
B2 6:23

Future Tense

§299. a. In the protasis of conditional sentences, after the particle הֵן, the SC can be used to express future tense with epistemic modality (see §422b).

    b. After the particle לָהֵן (§423) the SC can also be used as a future-modal:

לָא נְהַשְׁכַּח לְדָנִיֵּאל דְּנָה כָּל־עִלָּא לָהֵן הַשְׁכַּחְנָה עֲלוֹהִי בְּדָת אֱלָהֵהּ

we will not find any ground for condemnation of this Daniel unless *we find something* against him in the law of his god
Dan 6:6

TAM FEATURES OF THE PREFIX CONJUGATION (INDICATIVE)

For the inflections of the prefix conjugation, see §213.

Future Tense

§300. The indicative (non-jussive) form of the PC normally marks future tense, relative either to the time of speech or some other time inferred from the context.

The future tense is especially common in predictions:

ירתונה לכול עלמים

they (your seed) *will possess it* (the land) for all ages
1QapGen 21:12

וּבָתְרָךְ תְּקוּם מַלְכוּ אָחֳרִי

after you *will arise* another kingdom
Dan 2:39

ברה די אל יתאמר ובר עליון יקרונה

he *will be called* the son of God, *they will call* him son of the Most High
4Q246 1 ii 1

Modality

11

§301. a. In a great many cases, the PC indicative has a *modal* nuance. This nuance must be gleaned from context, as there is no special morphological or syntactic indicator of modality (§291b).

מַן־דִּי־לָא יִפֵּל וְיִסְגֻּד בַּהּ־שַׁעֲתָא יִתְרְמֵא לְגוֹא־אַתּוּן נוּרָא יָקִדְתָּא

whoever *does not fall and worship* [epistemic modality] at that moment *shall be thrown* [deontic modality] into the furnace of burning fire
Dan 3:6

מָאנֵי בֵית־אֱלָהָא . . . יַהֲתִיבוּן

they should return [deontic modality] the vessels of the house of God
Ez 6:5

כול דם לא תאכלון

you *must not eat* [deontic modality] any blood
1QapGen 11:17

[מ]ה ישפטון עקן עם עם אשה בשר עם סכין איש עם מ[לך]

how *could* wood *contend* [epistemic modality] with fire, meat with a knife, a man with a king?
C1 1:88 (Ahiqar)

b. A modal PC can appear in a context of past time:

וְלָא־בַטִּלוּ הִמּוֹ עַד־טַעְמָא לְדָרְיָוֶשׁ יְהָךְ וֶאֱדַיִן יְתִיבוּן נִשְׁתְּוָנָא

they did not stop them until the report *should go* to Darius and then an answer *be sent back*
Ez 5:5

ובעא מני די אתה ואצלה

he requested from me that *I might come and pray*
1QapGen 20:21

c. This is common in purpose clauses (see §§402, 405 with exemplification), denoting the modal action contemplated by the subject of the main clause verb.

Present Tense

§302. a. The PC can express present tense with the G stem of the root יכל/כהל "to be able":

תּוּכַל [תכול] פִּשְׁרִין לְמִפְשַׁר

you *are able* to give interpretations
Dan 5:16 (general present)

לא אכהל למפלח בבב היכלא   I *am not able* to serve in the gate of the palace
C1 1:17 (Ahiqar) (actual present, or possibly future: "I will not be able . . .")

כלא תכול למעבד   you *can* do everything
11QtgJob 37:4 (general present)

b. In elevated or archaic speech, the PC sometimes may express general present with other verbs.

וכל בתולן וכלאן די יעלן לגנון לא ישפרן מנהא   no virgins and brides who *enter* the bridal canopy are more beautiful than she
1QapGen 20:6 (although these verbs may be modal instead: "no virgins and brides who *might enter* the bridal canopy *could be more beautiful* than she")

חרב תדלח מין שפין בין רעין טבן   a sword *stirs up* quiet waters between good neighbors
C1 1:161 (or modal: "a sword can stir up . . .")

יקראון לקפא לבא   *they call* the sea-snake "*labbu*"
C1 1:165 (general present)

c. In the Qumran Job Targum, the PC is used to render the general present of Hebrew PC verbs:

יחאך על דחלא ולא יזוע ולא יתוב מן אנפי חרב   he *laughs* at fear and does not tremble, he *does not turn away* from the sword
11QtgJob 33:3–4 (MT Job 39:22 יִשְׂחַק לְפַחַד וְלֹא יֵחָת וְלֹא־יָשׁוּב מִפְּנֵי־חָרֶב)

d. Other than the instances with יכל/כהל, there are no clear cases of the PC expressing general or actual present in BA.[1]

Past Tense

Although mainly used for future-modal functions, the PC can sometimes refer to past time.

[1] The instances adduced by Li (2009: 101–103) are more readily understandable as modal (Dan 3:18, 4:14, 6:16, 7:14).

§303. The PC sometimes refers to *ongoing action* in the past:

תְּחֹתוֹהִי תַּטְלֵל חֵיוַת בָּרָא וּבְעַנְפוֹהִי יְדֻרוּן [יְדוּרָן]
צִפֲּרֵי שְׁמַיָּא וּמִנֵּהּ יִתְּזִין כָּל־בִּשְׂרָא

under (the tree) the wild beasts *found shade,* and in its branches the birds *dwelt* and from it all flesh *was fed*

Dan 4:9 (or "would find shade . . . would dwell . . . would be fed")

עִשְׂבָּא כְתוֹרִין יֵאכֻל וּמִטַּל שְׁמַיָּא גִּשְׁמֵהּ יִצְטַבַּע

he ate plants as the cattle, and his body *was bathed* from the dew of heaven

Dan 4:30 (or "would eat . . . would be bathed")

§304. a. In some contexts, the PC may express *past action that is not ongoing* (BA and QA only), e.g.:

חֵלֶם חֲזֵית וִידַחֲלִנַּנִי

I saw a dream and it *frightened* me

Dan 4:2

רְבָה אִילָנָא וּתְקִף וְרוּמֵהּ יִמְטֵא לִשְׁמַיָּא

the tree grew and became strong, and its height *reached* to heaven

Dan 4:8

מַנְדְּעִי יְתוּב עֲלַי . . . הַדְרִי וְזִוִי יְתוּב עֲלַי וְלִי
הַדָּבְרַי וְרַבְרְבָנַי יְבַעוֹן

my mind *returned* to me . . . my majesty and splendor *returned* to me, and my counselors and nobles *sought* me

Dan 4:33

בֵּאדַיִן מַלְכָּא בִּשְׁפַּרְפָּרָא יְקוּם בְּנָגְהָא
וּבְהִתְבְּהָלָה לְגֻבָּא דִי־אַרְיָוָתָא אֲזַל

Then the king *rose* at dawn, at first light, and in agitation went to the den of lions.

Dan 6:20

b. Although this use of the PC resembles the BH *wayyiqtol* (narrative preterite), it must be distinguished from it. BH *wayyiqtol* is the primary narrative tense, while the BA past-tense PC is used *alongside* the SC, which is the standard Aramaic narrative tense. Also, BH *wayyiqtol* is derived from the older Semitic short PC (represented in BA by the jussive, §222a), while the BA past-tense PC is derived from the Semitic long PC (in BA, the indicative PC) and, moreover, is not obligatorily preceded by the conjunction *wa*, as is the *wayyiqtol*.[2]

---

[2] The preterite PC sometimes used in the OA inscriptions of Zakkur, Deir ʿAllā, and Tel Dan was also derived from the short PC, and therefore apparently was not the ancestor of the form under discussion.

c. Since the PC is not marked for aspect (§290), it can be used for past action when the author wants to signify only the action in itself, without specifying aspect, with the time and nature of the action inferred from context and the neighboring verbs. Such occurrences are usually coordinated with the SC or participle of another verb, which do mark aspect. This is why some of the BA past-tense PCs refer to continuous action, as in §303 above (Li 2009: 105–110 argues that they all do), while others do not (as in §304).

d. The (infrequent) examples in QA, however, do in fact look like imitations of BH *wayyiqtol*; in 4Q551, the text is an Aramaizing of Gen 19:4–5 or Judg 19:22, which use the BH *wayyiqtol*.

עמי תמלל ולי תאמר

she *spoke* with me and *said* to me

1QapGen 2:13

ויתכנשון כל אנש קרתא. . . על ביתא וימרון לה

all the men of the city *gathered* . . . at the house and *said* to him

4Q551 1 4

e. There are no examples of past-tense PC in IA.

TAM FEATURES OF THE ACTIVE PARTICIPLE

§305. a. In general, the active participle, used predicatively (§379), is used for *present tense*, that is, to denote states, events, or processes happening at the time of speech or other contextually specified time.

b. The present tense in BA is a *relative tense*, that is, the tense of the verb is present relative to the time of the (quoted) speaker or the time specified by the narrator, although in absolute terms it may be in past time.

General Present

§306. *General present* refers to the "timeless" present, denoting states, events, or processes that are always or generally happening:

הוּא גָּלֵא עַמִּיקָתָא וּמְסַתְּרָתָא יָדַע מָה בַחֲשׁוֹכָא

he *reveals* deep and hidden things; he *knows* what is in darkness

Dan 2:22

פַּרְזְלָא מְהַדֵּק וְחָשֵׁל כֹּלָּא

iron *crushes* and *smashes* everything

Dan 2:40

Actual Present

§307. a. *Actual present* refers to non-recurring action taking place at the same time as the person is speaking (speech time). In many cases this corresponds to the English present progressive:

קַרְיְתָא מָרָדְתָּא וּבְאִישְׁתָּא בָּנַיִן   they *are building* the evil and rebellious city
Ez 4:12

יָדַע אֲנָה דִּי עִדָּנָא אַנְתּוּן זָבְנִין   I *know* that you *are buying* time
Dan 2:8

הָא־אֲנָה חָזֵה גֻּבְרִין אַרְבְּעָה שְׁרַיִן מַהְלְכִין   I *see* four men unbound *walking* in the fire
בְּגוֹא־נוּרָא   Dan 3:25

b. This includes action begun in the past and continuing at the time of the speaker:

וּמִן־אֱדַיִן וְעַד־כְּעַן מִתְבְּנֵא וְלָא שְׁלִם   from then until now (the temple) *has been (in the process of) being built* and is not finished
Ez 5:16

מן ירח תמוז שנת 14 דריהוש מלכא ועד זנה יומא   from the month of Tammuz, the 14th year of
אנחנה שקקן לבשן וצימין   Darius the king, until this day, we *have been wearing sackcloth and fasting*
A4 7:19–20 (Petition)

c. This may also include action which is habitual, if not actual, at speech time:

וְאֶשְׁתַּדּוּר עָבְדִין בְּגַוַּהּ מִן־יוֹמָת עָלְמָא   they *have been making* rebellion in it (Jerusalem) from days of old
Ez 4:15; cf. 4:19

Imminent Present

§308. The participle may denote actions that will happen a short time in the future (imminent present):

לָךְ טָרְדִין מִן־אֲנָשָׁא   they *are going to drive you away* from humankind
Dan 4:22

Past Progressive

§309. The past progressive denotes action that continues over a past interval with unspecified beginning or end. The action of the participle overlaps with whatever non-continuous action is described as occurring in the same interval. The progressive is therefore imperfective in aspect (§290).[3]

§310. a. Although the progressive action may take place in past time, the action is *present according to the viewpoint of the nearby non-participial verb*. The participle used in this way is here called *focused*, in that its action is focused on the action of an accompanying SC verb. It can often be translated by the English past progressive in a circumstantial clause.

בַּהּ־שַׁעֲתָה נְפַקוּ [נפקה] אֶצְבְּעָן דִּי יַד־אֱנָשׁ . . .
וּמַלְכָּא חָזֵה פַּס יְדָה דִּי כָתְבָה

at that moment fingers of a man's hand came out [SC]. . . and the king *was seeing* the portion of the hand that *was writing*
Dan 5:5

שָׁרִיו לְמִבְנֵא . . . וְעִמְּהוֹן נְבִיַּאיָּא [נבייא]דִּי־
אֱלָהָא מְסָעֲדִין לְהוֹן

they began [SC] to build . . . while with them the prophets of God *were supporting* them
Ez 5:2

ואמרת באתעצבא ודמעי נחתן

I said [SC] in distress while my tears *were coming down*
1QapGen 20:12

אדין מומאה מטאה עליכי וימאתי לי

then, the oath *coming* upon you, you swore [SC] to me
B2 8:4–5[4]

אתין לות איוב כל רחמוהי . . . ואכלו עמה לחם
בביתה

all his friends *coming* to Job . . . they ate [SC] with him a meal in his house
11QtgJob 38:4–6

See also Dan 5:6, 23.

b. The participle may also be used similarly in an object complement construction (§340b), which is a kind of embedded circumstantial copular clause (§374).

---

[3] In the section that follows, I am indebted to Bentein (2013); my *focused* and *non-focused* progressive correspond to his *focalized* and *durative* progressive, respectively.

[4] For a discussion of this passage, see Muraoka and Porten (2003: 204); Li (2009: 53–54).

חֲזָה מַלְכָּא עִיר וְקַדִּישׁ נָחִת מִן־שְׁמַיָּא	the king saw [SC] a watcher and holy one *coming down* from heaven Dan 4:20; cp. Dan 3:25
וְהַשְׁכַּחוּ לְדָנִיֵּאל בָּעֵא וּמִתְחַנַּן קֳדָם אֱלָהֵהּ	they found [SC] Daniel *making request and entreating* before his god Dan 6:12
ואשכח[ו ל[רעוא][ל י]תב קדם תרע דרתה	they found [SC] Reuel *sitting* before the gate of his courtyard 4Q197 4 iii 3

§311. The *non-focused progressive* extends over a longer interval that may encompass several other continuous actions and is not found in a circumstantial clause, as with the focused progressive (§310 above). In Daniel, the non-focused progressives occur together, with a plurality of participants, denoting ongoing actions that overlap each other:

בֵּאדַיִן מִתְכַּנְּשִׁין אֲחַשְׁדַּרְפְּנַיָּא . . . לַחֲנֻכַּת צַלְמָא . . . וְקָאֲמִין [וקימין] לָקֳבֵל צַלְמָא וְכָרוֹזָא קָרֵא בְחָיִל	then the satraps et al. . . . *were gathering* . . . to the dedication of the statue . . . and *were standing* before the statue and the herald *was calling* loudly Dan 3:3–4

The gathering and standing actions are distributed across a great number of participants, with multiple overlaps, with the process possibly repeated on several occasions. The author uses coordinated participles to express this situation.

כָּל־קֳבֵל דְּנָה בֵּהּ־זִמְנָא כְּדִי שָׁמְעִין כָּל־עַמְמַיָּא קָל קַרְנָא . . . נָפְלִין כָּל־עַמְמַיָּא . . . סָגְדִין לְצֶלֶם דַּהֲבָא	accordingly at that time, when all the peoples *were hearing* the sound of the horn, etc. . . . all the peoples *were falling* down . . . (and) *were worshipping* the statue of gold Dan 3:7

Again, we have a case of many overlapping actions by multiple participants.

בֵּאדַיִן נָפְקִין שַׁדְרַךְ . . . מִן־גּוֹא נוּרָא וּמִתְכַּנְּשִׁין אֲחַשְׁדַּרְפְּנַיָּא . . . חָזַיִן לְגֻבְרַיָּא אִלֵּךְ	then Shadrach et al. . . . *were coming out* of the fire and the satraps et al. . . . *were gathering* . . . *looking* at those men Dan 3:26–27

See also Dan 4:4, 5:8, 9. This seems to be a stylistic feature of the author of Daniel.

Habitual or Repeated Action

§312. The participle without הוי auxiliary (§313 below) is rarely used for *habitual action*, that is, action that is (deliberately) repeated (but does not run continuously) during a past interval of time.

מַלְכִין תַּקִּיפִין הֲווֹ עַל־יְרוּשְׁלֶם . . . וּמִדָּה בְלוֹ וַהֲלָךְ מִתְיְהֵב לְהוֹן
: mighty kings were over Jerusalem . . . and tax, toll, and tribute *would be given* to them
Ez 4:20

וְדָנִיֵּאל . . . עַל לְבַיְתֵהּ . . . וְזִמְנִין תְּלָתָה בְיוֹמָא הוּא בָּרֵךְ עַל־בִּרְכוֹהִי וּמְצַלֵּא וּמוֹדֵא קֳדָם אֱלָהֵהּ כָּל־קֳבֵל דִּי־הֲוָא עָבֵד מִן־קַדְמַת דְּנָה
: Daniel . . . went to his house . . . and three times in the day he *knelt on his knees and prayed and gave thanks* to his god, just as would do previously
Dan 6:11

In Dan 6:11, there is a contrast between the threefold repeated action of a single day (הוּא בָּרֵךְ) and the same threefold action customarily repeated over a long period (דִּי־הֲוָא עָבֵד, §313 below).

Participles with הוי *be* as Auxiliary (Periphrastic Construction)

§313. Just as the verb הוי "be" is used as a tensed copula in copular clauses (§373e), it may be used to indicate a specific tense or mood with predicative active participles (which syntactically are a type of predicate adjective, §376). This is the *periphrastic* construction.

a. The periphrastic construction with SC הוי indicates mainly past progressive (continuous) action. The relative order of הוי and the participle is not significant (*pace* Greenfield 1969; Li 2009: 93ff.).

עַל־הֵיכַל מַלְכוּתָא דִּי בָבֶל מְהַלֵּךְ הֲוָה
: *he was walking* on the royal palace of Babylon
Dan 4:26

הוית יתב בטורא די בית אל
: *I was dwelling* in the hill country of Beth-El
1QapGen 21:7

אנחנה עם נשין ובנין שקקן לבשן הוין
: we, with our wives and children, *have been wearing* sackcloth
A4 7:15 (Petition)

b. The SC הוי with participle can also function to indicate past *habitual* action:

לקבל זי קדמן פמון אבוהי הוה חשל
: just as previously Pamun his father *would pay/ used to pay*
A6 11:6

דִּי־הֲוָה צָבֵא הֲוָא קָטֵל וְדִי־הֲוָה צָבֵא הֲוָה מַחֵא   whomever *he wanted, he would kill*, and
      whomever *he wanted, he would keep alive*
      Dan 5:19

הויה בטנן מנהן   (the human women) *would become pregnant* from
      them (the watchers)
      4Q201 1 iii 16

c. The periphrastic construction with PC הוי indicates future imperfective (either continuous or habitual) action.

כסף ומרבי זי אהוה משלם לך   the silver and interest that *I shall keep paying* you
      B4 2:7

מִתְעָרְבִין לֶהֱוֹן . . . וְלָא־לֶהֱוֹן דָּבְקִין דְּנָה עִם־דְּנָה   *they will keep mixing* together . . . but *they will not adhere* to each other
      Dan 2:43

נִפְקְתָא תֶּהֱוֵא מִתְיַהֲבָא לְגֻבְרַיָּא אִלֵּךְ   the expenses *shall be continually given* to those
      men
      Ez 6:8 (deontic modal)

דלמא תהוה אמר די מן נכסי כול עתרה די אברם   lest *you go around saying*, Out of my possessions
      comes Abram's wealth
      1QapGen 22:22 (deontic modal)

d. The imperative of הוי can be used with a participle to enjoin a progressive (continuous) action:

הוא . . . אחדין בקושטא ואזלין בישירותא   *keep . . . holding on to* the truth and (*keep*) *walking*
      in uprightness (הוא impv mp)
      4Q542 1 i 8–9

הוי חזית על תשי ועל ברה   *keep looking* after Tashi and her son
      A2 3:11–12

§314. The use of הוי with the participle of a stative verb or with a passive participle is not ranked with the periphrastic construction but is straightforwardly a copular clause (§376), with the participle having adjectival force.

הֲוָת שָׁנְיָה מִן־כָּלְהֵון [כלהין]	(the fourth beast) *was different* from all of them Dan 7:19 (stative; not "was differing")
בַּיְתָא דִּי־הֲוָא בְנֵה מִקַּדְמַת דְּנָה	the house that *was built* previously Ezra 5:11 (passive)
כתיש הוית שנין שבע	I *was smitten* seven years 4Q242 1+3:3 (passive); the speaker was not continually being smitten, but his state was of someone who had been smitten

Participles with איתי

§315. Another kind of periphrastic construction with participles is formed by the combination of the existential particle אִיתַי with the active participle (§379). In such cases, אִיתַי serves as the copula, and a pronominal suffix joined to it expresses the subject. The function of the construction is to emphasize or expressively highlight the verbal action.

לֵאלָהַי לָא אִיתֵיכוֹן פָּלְחִין וּלְצֶלֶם דַּהֲבָא. . . לָא סָגְדִין	(is it true that) my gods *you indeed do not serve* and the golden image *you indeed do not worship*? Dan 3:14
לֵאלָהָיִךְ לָא־אִיתַיְנָא [איתנא] פָּלְחִין וּלְצֶלֶם דַּהֲבָא . . . לָא נִסְגֻּד	your gods *indeed we do not serve* and the golden image we shall not worship Dan 3:18

This construction is not attested in IA or QA, but is common in later dialects.

USE OF THE PASSIVE PARTICIPLES

§316. a. The purely passive participles – of the Gp, Dp, and Cp stems (§§224, 229, 235c) – function predicatively as adjectives. They imply the operation of a past action, but in terms of *Aktionsart* (§328), they are stative, while the participles of the T stems, though also usually passive in voice, are dynamic in *Aktionsart*.

לֶהֱוֵא שְׁמֵהּ דִּי־אֱלָהָא מְבָרַךְ	let the name of God be *blessed* Dan 2:20

מִלַּת מַלְכָּא מַחְצְפָה וְאַתּוּנָא אֵזֵה	the word of the king was *urgent* and the furnace *heated* Dan 3:22
חלבון די שימא על שמאל דרמשק	Helbon which is *located* to the north of Damascus 1QapGen 22:10 (lit., "is placed")

b. The G passive participle of עבד "do, make" is used to refer to the present condition or situation of something:

איך ביתא עביד	how is the family doing? A3 3:6 (lit., "done")
נשיא זילן כארמלה עבידין	our wives are in the condition of a widow A4 7:20

Some other apparently passive forms are best translated as active:

מַלְכָּא עֲשִׁית לַהֲקָמוּתֵהּ	the king *planned* to elevate him Dan 6:4
וּנְהִירָא [ונהורא] עִמֵּהּ שְׁרֵא	light *dwells* with him Dan 2:22

c. The passive participle can also be used in performative utterances (cp. §298), in which the utterance accomplishes the act it signifies:

בְּרִיךְ אֱלָהֲהוֹן דִּי־שַׁדְרַךְ מֵישַׁךְ וַעֲבֵד נְגוֹ	*blessed* be the god of Shadrach, Meshach, and Abed-nego Dan 3:28
מִנִּי שִׂים טְעֵם	from me *is* the order hereby *given* (as follows) Ez 6:8
ונכסיא כולהון שביקין לך	all the property is hereby *left* to you 1QapGen 22:19–20

VOLITIVE FORMS: JUSSIVE AND IMPERATIVE

The jussive form of the PC (the "short" PC) and the imperatives together constitute the volitive mood. As noted (§291a), the volitive forms express the will of the speaker that an action be done.

Jussive

§317. a. Sometimes the jussive expresses an indirect command, sometimes simply a desire or wish.

b. In the 3ms form, outside of the III-y verbs, it can be difficult to distinguish the affirmative jussive from the indicative PC used with deontic modality (§291c).

אֲנָה דָרְיָוֶשׁ שָׂמֶת טְעֵם אָסְפַּרְנָא יִתְעֲבִד   I Darius have so ordered; strictly *let it be done*
Ez 6:12

מִלְכִּי יִשְׁפַּר עֲלָיִךְ [עלך]   *may* my counsel *be pleasing* to you
Dan 4:24

מַלְכָּא חֶלְמָא יֵאמַר לְעַבְדוֹהִי   *let* the king *tell* the dream to his servants (or: the king *should/must tell* the dream to his servants [deontic modality])
Dan 2:7

c. The 3mp/2mp/2fs forms, the III-y singular forms ending in *-y*, forms with pronominal suffixes without *-inn-*, and the negative jussive are unambiguously jussive (§222).

דָּנִיֵּאל יִתְקְרֵי וּפִשְׁרָה יְהַחֲוֵה   *let* Daniel *be called* and he will tell the interpretation
Dan 5:12 (III-y 3ms)

אגורא זי יהו אלהא . . . יהעדו מן תמה   the temple of the god Yahu . . . *let them remove* from there
A4 7:6 (Petition) (3mp)

חֶלְמָא וּפִשְׁרֵא אַל־יְבַהֲלָךְ   *let not* the dream and its interpretation *disturb you*
Dan 4:16 (negative, 3ms with 2ms pronominal suffix); cf. Dan 5:10

עינין טבן אל יאכמו   *let* good eyes *not be dark*
C1 1:157 (Ahiqar) (negative, 3mp)

d. Since the imperative cannot be negated, the negative 2nd person jussive serves instead as a negative command (§388):

אל תקוצו ל[א]רזא   *do not* chop down the cedar
1QapGen 19:16 (2mp)

אל תצפי לה   *do not* worry about him
A2 3:4 (2fs)

לְחַכִּימֵי בָבֶל אַל־תְּהוֹבֵד   *do not* destroy the sages of Babylon
Dan 2:24 (2ms)

Imperatives

§318. a. The imperative forms express a command, although in certain contexts they express a wish or permission. Imperatives may be strung together with or without conjunctions.

מַלְכָּא לְעָלְמִין חֱיִי   O king, *live* forever
Dan 2:4 (ms)

הַעֵלְנִי קֳדָם מַלְכָּא   *bring me* to the king
Dan 2:24 (ms with 1cs suffix)

אֲזֶל־אֲחֵת הִמּוֹ בְּהֵיכְלָא   *go, put* them in the temple
Ezra 5:15 (ms)

קום הלך ואזל   *rise, walk,* and *go*
1QapGen 21:13 (ms)

ארקא זך זיליכי בני והבי למן זי רחמתי   that land is yours, *build* or *give* it to whomever you want
B2 3:19 (fs)

b. The particle נא (cp. BH נָא) is used infrequently in QA after imperatives to add expressivity or emphasis:

כען אזל נא עד למך   now *do go* to Lamech
4Q204 5 ii 29

שמע נא ואנה אמלל   *just listen* and I will speak
11QtgJob 37:6

INFINITIVES

§319. Infinitives do not have any TAM features as such and are subservient to finite verbs as either complements (§428) or adverbial adjuncts in purpose (§401) or temporal (§419) clauses. In addition to these functions, they also have other uses.

§320. a. The infinitive likely developed from a grammaticalized *verbal noun*, that is, a noun that names the verbal action abstractly (*nomen actionis*) like the gerund in English. The infinitive can still be used as a verbal noun in some contexts.

אַחֲוָיַת אֲחִידָן	*declaring* of riddles
	Dan 5:12

מְחַן עֲנָיִן	*showing mercy* to the poor
	Dan 4:24

לא בידי אנ[ש]א מנשא רגלהם	the *lifting* of their foot is not in the power of men
	C1 1:170 (Ahiqar)

ביום מפקך מן חרן	in the day of your *going forth* from Haran
	1QapGen 22:30

b. When the infinitive as verbal noun is used with a preposition, it can serve adverbially:

קָם בְּהִתְבְּהָלָה	he arose in *agitation*
	Dan 3:24 (tG of בהל)

אמרת באתעצבא	I said in *sadness*
	1QapGen 20:12 (tG/tD of עצב)

§321. a. Infinitives of the G stem verb אמר are often used to introduce direct speech.

כְּנֵמָא פִּתְגָמָא הֲתִיבוּנָא לְמֵמַר	thus they answered me, *saying*
	Ezra 5:11

שאיל דניאל לממר	he asked Daniel, *saying*
	4Q243 1 1

b. More common in IA is לאמר (*lə'amār*?) which may preserve the form of an archaic G stem infinitive without *m*:

אגרת שלח . . . לאמר	he sent a letter . . . *saying*
	A4 7:7 (Petition)

c. The particle לם, also used in IA to indicate direct speech, may be a shortened form of לאמר.[5] It can occur before a direct quotation or after the first word or words of a direct quotation:

---

[5] So CAL s.v. lm (accessed Jan. 11, 2021).

לם אגורא זי יהו אלהא . . . יהעדו — They said, That temple of the god Yaho . . . let them remove
A4 7:6 (Petition)

גהנת וסגדת לם אחיקר קדם אסרח[אד]ן — I bent and bowed (so said Ahiqar) before Esarhaddon
C1 1:13 (Ahiqar)

§322. Infinitives also can be used impersonally with לְא to express prohibitions (modal use).

כְּתָבָא דִּי לָא לְהַשְׁנָיָה — a writing that *is not to be changed*
Dan 6:9 (lit., "which one is not to change")

נִפְקְתָא תֶּהֱוֵא מִתְיַהֲבָא לְגֻבְרַיָּא אִלֵּךְ דִּי־לָא לְבַטָּלָא — the expenses shall be continually given to those men, *without cessation*
Ez 6:8 (lit., "which one is not to stop")

This construction is also found in inscriptional material from the Qumran period, e.g., the Uzziah burial plaque (Sukenik 1931, Albright 1931): לכה התית טמי עוזיה מלך יהודה ולא למפתח "I brought here the bones of Uzziah, king of Judah, and *it is not to be opened*" (lit., "and one is not to open").

CHAPTER 12

Verb Types

Valence, Voice, and Aktionsart

Verbs have different properties that affect the number and nature of the complements that they have, namely, valence, voice, and *Aktionsart*.

VALENCE

§323. Verbs differ in the number of nominal complements they require to make a complete predication. Aramaic verbs normally require a subject, but some verbs (the *intransitive*) do not take (or "govern") a direct object, while some (the *transitive*) govern one or more objects. Some verbs (here called *semi-transitive*) govern "oblique" objects, that is, nominal complements marked with a preposition, and others govern an infinitive complement or complement that is itself another clause. The number and type of complements governed by a verb is called its *valence*.

§324. a. *Causativity* is part of the landscape of valence, in that the lexical root of intransitive G stem verbs can be used transitively in the C(ausative) stem or sometimes in the D stem, e.g., סלק "go up" (G stem), "bring up" (C stem), or רבי "grow, become big" (G stem), "magnify, make big" (D stem). Hence the use of causative stems can increase valence.

b. The D and C stems can also causativize and increase the valence of already transitive verbs, e.g., אלף "learn X" (G stem, one direct object), "teach Y X, cause Y to learn X" (D stem, with two direct objects); חזי "see X" (G stem, one direct object), "show X to Y" (= "cause Y to see X," C stem, two direct objects).

c. The change of stem, however, may change meaning without adding valence, e.g., קטל "kill" (G stem), "kill more than one" (D stem), or מני "count" (G stem), "appoint" (D stem); all four verbs govern only one direct object.

VOICE

§325. Some verbs are related to other verbs by the category of voice. The typical sentence subject will act as the doer, initiator, or *agent* of an action denoted by a transitive verb, and the typical direct object will undergo that action as *patient*. That is the *active* voice. But the roles of agent and patient are separable from the grammatical roles of subject and object. In the *passive* voice, the patient plays the grammatical role of subject, and the agent is banished to a prepositional phrase, if it is expressed at all. Voice, then, has to do with the relationship of the subject to the verbal action.

Active and Passive Voice

§326. In Aramaic, voice is typically (but not obligatorily) associated with particular verbal stems (§208). The G, D, and C stems are *active*. The *passive* voice of the G stem is associated with the G internal passive (§224) or with the tG stem (§238), the passive of the D with the tD stem (§241), and the passive of the C with the C internal passive stem (§235; the tC stem is not highly productive, §243). In addition, G, D, and C have internal passive participles separate from the T stems. Hence, there is a systematic active–passive voice relationship between the stems.

Reflexive, Reciprocal, Middle Voice

§327. a. Besides the active and passive voices, Aramaic has three further voice categories: reflexive, reciprocal, and middle. In the *reflexive* voice, the agent (grammatical subject) voluntarily acts upon itself as patient; in the *reciprocal*, the agent acts upon the patient at the same time that the patient is acting upon the agent; in the *middle* voice, the subject fills the role of patient.

The *middle voice* is sometimes difficult to distinguish from the reflexive, and some authorities include reflexive and reciprocal under the category of middle voice. I here follow John Saeed's notion that middles "emphasize that the subject of the verb is affected by the action described by the verb" (2003: 172), especially with those intransitives where "the subject undergoes a non-volitional process or change of state."

b. All verbs in these voices are intransitive in valence. They are routinely associated with the T stems, especially the tD. Since these stems serve also to indicate passive voice, the differentiation of voice can sometimes be difficult. In the passive voice, the agent of the verb is other than the grammatical subject but "off stage," while in the reflexive and reciprocal the agent is usually "on stage" but playing a dual role as patient. In the middle voice, the agency of the subject is downplayed relative to its patienthood.

In the following chart, the categories of voice are aligned with the sentence categories of subject and object in terms of the semantic roles of agent and patient.

Semantic roles, grammatical subject, and object

12

Verb type	Agent	Patient	Participants in event
Active (trans)	Subject 1	Object 2	2
Passive	(Prep.) 2	Subject 1	2 (agent suppressed)
Active (intrans)	Subject 1	(none)	1
Reflexive	Subject 1	Subject 1	1
Reciprocal	Subject 1, 2	Subject 1, 2	2
Middle	(none)	Subject 1	1

AKTIONSART

§328. *Aktionsart* (German "type of action") refers to the division between *stative* and *dynamic* verbs, that is, verbs that express a state that is unchanging across some stretch of time, and verbs that describe an event or process.

Some stative verbs may become dynamic when they are used to describe the beginning of a state (*inceptive*) or a change of state (*inchoative*); some dynamic verbs expressing a change of position may become stative in certain usages (see קום below).

Aktionsart cuts across valence, in that stative and dynamic verbs may be either transitive or intransitive; however, a change of stem may sometimes mean a change in both *Aktionsart* and valence, as when a G stative intransitive verb becomes causative (dynamic) transitive in the D stem, e.g., G stem רבי means "to be big," the D stem of the same root "to make X big."

Aktionsart is aligned with the derivational stem system in that stative verbs are almost always in the G stem, whatever their valence.

VERB TYPES: INTRANSITIVE

§329. As noted, the hallmark of the intransitive verb is that it has no object. Therefore, an intransitive verb has no corresponding passive voice form.

§330. a. *Stative-inchoative.* Some verbs express either a state or a change of state in the G stem; they can change valence (become transitive) by a change of stem to D or C, although not every such verb has a corresponding D or C.

Some examples are ארך "be/become long" (G; C "lengthen X"), באש "be/become bad" (G; C "make X bad"), הוי "be/become" (G; no D or C), טאב "be/become good" (G),

רבי "be/become big" (G; D "magnify X, enlarge X"), תקף "be/become strong, hard" (G; D "strengthen X," C "hold, grip X"), etc.

רְבָה אִילָנָא the tree became large
Dan 4:8 (G stem)

מַלְכָּא לְדָנִיֵּאל רַבִּי the king made Daniel great
Dan 2:48 (D stem)

רוּחֵהּ תִּקְפַת his spirit became hard
Dan 5:20 (G stem)

לְתַקָּפָה אֱסָר to make strong a prohibition
Dan 6:8 (D stem)

b. Some verbs are stative-inchoative and appear with a prepositional complement; they can be transitivized with a change of stem. Examples are דמי "resemble" (G), with לְ (§§177ff.), דבק "adjoin" (G), with עִם (§189) or לְ, שׁוי "be/become equal/worth" (G; D "make X equal," with tD passive), with לְ or unmarked complement, שׁני "be different (from), change" (G; D/C "make X different," with tD passive), with מִן (§§182ff.).

דמה עלימא דן לטובי this lad *resembles* Tobit
4Q197 4 iii:5

אוצרא זי מלכא דבק לה the storehouse of the king *adjoins* it
B3 4:9

שָׁנְיָן דָּא מִן־דָּא (the beasts) *were different* one from the other
Dan 7:3

c. Some stative intransitive verbs require an infinitive verbal complement (§428), i.e., יכל/כהל "be able" (G), צבי (G) "want to." These do not change stem (or, accordingly, valence).

צְבִית לְיַצָּבָא עַל־חֵיוְתָא רְבִיעָיְתָא I *wanted to make certain* about the fourth beast
Dan 7:19

יְכֵלְתָּ לְמִגְלֵא רָזָה דְנָה *you are able to reveal* this secret
Dan 2:47

§331. a. Verbs expressing *change of location or other kinds of movement* are intransitive, but may sometimes require locative complement phrases headed by עַל/לְ "to" (§§177, 188), מִן "from" (§§182ff.), or בְּ "in" (§179). Such verbs are often made transitive in the C stem, retaining their locative complements along with adding direct objects (that is, they become transfer verbs; see below §339).

Examples are אזל "go" (G), אתי "come" (G; C "bring"), יתב "sit/dwell" (G; C "settle X"), מטי "reach/arrive" (G), נחת "go down" (G; C "bring down"), נפל "fall" (G), נפק "come out" (G; C "bring out"), סלק "go up" (G; C "bring up"), עלל "go into" (G; C "bring in"), קום "arise, stand" (G; D "make X permanent," C "set X up"), etc.

אֲנָה הֲוֵית יָתֵב בְּטוּרָא דִי בֵית אֵל	I was *dwelling in* the hill country of Beth-El 1QapGen 21:7 (G stem of יתב)
הוֹתֵב הִמּוֹ בְּקִרְיָה דִּי שָׁמְרָיִן	he *settled* them *in* a city of Samaria Ez 4:10 (C stem of יתב)

b. Some dynamic motion verbs may become stative when the subject "rests" in the final goal of the motion. For instance, קום (G stem) means "stand up, arise" (motion), but also "remain standing, endure" (stative). In such cases, the C stem may be causative of the motion, and the D stem causative of the state.

תְּקוּם מַלְכוּ אָחֳרִי	another kingdom shall *arise* Dan 2:39 (G stem of קום)
הִיא תְּקוּם לְעָלְמַיָּא	it will *stand* (last) forever Dan 2:44 (G stem of קום)
צַלְמָא דִּי הֲקֵים נְבוּכַדְנֶצַּר	the image that Nebuchadnezzar *raised* Dan 3:3 (C stem of קום, causative of motion)
לְקַיָּמָה קְיָם	to *confirm* a statute Dan 6:8 (D stem of קום, causative of state)

c. Some motion verbs have different senses that govern different prepositional complements, e.g., קרב with לְ (G) "be/become near, approach," קרב with בְּ (G) "touch X" (D or C "bring near, offer X," corresponding to the first G sense).

קְרֵב נְבוּכַדְנֶצַּר לִתְרַע אַתּוּן נוּרָא יָקִדְתָּא
Nebuchadnezzar *came near to* the entrance of the furnace of burning fire
Dan 3:26

לא יכל למקרב בהא
he was not able to *touch* her
1QapGen 20:17

d. Sometimes the goal or path of motion verbs is unmarked instead of marked with לְ:

אזלן עמה מצרין
they are *going* with him *to* Egypt
A6 9:4

לא יעלון תרעיה
they will not *go through* its gates
4Q213 1 ii+2:1

סלקו ארחא די מדברא
they went up *by* the road of the wilderness
1QapGen 21:28

Middle, Reflexive, or Reciprocal Voice Intransitives

§332. The middle voice is limited to the G stem and the T stems. The T stems, as well as expressing passive voice, may also be the vehicle for middle, reflexive, and reciprocal voice verbs.

§333. a. Intransitive G stem verbs in the middle voice express a change of state only and will change voice (becoming active) and valency (becoming transitive) with a change of stem, e.g., אבד "perish" (G; D/C "destroy X"), בלי "decay" (G; D "wear X out"), דקק "X break apart" (G; C "smash X"), etc.

כל נכסין זי קנה אבדו
all the possessions he had gotten *perished*
A4 7:16 (Petition) (G stem of אבד)

לְחַכִּימֵי בָבֶל אַל־תְּהוֹבֵד
do not *destroy* the sages of Babylon
Dan 2:24 (C stem of אבד)

דָּקוּ כַחֲדָה פַּרְזְלָא חַסְפָּא נְחָשָׁא כַּסְפָּא וְדַהֲבָא
the iron, clay, bronze, silver and gold *broke apart* all at once (G stem of דקק)
Dan 2:35

הַדֵּקֶת פַּרְזְלָא נְחָשָׁא חַסְפָּא כַּסְפָּא וְדַהֲבָא
it *smashed* the iron, bronze, clay, silver, and gold
Dan 2:45 (C stem of דקק)

b. T stem middle voice verbs, like those of the G stem, express a change of state without causation by an agent.

Examples are קום "remain alive, endure" (tD); קרם "become hard" (tG); עצב "become sad" (tG); שמם (tR) "be appalled, dumbfounded"; תמה "be amazed" (tG), etc.

עליהן מתקימין	their leaves *endure* 4Q201 1 ii 5
כא[בן] מין התקרמו	like a stone the waters *harden* 11QtgJob 31:7
אֶשְׁתּוֹמַם כְּשָׁעָה חֲדָה	he was *stunned* for a moment Dan 4:16
אתמה על כול שפרהא	he was *amazed* at all her beauty (tG of תמה) 1QapGen 20:9

§334. a. Examples of reflexive verbs (§327) are נשא "raise oneself" (tD); נצח "excel, distinguish oneself" (tD; Dan 6:4; A6 10:4); חנן "ask mercy for oneself" (tD; Dan 6:12, 1QapGen 20:12, 11QtgJob 35:6); רום "exalt oneself" (tD; Dan 5:23); שׂדר "exert oneself" (tD; Dan 6:15); נדב "volunteer" (tD; Ez 7:13);[1] גבה "rise high (in the air)" (tG[?]; 11QtgJob 33:8); פני "turn oneself" (tG); and so on.

אתפנית למחזה זיתא	I *turned* to see the olive tree 1QapGen 13:13
עַל מָרֵא־שְׁמַיָּא הִתְרוֹמַמְתָּ	against the lord of heaven you *exalted yourself* Dan 5:23
קִרְיְתָא דָךְ . . . עַל־מַלְכִין מִתְנַשְּׂאָה	that city *lifts itself up* (revolts) against kings Ez 4:19

b. Verbs indicating a *voluntary psychological experience or disposition* are a subset of reflexives. They appear in T stems and may have a nominal complement denoting the focus of the disposition.

---

[1] Besides the reflexive sense in Ez 7:13, this verb has a second sense, "donate," that is transitive as in §339 (transfer) above; see Ez 7:15, 16.

שֵׁיזִב לְעַבְדוֹהִי דִּי הִתְרְחִצוּ עֲלוֹהִי	he saved his servants who *trusted* in him Dan 3:28 (tG stem of רחץ)
כֹּל שָׁלְטָנַיָּא לֵהּ יִפְלְחוּן וְיִשְׁתַּמְּעוּן	all dominions shall serve him and *obey* him Dan 7:27 (tD stem of שמע)
עליכי מתכל אנה	I *trust* in you A2 7:2 (tG stem of תכל)
אתעשת על אגורא זך	*take thought* for that temple A4 7:23 (tG or tD stem of עשת)
[א]ל֯ תֿתאבל בֿשֿק֯[י]ן֯	do not *mourn* in sackcloth 4Q541 24 ii 2 (tD stem of אבל)

§335. Examples of reciprocal verbs (§327) are זמן "meet" (tD); ערב "mix together" (tD); יעט "agree together" (tD; Dan 6:8); שׂרר "strive with" (tD; 4Q531 22 5); כנש "gather together" (tD; Dan 3:3, 27); and others.

פַּרְזְלָא לָא מִתְעָרַב עִם־חַסְפָּא	iron does not *mix with* clay Dan 2:43 (tD stem of ערב)
קרית לבני ולבני בני ולנשי כולנא ולבנתהון ואתכנשנא כחדא	I called my sons and my sons' sons and the wives of all of us and their daughters and we *gathered* together 1QapGen 12:16 (tD stem of כנש)
כול אלן אזדמנו כחדא לקרב	all these *met together* for war 1QapGen 21:25 (tD stem of זמן)
[ולא] מֿשכח אנה עמן לאשתררה	I am not able *to strive* with them 4Q531 22 5

The voice of some T stems is difficult to identify:

אתעירת בליליא מן שנתי	I *awoke* (or *was awakened*) in the night from my sleep 1QapGen 19:17 (עור, tG)

Others may change voice depending on the context:

אתחזי לי אלהא בחזוא די ליליא   God *appeared* [חזי, tG reflexive] to me in a vision of the night
1QapGen 21:8

כמותא זי ל[א מתחזה   like death that is *not seen* [חזי, tG passive]
C1 1:90

The "Ethical Dative"

§336. With verbs of motion or (less frequently) other verb types, the subject is sometimes expressed as a pronominal suffix on ל immediately following the verb. This construction is comparable to both middle and reflexive voice and signifies a heightened participation of the subject in the verbal action. However, it is not reflexive, in that the verbal action is not directed toward the subject, nor is it purely middle (as here defined, §327a), in that the subject's agency is increased, not reduced. It is naturally favored by the volitive mood. It may be translated with a paraphrase or left untranslated:

תהך לה אן זי צבית   she may go wherever she wishes (or "she may readily go . . .")
B2 6:25

עדי לך מן כול מדינת מצרין   depart from all the cities of Egypt (or "get out immediately . . .")
1QapGen 20:27–28

חזו לכן לדגלי [קיטה]   look at the signs of [summer] (or "look intently . . .")
4Q201 1 ii 6–7

The expression "ethical dative" for this construction is inaccurate but by now well established as a label for this construction, and it can continue to serve in that capacity. (See Contini 1998, Fassberg 2018.)

TRANSITIVE VERBS

§337. Transitive verbs govern a direct object noun or noun phrase (§359), and some may govern a prepositional phrase as well. Transitive G stem verbs, when converted to the C stem or D stem, may retain the same valence with a change of meaning or increase valence to govern two direct objects.

Transitive verbs of D or C stems that have a corresponding intransitive G verb can become passive in the appropriate stem.

§338. a. Examples of transitive verbs with a direct object, e.g., אזי "heat X" (G, with tG passive), אכל "eat" X (G), בני "build X" (G, with tG passive), זבן "buy X" (G, and D "sell X"), חזי "see X" (G, with tG passive, C "show X Y," with two direct objects), חתם "seal" X (G), לבש "wear X" (G, with C "clothe X (with) Y," with two objects), מלי "fill X," with one object (G, tG passive [§342b], D "fill X (with) Y," with two objects), מני "count X" (G, with pass. ptcp., D "appoint X"), עבד "do/make X" (G, with tG passive), קטל "kill X" (G, with tG passive, D "kill many X," with tD passive), etc.

נְבוּכַדְנֶצַּר מַלְכָּא עֲבַד צְלֵם דִּי־דְהַב
Nebuchadnezzar the king *made* an image of gold
Dan 3:1 (G stem)

עִשְׂבָּא כְתוֹרִין יַאכֻל
he *ate* grass like cattle
Dan 4:30 (G stem)

אחזיני בית דרג
he *showed* me a staircase
4Q554 1 iii:19 (C stem) (two direct objects)

b. Some D stem verbs are transitive with no corresponding G: בדר "scatter X," בקר "search X" (with tD passive), חבל "harm X" (with tD passive), מגר "overthrow X," צבע "drench X" (with tD passive), שבח "praise X," etc.

c. Transitive C stem verbs with no corresponding G stem are less common, e.g., חסן "take possession of inheritance," יסף "add X to" (with tC passive), נצל "rescue X," צלח "prosper X," שכח "find X" (with tG [!] passive).

d. Stative transitive, with single object: ידע "know X" (G, with pass. ptcp., C "make X know Y," with two objects), רחם "love X" (G; D "have pity on X"); שׂני "hate X" (G).

שנאת לאסחור בעלי
I *hate* Eshor my husband
B2 6:23

בגסרו ידע טעמא זנה
Bagasraw *knows* this order
A6 8:4

§339. a. *Transfer* verbs are transitives with a direct object and a locative prepositional phrase complement, e.g., טרד "drive out X (from)" (G, with pass. ptcp.) with מִן (§§182ff.), רמי "throw X (into, at)" (G, with G passive and tG passive) with לְ or לְגוֹא (§178g), יבל "bring X (to)" (G, C), with לְ, ישׁר "send X (to)" (C) with לְ, שׂים "place, put X (on)" (G, with Gp and tG passive, "be put/given by/from," with עַל (§188) or לְ, שׁוי "put, give X (to)" (D) with עַל, שׁלח "send X (to)" (G, with tG passive; D "release X"), with לְ or עַל; שׁלם "hand over X (to)" (C, Dan 5:26), and the C stems of motion verbs: עלל "bring

X (into)," with קֳדָם for לְ (§203b); סלק "bring up X (from)," with מֶן; אתי "bring X (to)," and others.

הַנְעֵל לְדָנִיֵּאל קֳדָם מַלְכָּא   he *brought in* Daniel *before* the king
Dan 2:25 (C stem of עלל)

הֲלָא גֻבְרִין תְּלָתָה רְמֵינָא לְגוֹא־נוּרָא   did we not *throw* three men *into* the fire?
Dan 3:24 (G stem of רמי)

b. In this class are transitive verbs of giving with a direct object and indirect (recipient) object marked with לְ, typically the suppletive pair יהב/נתן "give X (to) Y" (G, with G internal passive and tG passive for יהב).

יָהֵב חָכְמְתָא לְחַכִּימִין   he *gives* wisdom *to* the wise
Dan 2:21

לזרעך אנתן כול ארעא דא   *to* your seed I will *give* all this land
1QapGen 21:12

c. Verbs of *communication* can also be considered as transfer verbs, with direct speech or clause complements as the direct object and the addressee as indirect object marked with לְ, e.g., אמר "say X (to) Y" (G, with tG passive), קרי "call X to Y = give name X to Y" (one sense of G, with tG passive), with the name as direct object and the named as indirect object; חוי "tell X (to) Y" (D or C, no passive), ידע "tell X to Y (= cause X to know Y)" (C stem), שׁעי "tell/relate X (to)" (tD).

מִלְתָא הוֹדַע אַרְיוֹךְ לְדָנִיֵּאל   Arioch *told* the matter *to* Daniel (caused Daniel
     to know the matter)
Dan 2:15 (C stem of ידע)

קרין לדרומא דרום   they *give the name* "darom" *to* the south
4Q210 1 ii:15 (G stem of קרי)

וַאֲמַר לְאַרְיוֹךְ . . . עַל־מָה . . .   he *said to* Arioch . . . "why . . . ?"
Dan 2:15 (G stem of אמר)

d. Verbs of *request* have a similar structure, with the request as direct object and the grantor of the request marked with מֶן or with לְ:

שְׁמָהָתְהֹם שְׁאֵלְנָא לְהֹם   we *asked* (of) *them* their names
Ez 5:10 (G stem of שאל)

וּבְעָה מִן־מַלְכָּא דִּי זְמָן יִנְתֶּן־לֵהּ   he *requested from* the king *that* he would give him a time
Dan 2:16 (G stem of בעי)

In other contexts, the verb שאל (G) may govern two direct objects, one of them direct discourse: שאלתה מן שמך "I asked *him*, What is your name?" (4Q552 1 ii 5).

§340. a. Transitive verbs may govern a direct object plus a noun phrase as object (resultative) complement, i.e., verbs of transformation, e.g., עבד in one of its senses, "make X into Y" (G, with tG passive), שוי "make X the same as Y" (D, with tD passive), שים in one of its senses, "make X into Y" (G, with tG passive). The resultative complement remains after passivization.

למעבדה עבד   to make him a slave
B3 9:7

שוית דחשת ביתה   I made the steppe his home
11QtgJob 32:5

בַּיְתֵהּ נְוָלוּ יִתְעֲבֵד   his house shall be made a latrine (passivization of "they shall make his house a latrine")
Ez 6:11

מַלְכָּא שָׂם־שְׁמֵהּ בֵּלְטְשַׁאצַּר   the king made his name "Belteshazzar"
Dan 5:12

b. Of the same general type are verbs governing direct objects plus predicate phrases as object complements, e.g., שכח "find X to be Y" (C, tG passive), חזי (G) "see X to be Y, see X Y-ing" (§310b).

הַשְׁכַּחוּ לְדָנִיֵּאל בָּעֵא וּמִתְחַנַּן   they *found* Daniel *making* request and *entreating*
Dan 6:12

חֲזַיְתָה פַּרְזְלָא מְעָרַב בַּחֲסַף טִינָא   you *saw* the iron *mixed* with mud clay
Dan 2:41

§341. Transitive verbs with clauses as direct object complements are typically verbs of *perception*, like חזי "see" (G), שׁמע "hear" (G); *cognition*, like ידע "know" (G); and *speaking*, like אמר "say." Their object clauses are introduced by the particle דִּי (§426b), or, in the case of direct quotation, with speaking verbs, no marker at all:

חֲזֵיתוֹן דִּי אַזְדָּא מִנִּי מִלְּתָא   you *have seen that* the matter from me is certain
Dan 2:8

שמע מלך סודם די אתיב אברם כול שביתא   the king of Sodom *heard that* Abram brought back all the captives
1QapGen 22:12

אִנְדַּע דִּי פִשְׁרֵהּ תְּהַחֲוֻנַּנִי   I will *know that* its interpretation you can tell me
Dan 2:9

אֲמַר לֶהֱוֵא שְׁמֵהּ דִּי־אֱלָהָא מְבָרַךְ   he *said,* "Let the name of God be blessed"
Dan 2:20

SEMI-TRANSITIVE VERBS

§342. a. Verbs whose object is introduced with בְּ are like transitive verbs, in that the object is required for full expression of the sense; but unlike, in that the "oblique" object cannot become the subject of a passive verb. The preposition is essentially meaningless. Examples are שׁלט "rule, control" (G; C "let or cause to rule"), אחד "hold on to" (G), קרב "touch" (G), שׂכל "look at" (tD), בין "consider" (tD).

תִּשְׁלַט בְּכָל־אַרְעָא   it shall *rule* all the earth
Dan 2:39

אחדו בממר יעקוב   *hold on to* the command of Jacob
4Q542 1 i 7

מִשְׁתַּכַּל הֲוֵית בְּקַרְנַיָּא   I was *looking at* the horns
Dan 7:8

Some semi-transitive verbs have different meanings with different complements, e.g., אחד "seize" (G, fully transitive), קרב "approach" (G, intransitive).

b. The stative verb מלי (G) "fill, be full" may govern a noun or noun phrase that is unmarked like an object, although that nominal cannot become the subject of a passive verb; instead, it remains as an unmarked complement after passivization.

אל תמלי לבת   don't be full (of) anger
A3 3:10 (G jussive)

ארעא כולהא מליא דתא ועש[ב] ועבור   the whole land was full (of) grass, plants, and grain
1QapGen 11:12 (G active ptcp)

נְבוּכַדְנֶצַּר הִתְמְלִי חֱמָא   Nebuchadnezzar was filled (with) *rage*
Dan 3:19 (tG passive)

c. Other verbs have similar constructions, with unmarked complements that are not full-fledged direct objects:

יחסר נכסין זעירא   the younger will be lacking (in) possessions
4Q540 1 1 (G active of חסר)

מין לא חסרה   (the well) is not lacking (in) water
A4 5:7

In the passive alternation, such complements remain in place as unmarked complements:

ארעא חפית מין   the earth was covered (by) water
4Q206 4 i:18 (G passive), cp. מיא חפו עליהון 4Q206 4 iii:15

CHAPTER 13
Adverbs and Adverbial Phrases

13

§343. Adverbs as such have no distinctive patterns or bases, and a breakdown of adverbial "shapes" would be unrewarding. Some adverbial expressions draw their form from other word classes such as adjectives and nouns, and only in such cases do they have a relation to triliteral derivation. Others are loanwords or prepositional phrases.

ADVERBIAL FORM
§344. There are some adverbial sufformatives, however, that are worthy of attention:

Adverbial sufformatives

Suffix	Example and gloss	Remarks
unstressed final אָ -ā	יַתִּירָא "exceedingly" (Dan 3:22)	added to adjective *yattīr* "excessive"
	עֵלָּא "upward" (Dan 6:3)	added to (unattested) noun *ʕēl* "height"
	לעלא often in QA	
	אַרְעָ K, אַרעא "downward" (Q Dan 2:39); should be read *ʔárʕā*	added to noun *ʔarʕ* "earth"
	להלא "thither" ("there-ward") (QA)	added to deictic element *hl*
	אָסְפַּרְנָא "completely" (Ez 5:8)	loanword from Persian
	אספרן IA	
	כְּנֵמָא "thusly" (Ez 4:8)	perhaps כֵּן + מָא
	כנמ IA	
	ברא "outwards, outside" (QA *bárrā*)	added to noun *barr* "field, outdoors"
	בר IA	
-ūt	תִּנְיָנוּת "once again" (Dan 2:7)	from ordinal number *tinyān*, "second"
	cp. תניאני QA (1QapGen 21:1)	
-īt	אֲרָמִית "in Aramaic" (Dan 2:4)	from proper name אֲרָם "Aram"
-āyit	גנבית "dishonestly, like a thief" (IA)	from *gannāb*, "thief"
-t	רחמת "without cost, *gratis*" (IA)	from *rḥm* "to love"
	טְוָת "fasting" (Dan 6:19)	from *ṭwy* "to fast"

213

a. It is likely that Aramaic adverbial -ה is cognate to Hebrew directional הָ֫- -ה. Most Aramaic instances do have a directional force.

b. It is disputed whether the frequent כֹּלָּא *kóllɔ*, with penultimate stress, is an instance of adverbial *-ה. In IA, there are some instances which are amenable to an adverbial translation such as "completely, totally" (Muraoka & Porten 2003: 93), and perhaps one in BA: פַּרְזְלָא מְהַדֵּק וְחָשֵׁל כֹּלָּא "as iron that crushes and smashes *completely*" (Dan 2:40). In general, however, despite the anomalous stress pattern, the final -ה functions more like the determined state ending and כֹּלָּא conveys a meaning such as "all, everything" (Fitzmyer 1957).

§345. Sometimes adjectives are used adverbially in the 1st decl. absolute state (see also below, §347): נכסי[א זיל]י חסין טרו "guard *well* my possessions" (A6 10:6, *ḥassīn* "strong"); אל תסתכל כביר "do not look too hard" (C 1 1:147, *kabbīr* "large").

ADVERBIAL FUNCTION

§346. Adverbs and adverbial phrases modify either (1) adjectives or adjectival verbs or (2) the verbal action, outside the complements of the verb itself.

Degree Adverbs

§347. Some adverbs are limited to modifying scalar properties in a verb or adjective, that is, words that can express in some way a property that can increase or decrease in degree.

a. The word שַׂגִּיא (QA שגי, סגיא) is actually an adjective, "much, many, numerous," used as an adverb "very." It modifies adjectives or verbs that express scalar properties:

מַלְכָּא בֵלְשַׁאצַּר שַׂגִּיא מִתְבָּהַל	King Belshazzar was *very* agitated Dan 5:9, cp. Dan 6:15, 24, 7:28
שגיא סנחאריב מלכא רחמני	Sennacherib the king loved me *greatly* C 1 1:51 (Ahiqar)
ארחקת שגיא מנה	I was taken *very* far from it 4Q206 1 xxvi 20
שַׂגִּיא צַלְמָא דִּכֵּן רַב	that image was *very* large Dan 2:31[1]
אנת אחתי שגיא חכים	you, my sister, are *very* wise KAI 264 (Arebsun stele)

---

[1] The Masoretic cantillation marks join שׂגיא to the previous clause, but this is improbable.

b. In QA, the particle לחדא (cp. JLA לַחֲדָא) is frequent for adverbial modification of adjectives, like "very": בנכסין שגיאין לחדא "with very many possessions" (1QapGen 20:33); שפירא לחדא "very beautiful" (4Q197 4 iii 1).

c. The adjective יַתִּיר "excellent, excessive" is pressed into service adverbially in BA and QA (for the penultimate accent, see above): אַתּוּנָא אֵזֵה יַתִּירָא "the furnace was heated *exceedingly*" (Dan 3:22); תַּקִּיפָא יַתִּירָא "*exceedingly* strong" (Dan 7:7; 1QapGen 19:23, fragmentary).

d. The interrogatives מָה "what?" and כְּמָה "how much?" are used adverbially with adjectives, in exclamations:

אָתוֹהִי כְּמָה רַבְרְבִין וְתִמְהוֹהִי כְּמָה תַקִּיפִין	*how* great are his signs! and *how* mighty are his wonders! Dan 3:33
כמא יאין כפיהא ומא אריכן וקטינן כול אצבעת ידיהא	*how* beautiful are her hands! and *how* long and fine are the fingers of her hands! 1QapGen 20:5

Other Adverbs

§348. Adverbs modify verbal action, as noted, mainly by fixing the time, manner, and location of the action. Prepositional phrases often function adverbially (see Chapter 9), as do some noun phrases (§§352ff.), but there are also lexical adverbs. These do not inflect (for unstressed final -ā, see above) and do not constitute a morphologically unified group. Semantically, they are often deictic, i.e., they depend on the situation of the speaker.

§349. a. In the dialects considered in this grammar, the notions of *here* and *there* are expressed as follows:

	Here	There
IA	תנה	תמה
BA	כָּה	תַּמָּה
QA	תנה, תנא, כה	תמה, תמן

QA also has להכא "hither": להכא אתית "I have come hither" (1QapGen 2:25).
IA texts may also use בזנה "in this (place)" instead of תנה.

b. The interrogative אָן "where?" can be used adverbially, e.g., תהך לה אן זי צבית "she may go where she wishes" (B2 6:25).[2]

---

[2] For the Hebraism מנאין, מאין "whence/where" in QA, see DQA 131, 143.

c. With the adverbial ending *-ā*, locational adverbs can combine with prepositions: עֵלָּא מִנְּהוֹן "above them" (Dan 6:3, figuratively), לעלא מנה "above him" (C1 1:162, Ahiqar, with redundant ל); לעלא מן כולהן "(her beauty is) above all of them" (1QapGen 20:7); להלא מן נחל[י]א "beyond the valleys" (4Q204 1 xii 25).

e. With the penultimate *-ā* adverbial ending, בַּר "outside, out-of-doors" becomes directional "outward": הנפקה ברא "(a broken vessel) lets it go *out*" (C1 1:93, Ahiqar). בָּרָא is also used with מִן as a compound preposition (§192).

§350. a. The deictic adverbs כְּעַן (כְּעֶנֶת, כְּעֶת) "now" and אֱדַיִן (בֵּאדַיִן) "then" are usually employed as discourse conjunctions in BA and QA (§§430–31), but they also can temporally modify verbal action:

| מִן־אֱדַיִן וְעַד־כְּעַן מִתְבְּנֵא וְלָא שְׁלִם | from *then* until *now* it is under construction and not complete
Ez 5:16; cf. 1QapGen 19:8, 12 |
| אברם באדין הוא יתב בחברון | Abram *at that time* was dwelling in Hebron
1QapGen 22:2–3 |

אדין indicates time (instead of discourse narrative sequence) in IA (§431b).

b. Time relative to another implied time is indicated by the adverbs כְּבָר "already" and עוֹד "still, again."

| די אכלו כבר עולימי | that which my servants have eaten *already*
1QapGen 22:23 |
| עוֹד מִלְּתָא בְּפֻם מַלְכָּא | the word was *still* in the mouth of the king
Dan 4:28 |

Both lexemes, well known in later dialects, are sparsely attested in clear contexts in our corpora.

c. Orientation by day is denoted by מחר (IA) "tomorrow" (JLA מְחַר), אתמל (IA) "yesterday" (cp. JLA אִתְמָלֵי, BH אֶתְמוֹל), and יומא זנה (IA), יומא דן (QA) "this day, today."

d. The *tantum plurale* noun (§92) קדמין is used in IA alone or with prepositions מן לקדמן, קדמן for "previously"; לקדמין is used in QA for "first in a series") (see JLA קַדְמִין).

בנה הוה מן קדמן קדם כנבוזי	it had been built *previously* before Cambyses A4 9:4–5
למבניה באתרה כזי הוה לקדמן	to build it in its place just as it was *previously* A4 9:8
שאלו שלמה לקדמין	they greeted him *first of all* 4Q197 4 iii 3

In the IA Bactrian letters, the form קדמנ "previously" appears, e.g., איך זי קדמנ מני שים טעם "as I previously had ordered" (Bactrian letter 5:2); it may be קדמן with enclitic *-m(a)*.

e. Combinations with the preposition קֳדָמַת "before" (§204) are also found: בַּיְתָא דִּי־הֲוָא בְנֵה מִקַּדְמַת דְּנָה "the house that was built previously" (Ez 5:11; Dan 6:11; קדמת זנה, A4 7:17 [Petition]).

f. Adverbs formed from the ordinal תִּנְיָן "second" denote "second in a series": עֲנוֹ תִנְיָנוּת "they answered *a second time*" (Dan 2:7); בניתה תניאני "I built it (the altar) *a second time*" (1QapGen 21:1).

g. Time duration is indicated by prepositional phrases, often with עלם: מַלְכָּא לְעָלְמִין חֱיִי "O king, live *forever*" (Dan 2:4 etc.); לְעָלְמִין לָא תִתְחַבַּל "it will *never* be destroyed" (Dan 2:44); מן יומא זנה ועד עלם "from this day forth and *forever*" (B2 3:9); חדה ושריר הוי בכל עדן "be happy and healthy *always*" (A4 7:3, Petition); see also עַד־זְמַן וְעִדָּן "for a time and a season" (Dan 7:12); and so on.

h. The notion of *sometimes, occasionally* is indicated by the bare plural of זְמַן "time": זמנין תעמל וזמנין תנוח "*sometimes* you will labor and *sometimes* you will rest" (1Q21 3).

§351. Most adverbial modification of *manner* is the work of prepositional phrases (Chapter 9); however, there are a few indeclinable words that function as manner adverbs.

a. The notion *thus, so, in this way*, referring to something that precedes or follows, is indicated by the particle כֵּן (in BA usually with אמר "say"). Sometimes it is coordinated with a conjunction meaning "as" or "like."

כֵּן אֲמַר	*thus* he said
	Dan 7:23
הן כן עבדו	if *thus* it is done
	A4 7:27 (Petition)
לקבל זי אנה עבדת לך כן אפו עבד לי	*as* I have done for you, *so* also do for me
	C1 1:52 (Ahiqar)
כזיקיא די חזיתא כן מלכותהן תהוה	*like* the meteors that you saw, *so* shall be their reign
	4Q246 1 ii 1–2

b. The particle כְּנֵמָא, with penultimate stress, appears to be derived from כֵּן with enclitic מָא added: כְּנֵמָא אֲמַרְנָא לְהֹם "*thus* we said to them" (Ez 5:9); הן כנם הו כמליא אלה "if *so* it is according to these words" (A6 11:3).

c. The phrase כִּדְנָה (כְּ + דְּנָה) or כזנה (IA) or כדן (QA) is sometimes found in preference to כֵּן: לָא מקרא אִיתַי אֱלָהּ אָחֳרָן דִּי־יִכֻּל לְהַצָּלָה כִּדְנָה "there is no other god who can save *like this*" (Dan 3:29),

אַרמית כזנה, "a legend in Aramaic *as follows*" (B2 11:6), כדן אחזיני, "*thus* he showed me" (4Q554 1 ii 14); and the like.

    d. Other manner adverbs of note:

        כַּחֲדָה "as one, together": דָּקוּ כַחֲדָה פַּרְזְלָא חַסְפָּא נְחָשָׁא כַּסְפָּא וְדַהֲבָא "the iron, pottery, bronze, silver, and gold broke apart *as one*" (Dan 2:35); כול אלן אזדמנו כחדא לקרב "all these met *together* for war" (1QapGen 21:25); etc.

        לעובע "quickly" (QA; IA :לעבק): שלח לעובע דברהא "he sent quickly" (1QapGen 20:9); אל תקום חת לעבק "don't stop, go down quickly" (A3 8:13); etc. (For the variation in consonants, see §37.)

The following adverbs are loans from Persian (§122):

אָסְפַּרְנָא "diligently, completely": אָסְפַּרְנָא יִתְעֲבִד "let it be done diligently" (Ez 6:12 and elsewhere); אספרן (A6 13:4); אספרן הנעל לקבל זי חיב אנת "bring it in full as you are obligated" (Bactrian Letter A6:8 [Naveh & Shaked 2012: 112]).

אַדְרַזְדָּא "well, diligently": כָּל־דִּי מִן־טַעַם אֱלָהּ שְׁמַיָּא יִתְעֲבֵד אַדְרַזְדָּא "everything under the auspices of the God of heaven should be done diligently" (Ez 7:23).

Adverbial Noun Phrases

§352. An unmarked noun phrase (one not introduced by a preposition) can serve in an adverbial function. Such adverbial noun phrases (also called adverbial "accusatives") are to be distinguished from unmarked direct objects or other unmarked verbal complements (§§342b, 359). Adverbial noun phrases are not core elements of the verbal predication but, like adverbs or prepositional phrases, modify it in various ways.

    a. *Temporal.* זִמְנִין תְּלָתָה בְיוֹמָא "(he was praying) *three times* in that day" (Dan 6:11), תרתין שנין בתר מבולא "(Arpachshad was born) *two years* after the Deluge" (1QapGen 12:10), מחר או יום אחרן "(I shall not reclaim it) *tomorrow or another day*" (B2 3:18); and the like.

    b. *Specification.* הוּא מִתְבְּנֵא אֶבֶן גְּלָל "it is being built (of) choice stone" (Ez 5:8).

    c. *Manner.* קושטא כול יומי דברת "all my days I lived *righteously*" (1QapGen 6:2).

    d. *Location.* מדנה חורן ושניר "*east* of Hauran and Senir" (1QapGen 21:12); מערב לביתא זילך "*west* of your house" (B2 4:3).

    e. *Extent.* אֲמַר לְמֵזֵא לְאַתּוּנָא חַד־שִׁבְעָה עַל דִּי חֲזֵה לְמֵזְיֵהּ "he said to heat the furnace *seven times more* than it was proper to heat it" (Dan 3:19); כסה פלג שביע "(the moon) is *half a seventh* covered" (4Q209 2 ii 7); ארכה משחה חדה קנין תרין בתרין "its length was one measurement, *two rods by two*" (4Q554 1 iii 20).

CHAPTER 14
Clauses

§353. A clause consists of a subject and a predicate. The subject is always a noun or noun phrase, or a verbal element used as a noun. The predicate, in a verbal clause, consists of the verb and its complements (Chapter 12); in a copular clause, it consists of the copula (expressed or unexpressed) and a noun/noun phrase, adjective/adjective phrase, or a prepositional phrase (§373). These are the core elements of a clause. Existential clauses with אִיתַי (§380) and presentative constructions (§382), however, do not have subjects.

Non-core elements or adjuncts are adverbs (Chapter 13), prepositional phrases used adverbially (Chapter 9), and conjunctions or half-conjunctions (§§429ff.). These "adjuncts" could be removed without affecting the basic predication; their role is to describe conditions under which the predication takes place or to indicate how the clause is related to other clauses or the discourse as a whole.

Clauses can be linked together (Chapters 17 and 18) or embedded in another clause as part of a core clause element (§426).

VERBAL CLAUSES
Subject
§354. Verbal clauses, as adumbrated above, have a predicate consisting of the verb and its complements; the verb is governed by a subject.

§355. a. *Subject–predicate agreement.* The subject *governs* the verb in that a finite verb must agree with the nominal subject in number, person, and gender, that is, must have the equivalent verbal inflections for those categories. Participial and adjectival predicates (§§375ff.) cannot be inflected for person, but must agree with the subject in number and gender.

b. In rare cases, the verb may be inflected by *attraction* to the noun closest in position, even if that noun is not the head of the phrase, e.g., the Ketiv in Dan 3:19 וּצְלֵם אַנְפּוֹהִי אֶשְׁתַּנּוּ "the visage [sg.] of his face [pl.] changed [pl.]."

c. When the subject is a compound noun phrase (§142), the verb may be in the singular, agreeing in gender with the first member of the phrase:

219

חֶלְמָא וּפִשְׁרֵא אַל־יְבַהֲלָךְ	let the dream (ms) and its interpretation not disturb you Dan 4:16 (3ms verb)
אזלת אנה וצחא בר פחה	I and Seha son of Peho went A3 6:2 (1cs verb)
יתוך מנכה מכתשא דן ורוח שחלניא	this plague (ms) and spirit of putridity will depart from you 1QapGen 20:26 (3ms verb)

§356. *Pronominal subject and dropped subject.* Because of inflectional agreement, an independent personal pronoun – which also agrees with its nominal antecedent – is usually superfluous as subject of a finite verb, and frequently there is no explicit subject if it can be identified from context. When the pronoun is present, it is mainly used for emphasis or contrast, as in the following examples:

כלהן עבדין ממרה ואנתן שניתן עבדכן	*they* all do his bidding, but *you* have perverted your action 4Q201 1 ii 12
בָּבֶל רַבְּתָא דִּי־אֲנָה בֱנַיְתַהּ לְבֵית מַלְכוּ	great Babylon, which *I myself* have built into a royal house Dan 4:27
בני המו ישלמון לך כספא זנה ומרביתה	my children, (it is) *they* (who) shall pay you this money and its interest B3 1:15

§357. *Impersonal constructions.* In some cases, the subject of third person finite verbs is intentionally left unidentifiable. Such "impersonal" constructions are semantically equivalent to passives (§326), like English impersonal *they*:

עִשְׂבָּא כְתוֹרִין לָךְ יְטַעֲמוּן	*they shall feed you* grass like oxen Dan 4:22 (= you shall be fed)
בר עליון יקרונה	*they shall call him* "son of the Most High" 4Q246 1 ii 1 (= he shall be called)
יְבַקַּר בִּסְפַר־דָּכְרָנַיָּא	*one should search* in the book of records Ez 4:15 (= search should be made)

| מנחה ולבו[נ]ה ועלוה לא עבדו באגורא זך | meal offering, incense, and burnt offering *they have not made* in that temple |
| | A4 7:21–22 (Petition) (= have not been made) |

See also Dan 2:30, 4:29, 5:21, 7:26, Ez 6:5.

§358. a. *Subject-less participles.* Predicative participles (§§305ff.), as non-finite verbs, normally require an overt subject, but if the subject is readily identifiable from the context, they may appear without it.

| מְשֵׁיזִב וּמַצִּל וְעָבֵד אָתִין וְתִמְהִין | (God) saves and rescues and does signs and wonders |
| | Dan 6:28 |

| קַרְיְתָא מָרָדְתָּא וּבְאִישְׁתָּא בָּנַיִן | the wicked and rebellious city (those Jews) are rebuilding |
| | Ez 4:12 |

b. In many cases, these participles are impersonal quasi-passives, as with finite verbs (§357 above), with intentionally unidentifiable subject:

| לְכוֹן אָמְרִין | to you (they) command |
| | Dan 3:4 (= it is commanded) |

| לָךְ טָרְדִין מִן־אֲנָשָׁא | (they) will drive you away from men |
| | Dan 4:22, cf. 4:29 (=you will be driven away) |

| אֲתַר דִּי־דָבְחִין דִּבְחִין | the place where (they) make sacrifices |
| | Ez 6:3 (= sacrifices are made) |

| וקרין לדרומא דרום | (they) call the south "darom" |
| | 4Q209 23 3 (= the south is called) |

| לא שבקן לן למבניה | (they) do not allow us to build it |
| | A4 7:23 (Petition) (= we are not allowed) |

c. The G passive participles may also be used without an overt subject:

| שְׁלִיחַ לְבַקָּרָא עַל־יְהוּד וְלִירוּשְׁלֶם | (you) *are sent* to oversee Judea and Jerusalem |
| | Ez 7:14 |

יִתְנְסַח אָע מִן־בַּיְתֵהּ וּזְקִיף יִתְמְחֵא עֲלֹהִי   wood shall be pulled out of his house and (it) *being erected*, he shall be impaled on it
Ez 6:11

הן פקיד לך   if (something) *is commanded* to you
C1 1:87 (Ahiqar)

d. The deletion of the subject in *a* and *b* above and in §357 should not be confused with naturally subject-less verbs:

שַׂגִּיא בְּאֵשׁ עֲלֹוהִי   it was very displeasing to him
Dan 6:15

שַׂגִּיא טְאֵב עֲלֹוהִי   it was very pleasing to him
Dan 6:24

Object

With transitive verbs, objects are obligatory constituents in a clause.

§359. a. *Direct object marking*. The direct object is either unmarked by a preposition (i.e., is a bare noun or noun phrase) or may be introduced with the preposition לְ, most often when the object is definite and animate. The object-marking לְ is essentially meaningless, unlike the adverbial לְ, which usually has a definite contextual meaning (§§177ff., with exemplification).

b. The particle יָת (§186) can also mark a definite direct object, although it is rare in our dialects. It appears once in Daniel (3:12) and a handful of times in QA, e.g., אלהא ברך ית א[יו]ב "God blessed Job" (11QtgJob 38:9; see *DQA* 107). The use of יָת is regular in JLA as a translation of the Hebrew object marker אֵת.

§360. *Dropped object pronoun*. Like the subject pronoun, the object pronoun can sometimes be omitted, especially if it would appear in the second of coordinated sentences (§393):

יהוי זבן גשרן ושבק בבתה   let him buy beams and leave (them) in the house
A2 2:14–15

אתיב אברם כול נכסיא וכול שביתא ויהב למלך סודם   Abram brought back all the possessions and all the captives and gave (them) to the king of Sodom
1QapGen 22:24–25

וְהַיְתִיו לְדָנִיֵּאל וּרְמֹו לְגֻבָּא דִּי אַרְיָוָתָא   they brought Daniel and threw (him) into the den of lions
Dan 6:17

§361. *Cognate object.* Some verbs may govern a cognate object, that is, an object noun derived from the same root as the verb (also called cognate accusative or *figura etymologica*). The object is often in the absolute state (indefinite).

כָּל־דִּי־יִבְעֵה בָעוּ   all who make a request (lit., "request a request")
Dan 6:8

תּוּכַל [תיכול] פִּשְׁרִין לְמִפְשַׁר   you are able to give interpretations
            (lit., "interpret interpretations")
Dan 5:16

טענוך לי מומאה למומא   they required you to swear an oath to me
            (lit., "swear a swearing")
B2 2:6

חלמת אנה אברם חלם   I, Abram, had a dream (lit., "dreamed a dream")
1QapGen 19:14

Word Order and Related Issues

§362. a. Word order at the clause level in BA is *free*, in that there is no single *obligatory* order of subject (S), verb (V), and object (O). It does not mean that the order is arbitrary, although the forces favoring one order rather than another are not agreed upon.

    b. The subject tends to come first, before the other elements, but may occur in other positions as well. Unlike Biblical Hebrew prose, in which the verb must occur in first or second position, in BA the verb may occur in the final position, after the other elements, including adverbial phrases.

§363. The default order of the ancestor language was probably Verb–Subject–Object (VSO). The frequent SVO order in BA can be understood as a move to the first position of the subject out of an original VSO (VSO > SVO), and the frequent SOV order can be understood as a regressive movement of the verb from the same original pattern (VSO > SOV). Various explanations, both diachronic (historical) and synchronic (language-internal), have been offered for these movements (for a recent overview of some issues, see Noonan 2020: 181–200). It is possible that historically the SOV word order is due to the influence of Akkadian and Persian, which have prevailing SOV orders.

§364. Free word order is also a characteristic of IA and QA, although the frequency of particular patterns differs by sub-corpora. For special discussion of the word order of these dialects, see, for IA Folmer (1995: 521–588), Muraoka and Porten (2003: 296–313); for QA, Chandler (2001), Muraoka (2012: 241–251), Schattner-Rieser (2004: 132–135).

Survey of Word Order Types

§365. a. Only sentences with transitive verbs (§§337ff.) can have all three elements. All of the six possible combinations occur in BA, but, as noted, VSO, SVO, and SOV are the most common. (The object pronominal suffix is necessarily attached to the verb by morphological rule and is not included in word-order counts.)

b. Sentences with all three elements are rarer than those with two (SV, VS, OV, VO), which are all amply exemplified in the sources. Sentences with verbs in the final position are common.

c. *Verb–Subject–Object.*

הַרְגִּזוּ אֲבָהֳתַנָא לֶאֱלָהּ שְׁמַיָּא   our fathers angered the God of heaven
Ez 5:12

כתב פלטיה בר אחיו ספרא זנה   Pelatiah son of Ahio wrote this document
B2 1:15

דבר מלך עילם לכול חברוהי   the king of Elam led all his allies
1QapGen 21:27–28

d. *Subject–Verb–Object.*

נְבוּכַדְנֶצַּר מַלְכָּא עֲבַד צְלֵם דִּי־דְהַב   Nebuchadnezzar the king made an image of gold
Dan 3:1

ארתוהי ידע טעמא זנה   Artavahya knows this order
A6 13:5

לוט קנה לה נכסין שגיאין   Lot acquired for himself many possessions
1QapGen 20:34

e. *Subject–Object–Verb.*

דָּנִיֵּאל חֵלֶם חֲזָה   Daniel saw a dream
Dan 7:1

פַּחַת יְהוּדָיֵא וּלְשָׂבֵי יְהוּדָיֵא בֵּית־אֱלָהָא דֵךְ יִבְנוֹן   the governor of the Judeans and the elders of the Judeans shall build that house of God
Ez 6:7

כמריא זי חנוב אלך ברא זך סכרו | those priests of Khnub stopped up that well
A4 5:8

f. Object–Verb–Subject (rare).

מִלְּתָא הוֹדַע אַרְיוֹךְ לְדָנִיֵּאל | Arioch made the matter known to Daniel
Dan 2:15

פִּתְגָמָא שְׁלַח מַלְכָּא | the king sent the answer
Ez 4:17

אנשא לא ידע איש | a man cannot know humankind
C1 1:164 (Ahiqar)

g. Object–Subject–Verb (rare).

לִי הַדָּבְרַי וְרַבְרְבָנַי יְבַעוֹן | my counselors and nobles sought me
Dan 4:33

שלם מראן אלה שמיא ישאל | may the God of heaven seek the health
of our lord
A4 7:1 (Petition)

h. Verb–Object–Subject (rare). The independent 3mp pronouns הִמּוֹן/אִנּוּן (§124) used as objects invariably follow the verb and are constrained by the necessarily post-verbal order of pronominal suffixes. Excluding these cases, there is apparently only one example of Verb–Object–Subject order in the sources: וִיקַבְּלוּן מַלְכוּתָא קַדִּישֵׁי עֶלְיוֹנִין "the holy ones of the Most High shall receive the kingship" (Dan 7:18).

Objects with Infinitives

§366. Direct objects governed by infinitives often precede those infinitives:

לְדָנִיֵּאל אֲמַר לְהַנְסָקָה מִן־גֻּבָּא | *Daniel* he commanded to *bring up* from the pit
(= he commanded *to bring up* Daniel)
Dan 6:24; *Daniel* is the object of *bring up* (לְהַנְסָקָה)

מַן־שָׂם לְכֹם טְעֵם בַּיְתָא דְנָה לִבְּנֵא וְאֻשַּׁרְנָא דְנָה לְשַׁכְלָלָה | who ordered you *this house to build* and *this structure to complete?*
Ez 5:3

פגרה זי אחיקר זנה למחזה	(he will send others) the *body* of this Ahiqar *to see*
	C1 1:63 (Ahiqar)

אל תמחלו חכמתא למאלף	do not neglect *wisdom to study*
	4Q213 1 i 13

The order Object–Infinitive is more frequent in BA than in IA or QA.

Other Sentence Elements

§367. a. Conjunctions and half-conjunctions (§§429ff.) necessarily come first or second in the sentence.

b. When serving as a complement with transfer verbs (§339), ל with pron. suff. usually comes directly after the verb; when it introduces the direct object (§359), it may occur before the verb.

Extraposition

§368. There may be further constituents attached to the clause, usually preceding the entire clause, which are neither core elements, adverbials, nor conjunctions. Such constituents are said to be *extraposed*.

When these elements are referred to within the clause by a pronoun, then the term *left-dislocation* is used; when the clause makes a comment on a preceding element that is not resumed by a pronoun, I use the term *topicalization*.

§369. *Left-dislocation*[1] refers to a nominal phrase preceding the clause proper that is resumed within the clause by a pronoun. This phenomenon is also called *casus pendens* or nominative absolute.

גֻּבְרַיָּא אִלֵּךְ דִּי הַסִּקוּ לְשַׁדְרַךְ מֵישַׁךְ וַעֲבֵד נְגוֹ קַטִּל	those men who brought up Shadrach,
הִמּוֹן שְׁבִיבָא דִּי נוּרָא	Meshach, and Abed-nego – the flame of
	fire killed *them*
	Dan 3:22

---

[1] The term "left-dislocation" originated with scholars studying languages written from left to right; hence "left-dislocation" amounts to "front-dislocation." The term is established and may be retained as a non-literal label with languages written right to left.

וְעמודיא זי אבנא זי הוו תמה תברו המו	the pillars of stone that were there – they broke *them* A4 7:9 (Petition)
דרגא די סלק לידה פתיה אמין ארבע	the stair that goes up beside it – *its* width is four cubits 5Q15 1 ii 5 (New Jerusalem)

§370. *Topicalization*, as used in this grammar, refers to a nominal phrase preceding the clause, which comments on or explains the nominal constituent, without a resumptive pronoun.

חֵיוְתָא רְבִיעָיְתָא מַלְכוּ רְבִיעָיָא [רביעאה] תֶּהֱוֵא בְאַרְעָא	the fourth beast – there shall be a fourth kingdom in the earth Dan 7:23
וְדִי־חֲזַיְתָה רַגְלַיָּא וְאֶצְבְּעָתָא מִנְּהֵון [מנהן] חֲסַף דִּי־פֶחָר וּמִנְּהֵון [ומנהן] פַּרְזֶל מַלְכוּ פְלִיגָה תֶּהֱוֵה	what you saw, the feet and toes, some of them potter's clay and some of them iron – it will be a divided kingdom Dan 2:41
צבות ביתא זילי זי פסמשך יאמר לך . . . זכי אשתמעו לה ועבדו כן	the matter of my house that Psamshek will say to you . . . that (matter) – obey him and do thus A6 8:2

§371. All *titles* are a species of extraposition, for which the discourse following provides the comment.

מלי כתבא די אמר מיכאל	the words of the book that Michael spoke 4Q529 1 1
פרשגן כתב מלי חזות עמרם	a copy of the book of the words of Amram 4Q543 1a–c 1
פַּרְשֶׁגֶן אִגַּרְתָּא דִּי־שְׁלַח תַּתְּנַי	a copy of the letter that Tattenai sent Ez 5:6
מלי אחיקר שמה ספר חכים ומהיר	the words of one named Ahiqar, a wise and fluent scribe C1 1:1 (Ahiqar)

§372. Some extraposed phrases typically provide fuller identification, in a kind of *parenthesis*, about the antecedents of pronouns or participants in the verbal action. They may occur within or at the end of clauses.

אֶתְכְּרִיַּת רוּחִי אֲנָה דָנִיֵּאל   my spirit – I, Daniel – was distressed
Dan 7:15

וּמִנִּי אֲנָה אַרְתַּחְשַׁסְתְּא מַלְכָּא שִׂים טְעֵם   from me – I, Artaxerxes the king – was given an order
Ez 7:21

הא זנה חלקא זי מטאך בחלק אנת ידניה   behold, this is the portion that comes to you as a portion –
you, Jedoniah
B2 11:3

COPULAR CLAUSES

§373. a. Copular clauses consist of subject (typically a noun or noun phrase), non-verbal predicate (that is, a noun phrase, adjective phrase, or prepositional phrase), and a copula, that is, a linking element corresponding to the English verb *to be*.

    b. In the most usual type of copular clause, the linking element is only implied and not expressed overtly in the sentence; the subject and predicate are simply juxtaposed.

    c. However, the copula may sometimes be expressed by a personal pronoun, the existential particle איתי, or the verb הוי "to be."

    d. The usual word order for the copular clause is Subject–Predicate; however, the order Predicate–Subject is not uncommon.

    e. In the absence of a finite verb, the tense of the copular clause is inferred from the context. When הוי serves as copula, it determines the tense.

Copular clauses fall into three main types.

Noun or Adjective Predicate in Absolute State

§374. In this most common type, the subject is a definite (§85) noun/noun phrase or an independent pronoun.

§375. a. When the predicate is an *indefinite noun or noun phrase in the absolute state* (§86), it denotes the general category that the subject is included in. This "inclusion" type is also called a clause of *classification*, since the predicate refers to a class of entity, not a particular entity.

מַלְכוּתֵהּ מַלְכוּת עָלַם   his kingdom is *an eternal kingdom*
Dan 3:33

קַרְיְתָא דָךְ קַרְיָא מָרָדָא   this city is *a rebellious city*
Ez 4:15

אנתה מרה ושליט על כולא   you are *lord and ruler over all*
1QapGen 20:13

b. An independent relative clause (§150) may occur in the predicate slot. The predicate is an implied indefinite noun.

וּמַלְכוּתֵהּ דִּי־לָא תִתְחַבַּל   his kingdom is *(one) that will not be destroyed*
Dan 6:27

c. A דִי genitive of material (§161) can also be the predicate, again with an implied indefinite noun as underlying predicate:

רֵאשֵׁהּ דִּי־דְהַב טָב   its head was *(a head) of fine gold*
Dan 2:32

d. Interrogative pronouns (§138) are used as predicate nouns (not common in the corpora):

מַן־אִנּוּן שְׁמָהָת גֻּבְרַיָּא   *what* (lit., "who") are the names of those men?
Ez 5:4 (with pronominal copula)

מן שמך   *what* (lit., "who") is your name?
4Q552 1 ii 5

§376. a. The predicate can be an *adjective in the absolute state* (§86) and agrees with the subject in number and gender. The most common variety has a definite noun subject. This construction asserts that the subject has a particular property denoted by the adjective:

עָפְיֵהּ שַׁפִּיר   its foliage was *beautiful*
Dan 4:9

מְהֵימַן הוּא   *faithful* was he
Dan 6:5

עליא שפרהא לעלא מן כולהן   *high* is her beauty above all of them
1QapGen 20:7

הִי עריה   she was *cold*
C1 1:166 (Ahiqar)

b. Pronominal copulas are sometimes used in this type of copular clause:

חֲדָה־הִיא דָתְכוֹן   *one* is your sentence (= there is only one sentence
         for you)
Dan 2:9

c. Cases of indefinite subject are uncommon:

רכיך ממלל מלך   *soft* is a king's speech
C1 1:84 (Ahiqar)

d. When pronominal suffixes are added to the existential particle אִיתַי (§380), it serves as a
copula:

הֵן אִיתֵיכוֹן עֲתִידִין   if you are *ready* (2mp suffix)
Dan 3:15

This is more common with participial predicates.

e. The participle used predicatively also belongs to the predicate adjective type and will be
treated below (§379).

Prepositional Phrase Predicate

§377. a. When the predicate is a *prepositional phrase*, the clause describes the relationship the subject
has to some other entity, denoted by the object of the preposition. In this subtype, the subject
can be definite (§85) or indefinite (a noun or noun phrase in the absolute state).

קַדְמָיְתָא כְאַרְיֵה   the first one was *like a lion*
Dan 7:4

בִּירוּשְׁלֶם מִשְׁכְּנֵה   *in Jerusalem* is his dwelling
Ez 7:15

חכמא שגיא עמהא   much wisdom is *with her*
1QapGen 20:7

b. When the preposition is לְ or דִּי־לְ (דיל or זיל, §159) the subject is possessed by the object of the preposition:

וְאַרְבְּעָה רֵאשִׁין לְחֵיוְתָא   four heads were *to the beast* (= the beast had four heads)
Dan 7:6

אגרא זך זילך הי   that wall is *yours*
B2 1:4 (with pronominal copula)

c. Copular הוי is more common with this type than the others:

וְעֵין אֱלָהֲהֹם הֲוָת עַל־שָׂבֵי יְהוּדָיֵא   the eye of their god was on the elders of the Judeans
Ez 5:5

מַלְכוּ רְבִיעָיָא [רביעאה] תֶּהֱוֵא בְאַרְעָא   a fourth kingdom shall be in the earth
Dan 7:23

כזי יוזא הוה במצרין   when the unrest was in Egypt
A6 11:4

d. See also the construction with the existential particle איתי (§380d).

e. The infinitive functioning as a noun (§320) can appear as subject: לא בידיך מנשא רגלך למנחתותה "to lift up your foot or set it down is not in your power" (C1 1:171, Ahiqar)

Subject and Predicate Both Definite, or Both Indefinite

§378. a. In this construction, both subject and predicate are nominal (or pronominal) constituents. The predicate identifies the subject with some other referent, denoting a particular entity, not a class of entity. The construction as a whole is thus an equative clause, or clause of *identification*.

שְׁמֵהּ בֵּלְטְשַׁאצַּר   his name was "*Belteshazzar*"
Dan 4:16

דְּנָה פִּשְׁרָא   *this* is the interpretation
Dan 4:21

אחי הוא   he is *my brother*
1QapGen 19:20

b. The use of pronominal copula is common with this type:

אֲנַחְנָא *הִמּוֹ* עַבְדוֹהִי דִי־אֱלָהּ שְׁמַיָּא   we are *the servants of the god of heaven*
Ez 5:11

ארה לא אחי *הו* חרוץ   behold, is not Harus *my brother?*
A2 3:8

אנה *הו* אחיקר   I am *Ahiqar*
C1 1:46 (Ahiqar)

c. Clauses with indefinite subject and indefinite predicate are rare:

צנפר הי מלה   an utterance is *a bird*
C1 1:82 (Ahiqar) (pronominal copula)

Participial Predicates

§379. a. Syntactically, participial predicates are a type of predicate adjective (§376), agreeing with the subject in number and gender. However, the participle expresses not a stative property but rather verbal action, usually with imperfective aspect in the (relative) present tense (§305b). As with the other predicates, the copula is usually implied, rather than explicit.

b. The pronominal copula does not appear with a participial predicate, but the verbal copula with הוי and the copula with איתי are sometimes used (the periphrastic constructions, §§313, 315).

c The role of the participle in the verbal system is dealt with elsewhere; here only some structural aspects are highlighted.

d. The syntax does not require a particular word order in this construction. The word order with the participial predicate, as with the other predicate adjectives, is usually Subject–Predicate, but the reverse order is also found, particularly when the action is in the narrative foreground.

עֲנֵה מַלְכָּא וְאָמַר   the king answered and said
Dan 2:5 (Predicate–Subject)

בֵּאדַיִן עָלְלִין [עלין] חַרְטֻמַיָּא . . .   then the magicians etc. were entering
Dan 4:4 (Predicate–Subject)

e. When two or more participial predicates appear in coordinated clauses (§393), one subject may suffice for the series.

וְהוּא מְהַשְׁנֵא עִדָּנַיָּא וְזִמְנַיָּא מְהַעְדֵּה מַלְכִין וּמְהָקֵים מַלְכִין	*he* changes seasons and times, removes kings and sets up kings Dan 2:21
בֵּאדַיִן מִתְכַּנְּשִׁין אֲחַשְׁדַּרְפְּנַיָּא . . . וְקָאֲמִין [וקימין] לָקֳבֵל צַלְמָא	then the *satraps* etc. were gathering . . . and standing before the statue Dan 3:3; see also 3:7, 27; 4:34
נגדו מלכיא . . . למדיתון ושבין ובזין ומחין וקטלין	the *kings* went . . . to their country, taking captives and plundering and smiting and killing 1QapGen 22:4
אנחנה . . . שקקן לבשן הוין וצימין ומצלין ליהו	*we* . . . have been wearing sackcloth and fasting and praying to Yaho A4 7:15 (Petition) (with verbal copula)

This is not to be confused with the omission of the subject with the "impersonal" participle (§358).

EXISTENTIAL CLAUSES

The existential clauses assert the existence, or more precisely the presence, of an entity in a place or in a particular relation.

§380. a. The existential particle אִיתַי serves as a predicator of existence, that is, it asserts that something is present in a particular place or stands in a particular relation; more rarely, it expresses existence *simpliciter*, that is, that something just exists or is present. The negative form is לָא אִיתַי. As with the copular clause, the tense of the existential clause is determined by the context.

b. This construction is analogous to constructions like English *there is/are*, German *es gibt*, or French *il y a*. Unlike these constructions, however, it has no "dummy" (semantically empty) subject; indeed, it has no subject at all. The only obligatory complement to אִיתַי is an indefinite noun (absolute state) accompanied in many cases by a prepositional phrase. Here the noun/noun phrase is called the *existential complement*.

אִיתַי אֱלָהּ בִּשְׁמַיָּא	there is *a god* in heaven Dan 2:28
אִיתַי גְּבַר בְּמַלְכוּתָךְ	there is *a man* in your kingdom Dan 5:11
הן איתי כסף הבי עלוהי	if there is *money*, give (it) to him A3 4:4

c. The existential complement may be an independent relative clause (§150) with indefinite meaning:

לא איתי זי יקיר מן נכ[ר]ן   there is not (anyone) who is more burdensome
          than a foreigner
          C1 1:159 (Ahiqar)

לָא אִיתַי דִּי־יְמַחֵא בִידֵהּ   there is not (anyone) who can strike at his hand
          Dan 4:32

d. When combined with the preposition לְ, the meaning is that the existential complement is possessed by the object of the preposition (compare §377b), like English *have*:

חֲלָק ... לָא אִיתַי לָךְ   *a portion* ... there will not be to you
          (= you will have no portion)
          Ez 4:16

איתי לה ברא שפירא   there is to him *a beautiful daughter*
          (= he has a beautiful daughter)
          4Q197 4 i 17

איתי לי אנתה אחרה   there is to me *another wife* (= I have another wife)
          B2 6:32

כל זי איתי לה   *all* that there is to me (= all that I have)
          B2 6:19

האיתי למטרא אב   is there to the rain *a father*? (= has the rain a father?)
          11QtgJob 31:5

e. A variant short form אית or את appears in some IA documents; in later dialects it becomes the standard form (see Porten & Lund 2002: 11–12). The contracted negated form לת (< לָא אִית, cp. JLA לֵית) appears once in QA:

לת שלם לכן   there shall not be peace to you (= you shall have no peace)
          4Q201 1 ii 14

f. In addition to predicating existence or presence, איתי can be used to introduce a *new participant* into a discussion. In this usage, the existential complement may be definite.

אִיתַי גֻּבְרִין יְהוּדָאִין דִּי־מַנִּיתָ יָתְהוֹן	there are Judean men whom you have appointed (= as for certain Judean men . . .) Dan 3:12
אִיתי פמון שמ[ה א[בי	there is one named Pamun, my father (= as for one named Pamun . . .) A6 11:1

g. Finally, אִיתַי can mean "it is so, it is the case," introducing a clause:

הֵן אִיתַי דִּי־מִן־כּוֹרֶשׁ מַלְכָּא שִׂים טְעֵם	if it is the case that from king Cyrus an order was given Ez 5:17
איתי זי בפקד[ו] הפקדו	it is the case that they were placed on deposit B2 9:7

It is probable that אִיתַי in Dan 3:17 is an example of this usage:

הֵן אִיתַי אֱלָהַנָא דִּי־אֲנַחְנָא פָלְחִין	if it (the decree just mentioned) is the case, our god whom we worship . . . Dan 3:17

Others interpret this instance as a case of copular אִיתַי, but one would not expect copular אִיתַי without a pronominal suffix (§315).

§381. The tG stem of the root שׁכח can sometimes have existential force, that is, it indicates the existence or presence of a thing or trait in a location or person. Although the conventional gloss is "be found," the verb does not always imply that a search has been made.

כָל־אֲתַר לָא־הִשְׁתְּכַח לְהוֹן	no place was found for them (= they were no longer present) Dan 2:35
קָדָמוֹהִי זָכוּ הִשְׁתְּכַחַת לִי	before him innocence was found to me (= in his eyes I had innocence, was innocent) Dan 6:23
נַהִירוּ וְשָׂכְלְתָנוּ וְחָכְמָה כְּחָכְמַת־אֱלָהִין הִשְׁתְּכַחַת בֵּהּ	illumination and intelligence and wisdom like gods' wisdom was found in him (= illumination etc. was present in him) Dan 5:11 (see also Dan 5:12, 14)

כָּל־שָׁלוּ וּשְׁחִיתָה לָא הִשְׁתְּכַחַת עֲלוֹהִי	no negligence or corruption was found against him (= there was no negligence or corruption in him) Dan 6:5

The instance in Dan 6:5 might seem to favor a more typical idea of *finding after searching*, since it is expressly said that they were "trying to find a charge against Daniel." However, if הִשְׁתְּכַחַת is to be understood as "(not) being found after a search," then the phrase seems to be a pointless repetition of the phrase that preceded it, "they could not find any charge or corruption against him." However, the reason they could find no charge or corruption is not (tautologically) that no charge or corruption was found, but because there was no corruption in him. לָא הִשְׁתְּכַחַת is synonymous to לָא אִיתַי.

מנת משחא זי אשתכח	the portion of oil that was found, i.e., present C3.7A 2:4 (inventory)
כל שקר לא עוד ישתכח	no deceit shall be found (shall exist) any more 4Q537 1+2+3:2

PRESENTATIVE CONSTRUCTIONS

§382. Related to the existential constructions are those introduced with the presentative particles such as הָא, אֲלוּ, and אֲרוּ, all meaning something like English *behold, here is . . .*, Latin *ecce*, French *voilà*, and the like. They serve in general to highlight topics of immediate importance, to call attention to new facts or surprising things, or, after verbs of seeing, to introduce some new sight. With the exception of proverbial literature like those of Ahiqar, they are found only in direct discourse (and even Ahiqar's proverbs are framed as a personal wisdom instruction) or letters.

§383. The particle הָא is the standard presentative in Aramaic, although it appears but once in BA (Dan 3:25). It is used with simple nouns, noun phrases, or verbal clauses:

הָא־אֲנָה חָזֵה גֻּבְרִין אַרְבְּעָה	*behold*, I see four men Dan 3:25
כען הא אתין תמה עליכם	now, *behold*, they are coming there to you A4 3:5
הא שמהת גבריא זי אשתכחו בבבא	*here* are the names of the men who were found at the gate A4 4:6
[הוית] חזה והא מרזבין שבעה שפכין [מין]	I was seeing, and *behold*, seven spouts pouring water 4Q206 4 i 16

When used with pronouns or other deictic words, הָא adds greater emphasis:

הא זנה יקיר [קד]ם שמש — *indeed* this is precious before Shamash
C1 1:188 (Ahiqar)

לא הות ארק לדרגמן זילי הא אנה — it was not land of Dargaman (that is), mine, *that's me*
B2 2:7

§384. The particles אֲלוּ and אֲרוּ are often, but not exclusively, used in visionary contexts:

חָזֵה הֲוֵית וַאֲלוּ אִילָן בְּגוֹא אַרְעָא — I was seeing, and *behold*, a tree in the midst of the earth
Dan 4:7

חָזֵה הֲוֵית וַאֲרוּ אָחֳרִי כִּנְמַר — I was seeing, and *behold*, another (beast) like a leopard
Dan 7:6

וארו לא איתי מנכון — *behold*, there is none among you (to refute Job)
11QtgJob 21:3 (MT וְהִנֵּה, Job 32:12)

In QA, ארו also has the meaning "because" (§412).

§385. a. In IA, the particle הלו is used in less formal documents:

הלו מחר לי למאזל [ל]ביתי — *behold*, tomorrow I have to go to my house
D7 1:9–10

כען הלו תאתא זי לך רבתא מטאת למגז — now, *behold*, your big ewe is ready to shear
D7 8:1–3

b. In one of the Hermopolis letters, the particle ארה is also used (cp. JLA אֲרֵי):

וכעת ארה ספר לה שלחתי — now, *look*, you have not sent a letter
A2 3:5

ארה לא אחי הו חרוץ — *look*, is Haruṣ not my brother?
A2 3:8

NEGATION

Negation is expressed by two particles in Aramaic.

§386. The negative particle לָא typically appears directly before the constituent that it is negating.

a. A *finite verbal form* with a negative particle לָא is part of the verbal nucleus; in other words, the negative particle shares the verbal slot with the verb itself. This category comprises the majority of usages.

b. In coordinated conditional sentences, the entire protasis may be dropped except for הֵן לָא (e.g., Dan 3:18).

c. When לָא appears in a *copular clause*, it may negate the subject or (normally) the predicate (including participial predicates):

לָא־חַשְׁחִין אֲנַחְנָה

we do not need
Dan 3:16

תרעא זך לא זילך הו

that gate is not yours
B2 1:2

לא חסרן הו לכם

it is not a loss for you
A4 3:9

d. *Prepositional phrases* may be negated, especially when a contrast is drawn:

בקושט עמי תמללין ולא בכדבין

in truth you should speak with me, and not with lies
1QapGen 2:7

e. When preceding *nouns and pronouns*, לָא may have a contrastive or emphatic nuance:

לא אנה כתבתה

it was *not I* that wrote it (lit., "not I wrote it")
B2 3:17

אלהא חיבנא ולא א[נש]

God has condemned us, and *not man*
11QtgJob 21:5

f. Before nouns, the expressions ולא and די לא are *quasi-prepositional*, meaning *without*:

דִּי־לָא שָׁלוּ

without negligence
Ez 6:9

די לא בנין

without sons
1QapGen 22:33

מנין שנוהי די לא סוף

the number of his years is *without* end
11QtgJob 28:4

וְלָא דין ולא דבב	*without* suit or process
	B2 3:14

Note also this use with prepositional phrases:

דִּי־לָא בִידַיִן	*without* by hands (= not by means of hands)
	Dan 2:34

In literary speech, לֹא alone may occur with this meaning:

גבר לא לב[ב]	a man *without* a mind
	C1 1:82 (Ahiqar)

§387. a. לָא with אִיתַי is used in the same way as אִיתַי alone (§380).

b. לָא with the infinitive is used modally (§322).

c. הֲלָא (with interrogative particle) does not negate sentence constituents, but applies to the whole sentence, usually in a rhetorical question (see §390b).

d. In one instance, לָא (spelled לָה) is used as a substantive: כְּלָה חֲשִׁיבִין "considered as *naught*" (Dan 4:32).

§388. The negative particle אַל is used only to negate jussives (§317):

לְחַכִּימֵי בָבֶל אַל־תְּהוֹבֵד	do not destroy the sages of Babylon
	Dan 2:24
אל תדחל אנה עמך	do not be afraid, I am with you
	1QapGen 22:30
בשגיא בנן לבבך אל יחדה	in many sons let your heart not rejoice
	C1 1:90 (Ahiqar)

INTERROGATIVE SENTENCES

§389. Interrogative sentences may be divided into *polar* questions (requiring *yes* or *no* as an answer) and *information-seeking* sentences using interrogative pronouns.

Polar Questions

§390. a. Polar questions are introduced with the interrogative particle הֲ (הַ before *ʾaleph* and consonants with *shewa*), in BA directly attached to the first word of the sentence:

הַיְכֵל לְשֵׁיזָבוּתָךְ מִן־אַרְיָוָתָא	was (your god) able to deliver you from the lions? Dan 6:21
השלם הוא	is he well? 4Q197 4 iii 7
האיתי למטרא אב	does the rain have a father? 11QtgJob 31:5
הא דרע כאלה איתי לך	do you have an arm like God? 11QtgJob 34:5, with הא = הֲ[2]

b. When attached to לָא (§386), the questioner expects a positive answer.

הֲלָא גֻבְרִין תְּלָתָא רְמֵינָא לְגוֹא־נוּרָא	did we not throw three men into the fire? Dan 3:24
הֲלָא דָא־הִיא בָּבֶל רַבְּתָא	is this not great Babylon? Dan 4:27 (rhetorical)

c. Sometimes a polar question is evident from context, without the use of הֲ, which is not attested in IA.

אַנְתְּה־[אנת]־הוּא דָנִיֵּאל	are you Daniel? Dan 5:13
ארה לא אחי הו חרוץ	look, is not Harus my brother? A2 3:8 (Hermopolis)

Information-Seeking Questions

§391. Interrogative particles introduce non-polar questions, which may sometimes be rhetorical. The particle is obligatorily at the beginning of the sentence if used in a question.

---

[2] The text should perhaps be emended to האדרע (cp. Ez 4:23).

a. מַן "who?"

מַן־שָׂם לְכֹם טְעֵם	who gave you an order? Ez 5:3
מן הו זי יקום קדמוהי	who is he who can stand before him? C1 1:91 (Ahiqar)
מן שם משחתה ... מן נגד עליה חוטא	who made its measurements? ... who stretched the line over it? 11QtgJob 30:3

מַן is often used as an indefinite pronoun with דִּי "whoever" (§151).

b. מָה or מָא "what?"

מָה עֲבַדְתְּ	what have you done? Dan 4:32
מה חסין הו מן חמר	what is stronger than wine? C1 1:174 (Ahiqar)
מא עבדתה לי	what have you done to me? 1QapGen 20:26
מא מידך יקבל	what will he receive from your hand? 11QtgJob 26:2

מָה can also mean "how?" in exclamations or rhetorical questions (cp. §347d):

[מ]ה ישפטון עקן עם אשה בשר עם סכין איש עם מ[לך]	how can wood dispute with fire, flesh with a knife, a man with a king? C1 1:88 (Ahiqar)
דרעיהא מא שפירן	her arms, how beautiful! 1QapGen 20:4

For the use of מָה in quantification ("any"), see §170; and as an indefinite pronoun ("whatever") in "light-headed" relative clauses, see §151.

מָה is used to form other interrogative words with prepositions:

עַל־מָה דָתָא מְהַחְצְפָה   *why* is the decree so harsh?
Dan 2:15

למא לי כל אלן   *to what purpose* do I have all these?
1QapGen 22:32–33

For למה "lest," see §406. For exclamatory כְּמָה, see §347d.

c. אן "where?"

אן הוית במעבדי ארעא   where were you when I made the earth?
11QtgJob 30:2

אן can be combined with מִן "from" to mean "whence? from where?"

מנאן אנתון אחי   where are you from, my brothers?
4Q197 4 iii 5

It can also be used as an indefinite pronoun with דִּי "wherever" (§349b).

d. איך "how?"

The particle איך "how" is sparsely attested: איך ביתא עביד "how is the household doing?" (A3 3:6).

e. אמת "when?"

The particle אמת "when" (cp. JLA אֵמַתִי, Syriac ܐܡܬܝ) is attested only in an indirect question: שלח לי אמת תעבדן פסח "send me *at what time* you are doing Passover" (D7 6:8–9, ostracon).

CHAPTER 15
Clause Combining

Coordination

§392. Coordination is to be distinguished from the mere succession of clauses; it refers to clauses that are joined with some kind of cohesion between them, whether semantic (e.g., dealing with the same events or entities, or the same causal forces) or structural (with, e.g., pronominal reference, parallel syntax). As in subordinate clauses (Chapter 16), one of the clauses comments on or proceeds in some way from the other, but syntactically both clauses are independent and could stand on their own. Typically, it is two clauses that are coordinated, but there are exceptions.

SIMPLE COORDINATION WITH וֹ

§393. The conjunction וֹ "and" joins clauses whose relationship is inferred from their contents and the surrounding context.

a. In the example below, the B-clause וּפִשְׁרָה נְהַחֲוֵה is linked to the A-clause both semantically (as a *consequence* of the A-clause) and grammatically (the object of the A-clause חֶלְמָא is referenced in the B clause by a 3ms pronominal suffix).

> מַלְכָּא חֶלְמָא יֵאמַר לְעַבְדוֹהִי וּפִשְׁרָה נְהַחֲוֵה let the king tell the dream to his servants, *and* we will tell its interpretation
>
> Dan 2:7 (condition, consequence)

b. In the next example, the action of the A-clause sets the stage for the B-clause, and the subject of the A clause carries over to the B clause. The action of the B-clause is the implicit *purpose* of the A-clause.

> קְרִבוּ גֻּבְרִין כַּשְׂדָּאִין וַאֲכַלוּ קַרְצֵיהוֹן דִּי יְהוּדָיֵא some Chaldean men drew near and slandered the Judeans
>
> Dan 3:8 (sequence)

c. The A-clause and the B-clause can be *parallel* in structure and meaning.

> לֵאלָהָיִךְ [לאלהך] לָא פָלְחִין וּלְצֶלֶם דַּהֲבָא דִּי your gods they do not serve *and* the golden image
> הֲקֵימְתָּ לָא סָגְדִין you set up they will not worship
>
> Dan 3:12 (synonymous parallel structure)

d. The B-clause gives the *fulfillment* of the desire described in the A-clause.

שְׁפַר קֳדָם דָּרְיָוֶשׁ וַהֲקִים עַל־מַלְכוּתָא
לַאֲחַשְׁדַּרְפְּנַיָּא מְאָה וְעֶשְׂרִין

it was pleasing to Darius *and* he set up over the
kingdom 120 satraps
Dan 6:2 (desire and fulfillment)

e. In some instances of coordination, the relationship of the two clauses is contextually *adversative*.

מאן טב כס[י]ן מלה בלבבה והו ז[י]תביר הנפקה
ברא

a good vessel hides a thing inside it, *but* one that is
broken lets it out
C1 1:93 (Ahiqar)

מִתְעָרְבִין לֶהֱוֹן בִּזְרַע אֲנָשָׁא וְלָא־לֶהֱוֹן דָּבְקִין דְּנָה
עִם־דְּנָה

they will mix together through human seed, *but*
they will not adhere one to the other
Dan 2:43

f. The B-clause can give *additional information* about something in the A-clause, or *circumstances* crucial to understanding the A-clause.

אברם שרא בעמק שוא והוא עמק מלכא

Abram camped in the Valley of Shaveh, *and* it is
the Valley of the King (= *which* is the Valley of
the King)
1QapGen 22:13–14 (background information)

לא יתלקח בדין וספרא זנה בידכי

it will not be accepted in court, *and* (= *while*) this
document is in your possession
B2 3:17 (accompanying circumstance)

g. Generally, the verbal forms in parallel A- and B-clauses have the same TAM features (Chapter 11); however, the past tense PC (§§303ff.) may be coordinated with the past tense SC (§292). In such cases, the PC clause gives a result of the action of the SC clause or action closely associated with it.

חֵלֶם חֲזֵית וִידַחֲלִנַּנִי

I saw a dream, *and* it frightened me
Dan 4:2 (action, result)

עַיְנַי לִשְׁמַיָּא נִטְלֵת וּמַנְדְּעִי עֲלַי יְתוּב

I lifted my eyes to heaven, *and* (= *after*) my reason
returned to me
Dan 4:31 (circumstantial)

Gapping

§394. The B-clause of coordinated parallel sentences (§294 and §393c above) may drop some parallel element, leaving a "gap" to be filled by inference from the A-clause. The gapped clause may be conjoined without וֹ.

וַחֲטָיָךְ [וחטאך] בְּצִדְקָה פְרֻק וַעֲוָיָתָךְ בְּמִחַן עֲנָיִן
your sins by charity remove, and your iniquities (*remove*) by having mercy on the poor
Dan 4:24

שְׁלֵה הֲוֵית בְּבֵיתִי וְרַעְנַן בְּהֵיכְלִי
at ease was I in my house, tranquil in my palace
Dan 4:1

[מ]ה ישפטון עקן עם אשה בשר עם סכין איש עם מ[לך]
how can wood dispute with fire, meat with a knife, a man with a king?
C1 1:88 (Ahiqar)

Asyndeton

§395. Verbs or entire clauses are sometimes coordinated without any conjunction (asyndeton). In such cases, the verbal actions are closely associated in time or manner.

שלח קרא לכול חכ'ימ['ין] מצרין
he sent, he summoned all the sages of Egypt (= he summoned by messenger)
1QapGen 20:18–19; cp. 1QapGen 21:21

בֵּאדַיִן חֶלְמָא כְתַב רֵאשׁ מִלִּין אֲמַר
then the dream he wrote, the beginning of matters he said (= . . . he wrote the dream, beginning as follows)
Dan 7:1

וּמִתְכַּנְּשִׁין אֲחַשְׁדַּרְפְּנַיָּא סִגְנַיָּא וּפַחֲוָתָא וְהַדָּבְרֵי מַלְכָּא חָזַיִן לְגֻבְרַיָּא אִלֵּךְ
the satraps, prefects and governors, and counselors of the king *were gathering (and) seeing* those men
Dan 3:27 (see §311)

הושרו יהיתו עלי אפריע
send (them), let them bring (them) to me quickly
A6 12:3

OTHER COORDINATING CONJUNCTIONS

§396. The particle בְּרַם "but, however" (BA and QA only) marks the B-clause as adversative, limiting the application of the A-clause:

גֹּדּוּ אִילָנָא וְחַבְּלוּהִי בְּרַם עִקַּר שָׁרְשׁוֹהִי בְּאַרְעָא שְׁבֻקוּ	chop down the tree and destroy it; *but* leave the core of its roots in the earth
	Dan 4:20
[י]הב לך ולבניך כולא למאכל . . . ברם כול דם לא תאכלון	he gave to you and to your sons everything to eat . . . *but* you shall eat no blood
	1QapGen 11:17

§397. The particle אוֹ "or" marks the B-clause as an *alternative* to the A-clause. In the attested cases, the alternative is not exclusive (as in Latin *vel*, not *aut*). (See also §142d.) In the following example, אוֹ occurs with both clauses.

או הא דרע כאלה איתי לך או בקל כותה תרעם	do you have an arm like God's, *or* will you thunder aloud like him?
	11QtgJob 34:5 (MT Job 40:9 has וְ with both clauses)

§398. The particle לָהֵן II (see also §434) can mark the B clause as preferred alternative to the negated A-clause. (See also its use in exceptive subordination, §423.)

לָא בְחָכְמָה דִּי־אִיתַי בִּי . . . רָזָא דְנָה גֱּלִי לִי לָהֵן עַל־דִּבְרַת דִּי פִשְׁרָא לְמַלְכָּא יְהוֹדְעוּן	*not* through the wisdom that is in me . . . was this secret revealed, *but rather* in order that the interpretation might be made known to the king (it was revealed)
	Dan 2:30 (with gapping, §394)
אנש לא שליט למשנתה ולמעבדה עבד להן ברי יהוה	*no one* shall have the right to mark him or make him a slave, *but rather* he shall be my son
	B3 9:8–9 (adoption contract)

CHAPTER 16
Clause Combining
Subordination

§399. The linking of a main clause to a second, dependent clause which modifies the main clause adverbially is subordination. The linking is usually marked by a subordinating conjunction, although in some cases a coordinating conjunction is used, and the subordination is semantic rather than syntactic.

PURPOSE CLAUSES

§400. The dependent purpose clause spells out the purpose or intended result of the action described in the main clause. In BA, purpose clauses are either (1) embedded in the main clause as an infinitive clause, or (2) introduced with דִּי as a subordinator followed by a verb in the prefix conjugation. There are also purpose clauses joined to the main clause with coordinating וְ instead of דִּי.

§401. a. The purpose clause can occur after the main verb, with the infinitive denoting the purposed action marked with לְ.

נְפַק לְקַטָּלָה לְחַכִּימֵי בָּבֶל	(Arioch) went out *to kill* the sages of Babylon Dan 2:14
שְׁמָהָתְהֹם שְׁאֵלְנָא לְהֹם לְהוֹדָעוּתָךְ	their names we asked of them *in order to inform* you Ez 5:10
שלח לה אל עליון רוח מכדש למכתשה	God Most High sent a spirit of plague *to afflict him* 1QapGen 20:16
אזלו לערקה זי דדרש למעבד קרב	they went towards Dadarsh *to do battle* C2 1:V.15

b. The infinitive לְהַשְׁנָיָה with לָא דִּי in Dan 6:9 is sometimes translated as a negative purpose clause (e.g., NRSV "so that it cannot be changed"), but is to be read as modal: "which one is not to change" (§322).

§402. a. Purpose clauses introduced with דִּי follow the main clause and have a verb in the PC.

מִנִּי שִׂים טְעֵם לְהַנְעָלָה קָדָמַי לְכֹל חַכִּימֵי בָבֶל דִּי־
פְּשַׁר חֶלְמָא יְהוֹדְעֻנַּנִי

I gave a command to bring before me all the sages of Babylon *so that they could tell me* the interpretation of the dream
Dan 4:3

שְׁלַחְנָא וְהוֹדַעְנָא לְמַלְכָּא דִּי יְבַקַּר בִּסְפַר־דָּכְרָנַיָּא

we have sent and informed the king *so that one may search* in the book of records
Ez 4:14–15

זף דגנא וחנטתא זי תאכל ותשבע

borrow grain and wheat *so that you may eat and be satisfied*
C1 1:129 (Ahiqar)

b. The jussive may be used in the purpose clause as well:

ברכתכי לפתח זי יחוני אפיך בשלם

I said a blessing for you to Ptah *so that he may show me* your face in good health
A2 1:2

c. Negative purpose (see also §406 below) can be expressed by דִּי לָא + the PC verb:

יְהַבוּ גֶשְׁמֵיהוֹן [גשמהון] דִּי לָא־יִפְלְחוּן וְלָא־
יִסְגְּדוּן לְכָל־אֱלָהּ לָהֵן לֵאלָהֲהוֹן

they gave their bodies *so that they would not worship or bow down* to any god except their god
Dan 3:28

§403. The purpose clause with infinitive and the purpose clause with דִּי can occur together in a *mixed construction*.

In Dan 5:15, the דִּי clause is followed by a purpose infinitive:

הֻעַלּוּ קָדָמַי חַכִּימַיָּא אָשְׁפַיָּא דִּי־כְתָבָה דְנָה יִקְרוֹן
וּפִשְׁרֵהּ לְהוֹדָעֻתַנִי

the sages and soothsayers were brought before me *so that they could read* this writing and to *make known* to me the interpretation
Dan 5:15

In Dan 2:17–18, the purpose infinitive is followed by the דִּי clause, which is dependent on it:

מִלְּתָא הוֹדַע וְרַחֲמִין לְמִבְעֵא מִן־קֳדָם אֱלָהּ שְׁמַיָּא
עַל־רָזָה דְּנָה דִּי לָא יְהֹבְדוּן דָּנִיֵּאל וְחַבְרוֹהִי

he made known (to his friends) the affair, *to seek mercy* from the God of heaven about this secret *so that Daniel and his friends should not perish*

§404. The prepositional compound עַל דְּבְרַת or עַד דְּבְרַת with דִּי also marks purpose clauses:

עַל־דְּבְרַת דִּי פִשְׁרָא לְמַלְכָּא יְהוֹדְעוּן (the secret was revealed to me) *in order that they might make known* the interpretation to the king
Dan 2:30

עַד־דְּבְרַת דִּי יִנְדְּעוּן חַיַּיָּא דִּי־שַׁלִּיט עִלָּיָא [עלאה] בְּמַלְכוּת אֲנָשָׁא [אנשא] (the decree is from the angels) *in order that the living would know* that the Most High rules in the realm of humankind
Dan 4:14

תחיבנני על דברת די תזכא will you make me guilty *so that you can be innocent?*
11QtgJob 34:4

§405. Sometimes a purpose clause occurs after a main clause without an overt sign of subordination, with simple coordination by ן and the verb in the PC. Instances in which the main clause is past tense are only found in BA; in IA and QA, the main clause has a volitive form.

בֵּלְשַׁאצַּר אֲמַר . . . לְהַיְתָיָה לְמָאנֵי דַהֲבָא וְכַסְפָּא . . . וְיִשְׁתּוֹן בְּהוֹן מַלְכָּא וְרַבְרְבָנוֹהִי שֵׁגְלָתֵהּ וּלְחֵנָתֵהּ Belshazzar commanded to bring the vessels of gold and silver *so they could drink* using them
Dan 5:2

קִרְבֵת עַל־חַד מִן־קָאֲמַיָּא וְיַצִּיבָא אֶבְעֵא־מִנֵּהּ עַל־כָּל־דְּנָה I approached one of those standing *so that I could ask* him the truth about all this
Dan 7:16

אֲמַר־לִי וּפְשַׁר מִלַּיָּא יְהוֹדְעִנַּנִי he spoke to me *so that he could tell me* the interpretation of the things
Dan 7:16

אשתעי לי חלמך ואנדע tell me your dream *that I may know it*
1QapGen 19:18

אמר למלכא וישלח אנתתה מנה speak to the king, *so that he will send away* the woman from him
1QapGen 20:23, cf. 20:28, 4Q197 4 ii 3, 4Q542 1 i 2

הוי יהבת עבר לוחפרע ויהוי זבן גשרן

keep giving grain to Wahpre *that* he may keep buying lumber

A2 2:14 (with the jussive)

§406. Negative purpose (*lest*), when the main clause action is performed to avert an action (see also §402c above), can be marked with the particle למה, sometimes preceded by די.

וּזְהִירִין הֱוֹו שָׁלוּ לְמֶעְבַּד עַל־דְּנָה לְמָה יִשְׂגֵּא חֲבָלָא לְהַנְזָקַת מַלְכִין

beware of acting negligently in this *lest* harm increase to the detriment of kings

Ez 4:22

יִתְעֲבֵד אָדְרַזְדָּא ... דִּי־לְמָה לֶהֱוֵא קְצַף עַל־מַלְכוּת מַלְכָּא וּבְנוֹהִי

let it be done diligently ..., *lest* there should be wrath on the realm of the king and his sons

Ez 7:23

אל תהרכב חטך לצדיק למה אלהיא יסגה בעדרה ויהתיבנהי עליך

do not aim your arrow at a righteous man, *lest* God come to his aid and turn it back on you

C1 1:126 (Ahiqar)

In QA, a form דלא (as §402c above) was changed by supralinear correction to דלמא:

דלˆמˆא תהוה אמר די מן נכסי כול עתרה די אברם

(I shall take nothing from you) *lest* you should go around saying, All Abram's wealth is from my possessions.

1QapGen 22:22

CAUSAL CLAUSES

§407. Causal clauses give the reason for the action described in the main clause, and are ordinarily introduced by a causal conjunction. There is considerable variety among the causal conjunctions; several are peculiar to one dialect.

§408. a. In BA, the most frequent causal conjunction is the compound form כָּל־קֳבֵל דִּי (see prepositions, §200d). כָּל־קֳבֵל דִּי in its causal sense introduces causal clauses, before or after the main clause. It can also serve to mark manner clauses (see §415b).

אֱדַיִן דָּנִיֵּאל דְּנָה הֲוָא מִתְנַצַּח עַל־סָרְכַיָּא וַאֲחַשְׁדַּרְפְּנַיָּא כָּל־קֳבֵל דִּי רוּחַ יַתִּירָא בֵּהּ

then this Daniel distinguished himself over the rulers and satraps, *because* an excellent mind was in him

Dan 6:4

כָּל־קֳבֵל דִּי־מְלַח הֵיכְלָא מְלַחְנָא ... שְׁלַחְנָא
וְהוֹדַעְנָא לְמַלְכָּא

because we partake of the salt of the palace, ...
we have sent and informed the king
Ez 4:14

See also Dan 2:8, 3:29, 4:15, 5:12, 6:5, 23, Ez 7:14. כלקובל appears in QA in broken contexts (see *DQA* 115). It is not attested in IA.

b. In Dan 2:10, כָּל־קֳבֵל דִּי marks a consequence ("therefore"), rather than a reason ("because"). It should perhaps be emended to כָּל־קֳבֵל דְּנָה (§200d).

לָא־אִיתַי אֲנָשׁ עַל־יַבֶּשְׁתָּא דִּי מִלַּת מַלְכָּא יוּכַל
לְהַחֲוָיָה כָּל־קֳבֵל דִּי כָּל־מֶלֶךְ רַב וְשַׁלִּיט מִלָּה
כִדְנָה לָא שְׁאֵל לְכָל־חַרְטֹם וְאָשַׁף וְכַשְׂדָּי

there is no one on earth who can tell what the king commands, *therefore* no king, leader, or ruler has asked such a thing of any magician, soothsayer, or Chaldean
Dan 2:10

c. In Dan 5:22, it marks a reason that was not followed (concessive *although*), rather than one that was followed (*because*).

לָא הַשְׁפֵּלְתְּ לִבְבָךְ כָּל־קֳבֵל דִּי כָל־דְּנָה יְדַעְתָּ

you have not humbled your heart, *although* you know all this
Dan 5:22

§409. a. The bare particle דִּי is sometimes used to mark causal clauses:

וְכָל־חֲבָל לָא־הִשְׁתְּכַח בֵּהּ דִּי הֵימִן בֵּאלָהֵהּ

no injury was found on him, *because* he trusted in his god
Dan 6:24

הוֹדַעְתַּנִי דִּי־בְעֵינָא מִנָּךְ דִּי־מִלַּת מַלְכָּא הוֹדַעְתֶּנָא

you have made known to me what we asked of you, *for* the matter of the king you have made known to us
Dan 2:23

b. In some cases, it is hard to tell if דִּי is used as a non-restrictive relative pronoun (§149) or as a causal conjunction:

וּלְחַי עָלְמָא שַׁבְּחֵת וְהַדְּרֵת דִּי שָׁלְטָנֵהּ שָׁלְטָן עָלַם

the living eternal one I blessed and praised, *for* his dominion is an eternal dominion (or: "*whose* dominion is an eternal dominion")
Dan 4:31; see also Dan 2:20, 3:28, 4:34, 6:27, 28

§410. The temporal conjunction מִן־דִּי (§421 below) can also be used to mark causal clauses:

מִן־דִּי הַרְגִּזוּ אֲבָהָתַנָא לֶאֱלָהּ שְׁמַיָּא יְהַב הִמּוֹ בְּיַד נְבוּכַדְנֶצַּר — *because* our fathers angered the God of heaven, he gave them into the hand of Nebuchadnezzar
Ez 5:12; see also Dan 3:22

מן די [הוית סב]ר די אלהין ה[וו] — *because* I used to think that they were gods
4Q242 1–3 8

§411. In QA, the preposition בדיל (§193) combined with די (JLA בְּדִיל) can mark causal clauses.

לא יכול רעואל למכליה מנך בדיל די הוא ידע [...] — Raguel cannot withhold her from you, *because* he knows ...
4Q197 4 ii 4

§412. In QA, the particle ארו, originally presentative (§384), has come to indicate causal clauses as well (compare JLA אֲרֵי, Jewish Palestinian Aramaic ארום).

ארו רב אלהא מן אנשא — *for* God is greater than man
11QtgJob 22:6 (MT Job 33:12 כִּי)

ולא יכלו כול אסיא . . . לאסיותה ארו הוא רוחא כתש לכולהון — none of the healers, etc. were able ... to heal him *because* that spirit had afflicted all of them
1QapGen 20:20

§413. The combined particle בדי (IA בזי) introduces causal clauses in QA and IA:

אתעשת על אגורא זך למבנה בזי לא שבקן לן למבניה — take thought to rebuild this temple, *because* they are not allowing us to rebuild it
A4 7:23 (Petition)

בדי מן תמן דנחין מאני שמיא — (they call the east *madnaḥ*), *because* the vessels of heaven shine (*dnḥyn*) from there
4Q209 23 7

§414. The particle כי (cp. BH כִּי) is used as a causal conjunction in IA, especially in the Ahiqar proverbs. It is most likely already an archaism in IA.

אל ידנח שמ[ש לה] כי גבר לחה הו — may Shamash not shine on him, *for* he is a bad man
C1 1:138 (Ahiqar)

MANNER CLAUSES

Manner clauses compare the way the main clause action is carried out to the action of the subordinate clause, by means of subordinating conjunctions.

§415. a. The expression לָקֳבֵל דִּי can be used to introduce manner clauses. The main clause may itself have a correlative manner adverb.

לָקֳבֵל דִּי־שְׁלַח דָּרְיָוֶשׁ מַלְכָּא כְּנֵמָא אָסְפַּרְנָא עֲבַדוּ	as Darius had sent, *so* they diligently did it Ez 6:13 (with correlative כְּנֵמָא)
לקבל זי אנה עבדת לך כן אפו עבד לי	as I have done for you, *so* then do for me C1 1:52 (Ahiqar) (with correlative כן)
למבניה . . . לקבל זי בנה הוה קדמין	to build it . . . *just as* it was built previously A4 7:25 (Petition)

b. So also כָּל־קֳבֵל דִּי (§408):

כָּל־קֳבֵל דִּי־הֲוָא עָבֵד מִן־קַדְמַת דְּנָה	(he prayed to his god), *just as* he used to do previously Dan 6:11. See also 2:40, 41, 45.

§416. The expression הֵא־כְדִי occurs once to introduce a manner clause:

לָא־לֶהֱוֹן דָּבְקִין דְּנָה עִם־דְּנָה הֵא־כְדִי פַרְזְלָא לָא מִתְעָרַב עִם־חַסְפָּא	they will not adhere to each other, *just as* iron does not mix with clay Dan 2:43

A Qumran text of Daniel reads הכא די (4Q112 3 ii+6:12), i.e., הֵכָא דִּי.

§417. In IA, כזי (= כְּ + דִּי) is used as a subordinating conjunction of manner (for its temporal use, see §418).

כזי עבד אנה לחרוץ כות תעבד בנת עלי	as I am doing for Harus, *so* may Banit do for me A2 3:7 (with correlative כות)
למבניה באתרה כזי הוה הוה לקדמן	(permission is given) to rebuild it in its place, *just as* it was previously A4 9:8

TEMPORAL CLAUSES

16

A temporal clause fixes the time of the main clause action by linking it to the time of the subordinate clause.

§418. The most common temporal subordinator is כְּדִי "when" (IA כזי), indicating that the action of the dependent clause is at the same time as the main clause.

| דָּנִיֵּאל כְּדִי יְדַע דִּי־רְשִׁים כְּתָבָא עַל לְבַיְתֵהּ | Daniel, *when* he knew that the writ was signed, entered his house |
| | Dan 6:11 |

| כזי יוזא הוה במצרין אבד עם נשי [ביתה] | *when* a revolt took place in Egypt, he perished with the household staff |
| | A6 11:4 |

| עדן יהוה נפלג המו | *when* the time comes, we shall divide them |
| | B2 11:13 |

| כדי אמות ערטלי אהך | *when* I die, I shall go naked |
| | 1QapGen 22:33 |

§419. A less frequent construction is the use of the infinitive governed by the prepositions בְּ or כְּ, followed by a subject or with a pronominal suffix as the subject.

| כְּמִקְרְבֵהּ לְגֻבָּא . . . בְּקָל עֲצִיב זְעִק | *as* he drew near to the den . . . he cried out in a sad voice |
| | Dan 6:21, cp. Dan 4:32 |

| אן הוית במעבדי ארעא | where were you *when* I made the earth? |
| | 11QtgJob 30:2 |

| במזהר כחדא כוכבי צפר | *when* the morning stars shine together |
| | 11QtgJob 30:4–5 |

This construction is unknown in IA, and reflects the influence of Biblical Hebrew in BA and QA.

§420. a. Subordination with עַד דִּי indicates that the main verb action takes place *until* the subordinate action takes place, or that the subordinate action occurs *during* the main verb action. If the main verb is negated, its action does not begin until the subordinate action is completed. (For prepositional עַד, see §187.)

חָזֵה הֲוַיְתָ עַד דִּי הִתְגְּזֶרֶת אֶבֶן	you were watching *while* a stone was cut out Dan 2:34
עִם־חֵיוַת בָּרָא חֲלָקֵהּ עַד דִּי־שִׁבְעָה עִדָּנִין יַחְלְפוּן עֲלוֹהִי	his portion is with the wild animals *until* (or *while*) seven seasons pass over him Dan 4:20
הן כן עבדו עד זי אגורא זך יתבנה	if so it is done *until* that temple is rebuilt A4 7:27 (Petition)
אתית ליד ימא עד די דבקת לטור תורא	I went along the sea *until* I reached the Mount of the Ox 1QapGen 21:16
לָא־מְטוֹ לְאַרְעִית גֻּבָּא עַד דִּי־שְׁלִטוּ בְהוֹן אַרְיָוָתָא	they did not reach the bottom of the pit *until* the lions had overpowered them Dan 6:25

b. עד can also be used without following דִּי. This is more common in IA.

אל תל[ו]ט יומא עד תחזה [לי]לה	do not curse the day *until* you see the night C1 1:80 (Ahiqar)
הוא רדף בתרהון עד דבק לדן	he pursued after them *until* he reached Dan 1QapGen 22:7

See also Ez 5:5 (§301b).

§421. The phrase מִן דִּי "after, since" (also used in causal clauses, §410) marks the main clause action as posterior to the subordinate clause action.

וחדא מן די תבת מן מצרין	one year (has passed) *since* you returned from Egypt 1QapGen 22:29
מִן־דִּי פַּרְשֶׁגֶן נִשְׁתְּוָנָא . . . קֱרִי . . . אֲזַלוּ בִבְהִילוּ לִירוּשְׁלֶם	*after* the copy of the letter . . . was read, . . . they went in haste to Jerusalem Ez 4:23
חנום הו עלין מן זי חנניה במצרין עד כען	Khnum is against us *since* Hananiah has been in Egypt until now A4 3:7

CONDITIONAL CLAUSES

Conditional clauses combine conditions in the (subordinate) protasis with consequences in the apodosis (main clause).

§422. a. The conditional clause is usually introduced with the particle הֵן (or אֵן)[1] for the protasis ("if" clause), and usually no particle marking the apodosis ("then" clause), although sometimes וֹ or אחר is used. Sometimes the meaning is concessive (*even if, although*) rather than conditional, as in C1 1:177 below.

הֵן חֶלְמָא וּפִשְׁרֵהּ תְּהַחֲוֹן מַתְּנָן וּנְבִזְבָּה וִיקָר שַׂגִּיא תְּקַבְּלוּן	*if* you tell the dream and its interpretation, (then) you shall receive gifts and reward and much honor Dan 2:6
הֵן קִרְיְתָא דָךְ תִּתְבְּנֵא וְשׁוּרַיָּה יִשְׁתַּכְלְלוּן מִנְדָּה־בְלוֹ וַהֲלָךְ לָא יִנְתְּנוּן	*if* that city is rebuilt and its walls completed, (then) tribute, tax, and toll will not be given Ez 4:13
החויני הן ידעת חכמה	tell me, *if* you have knowledge 11QtgJob 30:2
הן אמחאנך ברי לא תמות	*if* I should beat you, my son, (then) you will not die C1 1:177 (Ahiqar)

b. Although the PC is usually used in the protasis, the SC or participle may also be used with no difference in meaning:

הן נפקה טבה מן פם א[נשא טב] והן לחיה תנפק מ[ן] פמהם אלהן ילחון להם	if good comes out of [ptcp.] men's mouth, (then) it is well; but if evil should come [PC] from their mouth, (then) the gods will do evil to them C1 1:171–172 (Ahiqar) (participle, PC)
הן כליתך אנתן לך כסף	if I restrain [SC] you, (then) I must give you silver B2 1:7 (SC)

Folmer has suggested (1995: 403ff.) that in IA the SC is used in the protasis when הן immediately precedes, and the PC otherwise. Both conjugations express epistemic modality (§291b) in this context.

---

[1] The particle אם is used once in QA to mark the protasis (4Q318 8 9).

c. The particle הֵן can be used after the main clause, not to mark the protasis, but to indicate a *possible result*:

חֲטָיָךְ [חטאך] בְּצִדְקָה פְרֻק . . . הֵן תֶּהֱוֵא אַרְכָה לִשְׁלֵוְתָךְ	remove your sins by righteousness, . . . *so that perhaps* a prolongation of your comfort might come about Dan 4:24
קרא . . . אסי מצרין הן יכולון לאסיותה	he called . . . the healers of Egypt, *so that perhaps* they could heal him 1QapGen 20:19

d. הן can also be used to present alternatives, like *whether*:

הֵן לְמוֹת הֵן לִשְׁרֹשׁוּ [לשרשי] הֵן־לַעֲנָשׁ נִכְסִין וְלֶאֱסוּרִין	*whether* for death or for beating, *whether* for confiscation of property or confinement Ez 7:26
הן למכתש הן לארעא הן לכפן וחסרונה והן פתגם טוב	*whether* for plague, *whether* for the earth, *whether* for famine and want, or *whether* a decree of blessing 11QtgJob 29:3–4

e. The use of אן as a negative asseverative particle (to affirm an oath that something will not happen), as with Biblical Hebrew אִם, is due to the influence of the underlying Hebrew text in 1QapGen:

אן מן חוט עד ערקא דמסאן אן אסב מן כול די איתי לך	(I swear that) from thread to sandal-strap, I shall not take from anything that is yours 1QapGen 22:21–22 (cp. MT Gen 14:23)

§423. a. The negative conditional particle לָהֵן (לָא "not" + הֵן "if") "unless" ("if not") marks a condition that would prevent the main clause action from happening. If the main clause is itself negated, then לָהֵן marks an enabling condition.

לָא נְהַשְׁכַּח לְדָנִיֵּאל דְּנָה כָּל־עִלָּא לָהֵן הַשְׁכַּחְנָה עֲלוֹהִי בְּדָת אֱלָהֵהּ	we will not find any ground for condemnation of this Daniel *unless* we find something against him in the law of his god Dan 6:6

b. In many cases, the clause with לָהֵן is reduced to the portion of the negative condition that is targeted by the particle. In such cases, the most natural English translation is *except*:

אָחֳרָן לָא אִיתַי דִּי יְחַוִּנַּהּ קֳדָם מַלְכָּא לָהֵן אֱלָהִין	there is no other who can tell it to the king *except* *(if not)* the gods (= there is no other who can tell it to the king, if the gods do not tell it to the king) Dan 2:11 (complement of איתי)
כָּל־דִּי־יִבְעֵה בָעוּ מִן־כָּל־אֱלָהּ וֶאֱנָשׁ . . . לָהֵן מִנָּךְ	all who make a request from any god or man *except* *(if not)* from you Dan 6:8 (prepositional phrase)
[בר לא] איתי לה לה[ן] שרהֿ [ב]ל[חודי]ה	he has no (child) *except* Sarah alone 4Q197 4 i 18 (complement of איתי)
לא [ישא]ל [נמרא] שלם טביא להן למונק דמה	the leopard does not greet the gazelle *except* to suck its blood C1 1:167–168 (Ahiqar) (infinitive complement)

§424. The preposition בר מן *bárrā min* "aside from, except" (§192) is attested one time in IA as a conjunction before זי in the meaning *unless*: לא אכל אנצל לפלטי . . . בר מן זי אנת תתרך לאמה תמת "I am not able to reclaim Palti . . . *unless* you divorce his mother Tamet" (B3 3:14, marriage contract).

§425. A counterfactual condition, one that was not realized, is marked by הנלו (IA only; cf. JLA אִילוּ). It has the SC in the protasis and apodosis.

הנלו גלין אנפין על ארשם קדמן לכן לא כזנה הו[ה]	*if* we had revealed our face to Arsham previously, then it would not have been like this A4 2:8

CLAUSES AS EMBEDDED CONSTITUENTS

§426. Clauses that are constituents of a larger clause, instead of being conjoined in a separate clause, are embedded clauses: relative clauses, object clauses, and verbal complements.

a. Relative clauses modify nouns that are the head of a phrase; they are treated in the section on nouns and noun phrases (§148).

b. Clauses introduced by דְּ as complementizer may be the direct object of verbs of perceiving, knowing, or saying (exemplification in §341).

§427. A development of the complementizer use of דִּי is to introduce direct discourse after verbs of saying instead of indirect discourse.

אָמַר לְחַכִּימֵי בָבֶל דִּי כָל־אֱנָשׁ דִּי־יִקְרֵה כְּתָבָה he said to the sages of Babylon (that) "Any man who can
דְנָה וּפִשְׁרֵהּ יְחַוִּנַּנִי   read this writing and tell me its interpretation . . ."
Dan 5:7

אמרת שרי למלכא דאחי הוא   Sarai said to the king (that) "He is my brother"
1QapGen 20:9–10

§428. Some verbs govern other verbal clauses, most commonly headed by infinitives, as complements. This is to be distinguished from the use of infinitives in purpose clauses (§401).

a. This is most common with the G stem verb כהל/יכל "be able" (§§302a, 330c):

מִלַּת מַלְכָּא יוּכַל לְהַחֲוָיָה   (no man) is *able to tell* the matter of the king
Dan 2:10

לָא־כָהֲלִין כְּתָבָא לְמִקְרֵא וּפִשְׁרָא [וּפִשְׁרֵהּ]   they were not *able to read* the writing or *make known*
לְהוֹדָעָה   its interpretation
Dan 5:8 (governing two infinitives)

לא אכהל למפלח בבב היכלא   I am not *able to serve* in the gate of the palace
C1 1:17 (Ahiqar)

b. In IA, PC כהל/יכל more commonly governs a following PC verb with the same inflections, instead of an infinitive:

כדי תכלן תעבדן לה עבד אנה לה   as much as you would *be able to do* for him, I am
doing for him
A2 3:4–5 (both verbs G PC 2fs)

לא אכהל אגרנך דין ודבב   I will not *be able to instigate* suit or process against you
B2 2:12 (first verb G PC 1cs, second verb D PC 1cs)

יכל ישמע מלי קדשא   (who) *is able to hear* the words of the holy one?
4Q212 1 v 16 (both verbs G PC 3ms)

c. Besides the modal verb כהל/יכל, other modal verbs (signifying permission, obligation, necessity, desire, ability, etc.) govern infinitives:

מִנְדָּה בְלוֹ וַהֲלָךְ לָא שַׁלִּיט לְמִרְמֵא עֲלֵיהֹם — it is not *authorized to impose* tribute, custom, or toll on them
Ez 7:24

לָא־חַשְׁחִין אֲנַחְנָה עַל־דְּנָה פִּתְגָם לַהֲתָבוּתָךְ — We do not *need to give you an answer* about this
Dan 3:16

הֱוָא מִשְׁתַּדַּר לְהַצָּלוּתֵהּ — He was *trying to save* him
Dan 6:15

לא שבקן לן למבניה — They are not *allowing* us *to rebuild*
A4 7:23 (Petition)

d. In addition to modal verbs, *phasal* verbs (signifying the stages of an action) may govern infinitives:

שָׁרִיו לְמִבְנֵא בֵּית אֱלָהָא — They *began to build* the house of God
Ez 5:2

הוסף למדחל לאלהא — he *continued to fear* God
4Q198 1 1

וּבְעוֹ דָּנִיֵּאל וְחַבְרוֹהִי לְהִתְקְטָלָה — Daniel and his friends *were about to be killed*
Dan 2:13

כען הלו תאתא זי לך רבתא מטאת למגז — now, behold, your big ewe is *ready* to shear (lit., "has reached [time] to shear")
D7 8:1–3

e. The content of verbs of speaking or writing may be given in an infinitive:

הן יפקד לך מראך מין למנטר — if your lord *commands* you *to guard* water
C1 1:191 (Ahiqar)

אֲמַר לְכַפָּתָה לְשַׁדְרַךְ . . . לְמִרְמֵא לְאַתּוּן נוּרָא יָקִדְתָּא — he *said to bind* Shadrach et al. (and) *to throw* them into the furnace of burning fire
Dan 3:20

וּמִנִּי שִׂים טְעֵם לְהַנְעָלָה קָדָמַי לְכֹל חַכִּימֵי בָבֶל — I gave a *decree to bring* all the sages of Babylon to me
Dan 4:3

CHAPTER 17
Discourse Markers (Half-Conjunctions)

§429. Discourse markers, or half-conjunctions, do not link two sentences together. Rather, they link a sentence to a preceding discourse, logically or temporally. They may be combined with וֹ or precede subordinating conjunctions. In other contexts, they may serve as adverbs or as coordinating conjunctions. Unlike "full" coordinating conjunctions, they do not mark the B-clause of coordinated pairs.

§430. a. The particles כְּעַן, כְּעֶנֶת, כְּעֶת all mean "now," temporally, logically (introducing a consequence, "so now"), or introducing a new topic. Only כְּעַן is used in QA and in Daniel.

כְּעַן דָּנִיֵּאל יִתְקְרֵי וּפִשְׁרָה יְהַחֲוֵה	*now*, let Daniel be called and he will give the interpretation Dan 5:12, logical-temporal
וּכְעַן הֵן עַל־מַלְכָּא טָב	*so now*, if it is pleasing to the king Ez 5:17, logical
וכען אל תדחל אנה עמך	*so now*, fear not, I am with you 1QapGen 22:30, logical-temporal
כען עבדיך . . . כן אמרין	*therefore* your servants . . . say as follows A4 7:22 (Petition), logical

b. The verse-final placement of כְּעֶנֶת/כְּעֶת in MT Ezra (4:10, 11, 17, 7:12) obscures the function of these particles:

וּכְעֶנֶת: דְּנָה פַּרְשֶׁגֶן אִגַּרְתָּא דִּי שְׁלַחוּ	and now, this is the copy of the letter that they wrote Ezra 4:10–11, new topic
וּכְעֶנֶת: מִנִּי שִׂים טְעֵם	and now, from me a decree is given Ezra 7:12–13, new topic

261

§431. a. The frequent particles אֱדַיִן and בֵּאדַיִן mean "then, thereupon" and introduce new events into a narrative:

אֱדַיִן נְבוּכַדְנֶצַּר מַלְכָּא תְּוַהּ   *then* Nebuchadnezzar the king was astonished
    Dan 3:24

בֵּאדַיִן דָּרְיָוֶשׁ מַלְכָּא שָׂם טְעֵם   *then* Darius the king gave an order
    Ezra 6:1

באדין אתה עלי חרקנוש   *then* Horqanosh came to me
    1QapGen 20:21

b. In IA אֱדַיִן is used as a temporal adverb, "at that time," and only rarely as the discourse marker "thereupon" (באדין is not attested in IA). For "thereupon" in IA, see אחר (§435).

ב 24 למרחשון . . . אדין אמר ענני בר עזריה   on the 24th of Marheshwan . . . *at that time* said Anani son of Azariah
    B3 10:1

§432. The particle אַף "moreover, also," gives additional or summary material relevant to a preceding topic. Less frequently, it modifies particular words in a sentence (e.g., 11QtgJob 21:1 אף אנה "I too" = MT Job 32:10 אַף־אָנִי).

וְאַף קָדָמָיִךְ [קדמך] מַלְכָּא חֲבוּלָה לָא עַבְדֵת   *moreover*, O king, I have done no harm to you
    Dan 6:23

אף ללוט בר אחוהי פצא   he *also* rescued Lot his nephew
    1QapGen 22:11

מחאה לעלים כאיה לחנת אף לכל עבדיך אלפ[ן]   a blow for a servant, a rebuke for a maidservant – *indeed*, discipline for all your slaves
    C1 1:178 (Ahiqar)

§433. The particle לָהֵן (I) "therefore, so" introduces a sentence drawing a conclusion from the preceding discourse.

לָהֵן חֶלְמָא וּפִשְׁרֵהּ הַחֲוֹנִי   *so* tell me the dream and its interpretation
    Dan 2:6

להן אחדו בממר יעקוב   *therefore* hold on to the command of Jacob
    4Q542 1 i 7

§434. The exceptive quantifier לָהֵן (II) "except, unless" (§423) can serve as a discourse conjunction, "however, but," indicating a fact contrary to expectation, or a limitation of a generality.

לָהֵן מִן־דִּי הַרְגִּזוּ אֲבָהָתַנָא לֶאֱלָהּ שְׁמַיָּא

however, because our fathers angered the God of heaven (he put them into the power of Nebuchadnezzar)

Ez 5:12

להן ביתא זנך לא שליט אנת לזבנה

however, that house you do not have the right to sell

B2 4:6

§435. In IA, the particles אחר "then, after this" and קרבתא "immediately" are used to highlight new events.

אחר וידרנג זך לחיא אגרת שלח על נפין ברה

then that wicked Waidranga sent a letter to Naphaina his son

A4 7:6–7 (Petition)

קרבתא נבוסמסכן רביא אמר לכנותה

at once Nabusumiskun the servant said to his colleagues

C1 1:56 (Ahiqar)

###

CHAPTER 18

18

Reading Guide for Biblical Aramaic and Related Dialects

This guide is meant to direct the student through an inductive reading of Biblical Aramaic. For most effective use, consult the indicated sections of the textbook whenever they are mentioned, even if it seems repetitive. Repetition is the point.

DANIEL 3

v. 1–3 Before beginning to read, review the portions of the grammar introducing the orthography (§§21–33).

v. 1

נְבוּכַדְנֶצַּר מַלְכָּא עֲבַד צְלֵם דִּי־דְהַב רוּמֵהּ אַמִּין שִׁתִּין פְּתָיֵהּ אַמִּין שֵׁת אֲקִימֵהּ בְּבִקְעַת דּוּרָא בִּמְדִינַת בָּבֶל׃

Transliterate according to the conventions given in §21 and §23.

Read §25. Which words have *matres lectionis*?

Identify the letters בגדכפת. Why do some have *dagesh* (§28)?

Identify the vowel sign *shewa* (§74). Which ones are vocal and which silent?

v. 2

וּנְבוּכַדְנֶצַּר מַלְכָּא שְׁלַח לְמִכְנַשׁ ׀ לַאֲחַשְׁדַּרְפְּנַיָּא סִגְנַיָּא וּפַחֲוָתָא אֲדַרְגָּזְרַיָּא גְדָבְרַיָּא דְּתָבְרַיָּא תִּפְתָּיֵא וְכֹל שִׁלְטֹנֵי מְדִינָתָא לְמֵתֵא לַחֲנֻכַּת צַלְמָא דִּי הֲקֵים נְבוּכַדְנֶצַּר מַלְכָּא׃

Review §57. Syllabify the words of the verse by drawing a line between the syllables or by writing them separately in transliteration.

Begin to learn Rules 1 and 2 (§78). In your syllabification, which open syllables are stressed and which are not? (§§31, 56).

Identify the gutturals (§34c) and read over §§75–77.

Go back to v. 1 and syllabify, noting the vowels in each syllable.

v. 3

בֵּאדַ֡יִן מִֽתְכַּנְּשִׁ֡ין אֲחַשְׁדַּרְפְּנַיָּ֡א סִגְנַיָּ֣א וּֽפַחֲוָתָ֡א אֲדַרְגָּֽזְרַיָּא֩ גְדָ֨בְרַיָּ֤א דְּתָבְרַיָּא֙ תִּפְתָּיֵ֔א וְכֹ֖ל שִׁלְטֹנֵ֣י מְדִֽינָתָ֑א
לַחֲנֻכַּ֣ת צַלְמָ֔א דִּ֥י הֲקֵ֖ים נְבוּכַדְנֶצַּ֣ר מַלְכָּ֑א וְקָֽאֲמִין֙ [וְקָיְמִ֔ין] לָקֳבֵל֙ צַלְמָ֔א דִּ֥י הֲקֵ֖ים נְבוּכַדְנֶצַּֽר׃

Noun inflection. Read §§81–90. In this verse, pick out the nominal inflections that appear and identify them by declension.

Short and long vowels. Begin to familiarize yourself with §§61–71. In general, short vowels are indicated by vowel signs only and long vowels other than וֹ are accompanied by *matres lectionis*, but there are unpredictable exceptions (§27). The word שִׁלְטֹנֵי has a defective spelling. How do we know it is defective? (§64e).

Note the Ketiv-Qere variant (§33) in the word וְקָֽאֲמִין. Which word is Ketiv and which Qere?

Compare the absolute צְלֵם (v. 1) and צַלְמָא here. Read over §101.

vv. 1–3 inflection. The following section will review the first three verses and introduce verbal inflection.

v. 1

נְבוּכַדְנֶצַּ֣ר מַלְכָּ֗א עֲבַד֙ צְלֵ֣ם דִּֽי־דְהַ֔ב רוּמֵהּ֙ אַמִּ֣ין שִׁתִּ֔ין פְּתָיֵ֖הּ אַמִּ֣ין שֵׁ֑ת אֲקִימֵהּ֙ בְּבִקְעַ֣ת דּוּרָ֔א בִּמְדִינַ֖ת בָּבֶֽל׃

נְבוּכַדְנֶצַּר: *Nebuchadnezzar*, personal name. מַלְכָּא. *The king.*

עֲבַד: *Made.* Read §§207–219. This verb is G stem, 3ms (third masculine singular) from the root עבד. Why does this verb have a *ḥateph* vowel (§24) in the first syllable? (§78, Rule 4b).

צְלֵם דִּֽי־דְהַב: *An image of gold.* Both nouns are 1st declension, abs. state (§86). Although similar in vocalization, they have different underlying patterns. Read §98 and begin to familiarize yourself with the patterns in §§101ff. and §105.

The particle דִּי has many uses and you will run into it a lot. Here it is equivalent to English "of." See §135.

רוּמֵהּ אַמִּין שִׁתִּין: *Its height was sixty cubits.* The first sentence in the verse was a verbal clause; this one is a copular clause (sometimes called a verbless clause). Read over §373.

265

רוּמֵהּ: *Its height.* The suffix on the noun רוּם "height" is the 3ms suffix. On nouns, pronominal suffixes can be translated usually as possessives. See §128. Don't worry about memorizing paradigms at this point; you'll be seeing the most common suffixes many times.

אַמִּין: *Cubits.* The dictionary form of this word (i.e., the absolute singular) is אַמָּה; that is, the singular is of the 2nd declension, and the plural, as seen here, is of the 1st declension (§93). The gender is feminine and does not change according to declension.

שִׁתִּין: *Sixty.* See §166 and identify this form in Table 9. Cardinal numerals can occur either before or after the noun that they are quantifying.

פְּתָיֵהּ אַמִּין שֵׁת: *Its width was six cubits.* Compare the forms in this copular clause (§373) to the previous one. You will recognize the 3ms suffix on פְּתָיֵהּ and the word אַמִּין.

שֵׁת: *Six.* Compare with the word for "sixty" above and find this form in Table 9. What declension is this word? See §83 and §91d. Read over §164.

Cognate alert: The Hebrew word for "six" is שֵׁשׁ and "sixty" is שִׁשִּׁים. Read §38 and find the common phoneme from which each form descended.

אֲקִימֵהּ: *He set it up.* Start to get an idea of the stem system of Aramaic. This is a C stem verb (§232), 3ms of the suffix conjugation (SC) (see §212). Note the preformative א ʾaleph (for the "Aphˁel"); in most forms of the C stem SC, the preformative is ה. The root is קוּם, a "hollow" verb (§271).

The 3ms suffix on the verb here, like pronominal suffixes on verbs generally, indicates the direct object (§130).

בְּבִקְעַת דּוּרָא בִּמְדִינַת בָּבֶל: *In the plain of the wall, in the city of Babylon.* Note the construct forms ending in -*at* of the 2nd declension (§§87, 90). Read about the construct phrase in §153.

v. 2

וּנְבוּכַדְנֶצַּר מַלְכָּא שְׁלַח לְמִכְנַשׁ לַאֲחַשְׁדַּרְפְּנַיָּא סִגְנַיָּא וּפַחֲוָתָא אֲדַרְגָּזְרַיָּא גְּדָבְרַיָּא דְּתָבְרַיָּא תִּפְתָּיֵא וְכֹל שִׁלְטֹנֵי מְדִינָתָא לְמֵתֵא לַחֲנֻכַּת צַלְמָא דִּי הֲקֵים נְבוּכַדְנֶצַּר מַלְכָּא:

שְׁלַח: *He sent.* Compare this form with עֲבַד in v. 1 and review §§215–217.

לְמִכְנַשׁ: *To gather.* For the infinitive of the G stem, see §225.

לֵאֲחַשְׁדַּרְפְּנַיָּא סִגְנַיָּא וּפַחֲוָתָא אֲדַרְגָּזְרַיָּא גְדָבְרַיָּא דְּתָבְרַיָּא תִּפְתָּיֵא: *The satraps, prefects, and governors, the counselors, treasurers, legal experts, magistrates.* Most of these nouns are words borrowed from Persian or Akkadian with Aramaic nominal inflections (§122). תִּפְתָּיֵא is inflected like a gentilic (§97). Look up the words in HALOT or LBA.

Compare the לְ preposition on לְמִכְנַשׁ and לֵאֲחַשְׁדַּרְפְּנַיָּא. How do you account for the difference in vowel? (§76b).

Note also that the לְ on לְמִכְנַשׁ and לֵאֲחַשְׁדַּרְפְּנַיָּא has different functions (§§178f, 359a).

The list of nouns beginning with לֵאֲחַשְׁדַּרְפְּנַיָּא and ending with מְדִינָתָא forms a single constituent (that is, a word or groups of words functioning as a unit to fill one grammatical role in the sentence). This is a compound noun phrase (§142) serving as direct object.

וְכֹל שִׁלְטֹנֵי מְדִינָתָא: *And all the rulers of the provinces.* This is a series of three nouns forming a construct phrase (review the construct noun phrase in §§153ff.). Identify the noun declensions for each word.

לְמֵתֵא לַחֲנֻכַּת צַלְמָא: *To come to the dedication of the image.* לְמֵתֵא is also an infinitive, from the weak root אתי, G stem "come." See §225 again. We will deal with weak roots (roots with one or more unstable consonants) in greater depth later.

לַחֲנֻכַּת צַלְמָא: Compare to בְּבִקְעַת דּוּרָא בִּמְדִינַת בָּבֶל above and review §90 and §153. Identify the noun declensions.

דִּי הֲקֵים נְבוּכַדְנֶצַּר מַלְכָּא: *Which king Nebuchadnezzar set up.* Here is דִּי again, this time as the relative pronoun (§135) instead of as the genitive "of." It introduces a relative clause. Read over §148.

הֲקֵים: Compare to אֲקִימֵהּ in v. 1. The parsing is the same (C stem SC 3ms < the root קום), but without the 3ms pronominal suffix and with preformative ה instead of א. Review §232.

v. 3

בֵּאדַיִן מִתְכַּנְּשִׁין אֲחַשְׁדַּרְפְּנַיָּא סִגְנַיָּא וּפַחֲוָתָא אֲדַרְגָּזְרַיָּא גְדָבְרַיָּא דְּתָבְרַיָּא תִּפְתָּיֵא וְכֹל שִׁלְטֹנֵי מְדִינָתָא לַחֲנֻכַּת צַלְמָא דִּי הֲקֵים נְבוּכַדְנֶצַּר מַלְכָּא וְקָאֲמִין [וקימין] לָקֳבֵל צַלְמָא דִּי הֲקֵים נְבוּכַדְנֶצַּר:

בֵּאדַ֫יִן מִתְכַּנְּשִׁין אֲחַשְׁדַּרְפְּנַיָּא ... מְדִינָתָא: *Then were gathering the satraps. etc.* (as in v. 2).

בֵּאדַ֫יִן: See §431. We will meet this word many times.

מִתְכַּנְּשִׁין: What is the inflection? See §89. The form is a participle of the tD stem (§242). This stem often has a passive, reflexive, or reciprocal meaning (§327), and the participle is often past progressive in tense (§309), as it is here.

The nouns that follow the participle are the subject of the sentence. In this sentence, the participles play the role of predicate adjective in a copular clause (§§373, 379) and agree with the subject (§355).

דִּי הֲקִים: Once again, דִּי. What is its role? See previous verse.

[וְקָאֲמִין [וקימין: *And were standing.* Compare this ending with that of מִתְכַּנְּשִׁין (§89). This is another participle, of the G stem. See §223. The long vowel ō under the first root letter, in this case ק, is diagnostic of the G stem participle. For the G stem participle in hollow verbs, see §273.

Note the difference in *valence* between the G stem of קום (intransitive) and the C stem (transitive). Read §323.

לָקֳבֵל: *Facing.* For this prepositional form, see §200.

> REVIEW: Verbal forms: עֲבַד, שְׁלַח, הֲקִים; לְמֶתָא, לְמִכְבַּשׁ, מִתְכַּנְּשִׁין, קָיְמִין (Qere). Suffixes: רוּמֵהּ, אֲקִימֵהּ, פְּתָיֵהּ. Particles: דִּי, לְ, בְּ, לָקֳבֵל.

v. 4

וְכָרוֹזָא קָרֵא בְחָ֑יִל לְכוֹן אָמְרִין עַמְמַיָּא אֻמַּיָּא וְלִשָּׁנַיָּא:

> REVIEW: Transliterate the verse, and note the syllabification.

וְכָרוֹזָא קָרֵא בְחָ֑יִל: *And the herald called out/was calling out loudly* (lit., "with force"). וְכָרוֹזָא: For the noun pattern, see §109. קָרֵא: Note again the long ō in the first syllable and read §223 again. G stem participle ms, from the root קרי "say aloud, call." The final *y* of the root is "weak" (unstable) and is not present throughout the paradigm; the final *ʾaleph* in the orthography is not part of the root, but is a *mater* (§261; review §25). בְחָ֑יִל: Preposition בְּ and the noun חַ֫יִל

"strength, force." Read §179e. For the noun pattern, see §103; for the pausal vocalization here, see §32.

לְכוֹן אֲמְרִין: *To you it is commanded.* לְכוֹן: Preposition לְ with 2mp pronominal suffix. For the suffix, see §128; for the use of לְ, see §177b. Frequently used prepositions have very general meanings and are best observed in context. Don't make an effort to memorize the meanings; you'll pick them up inductively over time.

אֲמְרִין: Compare with קָיְמִין above. What form is this? (§223) For the "impersonal" use of the participle, see §358b. The G stem of אמר means not only "say" but also "command."

עֲמְמַיָּא אֻמַיָּא וְלִשָּׁנַיָּא: *O peoples, tribes, and tongues.* What nominal ending is this? (§89) For the vocative use of the determined state, see §85e. For the form of עֲמַמַיָּא, see §104.

v. 5

בְּעִדָּנָא דִּי־תִשְׁמְעוּן קָל קַרְנָא מַשְׁרוֹקִיתָא קִיתָרוֹס [קתרוס] סַבְּכָא פְּסַנְתֵּרִין סוּמְפֹּנְיָה וְכֹל זְנֵי זְמָרָא תִּפְּלוּן וְתִסְגְּדוּן לְצֶלֶם דַּהֲבָא דִּי הֲקֵים נְבוּכַדְנֶצַּר מַלְכָּא:

בְּעִדָּנָא דִּי־תִשְׁמְעוּן: *At the time that you hear.* בְּעִדָּנָא: Prep. בְּ + noun עִדָּן "time"; for the pattern, see §110. דִּי־תִשְׁמְעוּן: די in its role as relative pronoun (§135), introducing a relative clause (§148). תִשְׁמְעוּן: Up to now we've only seen suffix conjugation (SC) verbs and participles; this is a prefix conjugation (PC) verb (see §213). PC verbs have prefixes as well as suffixes for inflection. In Aramaic, the function of the PC is mainly for future tense plus modality (see §291b). This form is the G stem 2mp from the root שמע "hear."

קָל קַרְנָא מַשְׁרוֹקִיתָא קַיתְרוֹס [קתרוס] סַבְּכָא פְּסַנְתֵּרִין סוּמְפֹּנְיָה וְכֹל זְנֵי זְמָרָא: *The sound of the horn, pipe, lyre, trigon, harp, bagpipe, and all kinds of musical instruments.* This long phrase is one constituent, being the direct object of the verb תִשְׁמְעוּן. In structure it is a construct phrase (read §153), of which קָל "sound" is the head noun, and all of the following words are a compound noun phrase (§142), serving as the dependent part of the construct phrase. Read §154b.

קַרְנָא: Compare to מַלְכָּא and צַלְמָא and review §101a. The gender of this noun is feminine.

מַשְׁרוֹקִיתָא: What declension is this noun? §90d.

קַיתְרוֹס [קתרוס] סַבְּכָא פְּסַנְתֵּרִין סוּמְפֹּנְיָה: These are loanwords from Greek (§122) and are not inflected with Aramaic declensional endings, despite their appearance. They are best studied in a lexicon (see HALOT and the commentaries for more detailed information). Note the Ketiv-Qere and review §33.

וְכֹל זְנֵי זְמָרָא: Compare to וְכֹל שִׁלְטֹנֵי מְדִינָתָא above. A construct phrase, as a nominal constituent, can be a part of a compound phrase; that is, phrases can be embedded in other phrases. זְנֵי: 1st decl. cstr. pl. of זַן "kind," a Persian loanword (§122). זְמָרָא: *qaṭāl* noun pattern (§108).

תִּפְּלוּן וְתִסְגְּדוּן לְצֶלֶם דַּהֲבָא: *You must fall down and worship the image of gold.* Compare תִּפְּלוּן וְתִסְגְּדוּן to תִּשְׁמְעוּן above and review §220. You should be able to identify the root of תִסְגְּדוּן; what about תִּפְּלוּן? See §42 and §253. The root is נפל, G stem "fall": *tinpəlūn > tippəlūn*.

לְצֶלֶם דַּהֲבָא: Prep. לְ + construct noun phrase. Compare to צְלֶם דִּי־דְהַב in v. 1. Compare צְלֵם, צֶלֶם, and צַלְמָא and review §101. דַּהֲבָא: Compare to דְהַב and review §105. Why is there a *hateph* vowel in דַּהֲבָא? Review §76a. Why would this syllable normally be closed? Review Rule 2, §78 (syncopation).

v. 6

וּמַן־דִּי־לָא יִפֵּל וְיִסְגֻּד בַּהּ־שַׁעֲתָא יִתְרְמֵא לְגוֹא־אַתּוּן נוּרָא יָקִדְתָּא:

וּמַן־דִּי־לָא יִפֵּל וְיִסְגֻּד: *And whoever does not fall down and worship.* The word מַן means "who"; when combined with דִּי it means "whoever." See §151. The principal negative particle is לָא; in this sentence it negates the two following verbs (§386). יִפֵּל וְיִסְגֻּד: Compare with תִּפְּלוּן וְתִסְגְּדוּן above and review the table at §220. What forms are these? See also §253. The theme vowel (§210) in each verb is what? Why does the theme vowel not appear in תִּפְּלוּן וְתִסְגְּדוּן? (§78, Rule 1).

יִפֵּל וְיִסְגֻּד: These PC verbs are modal (§301); specifically, *epistemic* modality (§291b). The event may or may not happen (=epistemic).

בַּהּ־שַׁעֲתָא יִתְרְמֵא: *At that very moment shall be thrown.* בַּהּ: Prep. בְּ and the 3fs pronominal suffix (§128). Lit., "in it." The 3fs suffix refers ahead by "anticipation" to the following word שַׁעֲתָא. Identify the form (§90). For the noun שָׁעָה "moment, hour," see §100. The *patah* in the first syllable is irregular.

בַּהּ־שַׁעֲתָא: "in it, the moment" is idiomatic for "at that very moment" (§175d). יִתְרְמֵא: Compare with יִפֵּל וְיִסְגֻּד above. The T stems (§237) are frequently passive in meaning. This is tG PC 3ms (§238), passive of the G stem root רמי "throw." This is a III-y weak verb (§266b), which we will cover in more detail later.

לְגוֹא־אַתּוּן נוּרָא יָקֶדְתָּא: *Into the furnace of burning fire.* לְגוֹא: Prep. לְ + noun גוּ "interior"; the combination yields a derived preposition (§178g) "into" (lit., "to in"). Note that *-aw-* of the noun contracts to ō, and read §72. (The "silent" א on the end of the word is not etymological (§26c)). אַתּוּן נוּרָא יָקֶדְתָּא: Construct phrase, head noun אַתּוּן, dependent on noun phrase consisting in turn of a head-modifier construction, with the head word נוּרָא "fire" modified by יָקֶדְתָּא. Note the long ō under the *y* of יָקֶדְתָּא; what kind of form is this? §148d and §223. Based on the inflection of יָקֶדְתָּא, what is the gender of נוּרָא?

REVIEW: Additional verbs יָקֶדְתָּא יִתְרְמֵא יִסְגֻד יִפֵּל תִּסְגְּדוּן תִּפְּלוּן תִּשְׁמְעוּן אָמְרִין קָרֵא .

> Exercise: (1) Write out all the PC forms of the G stem of the roots סגד and נפל, with vowel points. (See the table in §220.) (2) נוּרָא יָקֶדְתָּא is in the determined state; write out the same phrase in the absolute state. (3) Identify all the construct noun phrases found in vv. 1–6.

COGNATES: The Hebrew cognates to קָל and לָא are קוֹל and לֹא (§67e). Can you identify any other instances above of Aramaic ō ◌ָ = Hebrew ō?

v. 7

כָּל־קֳבֵל דְּנָה בֵּהּ־זִמְנָא כְּדִי שָׁמְעִין כָּל־עַמְמַיָּא קָל קַרְנָא מַשְׁרוֹקִיתָא קִיתָרוֹס [קתרוס] שַׂבְּכָא פְּסַנְטֵרִין וְכֹל זְנֵי זְמָרָא נָפְלִין כָּל־עַמְמַיָּא אֻמַיָּא וְלִשָּׁנַיָּא סָגְדִין לְצֶלֶם דַּהֲבָא דִּי הֲקֵים נְבוּכַדְנֶצַּר מַלְכָּא:

כָּל־קֳבֵל דְּנָה בֵּהּ־זִמְנָא כְּדִי שָׁמְעִין כָּל־עַמְמַיָּא: *Accordingly, at that exact time, when all the peoples heard (were hearing).* כָּל־קֳבֵל is related to לְקֳבֵל above (v. 3) by the addition of the preposition כְּ. The meaning "facing opposite X" (לְקֳבֵל) develops into "corresponding to X," so that כָּל־קֳבֵל דְּנָה means "accordingly, because of this." We will meet כל קבל again. (See §76b and §200d.)

בֵּהּ־זִמְנָא: Lit., "in it, the time." This is the same sort of construction seen in בַּהּ־שַׁעֲתָא above, with almost identical meaning. What is the suffix in בֵּהּ? (§128) What therefore is the gender of זִמְנָא?

כְּדִי is composed of כְּ and דִי, the idiomatic meaning being "when," "at the time that." See §418.

שָׁמְעִין: Compare with אָמְרִין and קָיְמִין above. What is this form? §223. Compare with תִּשְׁמְעוּן (v. 5). עַמְמַיָּא: see v. 4.

> WORD ORDER: Note that so far we have seen sentences where the subject comes first (v. 1, 2, 4) and those in which the verb comes before the subject (v. 2, 3, and here). Word order in Biblical Aramaic is free in the sense that no one order is obligatory; take a look at §362.

קֵל קַרְנָא: For this and the nouns which follow, see v. 5 above, although סומפניה is missing here, and פְּסַנְטֵרִין is spelled differently. Borrowed words are sometimes inconsistent in their spelling.

נָפְלִין כָּל־עַמְמַיָּא אֻמַיָּא וְלִשָּׁנַיָּא סָגְדִין לְצֶלֶם דַּהֲבָא: *All the people, tribes, and tongues were falling down, worshipping the image of gold.* The forms נפלין and סגדין should give you no trouble at this point. (§223) For the verbal meaning, read over §311.

עַמְמַיָּא אֻמַיָּא וְלִשָּׁנַיָּא: See v. 4. Anomalously, אֻמַיָּא has no *dagesh* (§28) as it does in v. 4. Why is it anomalous? (§78, Rule 1).

v. 8

כָּל־קֳבֵל דְּנָה בֵּהּ־זִמְנָא קְרִבוּ גֻּבְרִין כַּשְׂדָּאִין וַאֲכַלוּ קַרְצֵיהוֹן דִּי יְהוּדָיֵא:

כָּל־קֳבֵל דְּנָה בֵּהּ־זִמְנָא: Exactly as in the previous verse.

קְרִבוּ גֻּבְרִין כַּשְׂדָּאִין: *Chaldean men approached.* Again we have the verb (קְרִבוּ) preceding the subject. This is our first SC verb in the plural; note the penultimate accent and the *i*-theme vowel (§§210, 218): G stem SC 3mp from קרב "approach, draw near."

גֻּבְרִין כַּשְׂדָּאִין: A noun phrase consisting of noun (גֻּבְרִין) + attributive adjective (כַּשְׂדָּאִין). What is the declension, number, and state of גֻּבְרִין? For the plural of *qVṭl* nouns, see §102. The dictionary form is גְּבַר "man." כַּשְׂדָּאִין: For the mp form of adjectives ending in -ɔ̄y, see §97.

וַאֲכַלוּ קַרְצֵיהוֹן דִּי יְהוּדָיֵא: *They accused the Judeans.* The combination of the verb אֲכַל "eat" and the noun קְרַץ "piece (?)" means "to accuse" and is idiomatic, that is, the meaning of the phrase is not derivable from its parts.

אֲכַלוּ: Compare to קְרִבוּ, and read §217. Both verbs are G stem SC 3mp, this one from the root אכל.

קַרְצֵיהוֹן: What is the suffix on this word? Read over §129. Add 3mp הוֹן to the list of suffixes encountered: 3ms (v. 1), 2mp (v. 4), 3fs (v. 6).

קַרְצֵיהוֹן דִּי יְהוּדָיֵא: A genitive phrase with דִּי with a suffix on the head noun (§162). Lit., "their pieces (?) of the Judeans."

So far we have seen all the principal forms of the genitive phrase: construct (e.g., זְנֵי זְמָרָא, review §153), periphrastic genitive with דִּי (e.g., צְלֵם דִּי דְהַב, review §160), and periphrastic genitive with דִּי and suffixed head noun (§162).

יְהוּדָיֵא: This is also a gentilic adjective, like כַּשְׂדָּאֵין above. For the form of the plural ending, see §97.

v. 9

עֲנוֹ וְאָמְרִין לִנְבוּכַדְנֶצַּר מַלְכָּא מַלְכָּא לְעָלְמִין חֱיִי:

עֲנוֹ וְאָמְרִין: *They answered and said.* אָמְרִין you have seen before (v. 4), but what is עֲנוֹ? Take a look at §256. The ending וֹ *ō* is the 3mp SC ending on III-*y* verbs, that is, verbs whose third root letter is *y*, to be compared to the usual וּ *-ū* ending on other roots (as in קְרִבוּ and אֲכַלוּ). The parsing is G SC 3mp from the root ענה. Other forms from III-*y* roots we have seen are קְרָא (v. 4), לְמֵתֵא (v. 2), יִתְרְמֵא (v. 6).

For the expression, "answered and said," see §295.

מַלְכָּא לְעָלְמִין חֱיִי: *O king, live forever!* מַלְכָּא: For the vocative, see again §85e. לְעָלְמִין: Prep. לְ + the noun עָלַם "unlimited time, age." Why does the *patah* in the second syllable become *shewa* when ין -*īn* is added? (§78, Rule 1). "For ages," "forever." §350g. חֱיִי: G stem ms imperative from the root חיי "live." Read §222 and §260. Add this to your collection of III-*y* root forms.

REVIEW: Suffixes הוֹן, כוֹן, ־ַה, ־ֵה. Suffix conjugation: עֲבַד, אֲקִימָה, הָקֵים, שְׁלַח, קְרִבוּ, אֲכַלוּ, עֲנוֹ.

v. 10

אַנְתְּה [אנת] מַלְכָּא שָׂמְתָּ טְעֵם דִּי כָל־אֱנָשׁ דִּי־יִשְׁמַע קָל קַרְנָא מַשְׁרוֹקִיתָא קַיתְרֹוס [קתרס] שַׂבְּכָא פְּסַנְתֵּרִין וְסִיפֹּנְיָה [וסופניה] וְכֹל זְנֵי זְמָרָא יִפֵּל וְיִסְגֻּד לְצֶלֶם דַּהֲבָא:

אַנְתְּה [אנת] מַלְכָּא שָׂמְתָּ טְעֵם: *You, O king, gave a decree.* אַנְתְּה, 2ms independent personal pronoun. See §124. The Ketiv-Qere (§33) tells us that the reading tradition pronounces this as *ʾant*; the Ketiv preserves the ancient pronunciation *ʾantā*.

שָׂמְתָּ: Another SC verb; the inflectional sufformative -*tā* is 2ms. See §212c for the inflection. The root שׂים is "hollow," like קוּם with הָקֵים (§272). So far the inflections of the SC we have seen are 3ms (zero, as in שְׁלַח), 3mp (-*ū* as in אֲכַלוּ, -*ō* as in עֲנוֹ), and now 2ms -*tā*. G SC 2ms < שׂים "give, put, place."

טְעֵם: Review §101b, d; this frequent noun is of the **qaṭl* type, with stress shift to the separating vowel. For the *dagesh* in the first letter, see §28c.

דִּי כָל־אֱנָשׁ דִּי־יִשְׁמַע: *That every person who will hear.* Another use of דִּי is introducing a clause that is a direct object (see §341), as in the first occurrence here. כָל־אֱנָשׁ: We have encountered the quantifier כֹּל in vv. 2, 3, 5, 7 (3 times), and here. The underlying base is *kul(l)* (see §104). אֱנָשׁ: *qiṭāl* noun pattern (§108); here, "person, individual."

דִּי־יִשְׁמַע: What use of די? Review §135 and §148. יִשְׁמַע: Compare יִפֵּל, יִסְגֻּד, יִתְרְמֵא (v. 6). What form is this? §213.

יִפֵּל וְיִסְגֻּד לְצֶלֶם דַּהֲבָא and the words following are as in v. 6 (with some spelling variations). קָל קַרְנָא Compare to v. 5 and translate.

v. 11
Compare v. 11 to v. 6 and translate.

v. 12
אִיתַי גֻּבְרִין יְהוּדָאיִן דִּי־מַנִּיתָ יָתְהוֹן עַל־עֲבִידַת מְדִינַת בָּבֶל שַׁדְרַךְ מֵישַׁךְ וַעֲבֵד נְגוֹ גֻּבְרַיָּא אִלֵּךְ לָא־שָׂמוּ
עֲלָיךְ [עֲלָךְ] מַלְכָּא טְעֵם לֵאלָהָיךְ [לֵאלָהָךְ] לָא פָלְחִין וּלְצֶלֶם דַּהֲבָא דִּי הֲקֵימְתָּ לָא סָגְדִין: ס

אִיתַי גֻּבְרִין יְהוּדָאיִן: *There are Judean men.* אִיתַי is the existential particle (see §380) and expresses the same idea as English "there is/are," Hebrew יֵשׁ, etc. The complement of אִיתַי is normally a noun or noun phrase in the absolute state. גֻּבְרִין: See v. 8. יְהוּדָאיִן: See יְהוּדָיֵא v. 8 and review §97. (We expect יְהוּדָאיִן, as in כַּשְׂדָּאיִן.)

דִּי־מַנִּיתָ יָתְהוֹן עַל־עֲבִידַת מְדִינַת בָּבֶל: *Whom you have appointed over the work of the city of Babylon.* דִּי־מַנִּיתָ יָתְהוֹן: די as relative pronoun. מַנִּיתָ: Compare the inflection on שָׂמְתָ above (v. 10). This is another SC 2ms form, this time of the D stem (read through §227). The hallmark of the D stem is the *d*oubled middle root letter, in this case נ. This is also a III-y weak root (§263), מני "appoint" (D stem; G stem "count").

יָתְהוֹן: You may recognize הוֹן as the 3mp suffix (cp. קַרְצֵיהוֹן v. 8). The preposition יָת has no semantic content and only is used to indicate a definite direct object (§359b). יָתְהוֹן here is a "shadow" pronoun of the object that the די clause is modifying; read §148a, c.

עַל־עֲבִידַת מְדִינַת בָּבֶל: Preposition עַל (§188e) + construct phrase of three nouns (review §154b). For the latter two nouns, see v. 1. עבידה: *qaṭīl-at* noun pattern (§108).

שַׁדְרַךְ מֵישַׁךְ וַעֲבֵד נְגוֹ: For these proper names, see the lexicons and the commentaries. "Shadrach, Meshach, and Abed-nego."

גֻּבְרַיָּא אִלֵּךְ לָא־שָׂמוּ עֲלָיךְ [עֲלָךְ] מַלְכָּא טְעֵם: *Those men have not followed your order, O king.* גֻּבְרַיָּא: Cp. גֻּבְרִין v. 8 above. What form? אִלֵּךְ: See §136. שָׂמוּ: Compare with קְרִבוּ, אֲכַלוּ (v. 8), and שָׂמְתָ (v. 10). What form? See §§212, 272a. Parse.

[עלך] עֲלָיךְ: Prep. עַל (as above) + 2ms pron. suff., second series (§129). Note that some prepositions are inflected like 1st decl. plural nouns when suffixes are added. The *y* of the Ketiv is a remnant of a time when it was pronounced: *ʿaláyk(ā)*. The Qere עֲלָךְ is the same as later JLA.

טְעֵם: See v. 10 above. Lit., "they have not put on you, O king, decree" = idiomatically, "they have not followed your decree."

לֵאלָהָיךְ [לאלהך] לָא פָלְחִין: *Your gods they do not serve.* Again note the Ketiv-Qere variant with the 2ms suffix. The noun אֱלָה "god" (§63f, and review §108a) is plural before the suffix. For the vocalization *lē-* at the beginning of the word, see §48. Transliterate *lēlɔhɔ̄k*. The לְ indicates the direct object (§359).

פָלְחִין. Cf. אָמְרִין, שָׁמְעִין, נָפְלִין, סָגְדִין. What form? §223. For participles without subjects, see §358a.

וּלְצֶלֶם דַּהֲבָא דִּי הֲקֵימְתָּ לָא סָגְדִין: Compare הֲקֵימְתָּ to מַנִּיתָ, שָׂמְתָּ, and הֲקֵים, and translate the sentence.

> Exercise: Consider the vowel sign *qameṣ* ָ in the following words: כָּל־קֳבֵל, לָא, בָּבֶל, לְעָלְמִין, שָׂמוּ, וְכָרוֹזָא. Which would you transliterate as long *ɔ̄* and which short *ɔ*? Review §67 and §64c.

v. 13

בֵּאדַיִן נְבוּכַדְנֶצַּר בִּרְגַז וַחֲמָה אֲמַר לְהַיְתָיָה לְשַׁדְרַךְ מֵישַׁךְ וַעֲבֵד נְגוֹ בֵּאדַיִן גֻּבְרַיָּא אִלֵּךְ הֵיתָיוּ קֳדָם מַלְכָּא:

בֵּאדַיִן נְבוּכַדְנֶצַּר בִּרְגַז וַחֲמָה אֲמַר: *Then Nebuchadnezzar in anger and wrath commanded.* בֵּאדַיִן: See v. 3. בִּרְגַז וַחֲמָה: Prep. בְּ + compound noun phrase (§142). אֲמַר: We've seen the participle (אמרין); this is the SC. The parsing should give you no trouble. Why is there a *ḥaṭeph* vowel under the *ʾaleph*? (§219).

לְהַיְתָיָה לְשַׁדְרַךְ מֵישַׁךְ וַעֲבֵד נְגוֹ: *To bring Shadrach, Meshach, and Abed-nego.* לְהַיְתָיָה is the C stem infinitive from the root אתי (§283b). The G stem inf. was encountered in v. 2 (לְמֵתֵא). For the relation of the C stem to the G stem, read over §§323–324. We'll be seeing more of אתי.

בֵּאדַיִן גֻּבְרַיָּא אִלֵּךְ הֵיתָיוּ קֳדָם מַלְכָּא: For the first three words see previous verses. הֵיתָיוּ: The ending *-ū* will probably ring a bell (SC 3mp). The stem is Cp (causative passive), vocalized irregularly. Note §235 and §283c. Such infrequent irregular forms should be noted but not necessarily memorized.

קְדָם: Read §203, especially b. Translate the entire sentence.

v. 14

עֲנֵה נְבֻכַדְנֶצַּר וְאָמַר לְהֹון הַצְדָּא שַׁדְרַךְ מֵישַׁךְ וַעֲבֵד נְגֹו לֵאלָהַי לָא אִיתֵיכוֹן פָּלְחִין וּלְצֶלֶם דַּהֲבָא דִּי הֲקֵימֶת לָא סָגְדִין:

עֲנֵה נְבֻכַדְנֶצַּר וְאָמַר לְהֹון: *N. answered and said to them.* For עֲנֵה וְאָמַר, compare עֲנֹו וְאָמְרִין above v. 9. The *qameṣ* ◌ָ in the first syllable indicates the G stem participle – ms in this case, like קָרֵא in v. 4. The second syllable vowel is normally an *i*-class vowel (§223), so why does אָמַר have short *a*? (§78, Rule 4a). לְהֹון: Compare קַרְצֵיהֹון (v. 8), יָתְהֹון (v. 12), לְכֹון (v. 4).

הַצְדָּא שַׁדְרַךְ מֵישַׁךְ וַעֲבֵד נְגֹו לֵאלָהַי לָא אִיתֵיכוֹן פָּלְחִין: *Is it so, Shadrach, Meshach, and Abed-nego? My gods you really are not serving?* הַצְדָּא – not a common expression – is composed of the interrogative particle הֲ (see §390) and adverb צְדָא "in truth." לֵאלָהַי לָא אִיתֵיכוֹן פָּלְחִין: Cp. v. 12. לֵאלָהַי: For the suffixal ending *-ay*, see §129. לָא אִיתֵיכוֹן: For אִיתי, see v. 12; but here it serves as copula (the "be, is, are" word) and the suffix כון (2mp) as the subject of the copular clause (§345).

וּלְצֶלֶם דַּהֲבָא דִּי הֲקֵימֶת לָא סָגְדִין: Compare v. 5, v. 12. For הֲקֵימֶת, cp. הָקֵים (SC 3ms, v. 2, etc.), הֲקֵימְתָ (SC 2ms, v. 12). This is 1cs (see §§60b, 277).

v. 15a

כְּעַן הֵן אִיתֵיכוֹן עֲתִידִין דִּי בְעִדָּנָא דִּי־תִשְׁמְעֹון קָל קַרְנָא מַשְׁרוֹקִיתָא קַיתְרוֹס [קתרס] שַׂבְּכָא פְּסַנְתֵּרִין וְסוּמְפֹּנְיָה וְכֹל זְנֵי זְמָרָא תִּפְּלֹון וְתִסְגְּדוּן לְצַלְמָא דִי־עַבְדֵת

כְּעַן הֵן אִיתֵיכוֹן עֲתִידִין: *Now, are you indeed ready. . . ?* כְּעַן: A particle connecting parts of a discourse; see §430. הֵן is the normal conditional particle "if," but here it seems to be used more like an interrogative (if it is a conditional protasis, there is no apodosis to follow). עֲתִידִין: **qaṭīl* pattern adjective (§108); "prepared, ready." אִיתֵיכוֹן עֲתִידִין is like לָא אִיתֵיכוֹן פָּלְחִין in the previous verse.

For the balance of v. 15a, see v. 5 above.

לְצַלְמָא דִי־עַבְדֵת: *the image I have made.* עַבְדֵת: The first SC 1cs form in this chapter was הֲקֵימֶת in the previous verse; this is the second. Note the final *-eṯ* or *-ɛṯ* in the two verbs and cf. §237b. G stem SC 1cs < עבד (see v. 1 for the 3ms).

v. 15b

וְהֵן לָא תִסְגְּדוּן בַּהּ־שַׁעֲתָה תִתְרְמֹון לְגֹוא־אַתּוּן נוּרָא יָקִדְתָּא וּמַן־הוּא אֱלָהּ דִּי יְשֵׁיזְבִנְכֹון מִן־יְדָי:

וְהֵן לָא תִסְגְּדוּן בַּהּ־שַׁעֲתָה תִתְרְמֹון: *And if you do not worship, at that very moment you will be thrown.* הֵן: Cf. v. 15a. תִסְגְּדוּן: Cf. v. 5. בַּהּ־שַׁעֲתָה: Cf. v. 6. תִתְרְמֹון: Cp. תִשְׁמְעוּן, תִּפְּלוּן, תִסְגְּדוּן, etc., and יִתְרְמֵא הֵן:

(vv. 6, 11). The final *-ōn* instead of *-ūn* is typical of the III-y verbs (§266). Parsing tG stem PC 2mp < רמי.

וּמַן־הוּא אֱלָהּ דִּי יְשֵׁיזְבִנְכוֹן מִן־יְדָי: *And who is a god who could save you from my hands?* We've seen מַן in vv. 6 and 11 paired with דִּי to mean "whoever"; here it appears in its interrogative meaning (§138, §391). הוּא is the 3ms independent personal pronoun (§124). Here it is used as a substitute for the copula (§§373c, 378). אֱלָהּ: ms absolute, cf. לֵאלָהָיךְ v. 12, לֵאלָהַי v. 14.

דֵּי is a mispointed דִּי in the Leningrad Codex. יְשֵׁיזְבִנְכוֹן: Read §288; identify the base form. The inflectional prefix *y-* is familiar from יִפֵּל, יִסְגֵּד, יִתְרְמֵא, יִשְׁמַע above, and the pronominal suffix כוֹן from לְכוֹן v. 4, אִיתֵיכוֹן v. 14. Here it serves as a direct object. For the "energic" morpheme *-in(n)-* before the suffix, read §130a. מִן־יְדָי: Prep. מִן (§182) + 1st decl. plural noun יַד "hand" with 1cs pron. suff. *-ɔy.* Cp. the suffix on לֵאלָהַי v. 14; why does this one have *qameṣ*? (§32)

> Exercise: Read the apparatus for this verse in BHS, and paraphrase the readings in English.

v. 16

עֲנוֹ שַׁדְרַךְ מֵישַׁךְ וַעֲבֵד נְגוֹ וְאָמְרִין לְמַלְכָּא נְבוּכַדְנֶצַּר לָא־חַשְׁחִין אֲנַחְנָה עַל־דְּנָה פִּתְגָם לַהֲתָבוּתָךְ:

עֲנוֹ שַׁדְרַךְ מֵישַׁךְ וַעֲבֵד נְגוֹ וְאָמְרִין לְמַלְכָּא: You should have no trouble with this.

לָא־חַשְׁחִין אֲנַחְנָה: *We do not need.* חַשְׁחִין is mp adj. from חשׁח "need, having necessity," a stative verb (§328). It is the predicate (§376) to אֲנַחְנָה, the 1cp independent personal pronoun (§124).

עַל־דְּנָה פִּתְגָם לַהֲתָבוּתָךְ: *To answer you concerning this.* Lit., "concerning this an answer to return to you." עַל־דְּנָה: Prep. עַל (§188i) + דנה, ms demonstrative pronoun (§136). פִּתְגָם: "word, statement," from Persian (§122).

לַהֲתָבוּתָךְ: לְ + C stem infinitive from the hollow root תוב + 2ms pron. suff. For the strong root C infinitive, see §234b; for the hollow verb C infinitive, see §277f. When a derived stem infinitive has a pronominal suffix, the final הֹ is replaced by וּת before the suffix: לַהֲתָבָה + 2ms suffix = לַהֲתָבוּתָךְ (§133b).

In the G stem, the root תוב "return" is intransitive; in the C stem, it becomes transitive, "cause X to return (to)" (§§323–324). The combination of C stem תוב + פתגם "to cause a word to return" conventionally means "reply, respond"; in later Aramaic, פתגם is often dropped and C stem תוב by itself just means "respond, answer." As for the word order, note that objects often come before their verbs, even (or especially) with infinitives (§366).

v. 17

הֵן אִיתַי אֱלָהַנָא דִּי־אֲנַחְנָא פָלְחִין יָכֵל לְשֵׁיזָבוּתַנָא מִן־אַתּוּן נוּרָא יָקִדְתָּא וּמִן־יְדָךְ מַלְכָּא יְשֵׁיזִב:

הֵן אִיתַי: *If it is so*. In v. 12, איתי was used as an existential particle; in vv. 14–15 as a copula; here it introduces an implied clause: "if (what you say) is so" (see §380g).

אֱלָהַנָא דִּי־אֲנַחְנָא פָלְחִין יָכֵל לְשֵׁיזָבוּתַנָא: *Our god whom we worship is able to save us.* אלה (vv. 12, 14, 15) with 1cp pron. suff. (§128). אֲנַחְנָא: Cp. אֲנַחְנָה in the previous verse. יָכֵל: long *ō* under the *y* signifies what form? §223. For the G stem of יכל, see §330c, §428a. Note that here short *i* remains in the closed stressed syllable (§63c). לְשֵׁיזָבוּתַנָא: Prep. לְ + infinitive of שׁיזב + 1cp pron. suff. For the pre-suffixal form of the infinitive, cf. the remarks above on לַהֲתָבוּתָךְ. What would the form without the suffix be?

וּמִן־יְדָךְ מַלְכָּא יְשֵׁיזִב: Translate. Note the 2ms suffix on יְדָ, and see §128 and §129. The suffix ־ָךְ can appear on singular or plural 1st decl. nouns. Which is it here? יְשֵׁיזִב: Cp. יְשֵׁיזְבִנְכוֹן in v. 15.

> Exercise: Read over §56, especially §56d. Review vv. 14–17 and find all the words with *penultimate* stress.

v. 18

וְהֵן לָא יְדִיעַ לֶהֱוֵא־לָךְ מַלְכָּא דִּי לֵאלָהָיךְ [לאלהך] לָא־אִיתַיְנָא [איתנא] פָלְחִין וּלְצֶלֶם דַּהֲבָא דִּי הֲקֵימְתָּ לָא נִסְגֻּד:

וְהֵן לָא יְדִיעַ לֶהֱוֵא־לָךְ מַלְכָּא: *And if not, let it be known to you, O king.* יְדִיעַ: G stem passive participle (§224), used performatively (§316c). לֶהֱוֵא: G stem PC 3ms from the root הוי "to be." Read §268. לָךְ should give you no trouble at this point. The subject of לֶהֱוֵא can be taken as the relative clause that follows: active "I know that X (is true)," passive "that X (is true) is known" (cf. §326).

For לֵאלָהָיךְ [לאלהך], see above v. 12. (Note, by the way, that the Leningrad Codex does not have a full Ketiv-Qere here; its masorah for לֵאלָהָיךְ says יתיר י "superfluous *y*.")

לָא־אִיתַיְנָא [איתנא]: איתי copula + 1cp pron. suff. as subject, as in איתיכון above vv. 14, 15 (§129). נִסְגֻּד: Cp. יסגד v. 6 and see §220. Translate the whole verse.

v. 19

בֵּאדַיִן נְבוּכַדְנֶצַּר הִתְמְלִי חֱמָא וּצְלֵם אַנְפּוֹהִי אֶשְׁתַּנּוּ [אשתני] עַל־שַׁדְרַךְ מֵישַׁךְ וַעֲבֵד נְגוֹ עָנֵה וְאָמַר לְמֵזֵא לְאַתּוּנָא חַד־שִׁבְעָה עַל דִּי חֲזֵה לְמֵזְיֵהּ:

הִתְמְלִי חֱמָא וּצְלֵם אַנְפּֿוֹהִי אֶשְׁתַּנּוֹ [אשתני]: *He was filled with rage and the visage of his face was changed.*

הִתְמְלִי: Compare with יִתְרְמֵא (vv. 6, 11), תִּתְרְמוֹן (v. 15). This form is SC of the tG stem (§239 for strong roots; §266a–b for III-y roots). Parsing: tG SC 3ms from מלי. חֱמָא: "rage," spelled חֵמָה in v. 13. For the sentence structure, see §342b. וּצְלֵם אַנְפּֿוֹהִי: The noun צלם is familiar by now; here it means "facial features" or the like.

אַנְפּֿוֹהִי: For the ending וֹהִי *-ôhī*, see §129. To find the absolute form of a word with such a suffix, replace the suffix with 1st decl. mp ין ◌ *-īn.* אַנְפִּין "face" is *tantum plurale* (§92), like Hebrew פָּנִים (the words are not etymologically related).

אֶשְׁתַּנּוֹ [אשתני]: The verb אֶשְׁתַּנּוֹ (Qere) has undergone metathesis (§53). Note the *dagesh forte* in the נ and see §241c and §267. This is tD stem SC 3ms from שני. See also §50b for the ʾaleph preformative. The Ketiv with final *w* could be parsed as 3mp (cf. §257b) due to attraction, §355b.

לְמֵזֵא לְאַתּוּנָא חַד־שִׁבְעָה עַל דִּי חֲזֵה לְמֵזְיֵהּ: *To heat the furnace sevenfold more than was usual to heat it.* For לְמֵזֵא, cp. לְמֵתָא, v. 2. G stem infinitive from אזי "heat" (§284). לְאַתּוּנָא: For prep. לְ on the direct object, review §359a.

חַד־שִׁבְעָה: *Sevenfold* (lit., "one seven"). For the cardinal numbers, review Table 9 and see §164i. Prep. עַל (§188). The complement of the preposition is the independent relative phrase דִּי חֲזֵה לְמֵזְיֵהּ (§150). חֲזֵה: G passive participle (§224), III-y root (§262a), from the root חזי "see." Idiomatically, what is "seen" (חֲזֵה) is what is "usual" and "proper." לְמֵזְיֵהּ is לְמֵזֵא with what suffix?

v. 20

וּלְגֻבְרִין גִּבָּרֵי־חַיִל דִּי בְחַיְלֵהּ אֲמַר לְכַפָּתָה לְשַׁדְרַךְ מֵישַׁךְ וַעֲבֵד נְגוֹ לְמִרְמֵא לְאַתּוּן נוּרָא יָקִדְתָּא:

וּלְגֻבְרִין גִּבָּרֵי־חַיִל דִּי בְחַיְלֵהּ: *(He said) to some men, warriors who were in his army.* גֻבְרִין: Cf. vv. 8, 12, etc. גִּבָּרֵי־חַיִל: Construct phrase (§153) in apposition (§143) to גֻבְרִין. גִּבָּר: **qiṭṭāl* noun pattern (§110); "mighty one." חַיִל: Cf. v. 4 and review §102. גִּבָּרֵי־חַיִל is a calque (loan translation) of Hebrew גִּבּוֹרֵי חַיִל. דִּי בְחַיְלֵהּ: A relative clause with prepositional phrase (§148). Here חַיִל has the meaning "army."

לְכַפָּתָה לְשַׁדְרַךְ מֵישַׁךְ וַעֲבֵד נְגוֹ לְמִרְמֵא: *To bind Shadrach, Meshach, and Abed-nego, to throw (them).* לְכַפָּתָה: D stem infinitive (§230) from כפת. לְשַׁדְרַךְ: What is the function of the לְ? §177c. לְמִרְמֵא: The root רמי we've seen in vv. 6, 11, 15; also we've seen forms like לְמִכְנַשׁ (v. 2), לְמֵתָא (v. 2), (v. 19). Parse the verb (§261c).

Note that a direct object pronoun can be omitted under certain circumstances (§360).

v. 21

בֵּאדַ֗יִן גֻּבְרַיָּ֣א אִלֵּ֗ךְ כְּפִ֙תוּ֙ בְּסַרְבָּלֵיהוֹן֙ פַּטִּישֵׁיהוֹן [פטשיהון] וְכַרְבְּלָתְהוֹן֙ וּלְבֻשֵׁיהֹ֑ון וּרְמִ֕יו לְגֽוֹא־אַתּ֥וּן נוּרָ֖א יָקִֽדְתָּֽא׃

כְּפִ֙תוּ֙ בְּסַרְבָּלֵיהוֹן. *They were bound while in their clothes, etc.* כְּפִ֙תוּ looks like קְרִבוּ (v. 8), that is, an *i*-theme G stem verb (§218); however, in fact it is a G passive SC (§224) spelled defectively (§27). We would expect the spelling כְּפִיתוּ. סַרְבָּלֵיהוֹן: סַרְבָּל "pants" (Persian loanword) + 3mp pron. suff. (§129). פַּטִּישֵׁיהוֹן: Another word for "pants," possibly a gloss? וְכַרְבְּלָתְהוֹן: "and their headgear," Persian loanword. All the words from Persian have been inflected like Aramaic words. לְבֻשֵׁיהֹון: "and their clothing." Note again the defective orthography in לְבֻשׁ (instead of לְבוּשׁ). What tells you that this spelling is defective? Review §78, Rule 1. Violation of this rule indicates that the vowel is in fact long, not short.

וּרְמִ֕יו: *They were thrown.* Parsed like כְּפִ֙תוּ above (see §262). What is the root?

v. 22

כָּל־קֳבֵ֣ל דְּנָ֗ה מִן־דִּ֤י מִלַּ֣ת מַלְכָּא֙ מַחְצְפָ֔ה וְאַתּוּנָ֖א אֵזֵ֣ה יַתִּ֑ירָא גֻּבְרַיָּ֣א אִלֵּ֗ךְ דִּ֤י הַסִּ֙קוּ֙ לְשַׁדְרַ֤ךְ מֵישַׁךְ֙ וַעֲבֵ֣ד נְג֔וֹ קַטִּ֣ל הִמּ֔וֹן שְׁבִיבָ֖א דִּ֥י נוּרָֽא

כָּל־קֳבֵ֣ל דְּנָ֗ה מִן־דִּ֤י מִלַּ֣ת מַלְכָּא֙ מַחְצְפָ֔ה: *Accordingly, since the word of the king was urgent.* כָּל־קֳבֵ֣ל דְּנָ֗ה: See v. 7. מִן־דִּ֤י: "since, because" (§410). מִלַּ֣ת: *qill-at* noun pattern (§104); "word, command." The construct phrase מִלַּ֣ת מַלְכָּא֙ is the subject of a copular clause (review §376); the predicate follows. מַחְצְפָ֔ה: Adjectival predicate, agreeing with the subject (the head noun of the construct phrase) in number and gender. This adjective is a C passive participle (§235c). In this instance, the *h* of the C/Cp stems has elided: *məhahṣəpɔ > *maḥṣəpɔ*, from the root חצף (C stem "urge," Cp ptcp "urgent, insistent").

וְאַתּוּנָ֖א אֵזֵ֣ה יַתִּ֑ירָא: *And the furnace was heated exceedingly.* אֵזֵ֣ה: We expect a *ḥateph* vowel in the first syllable (§75c, e; §78, Rule 4b). The root אזה we've seen in infinitival form in v. 19; what form is it here? Compare to חֲזֵה in v. 19. יַתִּ֑ירָא: See §344.

גֻּבְרַיָּ֣א אִלֵּ֗ךְ דִּ֤י הַסִּ֙קוּ֙ לְשַׁדְרַ֤ךְ מֵישַׁךְ֙ וַעֲבֵ֣ד נְג֔וֹ קַטִּ֣ל הִמּ֔וֹן שְׁבִיבָ֖א דִּ֥י נוּרָֽא: *Those men who brought up Shadrach, Meshach, and Abed-nego – the flame of the fire killed them.* First of all, note the overall structure of this sentence, and read section §369 (left-dislocation).

הַסִּ֙קוּ֙: The root סלק uniquely shows assimilation of ל to preceding ס when inflection brings them together, as here. The C stem of the root brings the first two root letters together in the base *hasliq, which then changes to *hassiq* (§§43, 287). This occurrence is the SC 3mp.

קְטַל הִמּוֹן: Since the phrase headed by גֻּבְרַיָּא is dislocated, it is resumed in the main clause by the 3mp independent personal pronoun הִמּוֹן. In Aramaic, there is no 3mp pron. suff. on verbs, and the independent pronoun is used instead, as here (§130d). קַטֵּל: We've seen the D stem verbs מַנִּית (v. 12) and לְכַפָּתָה (v. 20). This is literally a paradigm form of the strong root SC (§227).

שְׁבִיבָא דִּי נוּרָא: Periphrastic genitive (§160) with דִי. שְׁבִיבָא: *qaṭīl noun pattern (§108); "flame."

v. 23

וְגֻבְרַיָּא אִלֵּךְ תְּלָתֵּהוֹן שַׁדְרַךְ מֵישַׁךְ וַעֲבֵד נְגוֹ נְפַלוּ לְגוֹא־אַתּוּן־נוּרָא יָקֶדְתָּא מְכַפְּתִין:

וְגֻבְרַיָּא אִלֵּךְ תְּלָתֵּהוֹן שַׁדְרַךְ מֵישַׁךְ וַעֲבֵד נְגוֹ: *And those men, the three of them, Shadrach, Meshach, and Abed-nego.* תְּלָתֵּהוֹן: See §158b, and review cardinal numbers (§166).

נְפַלוּ . . . מְכַפְּתִין: *They fell . . . bound.* נְפַלוּ: Should be recognizable; if not, review §217. מְכַפְּתִין: The doubled middle root letter indicates D stem; however, the active D stem does not suit the context. This form is the D passive participle (§229).

v. 24

אֱדַיִן נְבוּכַדְנֶצַּר מַלְכָּא תְּוַהּ וְקָם בְּהִתְבְּהָלָה עָנֵה וְאָמַר לְהַדָּבְרוֹהִי הֲלָא גֻבְרִין תְּלָתָא רְמֵינָא לְגוֹא־נוּרָא מְכַפְּתִין עָנַיִן וְאָמְרִין לְמַלְכָּא יַצִּיבָא מַלְכָּא:

אֱדַיִן נְבוּכַדְנֶצַּר מַלְכָּא תְּוַהּ וְקָם בְּהִתְבְּהָלָה: *Then king N. was amazed and stood up in agitation.* תְּוַהּ: The root letters of this verb are all strong (stable), with consonantal ו and ה. G stem SC 3ms from the root תוה. The *mappiq* (§29b) in the *h* indicates that it is consonantal, and not a *mater.* קָם: Cp. שָׂמְתָּ (v. 10) and שָׂמוּ (v. 12); review §272a. The root קום is no doubt familiar by now.

בְּהִתְבְּהָלָה: The ◌ָה ◌ֲ ַ*ā-ā* ending has been met with in לְהֵיתָיָה (v. 13), לְכַפָּתָה (v. 20). This is the ending of non-G stem infinitives. Before suffixes, non-G stem or "derived" stem infinitives have the ending ◌ ◌וּת *-ūt-* (e.g., לַהֲתָבוּתָךְ v. 16, לְשֵׁיזָבוּתַנָא v. 17; see §230a–b). Here the infinitive is used as an abstract verbal noun (§320).

עָנֵה וְאָמַר לְהַדָּבְרוֹהִי: *He answered and said to his officials.* Review §295. לְהַדָּבְרוֹהִי: For the וֹהִי ending, see above re: אַנְפּוֹהִי (v. 19). Persian loanword.

הֲלָא גֻבְרִין תְּלָתָא רְמֵינָא: *Did we not cast three men?* הֲלָא: The interrogative הֲ + the negator לָא (see §§390a–b, 387c). גֻבְרִין תְּלָתָא: For the cardinal number, review §164, Table 9; and §166a–b. רְמֵינָא: For this root, we've seen the following forms: יִתְרְמֵא (vv. 6, 11), תִּתְרְמוֹן (v. 15), לְמִרְמֵא (v. 20), רְמִיו (v. 21). See §256e and parse.

18

עֲנוֹ וְאָמְרִין לְמַלְכָּא יַצִּיבָא מַלְכָּא: *They answered and said to the king, Yes, O king.* עֲנוֹ: The ָ (qames) under the ʿayin points to G stem participle, and the ◌ִין -áyin is peculiar to the mp inflection of III-y root participles, both active and passive (§261a). עֲנוֹ וְאָמְרִין is the plural form of the frequent עֲנֵה וְאָמַר. Review §295 if needed. יַצִּיבָא: "Certain," an adjective of the qattîl type (§110b).

> **v. 25**
>
> עָנֵה וְאָמַר הָא־אֲנָה חָזֵה גֻּבְרִין אַרְבְּעָה שְׁרַיִן מַהְלְכִין בְּגוֹא־נוּרָא וַחֲבָל לָא־אִיתַי בְּהוֹן וְרֵוֵהּ דִּי רְבִיעָיָא [רביעאה] דָּמֵה לְבַר־אֱלָהִין:

הָא־אֲנָה חָזֵה: *Behold, I see.* For the particle הָא, see §383. אֲנָה: 1cs independent personal pronoun (§124). Identify the other independent pronouns encountered thus far in vv. 10, 15, 16, 17, and 22. חָזֵה: Cp. חֲזָה (v. 19) and §261a. The participle expresses the present tense (§305a–b, §307).

גֻּבְרִין אַרְבְּעָה שְׁרַיִן מַהְלְכִין בְּגוֹא־נוּרָא: *Four men unbound walking within the fire.* For אַרְבְּעָה, cp. גֻּבְרִין תְּלָתָא in the previous verse. שְׁרַיִן: Note again the ◌ִין ending; cf. עֲנוֹ in the previous verse. There is no qames under the first radical, so the form is not G stem active ptcp. See §224a and §262a. G passive ptcp mp from the root שרי "loose."

מַהְלְכִין: The preformative מ־ combined with the mp inflection ◌ִין points to a ptcp of the derived stems. Which stem? The middle radical is not doubled, therefore not D stem; there is no -it- preformative, so not tG or tD. See §234. בְּגוֹא: גו + בְּ "within" (§179b); for the final א, see §26c.

וַחֲבָל לָא־אִיתַי בְּהוֹן: *And there is no damage on them.* חֲבָל: a qaṭāl pattern noun (§108a). לָא־אִיתַי: Review §380a, b. בְּהוֹן: בְּ and הוֹן are both known to you.

וְרֵוֵהּ דִּי רְבִיעָיָא [רביעאה] דָּמֵה לְבַר־אֱלָהִין: *And the appearance of the fourth resembles a divine being.* For רֵו, see §63d and §100. Note the suffix and see §162. For the dependent noun רביעאה, cf. §97a and §145c. דָּמֵה: What form? For the root דמי + לְ, see §330b. בַּר־אֱלָהִין: For the frequent בַּר "son," see §99. בר אלהין, idiomatically = "a member of the category *divinity*." The three men are accompanied by an angel.

> **v. 26**
>
> בֵּאדַיִן קְרֵב נְבוּכַדְנֶצַּר לִתְרַע אַתּוּן נוּרָא יָקִדְתָּא עָנֵה וְאָמַר שַׁדְרַךְ מֵישַׁךְ וַעֲבֵד־נְגוֹ עַבְדוֹהִי דִּי־אֱלָהָא עִלָּיָא [עלאה] פֻּקוּ וֶאֱתוֹ בֵּאדַיִן נָפְקִין שַׁדְרַךְ מֵישַׁךְ וַעֲבֵד נְגוֹ מִן־גּוֹא נוּרָא:

בֵּאדַיִן קְרֵב נְבוּכַדְנֶצַּר לִתְרַע אַתּוּן נוּרָא יָקִדְתָּא: *Then N. approached the gate of the furnace of burning fire.* קְרֵב: Cp. קָרִבוּ v. 8, and review §218. תְּרַע: *qaṭl pattern noun (§101b, c); "gate." לִתְרַע: For the vocalization, see §176a. לִתְרַע אַתּוּן נוּרָא יָקִדְתָּא: Note that the head word תרע in construct governs a dependent noun phrase אתון נורא יקדתא that is itself a construct phrase, whose dependent noun נוּרָא is modified by an attributive participle יָקִדְתָּא. Review §154b.

282

עַבְדּוֹהִי דִּי־אֱלָהָא עִלָּיָא [עלאה] פֻּקוּ וֶאֱתוֹ: *Servants of the most high God, come out and come here!* עַבְדוֹהִי: mp with 3ms pron. suff., from עֲבַד "slave, servant." For the suffix, review once more §129. עֲבַד is a noun of the *qaṭl* pattern, whose plural forms have a bisyllabic base (§102).

עַבְדוֹהִי דִּי־אֱלָהָא עִלָּיָא [עלאה]: Once more, a periphrastic genitive with "anticipatory" pronominal suffix on the head word, like קרציהון די יהודיא (v. 8) and רוח די רביעאה (v. 25). Review §162. עִלָּיָא [עלאה]: Adjective with -ɔy ending (§97a).

פֻּקוּ וֶאֱתוֹ בֵּאדַיִן נָפְקִין: *Come out and come here! Then they came out.* פֻּקוּ: Read §253b. G stem impv mp from נפק. וֶאֱתוֹ: For the vowel ε on the conjunction ו, see §76b. For the form of the verb, see §260. G stem impv mp from אתי. Cp. חֱיִי (v. 9). נָפְקִין: For the function of the ptcp in this verse, see §311; it shares a narrative time-frame with the ptcps. in the next verse.

3:27

וּמִתְכַּנְּשִׁין אֲחַשְׁדַּרְפְּנַיָּא סִגְנַיָּא וּפַחֲוָתָא וְהַדָּבְרֵי מַלְכָּא חָזַיִן לְגֻבְרַיָּא אִלֵּךְ דִּי לָא־שְׁלֵט נוּרָא בְּגֶשְׁמְהוֹן
וּשְׂעַר רֵאשְׁהוֹן לָא הִתְחָרַךְ וְסָרְבָּלֵיהוֹן לָא שְׁנוֹ וְרֵיחַ נוּר לָא עֲדָת בְּהוֹן:

וּמִתְכַּנְּשִׁין אֲחַשְׁדַּרְפְּנַיָּא סִגְנַיָּא וּפַחֲוָתָא וְהַדָּבְרֵי מַלְכָּא. *The satraps, prefects, and governors, and the officials of the king gathered.* מִתְכַּנְּשִׁין: First seen in v. 3. The nouns following have been encountered previously.

חָזַיִן לְגֻבְרַיָּא אִלֵּךְ דִּי לָא־שְׁלֵט נוּרָא בְּגֶשְׁמְהוֹן: *They saw those men, that the fire had no power over their body.* חָזַיִן: The -áyin ending once again; see עָנַיִן (v. 24), שָׁרַיִן (v. 25). Parse (§261a). דִּי: Here introduces the clausal object of חָזַיִן (§341). לָא־שְׁלֵט: The G stem verb has an *i*-theme, like קְרֵב (§218). This one governs a בְּ prepositional phrase ("semi-transitive," §342a). בְּגֶשְׁמְהוֹן: *qiṭl pattern noun (cf. §101a). Identify the pronominal suffix.

Note that the gender of נוּרָא in this sentence is masculine (the verb that agrees with it [§355] is 3ms) instead of feminine as in נורא יקדתא.

וּשְׂעַר רֵאשְׁהוֹן לָא הִתְחָרַךְ: *The hair of their head was not singed.* שְׂעַר: *qiṭal pattern noun (§105); "hair." It is in construct with suffixed noun רֵאשׁ, in origin a *qiṭl noun, but with quiescence of ʾaleph (§47). הִתְחָרַךְ: Recognizable as a T stem (tG or tD) by the *hit-* preformative (§237a, b). The tD stem, unlike the tG, will always have a full vowel *a* or *ɔ* following the first root letter, as here. tD stem SC 3ms from חרך, with compensatory lengthening (§77c). For the passive meaning, see §241a.

וְסָרְבָּלֵיהוֹן לָא שְׁנוֹ: *Their pants did not alter.* For שְׁנוֹ, cp. עֲנוֹ (vv. 9, 16), and review §256c. For the root שני, cp. אֶשְׁתַּנִּי (v. 19). For the G stem meaning, cf. §330b.

וְרֵיחַ נוּר לָא עֲדָת בְּהוֹן: *The odor of fire did not pass into them.* רֵיחַ: *qēl noun pattern (§100), with *pataḥ furtivum* (§76c). עֲדָת: III-y root; see §58a and §256b. G stem SC 3fs from עדי. Since רֵיחַ is ms, the gender of the verb has been affected by attraction (§355b) to נוּר (fs).

v. 28

עָנֵה נְבוּכַדְנֶצַּר וְאָמַר בְּרִיךְ אֱלָהֲהוֹן דִּי־שַׁדְרַךְ מֵישַׁךְ וַעֲבֵד נְגוֹ דִּי־שְׁלַח מַלְאֲכֵהּ וְשֵׁיזִב לְעַבְדוֹהִי דִּי הִתְרְחִצוּ עֲלוֹהִי וּמִלַּת מַלְכָּא שַׁנִּיו וִיהַבוּ גֶשְׁמְיהוֹן [גשמהון] דִּי לָא־יִפְלְחוּן וְלָא־יִסְגְּדוּן לְכָל־אֱלָהּ לָהֵן לֵאלָהֲהוֹן:

בְּרִיךְ אֱלָהֲהוֹן דִּי־שַׁדְרַךְ מֵישַׁךְ וַעֲבֵד נְגוֹ: *Blessed be the god of Shadrach et al.* For בְּרִיךְ, see §224a, §316c. אֱלָהֲהוֹן דִּי־שַׁדְרַךְ: Yet another case of די genitive with suffixed head word (§162). אֱלָהֲהוֹן: Why does the ה of אלה have a *ḥaṭeph shewa* (§78, Rule 4b)?

דִּי־שְׁלַח מַלְאֲכֵהּ וְשֵׁיזִב לְעַבְדוֹהִי: *Who (or because) he sent his angel and saved his servants.* דִּי: In certain contexts, דִּי can be ambiguous between a relative pronoun (§135) and a conjunction (§409a, b), as it is here. שְׁלַח: Cf. v. 2. מַלְאֲכֵהּ: *maqtal noun pattern (§117). וְשֵׁיזִב: cf. vv. 15, 17. לְעַבְדוֹהִי: What is the function of לְ? §359a.

דִּי הִתְרְחִצוּ עֲלוֹהִי וּמִלַּת מַלְכָּא שַׁנִּיו: *Who (or because) they trusted in him and disobeyed* (lit., "changed") *the king's order.* דִּי: For the ambiguity, see the remarks just above. הִתְרְחִצוּ: Cp. to הִתְמְלִי (v. 19) above. A diagnostic trait of the tG stem is the reduced vowel following the first root letter (review §239). Parse, and see §334b. וּמִלַּת מַלְכָּא: v. 22. שַׁנִּיו: Cp. אֶשְׁתַּנִּי (v. 19; Qere), שְׁנוֹ (v. 27). The doubled middle root letter indicates what stem (§227)? As for the -*iw* ending, see §263b. שְׁנוֹ is intransitive, שַׁנִּיו transitive; see §330a, b.

וִיהַבוּ גֶשְׁמְיהוֹן [גשמהון] דִּי לָא־יִפְלְחוּן וְלָא־יִסְגְּדוּן לְכָל־אֱלָהּ לָהֵן לֵאלָהֲהוֹן: *They gave their body so that they would not serve or worship any god but their god.* וִיהַבוּ: For initial וִי when the conjunction is added, see §52d. The G stem verb יהב "give" is used in the SC and ptcp (active and passive) only; the G stem verb נתן (same meaning) is used in the PC and infinitive. I-y roots in the SC are strong; see §249. גֶשְׁמְיהוֹן: Cf. v. 27. Here the Ketiv has an extraneous י (in fact, the Leningrad Codex has no Qere, only a note יתיר י "superfluous *yodh*").[1]

דִּי לָא־יִפְלְחוּן: See §402c for negative purpose clauses. לְכָל־אֱלָהּ לָהֵן לֵאלָהֲהוֹן: For the use of כל, see §167a–c. For להן, see §423b.

---

[1] The *yodh* in Leningrad in fact is written above the line, not in line with the other letters.

v. 29

וּמִנִּי שִׂים טְעֵם דִּי כָל־עַם אֻמָּה וְלִשָּׁן דִּי־יֵאמַר שָׁלֵה [שׁלו] עַל אֱלָהֲהוֹן דִּי־שַׁדְרַךְ מֵישַׁךְ וַעֲבֵד נְגוֹא הַדָּמִין יִתְעֲבֵד וּבַיְתֵהּ נְוָלִי יִשְׁתַּוֵּה כָּל־קֳבֵל דִּי לָא אִיתַי אֱלָה אָחֳרָן דִּי־יִכֻּל לְהַצָּלָה כִּדְנָה׃

וּמִנִּי שִׂים טְעֵם: *From me is hereby given an order.* The combination of שׂים with טעם has been seen in vv. 12, 29; here שִׂים is the G passive participle, used as a performative utterance (§316c). See also §273c.

דִּי כָל־עַם אֻמָּה וְלִשָּׁן דִּי־יֵאמַר שָׁלֵה [שׁלו]: *That any people, tribe, or tongue that might utter blasphemy.* עַם אֻמָּה וְלִשָּׁן: Cf. the plural forms of these words in vv. 4, 7. For the noun pattern of אֻמָּה, see §104; for לִשָּׁן, see §110. יֵאמַר: The G stem verb אמר has been encountered in the ptcp forms אָמְרִין, אָמַר, and SC 3ms אֲמַר (v. 20). For this form, see §246a. The function here is modal (§291b and §301).

The Ketiv consonants שלה most likely signified שָׁלֵה, a loanword from Akkadian *šillatu*, "blasphemy," as the BHS apparatus indicates. The Qere favors instead שָׁלוּ "error due to negligence" (as in Dan 6:5).

הַדָּמִין יִתְעֲבֵד וּבַיְתֵהּ נְוָלִי יִשְׁתַּוֵּה. *Shall be dismembered* (lit., "shall be made limbs") *and his house shall be made equivalent to a latrine.* הַדָּמִין: For the *qaṭṭāl noun pattern, see §110. יִתְעֲבֵד: Cp. with יִתְרְמֵא (vv. 6, 11). If the tG base is -itqaṭil-, why does יִתְעֲבֵד have a reduced vowel after the ʿayin? (§78, Rule 1). Why does it have e instead of i in the last syllable? (§78, Rule 7). For the syntax, see §340a.

וּבַיְתֵהּ: Review vocalization of proclitic וְ (§52c). בַיְתֵהּ: Cp. with חֵילָה v. 20, and review §103. נְוָלִי: See the entry נְוָלוּ in HALOT (unknown origin, "dunghill"). יִשְׁתַּוֵּה: For metathesis, cp. אֶשְׁתַּנִּי (v. 19). What is the root? For the vocalization, see §267. The root שׁוי is stative and intransitive in the G stem ("be equal"), transitive in the D stem ("make X equal"), and passive of the D in the tD ("X be made equal"). See §330b.

כָּל־קֳבֵל דִּי לָא אִיתַי אֱלָה אָחֳרָן: *Because there is no other god.* כָּל־קֳבֵל דִּי: See §408a. לָא אִיתַי: Review §380a, b. אָחֳרָן: *Other,* see §116.

דִּי־יִכֻּל לְהַצָּלָה כִּדְנָה: *Who is able to deliver like this one.* יִכֻּל: For the form of I-y weak roots, see §250a. G stem PC 3ms from יכל "be able." לְהַצָּלָה: Cp. לְהַיְתָיָה (v. 13; C stem inf). In I-n verbs (§254), the first root consonant n can assimilate to the following consonant (§78, Rule 11a); here *hanṣɔlɔ > *haṣṣɔlɔ*, from the root נצל. כִּדְנָה: Prep. כְּ + demonstrative ms pron. דְּנָה (§136): "like this"; see §351c.

v. 30

בֵּאדַ֗יִן מַלְכָּ֡א הַצְלַ֣ח לְשַׁדְרַ֤ךְ מֵישַׁךְ֙ וַעֲבֵ֣ד נְג֔וֹ בִּמְדִינַ֖ת בָּבֶֽל׃

הַצְלַח: *Advanced (prospered).* For the *a* theme vowel, see §75a (§78, Rule 4a). For the C stem SC, see §233. C stem SC 3ms from צלח.

The last three verses of Dan 3 in the MT actually belong to the following narrative and in English translations are included in Dan 4 (as vv. 1–3). Accordingly, Dan 3:31–33 will be included in the reading guide for Dan 4.

READING 2: DANIEL 6

v. 1

וְדָרְיָ֨וֶשׁ֙ מָֽדָיָ֔א [מדאה] קַבֵּ֖ל מַלְכוּתָ֑א כְּבַ֥ר שְׁנִ֖ין שִׁתִּ֥ין וְתַרְתֵּֽין׃

וְדָרְיָ֨וֶשׁ֙ מָֽדָיָ֔א [מדאה] קַבֵּ֖ל מַלְכוּתָ֑א: *And Darius the Mede received the kingdom.* מָדָיָא: The Qere is to be read as מֵדָאָה; cp. עִלָּאָה (Dan 3:26) and review the gentilic endings in §97a. קַבֵּל: Strong verb; parse (§227). מַלְכוּתָא: Abs. is מַלְכוּ, see §113.

כְּבַר שְׁנִין שִׁתִּין וְתַרְתֵּין: *About sixty-two years of age.* Prep. כְּ (§181) + בַּר "son." בַּר in construct with שְׁנִין "years" denotes the age of a person. For the nominal pattern, see §99. שְׁנִין: Mixed declension noun (§93), fem. gender. שִׁתִּין וְתַרְתֵּין: For שִׁתִּין, see Dan 3:1; see §164. תַּרְתֵּין: See again Table 9, and cf. §164c. For the structure of the numeral, see §164h.

v. 2

שְׁפַר֙ קֳדָ֣ם דָּרְיָ֔וֶשׁ וַהֲקִים֙ עַל־מַלְכוּתָ֔א לַאֲחַשְׁדַּרְפְּנַיָּ֖א מְאָ֣ה וְעֶשְׂרִ֑ין דִּ֥י לֶהֱוֺ֖ן בְּכָל־מַלְכוּתָֽא׃

שְׁפַר קֳדָם דָּרְיָוֶשׁ: *It was pleasing to Darius.* שְׁפַר: G stem, "be pleasing," stative. The subject is impersonal and refers to the action contemplated, spelled out in the next clause (cf. coordination; §393d).

וַהֲקִים֙ עַל־מַלְכוּתָ֔א לַאֲחַשְׁדַּרְפְּנַיָּ֖א מְאָ֣ה וְעֶשְׂרִ֑ין: *He set up over the kingdom the one hundred and twenty satraps.* וַהֲקִים: Cp. הֲקֵים in Dan 3 (§277). עַל־מַלְכוּתָא: Prep. עַל; see §188e. לַאֲחַשְׁדַּרְפְּנַיָּא: See Dan 3:2; for the preposition, review §177c. מְאָה וְעֶשְׂרִין: See §164g, h, and Table 9.

דִּי לֶהֱוֺן בְּכָל־מַלְכוּתָא: *Who (or so that) they should be in all the kingdom.* The ambiguity of דִּי strikes again. This could be a relative pronoun (§135 and §148) or a conjunction introducing a purpose clause (§402). לֶהֱוֺן: See §268 and parse. Transliterate; note the defective spelling in the last syllable (we expect לֶהֱוֹון).

v. 3

וְעֵלָּא מִנְּהוֹן סָרְכִין תְּלָתָה דִּי דָנִיֵּאל חַד־מִנְּהוֹן דִּי־לֶהֱוֹן אֲחַשְׁדַּרְפְּנַיָּא אִלֵּין יָהֲבִין לְהוֹן טַעְמָא וּמַלְכָּא לָא־לֶהֱוֵא נָזִק:

וְעֵלָּא מִנְּהוֹן סָרְכִין תְּלָתָה: *And above them, three overseers.* For עֵלָּא, see §344. עֵלָּא מִן lit., "upwards from" = "above." מִנְּהוֹן: See §182c. סָרְכִין: A nominalized G stem participle (§172b) from סרך "follow closely." סָרְכִין תְּלָתָה: Cp. גֻּבְרִין תְּלָתָא (Dan 3:24) and review §166a.

דִּי דָנִיֵּאל חַד־מִנְּהוֹן: *Of whom Daniel was one* (lit., "who Daniel was one of them"). For the resumptive pronoun, review §148b. For the numeral חַד, see Dan 3:19 and §164, Table 9; §166d.

דִּי־לֶהֱוֹן אֲחַשְׁדַּרְפְּנַיָּא אִלֵּין יָהֲבִין לְהוֹן טַעְמָא: *To whom these satraps would give account* (lit., "who ... would give to them account"). לֶהֱוֹן ... יָהֲבִין: For the linkage of הוי with the ptcp (periphrastic), see §313c. לֶהֱוֹן as in the previous verse. יָהֲבִין: Recognizable as a G stem ptcp. How do you account for the *ḥaṭeph* vowel with ה? (Review §75c.) לְהוֹן: Another resumptive pronoun in a relative clause (§148b). טַעְמָא: Cf. טְעֵם (Dan 3:10, 12, 29) and compare צְלֵם, צַלְמָא. Review §101b, d if needed.

וּמַלְכָּא לָא־לֶהֱוֵא נָזִק: *And the king would not be bothered.* לֶהֱוֵא נָזִק: Another periphrastic construction; see previous clause. נָזִק: For the short *i* in the second syllable, see §63a, c; also §32 on pause. נזק: G stem stative (§328), "be annoyed, bothered."

v. 4

אֱדַיִן דָּנִיֵּאל דְּנָה הֲוָא מִתְנַצַּח עַל־סָרְכַיָּא וַאֲחַשְׁדַּרְפְּנַיָּא כָּל־קֳבֵל דִּי רוּחַ יַתִּירָא בֵּהּ וּמַלְכָּא עֲשִׁית לַהֲקָמוּתֵהּ עַל־כָּל־מַלְכוּתָא:

אֱדַיִן דָּנִיֵּאל דְּנָה הֲוָא מִתְנַצַּח: *Then this Daniel was distinguishing himself.* הֲוָא מִתְנַצַּח: Once again, the periphrastic construction. For הֲוָא, review §256a. For reflexive verbs, see §334. מִתְנַצַּח: Parse.

כָּל־קֳבֵל דִּי רוּחַ יַתִּירָא בֵּהּ: *Because an excellent spirit was in him.* כָּל־קֳבֵל דִּי: Cf. Dan 3:29. רוּחַ יַתִּירָא: Noun (fs) with attributive adj. (fs). רוּחַ is 1st decl., fem.; יַתִּירָא is 2nd decl. of the pattern *qaṭṭîl* (§110b). For the attributive relation, see §145. רוּחַ יַתִּירָא בֵּהּ: For copular clauses of this type, see §377.

וּמַלְכָּא עֲשִׁית לַהֲקָמוּתֵהּ עַל־כָּל־מַלְכוּתָא: *The king planned to raise him up over all the kingdom.* עֲשִׁית: This looks like a G passive SC (§224b), but it has an active meaning (§316b). לַהֲקָמוּתֵהּ: Cp. לַהֲתָבוּתָךְ (Dan 3:16). Review §277f; for the ending before suffixes, see §234b. Parse.

v. 5

אֱדַיִן סָרְכַיָּא וַאֲחַשְׁדַּרְפְּנַיָּא הֲווֹ בָעַיִן עִלָּה לְהַשְׁכָּחָה לְדָנִיֵּאל מִצַּד מַלְכוּתָא וְכָל־עִלָּה וּשְׁחִיתָה לָא־יָכְלִין לְהַשְׁכָּחָה כָּל־קֳבֵל דִּי־מְהֵימַן הוּא וְכָל־שָׁלוּ וּשְׁחִיתָה לָא הִשְׁתְּכַחַת עֲלוֹהִי:

אֱדַיִן סָרְכַיָּא וַאֲחַשְׁדַּרְפְּנַיָּא הֲוֹ בָעַיִן עִלָּה לְהַשְׁכָּחָה לְדָנִיֵּאל מִצַּד מַלְכוּתָא: *Then the overseers and satraps kept seeking to find a charge against Daniel from the side of the kingdom.* הֲוֹ: Cp. עֲנוֹ (Dan 3:9), שְׁנוֹ (Dan 3:27), and הֲוֵא in the previous v. Parse. בָעַיִן: Cp. עֲנַיִן (Dan 3:24), חָזַיִן (Dan 3:27), and parse. What kind of construction is הֲוֹ בָעַיִן?

לְהַשְׁכָּחָה: If needed, review §234b and parse. עִלָּה לְהַשְׁכָּחָה: This could be confusing. Cp. פִּתְגָם לַהֲתָבוּתָךְ (Dan 3:16) and review §366. לְדָנִיֵּאל: See §178a. מִצַּד: Prep. מִן, cf. §182a. צַד: *qall* pattern (§104).

וְכָל־עִלָּה וּשְׁחִיתָה לָא־יָכְלִין לְהַשְׁכָּחָה: *But no charge or corruption were they able to find.* For the adversative ("but") relation of the clauses, see §393e. עִלָּה: *qill-at* pattern (again §104). שְׁחִיתָה: *qatīl-at* pattern (§108). יָכְלִין: The form is familiar by now; for the root, cf. יָכֵל (Dan 3:17), יֻכַּל (Dan 3:29). The verb יכל routinely governs an infinitive complement (§330c and §428a). The implied tense of יָכְלִין is conveyed by הֲוֹ of the previous clause, which also gives the subject: "the overseers and satraps were seeking . . . and (they were) not able to find."

כָּל . . . לֹא: For negation with the quantifier כֹּל, see §167c. Again, the object (כָל־עִלָּה וּשְׁחִיתָה) of the infinitive (לְהַשְׁכָּחָה) appears before it (§366).

כָּל־קֳבֵל דִּי־מְהֵימַן הוּא: *Because he was trustworthy.* See §376a (copular clauses). For מְהֵימַן, see §288b.

וְכָל־שָׁלוּ וּשְׁחִיתָה לָא הִשְׁתְּכַחַת עֲלוֹהִי: *And no negligence or corruption was there against him.* שָׁלוּ: Cf. Dan 3:29. For the noun pattern, see §113. הִשְׁתְּכַחַת: Review §53 and §78 (Rule 10a). What is the root? The stem? The stress is penultimate, contrary to the default (§56b, c) and to diachronic development (§56a); this irregularity may be the result of JLA influence (which has penultimate stress in the SC 3fs).

הִשְׁתְּכַחַת, cont.: Note the original *i* of the stem has become *a* (§75a). For the semantics, see §381. עֲלוֹהִי: Cf. Dan 3:28. This prep. takes suffixes as a 1st decl. plural noun.

v. 6

אֱדַיִן גֻּבְרַיָּא אִלֵּךְ אָמְרִין דִּי לָא נְהַשְׁכַּח לְדָנִיֵּאל דְּנָה כָּל־עִלָּה לָהֵן הַשְׁכַּחְנָא עֲלוֹהִי בְּדָת אֱלָהֵהּ:

דִּי לָא נְהַשְׁכַּח לְדָנִיֵּאל דְּנָה כָּל־עִלָּה: *We shall not find against this Daniel any charge.* דִּי: See §426b. נְהַשְׁכַּח: Review §233.

לָהֵן הַשְׁכַּחְנָא עֲלוֹהִי בְּדָת אֱלָהֵהּ: *Unless we find (a charge) against him in the law of his god.* For the use of לָהֵן, see §423a. הַשְׁכַּחְנָא: C stem SC 1cp from שׁכח; see §299 for the use of the SC. דָּת: Persian loanword (§122), "law, decree."

v. 7

אֱדַ֗יִן סָרְכַיָּ֣א וַאֲחַשְׁדַּרְפְּנַיָּ֗א אִלֵּ֛ן הַרְגִּ֥שׁוּ עַל־מַלְכָּ֑א וְכֵ֣ן אָמְרִ֣ין לֵ֔הּ דָּרְיָ֥וֶשׁ מַלְכָּ֖א לְעָלְמִ֥ין חֱיִֽי׃

אֱדַ֗יִן סָרְכַיָּ֣א וַאֲחַשְׁדַּרְפְּנַיָּ֗א אִלֵּ֛ן הַרְגִּ֥שׁוּ עַל־מַלְכָּ֑א: *Then these overseers and satraps went in a group (?) to the king.* אִלֵּן: Cf. אִלֵּין (Dan 6:3). הַרְגִּשׁוּ: Should be easy to parse; if not, review §233. The meaning is disputed; HALOT gives "to enter in a crowd."

The balance of the verse should present no difficulties.

v. 8

אִתְיָעַ֜טוּ כֹּ֣ל ׀ סָרְכֵ֣י מַלְכוּתָ֗א סִגְנַיָּ֤א וַֽאֲחַשְׁדַּרְפְּנַיָּא֙ הַדָּֽבְרַיָּ֣א וּפַחֲוָתָ֔א לְקַיָּמָ֤ה קְיָם֙ מַלְכָּ֔א וּלְתַקָּפָ֖ה אֱסָ֑ר דִּ֣י כָל־דִּֽי־יִבְעֵ֣א בָ֠עוּ מִן־כָּל־אֱלָ֨הּ וֶאֱנָ֜שׁ עַד־יוֹמִ֣ין תְּלָתִ֗ין לָהֵן֙ מִנָּ֣ךְ מַלְכָּ֔א יִתְרְמֵ֕א לְגֹ֖ב אַרְיָוָתָֽא׃

אִתְיָעַ֜טוּ כֹּ֣ל ׀ סָרְכֵ֣י מַלְכוּתָ֗א סִגְנַיָּ֤א וַֽאֲחַשְׁדַּרְפְּנַיָּא֙ הַדָּֽבְרַיָּ֣א וּפַחֲוָתָ֔א: *All the overseers of the kingdom, the prefects and satraps, the officials and governors, have agreed together.* אִתְיָעַטוּ: For אִתְ instead of הִתְ as a T stem preformative, see §237b. For the vowel ◌ְ ֹ under the י, see §77c. Parse. סָרְכֵי: Cp. סָרְכִין (Dan 6:3), סָרְכַיָּא (Dan 6:4) to review 1st decl. pl. endings.

לְקַיָּמָ֤ה קְיָם֙ מַלְכָּ֔א וּלְתַקָּפָ֖ה אֱסָ֑ר: *To confirm a statute and to strengthen a prohibition.* לְקַיָּמָה: See §275 and parse. For the use of the D stem with this root, see §331b and §231b. קְיָם: *qiṭāl* noun pattern (§108). וּלְתַקָּפָה: Parse. אֱסָר: Another *qiṭāl* pattern noun.

דִּ֣י כָל־דִּֽי־יִבְעֵ֣א בָ֠עוּ מִן־כָּל־אֱלָ֨הּ וֶאֱנָ֜שׁ עַד־יוֹמִ֣ין תְּלָתִ֗ין: *That anyone who makes a request of any god or man for thirty days.* What use of דִּי? Clause complement after implied speech contained in the edict (§341). יִבְעֵה: Cp. יִתְרְמֵא (Dan 3:6), לֶהֱוֵא (Dan 3:18). For the final -ē, see §58c. Review §258. For the root, cp. בָעַיִן (Dan 6:5) above. Parse. בָּעוּ: *qālū* noun pattern (§113); "request." Note that the verb and its object are from the same root, and see §361. אֱנָשׁ: Cf. Dan 3:10.

עַד־יוֹמִין תְּלָתִין: עַד: Prep.; see §187b. יוֹם "day"; note §71a. The form יוֹם is invariable throughout inflection, unlike Hebrew יוֹם sg., יָמִים pl. תְּלָתִין: Review numerals at §164f, Table 9.

לָהֵן֙ מִנָּ֣ךְ מַלְכָּ֔א יִתְרְמֵ֕א לְגֹ֖ב אַרְיָוָתָֽא: *Except from you, O king, shall be thrown into the pit of lions.* לָהֵן: Cf. Dan 3:28, 6:6. מִנָּךְ: Cp. מִנִּי Dan 3:29 and review pronominal suffixes (§128). גֹּב: *qull* noun pattern (§104); "pit." Note that the original *u* changes to *o* (§78, Rule 7) when the word is without suffixes. אַרְיָוָתָא: What kind of plural ending? Review §90a, and see §96. The abs./cstr. form is אַרְיֵה.

v. 9

כְּעַ֣ן מַלְכָּ֔א תְּקִ֥ים אֱסָרָ֖א וְתִרְשֻׁ֣ם כְּתָבָ֑א דִּ֣י לָ֧א לְהַשְׁנָיָ֛ה כְּדָת־מָדַ֥י וּפָרַ֖ס דִּי־לָ֥א תֶעְדֵּֽא׃

כְּעַן מַלְכָּא תְּקֵים אֱסָרָא וְתִרְשֻׁם כְּתָבָא: *So now, O king, you must establish the prohibition and sign the writ.* כְּעַן: "now"; see §430a. תְּקֵים: See §277d; this is an "Aphˁel" C stem, 2ms.[2] תִּרְשֻׁם: For the form, review §220. Both תְּקֵים and תִּרְשֻׁם are PC 2ms expressing deontic modality (§291b). The edict was not drafted by the king, but he must consent and put his name to it for it to be valid. כְּתָבָא: Another *qiṭāl* pattern (§108); "writing, document."

דִּי לָא לְהַשְׁנָיָה כְּדָת־מָדַי וּפָרַס דִּי־לָא תֶעְדֵּא: *Which is not to be changed, like the law of Media and Persia, which does not pass away.* לְהַשְׁנָיָה: Cp. לְהַיְתָיָה Dan 3:13 and parse. For this use of the infinitive, see §322. מָדַי וּפָרַס: A compound noun phrase (§142) can be the dependent part of a construct phrase (§154b). תֶעְדֵּא: For the root, cp. עֲדָת (Dan 3:27). For the ε after the prefix, see §75b.

v. 10

כָּל־קֳבֵל דְּנָה מַלְכָּא דָּרְיָוֶשׁ רְשַׁם כְּתָבָא וֶאֱסָרָא:

רְשַׁם: *He signed.* Cp. תִּרְשֻׁם in previous verse and parse (easy and fun). For the common word order SVO (Subject, Verb, Object), read §§362ff. וֶאֱסָרָא: For the ε vowel with the ו conjunction, see §76b.

v. 11

וְדָנִיֵּאל כְּדִי יְדַע דִּי־רְשִׁים כְּתָבָא עַל לְבַיְתֵהּ וְכַוִּין פְּתִיחָן לֵהּ בְּעִלִּיתֵהּ נֶגֶד יְרוּשְׁלֶם וְזִמְנִין תְּלָתָה בְיוֹמָא הוּא ׀ בָּרֵךְ עַל־בִּרְכֹוהִי וּמְצַלֵּא וּמוֹדֵא קֳדָם אֱלָהֵהּ כָּל־קֳבֵל דִּי־הֲוָא עָבֵד מִן־קַדְמַת דְּנָה:

וְדָנִיֵּאל כְּדִי יְדַע דִּי־רְשִׁים כְּתָבָא: *And Daniel, when he knew that the writ was signed.* כְּדִי: Cp. Dan 3:7 and review §418. יְדַע: A root last encountered in יְדִיעַ (Dan 3:18) and familiar from Hebrew. רְשִׁים: Review §224b.

עַל לְבַיְתֵהּ וְכַוִּין פְּתִיחָן לֵהּ בְּעִלִּיתֵהּ נֶגֶד יְרוּשְׁלֶם: *He entered his house, and he had windows open in his upper room facing Jerusalem.* עַל: Not the prep., but a finite verb; see §279. לְבַיְתֵהּ: See Dan 3:29. וְכַוִּין פְּתִיחָן: Judging by the inflection of פְּתִיחָן, what gender is כַוִּין? Review §90a, §91a–c. כַוִּין: Sg. כַּוָּה "window," *qall-at* noun pattern (§104). פְּתִיחָן: §224 again.

לֵהּ: For the predicative use of the prep., see §377b. עִלִּיתֵהּ: *qill-ī(t)* noun pattern (§114). נֶגֶד: Hebrew prep.; see §201.

וְזִמְנִין תְּלָתָה בְיוֹמָא הוּא בָּרֵךְ עַל־בִּרְכֹוהִי: *And three times in the day he knelt on his knees.* זִמְנִין: Cf. זְמָא (Dan 3:7, etc.). תְּלָתָה: as in Dan 3:24, 6:3. יוֹמָא: Cf. יוֹמֵין above, 6:8. הוּא בָּרֵךְ: as in 6:5, etc.; what form is בָּרֵךְ? This root in the G stem means "kneel." הוּא should perhaps be corrected to הֲוָא, yielding a periphrastic construction (as in the BHS apparatus), but see §312. בִּרְכֹוהִי: *qiṭl* noun pattern (§102); "knee."

---

[2] It is tempting to emend the vowel points to produce a D stem תַּקֵּים "confirm, verify," which seems to fit better.

וּמְצַלֵּא וּמוֹדֵא קֳדָם אֱלָהֵהּ כָּל־קֳבֵל דִּי־הֲוָא עָבֵד מִן־קַדְמַת דְּנָה: *And was praying and giving thanks to his god just as he used to do before.* מְצַלֵּא: Note the *m* here and in מִתְכַּנְּשִׁין (Dan 3:3), מַחְצְפָה (Dan 3:22), מַהְלְכִין (Dan 3:25), מִתְנַצַּח (Dan 6:4), and observe that preformative *m* is a feature of all *non-G stem participles*. What does the geminated middle root letter tell you? See §264. מוֹדֵא: Another non-G stem participle; see §285b. Parse.

קֳדָם אֱלָהֵהּ: Prep. קֳדָם as in Dan 3:13, 6:2. Review §203a. כָּל־קֳבֵל דִּי: We have seen this meaning "because," but here "just as" (§415b). הֲוָא עָבֵד: Auxiliary הוי; review §313b. עָבֵד: Cf. עֲבַד (Dan 3:1), עַבְדְּת (Dan 3:15). Parse. מִן־קַדְמַת דְּנָה: For קַדְמַת, see §204 and §350e.

v. 12

אֱדַיִן גֻּבְרַיָּא אִלֵּךְ הַרְגִּשׁוּ וְהַשְׁכַּחוּ לְדָנִיֵּאל בָּעֵא וּמִתְחַנַּן קֳדָם אֱלָהֵהּ:

הַרְגִּשׁוּ: As above, 6:7. וְהַשְׁכַּחוּ: Cp. 6:5, 6 for previous instances of the verb. לְדָנִיֵּאל: What use of לְ? §359a.

בָּעֵא וּמִתְחַנַּן קֳדָם אֱלָהֵהּ: *Making petition and entreating to his god.* בָּעֵא: What kind of weak verb? §261a. מִתְחַנַּן: Review the previous verse on non-G stem participles. See §280.

v. 13

בֵּאדַיִן קְרִבוּ וְאָמְרִין קֳדָם־מַלְכָּא עַל־אֱסָר מַלְכָּא הֲלָא אֱסָר רְשַׁמְתָּ דִּי כָל־אֱנָשׁ דִּי־יִבְעֵה מִן־כָּל־אֱלָהּ וֶאֱנָשׁ עַד־יוֹמִין תְּלָתִין לָהֵן מִנָּךְ מַלְכָּא יִתְרְמֵא לְגוֹב אַרְיָוָתָא עָנֵה מַלְכָּא וְאָמַר יַצִּיבָא מִלְּתָא כְּדָת־מָדַי וּפָרַס דִּי־לָא תֶעְדֵּא:

Most of the words and expressions in this verse can be found in vv. 8–9. הֲלָא: Cf. Dan 3:24. כָּל־אֱנָשׁ דִּי: Cp. Dan 3:10. יַצִּיבָא: Cf. Dan 3:24. מִלְּתָא: Cp. מִלַּת (Dan 3:22), 28; *qill-at* noun pattern (review §104). יַצִּיבָא מִלְּתָא: Copular clause; see §376.

v. 14

בֵּאדַיִן עֲנוֹ וְאָמְרִין קֳדָם מַלְכָּא דִּי דָנִיֵּאל דִּי מִן־בְּנֵי גָלוּתָא דִּי יְהוּד לָא־שָׂם עֲלָיִךְ [עלך] מַלְכָּא טְעֵם וְעַל־אֱסָרָא דִּי רְשַׁמְתָּ וְזִמְנִין תְּלָתָה בְּיוֹמָא בָּעֵא בָּעוּתֵהּ:

דָנִיֵּאל דִּי מִן־בְּנֵי גָלוּתָא דִּי יְהוּד: *Daniel, who is from the sons of the exile of Judah.* בְּנֵי: The mp cstr. of בַּר (Dan 3:25, 6:1). For this irregular plural form, see §94. גָלוּתָא: *qāl-ū(t)* noun pattern (§113). יְהוּד: Proper noun, "Judah." בְּנֵי גָלוּתָא דִּי יְהוּד: Cstr. phrase (§153) as head component of periphrastic genitive (§160).

לָא־שָׂם עֲלָיִךְ [עלך] מַלְכָּא טְעֵם: Cf. Dan 3:12.

וְעַל־אֱסָרָא דִּי רְשַׁמְתָּ: *Or the prohibition that you signed.* Prep. phrase headed by עַל is coordinated with עֲלָיִךְ from the previous clause: "he paid no attention to you . . . or to the prohibition." יִבְעֵה בָעוּ: Cp. 6:11. בָּעֵא בָּעוּתֵהּ: Cp. 6:8 וְזִמְנִין תְּלָתָה בְּיוֹמָא.

v. 15

אֱדַ֜יִן מַלְכָּ֗א כְּדִ֤י מִלְּתָא֙ שְׁמַ֔ע שַׂגִּ֥יא בְּאֵ֖שׁ עֲל֑וֹהִי וְעַ֧ל דָּנִיֵּ֛אל שָׂ֥ם בָּ֖ל לְשֵׁיזָב֑וּתֵהּ וְעַד֙ מֶעָלֵ֣י שִׁמְשָׁ֔א הֲוָ֥א מִשְׁתַּדַּ֖ר לְהַצָּלוּתֵֽהּ׃

כְּדִ֤י מִלְּתָא֙ שְׁמַ֔ע: *When he heard the word.* כְּדִ֤י: Cf. 3:7, 6:11. מִלְּתָא: Cf. 6:13. Note Object–Verb word order.

שַׂגִּ֥יא בְּאֵ֖שׁ עֲל֑וֹהִי: *It was very displeasing to him.* שַׂגִּיא: Adj. used adverbially (§347a); *qaṭṭil pattern (§110). בְּאֵשׁ: G stem, *i*-theme, stative verb (§330); cp. שְׁפַר (Dan 6:2).

וְעַ֧ל דָּנִיֵּ֛אל שָׂ֥ם בָּ֖ל לְשֵׁיזָב֑וּתֵהּ: *On Daniel he set his mind to save him.* Prep. עַל; see §188b. שָׂם: Cf. Dan 6:14, etc. בָּל: *qɔl noun pattern (§100); "mind." לְשֵׁיזָבוּתֵהּ: Cp. לְשֵׁיזָבוּתָנָא (Dan 3:17).

וְעַד֙ מֶעָלֵ֣י שִׁמְשָׁ֔א הֲוָ֥א מִשְׁתַּדַּ֖ר לְהַצָּלוּתֵהּ: *Until sunset he kept trying to rescue him.* מֶעָלֵי: Noun with *mV*-preformative (§117); "entering" of the sun = sunset. שִׁמְשָׁא: *qiṭl noun pattern (§101). הֲוָ֥א מִשְׁתַּדַּ֖ר: Another case of הֲוָא as auxiliary (§313). מִשְׁתַּדַּר: Cf. the remarks on מְצַלֵּא in v. 11. Review §78, Rule 10, and parse. לְהַצָּלוּתֵהּ: Cp. לְהַצָּלָה (Dan 3:29). Review §254 on I-*n* roots, C stem.

v. 16

בֵּאדַ֨יִן֙ גֻּבְרַיָּ֣א אִלֵּ֔ךְ הַרְגִּ֖שׁוּ עַל־מַלְכָּ֑א וְאָמְרִ֣ין לְמַלְכָּ֗א דַּ֤ע מַלְכָּא֙ דִּֽי־דָת֤ לְמָדַי֙ וּפָרַ֔ס דִּֽי־כָל־אֱסָ֥ר וּקְיָ֛ם דִּֽי־מַלְכָּ֥א יְהָקֵ֖ים לָ֥א לְהַשְׁנָיָֽה׃

דַּע: See §250g. דִּֽי־דָת֤ לְמָדַי֙ וּפָרַ֔ס דִּֽי־כָל־אֱסָ֥ר: *A law of Media and Persia is that every prohibition, etc.* The words דת למדי ופרס could be a copular clause ("Media and Persia have a law," §377b), but more likely a periphrastic genitive (§163).

דִּֽי־מַלְכָּ֥א יְהָקֵ֖ים לָ֥א לְהַשְׁנָיָֽה: *Which the king may establish is not to be changed.* יְהָקֵים: See §277c, and cp. 6:9 תְּקִים above. לָ֥א לְהַשְׁנָיָֽה: Cf. Dan 6:9 above.

v. 17

בֵּאדַ֜יִן מַלְכָּ֣א אֲמַ֗ר וְהַיְתִיו֙ לְדָ֣נִיֵּ֔אל וּרְמ֕וֹ לְגֻבָּ֖א דִּ֣י אַרְיָוָתָ֑א עָנֵ֤ה מַלְכָּא֙ וְאָמַ֣ר לְדָנִיֵּ֔אל אֱלָהָ֗ךְ דִּ֣י אַנְתָּה֙ [אנת] פָּֽלַֽח־לֵהּ֙ בִּתְדִירָ֔א ה֖וּא יְשֵׁיזְבִנָּֽךְ׃

וְהַיְתִיו֙: *They brought Daniel and threw him into the pit of lions.* וְהַיְתִיו: Cp. לְהַיְתָיָה (Dan 3:13), and see §283a. Parse. וּרְמוֹ: The root should be familiar; review §256c. Parse. Where is the object? See §360. לְגֻבָּ֖א דִּ֣י אַרְיָוָתָ֑א: Cp. לְגֹב אַרְיָוָתָא, 6:8, 13.

אֱלָהָ֗ךְ דִּ֣י אַנְתָּה֙ [אנת] פָּֽלַֽח־לֵהּ֙ בִּתְדִירָ֔א ה֖וּא יְשֵׁיזְבִנָּֽךְ: *Your god whom you serve regularly – he must save you.* אַנְתָּה: Cf. 3:10. פָּלַח: Cp. פָּלְחִין (Dan 3:12); why is there short *a* in the second syllable? Review §75a. פָּֽלַֽח־לֵהּ: Review §148a and explain the suffix on the prep. phrase. בִּתְדִירָא: בְּ + תְּדִיר *qaṭil noun pattern (§108); *in regularity* = "regularly."

הוּא יְשֵׁיזְבִנְכֵן: Review §369; what role does הוּא play? יְשֵׁיזְבִנְכוֹן: Cf. יְשֵׁיזְבִנְכֵן (Dan 3:15) and review §130a. The meaning here is modal (deontic), not volitive, as many English translations have it: not "may your god deliver you," but "your god (not I) must deliver you." See again §130b.

v. 18

וְהֵיתָיִת אֶבֶן חֲדָה וְשֻׂמַת עַל־פֻּם גֻּבָּא וְחַתְמַהּ מַלְכָּא בְּעִזְקְתֵהּ וּבְעִזְקָת רַבְרְבָנוֹהִי דִּי לָא־תִשְׁנֵא צְבוּ בְּדָנִיֵּאל:

וְהֵיתָיִת אֶבֶן חֲדָה וְשֻׂמַת עַל־פֻּם גֻּבָּא: And a stone was brought and placed on the mouth of the pit. וְהֵיתָיִת: See §283c. אֶבֶן: *qatl noun pattern (§101c; Hebrew segholate type). חֲדָה: See §166d.

וְשֻׂמַת: See §273c. פֻּם: *qull noun pattern (§104).

וְחַתְמַהּ מַלְכָּא בְּעִזְקְתֵהּ וּבְעִזְקָת רַבְרְבָנוֹהִי: And the king sealed it with his signet and with the signets of his nobles. וְחַתְמַהּ: G stem SC 3ms + 3fs suffix. The theme vowel of the verb syncopates through the operation of Rule 2 (§78): ḥatam-ah > ḥatmah. בְּעִזְקְתֵהּ: בְּ instrumental (§179e) with noun of *qitl-at pattern (§101). Double prep. phrase; see §142b.

דִּי לָא־תִשְׁנֵא צְבוּ בְּדָנִיֵּאל: So that nothing regarding Daniel should change. דִּי לָא־תִשְׁנֵא: See §402. תִשְׁנֵא: Cp. 6:9 תְּעֵדֵא, 6:13 יִבְעֵה. Parse and see §330b. צְבוּ: *qal-ū(t) noun pattern (§113); "matter, thing."

v. 19

אֱדַיִן אֲזַל מַלְכָּא לְהֵיכְלֵהּ וּבָת טְוָת וְדַחֲוָן לָא־הַנְעֵל קָדָמוֹהִי וְשִׁנְתֵּהּ נַדַּת עֲלוֹהִי:

אֱדַיִן אֲזַל מַלְכָּא לְהֵיכְלֵהּ וּבָת טְוָת: Then the king went to his palace and spent the night fasting. אֲזַל: "to go," G stem, common verb of motion (§331a). לְהֵיכְלֵהּ: הֵיכַל "palace," Akkadian loanword (ekallum via Sumerian É.GAL). וּבָת: Cp. קָם (Dan 3:24), שָׂם (Dan 6:14). Cf. §272a; root בית "spend the night." טְוָת: Adv.; see §344, "fasting."

וְדַחֲוָן לָא־הַנְעֵל קָדָמוֹהִי: And entertainments (?) he did not have brought before him. דַּחֲוָן is obscure; it may be derived from the root דחי "delay, push away," meaning "distractions, diversions, entertainment." The pl. inflection is 2nd decl. הַנְעֵל: The root is עלל (cf. עַל in 6:11). For this form, see §281a. "He did not cause refreshments to come in" = he did not ask or order refreshments (or whatever) to be brought. קָדָמוֹהִי: Again, see §203b.

וְשִׁנְתֵּהּ נַדַּת עֲלוֹהִי: And his sleep wavered to him. שִׁנְתֵּהּ: *qil-t noun pattern (§99). Note the non-assimilation (nasalization?) of the n (§42). נַדַּת: Root נדד, see §279a. Although usually glossed as "flee," the root more likely means "be unsteady, waver" or the like; it is often found with "sleep" and in some dialects the combination ndd + šnh just means "to have restless sleep." עֲלוֹהִי: See §188g.

v. 20

בֵּאדַיִן מַלְכָּא בִּשְׁפַּרְפָּרָא יְקוּם בְּנָגְהָא וּבְהִתְבְּהָלָה לְגֻבָּא דִי־אַרְיָוָתָא אֲזַל:

שְׁפַּרְפָּרָא בֵּאדַיִן מַלְכָּא בִּשְׁפַּרְפָּרָא יְקוּם בְּנָגְהָא: *Then the king arose at dawn, at first light.* שְׁפַּרְפָּרָא: Pattern with reduplication (§120). יְקוּם: A familiar root; see §272a. This is PC, but with a past meaning. Read §304. נָגְהָא: *qutl* pattern (§101). Transliterate *nɔghɔ*; "first light of dawn."

וּבְהִתְבְּהָלָה לְגֻבָּא דִי־אַרְיָוָתָא אֲזַל: *And in agitation to the pit of lions he went.* הִתְבְּהָלָה: What kind of form? Cf. Dan 3:24 above, and review §240b. For the use with prep., see §320b. אֲזַל: As in v. 19 above.

v. 21

וּכְמִקְרְבֵהּ לְגֻבָּא לְדָנִיֵּאל בְּקָל עֲצִיב זְעִק עָנֵה מַלְכָּא וְאָמַר לְדָנִיֵּאל דָּנִיֵּאל עֲבֵד אֱלָהָא חַיָּא אֱלָהָךְ דִּי אַנְתְּה [אנת] פָּלַח־לֵהּ בִּתְדִירָא הַיְכֵל לְשֵׁיזָבוּתָךְ מִן־אַרְיָוָתָא:

וּכְמִקְרְבֵהּ לְגֻבָּא לְדָנִיֵּאל בְּקָל עֲצִיב זְעִק: *And when he drew near to the pit, to Daniel in a sad voice he cried out.* כְמִקְרְבֵהּ: What form? Cp. לְמִכְנַשׁ (Dan 3:2), לְמֵזֵיה (Dan 3:19). Parse. For the syntax, see §419. בְּקָל: Cf. Dan 3:5, etc. עֲצִיב: *qatīl* pattern, adjective (§108a); "sad." זְעִק: *i*-theme G stem SC 3ms (review §218), "cry out."

עֲבֵד אֱלָהָא חַיָּא: *Servant of the living God.* עֲבֵד: *qatl* noun pattern (§101b). Cp. עֲבְדוֹהִי דִי־אֱלָהָא עִלָּיָא (Dan 3:26). חַיָּא: *qall* pattern adjective (review §104); "living." The abs. sing. is חַי; see §78, Rule 12b.

אֱלָהָךְ . . . בִּתְדִירָא: Cf. 6:17. הַיְכֵל לְשֵׁיזָבוּתָךְ: *Was he able to save you?* הַיְכֵל: Interrogative particle; see §390a. יְכִל: another *i*-theme verb (§218). לְשֵׁיזָבוּתָךְ: This is now old hat to you after learning לְשֵׁיזָבוּתַנָא (Dan 3:17), לְשֵׁיזָבוּתֵהּ (Dan 6:15). For the inf. complement, see §330c.

v. 22

אֱדַיִן דָּנִיֵּאל עִם־מַלְכָּא מַלִּל מַלְכָּא לְעָלְמִין חֱיִי:

עִם־מַלְכָּא מַלִּל: *Spoke with the king.* Prep. עִם (§189c). מַלִּל: Geminate verb, but strong in the D stem (§227). מַלְכָּא לְעָלְמִין חֱיִי: Cf. Dan 3:9, 6:7.

v. 23

אֱלָהִי שְׁלַח מַלְאֲכֵהּ וּסֲגַר פֻּם אַרְיָוָתָא וְלָא חַבְּלוּנִי כָּל־קֳבֵל דִּי קֳדָמוֹהִי זָכוּ הִשְׁתְּכַחַת לִי וְאַף קָדָמָיִךְ [קדמך] מַלְכָּא חֲבוּלָה לָא עַבְדֵת:

אֱלָהִי שְׁלַח מַלְאֲכֵהּ וּסֲגַר פֻּם אַרְיָוָתָא וְלָא חַבְּלוּנִי: *My god sent his angel and closed the mouth of the lions and they did not hurt me.* אֱלָהִי: For the suffix, review §128. שְׁלַח: Cf. Dan 3:2, 28. וּסֲגַר: The *ḥaṭeph* vowel under ס is unusual (§75d). G stem SC, "to close." פֻּם: Cf. 6:18. חַבְּלוּנִי: For the suffix *-nī*, see §130c. The addition of the suffix changes the stress pattern of the word: *ḥabbílū + nī > ḥabbilū́nī > ḥabbəlū́nī* (§78, Rule 1). Parse.

קֳדָמֹ֫והִי זָכוּ הִשְׁתְּכַחַת לִי: *Before him innocence was found to me* (i.e., in his eyes I had innocence). קֳדָמֹ֫והִי: Irregularly, the short *qameṣ* in the first syllable did not reduce; transliterate *qŏdɔ̄mṓhī* (§64g) (likewise in 6:19). זָכוּ: **qāl-ū(t)* noun pattern (§113); "innocence." הִשְׁתְּכַחַת: Cp. 6:5 above. לִי: לְ of possession (§177f). הִשְׁתְּכַחַת: This verb often has an existential nuance (§381), synonymous with אִיתַי. זכו איתי לי = זכו השתכחת לי.

וְאַף קָֽדָמָיִךְ [קדמך] מַלְכָּא חֲבוּלָה לָא עַבְדֵת: *And also to you, O king, I have done no crime.* קָֽדָמָיִךְ: Cf. עֲלָיִךְ (Dan 3:12, etc.). Review §203b. חֲבוּלָה: *qaṭūl-at noun pattern (§108). Cp. חֲבָל (Dan 3:25). עַבְדֵת: As in Dan 3:15.

v. 24

בֵּאדַיִן מַלְכָּא שַׂגִּיא טְאֵב עֲלֹוהִי וּלְדָנִיֵּאל אֲמַר לְהַנְסָקָה מִן־גֻּבָּא וְהֻסַּק דָּנִיֵּאל מִן־גֻּבָּא וְכָל־חֲבָל לָא־
הִשְׁתְּכַח בֵּהּ דִּי הֵימִן בֵּאלָהֵהּ:

מַלְכָּא שַׂגִּיא טְאֵב עֲלֹוהִי: *The king – it was very pleasing to him.* Another case of left-dislocation (§369). שַׂגִּיא: Cf. 6:15. טְאֵב: Stative, *i*-theme SC (§330a). Like בְּאֵשׁ in 6:15, it has no subject, or only a vague one (§358c).

וּלְדָנִיֵּאל אֲמַר לְהַנְסָקָה מִן־גֻּבָּא: *And he commanded to bring up Daniel from the pit.* לְהַנְסָקָה: Inf. of C stem, but which root? See §43 and §287. Cp. הַסִּקוּ (Dan 3:22). For the word order, see §366.

וְהֻסַּק דָּנִיֵּאל מִן־גֻּבָּא: *And Daniel was brought up from the pit.* הֻסַּק: The nasalization of לְהַנְסָקָה is not found in this form (§287 again): *hussaq < *huslaq.*

וְכָל־חֲבָל לָא־הִשְׁתְּכַח בֵּהּ דִּי הֵימִן בֵּאלָהֵהּ: *No harm was found on him, for he believed in his god.* חֲבָל: Cf. Dan 3:25. For the whole phrase, cp. חֲבָל לָא־אִיתַי בְּהוֹן (Dan 3:25). This again is the existential use of השתכח (§381). דִּי: Conjunctive; see §409a. הֵימִן: See §288b. בֵּאלָהֵהּ: For the vocalization, note §48.

v. 25

וַאֲמַר מַלְכָּא וְהַיְתִיו גֻּבְרַיָּא אִלֵּךְ דִּי־אֲכַלוּ קַרְצֹ֫והִי דִּי דָנִיֵּאל וּלְגֹב אַרְיָוָתָא רְמֹו אִנּוּן בְּנֵיהֹון וּנְשֵׁיהֹון וְלָא־
מְטֹו לְאַרְעִית גֻּבָּא עַד דִּי־שְׁלִטוּ בְהֹון אַרְיָוָתָא וְכָל־גַּרְמֵיהֹון הַדִּקוּ:

וַאֲמַר מַלְכָּא וְהַיְתִיו: See 6:17 above. דִּי־אֲכַלוּ קַרְצֹ֫והִי דִּי דָנִיֵּאל: Cf. Dan 3:8. וּלְגֹב אַרְיָוָתָא רְמֹו: Cf. 6:17. The disjunctive accent on רְמֹו suggests that the following words are not the object. אִנּוּן בְּנֵיהֹון וּנְשֵׁיהֹון: אִנּוּן: Indep. pron. 3mp (§124). בְּנֵיהֹון: Irregular plural of בַּר (§94). וּנְשֵׁיהֹון: Irregular plural of אִנְתָּה "woman, wife." Translate: "they threw (them) – they, their children, and their wives."

18

וְלָא־מְטוֹ לְאַרְעִית גֻּבָּא עַד דִּי־שְׁלֵטוּ בְהוֹן אַרְיָוָתָא וְכָל־גַּרְמֵיהוֹן הַדִּקוּ: *They did not reach the bottom of the pit until the lions had overpowered them, and crushed all their bones.* מְטוֹ: G SC 3mp from מטא "reach, arrive." Review §256c. לְאַרְעִית: *-ī(t)* noun pattern (§114).

עַד דִּי: See §420. שְׁלֵטוּ בְהוֹן אַרְיָוָתָא: Cp. לָא־שְׁלֵט נוּרָא בְּגֶשְׁמְהוֹן (Dan 3:27). גַּרְמֵיהוֹן: *qatl* noun pattern (§101); cp. BH גֶּרֶם "bone." הַדִּקוּ: C stem SC, geminate verb דקק; see §281a.

v. 26

בֵּאדַיִן דָּרְיָוֶשׁ מַלְכָּא כְּתַב לְכָל־עַמְמַיָּא אֻמַּיָּא וְלִשָּׁנַיָּא דִּי־דָאֲרִין [דירין] בְּכָל־אַרְעָא שְׁלָמְכוֹן יִשְׂגֵּא:

עַמְמַיָּא אֻמַּיָּא וְלִשָּׁנַיָּא: כְּתַב: G stem SC, strong verb. Easy and fun to parse. עַמְמַיָּא אֻמַּיָּא וְלִשָּׁנַיָּא: Cf. Dan 3:4, 7. דָאֲרִין [דירין]: G stem ptcp, root דור "dwell." For the Ketiv-Qere, cf. וְקָאֲמִין [וקימין] in Dan 3:3 and references cited there. אַרְעָא: *qatl* noun pattern (cf. §101); "land, earth"; cp. BH אֶרֶץ and cf. §38.

שְׁלָמְכוֹן יִשְׂגֵּא: *May your peace be multiplied.* שְׁלָמְכוֹן: *qatāl* noun pattern (§108). For the suffix, cf. לְכוֹן (Dan 3:4, etc.), and review §128c. יִשְׂגֵּא: G stem PC from the root שׂגי "increase, be much/many" (cp. the related adj. שַׂגִּיא). Parse.

v. 27

מִן־קֳדָמַי שִׂים טְעֵם דִּי ׀ בְּכָל־שָׁלְטָן מַלְכוּתִי לֶהֱוֹן זָאֲעִין [זיעין] וְדָחֲלִין מִן־קֳדָם אֱלָהֵהּ דִּי־דָנִיֵּאל ׀ דִּי־הוּא אֱלָהָא חַיָּא וְקַיָּם לְעָלְמִין וּמַלְכוּתֵהּ דִּי־לָא תִתְחַבַּל וְשָׁלְטָנֵהּ עַד־סוֹפָא:

מִן־קֳדָמַי שִׂים טְעֵם: Prep. מִן־קֳדָם is the "honorific" equivalent of מִן (§203d). שִׂים טְעֵם: Cf. Dan 3:29. שָׁלְטָן: *qutlān* noun pattern (§115); "dominion," cstr. sg. מַלְכוּתִי: Cf. מַלְכוּתָא (6:1, etc.).

לֶהֱוֹן זָאֲעִין [זיעין] וְדָחֲלִין מִן־קֳדָם אֱלָהֵהּ דִּי־דָנִיֵּאל: *They shall tremble and be afraid of the god of Daniel.* לֶהֱוֹן: Cf. 6:2, 3. זָאֲעִין [זיעין]: G stem ptcp from hollow root זוע; see again §273a. דָחֲלִין: G ptcp, with reduction to *ḥateph patah* after ח (§75c), from דחל "to fear." For the use of הוי with the ptcp, review §313c. אֱלָהֵהּ דִּי־דָנִיֵּאל: Once again, the anticipatory pronoun construction (§162).

דִּי־הוּא ׀ אֱלָהָא חַיָּא וְקַיָּם לְעָלְמִין: *For he is the living god and (one who) endures forever.* דִּי is again here conjunctive ("for, because"), or possibly relative (§149). אֱלָהָא חַיָּא: Cf. 6:21. קַיָּם: *qattāl* adjectival pattern (§110b); from the root קום; "enduring." לְעָלְמִין: Cf. Dan 3:9, etc.

וּמַלְכוּתֵהּ דִּי־לָא תִתְחַבַּל וְשָׁלְטָנֵהּ עַד־סוֹפָא: *And his kingdom is one that will not be destroyed, and his dominion is to the end.* דִּי־לָא תִתְחַבַּל: An independent ("headless") relative clause (§150) used as a predicate of a copular clause (§375b). סוֹפָא: *qōl* noun pattern (§100).

v. 28

מְשֵׁיזֵב וּמַצִּל וְעָבֵד אָתִין וְתִמְהִין בִּשְׁמַיָּא וּבְאַרְעָא דִּי שֵׁיזִב לְדָנִיֵּאל מִן־יַד אַרְיָוָתָא:

296

מְשֵׁיזֵב וּמַצִּל וְעָבֵד אָתִין וְתִמְהִין בִּשְׁמַיָּא וּבְאַרְעָא: *(He) saves and delivers and does signs and wonders in heaven and on earth.* מְשֵׁיזֵב: Ptcp of שׁיזב, cf. Dan 3:15, 17, 28, etc. וּמַצִּל: Ptcp, cf. לְהַצָּלָה (Dan 3:29), לְהַצָּלוּתֵהּ (Dan 6:15). וְעָבֵד: Cf. Dan 6:11. For the omission of subject, see §358a.

אָתִין: *qāl* noun pattern (§100); "sign." וְתִמְהִין: *qiṭl* noun pattern (§101). שְׁמַיָּא: Form with pseudo-dual ending (§95c), always appearing with the 1st decl. pl. det. ending in BA. וּבְאַרְעָא: Cf. v. 26. For the use of בְּ with both nouns, see §142b.

דִּי שֵׁיזִב לְדָנִיֵּאל מִן־יַד אַרְיָוָתָא: For the phrasing, cp. דִּי יְשֵׁיזְבִנְכוֹן מִן־יְדָי (Dan 3:15).

v. 29

וְדָנִיֵּאל דְּנָה הַצְלַח בְּמַלְכוּת דָּרְיָוֶשׁ וּבְמַלְכוּת כּוֹרֶשׁ פָּרְסָיָא [פרסאה]:

הַצְלַח: Cf. Dan 3:30 (although here intransitive). כּוֹרֶשׁ: Proper name, "Cyrus." [פרסאה] פָּרְסָיָא: Adj., "Persian."

READING 3: DANIEL 3:31–4:34

3:31

נְבוּכַדְנֶצַּר מַלְכָּא לְכָל־עַמְמַיָּא אֻמַּיָּא וְלִשָּׁנַיָּא דִּי־דָארִין [דירין] בְּכָל־אַרְעָא שְׁלָמְכוֹן יִשְׂגֵּא:

This sentence is the *praescriptio* (address) of a letter, which provides the framework for the story which follows. A typical structure of a *praescriptio* is "X to Y, greetings [or other salutation]" (Fitzmyer 1974).

לְכָל־עַמְמַיָּא אֻמַּיָּא וְלִשָּׁנַיָּא: Cp. Dan 3:4, 6:26, etc. דִּי־דָארִין [דירין]: Cf. Dan 6:26. שְׁלָמְכוֹן יִשְׂגֵּא: Cf. Dan 6:26.

3:32

אָתַיָּא וְתִמְהַיָּא דִּי עֲבַד עִמִּי אֱלָהָא עִלָּיָא [עלאה] שְׁפַר קָדָמַי לְהַחֲוָיָה:

אָתַיָּא וְתִמְהַיָּא: Cp. אָתִין וְתִמְהִין (Dan 6:28). עֲבַד: Cf. Dan 3:1. עִמִּי: Before suffixes, prep. עִם (§189a) has a geminate *m*. [עלאה] עִלָּיָא: Cf. Dan 3:26. שְׁפַר: Cf. Dan 6:2. לְהַחֲוָיָה: Cp. to לְהַיְתָיָה (Dan 3:13), לְהַשְׁנָיָה (Dan 6:9). C stem of חוי "tell, relate." Note the secondary opening (§76a).

3:33

אָתוֹהִי כְּמָה רַבְרְבִין וְתִמְהוֹהִי כְּמָה תַקִּיפִין מַלְכוּתֵהּ מַלְכוּת עָלַם וְשָׁלְטָנֵהּ עִם־דָּר וְדָר:

אָתוֹהִי כְּמָה רַבְרְבִין וְתִמְהוֹהִי כְּמָה תַקִּיפִין: *How great are his signs, how mighty are his wonders!* Two copular clauses with predicate adjectives (§376). כְּמָה: See §347d. רַבְרְבִין: Pl. adj. רַב "great," with reduplication (§120). When רַב means "great," the plural is רַבְרְבִין; when it means "noble, chief," the plural is רִבְרְבָנִין (cp. רַבְרְבָנוֹהִי Dan 6:18). תַקִּיפִין: *qaṭṭīl* adjective pattern (§110b). Cp. the verbal form לְתַקָּפָה (Dan 6:8).

מַלְכוּתֵהּ. מַלְכוּתָא מַלְכוּת עָלַם וְשָׁלְטָנֵהּ עִם־דָּר וְדָר‎ :מַלְכוּתָא Cf. (Dan 6:1, etc.). For the cstr. מַלְכוּת, review §113. עָלַם: Cf. לְעָלְמִין (Dan 3:9, etc.). *qāṭal noun pattern (§107). For the meaning of the cstr. phrase, see §156. וְשָׁלְטָנֵהּ: Cf. Dan 6:27. עִם־דָּר וְדָר: For repetition to express distributivity ("each"), see §169c. דָּר: *qāl noun pattern (§100).

4:1

אֲנָה נְבוּכַדְנֶצַּר שְׁלֵה הֲוֵית בְּבֵיתִי וְרַעְנַן בְּהֵיכְלִי:

אֲנָה: Cf. Dan 3:25. שְׁלֵה הֲוֵית: *I was at ease.* שְׁלֵה: *qaṭil pattern adjective, from final y root (שלי) (§106). הֲוֵית: G stem SC 1cs from הוי, cf. §256e (hǝwēṯ < *hawayt). Copular clause with הוי and pred. adj. (§376). בְּבֵיתִי: Cp. בַיְתֵהּ (Dan 3:29, 6:11); see §73b.

רַעְנַן: *qaṭlal pattern (§120); "tranquil." בְּהֵיכְלִי: Cp. לְהֵיכְלֵהּ (Dan 6:19). For coordination and gapping, see §394.

4:2

חֵלֶם חֲזֵית וִידַחֲלִנַּנִי וְהַרְהֹרִין עַל־מִשְׁכְּבִי וְחֶזְוֵי רֵאשִׁי יְבַהֲלֻנַּנִי:

חֵלֶם חֲזֵית וִידַחֲלִנַּנִי: *A dream I saw and it frightened me.* חֵלֶם: *qiṭl pattern (§101a); "dream." חֲזֵית: Cp. הֲוֵית in previous verse and parse; cp. חֲזֵה (Dan 3:25, etc.). וִידַחֲלִנַּנִי: D stem PC; middle ח does not accept dagesh (§77a, b). The ending -innáni is the "energic" -inn- plus the 1cs pron. suff. -ání (§130a, c). Note the following: *wǝ + yǝdaḥ(ḥ)el + inn + ání, where wǝ + yǝ yields wī (§52d) and the e reduces to ǎ (§75b and §78, Rule 4b). Transliterate as wīdaḥ(ḥ)ǎlinnáni. This is another example of PC used of past time; cp. יְקוּם (Dan 6:20), and review §304.

וְהַרְהֹרִין עַל־מִשְׁכְּבִי וְחֶזְוֵי רֵאשִׁי יְבַהֲלֻנַּנִי: *And thoughts on my bed and visions of my head disturbed me.* הַרְהֹרִין: Reduplicative pattern (§120); "bothersome thoughts." מִשְׁכְּבִי: *miqṭal pattern (§117). חֶזְוֵי: *qiṭl pattern; cf. חֵלֶם above, cstr. pl. רֵאשִׁי: Originally *qiṭl pattern, now *qēl pattern, with 1cs pron. suff. יְבַהֲלֻנַּנִי: Cp. to וִידַחֲלִנַּנִי above. D stem PC 3mp with 1cs suffix: *yǝbah(ḥ)ǝlūn-n-áni. The energic morpheme (review §130a) is simply -n- after the 3mp ending -ūn, here written defectively (§27), i.e., we expect ־לוּנַּ instead of ־לֻנַּ. Another PC used as past tense.

4.3

וּמִנִּי שִׂים טְעֵם לְהַנְעָלָה קָדָמַי לְכֹל חַכִּימֵי בָבֶל דִּי־פְשַׁר חֶלְמָא יְהֹודְעֻנַּנִי:

וּמִנִּי שִׂים טְעֵם: Cf. Dan 3:29, 6:27. לְהַנְעָלָה קָדָמַי לְכֹל חַכִּימֵי בָבֶל. *To bring to me all the sages of Babylon.* לְהַנְעָלָה: Cp. הַנְעֵל (Dan 6:19) and review §281a. קָדָמַי: Cf. Dan 3:32. לְכֹל: לְ as object marker (§177c). Note that the C stem of this root has two verbal complements: direct object לְכֹל חַכִּימֵי בָבֶל and locative preposition קָדָמַי (§339a). חַכִּימֵי: *qaṭṭīl pattern (§110b).

298

דִּי־פְשַׁר חֶלְמָא יְהוֹדְעַנַּנִי: *So that they would tell me the interpretation of the dream.* דִּי conjunctive, introducing purpose clause (§402a). פְשַׁר: **qiṭl* pattern (§101b). חֶלְמָא: Cf. חֵלֶם in 4:2 above. For ḥɛlmɔ̄ instead of *ḥilmɔ̄*, see §75b.

יְהוֹדְעַנַּנִי: Cp. יְבַהֲלֻנַּנִי in previous verse. The ה after י prefix of PC indicates C stem (Haphʿel pattern); וֹ after ה indicates I-y root (§251a); C PC 3mp with 1cs suffix from ידע: yəhōdəʿūn-n-ánī, with energic morpheme once again abridged to -n- after -ūn (§130a). Note two direct objects in the C stem: (1) the 1cs suffix, and (2) פְשַׁר חֶלְמָא, with stem change increasing valence by causativity (G ידע transitive, one object, C transitive with two objects). See §323–324.

4:4

> בֵּאדַיִן עָלֲלִין [עללין] חַרְטֻמַיָּא אָשְׁפַיָּא כַּשְׂדָּיֵא [כשדאי] וְגָזְרַיָּא וְחֶלְמָא אָמַר אֲנָה קֳדָמֵיהוֹן וּפִשְׁרֵהּ לָא־מְהוֹדְעִין לִי:

עָלֲלִין [עללין] חַרְטֻמַיָּא אָשְׁפַיָּא כַּשְׂדָּיֵא וְגָזְרַיָּא [כשדאי]: *The magicians, enchanters, Chaldeans, and diviners entered.* [עללין] עָלֲלִין: G stem geminate verb עלל; what form? §279f. For the following nouns (loanwords), consult the lexicons. [כשדאי] כַּשְׂדָּיֵא: The gentilic adjective with -ɔ̄y ending has a variation in the Ketiv-Qere, with ◌ָיֵ⁻ -ɔ̄yē Ketiv and ◌ָאֵ⁻ -ɔ̄ʔē Qere (§97b).

וְחֶלְמָא אָמַר אֲנָה קֳדָמֵיהוֹן וּפִשְׁרֵהּ לָא־מְהוֹדְעִין לִי: *I kept saying the dream to them, but its interpretation they did not tell me.* אָמַר: Cf. Dan 3:14, etc. קֳדָמֵיהוֹן: For the suffix, review §129. פִשְׁרֵהּ: Cf. פְשַׁר in previous verse. מְהוֹדְעִין: Cp. יְהוֹדְעַנַּנִי in previous verse. Preformative *m* indicates what form? Parse.

The coordination of ptcps. indicates multiple overlapping actions; review §311.

4:5

> עַד אָחֳרֵין עַל קֳדָמַי דָּנִיֵּאל דִּי־שְׁמֵהּ בֵּלְטְשַׁאצַּר כְּשֻׁם אֱלָהִי וְדִי רוּחַ־אֱלָהִין קַדִּישִׁין בֵּהּ וְחֶלְמָא קֳדָמוֹהִי אַמְרֵת:

עַד אָחֳרֵין: Adv., see §116c. עַל: Verb, cf. Dan 6:11. שְׁמֵהּ: **qul* pattern (§99) + 3ms pron. suff.; "name." בֵּלְטְשַׁאצַּר: "Belteshazzar," proper name. אֱלָהִי: Cf. Dan 6:23.

וְדִי רוּחַ־אֱלָהִין קַדִּישִׁין בֵּהּ: *In whom was a spirit of (the) holy gods.* וְדִי: Introducing a second non-restrictive relative clause (§149). רוּחַ: Cf. Dan 6:4. קַדִּישִׁין: **qaṭṭīl* pattern adjective (§110); "holy," used attributively (§145). בֵּהּ: The suffix is resumptive (review §148b), as it is on שְׁמֵהּ. אַמְרֵת: Cp. עַבְדֵת (Dan 3:15) and parse.

4:6

> בֵּלְטְשַׁאצַּר רַב חַרְטֻמַיָּא דִּי | אֲנָה יִדְעֵת דִּי רוּחַ אֱלָהִין קַדִּישִׁין בָּךְ וְכָל־רָז לָא־אָנֵס לָךְ חֶזְוֵי חֶלְמִי דִי־חֲזֵית וּפִשְׁרֵהּ אֱמַר:

18

299

רַב: *qall* pattern (§104); "ruler, chief." יְדְעָת: Cp. עַבְדַת (Dan 3:15), אָמְרֵת (Dan 4:5). Parse. For tense, see §297.

וְכָל־רָז לָא־אָנֵס לָךְ: *No mystery is too difficult for you.* רָז: *qāl* pattern (§100); Persian loanword. אָנֵס: What part of speech? G stem אנס "constrain, put pressure on" > "to be difficult." For כל + לא, see again §167c. חֶזְוֵי: Cf. 4:2 above. חֶלְמֵי דִי־חֲזֵית: Cp. 4:2 חֵלֶם חֲזֵית above. וּפִשְׁרֵהּ: Cf. 4:4 above. אֱמַר: See §246d.

4:7

וְחֶזְוֵי רֵאשִׁי עַל־מִשְׁכְּבִי חָזֵה הֲוֵית וַאֲלוּ אִילָן בְּגוֹא אַרְעָא וְרוּמֵהּ שַׂגִּיא:

חָזֵה הֲוֵית: *I was seeing.* For the use of הוי as auxiliary, review §313a. וַאֲלוּ: Presentative particle (§384). אִילָן: *qīṭāl* noun pattern (§109); "tree." Absolute state; review §86a. בְּגוֹא: Cf. Dan 3:25. אַרְעָא: Cf. Dan 3:31, 6:26. וְרוּמֵהּ: Cf. Dan 3:1. שַׂגִּיא: Cf. Dan 6:15, 24; here it is used adjectivally ("great, high").

4:8

רְבָה אִילָנָא וּתְקֵף וְרוּמֵהּ יִמְטֵא לִשְׁמַיָּא וַחֲזוֹתֵהּ לְסוֹף כָּל־אַרְעָא:

רְבָה אִילָנָא וּתְקֵף: *The tree grew large and sturdy.* רְבָה: Cp. הֲוָא (Dan 6:4) and see §256a. "Be/become big" (§330a). וּתְקֵף: *i*-theme G stem (§218); also stative-inchoative (§330).

וְרוּמֵהּ יִמְטֵא לִשְׁמַיָּא וַחֲזוֹתֵהּ לְסוֹף כָּל־אַרְעָא: *Its height reached to heaven and its crown to the end of all the earth.* יִמְטֵא: Cp. יִשְׂגֵּא (Dan 3:31), לֶהֱוָא (Dan 3:18), יִבְעֵה (Dan 6:8), תִּשְׁנֵא (Dan 6:18) and parse. Review §258a. PC for past tense again; review §304. חֲזוֹתֵהּ: *qaṭal-t* pattern (§105). The root is חזי, originally *ḥzw*; cp. חֲזָוָא. The spreading crown of a tree is its most visible feature. לְסוֹף: Cf. Dan 6:27.

4:9

עָפְיֵהּ שַׁפִּיר וְאִנְבֵּהּ שַׂגִּיא וּמָזוֹן לְכֹלָּא־בֵהּ תְּחֹתוֹהִי תַּטְלֵל | חֵיוַת בָּרָא וּבְעַנְפוֹהִי יְדֻרוּן [ידורן] צִפֲּרֵי שְׁמַיָּא וּמִנֵּהּ יִתְּזִין כָּל־בִּשְׂרָא:

עָפְיֵהּ שַׁפִּיר וְאִנְבֵּהּ שַׂגִּיא וּמָזוֹן לְכֹלָּא־בֵהּ: *Its foliage was beautiful, and its fruit abundant, and food for all was on it.* עָפְיֵהּ: *quṭl* noun pattern (§101e). שַׁפִּיר: *qaṭṭīl* pattern (§110b). אִנְבֵּהּ: *qiṭl* pattern (§101). שַׂגִּיא: Used adjectivally again, "abundant, numerous." מָזוֹן: *qāṭōl* pattern (§109): The form is derived from the verbal root זון "eat, feed" (G stem). כֹּל: לְכֹלָּא־בֵהּ + det. state suffix -ָּ routinely has penultimate stress with this word; cf. §344b.

Three copular clauses begin the verse: two with adjectival predicates (שַׁפִּיר, שַׂגִּיא), one with prepositional predicate (בֵהּ). Review sections §376 and §377.

תַּטְלֵל: תְּחֹתוֹהִי תַּטְלֵל | חֵיוַת בָּרָא: *Under it the wild animals would find shade.* Prep. תְּחוֹת (§205). חֵיוַת: *qayl-at* pattern (§103); "animal" (collective sg.). בָּרָא: *qall* noun pattern (§104), with compensatory lengthening (§77c); "field, countryside." חֵיוַת בָּרָא: A standard collocation referring to wild, non-domesticated animals.

עַנְפּוֹהִי: וּבְעַנְפּוֹהִי יְדֻרוּן [ידורן] צִפֲּרֵי שְׁמַיָּא: *In its branches the birds of heaven would dwell.* עַנְפּוֹהִי: *qaṭal* noun pattern (§105); "branch." יְדֻרוּן [ידורן]: The Ketiv suggests *yədurun*, G stem 3mp from דור "dwell, sojourn," the Qere equivalent 3fp form *yədurɔn*; see §272a. Again, the PC refers to habitual action. צִפֲּרֵי (Leningrad Codex): *qiṭṭal* pattern (§111); feminine gender with 1st decl. inflection; see §91b. שְׁמַיָּא: Cp. בִּשְׁמַיָּא (Dan 6:28).

יִתְּזֵין: וּמִנַּהּ יִתְּזֵין כָל־בִּשְׂרָא. מִנַּהּ: Cf. מִנִּי (Dan 3:29, 4:3), מִנְּהוֹן (Dan 6:3), מִנָּךְ (Dan 6:8). Translate. יִתְּזֵין: tG PC 3ms from זון; see §274. The tG usually has passive meaning (§238). בִּשְׂרָא: *qaṭal* pattern (§105b); "flesh" (collective).

Dan 4:10

חָזֵה הֲוֵית בְּחֶזְוֵי רֵאשִׁי עַל־מִשְׁכְּבִי וַאֲלוּ עִיר וְקַדִּישׁ מִן־שְׁמַיָּא נָחֵת:

חָזֵה הֲוֵית: Cf. 4:7. בְּחֶזְוֵי רֵאשִׁי עַל־מִשְׁכְּבִי: Cf. Dan 4:2. וַאֲלוּ: Cf. Dan 4:7. עִיר: *qil* pattern (§100); from the root עור (G, "be wakeful"), "vigilant angel." קַדִּישׁ: Cf. קַדִּישִׁין (Dan 4:5). עִיר וְקַדִּישׁ: Not two figures, but one (RSV: "a watcher, a holy one"); see §143c. The conventional translation "watcher" is derived from the archaic meaning of English *watch*, "to stay awake, alert," e.g., "watch and pray"). נָחֵת: For the syntax, see §310b and cf. §340b. G stem of נחת "come down"; parse.

Dan 4:11

קָרֵא בְחַיִל וְכֵן אָמַר גֹּדּוּ אִילָנָא וְקַצִּצוּ עַנְפוֹהִי אַתַּרוּ עָפְיֵהּ וּבַדַּרוּ אִנְבֵּהּ תְּנֻד חֵיוְתָא מִן־תַּחְתּוֹהִי וְצִפֲּרַיָּא מִן־עַנְפוֹהִי:

קָרֵא בְחַיִל: Cf. Dan 3:4. וְכֵן אָמַר: Cp. כֵּן אָמְרִין (Dan 6:7).

גֹּדּוּ אִילָנָא וְקַצִּצוּ עַנְפוֹהִי: *Cut down the tree and cut off its branches.* גֹּדּוּ: G stem impv from the geminate root גדד (§279e). קַצִּצוּ: D stem impv from the geminate root קצץ; as a rule, geminate roots are strong in the D/tD stems (§280). Both forms are mp. עַנְפוֹהִי: Cf. Dan 4:9.

אַתַּרוּ עָפְיֵהּ וּבַדַּרוּ אִנְבֵּהּ: *Make its foliage drop off and scatter its fruit.* אַתַּרוּ: C stem impv, Aphʿel type (§232b). What is the root? §254. Why is the theme vowel *a*? (§78, Rule 4a). The "original" form is *hantiru*; with change of *ha-* to *ʾa-* (*ʾantiru*), assimilation of *n* (*ʾattiru*) (§42), and change of *i* theme to *a* (*ʾattárū*). Root נתר (G: "to fall [of leaves]", C: "to make leaves fall"). עָפְיֵהּ: Cf. Dan 4:9. וּבַדַּרוּ: D stem impv, "scatter." Cp. קַצִּצוּ and note again the influence of *r* on the theme vowel. אָנְבֵּהּ: Cf. 4:9.

תְּנֻד חֵיוְתָא מִן־תַּחְתּוֹהִי וְצִפְּרַיָּא מִן־עַנְפּוֹהִי: *Let the beasts depart from beneath it, and the birds from its branches.* תְּנֻד: Defective spelling for תְּנוּד "wander, move away" (see §272). Contextually, the form is jussive. חֵיוְתָא: Cp. חֵיוַת (Dan 4:9). מִן־תַּחְתּוֹהִי: Cp. תְּחֹתוֹהִי (Dan 4:9); the vocalization here is a Hebraism. צִפְּרַיָּא: Cp. 4:9 צִפְּרֵי.

וְצִפְּרַיָּא מִן־עַנְפּוֹהִי: For the absence of a verb, see §394.

4:12

בְּרַם עִקַּר שָׁרְשׁוֹהִי בְּאַרְעָא שְׁבֻקוּ וּבֶאֱסוּר דִּי־פַרְזֶל וּנְחָשׁ בְּדִתְאָא דִּי בָרָא וּבְטַל שְׁמַיָּא יִצְטַבַּע וְעִם־חֵיוְתָא חֲלָקֵהּ בַּעֲשַׂב אַרְעָא:

בְּרַם עִקַּר שָׁרְשׁוֹהִי בְּאַרְעָא שְׁבֻקוּ: *But the core of its roots leave in the earth.* בְּרַם: See §396. עִקַּר: **qiṭṭal* pattern in the MS, but properly a **qiṭṭāl* noun (§110); "core of a root system" (CAL). שָׁרְשׁוֹהִי: **quṭl* pattern (§101). Cp. Heb. שֹׁרֶשׁ "root." שְׁבֻקוּ: "Leave, abandon." Review §222. Parse.

וּבֶאֱסוּר דִּי־פַרְזֶל וּנְחָשׁ בְּדִתְאָא דִּי בָרָא: *And in a band of iron and bronze in the grass of the field (leave it).* אֱסוּר: **qiṭūl* pattern (§108). דִּי־פַרְזֶל וּנְחָשׁ: Genitive of material (§161). פַרְזֶל: "iron," cp. Heb. בַּרְזֶל. נְחָשׁ: **quṭāl* pattern (§108); "copper, bronze." בְּדִתְאָא: Prep. בְּ + **qiṭl* pattern noun (§101). Cp. Heb. דֶּשֶׁא. בָרָא: Cf. 4:9.

וּבְטַל שְׁמַיָּא יִצְטַבַּע וְעִם־חֵיוְתָא חֲלָקֵהּ בַּעֲשַׂב אַרְעָא: *And by the dew of heaven let him be drenched, and with the beasts his portion will be in the plants of the earth.* וּבְטַל: Prep. בְּ + טַל, **qall* pattern (§104); "dew." יִצְטַבַּע: tD stem; see §44, PC 3ms from the root צבע "be drenched, wet." For the passive meaning of the tD, see §237a. חֵיוְתָא: Cf. 4:11. חֲלָקֵהּ: **qaṭāl* pattern (§108); "allotted portion." בַּעֲשַׂב: Prep. בְּ + עֲשַׂב, **qiṭl* pattern (§101b); "plants," cp. Heb. עֵשֶׂב. Explain why the prep. has a *pataḥ* (§76b).

4:13

לִבְבֵהּ מִן־אֲנָושָׁא [אנשא] יְשַׁנּוֹן וּלְבַב חֵיוָה יִתְיְהִב לֵהּ וְשִׁבְעָה עִדָּנִין יַחְלְפוּן עֲלוֹהִי:

לִבְבֵהּ מִן־אֲנָושָׁא [אנשא] יְשַׁנּוֹן: *His mind will be altered from the human race.* לִבְבֵהּ: **qiṭal* pattern (§105); "mind, heart." אֲנָושָׁא [אנשא]: Qere, cf. אֱנָשׁ (Dan 3:10); **qiṭāl* pattern (§108); abs. sg. אֱנָשׁ "human," אֲנָשָׁא "humanity, humankind" (generic; see §85c). The Ketiv reflects a pronunciation like Heb. אֱנוֹשׁ. For the meaning of prep. מִן, see §183b. יְשַׁנּוֹן: For the inflection, review §263c. D stem PC 3mp from the root שׁנ. For the equation *impersonal plural verb = passive*, see §357. Cp. the D stem SC 3mp שַׁנִּיו in Dan 3:28.

302

וּלְבַב חֵיוָה יִתְיְהֵב לֵהּ וְשִׁבְעָה עִדָּנִין יַחְלְפוּן עֲלוֹהִי: *And the mind of a beast will be given to him, and seven periods will pass over him.* חֵיוָה: Cp. חֵיוַת (Dan 4:9), חֵיוָתָא (Dan 4:11), and review §90a. יִתְיְהֵב: Cp. יְהַבוּ (Dan 3:28), יְהַבְין (Dan 6:3). What form? See §239. Parse.

שִׁבְעָה: Cf. Dan 3:19, and §166a, b. עִדָּנִין: Cp. עִדָּנָא (Dan 3:5). יַחְלְפוּן: Cp. יְפְלְחוּן, יִסְגְּדוּן (Dan 3:28, etc.) and parse. Why does the preformative have *a*? See §78, Rule 4a, "pass by." עֲלוֹהִי: Cf. Dan 3:28, 6:5, etc.

4:14

בִּגְזֵרַת עִירִין פִּתְגָמָא וּמֵאמַר קַדִּישִׁין שְׁאֵלְתָא עַד־דִּבְרַת דִּי יִנְדְּעוּן חַיַּיָּא דִּי־שַׁלִּיט עִלָּיָא [עלאה] בְּמַלְכוּת אֱנוּשָׁא [אנשא] וּלְמַן־דִּי יִצְבֵּא יִתְּנִנַּהּ וּשְׁפַל אֲנָשִׁים יְקִים עֲלַיהּ [עלה] :

בִּגְזֵרַת עִירִין פִּתְגָמָא וּמֵאמַר קַדִּישִׁין שְׁאֵלְתָא: *By angelic decision is the decree, and the matter is a command of the holy ones.* בִּגְזֵרַת: Prep. בְּ + *qaṭēl-at noun pattern (§108b); "decision." עִירִין: Cf. Dan 4:10. פִּתְגָמָא: Cf. Dan 3:16: here "decree, statement." וּמֵאמַר: By derivation, a G stem inf. from אמר (see §246a), used as a substantive, "utterance, command." Cp. יֵאמַר (Dan 3:29). קַדִּישִׁין: Cf. Dan 4:5. שְׁאֵלְתָא: Another *qaṭēl-at form (cf. *supra*); "question, matter."

עַד־דִּבְרַת דִּי יִנְדְּעוּן חַיַּיָּא דִּי־שַׁלִּיט עִלָּיָא [עלאה] בְּמַלְכוּת אֱנוּשָׁא [אנשא]: *So that the living may know that the Most High rules in the realm of humankind.* עַד־דִּבְרַת דִּי: For purpose clauses, see §404. יִנְדְּעוּן: See §250d. The root you know; parse. For deontic modality, review §291b, c. חַיַּיָּא: Cf. חַיָּא (Dan 6:21). The present form is 1st decl. pl. det., adj. used as noun (§172).

דִּי is used here as a complementizer (§341). שַׁלִּיט: *qaṭṭīl pattern (§110b); adj., "having authority." Its root שלט occurred verbally in Dan 3:27, 6:25, and in the noun שָׁלְטָן (Dan 3:33, 6:27). עִלָּיָא [עלאה]: Cf. Dan 3:26. אֱנוּשָׁא [אנשא]: See previous verse.

וּלְמַן־דִּי יִצְבֵּא יִתְּנִנַּהּ וּשְׁפַל אֲנָשִׁים יְקִים עֲלַיהּ [עלה]: *And to whomever he may desire he will give it, and a lowly person he may raise over it.* מַן־דִּי has been seen in Dan 3:6, 11, etc.; here with prep. לְ (§177b). יִצְבֵּא: Should be recognizable as a G stem III-*y* PC verb; "to wish, desire." Parse. The modality is epistemic (§291b). יִתְּנִנַּהּ: G stem PC 3ms + 3fs pron. suff. from נתן "to give." Review I-n roots (§252a; §253a). For the pron. suff., review §130a. The composition is *yitten + inn + ah*, with Rule 1 (§78) operating on the theme vowel *e*. Transliterate the final form.

וּשְׁפַל: *qaṭal pattern (§105); "low, mean." אֲנָשִׁים: A clear Hebraism, with *-īm* pl. ending, and lengthened rather than reduced vowel before the stress. Aramaic does not normally pluralize אנש "people." יְקִים: Cp. תְּקִים (Dan 6:9) and parse. עֲלַיהּ [עלה]: Prep. עַל + 3fs pron. suff.; for the Ketiv-Qere, see §73c and §129.

4:15

דְּנָה חֶלְמָא חֲזֵית אֲנָה מַלְכָּא נְבוּכַדְנֶצַּר וְאַנְתָּה [ואנת] בֵּלְטְשַׁאצַּר פִּשְׁרֵא ׀ אֱמַר כָּל־קֳבֵל דִּי ׀ כָּל־חַכִּימֵי מַלְכוּתִי לָא־יָכְלִין פִּשְׁרָא לְהוֹדָעוּתַנִי וְאַנְתָּה [ואנת] כָּהֵל דִּי רוּחַ־אֱלָהִין קַדִּישִׁין בָּךְ:

דְּנָה חֶלְמָא חֲזֵית אֲנָה מַלְכָּא נְבוּכַדְנֶצַּר וְאַנְתָּה [ואנת] בֵּלְטְשַׁאצַּר פִּשְׁרֵא ׀ אֱמַר: *This dream I saw – I, king Nebuchadnezzar. And you, Belteshazzar, tell its interpretation.* דְּנָה חֶלְמָא: See §146. [ואנת] וְאַנְתָּה: Cf. Dan 3:10, etc. פִּשְׁרֵא: We expect a Ketiv-Qere note here, but it is lacking in the Leningrad Codex. The consonants suggest פִּשְׁרָא, the vowels פִּשְׁרֵה. אֱמַר: Cf. 4:6 above.

כָּל־חַכִּימֵי מַלְכוּתִי לָא־יָכְלִין פִּשְׁרָא לְהוֹדָעוּתַנִי וְאַנְתָּה [ואנת] כָּהֵל: *None of the sages of my kingdom are able to make known to me the interpretation, but you can.* כָּל־חַכִּימֵי: Cf. 4:3 above. יָכְלִין: Cf. Dan 6:5. לְהוֹדָעוּתַנִי (Leningrad לְהוֹדָעֻתַנִי): Cp. יְהוֹדְעַנִּי (Dan 4:3), מְהוֹדְעִין (Dan 4:4), What form is this? §251a and §133b. The order Object–Infinitive is routine (§366). כָּהֵל: The root כהל is a variant of יכל. What form?

4:16

אֱדַיִן דָּנִיֵּאל דִּי־שְׁמֵהּ בֵּלְטְשַׁאצַּר אֶשְׁתּוֹמַם כְּשָׁעָה חֲדָה וְרַעְיֹנֹהִי יְבַהֲלֻנֵּהּ עָנֵה מַלְכָּא וְאָמַר בֵּלְטְשַׁאצַּר חֶלְמָא וּפִשְׁרֵא אַל־יְבַהֲלָךְ עָנֵה בֵלְטְשַׁאצַּר וְאָמַר מָרִאי חֶלְמָא לְשָׂנְאָיִךְ [לשנאך] וּפִשְׁרֵהּ לְעָרָיִךְ [לערך]:

אֶשְׁתּוֹמַם כְּשָׁעָה חֲדָה וְרַעְיֹנֹהִי יְבַהֲלֻנֵּהּ: *Was astonished for a moment, and his thoughts disturbed him.* אֶשְׁתּוֹמַם: For the tL stem, see §236. tL stem SC 3ms from שׁמם "be desolate, dismayed." שָׁעָה: *qāl-at* pattern (§100); "moment, hour, short amount of time." וְרַעְיֹנֹהִי: *qitlōn* pattern (§115) with *ri'yōn > ra'yōn* (§78, Rule 4a); "thought, idea." The spelling is doubly defective (§64e and §71d). יְבַהֲלֻנֵּהּ: Cp. 4:2 יְבַהֲלַנִּי above; parse and transliterate.

חֶלְמָא וּפִשְׁרֵא אַל־יְבַהֲלָךְ: *Let the dream and its interpretation not disturb you.* וּפִשְׁרֵא: Cf. 4:15. אַל: See §388. The presence of this particle always indicates that the following verb is jussive. יְבַהֲלָךְ: D stem jussive 3ms with 2ms suffix. The jussive never has energic *n* before suffixes (§130b). Note that the verb is singular with a compound subject (§355c).

מָרִאי [מרי] חֶלְמָא לְשָׂנְאָיִךְ [לשנאך] וּפִשְׁרֵהּ לְעָרָיִךְ [לערך]: *My lord, the dream is for your enemies, and its interpretation for your foes.* מָרִאי [מרי]: *qātil* pattern, with final *'aleph* (§107); *māri' > mōrē*. In the Qere vocalization, the א is not pronounced (see §48). שָׂנֵא [לשנאך] לְשָׂנְאָיִךְ: "enemy" is a G stem participle turned noun (§172b). For the Ketiv-Qere of the 2ms suffix, see §129f. [לערך] לְעָרָיִךְ: *qāl* noun pattern (§100); "enemy, foe."

4:17

אִילָנָא דִּי חֲזַיְתָ דִּי רְבָה וּתְקִף וְרוּמֵהּ יִמְטֵא לִשְׁמַיָּא וַחֲזוֹתֵהּ לְכָל־אַרְעָא:

חֲזַיְתָ: See §256e and cp. חֲזֵית (4:2, 6, 15). Parse. For the rest of the verse, see 4:8.

4:18

וְעָפְיֵהּ שַׁפִּיר וְאִנְבֵּהּ שַׂגִּיא וּמָזוֹן לְכֹלָּא־בֵהּ תְּחֹתוֹהִי תְּדוּר חֵיוַת בָּרָא וּבְעַנְפוֹהִי יִשְׁכְּנָן צִפֲּרֵי שְׁמַיָּא:

יִשְׁכְּנֵן: See .(Dan 4:9) יְדֻרוּן [ידורן] .Cp :תְּדוּר .(Dan 4:9) תַּטְלֵל חֵיוַת בָּרָא Cp. :תְּדוּר חֵיוַת בָּרָא
§220 and parse. "Dwell," a synonym of G stem דוּר. For the verse as a whole, cp. 4:9 above.

4:19

אַנְתְּה־[אנת]־הוּא מַלְכָּא דִּי רְבַית [רבת] וּתְקֵפְתְּ וּרְבוּתָךְ רְבָת וּמְטָת לִשְׁמַיָּא וְשָׁלְטָנָךְ לְסוֹף אַרְעָא:

אַנְתְּה־[אנת]־הוּא מַלְכָּא דִּי רְבַית [רבת] וּתְקֵפְתְּ: *You, O king, are the one who grew tall and strong.*
אַנְתְּה־[אנת]־הוּא: Review §378a, b; הוּא expresses the copula. דִּי רְבַית: See §150, for independent
relative clause. רְבַית [רבת]: This Ketiv-Qere is something of a puzzle. The form is G stem SC
2ms from רבי (cp. רְבָה Dan 4:8, 17). The expected form is רְבֵית / רְבַיְתָ, both agreeing with the
Ketiv. The Qere (actually a note יַתִּיר י "superfluous *yodh*" in the Leningrad MS) has רבת, which
is anomalous; there may be a confusion with the following רבת. וּתְקֵפְתְּ: Cp. וּתְקִף (Dan 4:8, 17).

וּרְבוּתָךְ רְבָת וּמְטָת לִשְׁמַיָּא וְשָׁלְטָנָךְ לְסוֹף אַרְעָא: *Your greatness grew and reached heaven, and your*
dominion to the end of the earth. וּרְבוּתָךְ: *qal-ū(t) pattern (§113); with 2ms suff. רְבָת: Cp. עֲדָת
(Dan 3:27) and review §256b. וּמְטָת: Cp. יְמְטֵא (Dan 4:8, etc.), and parse. וְשָׁלְטָנָךְ: Cp. שָׁלְטָנֵהּ (Dan
3:33). לְסוֹף אַרְעָא: Cf. 4:8 above.

4:20

וְדִי חֲזָה מַלְכָּא עִיר וְקַדִּישׁ נָחֵת ׀ מִן־שְׁמַיָּא וְאָמַר גֹּדּוּ אִילָנָא וְחַבְּלוּהִי בְּרַם עִקַּר שָׁרְשׁוֹהִי בְּאַרְעָא שְׁבֻקוּ
וּבֶאֱסוּר דִּי־פַרְזֶל וּנְחָשׁ בְּדִתְאָא דִּי בָרָא וּבְטַל שְׁמַיָּא יִצְטַבַּע וְעִם־חֵיוַת בָּרָא חֲלָקֵהּ עַד דִּי־שִׁבְעָה עִדָּנִין
יַחְלְפוּן עֲלוֹהִי:

וְדִי חֲזָה מַלְכָּא: *As for that which the king saw.* A topically fronted phrase; see §370. The rest of the
verse, for which cf. 4:10–13 above, is appositional to the topical independent relative clause
(§150g). וְחַבְּלוּהִי: Cp. חַבְּלוּנִי (Dan 6:23); this is impv (§227g). Parse. עַד דִּי: Cf. Dan 6:25.

4:21

דְּנָה פִשְׁרָא מַלְכָּא וּגְזֵרַת עִלָּיָא [עלאה] הִיא דִּי מְטָת עַל־מָרְאִי [מרי] מַלְכָּא:

וּגְזֵרַת עִלָּיָא [עלאה] הִיא: *It is the decree of the Most High.* וּגְזֵרַת: Cf. 4:14 above. Copular clause,
identification (§378). The subject is הִיא; see §124.

מְטָת: Cf. 4:19 above. The subject is גְזֵרַת. מָרְאִי [מרי]: Cf. 4:16 above. מָרְאִי [מרי] מַלְכָּא. Apposition
(§143).

4:22

וְלָךְ טָרְדִין מִן־אֲנָשָׁא וְעִם־חֵיוַת בָּרָא לֶהֱוֵה מְדֹרָךְ וְעִשְׂבָּא כְתוֹרִין ׀ לָךְ יְטַעֲמוּן וּמִטַּל שְׁמַיָּא לָךְ מְצַבְּעִין
וְשִׁבְעָה עִדָּנִין יַחְלְפוּן עֲלֶיךְ [עלך] עַד דִּי־תִנְדַּע דִּי־שַׁלִּיט עִלָּיָא [עלאה] בְּמַלְכוּת אֲנָשָׁא וּלְמַן־דִּי יִצְבֵּא
יִתְּנִנַּהּ:

18

וְלָךְ טָֽרְדִין מִן־אֲנָשָׁא וְעִם־חֵיוַת בָּרָא לֶהֱוֵה מְדֹרָךְ: *And you will be driven away from humanity and your dwelling will be with the wild animals.* וְלָךְ: לֹ with the direct object; review §177c. טָֽרְדִין: For the form, cp. אָמְרִין (Dan 3:4), שָׁמְעִין (Dan 3:7, etc.), and parse. For the construction, see §358b. For the tense, see §308 (imminent present). מִן־אֲנָשָׁא: Cp. 4:13 above. וְעִם־חֵיוַת בָּרָא: Cp. 4:20 above. לֶהֱוֵה: Cp. לֶהֱוֵא (Dan 3:18, etc.). מְדֹרָךְ: *maqōl* pattern (§117), written defectively (§64e), with 2ms pron. suff.; "dwelling."

וְעִשְׂבָּא כְתוֹרִין לָךְ יְטַעֲמוּן וּמִטַּל שְׁמַיָּא לָךְ מְצַבְּעִין: *And you shall be fed plants like cattle and you shall be drenched by the dew of heaven.* וְעִשְׂבָּא: Cf. 4:12 עֲשַׂב above. כְתוֹרִין: *qōl* (< *qawl*) pattern (§100), 1st decl. pl., with prep. כְ; "bull, ox." יְטַעֲמוּן: "To feed (provide food)"; *shewa* with preformative and *pataḥ* under the first root letter indicate what stem? §227a, f.

וּמִטַּל שְׁמַיָּא: Cf. 4:12 above. מְצַבְּעִין: Cf. יִצְטַבַּע 4:12 above. What form is this? Once again, the impersonal construction with the imminent present. [עלך] וְשִׁבְעָה עִדָּנִין יַחְלְפוּן עֲלָיִךְ: Cf. 4:13 above.

4:14 = יִתְבְּנֵה וּלְמַן־דִּי יִצְבֵּא: עַד דִּי־תִנְדַּע דִּי־שַׁלִּיט עִלָּיָא [עלאה] בְּמַלְכוּת אֲנָשָׁא: Cp. 4:14 above. Translate. above.

4:23

וְדִי אֲמַרוּ לְמִשְׁבַּק עִקַּר שָׁרְשׁוֹהִי דִּי אִֽילָנָא מַלְכוּתָךְ לָךְ קַיָּמָא מִן־דִּי תִנְדַּע דִּי שַׁלִּטִן שְׁמַיָּא:

וְדִי אֲמַרוּ לְמִשְׁבַּק עִקַּר שָׁרְשׁוֹהִי דִּי אִֽילָנָא: *And what they said, to leave the core of the roots of the tree.* Again, an extraposed phrase (§370a). אֲמַרוּ: Cp. אֲמַר (Dan 3:13) and parse; review §357. "What they said" = "what was said." לְמִשְׁבַּק: Cp. שְׁבַקוּ (Dan 4:12), לְמִכְנַשׁ (Dan 3:2), and parse. עִקַּר שָׁרְשׁוֹהִי דִּי אִֽילָנָא: Noun in construct with a noun phrase formed with genitive דִּי (§154b and §162a).

מַלְכוּתָךְ לָךְ קַיָּמָא מִן־דִּי תִנְדַּע דִּי שַׁלִּטִן שְׁמַיָּא: *Your kingdom endures for you after you know that Heaven rules.* קַיָּמָא: Cf. קַיָּם (Dan 6:27). Here the 2nd decl. ending is spelled with אָ◌, so this is absolute state (§90b). What kind of clause? §376a. מִן־דִּי: See §421, temporal clause. שַׁלִּטִן: Cp. שַׁלִּיט (Dan 4:14, etc., above) and note the doubly defective spelling (§68b). שְׁמַיָּא: Here used as a reverential euphemism for God.

4:24

לָהֵן מַלְכָּא מִלְכִּי יִשְׁפַּר עֲלָיִךְ [עלך] וַחֲטָיָךְ [וחטאך] בְּצִדְקָה פְרֻק וַעֲוָיָתָךְ בְּמִחַן עֲנָיִן הֵן תֶּהֱוֵה אַרְכָה לִשְׁלֵוְתָךְ:

לָהֵן מַלְכָּא מִלְכִּי יִשְׁפַּר עֲלָיִךְ [עלך]: *Therefore, O king, may my counsel be pleasing to you.* לָהֵן: Here = "therefore" (§433). מִלְכִּי: *qiṭl* pattern (§101); "counsel." יִשְׁפַּר: Cp. שְׁפַר (Dan 3:32, etc.). Prep. עַל (§188f), with שְׁפַר; see §330b.

וַחֲטָיָךְ [וחטאך] בְּצִדְקָה פְרֻק וַעֲוָיָתָךְ בְּמִחַן עֲנָיִן: *Your sins by righteousness remove, and your iniquities by showing compassion to the poor.* וַחֲטָיָךְ: *qaṭāl* pattern (§108); "sin," with 2ms pron. suff. (§129). בְּצִדְקָה: Prep. בְ (§179e), with *qiṭlat* (< *qaṭalat*) pattern noun (§105); "righteousness" (or "almsgiving"). פְרֻק: "Remove, unload"; see §222 to review the imperative.

עֲוָיָתָךְ: Singular or plural? Note the vowel before ת and review §90a. *qaṭal-at* pattern (§108); "iniquity." בְּמִחַן: Again instrumental בְ, this time with G stem inf. from the root חנן; see §279g. For the virtual doubling of the ח, see §77b. The infinitive is used as a verbal noun (§320). עֲנָיִן: *qaṭē (*qaṭil) pattern (§106); adj. עֲנֵה "poor, afflicted." For the plural form, see §58d. The יִן ending has become יִן in pause (§32).

For the structure of the last two clauses, review gapping (§394).

הֵן תֶּהֱוֵא אַרְכָה לִשְׁלֵוְתָךְ: *So that perhaps there might be a prolongation for your comfort.* הֵן: Cf. Dan 3:15, 17. For this use of the particle, see §422c. תֶּהֱוֵא: review other like forms in Dan 3:18, 4:22, 6:2, 3, 27, with תֶעְדֵּא (Dan 6:9), and parse. אַרְכָה: *qaṭalat* pattern (§105); "lengthening, prolongation." Note also the operation of Rule 2a (§78) and spirantization (Rule 6). לִשְׁלֵוְתָךְ: Prep. לְ (§178a), with *qaṭēlat* pattern (§108b); "prosperity, tranquility."

4:25–26

כֹּלָּא מְטָא עַל־נְבוּכַדְנֶצַּר מַלְכָּא:
לִקְצָת יַרְחִין תְּרֵי־עֲשַׂר עַל־הֵיכַל מַלְכוּתָא דִּי בָבֶל מְהַלֵּךְ הֲוָה:

כֹּלָּא: Cf. Dan 4:9, 18; for the anomalous penultimate stress, see §344b. מְטָא: Cp. מְטָת (Dan 4:19, 21 above), and parse. For conjunctive *dagesh*, see §28c.

לִקְצָת יַרְחִין תְּרֵי־עֲשַׂר: *At the end of twelve months.* לִקְצָת: Prep. לְ (§178b) and *qaṭalat* pattern noun (from *qaṣayat > qaṣāt) (§105); here "end"; elsewhere "part, portion."[3] יַרְחִין: *qaṭl* pattern (§101); "month." תְּרֵי־עֲשַׂר: Review cardinal numbers (§164e, Table 9, and §166a).

עַל־הֵיכַל מַלְכוּתָא דִּי בָבֶל מְהַלֵּךְ הֲוָה: *On the royal palace of Babylon he was walking.* הֵיכַל: Cf. Dan 6:19. הֵיכַל מַלְכוּתָא: Noun in construct with an abstract noun can be equivalent to an attribute: "the palace of the kingdom" = the royal palace (§156). ה׳ מ׳ דִּי בָבֶל: Cstr. phrase in periphrastic genitive construction, review §160. מְהַלֵּךְ: Cp. מְצַלֵּא (Dan 6:11) and מַהְלְכִין (Dan 3:25) and comments made thereon. Parse. מ׳ הֲוָה: See §313a again.

---

[3] Two verbal roots influence the meaning of this noun: G stem קצי "break into pieces" and G/D stem קצץ "cut up, off." Construed from the first (the actual etymological root), it means "part"; from the second, "end."

4:27

עֲנֵה מַלְכָּא וְאָמַר הֲלָא דָא־הִיא בָּבֶל רַבְּתָא דִּי־אֲנָה בֱנַיְתַהּ לְבֵית מַלְכוּ בִּתְקַף חִסְנִי וְלִיקָר הַדְרִי׃

הֲלָא דָא־הִיא בָּבֶל רַבְּתָא: *Is this not great Babylon?* הֲלָא: Cf. Dan 3:24. דָא: See §136, "this." הִיא: Cf. Dan 4:21. רַבְּתָא: We've seen רַב in 4:6 as a noun, but it usually functions as an adjective. For the ending, see §90a, "great." Review §145. The copular clause is Subject (דא), Copula (היא), and Predicate (בָּבֶל רַבְּתָא). What type? See §378.

דִּי־אֲנָה בֱנַיְתַהּ לְבֵית מַלְכוּ: *Which I built (it) for a royal residence.* די relative. בֱנַיְתַהּ: G stem SC 1cs *banayt* + 3fs pron. suff -*ah*. We expect בְּנֵיתַהּ; the *ḥaṭeph* vowel is unexpected. Cp. other 1cs forms from weak roots: הֲוֵית (Dan 4:1), חֲזֵית (4:2, etc.). The original diphthong does not contract here (see §73a). For the syntax of the resumptive pronoun, see §148a, c. What does the 3fs suffix refer to? לְבֵית מַלְכוּ: For בית, cf. Dan 4:1; for מלכו, see Dan 3:33, 4:14, etc. Review §90d. בית מ': For the attributive use of the genitive, cf. previous verse.

בִּתְקַף חִסְנִי וְלִיקָר הַדְרִי: *By the strength of my might and for the honor of my glory.* בִּתְקַף: Prep. בְּ (instrumental; §179e), with *quṭl* noun תְּקָף "strength" (§101d–e). (Some MSS have a variant reading בִּתְקֹף or בִּתְקוֹף with a different separating vowel.) חִסְנִי: *qiṭl* noun pattern (§101) with 1cs pron. suff.; "might." לִיקָר: Prep. לְ + יְקָר, *qaṭāl* pattern (§108a); "glory, honor." For the vocalization, see §176c. הַדְרִי: *qaṭal* pattern (§105); "splendor, glory."

4:28

עוֹד מִלְּתָא בְּפֻם מַלְכָּא קָל מִן־שְׁמַיָּא נְפַל לָךְ אָמְרִין נְבוּכַדְנֶצַּר מַלְכָּא מַלְכוּתָה עֲדָת מִנָּךְ׃

עוֹד מִלְּתָא בְּפֻם מַלְכָּא קָל מִן־שְׁמַיָּא נְפַל: *While the utterance was in the mouth of the king, a voice from heaven fell.* עוֹד: Temporal adv.; see §350b. מִלְּתָא: Cf. Dan 6:13, 15. בְּפֻם: Cf. Dan 6:18, 23. קָל: Cf. Dan 3:5, 7, etc. נְפַל: We've seen this root elsewhere in תִּפְּלוּן (Dan 3:5), יִפֵּל (Dan 3:6), נָפְלִין (Dan 3:7, etc.). Parse.

אָמְרִין: Review §358b. מַלְכוּתָה: What is the ending ָה? §85a and §90b. עֲדָת: Cf. Dan 3:27. With מִן, the verb means "pass from," with בְּ "pass into." What is the function of the SC here? See §298.

4:29

וּמִן־אֲנָשָׁא לָךְ טָרְדִין וְעִם־חֵיוַת בָּרָא מְדֹרָךְ עִשְׂבָּא כְתוֹרִין לָךְ יְטַעֲמוּן וְשִׁבְעָה עִדָּנִין יַחְלְפוּן עֲלַיִךְ [עֲלָךְ] עַד דִּי־תִנְדַּע דִּי־שַׁלִּיט עִלָּיָא [עִלָּאָה] בְּמַלְכוּת אֲנָשָׁא וּלְמַן־דִּי יִצְבֵּא יִתְּנִנַּהּ׃

Cf. Dan 4:22 above, which is almost identical to this verse.

4:30

בַּהּ־שַׁעֲתָא מִלְּתָא סָפַת עַל־נְבוּכַדְנֶצַּר וּמִן־אֲנָשָׁא טְרִיד וְעִשְׂבָּא כְתוֹרִין יֵאכֻל וּמִטַּל שְׁמַיָּא גִּשְׁמֵהּ יִצְטַבַּע עַד דִּי שַׂעְרֵהּ כְּנִשְׁרִין רְבָה וְטִפְרוֹהִי כְצִפְּרִין׃

בַּהּ־שַׁעֲתָא: Cf. Dan 3:6. סָפַת: Cp. קָם (Dan 3:24) and review §272a. Parse. "To end on X" = "to happen to X, come to fruition (of a prediction)." טְרִיד: Cp. רְשִׁים (Dan 6:11) and parse (cf. also טְרְדִין 4:22, 29). יֵאכֻל: Cp. יֵאמַר (Dan 3:29) and for the root cp. אֲכַלוּ (Dan 3:8, 6:25). See §246a. Parse. Here the PC signifies habitual action in the past (§303). וּמִטַּל שְׁמַיָּא: Cf. Dan 4:12, 20.

כְּנִשְׁרִין: גֻּשְׁמֵהּ Cp. גֶשְׁמְהוֹן (Dan 3:27, 28). יִצְטַבַּע: Cf. Dan 4:12, 20. עַד דִּי: Cf. 4:20, etc. שַׂעֲרֵהּ: Cf. Dan 3:27. Prep. כְּ + * qiṭl pattern noun (§101); "eagle, vulture." רְבָה: Cf. Dan 4:8, 17. טִפְרוֹהִי: * qiṭl pattern like the previous noun; with 3ms suff. on 1st decl. pl. ending; "nail, claw." כְּצִפְּרִין: Cf. Dan 4:9, etc.

4:31

וְלִקְצָת יוֹמַיָּא אֲנָה נְבוּכַדְנֶצַּר עַיְנַי לִשְׁמַיָּא נִטְלֵת וּמַנְדְּעִי עֲלַי יְתוּב וּלְעִלָּיָא [ולעלאה] בָּרְכֵת וּלְחַי עָלְמָא שַׁבְּחֵת וְהַדְּרֵת דִּי שָׁלְטָנֵהּ שָׁלְטָן עָלַם וּמַלְכוּתֵהּ עִם־דָּר וְדָר:

וְלִקְצָת יוֹמַיָּא: Cp. Dan 4:26. עַיְנַי: * qayl pattern (§103), pl. with 1cs suff.; "eye." נִטְלֵת: Cp. עַבְדֵת (Dan 3:15), אַמְרֵת (Dan 4:5), יְדַעֵת (Dan 4:6), and parse. "Lift up." מַנְדְּעִי: * maqṭal pattern (§117). What is the root? Review §54b and §250d. עֲלַי: Prep. עַל with 1cs suff.; see §188b. יְתוּב: See §272a, and cp. תְּדוּר (Dan 4:18), יְקוּם (Dan 6:20), and parse. Once again the PC is used for non-habitual past (§304).

וּלְעִלָּיָא [ולעלאה] בָּרְכֵת וּלְחַי עָלְמָא שַׁבְּחֵת וְהַדְּרֵת: *The Most High I blessed and the Eternal Living One I praised and glorified.* בָּרְכֵת: Note the vowel under ב and see §77c. D stem SC 1cs from ברך "bless." חַי עָלְמָא: Cstr. phrase; see §156, cp. מַלְכוּת עָלַם (Dan 3:33). חַי: Cp. חַיַּיָּא (Dan 4:14), and see §172. שַׁבְּחֵת: "Praise." Cp. to בָּרְכֵת and parse. וְהַדְּרֵת: Same parsing as the previous verbs; cp. the noun הדר in Dan 4:27.

דִּי שָׁלְטָנֵהּ שָׁלְטָן עָלַם וּמַלְכוּתֵהּ עִם־דָּר וְדָר. For the phrasing, cp. Dan 3:33. Translate.

4:32

וְכָל דָּאֲרֵי [דירי] אַרְעָא כְּלָה חֲשִׁיבִין וּכְמִצְבְּיֵהּ עָבֵד בְּחֵיל שְׁמַיָּא וְדָאֲרֵי [ודירי] אַרְעָא וְלָא אִיתַי דִּי־יְמַחֵא בִידֵהּ וְיֵאמַר לֵהּ מָה עֲבַדְתְּ:

דָּאֲרֵי [דירי]: Cf. Dan 3:31, 6:26. כְּלָה: כְּ + לָה (= לָא); see §387d. חֲשִׁיבִין: See §224. G stem חשב "think, consider," Gp "be considered." כְּלָה חֲשִׁיבִין: "considered as naught." וּכְמִצְבְּיֵהּ: Inf. used temporally; see §419, cp. Dan 6:21. מִצְבְּיֵהּ: See §261d; for the root, cf. יְצֵא (Dan 4:14); "as he desires." עָבֵד: Cf. Dan 6:11. For the syntax, review §358a.

בְּחֵיל: For חֵיל, cf. Dan 3:20, 4:11, etc.; here "host, army." וְלָא אִיתַי: Cf. Dan 3:25, 29. דִּי־יְמַחֵא בִידֵהּ: Independent ("headless") relative clause; see §150. יְמַחֵא: Verb, III-y root and guttural middle root letter; "hit, strike." Parse (see §263c and §77b). בִידֵהּ: For vocalization of בְּ, cp. לִיקָר Dan 4:27 and §52d; this is בְּ + יְדַה (yad + eh after Rule 1 [§78]). וְיֵאמַר: Cf. Dan 3:29. מָה: Interrogative pron. (§138 and §391b). עֲבַדְתְּ: SC 2ms can have תְּ or תָּא/תָּה endings (§212c).

18

4:33

בֵּהּ־זִמְנָא מַנְדְּעִי ׀ יְתוּב עֲלַי וְלִיקַר מַלְכוּתִי הַדְרִי וְזִיוִי[4] יְתוּב עֲלַי וְלִי הַדָּבְרַי וְרַבְרְבָנַי יְבַעוֹן וְעַל־מַלְכוּתִי הָתְקְנַת וּרְבוּ יַתִּירָה הוּסְפַת לִי:

בֵּהּ־זִמְנָא: Cf. Dan 3:7, 8. מַנְדְּעִי יְתוּב עֲלַי: Cf. Dan 4:31 above. וְלִיקַר מַלְכוּתִי הַדְרִי: Cp. 4:27 above. זִיוִי: * $q\bar{\imath}l$ pattern (§100). Actually, this noun is likely a loanword from Akkadian $z\bar{\imath}mu$, "splendor." הַדָּבְרַי: Cf. Dan 3:24, 27, etc. וְרַבְרְבָנַי: Cf. רַבְרְבָנוֹהִי (Dan 6:18). יְבַעוֹן: Prefixed יְ indicates PC; ending וֹן indicates what class of weak verb? See §263c, and note virtual doubling again (§77b). For the root, cf. בְּעָין (Dan 6:5), יִבְעֵה (6:8). The force of the D stem instead of the G here is not clear. "Consult, seek advice" (?).

הָתְקְנַת. For the form, see §235a, b. The 3fs form does not seem to fit the context, which demands 1cs instead; read הָתְקְנֵת *hŏtqanét*. Cp SC 1cs from תקן "I was established." וּרְבוּ: Cf. רְבוּתָךְ (Dan 4:19). יַתִּירָה: Cf. יַתִּירָא (Dan 3:22). What form is this? See §145. הוּסְפַת: Again the 3fs ending (§212). The ה preformative indicates C or Cp stem; see §52a, and §251d. Root יסף; "more greatness was added to me."

4:34

כְּעַן אֲנָה נְבֻכַדְנֶצַּר[5] מְשַׁבַּח וּמְרוֹמֵם וּמְהַדַּר לְמֶלֶךְ שְׁמַיָּא דִּי כָל־מַעֲבָדוֹהִי קְשֹׁט וְאֹרְחָתֵהּ דִּין וְדִי מַהְלְכִין בְּגֵוָה יָכֵל לְהַשְׁפָּלָה:

כְּעַן: Cf. Dan 3:15, 6:9. מְשַׁבַּח: Cp. שַׁבַּחֵת (Dan 4:31) above. וּמְרוֹמֵם: For the R stem, see §276; "exalt." וּמְהַדַּר: Cp. הַדְּרֵת (4:31) above. לְמֶלֶךְ: A common word, now encountered here in the cstr. form; see §101a, c. דִּי: Ambiguous between relative ("whose") or conjunctive ("because"); see §409b.

מַעֲבָדוֹהִי: * *maqtāl* pattern (§117); "deed." קְשֹׁט: * *qutl* pattern (§101d); "truth, righteousness." Abs. state with predicate nominative (§375). אֹרְחָתֵהּ: * *qutl* pattern as well, with 2nd decl. pl. ending, with 3ms suffix. אֹרַח "way." דִּין: * $q\bar{\imath}l$ pattern (cf. זִיו above.); "justice." Also predicate nominative.

וְדִי מַהְלְכִין בְּגֵוָה יָכֵל לְהַשְׁפָּלָה: *Those who walk in pride he is able to bring low.* וְדִי מַהְלְכִין: Independent relative clause; again see §150. מַהְלְכִין: Cf. Dan 3:25. גֵוָה: Originally * *qatl-at* form with א as second root letter; "pride." See §63d with §70c. יָכֵל: Review §358a. לְהַשְׁפָּלָה: For the root, cp. the noun שְׁפַל (Dan 4:14 above); "to bring low." Parse.

READING 4: DANIEL 7

7:1

בִּשְׁנַת חֲדָה לְבֵלְאשַׁצַּר מֶלֶךְ בָּבֶל דָּנִיֵּאל חֵלֶם חֲזָה וְחֶזְוֵי רֵאשֵׁהּ עַל־מִשְׁכְּבֵהּ בֵּאדַיִן חֶלְמָא כְתַב רֵאשׁ מִלִּין אֲמַר:

---

[4] Leningrad Codex has a defective spelling, זִוְ.   [5] Leningrad Codex נְבוּכַדְנֶצַּר.

בִּשְׁנַת חֲדָה: For this genitive construction, see §157b. "Year of one" = the first year. חֲדָה: Cf. Dan 4:16. לְבֵלְאשַׁצַּר: For לְ as a genitive particle, see §163. מֶלֶךְ: For the cstr. state, cf. Dan 4:34 and references there. חֵלֶם חֲזָה: Cp. חֵלֶם חֲזֵית (Dan 4:2). וְחֶזְוֵי רֵאשֵׁהּ עַל־מִשְׁכְּבֵהּ: Cp. Dan 4:2, 7. כְּתַב: Cf. Dan 6:26. מִלִּין: For the pl. form, see §93. רֵאשׁ מִלִּין = "the beginning of the discourse."

7:2

עָנֵה דָנִיֵּאל וְאָמַר חָזֵה הֲוֵית בְּחֶזְוִי עִם־לֵילְיָא וַאֲרוּ אַרְבַּע רוּחֵי שְׁמַיָּא מְגִיחָן לְיַמָּא רַבָּא:

חָזֵה הֲוֵית: Cf. Dan 4:7, 10. עִם־לֵילְיָא: For the use of עִם, see §189b. לֵילְיָא: For the class of final -ē nouns, see §96. The abs./cstr. form is לֵילִי "night." וַאֲרוּ: Cp. וַאֲלוּ (Dan 4:7) and see §384. אַרְבַּע: "Four." See §166, Table 9. רוּחֵי: here, "wind"; cf. Dan 4:5, 6:4. אַרְבַּע רוּחֵי שְׁמַיָּא: *the* four winds of heaven"; see §157a.

מְגִיחָן: The preformative *m-* and the ending *-ān* indicate a participle; see §277e. The root is גוח, here "arouse, agitate." יַמָּא: *qall* pattern (§104); "sea." לְיַמָּא רַבָּא: "The Great Sea," i.e., the Mediterranean.

7:3

וְאַרְבַּע חֵיוָן רַבְרְבָן סָלְקָן מִן־יַמָּא שָׁנְיָן דָּא מִן־דָּא:

חֵיוָן: Cp. חֵיוְתָא (Dan 4:11, etc.). Review §90, if necessary. רַבְרְבָן: Abs. pl. of רַב (§94). סָלְקָן: This root we have met before; cf. Dan 3:22, 6:24. This is G stem; what form? Visions often are described in the present tense. שָׁנְיָן: Same parsing as סָלְקָן, except for the root. See §331a. דָּא: See §136. For the syntax of the reciprocal relation, see §169d.

7:4

קַדְמָיְתָא כְאַרְיֵה וְגַפִּין דִּי־נְשַׁר לַהּ חָזֵה הֲוֵית עַד דִּי־מְּרִיטוּ גַפַּיהּ [גפה] וּנְטִילַת מִן־אַרְעָא וְעַל־רַגְלַיִן כֶּאֱנָשׁ הֳקִימַת וּלְבַב אֱנָשׁ יְהִיב לַהּ:

קַדְמָיְתָא: For the morphology, see §97, Table 8. For the syntax, see §165b. כְאַרְיֵה: The plural form was encountered in אַרְיָוָתָא (Dan 6:8). Review §96. For the copular clause type, review §377a. וְגַפִּין: *qall* pattern (§104); "wing." נְשַׁר: Cf. נִשְׁרִין (Dan 4:30). לַהּ: Predicate of copular clause; see §377b. דִּי־מְּרִיטוּ: conjunctive *dagesh* (§28c). See §224c, for the parsing; "pluck off." גַפַּיהּ [גפה]: For the suffix, review §129e.

וּנְטִילַת: Cp. נְטַלֶת (Dan 4:31), and see again §224c. וְעַל־רַגְלַיִן: For the use of עַל, see §188d. רַגְלַיִן: *qatl* pattern (§101), with dual ending (§95); "feet." כֶּאֱנָשׁ: For the vocalization, see §76b. הֳקִימַת: Cp. הָקֵים (Dan 3:2, etc.), and see §277i. Cp stem SC 3fs, from קום. וּלְבַב אֱנָשׁ: Cf. חֵיוָה (Dan 4:13). יְהִיב: For the root, cf. Dan 4:13, 6:3, and parse.

7:5

וַאֲרוּ חֵיוָה אָחֳרִי תִנְיָנָה דָּמְיָה לְדֹב וְלִשְׂטַר־חַד הֳקִמַת וּתְלָת עִלְעִין בְּפֻמַּהּ בֵּין שִׁנַּיהּ [שנה] וְכֵן אָמְרִין לַהּ קוּמִי אֲכֻלִי בְּשַׂר שַׂגִּיא:

וַאֲרוּ: Cf. 7:2 above. אָחֳרִי: "Another"; see §116a. תִנְיָנָה: Adj. ordinal number, "second"; see §164c, Table 9; attributive use (§145a). דָּמְיָה: Cp. שָׁנַיִן (7:3 above), and דָּמֵה (Dan 3:25). Parse. לְדֹב: For use of prep., see §330b. דֹּב: *qull* pattern (*dubb*) (§104); "bear."

שְׂטַר: *qaṭl* pattern (§101); "side." הֲקִמַת: Cf. הֲקֵימַת in previous verse. וּתְלָת: Cf. Dan 3:24, 6:3. What gender will the counted noun be? §166b. עִלְעִין: *qiṭl* pattern (§101); "rib"; see also §95b for the plural. בְּפֻמַּהּ: Cf. Dan 4:28, 6:18. בֵּין: Prep.; "between" (§194). [שנה] שִׁנַּיַּהּ: *qill* pattern (*šinn*) (§104); "teeth." For the Ketiv-Qere variation, cp. [גפה] גַּפַּיהּ in Dan 7:4 above. וְכֵן אָמְרִין לַהּ: Cf. Dan 6:7.

קוּמִי: Impv fs, see §272c. אֲכֻלִי: Also impv fs; see §222. For the root, cf. Dan 3:8, 4:30. בְּשַׂר: Cp. בִּשְׂרָא (Dan 4:9).

7:6

בָּאתַר דְּנָה חָזֵה הֲוֵית וַאֲרוּ אָחֳרִי כִּנְמַר וְלַהּ גַּפִּין אַרְבַּע דִּי־עוֹף עַל־גַּבַּיהּ [גבה] וְאַרְבְּעָה רֵאשִׁין לְחֵיוְתָא וְשָׁלְטָן יְהִיב לַהּ׃

בָּאתַר: Prep.; see §191. אָחֳרִי: Cf. 7:5 above. כִּנְמַר: Prep. כְּ with *qaṭil* pattern (*namir*); "leopard" (§105). For the change of *namir* > *namar*, recall §75a, Rule 4a (§78). For the vocalization, review §176a. גַּפִּין: Cf. 7:4 above. עוֹף: *qaṭl* pattern (*ʿawp*) (§101); "birds." This is a collective sg. (§84), referring to birds generically, while צִפֳּרִין is a regular plural. גַּפִּין אַרְבַּע דִּי־עוֹף "four wings of bird(-type)." גַּבַּיהּ: For the Ketiv-Qere variation, cp. [גפה] גַּפַּיהּ in 7:4 above; noun of *qall* pattern (*gabb*) (§104), pl. with sing. meaning (§84); "back."

וְאַרְבְּעָה רֵאשִׁין לְחֵיוְתָא: For the syntax, see §377b. יְהִיב לַהּ: Cf. Dan 7:4.

7:7

בָּאתַר דְּנָה חָזֵה הֲוֵית בְּחֶזְוֵי לֵילְיָא וַאֲרוּ חֵיוָה רְבִיעָיָה [רביעאה] דְּחִילָה וְאֵימְתָנִי וְתַקִּיפָא יַתִּירָא וְשַׁנַּיִן דִּי־פַרְזֶל לַהּ רַבְרְבָן אָכְלָה וּמַדְּקָה וּשְׁאָרָא בְּרַגְלַיהּ [ברגלה] רָפְסָה וְהִיא מְשַׁנְּיָה מִן־כָּל־חֵיוָתָא דִּי קָדָמַיהּ [קדמה] וְקַרְנַיִן עֲשַׂר לַהּ׃

חֵיוָה רְבִיעָיָה [רביעאה] דְּחִילָה וְאֵימְתָנִי וְתַקִּיפָא יַתִּירָא: *A fourth beast, frightful and terrible, and exceedingly strong.* רְבִיעָיָה: Cf. Dan 3:25. דְּחִילָה: *qaṭil* pattern (§108); "frightful"; for the root, cf. דָּחֲלִין (Dan 6:27). אֵימְתָנִי: Adj. with *-ān-ī* sufformative (§119); "terrible." וְתַקִּיפָא יַתִּירָא: The א ְ ending on תַּקִּיפָא is the 2nd decl. abs. sg., denoting feminine gender on adjectives (§90b). יַתִּירָא: Adv.; cf. Dan 3:22 and §347c.

וְשַׁנַּיִן דִּי־פַרְזֶל לַהּ רַבְרְבָן אָכְלָה וּמַדְּקָה וּשְׁאָרָא בְּרַגְלַיהּ [ברגלה] רָפְסָה: *And it had large teeth of iron; it was eating and crushing, and the residue with its feet it was trampling.* שַׁנַּיִן: Cf. Dan 7:5 above; this is the abs. dual form. דִּי־פַרְזֶל: Gen. of material (§161). פַּרְזֶל: Cf. Dan 4:12, etc. רְבִרְבָן: Attributive adj., modifying שִׁנַּיִן, occurring exceptionally after the predicate of the copular clause.

אָכְלָה: Ptcp without subject; see §358a. Parse. מַדֶּקָה: Cp. הַדִּקוּ (Dan 6:25). The root is דקק; what is the form? See §281d. The original short *i* of *maddiqɔ* has not reduced to *shewa*, as expected (§78, Rule 1), but to *ḥateph seghol* (§24, Table 3): *maddɛ̆qɔ*. שְׁאָרָא: *qaṭāl* pattern (§108); "remainder, residue." בְּרַגְלַיה [ברגלה]: For the Ketiv-Qere variation, cp. גֵּפַּיה [גפה] in 7:4 above, for the noun. רָפְסָה: Parse; G stem root; "trample."

וְהִיא מְשַׁנְּיָה מִן־כָּל־חֵיוָתָא דִּי קָדָמַיה [קדמה] וְקַרְנַיִן עֲשַׂר לַהּ: *And it was stranger than all the beasts that were before it, and it had ten horns.* מְשַׁנְּיָה: Cp. שַׁנִּיו (Dan 3:28), יִשַׁנּוֹן (Dan 4:13), שְׁנַיִן (Dan 7:3). The root is שני; the geminated middle root letter indicates what stem? The *m* preformative indicates what form? Morphologically, this could be active D stem ("change") or passive Dp stem ("changed"). Context favors the Dp. "Changed (for the worse), distorted" = "stranger, more monstrous." מִן־כָּל־חֵיוָתָא: Review §173 for the use of מִן. חֵיוָתָא: Cp. חֵיוָתָא (Dan 4:11, etc.), and explain the difference.

קַרְנַיִן: *qaṭl* noun pattern (§101), with dual ending; "horns." The dual here does not mean "two horns," but just "horns" (although animal horns usually come in pairs). עֲשַׂר: See §164, Table 9. This form is used with feminine gender nouns, hence קַרְנַיִן is fem.

7:8

מִשְׂתַּכַּל הֲוֵית בְּקַרְנַיָּא וַאֲלוּ קֶרֶן אָחֳרִי זְעֵירָה סִלְקָת בֵּינֵיהֵן [ביניהן] וּתְלָת מִן־קַרְנַיָּא קַדְמָיָתָא אֶתְעֲקַרוּ [אתעקרה] מִן־קֳדָמַיה [קדמה] וַאֲלוּ עַיְנִין כְּעַיְנֵי אֲנָשָׁא בְּקַרְנָא־דָא וּפֻם מְמַלִּל רַבְרְבָן:

מִשְׂתַּכַּל הֲוֵית בְּקַרְנַיָּא וַאֲלוּ קֶרֶן אָחֳרִי זְעֵירָה סִלְקָת בֵּינֵיהֵן [ביניהן]: *I was looking at the horns, and behold, a little other horn came up among them.* מִשְׂתַּכַּל הֲוֵית: Cp. חָזֵה הֲוֵית (7:2, etc.) above. What form is מִשְׂתַּכַּל? Cp. מִתְכַּנְּשִׁין (Dan 3:3), מִתְנַצַּח (Dan 6:4), מִתְחַנַּן (Dan 6:12), מִשְׁתַּדַּר (Dan 6:15). Review §53 and parse; "look at." The verb governs prep. בְּ; see §342a. קַרְנַיָּא: Cf. קַרְנַיִן, previous verse. וַאֲלוּ: As in Dan 4:7, 10, and not וַאֲרוּ as in 7:2, etc. קֶרֶן: For the form, review §101c. זְעֵירָה: *quṭayl* pattern (*zuʿayr*) (§112). סִלְקָת: For this G stem 3fs form, we expect final ת◌ as in נַדַּת (Dan 6:19) or (Dan 5:20). Some manuscripts, according to BHS, have סְלִקַת, as in 7:20 below.

בֵּינֵיהֵן [ביניהן]: The Ketiv has the 3mp pronoun הוֹן־, the Qere the 3fp הֵן־. The 3fp only occurs in the Qere in BA (§129g).

וּתְלָת מִן־קַרְנַיָּא קַדְמָיָתָא אֶתְעֲקַרוּ [אתעקרה] מִן־קֳדָמַיה [קדמה]: *Three of the first horns were uprooted before it.* וּתְלָת: Cf. 7:5 above. [אתעקרה] אֶתְעֲקַרוּ: אֶת preformative instead of אִת־ or הִת־ (§75b).

What kind of T stem? §239a. "Uproot," cp. עֲקַר (Dan 4:12, etc.). The Ketiv has the 3mp ending, the Qere the 3fp, as with the pron. suff. in [ביניהן] בֵּינֵיהֵ֑ן. [קדמה] מִן־קֳדָמַ֑יהּ: Cf. Dan 7:7 above.

קַרְנָא־דָא: Review §136 if needed. וּפֻם: Cf. Dan 4:28, 6:18. מְמַלִּל: Cp. מַלִּל (Dan 6:22) and parse. רַבְרְבָֽן: "Great (things)."Cf. 7:3 above, and see §172.

7:9

חָזֵ֣ה הֲוֵ֗ית עַ֣ד דִּ֤י כָרְסָוָן֙ רְמִ֔יו וְעַתִּ֥יק יוֹמִ֖ין יְתִ֑ב לְבוּשֵׁ֣הּ ׀ כִּתְלַ֣ג חִוָּ֗ר וּשְׂעַ֤ר רֵאשֵׁהּ֙ כַּעֲמַ֣ר נְקֵ֔א כָּרְסְיֵהּ֙ שְׁבִיבִ֣ין דִּי־נ֔וּר גַּלְגִּלּ֖וֹהִי נ֥וּר דָּלִֽק:

כָּרְסָוָ֙ן רְמִ֙יו וְעַתִּ֥יק יוֹמִ֖ין יְתִ֑ב: *Thrones were placed and one old in days sat down.* כָּרְסָוָ֙ן: Noun with final -*ē* in the singular; see §96. The plural follows the 2nd decl.; "thrones." רְמִ֙יו: Cf. Dan 3:21. G stem רמי can mean "place, put" as well as "throw" (cp. Greek βάλλω). עַתִּ֥יק: *qattīl* pattern adjective (§110b); "old, aged." יוֹמִ֖ין: Cf. Dan 6:8, 13. וְעַתִּ֥יק יוֹמִ֖ין: Cstr. phrase with adj. as head (§155). "Old one of days" = "old with respect to days." יְתִ֑ב: G stem, *i* theme SC (§218); "to sit, dwell."

לְבוּשֵׁ֣הּ ׀ כִּתְלַ֣ג חִוָּ֗ר וּשְׂעַ֤ר רֵאשֵׁהּ֙ כַּעֲמַ֣ר נְקֵ֔א: *His clothing was like white snow, and the hair of his head like pure wool.* לְבוּשֵׁ֣הּ: Cf. Dan 3:21. כִּתְלַ֣ג: Prep. + *qatl* pattern noun (*talg*) (§101b); "snow." חִוָּ֗ר: *qiṭṭāl* pattern adjective (§110). וּשְׂעַ֤ר רֵאשֵׁהּ֙: Cf. Dan 3:27. כַּעֲמַ֣ר: *qatl* pattern noun (*ʿamr*) (§101); "wool." נְקֵ֔א: *qatil* pattern adjective, from a III-y root (*naqiy* > *naqē*) (§106).[6]

כָּרְסְיֵהּ֙ שְׁבִיבִ֣ין דִּי־נ֔וּר גַּלְגִּלּ֖וֹהִי נ֥וּר דָּלִֽק: *His throne was flames of fire, its wheels were burning fire.* כָּרְסְיֵהּ֙: Cf. כָּרְסָוָ֙ן (Dan 7:9) above. שְׁבִיבִ֣ין דִּי־נ֔וּר: Cf. Dan 3:22. גַּלְגִּלּ֖וֹהִי: Reduplicated noun pattern (§120); "wheel." דָּלִֽק: Vowel pattern indicates what form? (§223); "to burn."

7:10

נְהַ֣ר דִּי־נ֗וּר נָגֵ֤ד וְנָפֵק֙ מִן־קֳדָמ֔וֹהִי אֶ֤לֶף אַלְפִים֙ [אלפין] יְשַׁמְּשׁוּנֵּ֔הּ וְרִבּ֥וֹ רִבְבָ֖ן [רבבן] קָֽדָמ֣וֹהִי יְקוּמ֑וּן דִּינָ֣א יְתִ֔ב וְסִפְרִ֖ין פְּתִֽיחוּ:

נְהַ֣ר: *qaṭal* noun pattern (§105a); "river." נָגֵ֤ד: For parsing, cp. דָּלִֽק above. Note the inconsistent application of Rule 7 (short vowel change; §78); "to flow, advance." וְנָפֵק֙: Cp. נָפְקִין (Dan 3:26). מִן־קֳדָמ֔וֹהִי: Review §203d. אֶ֤לֶף: *qatl* noun pattern (*ʾalp*) (§101c); cardinal number, "thousand" (§164g). אַלְפִים֙ [אלפין]: For the Ketiv-Qere variation, see §89b.

יְשַׁמְּשׁוּנֵּ֔הּ: *Shewa* under verb preformative, along with doubled middle root letter indicate what stem? (§227). For the ending -*ūnnēh*, cf. יְבַהֲלֻנַּ֑נִי (Dan 4:16). Parse. The PC here expresses continuous past action (§303).

---

[6] According to M. Sokoloff (1976), the word here means "lamb."

רִבּוֹ רִבְוָן [רבבן]: Unique final -ō pattern, perhaps of Hebrew/Canaanite origin (§71b). The pl. in the Ketiv may = רִבְוָן; Qere רִבְבָן, as if < *ribabān; "myriad, ten thousand." See §104. קֳדָמוֹהִי: Short vowel with q sometimes does not reduce (§64g): qŏdŏmôhī; contrast קֳדָמוֹהִי qŏdŏmôhī previously in the verse. יְקוּמוּן: Cp. יְקוּם (Dan 6:20), and parse. Again, the PC expresses continuous past action (§303).

דִּינָא יְתִב וְסִפְרִין פְּתִיחוּ. *The court sat and books were opened.* דִּינָא: Cp. דִּין (Dan 4:34); here = "court" instead of "justice." יְתִב: As in previous verse. סִפְרִין: *qiṭl* noun pattern (*sipr*) (§102); "book, document." פְּתִיחוּ: Cp. פְּתִיחָן (Dan 6:11); for this form cp. כְּפִתוּ (Dan 3:21), מְרִיטוּ (7:4), רְמִיו (7:9).

7:11

חָזֵה הֲוֵית בֵּאדַיִן מִן־קָל מִלַּיָּא רַבְרְבָתָא דִּי קַרְנָא מְמַלֱּלָה חָזֵה הֲוֵית עַד דִּי קְטִילַת חֵיוְתָא וְהוּבַד גִּשְׁמַהּ וִיהִיבַת לִיקֵדַת אֶשָּׁא:

מִלַּיָּא: Cp. מִלִּין (Dan 7:1, etc.). רַבְרְבָתָא: Cp. רַבְרְבָן (Dan 7:8, etc.). מְמַלֱּלָה: Cp. מְמַלִּל (7:8), and parse. The partial reduction of i to ĕ is unusual. קְטִילַת: Cp. נְטִילַת (Dan 7:4), and parse. וְהוּבַד: I-ʾaleph root אבד (see §248b); "to be destroyed." גִּשְׁמַהּ: Cp. גִּשְׁמֵהּ (Dan 4:30, etc.). וִיהִיבַת: Like קְטִילַת and נְטִילַת. לִיקֵדַת: Prep. לְ + *qaṭēlat* noun pattern (§108b); and for the root, cf. יְקִדְתָּא (Dan 3:6, etc.); "burning." אֶשָּׁא: *qill-at* noun pattern (§104); "fire."

7:12

וּשְׁאָר חֵיוָתָא הֶעְדִּיו שָׁלְטָנְהוֹן וְאַרְכָה בְחַיִּין יְהִיבַת לְהוֹן עַד־זְמַן וְעִדָּן:

וּשְׁאָר: Cf. 7:7 above. הֶעְדִּיו: For the root, cp. עֲדָת (Dan 3:27, etc.). For the ending ־ִיו, cp. שַׁנִּיו (Dan 3:28), הַיְתִיו (Dan 6:17, etc.). For the vocalizaton of the first syllable, review §75b. Parse. "To remove" (C stem changes valence of G stem, §324a). For the impersonal pl., review §357. וְאַרְכָה: Cf. Dan 4:24. בְחַיִּין: Prep. בְּ + *tantum plurale* abstract noun (§92); "life." Cp. the related adj. חַי "living." זְמַן: Cp. זִמְנָא (Dan 4:33, etc.). עִדָּן: Cp. עִדָּנִין (Dan 4:13, etc.).

7:13

חָזֵה הֲוֵית בְּחֶזְוֵי לֵילְיָא וַאֲרוּ עִם־עֲנָנֵי שְׁמַיָּא כְּבַר אֱנָשׁ אָתֵה הֲוָה וְעַד־עַתִּיק יוֹמַיָּא מְטָה וּקְדָמוֹהִי הַקְרְבוּהִי:

חָזֵה הֲוֵית בְּחֶזְוֵי לֵילְיָא וַאֲרוּ: = 7:7 above. עִם־עֲנָנֵי: Prep. עִם (§189b) + *qaṭāl* pattern noun (§108a); "cloud." כְּבַר אֱנָשׁ: Prep. כְּ + idiom בַּר אֱנָשׁ "son of humankind" = "human being." Cp. בַּר־אֱלָהִין (Dan 3:25) "son of gods" = "divine, supernatural being." For the use of the prep. phrase, see §147b.

אָתֵה: For the form, cp. עָנֵה (Dan 3:14), חָזֵה (Dan 3:25, etc.). Parse. For the combination with הֲוָה, review once again §313. עַתִּיק יוֹמַיָּא: Cf. 7:9 above. מְטָה: = מְטָא (Dan 4:25). הַקְרְבוּהִי: For the root, cf. קְרִבוּ (Dan 3:8, etc.). For the 3ms pron. suff., see §130. Parse the strong verb. "To present, bring to" (C stem). The impersonal construction is used once again (§357).

7:14

וְלֵהּ יְהִיב שָׁלְטָן וִיקָר וּמַלְכוּ וְכֹל עַמְמַיָּא אֻמַיָּא וְלִשָּׁנַיָּא לֵהּ יִפְלְחוּן שָׁלְטָנֵהּ שָׁלְטָן עָלַם דִּי־לָא יֶעְדֵּה וּמַלְכוּתֵהּ דִּי־לָא תִתְחַבַּל:

שָׁלְטָן וִיקָר וּמַלְכוּ: Compound noun phrase (§142). וּמַלְכוּ: Cp. מַלְכוּתָא (Dan 4:26, etc.). Review §90d. Note that the verb יְהִיב is singular with a compound subject (§355c). עַמְמַיָּא אֻמַיָּא וְלִשָּׁנַיָּא: Cf. Dan 3:7, 6:26, etc. יִפְלְחוּן: Cf. Dan 3:28. שָׁלְטָנֵהּ שָׁלְטָן עָלַם = Dan 4:31. יֶעְדֵּה: Parse; if necessary, review §258a. דִּי־לָא תִתְחַבַּל: Cf. Dan 6:27, independent rel. clause used as predicate (§375b).

7:15

אֶתְכְּרִיַּת רוּחִי אֲנָה דָנִיֵּאל בְּגוֹא נִדְנֶה וְחֶזְוֵי רֵאשִׁי יְבַהֲלֻנַּנִי:

אֶתְכְּרִיַּת: tG SC 3fs of III-y root (§266); כרי "to be distressed." אֲנָה דָנִיֵּאל: Parenthetical extraposition (§372). בְּגוֹא: Cf. Dan 3:25, 4:7. נִדְנֶה: Persian loanword "sheath"; some prefer to revocalize נִדְנַה (LBA 223 s.v.). וְחֶזְוֵי רֵאשִׁי יְבַהֲלֻנַּנִי = Dan 4:2.

7:16

קִרְבֵת עַל־חַד מִן־קָאֲמַיָּא וְיַצִּיבָא אֶבְעֵא־מִנֵּהּ עַל־כָּל־דְּנָה וַאֲמַר־לִי וּפְשַׁר מִלַּיָּא יְהוֹדְעִנַּנִי:

קִרְבֵת: Parse. עַל: For function, see §188c. מִן חַד: For the partitive, see §184b. קָאֲמַיָּא: See §273a; ptcp used as independent attributive adj. (§145c); "the (ones who were) standing." וְיַצִּיבָא: Cf. Dan 6:13; here final אַ◌ = det. state. אֶבְעֵא: Cf. יִבְעֵה (Dan 6:8, etc.). Parse. PC used in a purpose clause; see §405. מִנֵּהּ: For function of מִן, see §339d. וּפְשַׁר: Cf. Dan 4:3. יְהוֹדְעִנַּנִי: Cf. יְהוֹדְעִנַּנִי (Dan 4:3). Parse.

7:17

אִלֵּין חֵיוָתָא רַבְרְבָתָא דִּי אִנִּין אַרְבַּע אַרְבְּעָה מַלְכִין יְקוּמוּן מִן־אַרְעָא:

These great beasts, which are four – four kings shall arise from the earth. See §370. אִלֵּין: Cf. Dan 6:3. רַבְרְבָתָא: Cf. 7:11 above. אִנִּין: Independent pers. pron.; see §124. אַרְבַּע: Cardinal number as predicate of copular clause. מַלְכִין: For the plural of *qaṭl* nouns, see §102. יְקוּמוּן: Cf. 7:10 above; here the verb expresses future tense.

7:18

וִיקַבְּלוּן מַלְכוּתָא קַדִּישֵׁי עֶלְיוֹנִין וְיַחְסְנוּן מַלְכוּתָא עַד־עָלְמָא וְעַד עָלַם עָלְמַיָּא:

וִיקַבְּלוּן מַלְכוּתָא: Cp. קַבֵּל מַלְכוּתָא (Dan 6:1). עֶלְיוֹנִין: *qiṭlōn* pattern (*ʿilyōn) (§115); borrowed from Hebrew, "Most High." קַדִּישֵׁי עֶלְיוֹנִין: Cstr. phrase with double pl., i.e., the pl. ending is added to the dependent noun as well as the head noun: "Holy ones of the Most High" (not ". . . of the Most Highs").

וְיַחְסְנוּן: Because of the first root letter ח (Rule 4a, §78), this could be G stem (like יַחְלְפוּן Dan 4:13) or C stem (Aphʿel type). It is the latter (see below, Dan 7:22); "to inherit, come into possession"

(C stem). עַד־עָלְמָא: Cp. לְעָלְמִין (Dan 3:9, etc.), with the same meaning. וְעַד עָלַם עָלְמַיָּא: Rhetorical repetition for emphasis = "forever and ever and ever"; §350g.

7:19

אֱדַיִן צְבִית לְיַצָּבָא עַל־חֵיוְתָא רְבִיעָיְתָא דִּי־הֲוָת שָׁנְיָה מִן־כָּלְּהֵון [כלהין] דְּחִילָה יַתִּירָא שִׁנַּיָּה [שנה] דִּי־פַרְזֶל וְטִפְרַיַהּ [יתיר י] דִּי־נְחָשׁ אָכְלָה מַדְּקָה וּשְׁאָרָא בְּרַגְלַיַהּ [יתיר י] רָפְסָה:

צְבִית לְיַצָּבָא עַל־חֵיוְתָא רְבִיעָיְתָא: *I wanted to make certain about the fourth beast.* צְבִית: Verbs with III-y roots and *i* theme have different SC endings than those with *a* theme (§257); here -*īt*, not -*ēt*, "I wanted" (root צבי). לְיַצָּבָא: Cp. לְכַפָּתָה (Dan 3:20), לְקַיָּמָה (Dan 6:8), לְתַקָּפָה (Dan 6:8), and parse. See §231c, "to make certain." רְבִיעָיְתָא: Cf. 7:7 above; what form is this (§97)?

הֲוָת: Cp. עֲדָת (Dan 3:27), רְבַת (Dan 4:19), and parse. שָׁנְיָה: Cp. שָׁנַיִן (7:3) above, and parse. See §313. כָּלְּהֵון [כלהין]: The quantifier כֹּל is a **qull* pattern noun (§104). For the vocalization, review §64c. For the Ketiv-Qere variant, cf. 7:8 above. דְּחִילָה: Cf. 7:7 above. יַתִּירָא: Cf. 7:7 above.

שִׁנַּיָּה [שנה] דִּי־פַרְזֶל: Cf. 7:7 above. טִפְרַיַהּ: Cp. טִפְרוֹהִי (Dan 4:30). The note יתיר י "superfluous *yodh*" appears in the Leningrad Codex instead of Ketiv-Qere. נְחָשׁ: Cf. Dan 4:12; "bronze." For the balance of the verse, see 7:7 above.

7:20

וְעַל־קַרְנַיָּא עֲשַׂר דִּי בְרֵאשַׁהּ וְאָחֳרִי דִּי סִלְקָת וּנְפַלָו [ונפלה] מִן־קֳדָמַיַהּ [קדמה] תְּלָת וְקַרְנָא דִכֵּן וְעַיְנִין לַהּ וְפֻם מְמַלִּל רַבְרְבָן וְחֶזְוַהּ רַב מִן־חַבְרָתַהּ:

וְעַל־קַרְנַיָּא עֲשַׂר דִּי בְרֵאשַׁהּ: Again, see 7:7 above. אָחֳרִי: Cf. Dan 7:5, etc. סִלְקָת: Cp. סִלְקָת (7:8 above). וּנְפַלָו [ונפלה]: The same Ketiv-Qere alternation of verbal endings is found in 7:8 above. מִן־קֳדָמַיַהּ [קדמה]: As in 7:8 above. דִכֵּן: See §136. וְעַיְנִין לַהּ וְפֻם מְמַלִּל רַבְרְבָן: Cf. 7:8 above.

וְחֶזְוַהּ רַב מִן־חַבְרָתַהּ: *And its appearance was greater than the others.* חֶזְוַהּ: Cp. חֶזְוִי (7:2). Here the meaning is "appearance" rather than "vision." רַב מִן: To review the expression of the comparative, see §173. חַבְרָתַהּ: **qaṭil-at* pattern noun (**ḥabirat*), pl. with suff. (§105); "associate, other one."

The entire verse is extraposed, with the comment to follow (see §370).

7:21

חָזֵה הֲוֵית וְקַרְנָא דִכֵּן עָבְדָה קְרָב עִם־קַדִּישִׁין וְיָכְלָה לְהֹון:

עָבְדָה . . . וְיָכְלָה: Both forms should be easy to parse by now. קְרָב: **qaṭāl* pattern noun (§108); "war." וְיָכְלָה: In this context, without an inf. complement (§330c), "to overcome, prevail over." לְהֹון: לְ of direct object (§177c).

7:22

עַד דִּי־אֲתָה עַתִּיק יוֹמַיָּא וְדִינָא יְהִב לְקַדִּישֵׁי עֶלְיוֹנִין וְזִמְנָא מְטָה וּמַלְכוּתָא הֶחֱסִנוּ קַדִּישִׁין:

אֲתָה: Cp. אֲתָה (7:13 above, etc.), and חֲזָה (Dan 4:20), הֲוָה (Dan 4:26, etc.). Parse. וְדִינָא: Cf. 7:10; here, "judgment." יְהִב: Cp. יְהִיב (7:6 above) and note defective writing (§27). לְקַדִּישֵׁי עֶלְיוֹנִין: Cf. 7:18 above. מְטָה: Cf. 7:13 above. הֶחֱסִנוּ: Cp. יַחְסְנוּן (7:18 above). Parse and note the vocalization (§75b).

7:23

כֵּן אֲמַר חֵיוְתָא רְבִיעָיְתָא מַלְכוּ רְבִיעָיָא [רביעאה] תֶּהֱוֵא בְאַרְעָא דִּי תִשְׁנֵא מִן־כָּל־מַלְכְוָתָא וְתֵאכֻל כָּל־אַרְעָא וּתְדוּשִׁנַּהּ וְתַדְּקִנַּהּ:

חֵיוְתָא רְבִיעָיְתָא: Cf. 7:19; here extraposed (§370). [רביעאה] מַלְכוּ רְבִיעָיָא: Cf. Dan 2:40. תִשְׁנֵא: Cf. Dan 6:18; there, "to change" (inchoative, "become different"); here, "to be different" (stative). See §330. מַלְכְוָתָא: For the plural of this noun type, see §90d. תֵאכֻל: Cp. יֵאכֻל (Dan 4:30). Parse. וּתְדוּשִׁנַּהּ: Hollow verb דושׁ, G stem; "to trample." Parse the form with its suffix. וְתַדְּקִנַּהּ: Cp. הַדִּקוּ (Dan 6:25); see §281a. Parse.

7:24

וְקַרְנַיָּא עֲשַׂר מִנַּהּ מַלְכוּתָה עַשְׂרָה מַלְכִין יְקֻמוּן וְאָחֳרָן יְקוּם אַחֲרֵיהוֹן וְהוּא יִשְׁנֵא מִן־קַדְמָיֵא וּתְלָתָה מַלְכִין יְהַשְׁפִּל:

וְקַרְנַיָּא עֲשַׂר: Cf. 7:20 above, extraposed phrase. מִנַּהּ מַלְכוּתָה: Pron. suff. on מִן is anticipatory (§175d), with emphatic nuance; "from that very kingdom." עַשְׂרָה: Again, 2nd decl. cardinal number with masc. noun (§91d, §164d). יְקֻמוּן = יְקוּמוּן; cf. 7:10 above, with defective orthography. וְאָחֳרָן: Cf. Dan 3:29, etc. יְקוּם: Cf. Dan 6:20. אַחֲרֵיהוֹן: Prep. with suff. (§190). וְהוּא: Overt expression of subject is emphatic (§356); "and he . . .," or equivalent to an English cleft sentence: "it is he that . . ." יִשְׁנֵא: Cp. תִשְׁנֵא (7:23).

קַדְמָיֵא: See §97, and cp. 2nd decl. pl. קַדְמָיָתָא (7:8 above). וּתְלָתָה מַלְכִין: Cf. remarks on cardinals above. יְהַשְׁפִּל: Cf. לְהַשְׁפָּלָה (Dan 4:34), and parse.

7:25

וּמִלִּין לְצַד עִלָּיָא [עלאה] יְמַלִּל וּלְקַדִּישֵׁי עֶלְיוֹנִין יְבַלֵּא וְיִסְבַּר לְהַשְׁנָיָה זִמְנִין וְדָת וְיִתְיַהֲבוּן בִּידֵהּ עַד־עִדָּן וְעִדָּנִין וּפְלַג עִדָּן:

וּמִלִּין: Cf. Dan 7:1, etc. לְצַד: Prep. לְ + צַד, *qall* pattern noun (§104); "side." The combination לְצַד means "toward," but in this context must mean "against, opposing." יְבַלֵּא: III-y root (§263), "to wear out = harass." Parse. וְיִסְבַּר: Parse. "Expect, suppose." לְהַשְׁנָיָה: Cf. Dan 6:9, 16. זִמְנִין: Cf. Dan 6:11; here, "set times of religious observance" (= Heb. מוֹעֵד). וְדָת: Cf. Dan 6:6, etc. Cp. וְיִתְיַהֲבוּן:

וּפְלַג: Dan 4:13. Parse. The subject is קַדִּישֵׁי עֶלְיוֹנִין. בִּידֵהּ: בְּ + יַד + ◌ֵהּ; as in Dan 4:32 (§176). יִתְיְהִב *qaṭl pattern noun (*palg) (§164, Table 9); "half." The mysterious phrase is typical of oracular style.

7:26

וְדִינָא יִתֵּב וְשָׁלְטָנֵהּ יְהַעְדּוֹן לְהַשְׁמָדָה וּלְהוֹבָדָה עַד־סוֹפָא:

יִתֵּב: Cp. יְתִב 7:9, 10 above for the SC; here we have the PC; see §250a. Cf. 7:10 above. יְהַעְדּוֹן: The PC equivalent to SC הֶעְדִּיו in 7:12 above. לְהַשְׁמָדָה: Strong verb, "to destroy." Parse. וּלְהוֹבָדָה: I-ʾaleph roots generally have הוֹ hō- in the C stem base (§248). For the root, cp. הוּבַד (7:11 above). עַד־סוֹפָא: Cf. Dan 6:27.

7:27

וּמַלְכוּתָה וְשָׁלְטָנָא וּרְבוּתָא דִּי מַלְכְוָת תְּחוֹת כָּל־שְׁמַיָּא יְהִיבַת לְעַם קַדִּישֵׁי עֶלְיוֹנִין מַלְכוּתֵהּ מַלְכוּת עָלַם
וְכֹל שָׁלְטָנַיָּא לֵהּ יִפְלְחוּן וְיִשְׁתַּמְּעוּן:

וּרְבוּתָא: Cf. Dan 4:33. מַלְכְוָת: Cf. מַלְכְוָתָא (7:23 above); what form is this? תְּחוֹת: Cf. תְּחֹתוֹהִי (Dan 4:9, etc.). For the phrase, see §154b; approximately "the kingdoms of Under-heaven." יְהִיבַת: The subject is the compound וּמַלְכוּתָה וְשָׁלְטָנָא וּרְבוּתָא, with the first member determining agreement (§355c). It is unusual for SC to refer to future time; the coordination of the clauses may mean "the kingship . . . being given to the people . . ., its kingdom will be eternal," etc. מַלְכוּתֵהּ מַלְכוּת עָלַם = Dan 3:33. Here the 3ms suff. refers to עַם. יִפְלְחוּן: Cf. Dan 3:28 and 7:14 above. יִשְׁתַּמְּעוּן: Review §78, Rule 10. What is the root? The stem? Originally reflexive, "make oneself heedful" (cf. §334b).

7:28

עַד־כָּה סוֹפָא דִּי־מִלְּתָא אֲנָה דָנִיֵּאל שַׂגִּיא רַעְיוֹנַי יְבַהֲלֻנַּנִי וְזִיוַי יִשְׁתַּנּוֹן עֲלַי וּמִלְּתָא בְּלִבִּי נִטְרֵת:

כָּה: Locative adverb (§349). אֲנָה דָנִיֵּאל: Left-dislocated element; review §369. שַׂגִּיא: Adj. used as adv. (§347a). רַעְיוֹנַי: Cf. רַעְיֹנֹהִי (Dan 4:16, etc.). יְבַהֲלֻנַּנִי: As in 7:15 above. זִיוַי: Cf. זִיו (Dan 4:33); there "splendor," here in the plural, "countenance" (as in Dan 5:6, 9, 10). יִשְׁתַּנּוֹן: Cf. Dan 3:19 for the SC equivalent. Review metathesis (§78, Rule 10) and III-y PC (§267).

עֲלַי: Cf. Dan 4:31, 33. לִבִּי: *qill pattern noun, with 1cs suff. (§104); "heart." Cp. לְבַב (Dan 4:13, etc.), an alternate form of the same word. נִטְרֵת: Cp. יְדַעֵת (Dan 4:6), נִטְלֵת (Dan 4:31, etc.); "guard, keep." Parse.

READING 5: EZRA 4:24–5:17

This excerpt from the Book of Ezra includes a narrative about the rebuilding of the temple in Jerusalem and the letter sent by the Persian leaders of the province Beyond-the-River to King Darius.

4:24

בֵּאדַיִן בְּטֵלַת עֲבִידַת בֵּית־אֱלָהָא דִּי בִּירוּשְׁלֶם וַהֲוָת בָּטְלָא עַד שְׁנַת תַּרְתֵּין לְמַלְכוּת דָּרְיָוֶשׁ מֶלֶךְ־פָּרָס:

בֵּאדַיִן: Review §431. בְּטֵלַת: G stem 3fs, with anomalous vocalization (cf. §63d and §218). עֲבִידַת: Cf. Dan 3:12. בִּירוּשְׁלֶם: Cf. Dan 6:11. וַהֲוָת: Cf. Dan 7:19. בְּטְלָא: For the form, review §223 (here with final א for the 2nd decl. ending instead of ה). וַהֲוָת בָּטְלָא: The construction here is stative ("was in a state of cessation"); see §314. The preceding בְּטֵלַת is inchoative; "ceased" (§330a).

שְׁנַת תַּרְתֵּין: Cf. Dan 7:1, §157b. תַּרְתֵּין: Cf. Dan 6:1. לְמַלְכוּת: For the periphrastic use of לְ, see §163. דָּרְיָוֶשׁ: Cf. Dan 6:1. The Darius of this verse is Darius I Hystaspes (king from 522 BCE to 486 BCE).

5:1

> וְהִתְנַבִּי חַגַּי נְבִיאָה [נביא] וּזְכַרְיָה בַר־עִדּוֹא נְבִיאַיָּא [נביא] עַל־יְהוּדָיֵא דִּי בִיהוּד וּבִירוּשְׁלֶם בְּשֻׁם אֱלָהּ יִשְׂרָאֵל עֲלֵיהוֹן:

וְהִתְנַבִּי: tD stem SC 3ms, from III-y root (§267); "prophesy." חַגַּי: Proper name, "Haggai." נְבִיאָה [נביא]: *qatīl noun pattern, likely a Hebrew loanword (§108a); "prophet." The Ketiv suggests a pronunciation with (etymologically original) consonantal ʾaleph *nəbīʾā, and the Qere without: nəbīyā. זְכַרְיָה: Proper name, "Zechariah." נְבִיאַיָּא [נביא]: Again, the Ketiv with consonantal ʾaleph *nəbīʾayyā, the Qere without: nəbīyayyā. יְהוּדָיֵא: Cf. Dan 3:8, etc. בִיהוּד: Cf. Dan 6:14. For the vocalization, review §52d. בְּשֻׁם: Cf. כְּשֻׁם (Dan 4:5). אֱלָהּ: Cf. Dan 3:15, etc. Review §29b. יִשְׂרָאֵל: Proper name, "Israel." עֲלֵיהוֹן: Prep. עַל (§188e) + 3mp pron. suff. like a 1st decl. pl noun (§129).

Observe that the verb is singular with a subject consisting of a compound noun phrase (§355c).

5:2

> בֵּאדַיִן קָמוּ זְרֻבָּבֶל בַּר־שְׁאַלְתִּיאֵל וְיֵשׁוּעַ בַּר־יוֹצָדָק וְשָׁרִיו לְמִבְנֵא בֵּית אֱלָהָא דִּי בִירוּשְׁלֶם וְעִמְּהוֹן נְבִיאַיָּא [נביא] דִּי־אֱלָהָא מְסָעֲדִין לְהוֹן:

קָמוּ: Cp. קָם (Dan 3:24), and parse. זְרֻבָּבֶל: Proper name, "Zerubbabel." בַּר־שְׁאַלְתִּיאֵל: Proper name, "Shealtiel." יֵשׁוּעַ: Proper name, "Jeshua." יוֹצָדָק: Proper name, "Jozadak." שָׁרִיו: D stem PC, III-y verb; see §263b. For compensatory lengthening, review §77c. For the following infinitive, note §428d.

לְמִבְנֵא: G stem inf. with III-y root (§261c); cp. לְמִרְמֵא (Dan 3:20). עִמְּהוֹן: Prep. עִם (§189a) + 3mp pron. suff. מְסָעֲדִין: D stem mp ptcp, with compensatory lengthening (§77c) and partial reduction (§75c; §78, Rule 4b); "help, support," The participle functions as past progressive (§310a).

5:3

> בֵּהּ־זִמְנָא אֲתָה עֲלֵיהוֹן תַּתְּנַי פַּחַת עֲבַר־נַהֲרָה וּשְׁתַר בּוֹזְנַי וּכְנָוָתְהוֹן וְכֵן אָמְרִין לְהֹם מַן־שָׂם לְכֹם טְעֵם בַּיְתָא דְנָה לִבְּנֵא וְאֻשַּׁרְנָא דְנָה לְשַׁכְלָלָה:

בֵּהּ־זִמְנָא: As in Dan 3:7, etc. This expression is not attested in IA or QA. אֲתָה: As in Dan 7:22. תַּתְּנַי: Proper name, "Tattenai." פַּחַת: Cf. the plural form פַּחֲוָתָא in Dan 3:2, etc.; this is ms cstr. (Akkadian loanword). עֲבַר־נַהֲרָה: "Beyond-the-River," a name for the Transeuphratean

province of the Persian empire. עֲבַר: *qiṭl* noun pattern (§101); "other side, opposite bank." נַהֲרָה:
Cf. נְהַר (Dan 7:10). וּשְׁתַר בּוֹזְנַי: Proper name, "Shetar-boznai." וּכְנָוָתְהוֹן: Akkadian loanword
kinātu "colleague"; like פחת above, כנת was given Aramaic inflections of the 2nd declension
(§90e). Again, note the singular verb אֲתָה with the compound subject (§355c).

וְכֵן אָמְרִין: Cf. Dan 6:7. לְהֹם: With the older 3mp ending in -*m*; see §51. מַן: Cf. Dan 3:15, and see §391.
שָׂם: G stem SC 3ms, cp. שָׂמְתָּ (Dan 3:10), שָׂמוּ (Dan 3:12), and review §272a. לְכֹם: See again §51. טְעֵם: As
in Dan 3:12. בַּיְתָא: Cp. בַּיְתֵהּ (Dan 3:29), and see §73a. לְבְּנֵא: Probably an error for לְמִבְנֵא as in Ez 5:2
above. בַּיְתָא דְנָה לְבְּנֵא: See §366 for this and the following clause. אֲשַׁרְנָא: Persian loanword; "materials,
furnishings." לְשַׁכְלָלָה: Inf. of שכלל, borrowed from Akkadian (§288a); "restore, finish building."

5:4

אֱדַיִן כְּנֵמָא אֲמַרְנָא לְהֹם מַן־אִנּוּן שְׁמָהָת גֻּבְרַיָּא דִּי־דְנָה בִנְיָנָא בָּנַיִן:

כְּנֵמָא: Adverb of manner (§351b); "thus." אֲמַרְנָא: G stem SC 1cp; see §217. The context, however,
demands a third person form. Possibly the original text read אמרן (= ptcp אָמְרִין, as often in IA),
incorrectly resolved when the text was revised: "Thus *they* said." מַן: As in Ez 5:3 above; see §375d
for this use as a predicate. אִנּוּן: Cf. Dan 6:25; the later form of the 3mp independent pronoun
(§124). Here it is used as a copula; see §373c.

שְׁמָהָת: Pl. cstr. of שֵׁם; see §99. דְנָה בִנְיָנָא: Noun with demonstrative pronoun; review §146. בִּנְיָנָא:
qitl-ān noun pattern (§115). בָּנַיִן: Review §261a and parse.

5:5

וְעֵין אֱלָהֲהֹם הֲוָת עַל־שָׂבֵי יְהוּדָיֵא וְלָא־בַטִּלוּ הִמּוֹ עַד־טַעְמָא לְדָרְיָוֶשׁ יְהָךְ וֶאֱדַיִן יְתִיבוּן נִשְׁתְּוָנָא עַל־דְּנָה:

וְעֵין: Cf. עֵינֵי Dan 4:31, etc. Review §103. אֱלָהֲהֹם: Cp. אֱלָהֲהוֹן (Dan 3:28). הֲוָת: As in Ez 4:24
above. שָׂבֵי: *qāl* noun pattern, mp cstr. (§100); "elder." בַּטִּלוּ: D stem SC 3mp; for the root, cf.
בְּטֵלַת, בָּטְלָא in Ez 4:24. Review §330a. הִמּוֹ: Independent personal pron., 3mp (§124); cp. הִמּוֹן (Dan
3:22). The 3mp pron. is used as a direct object instead of a pron. suff. (§130d).

עַד: For the syntax of the clause, see §301b. טַעְמָא: Cf. Dan 6:3. יְהָךְ: G stem PC 3ms of the unique
root הוך (§272b). יְתִיבוּן: C stem PC 3mp; see §277a–d. For the verb, cp. לַהֲתָבוּתָךְ (Dan 3:16).
נִשְׁתְּוָנָא: Persian loanword; "document, letter."

5:6

פַּרְשֶׁגֶן אִגַּרְתָּא דִּי־שְׁלַח תַּתְּנַי ׀ פַּחַת עֲבַר־נַהֲרָה וּשְׁתַר בּוֹזְנַי וּכְנָוָתֵהּ אֲפַרְסְכָיֵא דִּי בַּעֲבַר נַהֲרָה עַל־דָּרְיָוֶשׁ
מַלְכָּא:

פַּרְשֶׁגֶן: Persian loanword; "copy." אִגַּרְתָּא: Akkadian loanword, Aramaized as 2nd decl. noun,
(§122); "letter." שְׁלַח: Cf. Dan 3:2, etc. For the names that follow, see Ez 5:3 above. וּכְנָוָתֵהּ: Cp.

כְּנָוָתְהוֹן in 5:3. אֲפַרְסְכָיֵא: Persian loanword, Aramaized in the MT as a gentilic adjective (§97a–b); "inquisitor" (?). Note again the singular verb שְׁלַח with the compound subject (§355c).

This entire verse is a species of "topical fronting," with the next verse constituting the comment (§370).

5:7

פִּתְגָמָא שְׁלַחוּ עֲלוֹהִי וְכִדְנָה כְּתִיב בְּגַוֵּהּ לְדָרְיָוֶשׁ מַלְכָּא שְׁלָמָא כֹּלָּא:

פִּתְגָמָא: Cf. Dan 3:16. שְׁלַחוּ: Here in the plural, without explicit subject (§356). וְכִדְנָה: Cf. Dan 3:29. כְּתִיב: Review §224c. בְּגַוֵּהּ: The word גַּו "interior" was previously encountered only in the cstr., e.g., בְּגוֹא (Dan 7:15); see §72; here with the 3ms pron. suff. The *praescriptio* (names of sender and recipient) follows. לְדָרְיָוֶשׁ: Prep. לְ in the *praescriptio* is characteristic of later texts, not of IA, which uses אל (§185) or על (§188b). שְׁלָמָא כֹּלָּא: Cp. this greeting to שְׁלָמְכוֹן יִשְׂגֵּא (Dan 6:26). The *praescriptio* and the greeting are both abridged in Ezra.

5:8

יְדִיעַ ׀ לֶהֱוֵא דִּי־אֲזַלְנָא לִיהוּד מְדִינְתָּא לְבֵית אֱלָהָא רַבָּא וְהוּא מִתְבְּנֵא אֶבֶן גְּלָל וְאָע מִתְּשָׂם בְּכֻתְלַיָּא וַעֲבִידְתָּא דָךְ אָסְפַּרְנָא מִתְעַבְדָא וּמַצְלַח בְּיֶדְהֹם:

יְדִיעַ ׀ לֶהֱוֵא ׀ לְמַלְכָּא: As in Dan 3:18. אֲזַלְנָא: Parse. לִיהוּד: Cp. בִיהוּד in Ez 5:1 above. מְדִינְתָּא: Cp. מְדִינַת (Dan 3:1, etc.), here in the det. state (see again §90a). לְבֵית אֱלָהָא רַבָּא: Review §154c. Formally either the head noun בית or the dependent אלהא could be modified by רבא, but contextually it is the dependent.

וְהוּא מִתְבְּנֵא: Actual present; see §307. מִתְבְּנֵא: See §266c and parse. אֶבֶן גְּלָל: For the adverbial specification, see §352b. אֶבֶן: Cf. Dan 6:18, here material, not an object. גְּלָל: *qaṭāl* noun pattern (§108a). The exact meaning is unknown, but must indicate high quality material; "choice (?) stone." אָע: For the etymology, see §46. (See also Dan 5:4, etc.) מִתְּשָׂם: Continuing the actual present tense; for the form, see §274. בְּכֻתְלַיָּא: *quṭl* noun pattern (§101); "wall." דָךְ: Distal fs demonstrative pron. (§136). אָסְפַּרְנָא: Persian loanword; "carefully, diligently" (with Aramaic adverbial suff.; §344).

מִתְעַבְדָא: Continuing the actual present; see §240a. Cp. יִתְעֲבֵד (Dan 3:29), and parse. מַצְלַח: *Pataḥ* under the *m* preformative indicates what stem? §234a. Note also the effect of ח in the last syllable (§75a; §78, Rule 4). בְּיֶדְהֹם: See §128d. The ε in יד "hand" is anomalous (unless based on Hebrew models; see Bauer & Leander 1981: 81).

5:9

אֱדַיִן שְׁאֵלְנָא לְשָׂבַיָּא אִלֵּךְ כְּנֵמָא אֲמַרְנָא לְהֹם מַן־שָׂם לְכֹם טְעֵם בַּיְתָא דְנָה לְמִבְנְיָה וְאֻשַּׁרְנָא דְנָה לְשַׁכְלָלָה:

שְׁאֵלְנָא: G SC 1cp, with *i*-theme (see §218); "ask." לְשָׂבַיָּא: Prep. לְ with verbs of communication (§339c); the direct object is the question that follows and is shared with אֲמַרְנָא. For the noun, cf. שָׂבֵי (Ez 5:5 above). כְּנֵמָא אֲמַרְנָא לְהֹם: As in Ez 5:4. For the balance of the verse, cf. 5:3. לְמִבְנְיָה: In place of לִבְנֵא in 5:3; here it must be revocalized as לְמִבְנְיֵה "to (re)build it," with 3ms pron. suff. (§261c–d).

5:10

וְאַף שְׁמָהָתְהֹם שְׁאֵלְנָא לְהֹם לְהוֹדָעוּתָךְ דִּי נִכְתֻּב שֻׁם־גֻּבְרַיָּא דִּי בְרָאשֵׁיהֹם:

וְאַף: Half-conjunction, as in Dan 6:23 (§432). שְׁמָהָתְהֹם: as in Ez 5:4. לְהוֹדָעוּתָךְ: Cp. לְהוֹדָעֻתַנִי (Dan 4:15), and review §251a. דִּי נִכְתֻּב: Introduces a purpose clause (§402). נִכְתֻּב: For the verb, cf. Dan 6:26, 7:1. See §220 and parse. בְרָאשֵׁיהֹם: Cp. רֵאשִׁין (Dan 7:6); the vocalization here is Hebraic, cp. JLA רֵישֵׁיהוֹן. The prep. בְּ here indicates role; "the men who were in (the position of) their leaders."

5:11

וּכְנֵמָא פִתְגָמָא הֲתִיבוּנָא לְמֵמַר אֲנַחְנָא הִמּוֹ עַבְדוֹהִי דִּי־אֱלָהּ שְׁמַיָּא וְאַרְעָא וּבָנַיִן בַּיְתָא דִּי־הֲוָא בְנֵה מִקַּדְמַת דְּנָה שְׁנִין שַׂגִּיאָן וּמֶלֶךְ לְיִשְׂרָאֵל רַב בְּנָהִי וְשַׁכְלְלֵהּ:

הֲתִיבוּנָא: C stem PC 3mp + 1cp pron. suff. Cp. יְתִיבוּן (Ez 5:5 above). The object פִּתְגָמָא precedes, and the pron. suff. is the indirect object: "thus they returned to us the statement" = thus they answered us. לְמֵמַר: G stem inf. from אמר, with elided א; cp. לְמֵאמַר (Dan 2:9); see §§47, 246a. "To say" = saying (introducing direct speech; §321a).

אֲנַחְנָא הִמּוֹ עַבְדוֹהִי דִּי־אֱלָהּ: Copular clause of identification (§378b). עַבְדוֹהִי: As in Dan 3:28. שְׁמַיָּא וְאַרְעָא: Periphrastic genitive with pronoun on head word (§162a). The dependent nominal is itself a cstr. phrase with a compound phrase as dependent (§160c). וּבָנַיִן: Participial predicate with implied subject אֲנַחְנָא from the previous clause; see §358a. The form should be readily identifiable.

דִּי־הֲוָא בְנֵה: See §314. For בְנֵה, review §262a. מִקַּדְמַת דְּנָה: Temporal adverb (§350e). שְׁנִין שַׂגִּיאָן: 1st decl. pl. noun with fem. gender, modified by pl. adj. in 2nd decl. (§91c). שְׁנִין: As in Dan 6:1. וּמֶלֶךְ לְיִשְׂרָאֵל רַב: Periphrastic genitive with לְ (§163). בְּנָהִי: G stem SC 3ms + 3ms pron. suff. The III-*y* verb *bᵊnɔ* ends in a vowel, which requires a suffix from the second series (§130). וְשַׁכְלְלֵהּ: Cp. לְשַׁכְלָלָה (Ez 5:3 above); here the SC 3ms + 3ms suffix. Since the SC verb ends in a consonant, it takes a suffix from the first series (§128).

5:12

לָהֵן מִן־דִּי הַרְגִּזוּ אֲבָהֳתַנָא לֶאֱלָהּ שְׁמַיָּא יְהַב הִמּוֹ בְּיַד נְבוּכַדְנֶצַּר מֶלֶךְ־בָּבֶל כַּסְדָּיָא [כסדאה] וּבַיְתָה דְּנָה סַתְרֵהּ וְעַמָּה הַגְלִי לְבָבֶל:

לָהֵן: Here the particle serves as a discourse marker (§434). מִן־דִּי: Introduces a causal clause (§410). הַרְגִּזוּ: C stem, strong verb; parse (§233). אֲבָהָתַנָא: *qal noun pattern, with pl. extended by ה (§99); "fathers." Cp. שְׁמָהָת (Ez 5:4 above); with 1cp suffix (§128). לֶאֱלָהּ: Prep. ל as direct object marker (§359a). יְהַב: G SC 3ms, "he gave." This begins the main clause.

הִמּוֹ: As in Ez 5:5, 11 above. בְּיַד: See §179b for the use of the prep. [כסדאה] כַּסְדָּיֵא: Cp. כַּשְׂדָּאִין (Dan 3:8), and see §40. For the Ketiv-Qere variation, review §97a. סַתְרֵהּ: G SC 3ms + 3ms pron. suff. (§130). Note the operation of Rule 2 (§78): *satar + eh > *sataréh > satreh. Again, we have a case of שׁ > ס, as with כַּסְדָּיֵא; "destroyed." וּבַיְתָה דְנָה סַתְרֵהּ: Left-dislocation (§369). עַמָּה: Cf. Dan 3:29, 7:27, in det. state. וּבַיְתָה, וְעַמָּה: Note the det. state suffix with ה instead of א (§85a). הַגְלִי: Review §265, and parse; "exiled."

5:13

בְּרַם בִּשְׁנַת חֲדָה לְכוֹרֶשׁ מַלְכָּא דִּי בָבֶל כּוֹרֶשׁ מַלְכָּא שָׂם טְעֵם בֵּית־אֱלָהָא דְנָה לִבְּנֵא:

בְּרַם: As in Dan 4:12, 20. בִּשְׁנַת חֲדָה: As in Dan 7:1. לְכוֹרֶשׁ: ל of genitive (§163). כּוֹרֶשׁ: Personal name, "Cyrus." מַלְכָּא דִּי בָבֶל: Review §160. שָׂם טְעֵם: As in Ez 5:3, 9 above. לִבְּנֵא: As in Ez 5:3.

5:14

וְאַף מָאנַיָּא דִי־בֵית־אֱלָהָא דִּי דַהֲבָה וְכַסְפָּא דִּי נְבוּכַדְנֶצַּר הַנְפֵּק מִן־הֵיכְלָא דִּי בִירוּשְׁלֶם וְהֵיבֵל הִמּוֹ לְהֵיכְלָא דִּי בָבֶל הַנְפֵּק הִמּוֹ כּוֹרֶשׁ מַלְכָּא מִן־הֵיכְלָא דִּי בָבֶל וִיהִיבוּ לְשֵׁשְׁבַּצַּר שְׁמֵהּ דִּי פֶחָה שָׂמֵהּ:

וְכַסְפָּא . . . מָאנַיָּא: *qāl noun pattern (§100). Originally *qaṭl; see §47 and §67d; "vessel." דִּי דַהֲבָה וְכַסְפָּא: Periphrastic genitive with another periphrastic genitive as head (§160c). דִּי דַהֲבָה וְכַסְפָּא: Genitive of material (§161). הַנְפֵּק: C stem SC 3ms; I-n root with unassimilated n is strong (§254); "bring/take out." הֵיכְלָא: Cp. הֵיכַל (Dan 4:26); here "temple" rather than "palace." הֵיבֵל: C stem SC 3ms from the root יבל; "carried." See §251b.

וְאַף . . . לְהֵיכְלָא דִּי בָבֶל: This long noun phrase is the extraposed element of a left-dislocation (see again §369); the main clause begins with הַנְפֵּק הִמּוֹ. וִיהִיבוּ: For this familiar root, cp. יְהַב in Ez 5:12 above, and see §224b. לְשֵׁשְׁבַּצַּר שְׁמֵהּ: See §143b. שֵׁשְׁבַּצַּר: Personal name, "Sheshbazzar." שְׁמֵהּ: As in Dan 4:5. פֶחָה שָׂמֵהּ: For the construction, see §340a; "he made him governor." פֶחָה: Cp. cstr. פַּחַת (Ez 5:3 above). שָׂמֵהּ: Cp. שָׂם (5:3 above), here with 3ms suffix.

5:15

וַאֲמַר־לֵהּ אֵלֶּה [אל] מָאנַיָּא שֵׂא אֵזֶל־אֲחֵת הִמּוֹ בְּהֵיכְלָא דִּי בִירוּשְׁלֶם וּבֵית אֱלָהָא יִתְבְּנֵא עַל־אַתְרֵהּ:

[אל] אֵלֶּה: Proximal demonstrative pron., IA form (§136); the Ketiv preserves a form with final unstressed vowel written (like אֵלֶּה Jer 10:11). The final vowel is omitted in the orthography of the Qere (§25). שֵׂא: G stem ms impv, I-n verb (§253b); "take, carry." אֵזֶל: G stem ms impv; see §246e. אֲחֵת: C stem ms impv, I-n root נחת; cf. §254. The ḥaṭeph vowel in the first syllable indicates that the *ḥ* has degeminated (or never geminated), and thus exposed the short vowel to reduction (§78, Rule 1): *ʾanḥet* > *ʾaḥḥet* > *ʾaḥet* > *ʾāḥet*. This also follows the pattern of JLA. יִתְבְּנֵא: Cp. יִתְרְמֵא (Dan 3:6), and parse. אַתְרֵהּ: *qaṭal* noun pattern (§105a) with 3ms suff.; "place."

5:16

אֱדַיִן שֵׁשְׁבַּצַּר דֵּךְ אֲתָא יְהַב אֻשַּׁיָּא דִּי־בֵית אֱלָהָא דִּי בִּירוּשְׁלֶם וּמִן־אֱדַיִן וְעַד־כְּעַן מִתְבְּנֵא וְלָא שְׁלִם:

דֵּךְ: Distal demonstrative pron.; "that" (see §136). אֲתָא יְהַב: Asyndeton (§395). אֲתָא: As in Ez 5:3 above. יְהַב: As in Ez 5:12 above. אֻשַּׁיָּא: *qull* noun pattern (§104); "foundation." וּמִן־אֱדַיִן וְעַד־כְּעַן: §350a. כְּעַן: Cf. Dan 3:15, etc. מִתְבְּנֵא: As in Ez 5:8 above. Review §358a. שְׁלִם: G stem SC, *i*-theme (§218); a stative SC with present meaning (§297); "be complete."

5:17

וּכְעַן הֵן עַל־מַלְכָּא טָב יִתְבַּקַּר בְּבֵית גִּנְזַיָּא דִּי־מַלְכָּא תַמָּה דִּי בְּבָבֶל הֵן אִיתַי דִּי־מִן־כּוֹרֶשׁ מַלְכָּא שִׂים טְעֵם
לְמִבְנֵא בֵּית־אֱלָהָא דֵךְ בִּירוּשְׁלֶם וּרְעוּת מַלְכָּא עַל־דְּנָה יִשְׁלַח עֲלֶינָא:

עַל־מַלְכָּא טָב: Copular clause (§376a) with implied subject; "if it (the following suggestion) is good to the king." טָב: *qāl* pattern adj. (§100). יִתְבַּקַּר: tD PC 3ms; see §241a. Again, with unexpressed subject, "let (it) be searched." גִּנְזַיָּא: Persian loanword, Aramaized as *qiṭl* (§101); "treasure, hidden thing." בְּבֵית גִּנְזַיָּא: Here, "archives." תַמָּה: Adverb of location (§349a); "there."

הֵן אִיתַי: See §380g. שִׂים טְעֵם: As in Dan 4:3, 6:27. רְעוּת: *qal-ū(t)* noun pattern (§113), sg. cstr.; "will, pleasure." עַל־דְּנָה: As in Dan 3:16. יִשְׁלַח: G stem jussive 3ms, with a familiar root (§317a). עֲלֶינָא: Prep. עַל + 1cp pron. suff. (§73c).

For the continuation of the narrative, read Ezra 6:1–18.

READING 6: PETITION TO REBUILD THE TEMPLE IN ELEPHANTINE (TAD A4.7)

In the year 410 BCE, the temple of the god YHW on Elephantine island was destroyed by a force of Egyptian soldiers, as we learn from the text given here, one of the most important found in the excavations at that location. In this letter, dated 407 BCE, the leaders of the Judean community, worshippers of YHW, ask the governor of Judah to use his influence in Egypt to aid their efforts to have the temple rebuilt. The description they give of the destruction of the edifice, its prior history, and the religion of the Judean community provide insight into the history of postexilic Judaism and are a valuable parallel to the narratives in Ezra.

The text surveyed here is evidently a first draft, and a more fragmentary second draft (TAD A4.8) was also found among the papyri, along with a memorandum (TAD A4.9) that the governor supported the rebuilding efforts. Besides the translations given in Cowley (1923; text with commentary) and Porten and Yardeni (1986; text and translation), readers may consult the translations in Lindenberger (2003; text and translation) and Porten (1996, 2003; translation with annotations). Muraoka (2013: 99–107) also gives the Aramaic text with commentary.[7]

Line 1

אל מראן בגוהי *ʾil mārīʾánā Bagavahya.* אל: Preposition; see §185. מראן: For the pron. suff., see §128. בגוהי: Persian name.

פחת יהוד *piḥat yahūd.* פחת: See Ezra 6:7; loanword from Akkadian *pī/āḫatu.* יהוד: See Dan 6:14, etc. For the nominal syntax of the address, see §143a.

עבדיך ידניה וכנותה *ʿabadaykā yadunyā wakanāwāteh.* עבדיך: See §102 for the nominal form; §129f for the suffix. ידניה : Hebrew name, considered by some to = יאזניה (Ezek 8:11), יזניה (Jer 40:8), but this is unlikely. כנותה: Akkadian loanword *kinātu*; see Ez 5:6 and elsewhere. It is declined in Aramaic as a 2nd decl. noun, masc. gender (§90e).

כהניא זי ביב בירתא *kāhinayyā dī bayeb bīrtā.* כהניא: Ezra 6:9, etc. זי: For the orthography, see §36a. BA דִּי. ביב: §179a. "Yeb" = Elephantine. בירתא: Yet another Akkadian loan (**birtu*); see Ezra 6:2. Again see §143a, for apposition.

Lines 1–2

שלם מראן אלה שמיא ישאל שגיא בכל עדן *šalām (2) mārīʾánā ʾilāh šamayyā yišʾal śaggīʾ bakul(l) ʿiddān.* שלם: Ezra 4:17, etc., and see §108. אלה שמיא: Ezra 5:11, etc. ישאל: Jussive verb, cf. Ez 5:9 שְׁאֵלְנָא; see §222. שגיא: Adjective used as adverb; see §347a. עדן: See Dan 3:5, etc., and see §110. For the word order (OSV) of the whole clause, see §365g. "May the God of heaven seek the welfare of our lord greatly at every time."

Lines 2–3

ולרחמן ישימנך קדם דריוהוש מלכא ובני ביתא *walaraḥamīn yaśīminnákā qudām darayavahuš malkā (3) wabanay baytā.* רחמן: Noun, *tantum plurale* (§92); cp. Dan 2:18. ישימנך: For the idiom "to put X for mercy," cp. BH Neh 1:11. For the suffix, see §130a. The mood is indicative (§291a and §130a–b), but the context favors a jussive nuance; "may he set you for mercy." קדם: Honorific preposition (§203b), governing the compound phrase (§175c). דריוהוש: Persian name, "Darius";

---

[7] For the text of the petition, see http://cal.huc.edu, in the section "Imperial/Official Aramaic," text section 23550 (Comprehensive Aramaic Lexicon).

cp. Dan 6:1, Ez 4:24, etc. וּבְנֵי בֵיתָא: Idiom meaning "princes" or "nobility." "May he place you for mercy before Darius the king and the sons of the house."

יתיר מן זי כען חד אלף *yattīr min dī kaʿan ḥad ʾalp.* יתיר: Dan 3:22, etc. This adverbial use could be vocalized *yattīrā*, with unstressed –*ā* ending (§344), not written word-finally (§56d). יתיר מן: For the comparative, see §173. כען: Dan 3:15, etc. חד אלף: For the multiplicative construction, cp. Dan 3:19 (§164i). "More than now a thousandfold."

וחין אריכן ינתן לך *waḥayyīn ʾarrīkīn yintin láka.* חין: Dan 7:12; another *tantum plurale* noun (§92). אריכן: *qaṭṭīl adjective (§110b) used attributively (§145); "long." In IA, the 1st decl. pl. ending is usually written defectively. Cf. Dan 2:16. ינתן: Presumably a jussive verb (§222). The *n* of the root is not assimilated (§78, Rule 11). "And long life may he give to you."

וחדה ושריר הוי בכל עדן *waḥādē wašarrīr hwī bakul(l) ʿiddān.* חדה: G stem active ptcp (§261), from the root חדי "rejoice." שריר: Adjective (§110b), "strong." הוי: G stem impv; cp. the forms in Ezra 4:22, 6:6. See §260. "Be joyful and strong at every time."

Line 4

כען עבדך ידניה וכנותה כן אמרן (4) *kaʾan ʿabdáka yadunyā wakanāwāteh kin ʾāmirīn.* עבדך : The singular, cp. line 1. כן אמרן: Cp. Dan 6:7, etc. כן: Manner adverb (§351a). אמרן: G stem mp ptcp. "Now your servant Y. and his colleagues say as follows."

בירח תמוז שנת 14 דריוהוש מלכא *bayarḥ tammūz šanat 14 darayavahuš malka.* בירח: Cp. Ez 6:15, Dan 4:26. תמוז: Babylonian month name, equivalent to June–July. 14 שנת: See §166c and §157b. The year indicated is 410 BCE. "In the month of Tammuz, the 14th year of King Darius."

Lines 4–5

כזי ארשם נפק ואזל על מלכא *kadī ʾaršama* (5) *napaq waʾazal ʿal malka.* כזי: Cp Dan. 6:15, etc., and see §418. ארשם: Arshama was the satrap (Persian provincial governor) of Egypt. נפק: G SC; see §217. אזל: Also G SC. על: Preposition, often used of motion toward a person (§188c). The satrap was not in the country when the events narrated took place. "When Arshama had left and gone to the king."

כמריא זי אלהא חנוב זי ביב בירתא *kumarayyā dī ʾilāhā ḥnub dī bayeb bīrta.* כמריא: *quṭl pattern noun (§102). "Priest." כמריא זי אלהא חנוב: Periphrastic genitive (§160). חנוב: The Egyptian god Khnum was the protector of the Nile River and depicted with the head of a ram. זי ביב בירתא: Relative clause (§148). "The priests of the god Khnum who is in Yeb the fortress."

Lines 5–6

המונית עם וידרנג זי פרתרך תנה הוה *hāmōnāyit ʿim Waidranga dī frataraka tanā* (6) *hawā.* המונית:
Possibly a Persian word, "in agreement with, in league with" (DNWSI 284), but the suffix looks
like an Aramaic adverbial ending (§344). וידרנג: Persian proper name. פרתרך: Persian word,
"governor" (DNWSI 945). Persian words are sometimes used in the papyri without Aramaic
inflection (§122). תנה: Locative adverb (§349a). הוה: Finite form (SC) used as copula (§373c). "In
league with Waidranga who was governor here."

לם אגורא זי יהו אלהא זי ביב בירתא יהעדו מן תמה *lam ʾēgūrā dī yahū ʾilāhā dī bayeb bīrtā yahaʿdaw
min tammā.* לם: Particle of direct speech (§321c). אגורא: Akkadian loanword, "temple" (from
Sumerian É.KUR). יהו: God of the Jews; cp. name element *yāhū* in BH. יהעדו: Jussive C stem
(§259 and §265c); final-weak verb from root עדי. Cp. Dan 7:26. Impersonal construction (§357).
תמה: Adverb (§349a); Ez 6:6, etc. "Said, The temple of Yahu the god that is in Yeb the fortress let
them remove from there."

Lines 6–7

אחר וידרנג זך לחיא אגרת שלח על נפין ברה *ʾaḥḥar Waidranga dik* (7) *laḥyā ʾiggart šalaḥ ʿal Nafaina
bareh.* אחר: Temporal adverb (§435). זך: Demonstrative pron. (§136) = BA דֵּךְ; cp. Ez 5:16. לחיא:
Adjective, attributive (§146b); perhaps **qaṭē* pattern (§106). אגרת: Akkadian loanword
(< **egirtu*); cf. Ez 4:11, etc. שלח: G SC; cf. Ez 5:6, etc. נפין: Persian proper name. ברה: For the
suffix, review §128. Observe the SOV word order, as in Akkadian and Persian (§§363, 365e).
"Then that wicked Waidranga sent a letter to his son Nafaina."

זי רב חיל הוה בסון בירתא לאמר *dī rab ḥayl hawā baSewen bīrtā laʾamār.* רב חיל: Written as one
word on the papyrus, as well as in later Aramaic dialects; "ruler of the army." בסון: Ancient name
of Aswan/Syene; cp. BH סְוֵנֶה (Ezek 29:10, 30:6). לאמר: An archaic G infinitive; see §321b. Note
that the relative clause is non-restrictive (§149). "Who was army commander in Syene the
fortress, saying."

Lines 7–8

אגורא זי [יהו אלהא ביב] בירתא ינדשו *ʾēgūrā dī [yahū ʾilāhā] bayeb* (8) *bīrtā yindúšū.* אגורא: This
noun phrase and its relative clause are the direct object. יהו אלהא ביב: The bracketed words are
from the "second draft" in TAD A4.8. ינדשו: I-n verb without assimilation (see §252); jussive
(review §222). "Let them demolish the temple of the god Yahu in Yeb the fortress."

אחר נפין [זך] דבר מצריא עם חילא אחרנן *ʾaḥḥar Nafaina dik dabar miṣrāyyē ʿim ḥaylā ʾuḥrānīn.* דבר:
Probably G stem, "lead, take"; the D stem would mean "guide, conduct" (review §231e). מצריא:

Gentilic plural; see §97. אחרנן: See §116b. "Then this Nafaina led the Egyptians with other troops."

אתו לבירת יב עם תליהם *ataw labīrat Yeb ʿim talayhum*. אתו: G SC, III-y verb; probably the diphthongs had not reduced at this time (§256c). תליהם: Meaning uncertain: "pick"? "axe"? (DNWSI 1216). The parallel text (A4.8) has זניהום "their tools." "They came to the fortress of Yeb with their axes."

Line 9

עלו באגורא זך נדשוהי עד ארעא (9) *ǵállū baʾēgūrā dik nadašûhī ʿad ʾarʿā*. עלו: G SC, geminate verb (§279). Note first consonant is transliterated as the velar fricative *ǵ*, rather than pharyngeal ʿ*ayin*, at this time both written with ע (§39). נדשוהי: Same verb (G SC 3mp) encountered in line 8 in jussive. For pron. suffix, see §131. ארעא: More frequently spelled ארקא in IA (§37). עלו . . . נדשוהי: Asyndeton (coordination of verbal clauses without conjunction) is widespread in Aramaic (§395). "They entered that temple, they demolished it to the ground."

ועמודיא זי אבנא זי הוו תמה תברו המו *waʿammūdayyā dī ʾabnā dī hawaw tammā tabbīrū hummū*. עמודיא: *qaṭṭūl noun pattern (§110). זי אבנא: Genitive of material (§161). זי: Second זי introduces relative clause. הוו: A verb you know by now: cp. אתו in line 8. תברו: Could be either G or D stem: "break." המו here used as direct object, as in Ez 5:5 (§130d). The construction is left-dislocation (§369). "The pillars of stone that were there – they broke them."

אף הוה *ʾap hawā*, אף: half-conjunction or discourse particle (§432). הוה: Not used here as copula, but as a lexical verb meaning "to happen." Translation: "also, it (the following) happened."

Lines 9–10

תרען זי אבן 5 בנין פסילה זי אבן זי הוו באגורא זך נדשו *taraʿīn dī ʾabn 5 banáyn pasīlā* (10) *dī ʾabn dī hawaw baʾēgurā dik nadášū*. תרען: For the word, see Dan 3:26, etc. *qaṭl noun pattern (§102). אבן: Cf. אבנא from line 9. בנין: G passive ptcp, III-y verb; see §262. פסילה: G passive ptcp in substantive meaning, "hewn (block)," as adverbial specification of previous verb (cp. Ez 5:8 מִתְבְּנֵא אֶבֶן גְּלָל; §352b). The noun phrase is lengthy: "Some five gates of stone, built of hewn (blocks) of stone, that were in that temple, they demolished."

Lines 10–11

ודשיהם קימן וצייריהם זי דששיא אלך נחש *wadaššayhum qāyimīn* (or: *qayyāmīn*) *waṣīrayhum* (11) *dī dašašayyā ʾillik nuḥāš*. דשיהם: *qall noun pattern (§104); "door"; so pl. *dašaš-* is expected (as in the next sentence). But later Aramaic has *daššīn*, and this may be a vernacular form. קימן: Either

G stem ptcp, hollow verb (§273), or, more likely, adjective of the *qaṭṭāl pattern (§110b, Dan 6:27); "lasting, enduring." צִירֵיהֶם: *qīl noun pattern (§100), "pivot of door"; mp cstr. with 3mp suffix (§129). וְצִירֵיהֶם זִי דְשִׁשָׁיא: Periphrastic genitive with anticipatory pronoun (§162). אִלֵּךְ: Distal demons. pron., common pl. (§136). נְחָשׁ: *quṭāl noun pattern (§108, Dan 4:12); "copper/bronze."

These circumstantial clauses are best taken in a concessive sense to the preceding sentence (§393f): "(They destroyed the gates,) *though* their doors were sturdy and the pivots of those doors bronze."

ומטלל עקהן זי ארז כלא *wamaṭlal ġaʿāhīn dī ʾarz kullā*. מטלל: *maqtal noun pattern (§117); "roof." Cp. the verb from the same root in Dan 4:9. עקהן: The word עק (protoform *ġiś) was probably pronounced *ġaʿ*; cp. QA עע. Later dissimilation (§46) led to BA אָע (Ez 5:8, etc.). The plural with *h* is an extension often found in bisyllabic nouns (§99). The plural may refer to "beams" or the like. ארז: *qaṭl noun pattern (§101); "cedar." כלא: Postpositive כל (§168), modifying the head of the phrase מטלל; "a roof of beams of cedar, all of it." The parallel second draft for this phrase has ומטלל אגורא זך כלא עקהן זי ארז "the roof of this temple, all beams of cedar."

Lines 11–12

{זי} עם שירית אשרנא ואחרן זי תמה הוה *dī ʿim šayārīt ʾuššarnā waʾuḥrān dī tammā* (12) *hawā*. {זי}: The parallel text at this point does not have זי, and the text reads better without it. שירית: Noun pattern with final *-īt (§114), possibly derived from the root שאר "remain," with palatalization of the ʾaleph: *šaʾārīt > *šayārīt. אשרנא: See Ez 5:3, 9. Persian loanword; "furnishings." ואחרן: See §116; in this context, ואחרן means "*et cetera*, and the rest" (DNWSI 42). "With the rest of the furniture and so on that was there."

כלא באשה שרפו *kullā baʾiššā śarápū*. אשה: Cf. Dan 7:11, for the instrumental use of the prep., see §179e. שרפו: G SC, "burn." In later Aramaic, the root is spelled סרף; see §40. "They burned everything with fire."

ומזרקיא זי זהבא וזי כספא ומנדעמתא זי הוה באגורא זך כלא לקחו *wamazraqayyā dī dahabā wadī kaspā wamandaʿmātā dī hawā baʾēgūrā dik kullā laqaḥū*. מזרקיא: *maqtal noun pattern (§117); cp. BH מִזְרָק "bowl." זהבא: Cp. Dan 3:1, etc.; here with the historical spelling with ז (§36a). זי זהבא וזי כספא: Genitive of material again; review §161. מנדעמתא: See §139a; here "the things." הוה: One might expect the 3mp verb. כלא: Postpositive כל again (§168). לקחו: G stem SC, 3mp. This verb is common in OA and IA (and Hebrew), but was replaced in later Aramaic by the G stem of נסב. "All the bowls of gold and silver and the items that were in that temple they took."

The long phrase ומזרקיא . . . כלא "all the bowls, etc." is the direct object of לקחו.

Line 13

ולנפשהום עבדו (13) *walanapš(a)hum ʿabádū.* נפשהום: *qaṭl noun pattern (§101); "self, soul." Sometimes the word is used with suffixes to signify "X's own"; here, "they made (these things) their own." הום: The 3mp pron. suff. with *plene* spelling (§27) is rare in IA. עבדו: The object pronoun is here omitted after the verb (§360).

ומן יומי מלך מצרין אבהין בנו אגורא זך ביב בירתא *wamin yawmay malk miṣrayn ʾabahaynā banaw ʾēgūrā dik bayeb bīrtā.* מן: Prep. with temporal meaning (§184c). יומי מלך: The parallel text in A4 8:12 has יום מלכי. מצרין: Proper noun, "Egypt." אבהין: In IA, the plural of אַב "father" is 1st declension, rather than 2nd declension (§93); here with 1cp pron. suff. (§129). בנו: G SC, III-y form (§58b). "But in the days of the king(s) of Egypt our fathers built that temple in Yeb the fortress."

וכזי כנבוזי על למצרין *wakadī kanbūzī ǵal(l) lamiṣrayn.* וכזי: Temporal conj. (§418). כנבוזי: Persian name, "Cambyses." על: G SC, geminate verb; see §279a. The first root letter is *ǵ*, written with ע (as in line 9; cf. §39). "When Cambyses entered Egypt."

Line 14

אגורא זך בנה השכחה (14) *ʾēgūrā dik banē haškiḥeh.* This is the main clause to which the temporal clause is subordinate. בנה: G passive ptcp from III-y root: **baniyu > banē* (see §262 and Ez 5:11). For the syntax, see §340b (object complement). השכחה: C stem SC + 3ms pron. suff.; see §131. The sentence displays left-dislocation (§369): "that temple – he found *it* built."

ואגורי אלהי מצרין כל מגרו *waʾēgūray ʾilāhay miṣrayn kullā maggírū.* ואגורי אלהי מצרין: Cstr. phrase with another cstr. phrase as dependent member (§154b). For the vocalization, note that the diphthong *ay had probably not contracted (§73b). כל: Postpositive כל; see again §168. This is likely a defective spelling of כלא. מגרו: D stem SC, 3mp (§227); cf. Ez 6:12. "And all the temples of the gods of Egypt they overthrew."

ואיש מנדעם באגורא זך לא חבל *waʾīš mandaʿam baʾēgūrā dik lā ḥabbil.* איש: *qīl noun pattern (§100). See also §139b; "man, someone." The noun is found in OA and IA, but in later Aramaic replaced by אנש or גבר. מנדעם: See §139a and above, line 12. חבל: D stem SC; cp. Dan 4:20, 6:23. The whole clause is contextually adversative to the previous clause (§393e). ". . . *but* no one harmed anything in that temple."

Line 15

וכזי כזנה עביד (15) *wakadī kadinā ʿabīd.* וכזי: Another temporal clause; see the previous line. כזנה: Cp. BA כְּדְנָה (§351c). עביד: G passive SC; review §224. "And when it was done like this" = since this was done.

אנחנה עם נשין ובנין שקקן לבשן הוין וצימן ומצלין ליהו מרא שמיא ʾanáḥnā ʿim našáynā wabanáynā śaqaqīn lābišīn hawáynā waṣāyimīn wamaṣallayn layāhū māriʾ šamayyā.

אנחנה: Independent pers. pron.; cf. Dan 3:16, etc.; in IA, often spelled defectively, as אנחן. נשין: Irregular plural (§94); cp. Dan 6:25. Here the *y* indicates the cstr. pl. ending -*ay*, not the 1st decl. suffix -*īn*, which is usually spelled defectively (ין־) in IA. ובנין: Another irregular plural; see again §94.

שקקן: *qall* noun pattern (§104). לבשן: G stem ptcp, with following הוין forming a periphrastic past progressive (§313a). הוין: G stem, SC 1cp; see §256e; probably the diphthong *-ay* is not contracted in IA. צימן: G stem mp ptcp from hollow verb צום "fast"; see §273a. מצלין: D stem active ptcp, III-*y* verb; see §263c; cp. Ez 6:10. In the periphrastic construction, more than one ptcp may be governed by a single הוי form: "We have been wearing . . . and fasting and praying." מרא שמיא: Cp. Dan 5:23. "We, with our wives and our children, have been wearing sackcloth and fasting and praying to Yahu, lord of heaven."

Line 16

זי החוין בוידרנג זך (16) *dī haḥwínā baWaidranga dik.* זי: Introducing a relative clause. החוין: C stem SC + 1cp pron. suff., III-*y* verb (see §265). The parallel text in A4 8:15 has the D stem חוינא (*ḥawwínā*) with the 1cp suff. written *plene.* בוידרנג זך: The combination of a perception verb plus complement introduced by בְּ means "triumph over" or "gloat over," as in (e.g.) Mesha stele הראני בכל שנאי "he let me triumph [lit., "he showed me"] over all my enemies" (KAI 181). So here, "who let us triumph over that Waidranga."

כלביא הנפקו כבלא מן רגלוהי *kalabayyā hanpíqū kablā min rigaláwhī.* Perhaps a proverb of some sort; the exact import is obscure. כלביא: *qatl* noun pattern (§102); mp det. "dog." הנפקו: Review §254. Cf. Dan 5:3, Ez 5:14, etc. כבלא: *qatl* noun pattern (§101); "fetter." The parallel text A4 8:15 reads plural כבלוהי *kabalawhī* here. רגלוהי: Cf. Dan 2:33, 7:4, etc. "The dogs made the fetter go out from his feet."

וכל נכסין זי קנה אבדו *wakul(l) nikasīn dī qanā ʾabádū.* נכסין: Akkadian loanword, but common in Aramaic; cp. Ez 7:26; in Hebrew, esp. in late texts. See §122. קנה: G SC 3ms, III-*y* verb; review §256a. אבדו: G SC 3mp, "perish." The agreement of verb is with נכסין (§167d). "All the property that he acquired perished."

Line 16–17

וכל גברין זי בעו באיש לאגורא זך כל קטילו וחזין בהום *wakul(l) gabarīn* (17) *dī baǵaw baʾīš laʾēgūrā dik kúllā qaṭílū waḥazáynā bahūm.* גברין: Cf. Dan 3:8, etc. בעו: G SC 3mp, III-*y* verb (§256c). The middle root letter is *ġ*, written with ע (§39); for the root, see Dan 6:5, etc. באיש: *qaṭīl pattern adjective (§108); cp. the feminine form Ez 4:12 and later in this line. In later Aramaic, the א elides: ביש < באיש (§48). כל: The parallel text A4 8:16 reads כלא. קטילו: G passive SC; review §224c. וחזין: G SC 1cp, III-*y* verb. וחזין בהום: For the meaning of the phrase, see above, line 16. "All men who sought harm for that temple were slain and we gloated over them."

Lines 17–18

אף קדמת דנה בעדן זי דא באיש^תא^ עביד לן *ʾap qadamat dīnā baʿiddān dī dā baʾištā* (18) *ʿabīd lánā*. אף: Discourse particle (§432). קדמת דנה: See §350e; cf. Ez 5:11. בעדן זי: See §152 for the absolute state noun used with relative clauses. דא באיש^תא^: Demonstrative pronoun; see §136b, and cp. Dan 7:8. Used attributively, the demon. pron. can appear either before or after the modified noun (§146). באיש^תא^: Adjective fs det used as a noun (§172a). The declensional ending is added above the line; the scribe at first just wrote באיש. עביד: G passive SC; see line 15. Although the subject באישתא is fem., this verb is masc.; this lack of agreement sometimes occurs with passive verbs (see line 20 below). לן = BA לַנָא (e.g., Ez 4:14), with defectively written 1cp pron. suff. The main clause follows this temporal clause. "Also, previously, when this harm was done to us."

אגרה שלחן <על> מראן ועל יהוחנן כהנא רבא *ʾiggarā šaláḥnā ʿal māriʾánā waʿal yāhūḥanan kāhinā rabbā*. אגרה: The same as אגרת in line 7. שלחן: G SC 1cp. <על>: This word was inadvertently left out; the parallel text has על זנה על. See §188c. יהוחנן: Possibly mentioned in Ez 10:6 (יְהוֹחָנָן). כהנא: Cp. Ez 7:12 etc. רבא: Cp. Dan 7:2. כהנא רבא: "The high priest." "We sent a letter to our lord and to Jehohanan the high priest."

Lines 18–19

וכנותה כהניא זי בירושלם ועל אוסתן אחוהי זי עני וחרי יהודיא *wakanāwāteh kāhinayyā dī baYerūšlēm waʿal ʾAvastana ʾaḥḥūhī* (19) *dī ʿAnanī waḥurray yahūdāyē*. כנותה: Cf. Ez 5:6 above, etc. ירושלם: "Jerusalem"; cf. BA יְרוּשְׁלֶם, Dan 6:11, Ez 5:1. אוסתן: Persian name borne by Jewish official. אחוהי: The presuffixal form of the word ends with -*ū* (§94), with 3ms pron. suff. Note that ה here likely indicates the velar fricative *ḥ* (§39). אחוהי זי עני: Periphrastic genitive with anticipatory suffix on the headword (§162). עני: Proper noun. חרי: *qull noun pattern (§104); "free, noble," here mp cstr. יהודיא: Cp. Dan 3:8, etc. "And his colleagues the priests who are in Jerusalem, and to Avastana, the brother of Anani, and the nobles of the Jews/Judeans."

אגרה חדה לא שלחו עלין *ʾiggarā ḥadā lā šaláḥū ʿaláynā*. חדה: Cardinal number; see §166d. שלחו עלין: Cp. lines 7, 18; = BA עֲלֶינָא, Ez 5:17, etc. "One letter they have not sent to us."

Lines 19–20

אף מן ירח תמוז שנת 14 דריוהוש מלכא ועד אזʌנה יומא *ʾap min yarḥ tammūz šanat 14 darayavahuš malkā (20) waʿad dinā yawmā.* ועד ... מן See §184c. ירח תמוז: See line 4. ועד אזʌנה: The *z* was added above the line. זנה יומא: Noun with demons. pron.; review §146. "So, from the month of Tammuz, the 14th year of King Darius until this day."

אנחנה שקקן לבשן וצימין *ʾanáḥnā śaqaqīn lābišīn waṣāyimīn.* Cp. to line 15; here the periphrastic past progressive is not used (see §307b). "We have been wearing sackcloth and fasting."

נשיא זילן כארמלה עבידין *našayyā dīlánā kaʾarmālā ʿabīdīn.* נשיא: Cp. form in line 15. זילן: Independent possessive; see §159. ארמלה: Rare noun with four root letters; see §121. עבידין: G passive ptcp; see §316b. This ptcp irregularly has 1st decl. inflection, although the gender of the subject is fem. "Our wives are in the condition of widows."

Lines 20–21

משח לא משחין וחמר לא שתין *mišḥ lā māšiḥīn (21) waḥamr lā šātayn.* משח: **qiṭl* noun pattern (§101); cp. מְשַׁח (Ez 7:22), JLA מִשְׁחָא "oil." משחין: G stem mp ptcp; "anoint." The parallel text A4 8:20 has משחן, possibly fp ptcp **māšiḥān.* וחמר: **qaṭl* noun pattern; cp. חַמְרָא "wine" (Dan 5:1). שתין: G stem mp ptcp, III-y verb; review §261. Neither participle has an overt subject; see §358. "(We) are not anointing (with) oil, and (we) are not drinking wine."

אף מן זכי ועד יום שנת 17 דריוהוש מלכא *ʾap min dikī waʿad yawm šanat 17 darayavahuš malkā.* מן זכי ... ועד יום: Again, temporal מן. זכי: Distal demonstrative pron. (see §136b); cp. JLA דִּיכֵי. The modified noun is missing; the parallel text has [מ]ן זך ע[ד]נא ועד ז[נה יומא] "from that time to this day" (A4 8:20). "From that (time) up to (this) day, the 17th year of King Darius."

Lines 21–22

מנחה ולבונה ועלוה לא עבדו באגורא זך *minḥā walibūnā waʿalāwā (22) lā ʿabádū baʾēgūrā dak.* מנחה: noun form is **qiṭl-at* (§101); "meal offering." Cf. Dan 2:46. לבונה: "Incense offering." Likely a West Semitic cultic word, cp. BH לְבוֹנָה. עלוה: **qaṭāl-at* noun pattern (§108a); "burnt offering." Perhaps originally **ʿalayat > ʿalā(t)* (§58a); cp. QA עלא (1QapGen 21:20). Cf. 2nd decl. pl. עֲלָוָן in Ez 6:9; עלואן (1QapGen 21:2). עבדו: G stem SC 3mp; see §357 for impersonal constructions. "They have not made a meal offering or an incense offering or a burnt offering in that temple."

כען עבדיך ידניה וכנותה ויהודיא כל בעלי יב כן אמריʌן *kaʿan ʿabadáykā Yadunyā wakanāwāteh wayahūdāyē kúllā baʿalay Yeb kin ʾāmirīn.* עבדיך ידניה וכנותה: As in line 1. כל: In the parallel text

(A4 8:22), the word is כלא. Review the functions of כל (§167). בעלי יב: For the lexeme, see Ez 4:8, etc. In this context, the meaning is "citizens" (DNWSI 184). אמרי^ן^: Actual present progressive use of the ptcp; "are saying, do say" (§307). "Now your servants Y. and his colleagues and all the Jews/Judeans, the citizens of Yeb, say thus."

Line 23

הן על מראן טב אתעשת על אגורא זך למבנה (23) *hin ʿal mariʾánā ṭāb ʾitʿašit ʿal ʾēgūrā dik lamibnē.* הן: Subordinating conjunction introducing protasis of conditional clause (§422a); cp. BA הֵן עַל. מראן טב: Almost the identical clause is found in Ez 5:17. הן על מלכא טב. אתעשת: Beginning of the apodosis, with tG (or possibly tD) ms impv verb, meaning "consider, think about" (see §334b). For the G stem, cf. עֲשִׂית (Dan 6:4). למבנה: G stem inf.; review §261c. "If it is pleasing to our lord, take thought for that temple, to rebuild (it)."

בזי לא שבקן לן למבניה *badī lā šābiqīn lánā lamibniyeh.* בזי: Causal conjunction (§413). שבקן: G stem mp ptcp, actual present, with unexpressed subject; see §358b. למבניה: G inf + 3ms pron. suff. "Because they are not allowing us to rebuild it."

Lines 23–24

חזי בעלי טבתך ורחמיך זי תנה במצרין *ḥzī baʿalay* (24) *ṭābātákā warāḥimáykā dī tanā bamiṣrayn.* חזי: G stem impv, III-y verb (cp. הוי in line 3 and review §260). טבתך: 2nd decl. sg. of ṭāb + 2ms pron suff. בעלי טבתך: Expression meaning perhaps "your friends, allies" (DNWSI 418). רחמיך: G mp ptcp that has become lexicalized as a noun "friend" (see §172b), here with 2ms pron suff. The reference is not to the letter writers, but to the Judean governor's supporters in the administration of Arshama. "See your allies and friends who are here in Egypt."

אגרה מנך ישתלח עליהום על אגורא זי יהו אלהא *ʾiggarā minnákā yištaliḥ ʿalayhūm ʿal ʾēgūrā dī Yāhū ʾilāhā.* The actual request begins here. אגרה: See lines 7, 18, 19. מנך: Review §182c. ישתלח: tG stem, jussive. Although the subject is fs, the verb is 3ms. עליהום: Prep. + 3mp pron. suff.; cp. עֲלֵיהוֹן Ez 5:1, etc., and review §51. Note the prep. עַל used in two different senses: direction (§188c) and object of attention (§188i). "Let a letter be sent from you to them about the temple of the god Yahu."

Line 25

למבניה ביב בירתא לקבל זי בנה הוה קדמין (25) *lamibniyeh bayeb bīrtā laqubl dī banē hawā qadamīn.* למבניה: As in line 23. לקבל זי: Introduces subordinate clause of manner; see §415a. Cp. BA לָקֳבֵל

(Dan 5:5, etc.). בנה: G passive ptcp. For the construction with הוה, note §314; cp. Ez 5:11. קדמין: See §350d. "To rebuild it in Yeb the fortress just as it was built before."

ומ<נ>חתא ולבונתא ועלותא יקרבון *wami(n)ḥātā walabūnatā waᶜalāwātā yaqarribūn.* מחתא: Det state pl. of מנחה above, line 21. The absence of *n* is inadvertent. The other nouns are also pl. יקרבון: D stem PC 3mp; a ה after the prefix was erased. This is another example of the impersonal construction; review §357. The clause is coordinated with the previous clause (§393a). "So that they can offer meal offerings and incense offerings and burnt offerings."

Line 26

על מדבחא זי יהו אלהא בשמך (26) *ᶜal madbiḥā dī Yahū ʾilāhā bašumákā.* מדבחא: Note the orthography, where ד is used for *d* < **ð*, instead of ז (§36a). Cp. מַדְבְּחָה in Ez 7:17. בשמך: Cp. בְּשֵׁם (Ez 5:1). "On the altar of the god Yahu in your name."

Lines 26–27

ונצלה עליך בכל עדן אנחנה ונשין ובנין ויהודיא כל זי תנה *wanaṣallē ᶜaláykā bakul(l) ᶜiddān ʾanáḥnā wanašáynā wabanáynā wayahūdāyē* (27) *kúllā dī tanā.* נצלה: D stem PC, III-y root (see §263c); for the verb, cf. Dan 6:11. אנחנה ונשין ובנין: See also line 15. ויהודיא כל: The parallel text for this sequence has יהודיא כלא (A4 8:26), as above, line 22. "And we will pray for you at every time, we and our wives and our children and all the Jews/Judeans who are here."

Lines 27–28

הן כן עבדו עד זי אגורא זך יתבנה וצדקה יהוה לך קדם יהו אלה שמיא *hin kin ᶜabádū ᶜad dī ʾēgūrā dik yitbanē waṣadaqā yihwē lákā qudām Yahū ʾilāh* (28) *šamayyā.* עבדו: G stem SC; modal use of SC in conditional sentence; see §299a and §422b. Here also the impersonal construction is used, with passive meaning: "if such they do" = if such would be done (see again §357). The parallel passage has תעבד "if you should do" (A4 8:26). עד זי: Here with the meaning "until" (§420). יתבנה: tG PC III-y root; cf. יִתְבְּנֵא (Ez 5:15). וצדקה: Apodosis begins here, with *waw* (§422a). צדקה: For the word, cp צִדְקָה (Dan 4:24 and §105b). יהוה: G stem PC, III-y verb. Note that IA does not use the PC with ל prefix used in later Jewish Aramaic (as in BA לֶהֱוֵה Dan 4:22). "If they do thus until that temple is built, then you will have righteousness before Yahu, the god of heaven."

מן גבר זי יקרב לה עלוה ודבחן *min gabr dī yaqarrib leh ᶜalāwā wadibaḥīn.* מן: Here with a comparative meaning, "more than" (§173). גבר: Cp. BA גְּבַר (Dan 2:25, etc.). יקרב: D stem PC, like יקרבון above, line 25. The PC expresses either epistemic modality ("a man who might offer") or general present ("a man who offers") (§301 and §302b). עלוה: See lines 21, 25. ודבחן: **qiṭl* noun pattern (§102); "sacrifice." Cp. דְּבָחִין in Ez 6:3, and observe the same root in מדבח, line 26. "More than a man who offers to him a burnt offering and sacrifices."

דמן כדמי כסף כנכרין 1 לף *damīn kadamay kasp kankarīn ḥad ʾalp.* דמן: Only occurs in the plural (*tantum plurale*; see §92), often spelled *plene* דמין; cp. JLA דְּמִין, MH דָּמִים; "price, value." Used here = "worth." דמן כדמי כסף: The parallel text (A4 8:27) has just דמי כסף. כנכרין: Reduplicated noun (§120), originally *karkar*, then *kakkar*, with nasalization (§54b). Cp. BA כַּכְּרִין, (Ez 7:22). לף1: The abbreviation לף1 may have been pronounced just ʾalp, as in the parallel text, which has אלף; cp. Dan 5:1, 7:10. Review cardinal numbers (§164g). The entire phrase is adverbial of specification (§352b). "(Whose) price is like the price of a thousand talents of silver" = a thousand talents of silver in value.

Lines 28–29

ועל זהב על זנה שלחן הודען ועל זהב על דינה (29) *waʿal dahab ʿal dinā* (29) *šaláḥnā hawdáʿnā.* זהב: Cf. line 12. זנה: Prep. phrases of uncertain import: "and about gold, about this." שלחן הודען: The verb שלח "send" is sometimes used immediately before another verb to indicate that the second action was accomplished by a message. "We sent, told" = we sent a message to tell. Compare QA שלחת קרית "I sent, called" = "I sent a message to summon" (1QapGen 21:21). Review §395. Parse the verbs. "Concerning gold, about this, we informed by message."

אף כלא מליא באגרה חדה שלחן ^בשמן^ על דליה ושלמיה *ʾap kullā millayyā baʾiggarā ḥadā šaláḥnā bašumánā ʿal Dalāyā waŠillemyā.* כלא מליא: Review §168. באגרה חדה: Cp. the same expression in line 19 and Ez 4:8. ^בשמן^: Added above the line. Cf. line 26. For the suffix, review §128. דליה: For this name, cp. BH דְּלָיָה, Ez 2:60, and elsewhere. שלמיה: Cp. BH שֶׁלֶמְיָה, Neh 3:30, and elsewhere. "Moreover, all the matters we have sent in a letter in our name to Delaiah and Shillemiah."

בני סנאבלט פ^ח^ת שמרין *banay sinʾuballiṭ piḥat šāmrayn.* סנאבלט: The same as Biblical סַנְבַלַּט. The name is Akkadian *Sin-uballiṭ*, although his sons have Hebrew names. פחת: See line 1. שמרין: Cp. BA שָׁמְרָיִן (Ez 4:10, 17). The whole phrase is appositional to the two previous personal names (§143a). "The sons of Sin-uballit (Sanballat), governor of Samaria."

Line 30

אף בזנה זי עביד לן ^כלא^ ארשם לא ידע (30) *ʾap badinā dī ʿabīd lánā kúllā ʾaršama lā yadaʿ.* בזנה: This usually means "here" in IA (§349a). זי עביד: Independent ("headless") relative clause (§150); "what was done to us." ^כלא^: Added above the line. In A4 8:29, the phrase reads כלא זי עביד לן, moving כלא to the head of the phrase. Note the rare Object-Subject-Verb word order (§365f). ארשם: See line 4 above. "Moreover, in this place, Arsham did not know what was done to us."

ב20 למרחשון שנת 17 דריהוש מלכא *ba-20 lamarḥišwān šanat 17 darayavahuš malkā,* מרחשון: The month name "Marheshwan" is of Akkadian provenance, as are all of the Judean month names. The year given, as noted above, is 407 BCE; the precise date in modern reckoning is November 25. For the rest, cp. line 1.

READING 7: SEVENTEEN PROVERBS OF AHIQAR

The story of Ahiqar is one of the taproot texts of Western civilization. Besides having a long life as a composition, being copied and rewritten in a dozen different languages, many of its themes and sayings are found in other texts, from the Talmud to Aesop's fables; Ahiqar himself appears as a character in the book of Tobit. The oldest version known to us was found among the Elephantine papyri, written in Aramaic. It consists of eleven papyrus sheets, mostly fragmentary, written over an erased economic text (palimpsest).

Ahiqar (אֲחִיקָר) was an Aramean sage who, according to the story, found fame in the Assyrian court of Sennacherib (reigned 705–681 BCE) and Esarhaddon (reigned 681–669 BCE). Childless, he adopted his nephew Nadin and trained him in wisdom; but Nadin, desiring Ahiqar's office, slandered him to the king, leading Esarhaddon to call for Ahiqar to be killed. The executioner, however, secretly hid Ahiqar and killed a prisoner in his place. When the king came to miss his counselor, Ahiqar returned and denounced Nadin's treachery. Nadin was executed and Ahiqar was restored to his position.

Besides the narrative, the Ahiqar legend includes a section of Ahiqar's proverbs, which are comparable to other Wisdom texts from the ancient Near East, including the biblical Book of Proverbs. They were first published by Sachau (1911) and were included in Cowley's collection (1923). The edition of Porten and Yardeni (TADC 1.1) reordered the columns on the basis of the recovered palimpsest text.

The following selection presents 17 of the better-preserved Aramaic proverbs included in the Elephantine text of Ahiqar. The line numbers are those of Porten and Yardeni, although the material readings are sometimes different.

80 ברי אל תלוט יומא עד תחזה לילה

    barī ʾal talūṭ yawmā ʿad tiḥzē laylē.

ברי: "My son," cf. בַּר (Dan 3:25), + 1cs pron. suff. אל: Review §388. תלוט: G stem jussive, 2ms, from hollow root לוט "curse" (§272). יומא: As in Dan 6:11. עד: Cf. §420 for conjunctive use. תחזה: Review §258 and parse. לילה: Cp. לֵילְיָא (Dan 7:2), and see §96; "night."

82 מן כל מנטרה טר פמך ועל זי ש[מעת] הוקר לבב
כי צנפר הי מלה ומשלחה גבר לא לב[ב]

min kul(l) manṭarā ṭar pummákā waʿal dī šamáʿtā hawqir libab
kī ṣinpar hī millā wamašalliḥah gabr lā libab.

מן כל מנטרה: See §184d. מנטרה: *maqtal-at* noun pattern (§117); "watching." טר: G stem ms impv, I-n verb; see §253b. For the root, cf. Dan 7:28. פמך: Cf. Dan 6:23, etc., with 2ms pron. suff. ועל: Cf. §188i. זי ש[מעת]: Independent relative (§150). שמעת: G stem SC 2ms; "concerning that which you have heard." הוקר: C stem ms impv, I-y root יקר; "make deaf, insensitive." See §251a. לבב: Cf. Dan 7:4, etc.; "make your mind deaf to what you have heard."

כי: Introduces causal clause (§414). צנפר: Cf. צִפְּרִין (Dan 4:30); here with nasalization (§54b). הי: 3fs personal pronoun (§125), used as copula (§378b–c). מלה: Cf. BA מִלָּה (Dan 2:10, 7:28, etc.), משלחה: D stem ms ptcp, with 3fs suffix; see §228. "Release, set free" (for the semantics, see §231f). גבר לא לב[ב]: Predicate nominal phrase (§375). לא לב[ב]: See §386f.

84 רכיך ממלל מלך שדק ועזיז הו מן סכין פמין

rakkīk mamlal malk
śadiq waʿazzīz hū min sakkīn pummayn.

רכיך: *qaṭṭīl* pattern adj. (§110); "soft." ממלל: *maqtal* noun pattern (§117); "speech"; cf. the verb מַלֵּל "speak" and מִלָּה "word." שדק: Adj. of uncertain pattern, possibly *qaṭil* (see §105); "sharp." עזיז: *qaṭṭīl* pattern adjective, like רכיך "strong." הו: 3ms personal pron. (§125); subject of copular clause (§376a). מן: Used comparatively (§173). סכין: *qaṭṭīl* noun pattern (§110); "knife." פמין: The ending is dual (§95); "a knife of two mouths" = a double-edged knife.

88 מה ישפטון עקן עם אשה בשר עם סכין איש עם [מלך]

mā yišpuṭūn ǵaʿin ʿim ʾiššā baśar ʿim sakkīn ʾīš ʿim malk

מה: Cf. §391b for the meaning "how." ישפטון: G stem; "dispute, argue"; parse. עקן: Cp. עקהן in the Petition (A4 7:11). עם: Indicates reciprocal action throughout the saying (§189c). אשה: Cf. A4 7:12 and אִשָּׁא (Dan 7:11). בשר: Cp. בְּשַׂר (Dan 7:5). סכין: As in the previous saying. איש: As in the Petition (A4 7:14).

89 טעמת אנזעררתא מררתא ו[טעמ]א חסין ולא איתי זי [מ]ריר מן ענוה

ṭaʿámit ʾanzaʿrārtā marrīratā waṭaʿmā hassīn walā ʾītay dī marrīr min
ʿanwā

טעמת: G stem SC 1cs; for the root, cp. יְטַעֲמוּן "taste" (Dan 4:22). אנזעררתא: Vocalization unknown, no doubt a loanword; cf. Syriac ʿazrārtā "medlar." מררתא: *qaṭṭīl pattern adjective (again see §110; here written defectively). אנזעררתא מררתא: "The bitter apple," or the like. טעמא: As in Dan 6:3 (if the restoration is correct); here = "taste." חסין: Another *qaṭṭīl adjective; "strong, sour." ולא איתי: As in Dan 4:32, etc. זי מ[ר]יר: Independent relative again (§150). מ[ר]יר מן: Comparative (§173). ענוה: Vocalization uncertain; "poverty."

91 מלך כרחמן אף קלה גבה ה[ו] מן הו זי יקום קדמוהי להן זי אל עמה

> malk karaḥmān ʾap qāleh gabih hū
> man hū dī yaqūm qudāmáwhī lāhin dī ʾil ʿimmeh

כרחמן: Prep. כְּ (§181) + *qaṭl-ān pattern adjective (§115); 1st decl. abs. Here a divine epithet, "the merciful one," perhaps a euphemism for any deity. אף: Cf. §432. קלה: Cf. קָל (Dan 3:5, etc.), with 3ms pron. suff. גבה: Adj., vocalization uncertain; "huge, overpowering." קלה גבה ה[ו]: Copular clause with pronominal copula (§376). מן: Interrogative מַן with rhetorical question (§391). מן הו זי: It is unclear whether הו is the head of the relative clause ("who (is) he who...") or the copula ("who is (he) who...") with independent relative following. יקום: As in Dan 7:24. קדמוהי: As in, e.g., Dan 4:5. להן: Conj.; see §423b. זי אל עמה: Independent relative clause; "(the one) whom (the god) El is with." אל: *qil noun pattern (§99); "god, the god El." "A king is like the Merciful, yes, and his voice is overpowering; who is he who can stand before him, except one with whom El is?"

93 מאן טב כס[י] מלה בלבבה והו ז[י]תביר הנפקה ברא

> mān ṭāb kassī millā balibabeh
> wahū dī tabīr hanpiqah bárrā

מאן: Cp. מָאנַיָּא (Ez 5:14). טב: As in Ez 5:17. [כס]י: D stem SC 3ms, III-y root כסי "hide" (§263). בלבבה: Cp לְבָבֵהּ (Dan 4:13), here "interior." הו זי: Personal pron. as head of relative clause; "he/the one which." תביר: G passive ptcp (§224); "broken." הנפקה: Cp. הַנְפֵּק Ez 5:14, here with 3fs pron. suff. ברא: See §344 for the adverbial ending: "out(wards)." For the verb tenses, see §296.

95 איש שפיר מדדה ולבבה טב כקר[י]ה חסינה זי מי[ן] בג[וה] איתי

> ʾīš šappīr madadeh walibabeh ṭāb
> kaqiryā ḥassīnā dī mayn bagawwah ʾītay

שפיר: As in Dan 4:9; a relative clause is implied (§148). מדדה: Vocalization uncertain, with 3ms pron. suff.; "stature, frame." ולבבה טב: Chiastic (ABBA) order with the previous clause (§393f). לבבה: Here, "mind." קריה: *qiṭl-at noun pattern (§101); cf. BA קִרְיָה (Ez 4:10, etc.); "city." חסינה: As in line 89 above, here fs. מי[ן]: With pseudo-dual ending (§95c); "water." בגוה: Cp. בְּגַוֵּהּ (Ez 5:7). זי מי[ן] בג[וה] איתי: Relative clause with resumptive pronoun (§148b); "a strong city that there is water *within it.*"

18

126 [אל תדרך ק]שתך ואל תהרכב חטך לצדיק למה אלהיא יסגה בעדרה ויהתיבנהי עליך

ʾal tidruk qaštákā waʾal taharkib ḥiṭṭákā laṣaddīq
lamā ʾilāhā yisgē baʿadreh wayahatībinníhī ʿaláykā

תדרך: G stem jussive 2ms, restored according to line 190 (not given here): דרך קשתה "to step on, tread"; to "tread the bow" is to bend the bow by stepping on one end in order to string it. קשתך: *qaṭl noun pattern (§101), here with 2ms pron. suff.; "bow." תהרכב: C stem jussive 2ms (cf. §233); "to mount." To "mount the arrow" is to notch it on the string in order to aim it. חטך: *qill noun pattern (§104); "arrow." צדיק: *qaṭṭīl pattern adj. (§110b); "righteous."

למה: Negative purpose (§406). אלהיא יסגה: The subject is pl., the verb sg. One of them must be emended. Since the verb that follows is also singular, the subject should probably be emended to sg. אלהא "the god/God." יסגה: G stem PC 3ms, III-y root סגי "to go/come." בעדרה: Prep. בְּ marking role (§179f). עדרה: *qaṭl noun pattern (§101), with 3ms pron. suff.; "aid, help." For the spelling with ד, see §36a. ויהתיבנהי: C stem PC 3ms + energic *n* + 3ms pron. suff. Cp. BA יְהָתִיבוּן (Ez 6:5). Review §277. The vocalization of the final segment נהי is uncertain; see §131a. "He will turn it back." עליך: Cp. Dan 3:12, and note QA עליכה (4Q531 5 4).

127 יה ברי הכצר כל כציר ועבד כל עבידה אדין תאכל ותשבע ותנתן לבניך

yā barī hakṣir kul(l) kaṣīr waʿabid kul(l) ʿabīdā
ʾidayn tiʾkul watiśbaʿ watintin labanáykā

יה: Particle of direct address; "O!" ברי: As in line 80 above. הכצר: C stem ms impv, root קצר* "harvest." For the change of *q > k*, see §45. כציר: *qaṭīl noun pattern (§108); cp. BH קָצִיר "harvest." עבד: G stem ms impv from a familiar root. עבידה: Cp. עֲבִידַת (Dan 3:12, etc.). אדין: See §431b. תאכל: G stem PC 2ms. Cp. יֵאכֻל (Dan 4:30, etc.). תשבע: G stem PC 2ms; "be filled, satisfied" (root שבע). תנתן: Cp. BA תִּנְתֵּן (Ez 7:20), without assimilation of *n* (§252a). לבניך: Review §94.

128 [הן ד]רגת קשתך והרכבת חטך לצדיק מנך חטא מן אלהן הו

hin darágtā qaštákā
waharkíbtā ḥiṭṭákā
laṣaddīq minnákā
ḥiṭ ʾ min ʾilāhīn hū

[ד]רגת: Restoration uncertain; the root דרג = דרך, as in line 126. G stem SC 2ms. This could be modal after הן (cf. §299a); "if you bend." קשתך: As in line 126. והרכבת: C stem SC 2ms; cp. תהרכב, line 126. חטך: As in line 126. לצדיק: As in line 126. לצדיק מנך: Here comparative; review §173. חטא: *qiṭl noun pattern (§101), or possibly *qaṭāl pattern (§108); "sin" or, more likely, "miss, stray shot." אלהן: Cp. אֱלָהִין (Dan 3:25). חטא מן אלהן הו: Copular clause with prep. predicate (§377), with pronominal copula.

138 [גבר זי] לא יתרומ<ם> בשם אבוהי ובשם אמה אל ידנח שמ[ש לה] כי גבר לחה הו

gabr dī lā yitromam bašum ʾabū́hī wabašum ʾimmeh
ʾal yidnaḥ šamaš leh kī gabr laḥē hū

<ם>יתרומ: tR stem PC 3ms (see §276), with reflexive meaning (§334); "exalt oneself, take pride" (cf. Dan 5:23). אבוהי: Cp. BA אֲבוּהִי (Dan 5:2). אמה: *qill* noun pattern (§104), with 3ms pron. suff.; "mother." ידנח: G stem jussive 3ms; "shine, rise (of sun)." שמש: Either *šamaš* "Shamash, sun-god" or *šimš*, *qiṭl* noun pattern (§101); "sun" (cf. Dan 6:15). כי: As in line 82. לחה: Cf. לחיא (A4 7:7; Petition). The whole proverb is a left-dislocated construction (§369).

140 [הן ברי] הוה לי שהד חמס ומן אפו צדקני

hin barī hawā lī śāhid ḥamas
waman ʾapū ṣaddiqánī

הוה: After הן, used modally (§422b). שהד: G stem ms ptcp, nominalized (§172b); "witness." Cp. BA שָׂהֲדוּתָא, "testimony" (Gen 31:47). חמס: *qaṭal* noun pattern (§105); "malice, crime." שהד חמס: Attributive genitive (§156); "false, malicious witness." ומן: Apodosis introduced by ן. אפו: Emphatic particle, vocalization uncertain; cf. BH אֵפוֹ "so, then." צדקני: D stem SC 3ms + 1cs pron. suff., with modal meaning. The D stem here is a "forensic" causative (cf. §231b): "to make just, innocent" > "to find innocent, acquit." "If my son becomes a false witness against me, who then would find me innocent?"

159 נשאית חלא וטענת מלח ולא איתי זי יקיר מן נכ[רי]

naśáyit ḥālā waṭaʿánit malḥ
walā ʾītay dī yaqqīr min nukrāy.

נשאית: G stem SC 1cs from נשא "lift, carry." This III-ʾaleph root has at least partially merged with the III-y roots; see §256e: *naśáʾit > naśáyit*. The א remains as a historical spelling (cf. §269). חלא: *qāl* noun pattern (§100); "sand." The det. state occurs with generic meaning (§85c). טענת: G stem SC 1cs from טען "load." מלח: *qiṭl* noun pattern (§101); cp. BA מְלַח "salt" (Ez 6:9, etc.). ולא איתי זי: As in line 89 above. יקיר: *qaṭṭīl* adj. pattern (§110b); "heavy, onerous." For the root, cp. יְקָר (Dan 7:14, etc.), and הוקר in line 82 above. יקיר מן: Comparative (§173). נכרי: Adj. with final *-āy* (§97d); "stranger, foreigner."

160 נשאית תבן ונסבת פרן ולא איתי זי קליל מן תותב

naśáyit tibn wanasíbit parrān
walā ʾītay dī qallīl min tawtab

נשאית: As in line 159. תבן: *qiṭl* noun pattern (§101); "straw." נסבת: G stem SC 1cs, *i*-theme (§218); "take, remove." פרן: *qall-at* noun pattern, pl. abs. (§104); "bran." ולא איתי זי: As in line 159. קליל: *qaṭṭīl* adj. pattern (§110b); "light." קליל מן: Comparative (§173). תותב: *ta-qṭāl* noun pattern (§118); "resident alien." "I have lifted straw and taken bran, but there is nothing lighter (of less consequence) than a resident alien."

161 חרב תדלח מין שפין בין רעין טבן

ḥarb tidlaḥ mayn šapayn bayn riʕayn ṭābīn

חרב: *qaṭl noun pattern (§101), fem.; "sword." תדלח: G stem PC 3fs; general present or modal (§301); "stir up, muddy." מין: As in line 95. שפין: *qaṭē pattern adj. (§106); "clear, pure." בין: Prep. (see §194). רעין: *qiṭē noun pattern (again §106); "friend." Cp. BH רֵעָה. טבן: Cf. line 93 above.

164 שגיאן [כ]וכב[י שמיא זי] שמהתהם לא ידע איש הא כן אנשא לא ידע איש

śaggīʔin kawkabay šamayyā dī šumāhāthum lā yādiʕ ʔiš

hā kin ʔināšā lā yādiʕ ʔiš

שגיאן: Cp. שַׂגִּיאָן (Ez 5:11); here 1st decl. pl. כוכבי: Cp. QA כוכבין (4Q201 1 iv 3); quadrilateral noun (§121); "star." שמהתהם: As in Ez 5:10. ידע: G stem ms ptcp. הא: See §383. אנשא: As in Dan 4:22, etc.; here, "humankind."

READING 8: GENESIS APOCRYPHON COLS. 21:23–22:26

The *Genesis Apocryphon* (1QapGen) is the longest surviving narrative in Jewish Aramaic from the Hellenistic period other than the tales of Daniel in the Hebrew Bible (§14). It was one of the scrolls in the original discovery made near the Dead Sea in 1947 in what is now called Qumran Cave 1. The scroll as discovered contained originally twenty-two columns, but much of the text is illegible or lost due to decay. Most of the readable portions of consecutive text come from cols. 19–22. In content, the original book contained tales of the patriarchs Lamech, Noah, and Abraham that are either expansions of the canonical biblical text of Genesis or else entirely new episodes.

The portion given here is from cols. 21–22 and consists of a retelling of Genesis 14, in which Abraham intervenes in an international military campaign to rescue his nephew Lot from captivity and meets the priest-king of Jerusalem, Melchizedek. A recent translation with text and commentary is that of Fitzmyer (2004); Machiela's text editions (2009, 2018) also contain translations. García-Martínez and Tigchelaar (2000) contain text and translation on facing pages.

The appendix (pp. 363–364) contains the Aramaic text as given below, with the addition of hypothetical Tiberian vocalization (§§17, 79).

21:23–24

(23) קדמת יומיא אלן אתה כדרלעומר מלך עילם אמרפל מלך בבל אריוך מלך כפתוך תדעל מלך
גוים די (24) הוא בין נהרין

קדמת: Prep. (§204). יומיא: As in Dan 7:13, etc. אלן: Cp. אֵלֶּין (Dan 6:3, etc.). אתה: As in Dan 7:22, etc. The verb is sg., with a compound subject (cf. §355c). כדרלעומר: Personal name, MT כְּדָרְלָעֹמֶר. עילם: Geographical name, MT עֵילָם, "Elam." אמרפל: Personal name, MT אַמְרָפֶל. אריוך: Personal name, MT אַרְיוֹךְ. כפתוך: Geographical name, "Cappadocia" (MT has אֶלָּסָר, "Ellasar"). תדעל: Personal name, MT תִּדְעָל. גוים: MT גּוֹיִם, to be understood as a name, "Goyim." די הוא: Relative clause, followed by pers. pron.; cf. §126. בין נהרין: Prep. phrase (§194), "between rivers," used as a name, i.e., "Mesopotamia." "Goyim, which is Mesopotamia."

21:24–25

ועבדו קרב עם ברע מלך סודם ועם ברשע מלך עומרם ועם שנאב מלך אדמא (25) ועם שמיאבד
מלך צבוין ועם מלך בלע

סודם. בֶּרַע: Personal name, MT בֶּרַע. עבדו: Cp. BA עֲבַדוּ (Ez 6:13). ועבדה קרב: Cp. ועבדו קרב (Dan 7:21). ברע: Personal name, MT בֶּרַע. סודם: Geographical name, MT סְדֹם; note the *mater lectionis*, and cp. the Greek Σόδομα. ברשע: Personal name, MT בִּרְשַׁע. עומרם: Geographical name, MT עֲמֹרָה (Greek Γομορρα), "Gomorrah." In this text, perhaps a rhyming pair, *Sodom / Gomorom* (see Fitzmyer 2004: 234 for a discussion of the final *m*). שנאב: Personal name, MT שִׁנְאָב. אדמא: Geographical name, MT אַדְמָה. שמיאבד: Personal name; cf. MT שֶׁמְאֵבֶר. The name here may be intentionally negative, perhaps שְׁמֵיֵאבַד "may (his) name perish" or the like. צבוין: Geographical name, MT צְבֹיִים. בלע: Personal name, MT בֶּלַע.

21:25

כול אלן אזדמנו כחדא לקרב לעמקא די סדיא

כול: This spelling with a *mater* is frequent in QA (§26b). אזדמנו: tD SC 3mp, from זמן "to meet"; note metathesis (§53; §78, Rule 10) and partial assimilation (§44b). כחדא: Adv. (§351d). לקרב: Prep. לְ of purpose (§178c). עמקא: **quṭl* noun pattern (§101); "valley." לעמקא: Prep. לְ of goal (§177d). סדיא: Geographical name; Aramaization of MT הַשִּׂדִּים (Gen 14:3), with ס for שׂ (§40).

21:25–26

ותקף מלך (26) עילם ומלכיא די עמה למלך סודם ולכול חברוהי ושויו עליהון מדא

ותקף: Cf. Dan 4:8, etc.; here with a transitive sense, "defeat, prevail over." עמה: Prep. עִם (§189a). Again note the singular verb with the compound subject (§355c). למלך: Prep. לְ of direct object (§177c). חברוהי: Cf. BA חַבְרוֹהִי (Dan 2:13, etc.). שויו: D stem SC 3mp (§263b); cp. BA שַׁוִּיו (Dan 5:21) Qere. Here, "to place, put." מדא: Cf. BA מִנְדָּה (Ez 4:13, 7:24), here with assimilation of *n* (§42; §78, Rule 11a); Akkadian loanword *mandattu* "tribute."

21:26–27

תרתי עשרה שנין הווא (27) יהבין מדתהון למלך עילם ובשנת תלת עשרה מרדו בה

שנין: תרתי עשרה: Review cardinal numerals (§164e); "twelve," fem., cp. masc. תְּרֵי־עֲשַׂר (Dan 4:26). As in Dan 6:1, etc. The whole phase is adverbial (§352a). הווא: G stem SC 3mp from הוי; cp. הֲווֹ

(Dan 6:5, etc.), here with (unpronounced) final א (§26c). יהבין: Cf. יְהָבִין (Dan 6:3). הווא יהבין: Past progressive; review §313a. מדתהון: Cf. מדא in previous sentence. ובשנת תלת עשרה: For the construction, see §157b. תלת עשרה: See once more §164e. מרדו: G stem SC 3mp; "they rebelled." For the root, cf. BA מְרַד (Ez 4:19); "rebellion." בה: Prep. בְּ marks the complement of the verb (§342a).

21:27–28

ובשנת ארבע עשרה דבר מלך עילם לכול (28) חברוהי וסלקו ארחא די מדברא

ובשנת ארבע עשרה: As in the previous sentence. דבר: G stem SC 3ms; "to take, lead," as in A4 7:8 above. חברוהי: As in line 26. סלקו: G SC 3mp; cf. BA סְלִקוּ (Dan 2:29, etc.). ארחא: Cp. אָרְחָתֵהּ (Dan 4:34); here 1st decl. sg. det. מדברא: *maqṭal noun pattern (§117); "desert, wilderness." ארחא די מדברא: Complement of motion verb (§331d).

21:28–30

והווא מחין ובזין מן פורת נהרא ומחו לרפאיא די בעשתרא (29) דקרנין ולזו^מ^זמיא די בעמן ולאימיא ד[י ב]שׁוה הקריות ולחוריא די בטורי גבל עד דבקו לאיל (30) פרן די במדברא

והווא מחין: Cp. הווא יהבין, lines 26–27. מחין: G stem ptcp mp, root מחי "to smite, attack." See again §261a. בזין: G stem ptcp mp, root בזז "to plunder"; see §279f. מן פורת נהרא: Prep. מֶן; cf. §184c. פורת: Geographical name, "Euphrates"; cp. MT פְּרָת. נהרא: As in Ez 5:3, etc. ומחו: G stem SC 3mp; cf. מחין. לרפאיא: Ethnic designation, "Rephaites"; cf. MT רְפָאִים (Gen 14:5). בעשתרא דקרנין: Geographical name; Aramaization of Hebrew עַשְׁתְּרֹת קַרְנַיִם "Ashteroth-karnaim." דקרנין: Note ד for די (§135c). קרנין: Cp. קַרְנַיִן (Dan 7:7, etc.). זו^מ^זמיא: Ethnic designation, "Zumzamites"; cp. MT הַזּוּזִים (Gen 14:5; also זַמְזֻמִּים (Deut 2:20). עמן: Geographical name, "Amman." אימיא: Ethnic designation, "Emites"; cp. MT הָאֵמִים (Gen 14:5).

שׁוה הקריות: Geographical name; cp. MT שָׁוֵה קִרְיָתָיִם "Shaveh-Kiriathaim" (Gen 14:5). הקריות: Cp. MT הַקְּרִיּוֹת "Kerioth" (Jer 48:41). חוריא: Ethnic designation, "Horites"; cp. MT הַחֹרִי (Gen 14:6). טורי: *qūl noun pattern (§100), 1st decl. pl. cstr.; "mountain," cp. BA טוּר (Dan 2:35). גבל: Geographical name, "Gebal"; cp. MT גְּבָל (Ps 83:8). עד: Temporal conj. (§420). דבקו: G stem SC 3mp, root דבק "reach, arrive at"; cf. BA Dan 2:43 ("adhere to"). לאיל פרן: Geographical name, "El Paran"; cp. MT אֵיל פָּארָן (Gen 14:6). במדברא: As in the previous sentence.

21:30

ותבו ומחו לעֵין [דינא ולאנש]א די בחצצן תמר [blank]

תבו: G stem SC 3mp, hollow root תוב "turn, return"; review §272. ומחו: As in line 28. לעֵין [דינא]: Geographical name, "spring of judgment" (assuming the restoration is correct), corresponding to MT עֵין מִשְׁפָּט (Gen 14:7). חצצן תמר: Geographical name; cf. MT חַצְצֹן תָּמָר "Hazazon-tamar."

21:31

(31) ונפק מלך סודם לעורעהֹון ומלך [עומרם ומ]לך אדמא ומלך צֹבֹואֹין ומלך בלע

לעורעהֹון: Cf. §199. The rest of the line should not be difficult.

21:31–32

וֹ[עֹ]בֹדֹ[וֹ] קרבא (32) בעמקא דֹ[י סדיא] לקובלי כֹדרל[עומר ומלכיא] די עמה

עבדו קרבא: As in line 24. לקובלי: An unusual form; cf. §200. The final *y* is evidently the pl. cstr. ending. עמה: Prep. עִם + 3ms pron. suff.

21:32–34

ואתבר מלך סודם וערק ומלך עומרםֹ (33) נפל וֹשֹגֹיאֹין [עמה . . .] וֹבֹזֹ מֹלֹך עילֹם כול נכסיא די סוֹדֹם ודי (34) [עו]מֹרֹ[ם . . .]

אתבר: tG SC 3ms, from root תבר "be broken > be defeated." The *t* of the preformative in this case has assimilated to the first root letter *t*; in Tiberian pointing, אִתְּבַר *ʾittəbar* (*ʾit* + *təbar*). סודם: Note two *matres lectionis* and cf. the notes at line 24. ערק: G stem SC 3ms, root ערק "to flee." נפל: Cf. BA נְפַל (Dan 4:28, etc.). שֹגֹיאֹין: 1st decl. pl. abs. of שַׂגִּיא (the reading follows Machiela et al. 2018: 142). בֹזֹ: G stem SC 3ms; for the root, see line 28 and §279a. נכסיא: Cp. BA נִכְסִין (Ez 7:26 and the Petition A4 7:16); "movable property." נכסיא די סודם ודי עומרם: Periphrastic genitive (§160) with two די-phrases as dependents.

The text between this sentence and the next is missing or illegible. The text continues at the top of column 22.

21:34–22:1

. . . וֹשֹבו לוט בר אחוי (22:1) די אברם די הוא יתב בסודם כחֹדֹא עמהון וכול נכסוהי

וֹשֹבו: G stem SC 3mp, root שבי "to take captive"; review §256c. לוט: Personal name, "Lot"; cp. MT לוֹט. אֹחוי די אברם: Periphrastic genitive with suffix on head word (§162). אחוי = אֲחוּהִי, אח "brother," with 3ms pron. suff. (§94). The elision of ה between vowels is regular in later dialects. אברם: Personal name, "Abram"; cp. MT אַבְרָם. "The son of the brother of Abram" = Abram's nephew. הוא יתב: Past progressive (§313a). הוא = הֲוָא, as in Dan 6:4. יתב: G stem ms ptcp; for the root, cf. יְתִב (Dan 7:9, etc.), but here meaning "dwell"; cf. BA יָתְבִין (Ez 4:17). כחדא: As in line 25 above. נכסוהי: Cf. line 33 above.

22:1–3

ואתה חד מן רעה (2) ענה די יהב אברם ללוט די פלט מן שביא על אברם ואברם באדין הוא (3) יתב בחברון

חד מן: See §184b; "one from" = one of. רעה: = רָעֵי "shepherd," G stem mp cstr. ptcp, from רעי "to graze"; the ptcp has become a noun (§172b). The use of ה for the pl. cstr. ending -*ē* is anomalous.

ענה: *qāl* noun pattern (§100) with 3ms pron. suff. (or perhaps def. state ending with ה instead of א); "flock." The word is cognate to BH צאן (§38). די: The second די introduces a further relative clause (non-restrictive; §149). פלט: G stem SC 3ms, "to escape." שביא: *qitl* noun pattern (§101) with det. state for abstraction (§85c); "state of captivity." על אברם: Prep. עַל; see §188c.

באדין: See §350a. This adverbial use is unusual in QA. הוא יתב: As in line 22:1. חברון: Geographical name, "Hebron"; cp. MT חֶבְרוֹן.

22:3–5

וחויה די שבי לוט בר אחוהי וכול נכסוהי ולא קטיל ודי (4) נגדו מלכיא ארחא חלתא רבתא למדיתון

ושבין ובזין ומחין וקטלין ואזלין (5) למדינת דרמשק

חויה: D stem SC 3ms + 3ms pron. suff., root חוי "to tell," as in BA נְחַוֵּא (Dan 2:4; PC 1cp). For suffixes, the verb is considered as ending in a consonant (i.e., *ḥawwiy* instead of *ḥawwī*, therefore *ḥawwiyeh* > *ḥawwəyeh*). See §132; "he told him." שבי: G passive SC 3ms; cf. §262b, "was taken captive." The verb is singular with a compound subject (§355c). קטיל: Review §224. ודי: Introduces another clause complement (§341). נגדו: G stem SC 3mp, root נגד "to advance, proceed" (cf. Dan 7:10).

ארחא: As in line 28 above. חלתא: *qill-at* noun pattern (§104); "valley." ארחא חלתא רבתא: We would expect די after ארחא to make a periphrastic genitive (§160). למדיתון = לְמְדִינָתְּהוֹן, with possible assimilation of *n* (§78, Rule 11a) and irregular elision of ה on the 3mp pron. suff.; "to their city." ושבין ובזין ומחין וקטלין ואזלין: These forms should be immediately recognizable by now; for the syntax, see §358a. דרמשק: Geographical name, "Damascus"; cp. MT דַּרְמֶשֶׂק (1 Chr 18:5, etc.). מדינת דרמשק: Here the construct phase relation (§153c) is appositional; "the city of Damascus," the city which is Damascus.

22:5–6

ובכא אברם על לוט בר אחוהי ואתחלם אברם וקם (6) ובחר מן עבדוהי גברין בחירין לקרב תלת מאא ותמניאת עשר

ובכא: G stem SC 3ms, root בכי "to weep." על לוט: Prep. עַל (§188i). אתחלם: tG SC 3ms, root חלם "to recover," reflexive voice; see §334b. בחר: G stem SC 3ms, "to choose." מן עבדוהי: Prep. מִן; see §184b (partitive). בחירין: What kind of ptcp? §224. Here the root indicates "tested, proven": men with known fighting prowess. תלת מאא ותמניאת עשר: Find all of the components of this compound number in §164. תמניאת: א is used in QA instead of י to separate contiguous vowels: *tamāniat* > *tamānī'at* (§49c).

22:6–8

וערנם (7) ואשכול וממרה נגדו עמה והוא רדף בתרהון עד דבק לדן ואשכח אנון (8) שרין בבקעת דן

ממרה: Personal name, "Arnem"; cf. MT עָנֵר. אשכול: Personal name, "Eshkol"; cf. MT אֶשְׁכֹּל. ממרה: Personal name, "Mamre"; cf. MT מַמְרֵא. נגדו: As in line 4 above. רדף: G stem ms ptcp, root רדף "to pursue." והוא רדף: See again §313a. בתרהון: Prep. ב(א)תר(§191). דבק: As in line 29 above. דן: Geographical name, "Dan"; cf. MT דָּן. אשכח: Cp. הַשְׁכַּחוּ (Dan 6:12), and parse. אנון: Cf. אִנּוּן (Dan 6:25, etc.). Note §132b. שרין: This could be G or G passive mp ptcp. Both can mean "encamped, staying in a place." For the syntax, see §340b. בקעת: As in Dan 3:1.

22:8–10

ורמה עליהון בליליא מן ארבע רוחיהון והוא קטל (9) בהון בליליא ותבר אנון והוא רדף להון
וכולהון הוא ערקין מן קודמוהי (10) עד דבקו לחלבון די שימא על שמאל דרמשק

רמה: Frequent in BA, e.g., רְמוֹ (Dan 6:25); here in the meaning "shoot arrows." עליהון: Cf. עֲלֵיהוֹן (Ez 5:1). בליליא: Cf. BA בְּלֵילְיָא (Dan 5:30). ארבע: Familiar from Dan 7:2 and elsewhere. רוחיהון: Cf. Dan 7:2, etc.; here in the meaning "side, direction." והוא: A scribal error for הוא (הֲוָא). והוא קטל: A frequent construction in this text. בהון: "In them," i.e., among them. ותבר: Cp. line 32 above; here G stem. אנון: As in the previous sentence.

והוא רדף: As in the previous sentence. להון: Prep. לְ (§177c). ערקין: Cf. line 32 above. מן קודמוהי: Review §203; here not reverentially, but literally "fleeing from before him." קודמוהי: Cp. קָדָמוֹהִי (Dan 4:5), and note §26b. חלבון: Geographical name, "Helbon"; cf. MT חֶלְבּוֹן (Ezek 27:18). שימא: G passive fs ptcp from שִׂים; cf. §273c. שמאל: "left," geographically "north"; in JLA texts סְמָל, in BH שְׂמֹאל.

22:10–12

ואצל מנהון כול די שבוא (11) וכול די בזו וכול טבתהון ואף ללוט בר אחוהי פצא וכול נכסוהי וכֹל
(12) שביתא די שבאו אתיב

אצל: C stem SC 3ms, root נצל; cf. ptcp מַצִּל (Dan 6:28); review §254. מנהון: See §183a. שבוא: Same as in line 34, here with final א (§26c). בזו: Cf. lines 21:33, 22:4, and parse. טבתהון: *qāl-at noun pattern (§100), here 2nd decl. pl.; cp. adj. טָב. "Goods," almost exactly in the English sense. ואף: Cf. §432. ללוט: What function does לְ have? (§359a) פצא: G stem SC 3ms, root פצי "to save, rescue." שביתא: *qaṭl-at noun pattern (§101), from root שבי; "group of captives," collective sing. (§84). שבאו: G passive SC 3mp, from שבי, with inserted א, §49c (= שְׁבָאוּ, cp. רְמִיו Dan 3:21). אתיב: Cp. BA הֲתִיב (Dan 2:14); "he brought back."

22:12–13

ושמע מלך סודם די אתיב אברם כול שביתא (13) וכול בזתא וסלק לעורעה

שמע: Parse. בזתא: *qill-at noun pattern (§104); "booty, spoil." לעורעה: Cp. לעורעהון in 21:31 above.

22:13–14

ואתה לשלם היא ירושלם ואברם שרא בעמק (14) שוא והוא עמק מלכא בקעת בית כרמא

שלם: Geographical name, "Salem"; cp. MT שָׁלֵם (Gen 14:18). היא ירושלם: Explanatory copular clause; see §378. שרא: As with שרין in 22:8 above, this could be שָׁרָא or שְׁרָא. עמק: Cf. lines 25, 32 above. שוא: Geographical name, "Shaveh"; cp. MT שָׁוֵה (Gen 14:17). והוא עמק מלכא: Cp. בית היא ירושלם. כרמא: Geographical name, "Beth-karma"; cf. MT בֵּית הַכֶּרֶם (Jer 6:1).

22:14–15

ומלכיצדק מלכא דשלם אנפק (15) מאכל ומשתה לאברם ולכול אנשא די עמה והוא הוא כהן לאל עליון

מלכיצדק: Personal name, "Melchizedek"; cp. MT מַלְכִּי־צֶדֶק (Gen 14:18). דשלם: Note again the proclitic ד for די in the periphrastic genitive, as in דקרנין line 29 above (§135c). אנפק = הַנְפֵּק (Ezra 5:14, etc.). מאכל: *miqtal noun pattern (§117), probably with elided ʾaleph (§47); "food," from root אכל. משתה: *miqtil noun pattern (see again §117); "drink," from root שתי (cf. Dan 5:10). אנשא: Here not generic ("humankind") but collective ("the men"). לאברם ולכול אנשא: See §142b.

הוא הוא: The first הוא is the pronoun, the second the verb: "he was." כהן: Cp. BA כָּהֲנָא (Ez 7:12); "priest." אל עליון: "God Most High"; cp. אֵל עֶלְיוֹן (Gen 14:18). כהן לאל עליון: Periphrastic genitive with לְ (§163).

22:15–17

וברך (16) ל[א]ברם ואמר בריך אברם לאל עליון מרה שמיא וארעא ובריך אל עליון (17) די סגר שנ̇איך בידך

וברך: Cf. BA בְּרַךְ (Dan 2:19, etc.). ל[א]ברם: לְ of direct object (§359a). בריך: G passive participle; cp. בְּרִיךְ (Dan 3:28, etc.). For the performative use, see §316c. לאל: לְ here indicates the source of the blessing. מרה: = BA מָרֵא "lord." The historical א has elided, and the final vowel -ē is marked with the mater ה. סגר: Cf. Dan 6:23; here, "hand over." שנ̇איך: Exactly as in Dan 4:16. בידך: Cf. Ez 5:12 for the same idiom, "to give/hand over into the hand/power."

22:17–18

ויהב לה מעשר מן כול נכסיא די מלך עילם וחברוהי (18) באדין קרב מלכא די סודם

מעשר: *maqtil noun pattern (§117); "tenth." קרב: As in Dan 3:26, etc.

22:18–20

ואמר לאברם מרי אברם (19) הב לי נפשא די איתי לי די שביא עמך די אצלתה מן מלך עילם ונכסיא (20) כולהון שביקין לך

מרי: As in the Qere of Dan 4:16, "my lord." הב: G stem ms impv; cf. BA הַב (Dan 5:17). See §250g. נפשא: *qatl noun pattern (§101), 1st decl. fem. sg.; here, "people," collective sg. איתי לי: See

§380d, "the people that are mine." שביא: G passive fs ptcp (§262a). אצלתה: Cf. אצל (22:10 above). Note the *plene* spelling of the 2ms ending (§212c). נכסיא כולהון: See §168b. שביקין: G passive mp ptcp, root שבק; cf. Dan 4:23, etc. Performative use (§316c): "The possessions are hereby left to you."

22:20–21

אדין אמר אברם למלך סודם מרים אנה (21) ידי יומא דן לאל עליון מרה שמיא וארעא

מרים: C stem ms ptcp; cf. BA מָרִים (Dan 5:19). Review §277e. ידי: Sg., with 1cs pron. suff. (§128). יומא דן: "today"; see §350c.

22:21–23

אן מן חוט עד ערקא דמסאן (22) אן אסב מן כול די איתי לך דל^מ^א תהוה אמר די מן נכסי כול עתרה די (23) אברם

אן: Conditional particle used in oath contexts (§422e). חוט: *qūl* noun pattern (§100); "thread." ערקא: *qaṭl-at* noun pattern (§101), here with א for final 2nd decl. abs. -ā; "strap." מסאן: *maqṭal* noun pattern (§117); in JLA, מְסָן (*masʔan > masān*); IA משאן (cf. §40); "shoe, sandal." ערקא דמסאן: With proclitic ד for די (§135c). מן חוט עד ערקא: Review §184c.

אסב: G stem PC 1cs, root נסב; cf. נסבת in the Ahiqar proverb above, line 160. "I shall not take," *commissive* modality (a kind of deontic modality [§291b] wherein the speaker commits him-/ herself to a course of action). דל^מ^א: The scribe first wrote דלא, then added supralinear *m* to create דלמא (see §406). תהוה אמר: Future habitual action (§313c). די: For this use of the particle, see §427.

נכסי: 1cs pron. suff. on 1st decl. pl. noun; cf. §129. עתרה: *quṭl* noun pattern (§101), with 3ms pron. suff.; "wealth." עתרה די אברם: Periphrastic genitive with suffix-marked head word (§162). מן נכסי כול עתרה: Prepositional predicate (§377).

22:23–24

ברא מן די אכלו כבר עולימי די עמי וברא מן חולק תלתת גבריא די (24) אזלו עמי אנון שליטין בחולקהון למנתן לך

ברא מן: For this prep., see §192. די אכלו: Independent relative (§150). "Except for that which . . ." כבר: Adv.; see §350b; cp. BH כְּבָר (Qoh 1:10, etc.). עולימי: *quṭayl* noun pattern (§112); "lad, servant." Here 1st decl. pl., with 1cs pron. suff. (cp. נכסי line 22 above). חולק: *quṭṭāl* noun pattern (§110); "portion." תלתת: 2nd decl. numeral, cstr.; see §166e. Cp. תְּלָתָה (Dan 6:11, etc.). תלתת גבריא: "the three men." אנון: As subject of a copular clause (§376). שליטין: Cf. שַׁלִּיטִין (Ezra 4:20, etc.), referring to *de jure* authority in a certain domain. בחולקהון: שַׁלִּיט functions as if it were the ptcp of שלט and governs the same oblique objects with בְּ (§342a). למנתן: G stem inf. cf. BA לְמִנְתַּן (Ez 7:20).

22:24–26

ואתיב אברם כול נכסיא וכול (25) שביתא ויהב למלך סודם וכול שביא די הואת עמה מן ארעא דא שבק (26) ושלח כולהון

שביתא: As in line 12. ויהב: Object is omitted, cf. §360. שביא: The same word in 2nd decl. abs. state. וכול שביא: Not "all the captives" (Machiela et al. 2018: 145), but "every group of captives." הואת: G stem SC 3fs; cp. BA הֲוָת (Dan 7:19, etc.), and see §26a. דא: Cf. Dan 4:27, etc. שלח: Likely D stem, "he released" (§231f).

READING 9: TARGUM JOB FROM QUMRAN, COLS. 37–38

Among the latest of the scrolls to be discovered, the Targum of Job from Qumran Cave 11 (11QtgJob) is the earliest example extant of Hebrew Scripture translated into Aramaic (§14). In rabbinic Judaism, the practice of reading the *targum* – the Aramaic translation – became a regular part of the synagogue service (§18); but the Qumran example does not seem to have served the same purpose. Instead, it appears to have been produced as an interpretive aid to one of the most difficult books of the Hebrew Bible.

Like most of the other Dead Sea Scrolls, the Job targum survives only in fragments; as with 1QapGen, only towards the end of the original scroll do we get a fair amount of consecutive text. The excerpt presented below contains the last two columns of text, with a rendering into Aramaic of parts of Job 42. García-Martínez and Tigchelaar (2000) contain text and translation of the targum.

Col. 37 (Job 42:1–6 + 40:5)

ענא איוב ואמר קדם אלהא ידעת די כלא 3
תכול למעבד ולא יתבצר מנך תקף וחכמה 4
הדה מללת ולא אתיב ותרתין ועליהן לא 5
אוסף שמע נא ואנה אמלל אשאלנך 6
והתיבני למשמע אדן שמעתך וכען עיני 7
חזתך על כן אתנסך ואתמהא ואהוא לעפר 8
וקטם 9

Line 3

ענא איוב ואמר: See §295. These could be ptcps. (as in BA) or SC (as in IA). ידעת: G stem SC 1cs; for the tense, see Dan 4:6 and §297. כלא: See §344b.

Line 4

תכול: Cp. יֻכַל (Dan 3:29); cf. §250a and parse. For the orthography, review §26b. למעבד: Review §428a. יתבצר: tG PC 3ms, root בצר "be lacking" (rendering the Heb. cognate). מנך: Cf. Dan 4:28, etc. תקף: Cf. Dan 4:27, etc. חכמה: *quṭl-at noun pattern (§101); cf. BA חָכְמָה (Dan 2:30); "wisdom." The verb is singular with a compound subject (§355c).

Line 5

חדה: Cf. Dan 4:16, etc.; see §166d. Here, חדה [מלה] "one (thing, word)." מללת: Cf. Dan 6:22 and parse. אתיב: C stem; PC or SC? Consider the context; cf. §277 (Dan 3:16, etc.). "I will not repeat." תרתין: Cf. Dan 6:1; here [מלין] תרתין "two (words, things)." עליהן: Note 3fp pron. suff.; see §129. This line translates Job 40:5.

Line 6

אוסף: C stem PC 1cs, root יסף "to add to"; cf. §251a. שמע: G stem ms impv. נא: See §318b. אמלל: Parse. אשאלנך: G stem PC 1cs + energic n + 2ms pron. suff. Review §130a, and cp. BA יִשְׁאֶלָנְכוֹן (Ez 7:21).

Line 7

והתיבני: C stem ms impv + 1cs pron. suff. Cp. הֵעֶלְנִי (Dan 2:24). Here, "to answer" (the parallel in 11QtgJob 34:3 reads התיבני פתגם "give back to me a word" = answer me), cf. Dan 3:16, Ez 5:11. למשמע: G stem inf. as *nomen actionis* (§320); "hearing." אדן: *quṭl noun pattern (§101); "ear." שמעתך: G stem SC 1cs + 2ms pron. suff. עיני: Sg., with 1cs pron. suff.; cp. pl. עַיְנֵי (Dan 4:31).

Line 8

חזתך: G stem SC 3fs + 2ms pron. suff. For the verbal form, review §256b. על כן: Cf. the MT at Job 42:6 עַל־כֵּן "therefore." אתנסך: tG PC 1cs, root נסך "to melt" (< "to be poured out"); for the middle voice, see §333b. The MT at Job 42:6 has אֶמְאַס ("I despise myself," NRSV), but the targum interprets as אמס "I melt." אתמהא: tG PC 1cs, root מהי "become like water." What voice? (§327). אהוא: Cp. BA לֶהֱוֵא and parse. For the verb tenses in the targum, see §302c. עפר: *qaṭal noun pattern (§105); "dust."

Line 9

קטם: *qiṭl noun pattern (§101); "ash."

Col. 38 (Job 42:10–12)

2 ושמע א[ל]הא בקלה די איוב ושבק

3 להון חטאיהון בדילה ותב אלהא לאיוב ברחמין

4 ויהב לה חד תרין בכל די הוא לה ואתין לות

5 איוב כל רחמוהי וכל אחוהי וכל ידעוהי ואכלו

6 עמה לחם בביתה ונחמוהי על כל באישתה די

7 היתי אלהא עלוהי ויהבו לה גבר אמרה חדה

8 וגבר קדש חד די דהב

18

Line 2

בקלה: Prep. בְּ + קָל + 3ms pron. suff.; ב + שמע: "to heed." איוב: Personal name, "Job"; cp. MT אִיּוֹב.
קלה די איוב: What kind of genitive? §162. וּשְׁבַק: Here, "to forgive."

Line 3

להון: See §178a. The pronoun refers to Job's comforters. חטאיהון: Cp. חֲטָאָךְ (Dan 4:24). בדילה:
§193. תב: Cp. תבו (1QapGen 21:30). רחמין: *tantum plurale* noun (§92 and Petition, line 2, above),
for abstraction; "mercy."

Line 4

חד תרין: Cp. חַד־שִׁבְעָה (Dan 3:19), and see §164i. בכל: Here בְּ = "in exchange for." הוא = הֲוָא. הוא לה:
See §177f; §377b. "All that was to him" = all that he had. אתין: Cp. בְּנַיִן Ez 5:4 and parse. לות:
See §197.

Line 5

רחמוהי: G stem mp ptcp, lexicalized as the noun "friend" (§172b), with 3ms pron. suff. (cf. line
24 of the Petition above). אחוהי: Cf. אחוהי (1QapGen 22:11); how do the two occurrences differ?
ידעוהי: Like רחמוהי, "acquaintances."

Line 6

לחם: *qaṭl* noun pattern (§101); cp. BA לְחֶם "bread, food" (Dan 5:1). נחמוהי: D stem SC 3mp +
3ms pron. suff.; "to console." For the suff., cf. §130. באישתה: Cp. BA בָּאִשְׁתָּא (Ez 4:12 and the
Elephantine petition, line 17 above).

353

Line 7

היתי: See §283a and cp. הַיְתִי (Dan 5:13, etc.). גבר: For this construction, see §169b. אמרה: *qiṭṭil-at* noun pattern (§111); "ewe lamb."

Line 8

וגבר: As in the previous line. קדש: *qaṭāl* noun pattern (§108); "nose-/ear-ring." די דהב: Genitive of material (§161).

APPENDICES

APPENDIX
Strong Verb Paradigm

A

	G stem	G stem *i*-theme	D stem	C stem	tG stem	tD stem
SC 3ms	קְטַל	קְטֵל / קְטֵל	קַטֵּל / קַטֵּל	הַקְטֵל / הַקְטֵל (אַקְ׳)	הִתְקְטֵל / הִתְקְטֵל (אִתְ׳)	הִתְקַטַּל
3fs	קִטְלַת	קִטְלַת	קַטְּלַת	הַקְטְלַת	הִתְקְטְלַת	הִתְקַטְּלַת
2ms	קְטַלְתְּ / ־תָּ	קְטֵלְתָּ	קַטֵּלְתָּ	הַקְטֵלְתָּ	הִתְקְטֵלְתָּ	הִתְקַטַּלְתָּ
2fs	קְטַלְתִּי	--	קַטֵּלְתִּי	הַקְטֵלְתִּי	הִתְקְטֵלְתִּי	הִתְקַטַּלְתִּי
1cs	קִטְלֵת		קַטְּלֵת	הַקְטְלֵת	הִתְקְטְלֵת	הִתְקַטְּלֵת
3mp	קְטַלוּ	קְטֵלוּ	קַטִּלוּ	הַקְטְלוּ	הִתְקְטִלוּ	הִתְקַטַּלוּ
3fp	קְטַלָה	קְטֵלָה	קַטִּלָה	הַקְטְלָה	הִתְקְטִלָה	הִתְקַטַּלָה
2mp	קְטַלְתּוּן	קְטֵלְתּוּן	קַטֵּלְתּוּן	הַקְטֵלְתּוּן	הִתְקְטֵלְתּוּן	הִתְקַטַּלְתּוּן
1cp	קְטַלְנָא	קְטֵלְנָא	קַטֵּלְנָא	הַקְטֵלְנָא	הִתְקְטֵלְנָא	הִתְקַטַּלְנָא
PC 3ms	יִקְטֵל	יִקְטַל	יְקַטֵּל	יְהַקְטֵל (יַק׳)	יִתְקְטֵל	יִתְקַטַּל
3fs	תִּקְטֵל	תִּקְטַל	תְּקַטֵּל	תְּהַקְטֵל	תִּתְקְטֵל	תִּתְקַטַּל
2ms	תִּקְטֵל	תִּקְטַל	תְּקַטֵּל	תְּהַקְטֵל	תִּתְקְטֵל	תִּתְקַטַּל
2fs	תִּקְטְלִין		תְּקַטְּלִין	תְּהַקְטְלִין	תִּתְקְטְלִין	תִּתְקַטְּלִין
1cs	אֶקְטֵל	אֶקְטַל	אֲקַטֵּל	אֲהַקְטֵל	אֶתְקְטֵל	אֶתְקַטַּל
3mp	יִקְטְלוּן		יְקַטְּלוּן	יְהַקְטְלוּן	יִתְקְטְלוּן	יִתְקַטְּלוּן
3fp	יִקְטְלָן		יְקַטְּלָן	יְהַקְטְלָן	יִתְקְטְלָן	יִתְקַטְּלָן
2mp	תִּקְטְלוּן		תְּקַטְּלוּן	תְּהַקְטְלוּן	תִּתְקְטְלוּן	תִּתְקַטְּלוּן
2fp	תִּקְטְלָן		תְּקַטְּלָן	תְּהַקְטְלָן	תִּתְקְטְלָן	תִּתְקַטְּלָן
1cp	נִקְטֵל	נִקְטַל	נְקַטֵּל	נְהַקְטֵל	נִתְקְטֵל	נִתְקַטַּל
Jussive						
2fs	תִּקְטְלִי		תְּקַטְּלִי	תְּהַקְטְלִי (תַּק׳)		
3mp	יִקְטְלוּ		יְקַטְּלוּ	יְהַקְטְלוּ		
2mp	תִּקְטְלוּ		תְּקַטְּלוּ	תְּהַקְטְלוּ		
Imperative						
ms	קְטֵל		קַטֵּל	הַקְטֵל		
fs	קְטֵלִי		קַטֵּלִי	הַקְטֵלִי		
mp	קְטֵלוּ		קַטֵּלוּ	הַקְטֵלוּ		

(*cont.*)

	G stem	G stem *i*-theme	D stem	C stem	tG stem	tD stem
Infinitive	(לְ)מִקְטַל	(לְ)מִקְטַל	(לְ)קַטָּלָה	(לְ)הַקְטָלָה	(לְ)הִתְקְטָלָה	(לְ)הִתְקַטָּלָה
Ptcp ms	קָטֵל / קְטִל		מְקַטֵּל	מְהַקְטֵל	מִתְקְטֵל	מִתְקַטַּל
fs	קָטְלָה		מְקַטְּלָה	מְהַקְטְלָה	מִתְקַטְּלָה	מִתְקַטְּלָה
mp	קָטְלִין		מְקַטְּלִין	מְהַקְטְלִין	מִתְקַטְּלִין	מִתְקַטְּלִין
fp	קָטְלָן		מְקַטְּלָן	מְהַקְטְלָן	מִתְקַטְּלָן	מִתְקַטְּלָן
Passive ptcp	קְטִיל		מְקַטַּל	מְהַקְטַל		

	Cp stem	Gp stem
PC 3ms	הָקְטַל	קְטִיל
3fs	הָקְטְלַת	קְטִילַת
2ms	–	קְטִילְתָּה
2fs	–	–
1cs	הָקְטְלֵת	קְטִילֵת
3mp	הָקְטַלוּ	קְטִילוּ

APPENDIX

III-y (Final-Weak) Verb Paradigm

	G stem	G stem *i*-theme	D stem	C stem	tG stem	tD stem
SC 3ms	בְּנָא	צְבִי	בַּנִּי	הַבְנִי (אב׳)	הִתְבְּנִי (את׳)	הִתְבַּנִּי (את׳)
3fs	בְּנָת	צְבִית	בַּנִּיַת	הַבְנִיַת	הִתְבְּנִיַת	etc. as D stem
2ms	בְּנַֽיְתָ	צְבִֽיְתָ	בַּנִּֽיְתָ	הַבְנִֽיְתָ	הִתְבְּנִֽיְתָ	
2fs	בְּנַֽיְתִי	צְבִֽיְתִי	בַּנִּֽיְתִי	הַבְנִֽיְתִי	הִתְבְּנִֽיְתִי	
1cs	בְּנֵית	צְבֵית	בַּנִּית	הַבְנִית	הִתְבְּנִית	
3mp	בְּנוֹ	צְבִיו	בַּנִּיו	הַבְנִיו	הִתְבְּנִיו	
3fp	בְּנָֽיָה	צְבָֽיָה	בַּנִּֽיָה	הַבְנִֽיָה	הִתְבְּנִֽיָה	
2mp	בְּנֵיתוּן	צְבֵיתוּן	בַּנִּיתוּן	הַבְנֵיתוּן	הִתְבְּנִיתוּן	
1cp	בְּנֵֽינָא	צְבֵֽינָא	בַּנִּֽינָא	הַבְנֵֽינָא	הִתְבְּנֵֽינָא	
PC 3ms	יִבְנֵא	יִצְבֵּא	יְבַנֵּא	יְהַבְנֵא (יב׳)	יִתְבְּנֵא	יִתְבַּנֵּא
3fs	תִּבְנֵא	etc.	תְּבַנֵּא	תְּהַבְנֵא	תִּתְבְּנֵא	etc. as D Stem
2ms	תִּבְנֵא		תְּבַנֵּא	תְּהַבְנֵא	תִּתְבְּנֵא	
2fs	תִּבְנֵין		תְּבַנֵּין	תְּהַבְנֵין	תִּתְבְּנֵין	
1cs	אֶבְנֵא		אֲבַנֵּא	אֲהַבְנֵא	אֶתְבְּנֵא	
3mp	יִבְנוֹן		יְבַנּוֹן	יְהַבְנוֹן	יִתְבְּנוֹן	
3fp	יִבְנְיָן		יְבַנְּיָן	יְהַבְנְיָן	יִתְבַּנְיָן	
2mp	תִּבְנוֹן		תְּבַנּוֹן	תְּהַבְנוֹן	תִּתְבְּנוֹן	
2fp	תִּבְנְיָן		תְּבַנְּיָן	תְּהַבְנְיָן	תִּתְבַּנְּיָן	
1cp	נִבְנֵא		נְבַנֵּא	נְהַבְנֵא	נִתְבְּנֵא	
Imperative						
ms	בְּנִי		בַּנִּי		הִתְבְּנִי	–
fs	בְּנָי		בַּנָּי		etc.	–
mp	בְּנוֹ		בַּנּוֹ	הַבְנוֹ		–
Infinitive	(לְ)מִבְנָא		(לְ)בַנָּיָה	(לְ)הַבְנָיָה	(לְ)הִתְבְּנָיָה	(לְ)הִתְבַּנָּיָה

(cont.)

	G stem	G stem *i*-theme	D stem	C stem	tG stem	tD stem
Ptcp ms	בָּנֵה		מְבַנֵּא	מְהַבְנֵא (מַבְ׳)	מִתְבְּנֵא	מִתְבַּנֵּא
fs	בָּנְיָה		מְבַנְּיָה	מְהַבְנְיָה	מִתְבַּנְיָה	etc. as D Stem
mp	בָּנַיִן		מְבַנִּין	מְהַבְנִין	מִתְבְּנַיִן	
fp	בָּנְיָן		מבַנְּיָן	מְהַבְנְיָן	מִתְבַּנְיָן	
Passive ptcp	בְּנֵה		מְבַנַּי ?	מְהַבְנַי ?	–	–

APPENDIX
Hollow Verb Paradigm

	G stem	C stem	tG stem
Suffix Conj.			
3ms	קָם	הֲקִים / הָקֵים	אִתְּשִׂים
3fs	קָמַת	הֲקִימַת	
2ms	קָֽמְתָּ	הֲקִימְתָּ	
2fs	קָֽמְתְּי		
1cs	קָֽמֵת	הֲקִימֵת	אתשׂימת
3mp	קָֽמוּ	הֲקִימוּ	
3fp	קָֽמָה	הֲקִימָה	
2mp	קַמְתּוּן	הֲקֵיבְתּוּן	
1cp	קָֽמְנָא	הֲקֵימְנָא	
Prefix Conj.			
3ms	יְקוּם (יְשִׂים)	יְהָקִים (יְקִים)	יִתְּשָׂם / ־שִׂים
3fs	תְּקוּם	etc.	
2ms	תְּקוּם		
2fs	תְּקוּמִין		
1cs	אֲקוּם		
3mp	יְקוּמוּן	יְהָקִימוּן (יְקִי׳)	יִתְּשָׂמוּן
3fp	יְקוּמָן		
2mp	תְּקוּמוּן		
2fp	תקומָן		
1cp	נְקוּם		
Jussive			
3ms	יְקוּם		
2fs	תְּקוּֽמִי		
3mp	יְקוּֽמוּ		
2mp	תְּקוּֽמוּ		
Imperative			
ms	קוּם		
fs	קוּֽמִי		
mp	קוּֽמוּ		

(cont.)

A

	G stem	C stem	tG stem
fp	–		
Infinitive	(לְ)מִקָם	(לְ)הָקָמָה	(לְ)אִתְּשָׂמָה ?
Active ptcp ms	קָאֵם	מְהָקֵים / מָקִים	מִתְּשָׂם
fs	קאמה		מתשמה
mp	קאמין (כ׳)	מְקִימִין	
	קָיְמִין (ק׳)		

SYNOPTIC PARADIGM, STRONG AND WEAK VERBS (MAJOR FORMS)

G Stem Suffix Conjugation

	Strong	I-n	I-aleph	I-y/w	III-y (a)	III-y (i)	Hollow	Geminate
3ms	קְטַל	נְטַל	אֲכַל	יְתֵב / יְתֶב	בְּנָא	צְבִי	קָם	דַּק
3fs	קִטְלַת	etc.	etc.	יִתְבַת	בְּנָת	צְבִיַת	קָ֫מַת	דַּקַת
		(strong)	(strong)					
2ms	קְטַלְתְּ /			יְתֵבְתְּ /	בְּנַיְתְ	צְבִיתְ	קָ֫מְתְּ	דַּקְתְּ
	קְטַ֫לְתְּ			יְתִבְתָּ				
1cs	קִטְלֵת			יִתְבֵת	בְּנֵית	צְבִית	קָ֫מֵת	דַּקֵת ?
3mp	קְטַ֫לוּ			יְתֵבוּ	בְּנוֹ	צְבִיו	קָ֫מוּ	דַּ֫קּוּ / דָּ֫קוּ
3fp	קְטַ֫לָה			יְתֵבָה	בְּנָיָה	צְבִיָה	קָ֫מָה	
2mp	קְטַלְתּוּן			יְתֶבְתּוּן	בְּנֵיתוּן	צְבִיתוּן	קַמְתּוּן	דַּקְתּוּן
1cp	קְטַ֫לְנָא			יְתֶ֫בְנָא	בְּנֶ֫ינָא	צְבִ֫ינָא	קַ֫מְנָא	דְּ֫קְנָא

G Stem Prefix Conjugation

	Strong	I-n	I-aleph	I-y/w	III-y	Hollow	Geminate
3ms	יִקְטֵל	יִטַל	יֵאכֻל	יִתֵּב / יִנְדַּע	יִבְנֵא	יְקוּם	יִדַּק
3fs	תִּקְטֵל	תִּטַל	תֵּאכֻל	תִּתֵּב / תִּנְדַּע	תִּבְנֵא	תְּקוּם	תִּדַּק
2ms	תִּקְטֵל	תִּטַל	תֵּאכֻל	תִּתֵּב / תִּנְדַּע	תִּבְנֵא	תְּקוּם	תִּדַּק
1cs	אֶקְטֵל	אֶטַל	אֵכֻל	אֶתֵּב ? / אֶנְדַּע	אֶבְנֵא	אֲקוּם	אֶדַּק

A

(cont.)

	Strong	I-n	I-aleph	I-y/w	III-y	Hollow	Geminate
3mp	יִקְטְלוּן	יִטְּלוּן	יֵאכְלוּן	יִתְּבוּן / יִנְדְּעוּן	יִבְנוֹן	יְקוּמוּן	יִדְּקוּן
3fp	יִקְטְלָן	יִטְּלָן	יֵאכְלָן	etc.	יִבְנְיָן	יְקוּמָן	etc.
2mp	תִּקְטְלוּן	תִּטְּלוּן	תֵּאכְלוּן		תִּבְנוֹן	תְּקוּמוּן	
2fp	תִּקְטְלָן	תִּטְּלָן	תֵּאכְלָן		תִּבְנְיָן	תְּקוּמָן	
1cp	נִקְטֻל	נִטֻּל	נֵאכֻל		נִבְנֵא	נְקוּם	

G Stem Jussive and Imperative

	Strong	I-n	I-aleph	I-y/w	III-y	Hollow	Geminate
3ms	יִקְטֻל	יִטֻּל	יֵאכֻל	יִתֵּב / יִנְדַּע	יִבְנֵי	יְקוּם	יִדֻּק
3fs	תִּקְטֻל	תִּטֻּל	תֵּאכֻל	תִּתֵּב / תִּנְדַּע	תִּבְנֵי	תְּקוּם	תִּדֻּק
2ms	תִּקְטֻל	תִּטֻּל	תֵּאכֻל	תִּתֵּב / תִּנְדַּע	תִּבְנֵי	תְּקוּם	תִּדֻּק
Imp. ms	קְטֻל	טֻל	אֱכֻל	תֵּב / דַּע	בְּנִי	קוּם	דֻּק
2fs	תִּקְטְלִי	תִּטְּלִי	תֵּאכְלִי	תִּתְּבִי / תִּנְדְּעִי	תִּבְנְי	תְּקוּמִי	תִּדְּקִי
imp fs	קְטֻלִי	טֻּלִי	אֱכֻלִי	תֵּבִי / דַּעִי	בְּנִי	קוּמִי	דֻּקִי
3mp	יִקְטְלוּ	יִטְּלוּ	יֵאכְלוּ	יִתְּבוּ / יִנְדְּעוּ	יִבְנוֹ	יְקוּמוּ	יִדְּקוּ
2mp	תִּקְטְלוּ	תִּטְּלוּ	תֵּאכְלוּ	תִּתְּבוּ / תִּנְדְּעוּ	תִּבְנוֹ	תְּקוּמוּ	תִּדְּקוּ
Imp. mp	קְטֻלוּ	טֻּלוּ	אֱכֻלוּ	תֵּבוּ / דַּעוּ	בְּנוֹ	קוּמוּ	דֻּקוּ

G Stem Infinitive and Participle

	Strong	I-n	I-aleph	I-y/w	III-y	Hollow	Geminate
Inf.	מִקְטַל	מִטַּל	מֵאכַל	מִנְדַּע	מִבְנֵא	מְקָם	מִדַּק
Act. Part.							
ms	קָטֵל / קָטֶל	נָטֵל	אָכֵל	יָתֵב / יָדַע	בָּנֵה	קָאֵם	דָּקֵק
fs	קָטְלָה	נָטְלָה	אָכְלָה	יָתְבָה	בָּנְיָה	קָאֲמָה	דָּקְקָה
mp	קָטְלִין	נָטְלִין	אָכְלִין	יָתְבִין	בָּנַיִן	קָיְמִין	דָּקְקִין / דָּקִין
fp	קָטְלָן	נָטְלָן	אָכְלָן	יָתְבָן	בָּנְיָן		
Pass. ms	קְטִיל	נְטִיל	אֲכִיל	יְדִיעַ	בְּנֵא	קִים	
mp	קְטִילִין	נְטִילִין	אֲכִילִין	יְדִיעִין	בְּנַיִן		

C Stem Suffix Conjugation

	Strong	I-n	I-aleph	I-y/w	III-y	Hollow	Geminate
3ms	הַקְטֵל	הַצֵּל	הוֹבֵד	הוֹתֵב	הַבְנִי	הֲקֵים	הַדֵּק
3fs	הַקְטְלַת	הַצְּלַת	הוֹבְדַת	הוֹתְבַת	הַבְנִיַת	הֲקֵימַת	הַדֵּקַת
2ms	הַקְטֵלְתָּ	הַצֵּלְתָּ	הוֹבֵדְתָּ	הוֹתֵבְתָּ	הַבְנִיתָ	הֲקֵימְתָּ	הַדֵּקְתָּ
1cs	הַקְטְלֵת	הַצֵּלֵת	הוֹבְדֵת	הוֹתְבֵת	הַבְנִית	הֲקֵימֵת	הַדֵּקֵת ?
3mp	הַקְטִלוּ	הַצִּלוּ	הוֹבְדוּ	הוֹתְבוּ	הַבְנִיו	הֲקֵימוּ	הַדִּקוּ
3fp	הַקְטִלָה	etc.	etc.	etc.	etc.	etc.	etc.
2mp	הַקְטֵלְתּוּן						
1cp	הַקְטֵלְנָא						

C Stem Prefix Conjugation

	Strong	I-n	I-aleph	I-y/w	III-y	Hollow	Geminate
3ms	יְהַקְטֵל	יְהַצֵּל	יְהוֹבֵד	יְהוֹתֵב	יְהַבְנֵא	יְהָקֵים / יְקֵים	יְהַדֵּק ?
3fs	תְּהַקְטֵל	etc.	etc.	etc.	etc.	etc.	etc.
2ms	תְּהַקְטֵל						
1cs	אֲהַקְטֵל						
3mp	יְהַקְטְלוּן	יְהַצְּלוּן	יְהוֹבְדוּן	יְהוֹתְבוּן	יְהַבְנוֹן	יְהָקֵימוּן / יְקֵימוּן	יְהַדְּקוּן ?
3fp	יְהַקְטְלָן	etc.	etc.	etc.	etc.	etc.	etc.
2mp	תְּהַקְטְלוּן						
	תְּהַקְטְלָן						
1cp	נְהַקְטֵל						

C Stem Infinitive and Participle

	Strong	I-n	I-aleph	I-y/w	III-y	Hollow	Geminate
Inf.	הַקְטָלָה	הַצָּלָה	הוֹבָדָה	הוֹתָבָה	הַבְנָיָה	הֲקָמָה	הַדָּקָה
Act. Part.							
ms	מְהַקְטֵל	מְהַצֵּל	מְהוֹבֵד	מְהוֹתֵב	מְהַבְנֵא	מְהָקֵים / מָקֵים	מְהַדֵּק
fs	מְהַקְטְלָה	מְהַצְּלָה	מְהוֹבְדָה	מְהוֹתְבָה	מְהַבְנְיָה	מְקֵימָה ?	מְהַדְּקָה
mp	מְהַקְטְלִין	מְהַצְּלִין	מְהוֹבְדִין	מְהוֹתְבִין	מְהַבְנַיִן	מְקֵימִין	מְהַדְּקִין
fp	מְהַקְטְלָן	מְהַצְּלָן	מְהוֹבְדָן	מְהוֹתְבָן	מְהַבְנְיָן	מְקֵימָן	מְהַדְּקָן
Pass. ms	מְהַקְטַל	מְהַצַּל	מְהוֹבַד	מְהוֹתַב	מְהַבְנַי	מֵקַם ?	מְהַדַּק

APPENDIX

A

Genesis Apocryphon 21:23–22:26 with Tiberian Vocalization

(21:23) קַדְמַת יוֹמַיָּא אִלֵּן אֲתָה כְּדָרְלָעוֹמֶר מֶלֶךְ עֵילָם אַמְרָפֶל מֶלֶךְ בָּבֶל אַרְיוֹךְ מֶלֶךְ כַּפְתוּךְ תִּדְעָל מֶלֶךְ גּוֹיִם דִּי (24) הוּא בֵּין

נַהֲרִין וַעֲבַדוּ קְרָב עִם בָּרַע מֶלֶךְ סוֹדֹם וְעִם בִּרְשַׁע מֶלֶךְ עוֹמְרָם וְעִם שִׁנְאָב מֶלֶךְ אַדְמָא (25) וְעִם שַׁמְיָאבַד מֶלֶךְ צְבוֹיִן וְעִם מֶלֶךְ

בָּלַע כֹּל אִלֵּן אִזְדַּמֵּנוּ כַּחֲדָא לִקְרָב לְעֵמְקָא דִּי סִדַּיָּא וּתְקַף מֶלֶךְ (26) עֵילָם וּמַלְכַיָּא דִּי עִמֵּהּ לְמָלֶךְ סוֹדֹם וּלְכוֹל חַבְרוֹהִי וְשַׁוִּיו

עֲלֵיהוֹן מַדָּא תַּרְתֵּי עֶשְׂרֵה שְׁנִין הֲווֹ (27) יָהֲבִין מַדַּתְהוֹן לְמָלֶךְ עֵילָם וּבִשְׁנַת תְּלָת עֶשְׂרֵה מְרַדוּ בֵהּ וּבִשְׁנַת אַרְבַּע עֶשְׂרֵה דְּבַר

מֶלֶךְ עֵילָם לְכוֹל (28) חַבְרוֹהִי וּסְלִקוּ אָרְחָא דִּי מַדְבְּרָא וַהֲווֹא מָחַיִן וּבָזִין מִן פּוּרַת נַהֲרָא וּמְחוֹ לִרְפָאַיָא דִּי בְּעַשְׁתְּרָא (29) דְּקַרְנַיִן

וּלְזוּזְמַזְמַיָּא דִּי בְּעַמָּן וּלְאֵימַיָּא דְּ[י בְּ]שָׁוֵ[ה הַקְּרָיוֹת וּלְחוֹרַיָּא דִּי בְּטוּרֵי גְבָל עַד דְּבָקוּ לְאֵיל (30) פָּרָן דִּי בְּמַדְבְּרָא וְתָבוּ וּמְחוֹ לְעֵו̇ן

דִּינָא [וְלֹאנָשׁ]א דִּי בְּחַצְצָן תָּמָר (31) וּנְפַק מֶלֶךְ סוֹדֹם לְעוּרְעָהֹו̇ן וּמֶלָךְ [עוֹמְרָם וּמֶ]לָךְ אַדְמָא וּמֶלָךְ צְבוֹאִין וּמֶלָךְ בָּלַע ו̇[עֲ]בַ̇דֹ[ו]

קְרָבָא (32) בְּעֵמְקָא דְּ[י סִדַּיָּא] לְקוּבְלֵי כְּדָרְלָ[עֹומֶר מֶלֶךְ עֵילָם וּמַלְכַיָּא] דִּי עִמֵּהּ וְאִתְּבַר מֶלֶךְ סוֹדֹם וַעֲרַק וּמֶלֶךְ עֹומְרָם (33)

נְפַל וְ[שַׁגִּיאִין עִמֵּהּ ...] וּבַז מֶלֶךְ עֵילָם כּוֹל נִכְסַיָּא דִּי סוֹדֹם וְדִי (34) [עֹו]מְרָ[ם ...] וּשְׁבוֹ לוֹט בַּר אֲחוּי

(22:1) דִּי אַבְרָם דִּי הֲוָא יָתֵב בְּסוֹדֹם כַּחֲדָא עִמְּהוֹן וְכוֹל נִכְסֹוהִי וַאֲתָה חַד מִן רָעֵה (2) עָנָה דִּי יְהַב אַבְרָם לְלוֹט דִּי

פְּלַט מִן שִׁבְיָא עַל אַבְרָם וְאַבְרָם בַּאדַיִן הֲוָא (3) יָתֵב בְּחֶבְרוֹן וַחֲזָיֵהּ דִּי שְׁבִי לוֹט בַּר אֲחוּהִי וְכוֹל נִכְסֹוהִי וְלָא קַטִיל וְדִי (4) נְגַדוּ

מַלְכַיָּא אָרְחָא חִלְתָא רַבְּתָא לִמְדִיתֹון וְשָׁבַיִן וּבָזִין וּמָחַיִן וְקָטְלִין וְאָזְלִין (5) לִמְדִינַת דַּרְמֶשֶׂק וּבְכָא אַבְרָם עַל לוֹט בַּר אֲחוּהִי

וְאִתְחַלַּם אַבְרָם וְקָם (6) וּבְחַר מִן עַבְדֹוהִי גַּבְּרִין בְּחִירִין לִקְרָב מְאָא וּתְמָנְיַאת עֲשַׂר וְעָרְנַם (7) וְאֶשְׁכֹּול וּמַמְרֵה נְגַדוּ עִמֵּהּ

וַהֲוָא רָדַף בָּתְרֵהוֹן עַד דְּבַק לְדָן וְאַשְׁכַּח אִנּוּן (8) שָׁרֵין בְּבִקְעַת דָּן וּרְמָה עֲלֵיהוֹן בְּלֵילְיָא מִן אַרְבַּע רוּחֵיהוֹן וַהֲוָא קָטֵל (9) בְּהוֹן

בְּלֵילְיָא וּתְבַר אִנּוּן וַהֲוָא רָדַף לְהוֹן וְכוּלְהוֹן הֲווֹא עָרְקִין מִן קוֹדְמֹוהִי (10) עַד דְּבָקוּ לְחֶלְבּוֹן דִּי שִׂימָא עַל שְׂמָאל דַּרְמֶשֶׂק וְאַצֵּל

מִנְּהוֹן כּוֹל דִּי שְׁבוֹא (11) וְכוֹל דִּי בַּזּוּ וְכוֹל טָבָתְהוֹן וְאַף לְלוֹט בַּר אֲחוּהִי פְּצָא וְכוֹל נִכְסֹוהִי וְכוֹל (12) שִׁבְיָתָא דִּי שְׁבָאוּ אֲתִיב

וּשְׁמַע מֶלֶךְ סוֹדֹם דִּי אֲתִיב אַבְרָם כּוֹל שִׁבְיָתָא (13) וְכוֹל בִּזְתָא וּסְלַק לְעוּרְעֵהּ וַאֲתָה לְשָׁלֵם הִיא יְרוּשְׁלֵם וְאַבְרָם שָׁרֵא בְּעֵמְק

(14) שָׁוֵא וְהוּא עֵמְק מַלְכָּא בְּקַעַת בֵּית כַּרְמָא וּמַלְכִּיצֶדֶק מַלְכָּא דִשָּׁלֵם אַנְפֵּק (15) מַאֲכַל וּמִשְׁתֵּה לְאַבְרָם וּלְכוֹל אֲנָשָׁא דִּי עִמֵּהּ

וְהוּא הֲוָא כָּהֵן לְאֵל עֶלְיוֹן וּבָרֵךְ (16) לְ[אַ]בְרָם וַאֲמַר בְּרִיךְ אַבְרָם לְאֵל עֶלְיוֹן מָרֵה שְׁמַיָּא וְאַרְעָא וּבְרִיךְ אֵל עֶלְיוֹן (17) דִּי סְגַר

שָׂנְאָיִךְ בִּידָךְ וִיהַב לֵהּ מַעְשַׂר מִן כּוֹל נִכְסַיָּא דִּי מָלֵךְ עֵילָם וְחַבְרוֹהִי (18) בֵּאדַיִן קְרֵב מַלְכָּא דִּי סֹודם וַאֲמַר לְאַבְרָם מְרִי אַבְרָם

(19) הַב לִי נַפְשָׁא דִּי אִיתַי לִי דִּי שְׁבְיָא עִמָּךְ דִּי אַצַּלְתָּה מִן מֶלֵךְ עֵילָם וְנִכְסַיָּא (20) כּוּלְהוֹן שְׁבִיקִין לָךְ אֱדַיִן אֲמַר אַבְרָם לְמֶלֵךְ

סֹודם מְרִים אֲנָה (21) יְדִי יוֹמָא דֵּן לְאֵל עֶלְיוֹן מָרֵה שְׁמַיָּא וְאַרְעָא אִן מִן חוּט עַד עֲרָקָא דִּמְסָאן (22) אַן אֶסַּב מִן כּוֹל דִּי אִיתַי לָךְ

דְּל^מָ^א תֶּהֱוֵה אֲמַר דִּי מִן נִכְסַי כּוֹל עֻתְרָה דִּי (23) אַבְרָם בָּרָא מִן דִּי אֲכַלוּ כְּבָר עוּלִימַי דִּי עִמִּי וּבָרָא מִן חוּלָק תְּלָתַת גֻּבְרַיָּא דִּי

(24) אָזַלוּ עִמִּי אִנּוּן שַׁלִּיטִין בְּחוּלְקָהוֹן לְמִנְתַּן לָךְ וַאֲתִיב אַבְרָם כּוֹל נִכְסַיָּא וְכוֹל (25) שְׁבְיָתָא וִיהַב לְמֶלֵךְ סֹודם וְכוֹל שַׁבְיָא דִּי

הֲוָאת עִמֵּהּ מִן אַרְעָה דָּא שְׁבַק (26) וְשַׁלַּח כּוּלְהוֹן

BIBLICAL ARAMAIC GLOSSARY

The following glossary is complete for all of Biblical Aramaic, including passages not included in the guided readings.

א

אַב	*n. m.* father (pl. w. suff. אֲבָהָתִי)
אֵב	*n. m.* fruit (w. suff. אִנְבֵּהּ)
אבד	*vb.* G: to perish; C: destroy
אֶבֶן	*n. f.* stone
אִגְּרָה	*n. f.* letter
אֱדַיִן	*adv./conj.* then (with prep. בֵּאדַיִן) (§431)
אֲדָר	*PN* Adar (month)
אִדַּר	*n. m.* threshing-floor
אֲדַרְגָּזַר	*n. m.* counsellor (Persian)
אַדְרַזְדָּא	*adv.* diligently (Persian)
אֶדְרָע	*n. f.* arm (= דְּרָע)
אַזְדָּא	*adj.* certain, established (Persian)
אזה	*vb.* G: to heat
אזל	*vb.* G: to go, walk
אָח	*n. m.* brother
אַחֲוָיַת	> חוי *vb.*
אֲחִידָה	*n. f.* riddle
אַחְמְתָא	*GN* Ecbatana
אַחֲרֵי	*prep.* after
אַחֲרִי	*n. f.* end
אָחֲרֵין	*adv.* finally
אָחֳרָן m., אָחֳרִי f.	*adj.* other, another (§116)
אֲחַשְׁדַּרְפַּן	*n. m.* satrap (Persian)
אִילָן	*n. m.* tree
אֵימְתָנִי	*adj.* frightful, terrible
אִיתַי	*existential part.* there is, are (§380)
אכל	*vb.* G: to eat, devour
אַל	*neg.* not (with jussive) (§388)
אֵל	*demon. pron.* these (Qere) (§136)
אֱלָהּ	*n. m.* god, God
אֵלֶּה	*demon. pron.* these (Ketiv) (§136)
אֲלוּ	*presentative part.* behold, lo! (§384)
אִלֵּין	*demon. pron.* these (§136)
אִלֵּךְ	*demon. pron.* those (§136)
אִלֵּן	> אִלֵּין
אֲלַף	*n. m.* thousand
אַמָּה	*n. f.* cubit (pl. אַמִּין)

367

אֻמָּה	*n. f.* tribe (det. pl. אֻמַּיָּא)
אמן	> הֵימַן
אמר	*vb.* G: to say, command
אִמַּר	*n. m.* lamb
אנב	> אֵב
אֲנָה	*pers. pron. 1cs* I, myself (§124)
אִנּוּן	*pers. pron. 3mp* they, those, them (§124)
אנוש	> אֱנָשׁ
אֲנַחְנָא	*pers. pron. 1cp* we (§124)
אִנִּין	*pers. pron. 3fp* they (§124)
אנס	*vb.* G: to trouble
אַנְפִּין	*n. m. pl.* face
אֱנָשׁ	*n. m.* human, humankind, group of people
אַנְתְּ	*pers. pron. 2ms* you (Qere) (§124)
אנתה	*pers. pron. 2ms* you (Ketiv) (§124)
אַנְתּוּן	*pers. pron. 2mp* you (§124)
אֱסוּר	*n. m.* fetter, chain
אָסְנַפַּר	*PN* Osnappar
אָסְפַּרְנָא	*adv.* exactly, strictly (Persian)
אֱסָר	*n. m.* ban, prohibition
אָע	*n. m.* wood (§46)
אַף	*conj.* also, moreover (§432)
אֲפָרְסִי	*adj. gent.* Persian (?)
אֲפַרְסְכָי	*adj.* inquisitor (?) (Persian)
אֲפַרְסַתְכָי	*adj.* prefect (?) (Persian)
אַפְתֹם	*adv.* surely (?)
אֶצְבַּע	*n. f.* finger (pl. אֶצְבְּעָן)
אַרְבַּע	*num. f.*, אַרְבְּעָה *m.* four (§164)
אַרְגְּוָן	*n. m.* purple wool (Akkadian)
אֲרוּ	*presentative part.* behold, lo! (§384)
אֹרַח	*n. f.* way (pl. w. suff. אֹרְחָתֵהּ)
אַרְיֵה	*n. m.* lion (det. pl. אַרְיָוָתָא) (§96)
אַרְיוֹךְ	*PN* Arioch
אֲרִיךְ	*adj.* proper (Persian)
אַרְכֻבָּה	*n. f.* knee
אַרְכָה	*n. f.* prolongation, extension
אַרְכְּוָי	*adj. gent.* Erechite
אֲרַע	*n. f.* earth, land
אַרְעִי	*n. f.* bottom
אֲרַק	*n. f.* earth, land (= אֲרַע)
אַרְתַּחְשַׁשְׁתְּא	*PN* Artaxerxes
אֹשׁ	*n. m.* foundation
אֶשָּׁא	*n. f.* fire
אָשַׁף	*n. m.* conjurer, enchanter (Akkadian)
אַשַּׁרְנָא	*n. m.* furnishings, material (Persian)
אֶשְׁתַּדּוּר	*n. m.* rebellion (Persian?)

אָת	*n. f.* sign (abs. pl. אָתִין)
אתי	*vb.* G: to come; C: bring; Cp: be brought (§282)
אַתּוּן	*n. m.* furnace
אֲתַר	*n. m.* place

ב

בְּ	*prep.* in, with, by (§179)
בְּאִישׁ	*adj.* bad, evil
באשׁ	*vb.* G: to be displeasing, bad
בָּתַר / בָּאתַר	*prep.* after (§191)
בָּבֶל	*GN* Babylon
בָּבְלִי	*adj. gent.* Babylonian
בדר	*vb.* D: to scatter
בְּהִילוּ	*n. f.* haste
בהל	*vb.* D: to upset, alarm; tD/tG: be upset, agitated
בטל	*vb.* G: to cease, be idle; D: to cause to cease
בַּי	*n. m.* house (cstr. בֵּית, abs. pl. בָּתִּין) (§94)
בֵּין	*prep.* between, among (§194)
בִּינָה	*n. f.* understanding
בִּירָה	*n. f.* fortress, capital (Akkadian)
בִּית	*vb.* G: to pass the night
בֵּית	> בַּי
בָּל	*n. m.* mind
בְּלוֹ	*n. m.* tribute (Akkadian)
בֵּלְטְשַׁאצַּר	*PN* Belteshazzar
בלי	*vb.* D: to wear out, wear down
בֵּלְשַׁאצַּר	*PN* Belshazzar
בני	*vb.* G: to build, tG: be built
בִּנְיָן	*n. m.* building
בנס	*vb.* G: to be angry, vexed
בָּעוּ	*n. f.* petition
בעי	*vb.* G: to seek, ask for, be about to; D: to search
בְּעֵל	*n. m.* owner, lord, commander
בִּקְעָה	*n. f.* plain
בקר	*vb.* D: to search, investigate; tD: be investigated
בַּר	*n. m.* son (pl. בְּנִין) (§94)
בַּר	*n. m.* field, outside, outdoors
בְּרִיךְ	*adj.* blessed (G passive ptcp.)
ברך	*vb.* G: to kneel; D: to bless
בְּרַךְ	*n. f.* knee (pl. with suffix בִּרְכוֹהִי)
בְּרַם	*conj.* but (§396)
בְּשַׂר	*n. m.* flesh
בַּת	*n. m.* bath, liquid measure (Hebrew)
בָּתַר	> בָּאתַר

G

ג

גַּב	*n. m.* side, flank
גֹּב	*n. m.* pit
גְּבוּרָה	*n. f.* might
גְּבַר	*n. m.* man, male (pl. גֻּבְרִין)
גִּבָּר	*n. m.* mighty one
גְּדָבַר	*n. m.* treasurer (Persian)
גדד	*vb.* G: to hew down
גַּו	*n. m.* interior; בְּגוֹא *prep.* within; לְגוֹא *prep.* into
גוב	> גֹּב
גֵּוָה	*n. f.* pride
גוח	*vb.* C: to stir up
גִּזְבַּר	*n. m.* treasurer (Persian)
גזר	*vb.* tG: to be cut
גָּזַר	*n. m.* diviner (G ptcp.)
גְּזֵרָה	*n. f.* decree (Hebrew)
גִּיר	*n. m.* chalk, plaster
גַּלְגַּל	*n. m.* wheel
גָּלוּ	*n. f.* exile
גלי	I *vb.* G: to reveal
גלי	II *vb.* C: to exile
גְּלָל	*n. m.* choice stone
גְּמִיר	*adj.* complete (G passive ptcp.; meaning obscure in Ez 7:12)
גְּנַז	*n. m.* treasure (Persian)
גַּף	*n. f.* wing of bird
גְּרַם	*n. f.* bone
גְּשֵׁם	*n. m.* body

ד

דְּ	*rel. pron.* > דִּי (via emendation of דְּהָוֵא (Ez 4:9 Ketiv) > דהי
דָּא	*demon. pron. fem. sg.* this (§136)
דֹּב	*n. m.* bear
דבח	*vb.* G: to sacrifice
דְּבַח	*n. m.* sacrifice
דבק	*vb.* G: to adhere to
דִּבְרָה	[*n. f.* cause, reason]; עַל דִּבְרַת *prep.* in order that
דְּהַב	*n. m.* gold
דַּהֲיֵ	*adj. gent.* Ez 4:9 דְּהָוֵא should be read דְּהוּא "that is"
דור	*vb.* G: to dwell
דוּר	*n. m.* wall (Akkadian) [formerly *GN* Dura]
דושׁ	*vb.* G: to trample
דַּחֲוָן	*n. f.* entertainments, distractions (?)
דחל	*vb.* G: to fear; D: frighten
דִּי	*rel. pron.* who, which; *complementizer* that; *conj.* because; *gen. part.* of; דִּי־ל possessive; דִּי־לְמָה
	conj. lest (§135)
דין	*vb.* G: to judge

דִּין	*n. m.* judgment, court
דִּינָי	*adj. gent.* Ezra 4:9 to be read דַּיָּנַיָּא judges
דַּיָּן	*n. m.* judge
דֵּךְ	*demon. pron. masc. sg.* that (§136)
דָּךְ	*demon. pron. fem. sg.* that (§136)
דִּכֵּן	*demon. pron. sg.* that (§136)
דְּכַר	*n. m.* ram
דִּכְרוֹן	*n. m.* memorandum, record (Hebrew)
דָּכְרָן	*n. m.* memorandum, record
דלק	*vb.* G: to burn (intrans.)
דמי	*vb.* G: to be like
דְּנָה	*demon. pron. masc. sg.* this (§136)
דָּנִיֵּאל	*PN* Daniel
דקק	*vb.* G: to break apart (intrans.); C: smash
דָּר	*n. m.* generation
דָּרְיָוֶשׁ	*PN* Darius
דְּרָע	*n. f.* arm
דָּת	*n. m.* decree, law (Persian)
דֶּתֶא	*n. m.* grass
דְּתָבַר	*n. m.* legal expert (Persian)

ה

הֲ	*interrog. part., introduces questions* (§390)
הָא	*presentative part.* lo! behold! (§383)
הָא	> הֵיךְ
הַדָּבַר	*n. m.* companion (Persian)
הַדָּם	*n. m.* member, limb (Persian)
הדר	*vb.* D: to glorify
הֲדַר	*n. m.* honor, majesty
הוּא	*pers. pron. masc.* he (§124)
הוי	*vb.* G: to be (PC לֶהֱוֵא) (§268)
ה(ו)ך	*vb.* G: to go (PC, inf.) (§272b)
הִיא	*pers. pron. fem.* she, it (§124)
הֵיךְ	*conj.* Dan 2:43 הֵיךְ דִּי = הֵא־כְדִי just as
הֵיכַל	*n. m.* palace, temple (Akkadian)
הימן	*vb.* Quad: to believe in (Hebrew) (§288b)
הך	> ה(ו)ך
הלך	*vb.* D: to walk around
הֲלָךְ	*n. m.* tribute (Akkadian)
הִמּוֹ	*pers. pron.* them (§124)
הִמּוֹן	*pers. pron.* them (§124)
הַמּוּנְכָא	*n. m.* chain (Ketiv) (Persian)
הַמְנִיכָא	Qere > הַמּוּנְכָא
הֵן	*conj.* if; whether (§422)
הַצְדָּא	*adv.* is it true?
הַרְהֹר	*n. m.* bad thought, imagination

G

ו

וְ	*conj.* and

ז

זבן	*vb.* G: to buy
זְהִיר	*adj.* cautious
זוד	*vb.* C: to act with arrogance
זון	*vb.* tG: to be fed
זוע	*vb.* G: to tremble
זִיו	*n. m.* countenance, radiance (Akkadian)
זָכוּ	*n. f.* innocence
זְכַרְיָה	*PN* Zechariah
זמן	*vb.* tD/tG: to meet together, conspire
זְמָן	*n. m.* time (det. sg. זִמְנָא) (Akkadian)
זְמָר	*n. m.* music, musical instruments
זַמָּר	*n. m.* singer
זַן	*n. m.* kind, sort (Persian)
זְעֵיר	*adj.* little, small
זעק	*vb.* G: to cry out
זקף	*vb.* G: to raise
זְרֻבָּבֶל	*PN* Zerubbabel
זְרַע	*n. m.* seed

ח

חֲבוּלָה	*n. f.* crime
חבל	*vb.* D: to destroy; tD: be destroyed
חֲבָל	*n. m.* harm, damage
חַבַּר	*n. m.* companion
חַבְרָה	*n. f.* companion
חַגַּי	*PN* Haggai
חַד	*num./adj.* one; a, an
חֲדֵה	*n. f.* breast (du. w. suff. חֲדוֹהִי)
חֶדְוָה	*n. f.* joy
חֲדַת	*adj.* new
חוט	> יחט
חוי	*vb.* D, C: to declare, make known
חִוָּר	*adj.* white
חֱזוּ	*n. m.* vision (det. חֶזְוָא)
חֲזוֹת	*n. f.* tree-top, crown
חזי	*vb.* G: to see
חֲטָי, חֲטָא	*n. m.* sin
חטי	*vb.* D: to remove sin
חַי	*adj.* living
חיי	*vb.* G: to live; C: make alive

חַיְוָה	n. f. animal, animals (collective sg.)
חַיִּין	n. m. pl. life
חַיִל	n. m. strength; army
חַכִּים	adj. wise; n. m. sage
חָכְמָה	n. f. wisdom
חֵלֶם	n. m. dream
חלף	vb. G: to pass
חֲלָק	n. m. share
חֲמָה /חֲמָא	n. f. rage
חֲמַר	n. m. wine
חִנְטָה	n. f. wheat (pl. חִנְטִין)
חֲנֻכָּה	n. f. dedication (Hebrew)
חנן	vb. G: to show mercy; tD: ask for mercy
חֲנַנְיָה	PN Hananiah
חַסִּיר	adj. wanting, lacking
חסן	vb. C: to take possession
חֱסֶן	n. m. power (det. חִסְנָא)
חֲסַף	n. m. pottery, earthenware
חצף	vb. Cp: to be made severe
חרב	vb. Cp: to be laid waste
חַרְטֹם	n. m. magician (Egyptian?)
חרך	vb. tD: to be singed
חֲרַץ	n. m. hip
חשׁב	vb. G: to think, esteem
חֲשׁוֹך	n. m. darkness
חשׁח	vb. G: to need
חַשְׁחָה	n. f. needed thing
חַשְׁחוּ	n. f. needs
חשׁל	vb. G: to shatter
חתם	vb. G: to seal

ט

טאב	vb. G: to be good
טָב	adj. good
טַבָּח	n. m. guard, executioner
טוּר	n. m. mountain
טְוָת	adv. fasting
טִין	n. m. clay
טַל	n. m. dew
טלל	vb. C: to take shelter
טעם	vb. D: to feed
טְעֵם	n. m. decree, sense, taste, influence
טְפַר	n. f. nail, claw
טרד	vb. G: to drive away
טַרְפְּלָי	adj. gent. Tripolite (?)

G

י

יבל	*vb.* C: to bring
יַבָּשָׁה	*n. f.* land, earth
יְגַר	*n. f.* heap
יַד	*n. f.* hand (du. יְדַיִן)
ידי	*vb.* C: to thank, praise
ידע	*vb.* G: to know; C: to tell
יהב	*vb.* G: to give (SC and impv. only)
יְהוּד	*GN* Judea
יְהוּדָי	*adj. gent.* Jew, Judean
יוֹם	*n. m.* day
יוֹצָדָק	*PN* Jozadak
יחט	*vb.* Gp: to be set down [Ezra 4:12 יַחִיטוּ is vocalized as a D stem with plene orthography; but vocalize rather Gp SC יְחִיטוּ]
יטב	*vb.* G: to be good, pleasing
יכל	*vb.* G: to be able
יַם	*n. m.* sea
יסף	*vb.* C: to add; Cp: to be added
יעט	*vb.* tD: to take counsel, agree
יָעֵט	*n. m.* adviser (G ptcp.)
יצב	*vb.* D: to make certain
יַצִּיב	*adj.* certain
יקד	*vb.* G: to burn (intrans.)
יְקֵדָה	*n. f.* burning (Hebrew?)
יַקִּיר	*adj.* noble, difficult
יְקָר	*n. m.* honor, glory
יְרוּשְׁלֶם	*GN* Jerusalem
יְרַח	*n. m.* month
יַרְכָה	*n. f.* thigh
יִשְׂרָאֵל	*GN* Israel
יֵשׁוּעַ	*PN* Jeshua
יָת	*prep.* direct object marker (§359b)
יתב	*vb.* G: to sit; C: settle
יַתִּיר	*adj.* exceeding; *adv.* יַתִּירָא very, exceedingly

כ

כְּ	*prep.* as, like (§181)
כִּדְבָה	*n. f.* falsehood
כְּדִי	*conj.* when (§418)
כָּה	*adv.* here (§349)
כהל	*vb.* G: to be able (also > יכל)
כָּהֵן	*n. m.* priest
כַּוָּה	*n. f.* window (pl. כַּוִּין)
כּוֹרֶשׁ	*PN* Cyrus
כַּחֲדָה	*adv.* together
כַּכַּר	*n. m.* talent

כֹּל	*n. m.* all (cstr. כָּל) (§167)
כלל	שׁכלל <
כְּמָה	*interrog.* how much
כֵּן	*adv.* thus (§351a)
כְּנֵמָא	*adv.* thus (§351b)
כנשׁ	*vb.* G: to gather (trans.); tD: to assemble (intrans.)
כְּנָת	*n. m.* colleague (Akkadian) (pl. with suff. כְּנָוָתֵהּ)
כַּסְדָּי	כַּשְׂדָּי <
כְּסַף	*n. m.* silver, money
כְּעַן	*adv.* now
כְּעֶת, כְּעֶנֶת	*adv.* now (= כְּעַן)
כפת	*vb.* D: to bind; to be bound
כֹּר	*n. m.* kor (dry measure)
כַּרְבְּלָה	*n. f.* hat (Akkadian)
כָּרוֹז	*n. m.* herald
כרז	*vb.* C: to announce
כרי	*vb.* tG: to be troubled
כָּרְסֵא	*n. m.* throne (Akkadian)
כַּשְׂדָּי	*adj. gent.* Chaldean
כתב	*vb.* G: to write
כְּתָב	*n. m.* writing; document
כְּתַל	*n. m.* wall (pl. det. כֻּתְלַיָּא)

ל

לְ	*prep.* for, to (§177)
לָא	*neg.* not, no (§386)
לָה	*n.* naught
לֵב	*n. m.* heart, mind
לְבַב	*n. m.* heart, mind
לְבוּשׁ	*n. m.* clothing
לבשׁ	*vb.* G: to wear; C: to clothe
לָהֵן	*conj.* therefore (§433)
לָהֵן	*conj.* except; however, rather (§§398, 423, 434)
לֵוָי	*adj. gent.* Levite
לְוָת	*prep.* unto (§197)
לְחֶם	*n. m.* feast
לְחֵנָה	*n. f.* concubine (Akkadian)
לֵילֵי	*n. m.* night (§96)
לְמָה	*conj.* lest (so that not) (§406)
לָקֳבֵל	קֳבֵל <
לִשָּׁן	*n. m.* tongue, language

מ

מְאָה	*num./n. f.* hundred; *du.* מָאתַיִן, two hundred
מֹאזַנְיָא	(מוזן) *n. f. du.* scale, balance (vocalized מֹאזַנְיָא Dan 5:27)
מֵאמַר	*n. m.* word, command

G

מָאן	*n. m.* vessel
מְגִלָּה	*n. f.* scroll
מגר	*vb.* D: to overthrow
מַדְבַּח	*n. m.* altar
מִדָּה	*n. f.* kind of tax (Akkadian) (= מִנְדָּה)
מְדוֹר	> מְדָר
מָדַי	*GN* Media
מָדַי	*adj. gent.* Median, Mede
מְדִינָה	*n. f.* province, city
מְדָר	*n. m.* dwelling-place (= מְדוֹר)
מָה	*interrog. pron.* what?; *with* דִּי whatever (§§138, 151, 170, 391b)
מְהֵימַן	*adj.* trustworthy, reliable
מוֹת	*n. m.* death
מָזוֹן	*n. m.* food
מחי	*vb.* G, D: to strike; tG: be impaled
מַחְלְקָה	*n. f.* division
מטי	*vb.* G: to reach, arrive
מִישָׁאֵל	*PN* Mishael
מֵישַׁךְ	*PN* Meshach
מַלְאַךְ	*n. m.* angel
מִלָּה	*n. f.* word, thing (pl. מִלִּין)
מלח	*vb.* G: to receive salt
מְלַח	*n. m.* salt
מלי	*vb.* G: to fill; tG: be filled (§342b)
מֶלֶךְ	*n. m.* king (det. מַלְכָּא)
מְלַךְ	*n. m.* counsel (w. suff. מִלְכִּי)
מַלְכָּה	*n. f.* queen
מַלְכוּ	*n. f.* kingship, realm
מלל	*vb.* D: to speak
מֵמַר	> מֵאמַר
מַן	*interrog. pron.* who?; מַן־דִּי whoever (§§138, 151, 391a)
מִן	*prep.* from; מִן דִּי *conj.* since, because (§§182, 410, 421)
מְנֵא	*n. m.* mina (weight)
מִנְדָּה	*n. f.* kind of tax (Akkadian) (= מִדָּה)
מַנְדַּע	*n. m.* knowledge, intellect
מִנְחָה	*n. f.* grain offering
מני	*vb.* G: to count; D: appoint
מִנְיָן	*n. m.* number
מַעֲבַד	*n. m.* doing, deed
מְעִין	*n. m. pl.* belly
מֶעָל	*n. m.* sunset
מָרֵא	*n. m.* lord
מָרַד	*adj.* rebellious
מְרַד	*n. m.* rebellion
מרט	*vb.* Gp: to be plucked off
מֹשֶׁה	*PN* Moses
מְשַׁח	*n. m.* oil

מִשְׁכַּב	*n. m.* bed
מִשְׁכַּן	*n. m.* tent, dwelling
מַשְׁרוֹקִי	*n. f.* pipe (musical instrument)
מִשְׁתֵּה	*n. m.* banquet
מַתְּנָה	*n. f.* gift

נ

נְבוּאָה	*n. f.* prophecy
נְבוּכַדְנֶצַּר	*PN* Nebuchadnezzar
נְבִזְבָּה	*n. f.* gift
נבי	*vb.* tD: to prophesy
נבי(א)	*n. m.* prophet
נֶבְרַשָׁה	*n. f.* lamp (Akkadian)
נגד	*vb.* G: to flow, advance
נֶגֶד	*prep.* facing, opposite (Hebrew) (§201)
נְגַהּ	*n. m.* daylight, dawn (det. נָגְהָא)
נגו	עבד נגו >
נדב	*vb.* tD: to contribute freely; volunteer
נִדְבָּךְ	*n. m.* row, course of stones (Akkadian)
נדד	*vb.* G: to waver, be agitated
נִדְנֶה	*n. m.* sheath (Persian)
נְהוֹר	*n. m.* light (Qere)
נְהִיר	*n. m.* light (Ketiv)
נַהִירוּ	*n. f.* illumination
נְהַר	*n. m.* river
נוד	*vb.* G: to wander off
נְוָלוּ	*n. f.* latrine (= נְוָלִי)
נְוָלִי	נְוָלוּ >
נוּר	*n. f./m.* fire
נזק	*vb.* G: to suffer harm; C: cause harm
נְחָשׁ	*n. m.* bronze, copper
נחת	*vb.* G: to go down; C: bring down; Cp: be brought down
נטל	*vb.* G: to lift up, take
נטר	*vb.* G: to keep, guard
נִיחוֹחַ	*n. m. pl.* fragrant sacrifice (Hebrew)
נִכְסִין	*n. m. pl.* movable property (Akkadian)
נְמַר	*n. m.* leopard
נסח	*vb.* tG: to tear out
נסך	*vb.* D: to pour out libation
נְסַךְ	*n. m.* libation
נפל	*vb.* G: to fall
נפק	*vb.* G: to go out; C: bring out
נִפְקָה	*n. f.* expenses
נִצְבָּה	*n. f.* stock, nature
נצח	*vb.* tD: to distinguish oneself
נצל	*vb.* C: to rescue

G

נְקֵא	*adj.* clean, pure [Sokoloff 1976: lamb]
נקשׁ	*vb.* G: to knock
נשׂא	*vb.* G: to lift, carry, take; tD: elevate oneself
נְשִׁין	*pl. of n. f.* אִנְתָּה woman, wife ($94)
נִשְׁמָה	*n. f.* breath
נְשַׁר	*n. m.* eagle
נִשְׁתְּוָן	*n. m.* document (Persian)
נְתִין	*n. m.* temple servant (Hebrew)
נתן	*vb.* G: to give (PC and inf. only)
נתר	*vb.* G: to fall (of leaves); C: cause to fall

ס

סַבְכָא	> שַׂבְכָא
סבל	*vb.* L: to support ($236)
סבר	*vb.* G: to think, intend
סגד	*vb.* G: to bow down
סְגַן	*n. m.* prefect (Akkadian)
סגר	*vb.* G: to shut
סובל	> סבל
סוּמְפֹּנְיָה	*n. f.* bagpipe (?) (Greek συμφωνία)
סוף	*vb.* G: to end, be fulfilled; C: to bring to an end
סוֹף	*n. m.* end
סִיפֹנְיָה	> סוּמְפֹּנְיָה
סלק	*vb.* G: to come up; C: bring up; Cp: be brought up
סעד	*vb.* D: to support
סָפַר	*n. m.* scribe
סְפַר	*n. m.* book
סַרְבָּל	*n. m.* pants (Persian)
סָרֵךְ	*n. m.* overseer (G ptcp.)
סתר	I *vb.* D: to hide
סתר	II *vb.* G: to tear down (< שׁתר)

ע

עבד	*vb.* G: to make, do; tG: be done
עֲבֵד	*n. m.* servant
עֲבֵד נְגוֹ	*PN* Abed-nego
עֲבִידָה	*n. f.* work, service
עֲבַר	*n. m.* other side; עֲבַר־נַהֲרָה GN Across-the-River, Transeuphrates
עַד	*prep./conj.* until, up to ($$187, 420)
עדי	*vb.* G: to pass on, depart; C: make go away
עִדּוֹא	*PN* Iddo
עִדָּן	*n. m.* time, season
עוֹד	*adv.* still
עֲוָיָה	*n. f.* iniquity
עוֹף	*n. m.* birds (collective sg.)

עוּר	*n. m.* chaff
עֵז	*n. f.* goat (abs. pl. עִזִּין)
עִזְקָה	*n. f.* signet ring
עֶזְרָא	*PN* Ezra
עֲזַרְיָה	*PN* Azariah
עֵטָה	*n. f.* counsel
עַיִן	*n. f.* eye (abs. pl. עֲיְנִין)
עִיר	*n. m.* watcher, angel
עַל	*prep.* upon, over, above (§188)
עֵלָּא	*adv.* upwards; + מִן above
עִלָּה	*n. f.* fault, ground for accusation
עֲלָוָה	*n. f.* burnt offering
עִלָּי	*adj.* high; עִלָּאָה (God) Most High
עִלִּי	*n. f.* roof chamber
עֶלְיוֹן	*n. m.* Most High (Hebrew)
עלל	*vb.* G: to enter; C: bring in; Cp.: be brought in
עָלַם	*n. m.* age, long time
עֵלְמָי	*adj. gent.* Elamite
עֲלַע	*n. f.* rib (abs. pl. עִלְעִין)
עַם	*n. m.* people (det. pl. עַמְמַיָּא)
עִם	*prep.* with (§189)
עַמִּיק	*adj.* deep
עֲמַר	*n. m.* wool
ענה	*vb.* G: to answer, speak up
עֲנֵה	*adj.* poor (abs. pl. עֲנָיִן)
עֲנָן	*n. m.* cloud
עֲנַף	*n. m.* branch
עֲנָשׁ	*n. m.* fine, punishment
עֳפִי	*n. m.* foliage
עֲצִיב	*adj.* sad
עקר	*vb.* tD: to be uprooted
עִקַּר	*n. m.* core of roots
עָר	*n. m.* enemy
ערב	*vb.* D: to mix; tD: be mixed
עֲרָד	*n. m.* wild donkey
עַרְוָה	*n. f.* dishonor, nakedness
עֲשַׂב	*n. m.* grass
עֲשַׂר, עֶשְׂרָה	*num.* ten, -teen
עֶשְׂרִין	*num.* twenty
עשׁת	*vb.* Gp: to take thought, plan
עֲתִיד	*adj.* ready
עַתִּיק	*adj.* old

פ

פֶּחָה	*n. m.* governor (Akkadian) (det. pl. פַּחֲוָתָא) (§90e)
פֶּחָר	*n. m.* potter

G

פְּטִישׁ	*n. m.* item of clothing (Persian?)
פְּלַג	*vb.* G: to divide
פְּלַג	*n. m.* half
פְּלֻגָּה	*n. f.* division
פְּלַח	*vb.* G: to worship, serve
פָּלְחָן	*n. m.* service
פֻּם	*n. m.* mouth
פַּס	*n. m.* palm of the hand
פְּסַנְתֵּרִין, פְּסַנְטֵרִין	*n. m.* harp (Greek ψαλτήριον)
פַּרְזֶל	*n. m.* iron
פְּרַס	*vb.* Gp: to be divided
פְּרֵס	*n. m.* half-mina (weight)
פָּרַס	GN Persia
פָּרְסִי	*adj. gent.* Persian
פְּרַק	*vb.* G: to remove, unload
פְּרַשׁ	*vb.* Dp: to be separated, clarified
פַּרְשֶׁגֶן	*n. m.* copy (Persian)
פְּשַׁר	*vb.* G: to interpret (read מְפַשַּׁר Dan 5:12 as מִפְשַׁר)
פְּשַׁר	*n. m.* interpretation
פִּתְגָם	*n. m.* message, word (Persian)
פְּתַח	*vb.* G: to open
פְּתָי	*n. m.* width

צ

צְבוּ	*n. f.* thing, matter
צְבִי	*vb.* G: to wish, want
צְבַע	*vb.* D: to drench; tD: be drenched
צַד	*n. m.* side
צְדָא	> הַצְדָא
צִדְקָה	*n. f.* righteousness, alms
צַוַּאר	*n. m.* neck
צְלַח	*vb.* C: to succeed, prosper
צְלִי	*vb.* D: to pray
צְלֵם	*n. m.* image (cstr. sg. צֶלֶם, det. צַלְמָא)
צְפִיר	*n. m.* male goat
צִפַּר	*n. f.* bird

ק

קְבַל	*vb.* D: to receive
קֳבֵל	*n. m.* [front] *prep* לָקֳבֵל. because of, in front of, corresponding to; *conj./prep.* כָּל־קֳבֵל because of, + דִּי because (§200)
קַדִּישׁ	*adj.* holy, holy one
קֳדָם	*prep.* before (§203)
קַדְמָה	[*n. f.* forepart] > מִן־קַדְמַת דְּנָה *adv.* formerly
קַדְמָי	*adj.* first

קוּם	*vb.* G: to arise, stand, endure, C: raise, Cp: be raised, D: make permanent
קְטַל	*vb.* G: to slay; D: slay many; tG/tD: be slain
קְטַר	*n. m.* joint, knot
קַיְט	*n. m.* summer
קְיָם	*n. m.* statute, agreement
קַיָּם	*adj.* enduring
קיתרוס	Ketiv, קַתְרֹס Qere *n. m.* lyre (Greek κίθαρις)
קָל	*n. m.* sound, voice
קְנִי	*vb.* G: to acquire
קְצַף	*vb.* G: to be angry
קְצַף	*n. m.* anger
קְצַץ	*vb.* D: to cut off
קְצָת	*n. f.* end, part
קְרֵב	*vb.* G: to approach; D: offer; C: bring near, offer
קְרָב	*n. m.* war
קְרִי	*vb.* G: to call, read; tG: be called
קִרְיָה	*n. f.* city
קֶרֶן	*n. f.* horn
קְרַץ	*n. m.* piece (?), in idiom אכל קרצין to speak calumny, accuse (< Akkadian *karṣi akālu*)
קְשֹׁט	*n. m.* truth, righteousness
קַתְרֹס	קיתרוס <

ר

רֵאשׁ	*n. m.* head
רַב	*adj.* great (pl. רַבְרְבִין); *n. m.* noble, ruler (pl. רַבְרְבָנִין)
רְבוּ	*n. f.* greatness
רִבּוֹ	*num./n. f.* ten thousand (pl. רִבְבָן Qere)
רְבִי	*vb.* G: to grow, D: make great
רְבִיעָי	*adj.* fourth
רַבְרְבָן	רַב <
רגז	*vb.* C: to make angry
רְגַז	*n. m.* anger
רְגַל	*n. f.* foot, leg
רגשׁ	*vb.* C: to go as a crowd (?)
רֵו	*n. m.* appearance
רוּחַ	*n. f.* spirit, wind
רוּם	*vb.* G: to be high, exalted; C: to make high, raise; R: exalt; tR: exalt oneself
רוּם	*n. m.* height
רָז	*n. m.* mystery (Persian)
רְחוּם	*PN* Rehum
רַחִיק	*adj.* far
רַחֲמִין	*n. m. pl.* compassion
רחץ	*vb.* tG: to trust
רֵיחַ	*n. m.* smell
רמי	*vb.* G: to throw, put; tG: be thrown, put

רְעוּ	*n. f.* will (cstr. רְעוּת)
רַעְיוֹן	*n. m.* thought
רַעֲנַן	*adj.* flourishing
רעע	*vb.* G: to break; D: smash
רפס	*vb.* G: to step on
רשם	*vb.* G: to sign, inscribe

שׂ

שָׂב	*n. m.* elder
סַבְּכָא, שַׂבְּכָא	*n. m.* kind of harp (Greek σαμβύκη?)
שׂגי	*vb.* G: to be much, many
שַׂגִּיא	*adj.* great, much; *adv.* very (§347a)
שָׂהֲדוּ	*n. f.* testimony
שְׂטַר	*n. m.* side
שׂים	*vb.* G: to set, make, place, Gp: be placed, issued (of decree); tG: be set, placed
שׂכל	*vb.* tD: to observe, watch
שָׂכְלְתָנוּ	*n. f.* insight
שָׂנֵא	*n. m.* enemy (G ptcp.)
שְׂעַר	*n. m.* hair (collective sg.)

שׁ

שׁאל	*vb.* G: to ask for something
שְׁאֵלָה	*n. f.* matter, question
שְׁאַלְתִּיאֵל	*PN* Shealtiel
שְׁאָר	*n. m.* remainder
שׁבח	*vb.* D: to praise
שְׁבַט	*n. m.* tribe
שְׁבִיב	*n. m.* flame
שִׁבְעָה	*num.* seven
שׁבק	*vb.* G: to leave; tG: be left
שׁבשׁ	*vb.* tD: to be perplexed
שֵׁגַל	*n. m.* royal consort (Akkadian)
שׁדר	*vb.* tD: to exert oneself
שַׁדְרַךְ	*PN* Shadrach
שׁוי	*vb.* G: to be equal, on same level; D: make equal; tD: be made like, equal
שׁוּר	*n. m.* wall
שׁוּשַׁנְכִי	*adj. gent.* Susian, of Susa
שְׁחִיתָה	*n. f.* fault, corruption
שׁיזב	*vb.* Quad: to deliver, save (Akkadian) (§288)
שׁיציא	*vb.* Quad.: to finish (Akkadian) (§288)
שׁכח	*vb.* C: to find; tG: be found, be present (§381)
שׁכלל	*vb.* Quad: to finish building; tQuad: be finished (Akkadian) (§288)
שׁכן	*vb.* G: to dwell; D: make dwell
שְׁלֵה	*adj.* tranquil

שְׁלָה	*n. f.* slander, blasphemy (Akkadian) [hypothetical original in Dan 3:29]
שָׁלוּ	*n. f.* error due to negligence
שַׁלְוָה	*n. f.* tranquillity (Hebrew)
שׁלח	*vb.* G: to send (esp. message)
שׁלט	*vb.* G: to rule; C: cause to rule, let rule
שָׁלְטָן	*n. m.* dominion
שִׁלְטוֹן	*n. m.* ruler
שַׁלִּיט	*adj.* having authority; *n. m.* ruler
שׁלם	*vb.* G: to be complete; C: make complete, hand over
שְׁלָם	*n. m.* peace
שֻׁם	*n. m.* name (pl. cstr. שְׁמָהָת)
שׁמד	*vb.* C: to destroy
שְׁמַיִן	*n. m.* sky, heavens, Heaven (= God) (det. שְׁמַיָּא)
שׁמם	*vb.* tL: to be appalled (§236)
שׁמע	*vb.* G: to hear; tD: submit oneself, obey
שָׁמְרָיִן	*GN* Samaria
שׁמשׁ	*vb.* D: to minister, serve
שְׁמַשׁ	*n. m.* sun
שִׁמְשַׁי	*PN* Shimshai
שֵׁן	*n. f.* tooth (du. שִׁנַּיִן)
שְׁנָה	*n. f.* year (pl. שְׁנִין)
שְׁנָה	*n. f.* sleep (w. suffix שִׁנְתֵּהּ)
שׁני	*vb.* G: to change (intr.); D, C: change, distort (trans.); tD: be changed
שָׁעָה	*n. f.* hour, moment
שָׁפֵט	*n. m.* judge (Hebrew) (G ptcp.)
שַׁפִּיר	*adj.* beautiful
שׁפל	*vb.* C: to make low, humble
שְׁפַל	*adj.* lowly
שׁפר	*vb.* G: to be pleasing
שְׁפַרְפָּר	*n. m.* dawn
שָׁק	*n. f.* leg, thigh
שׁרי	*vb.* G: to loosen (for מְשָׁרֵא in Dan 5:12 read מִשְׁרֵא); encamp, dwell; D: begin; tD: be loosened
שֹׁרֶשׁ	*n. m.* root
שְׁרֹשִׁי	*n. f.* corporal punishment (Persian) (שְׁרֹשׁוּ Ketiv)
שֵׁשְׁבַּצַּר	*PN* Sheshbazzar
שֵׁת	*num. f.* six
שׁתי	*vb.* G: to drink (SC 3mp אִשְׁתִּיו)
שִׁתִּין	*num.* sixty
שְׁתַר בּוֹזְנַי	*PN* Shethar-bozenai

ת

תְּבִיר	*adj.* fragile
תְּדִיר	[*n.* constancy] > *adv.* בִּתְדִירָא constantly
תוב	*vb.* G: to return (intrans.); C: to cause to return, answer
תוה	*vb.* G: to be astonished
תּוֹר	*n. m.* ox, bull

תְּחוֹת	*prep.* under (§205)
תְּלַג	*n. m.* snow
תְּלִיתָי	*adj.* third
תְּלָת	*num. f.*, תְּלָתָה *m.* three
תַּלְתָּא	*n. m.* triumvir, official of third rank
תְּלָתִין	*num.* thirty
תַּמָּה	*adv.* there
תְּמַה	*n. m.* wonder, miracle
תִּנְיָן	*adj.* second
תִּנְיָנוּת	*adv.* a second time
תִּפְתָּי	*n. m.* magistrate (Persian)
תַּקִּיף	*adj.* strong
תקל	*vb.* Gp: to be weighed
תְּקֵל	*n. m.* shekel (weight)
תקן	*vb.* Cp: to be established, made firm
תקף	*vb.* G: to become strong; D: make strong, valid
תְּקֹף	*n. m.* strength (det. תָּקְפָּא)
תְּרֵין	*num. m.*, תַּרְתֵּין *f.* two
תְּרֵי־עֲשַׂר	*num.* twelve (masc.)
תְּרַע	*n. m.* gate
תָּרָע	*n. m.* gatekeeper
תַּרְתֵּין	תְּרֵין >
תַּתְּנַי	*PN* Tattenai

Vocabulary for the Elephantine Petition and Ahiqar Proverbs (includes only vocabulary not already listed in the Biblical Aramaic glossary)

אגור	*n. m.* temple
אוסתן	*PN* Avastana
אחר	*part.* then, thereupon
איש	*n. m.* man, person
אל	*prep.* to
אל	*DN* El, God
אם	*n. f.* mother
אנזעררה	*n. f.* bitter apple (?)
אפו	*part.* then
ארז	*n. m.* cedar
אריך	*adj.* long
ארמלה	*n. f.* widow
ארשם	*PN* Arshama
בגוהי	*PN* Bagavahya
בזי	*conj.* because
בעל טבה	*n. m.* ally
גבה	*adj.* high
דבר	*vb.* G: to lead, take
דלח	*vb.* to trouble, stir up
דליה	*PN* Delaiah

דמין	*n. m. pl.* price, value
דנח	*vb.* G: to shine
דרג	*vb.* G: to bend
דריוהוש	*PN* Darius
דש	*n. m.* doorleaf
המונית	*adj.* in agreement (Persian)
וידרנג	*PN* Waidranga
זכי	*demonstrative pron.* this
חדה	*adj.* joyful
חט	*n. m.* arrow
חל	*n. m.* sand
חמס	*n. m.* malice, violence
חנוב	*DN* Khnum, Khnub
חר	*n. m.* noble, free person
חרב	*n. f.* sword
טען	*vb.* G: to load
יב	*GN* Yeb (Elephantine)
ידניה	*PN* Yedunya, Jedoniah
יה	*part.* O! (vocative particle)
יהו	*DN* Yahu/Yaho, god of the Judeans
יהוחנן	*PN* Jehohanan
יקר	*vb.* C: to make heavy, deaf
כבל	*n. m.* chain, fetter
כוכב	*n. m.* star
כי	*conj.* because, for
כלב	*n. m.* dog
כמר	*n. m.* priest
כנבוזי	*PN* Cambyses
כסי	*vb.* D: to cover
כציר	*n. m.* harvest (< קציר)
כצר	*vb.* C: to reap, harvest
לבונה	*n. f.* incense
לחי	*adj.* bad, wicked
לוט	*vb.* G: to curse
לם	*part.* direct speech marker
לקח	*vb.* G: to take
מדד	*n. m.* stature, physical frame
מזרק	*n. m.* bowl
מטלל	*n. m.* ceiling
ממלל	*n. m.* speech
מנדעם	*n. m.* thing
מנטרה	*n. f.* watching, guarding
מצרי	*adj. gent.* Egyptian
מצרין	*GN* Egypt
מרחשון	*n. m.* month name (Marheshwan)
מריר	*adj.* bitter
משח	*vb.* G: to anoint

G	נדש	*vb.* G: to demolish
	נכרי	*adj.* alien, foreigner
	נפין	*PN* Nafaina
	נפש	*n. f.* soul, self
	סגי	*vb.* G: to go
	סון	*GN* Syene
	סכין	*n. m.* knife
	סנאבלט	*PN* Sin-uballit, Sanballat
	עדר	*n. m.* help
	עזיז	*adj.* mighty, strong
	עמוד	*n. m.* column, pillar
	ענוה	*n. f.* poverty
	עננוי	*PN* Anani
	עק	*n. m.* wood (= אֵע)
	עשת	*vb.* tG: to contemplate a plan
	פסילה	*n. f.* cut stone (G passive ptcp.)
	פרה	*n. f.* bran, straw
	פרתרך	*n. m.* governor (Persian)
	צדיק	*adj.* righteous
	צדק	*vb.* D: to acquit, find innocent
	צום	*vb.* G: to fast
	ציר	*n. m.* pivot
	קדמן	*adv.* formerly
	קליל	*adj.* light, worthless
	קשת	*n. f.* bow
	רב חיל	*n. m.* general, troop commander
	רחם	*n. m.* friend (G ptcp.)
	רחמן	*adj.* merciful
	רכב	*vb.* C: to mount (trans.)
	רכיך	*adj.* soft
	רעי	*n. m.* companion
	שבע	*vb.* G: to be sated
	שדק	*adj.* sharp
	שהד	*n. m.* witness (G ptcp.)
	שק	*n. m.* sackcloth
	שרף	*vb.* G: to burn
	שירי	*n. f.* rest, remainder
	שלמיה	*PN* Shelemiah
	שפט	*vb.* G: to dispute
	שפי	*adj.* calm
	שריר	*adj.* firm, strong
	תבן	*n. m.* straw
	תבר	*vb.* G/D: to break
	תותב	*n. m.* resident alien
	תל	*n. m.* implement, weapon (?)
	תמוז	*n. m.* month name (Tammuz)
	תנה	*adv.* here

Additional Vocabulary for the Readings from the Genesis Apocryphon and Targum Job

G

אברם	*PN* Abram
אדמא	*GN* Admah
אדן	*n. f.* ear
איוב	*PN* Job
איל פרן	*GN* El-Paran
אימי	*adj. gent.* Emite
אל	*DN* El, God
אמרה	*n. f.* ewe lamb
אמרפל	*PN* Amraphel
אן	*conj.* if
אשכול	*PN* Eshkol
בדיל	*prep.* because of
בזה	*n. f.* plunder
בזז	*vb.* G: to plunder
בחר	*vb.* G: to choose
בכי	*vb.* G: to weep
בלע	*PN* Bela
בצר	*vb.* tG: to diminish, subtract
ברא מן	*prep.* except for, besides
ברע	*PN* Bera
ברשע	*PN* Birsha
גבל	*GN* Gebal
גוים	*GN* Goiim
דן	*demonstrative pron. masc.* this
דן	*GN* Dan
דרמשק	*GN* Damascus
הקריות	*GN* Hakerioth
זומזמי	*adj. gent.* Zamzummite
חברון	*GN* Hebron
חוט	*n. m.* thread
חולק	*n. m.* portion, share
חורי	*adj. gent.* Horite
חלבון	*GN* Helbon
חלה	*n. f.* valley
חלם	*vb.* tG: to recover
חצצן תמר	*GN* Hazazon-tamar
טבה	*n. f.* goodness, pl. goods
כבר	*adv.* already
כדרלעומר	*PN* Chedorlaomer
כפתוך	*GN* Cappadocia
כרמא	*GN* Karma
לוט	*PN* Lot
לעורע	*prep.* toward
מאכל	*n. m.* food
מדבר	*n. m.* wilderness

מהי	*vb.* tG: to become like water
מלכיצדק	*PN* Melchizedek
ממרה	*PN* Mamre
מסאן	*n. m.* shoe
מעשר	*n. m.* tithe
מרד	*vb.* G: to rebel
נא	*part.* expressive particle with imperative
נחם	*vb.* D: to comfort
נסך	*vb.* tD: to melt
סדיא	*GN* Siddim, Siddayya
סודם	*GN* Sodom
עולים	*n. m.* boy, servant
עומרם	*GN* Gomorrah
עתר	*n. m.* wealth
עילם	*GN* Elam
עמן	*GN* Amman
עמק	*n. m.* valley
ען	*n. f.* flock of sheep
עפר	*n. m.* dust
ערנם	*PN* Arnem
ערק	*vb.* G: to flee
ערקה	*n. f.* strap
עשׁתרא	*GN* Ashtera
פורת	*GN* Euphrates
פלט	*vb.* G: to escape
פצי	*vb.* G: to save, deliver
צבוין	*GN* Zeboiim
קדש	*n. m.* ring for nose or ear
קטם	*n. m.* ash
קרנין	*GN* Karnain
רדף	*vb.* G: to pursue
רחשׁ	*n. m.* creeping thing
רעה	*n. m.* shepherd (G ptcp.)
רפאי	*adj. gent.* Rephaite
שׂמאל	*n. m.* left, north
שׁבי	*vb.* G: to take captive
שׁבי	*n. m.* state of captivity
שׁביה	*n. f.* group of captives
שׁוא	*GN* Shaveh
שׁלם	*GN* Shalem, Salem
שׁמיאבד	*PN* Shumyebad
שׁנאב	*PN* Shinab
תדעל	*PN* Tid'al
תמניאת עשר	*num. m.* eighteen

BIBLIOGRAPHY

Abegg, M. G., Bowley, J. E., & Cook, E. M. (2003). *The Dead Sea Scrolls concordance, I: The non-biblical texts from Qumran.* Leiden: Brill.

Abraham, K., & Sokoloff, M. (2011). Aramaic loanwords in Akkadian – a reassessment of the proposals. *Archiv für Orientforschung, 52,* 22–76.

Albright, W. (1931). The discovery of an Aramaic inscription relating to King Uzziah. *Bulletin of the American Schools of Oriental Research, 44*(1), 8–10.

Baker, D. W. (1980). Further examples of the *waw-explicativum. Vetus Testamentum, 30*(2), 129–136.

Barr, J. (1989). Hebrew, Aramaic and Greek in the Hellenistic age. In *The Cambridge history of Judaism. Vol. 1: The Hellenistic Age* (ed. W. D. Davies and L. Finkelstein; Cambridge: Cambridge University Press), 79–114.

Bauer, H., & Leander, P. (1981 [1927]). *Grammatik des Biblisch-Aramäischen.* Hildesheim: Olms.

Beaulieu, P.-A. (2013). Aspects of Aramaic and Babylonian linguistic interaction in first millennium BC Iraq. *Journal of Language Contact, 6*(2), 358–378.

Bekins, P. (2020). *Inscriptions from the World of the Bible.* Peabody, MA: Hendrickson Academic.

Bentein, K. (2013). The syntax of the periphrastic progressive in the Septuagint and the New Testament. *Novum Testamentum, 55*(2), 168–192.

Beyer, K. (1984). *Die aramäischen Texte vom Toten Meer.* Göttingen: Vandenhoeck & Ruprecht.

Beyer, K. (1986). *The Aramaic language: Its distribution and subdivisions.* Tr. J. Healey. Göttingen: Vandenhoeck & Ruprecht.

Beyer, K. (1994). *Die aramäischen Texte vom Toten Meer. Ergänzungsband.* Göttingen: Vandenhoeck & Ruprecht.

Beyer, K. (2004). *Die aramäischen Texte vom Toten Meer. Band 2.* Vandenhoeck & Ruprecht.

Blake, F. R. (1950). The apparent interchange between *a* and *i* in Hebrew. *Journal of Near Eastern Studies, 9*(2), 76–83.

Blake, F. R. (1951). *A resurvey of Hebrew tenses, with an appendix: Hebrew influence on Biblical Aramaic.* Rome: Pontificium Institutum Biblicum.

Bresciani, E., & Kamil, M. (1966). *Le lettere aramaiche di Hermopoli.* Rome: Atti della Accademia Nazionale dei Lincei.

Brown, F., Driver, S. R., & Briggs, C. A. (1906). *A Hebrew and English lexicon of the Old Testament, with an appendix containing the Biblical Aramaic.* Oxford: Clarendon.

Contini, R. (1998). Considerazioni sul presunto "dativo etico" in aramaico pre-cristiano. In *Études sémitiques et samaritaines offertes à Jean Margain* (ed. C.-B. Amphoux; Lausanne: Ed. du Zèbre), 83–94.

Cook, E. M. (1986). Word order in the Aramaic of Daniel. *Afroasiatic Linguistics*, 9(3), 1–16.

Cook, E. M. (1989). "In the plain of the wall" (Dan. 3:1). *Journal of Biblical Literature*, 108(1), 115–116.

Cook, E. M. (1990). The orthography of final unstressed long vowels in Old and Imperial Aramaic. *Maarav*, 5, 53–67.

Cook, E. M. (1998). The Aramaic of the Dead Sea Scrolls. In *The Dead Sea Scrolls after fifty years: A comprehensive assessment* (ed. P. W. Flint and J. C. VanderKam; Leiden: Brill), 1: 359–378.

Cook, E. M. (2010). The causative internal passive in Qumran Aramaic. *Aramaic Studies*, 8(1–2), 5–12.

Cook, E. M. (2015). *Dictionary of Qumran Aramaic*. Winona Lake, IN: Eisenbrauns.

Cook, E. M. (2017). *Language contact and the genesis of Mishnaic Hebrew*. The Edward Ullendorff lectures in Semitic philology, fourth lecture. Cambridge: Faculty of Asian and Middle Eastern Studies, University of Cambridge.

Cowley, A. E. (1923). *Aramaic papyri of the fifth century B. C.* Oxford: Clarendon

Dalman, G. H. (1960 [1905]). *Grammatik des jüdisch-palästinischen Aramäisch.* Leipzig: Hinrichs.

Degen, R. (1969). *Altaramäische Grammatik der Inschriften des 10.-18. Jh.v. Chr.* Wiesbaden: Harrassowitz.

Dietrich, W., & Arnet, S. (2013). *Konzise und aktualisierte Ausgabe des Hebräischen und Aramäischen Lexikons zum Alten Testament.* Leiden: Brill.

Donner, H., & Röllig, W. (2002). *Kanaanäische und aramäische Inschriften I* (5th ed.). Wiesbaden: Harrassowitz.

Driver, G. R. (1954). *Aramaic documents of the fifth century B.C.* Oxford: Clarendon.

Driver, G. R. (1957). *Aramaic documents of the fifth century B.C.* (abridged and rev. ed.). Oxford: Clarendon.

Durkin, P. (2009). *The Oxford guide to etymology.* Oxford: Oxford University Press.

Dušek, J. (2013). Aramaic in the Persian period. *Hebrew Bible and Ancient Israel*, 2(2), 243–264.

Even-Shoshan, A. (1990). *Ḳonḳordantsyah ḥadashah le-Torah, Nevi'im u-Khetuvim: otsar leshon ha-Miḳra – 'Ivrit va-Aramit.* (rev. ed.). Jerusalem: Ḳiryat-sefer.

Fales, F. M. (1986). *Aramaic epigraphs on clay tablets of the Neo-Assyrian period.* Rome: Universita degli studi "La sapienza."

Fales, F. M., & Grassi, G. (2016). *L'aramaico antico.* Rome: Forum.

Fassberg, S. E. (2009). Vowel dissimilation in plural pronouns in Biblical Hebrew. *Orientalia*, 78 (3), 326–335.

Fassberg, S. E. (2018). The ethical dative in Aramaic. *Aramaic Studies*, 16(2), 101–116.

Fitzmyer, J. A. (1957). The syntax of כלא, כל in the Aramaic texts from Egypt and in Biblical Aramaic. *Biblica*, 38, 170–194.

Fitzmyer, J. A. (1974). Some notes on Aramaic epistolography. *Journal of Biblical Literature*, 93(2), 201–225.

Fitzmyer, J. A. (1979). The phases of the Aramaic language. In *A wandering Aramean: Collected Aramaic essays* (Chico, CA: Scholars Press), 57–84.

Fitzmyer, J. A. (2004). *The Genesis Apocryphon of Qumran Cave I* (3rd ed.). Biblia et orientalia 18/B. Rome: Pontifical Biblical Institute.

Fitzmyer, J. A. (2008). *A guide to the Dead Sea Scrolls and related literature* (rev. ed.). Grand Rapids: Eerdmans.

Fitzmyer, J. A., & Harrington, D. J. (1978). *A manual of Palestinian Aramaic texts*. Rome: Pontifical Biblical Institute.

Fitzmyer, J. A., & Kaufman, S. A. (1992). *An Aramaic bibliography*. Baltimore: Johns Hopkins University Press.

Folmer, M. L. (1995). *The Aramaic language in the Achaemenid period: A study in linguistic variation*. Leuven: Uitgeverij Peeters en Dép. Oosterse Studies.

García-Martínez, F., & Tigchelaar, E. J. C. (2000). *The Dead Sea Scrolls study edition*. Leiden: Brill.

Garr, W. R. (1990). On the alternation between construct and *dī* phrases in Biblical Aramaic. *Journal of Semitic Studies, 35*(2), 213–231.

Geller, M. (2006). Philology versus linguistics and Aramaic phonology. *Bulletin of the School of Oriental and African Studies, University of London, 69*(1), 79–89.

Gesenius, W., Kautzsch, E., & Cowley, A. E. (1910). *Gesenius' Hebrew Grammar* (ed. E. Kautzsch; tr. A. E. Cowley). Oxford: Clarendon.

Gibson, J. C. L. (1975). *Textbook of Syrian Semitic inscriptions. II. Aramaic Inscriptions*. Oxford: Clarendon.

Ginsberg, H. L. (1967). Biblical Aramaic. In *An Aramaic handbook*. Porta linguarum orientalium (ed. F. Rosenthal; Wiesbaden: Harrassowitz), I/1, 17–39 (text), I/2, 16–41 (glossary).

Greenfield, J. C. (1969). The "periphrastic imperative" in Aramaic and Hebrew. *Israel Exploration Journal, 19*(4), 199–210.

Greenfield, J. C. (1970). HAMARAKARA > ʾAMARKAL. In *W. B. Henning memorial volume* (ed. M. Boyce & I. Gershevitch. London: Lund Humphries), 180–186; reprinted in ʿAl Kanfei Yonah: Collected studies of Jonas C. Greenfield on Semitic philology (ed. S. Paul, M. Stone, & A. Pinnick; Leiden: Brill, 2001), 1: 68–74.

Greenfield, J. C. (1978). The dialects of early Aramaic. *Journal of Near Eastern Studies, 37*(2), 93–99.

Greenfield, J. C., & Naveh, J. (1984). Hebrew and Aramaic in the Persian period. In *The Cambridge history of Judaism I: The Persian period* (ed. W. D. Davies & L. Finkelstein; Cambridge: Cambridge University Press), 115–129.

Gzella, H., ed. (2018). *Theological dictionary of the Old Testament. Vol. 16: Aramaic dictionary*. Tr. M. Biddle. Grand Rapids: Eerdmans.

Hinz, W. (1975). *Altiranisches Sprachgut der Nebenüberlieferungen*. Wiesbaden: Harrassowitz.

Holm, T. (forthcoming). Papyrus Amherst 63. In *Aramaic literary texts: Writings from the ancient world*. Atlanta: SBL Press.

Hug, V. (1993). *Altaramäische Grammatik der Texte des 7. und 6. Jh.s v. Chr.* Heidelberg: Heidelberger Orientverlag.

Hoftijzer, J., & Jongeling, K. (1995). *Dictionary of the North-West Semitic inscriptions.* Leiden: Brill.

Huehnergard, J. (1987). The feminine plural jussive in Old Aramaic. *Zeitschrift der Deutschen Morgenländischen Gesellschaft, 137*(2), 266–277.

Huehnergard, J. (2005). Features of central Semitic. In *Biblical and Oriental essays in memory of William L. Moran* (ed. A. Gianto; Rome: Pontifical Biblical Institute), 155–203.

Hurvitz, A. (1968). The chronological significance of "Aramaisms" in Biblical Hebrew. *Israel Exploration Journal, 18,* 234–240.

Hurvitz, A. (2014). *A concise lexicon of late Biblical Hebrew: Linguistic innovations in the writings of the Second Temple period.* Leiden: Brill.

Johns, A. F. (1972). *A short grammar of Biblical Aramaic* (rev. ed.). Berrien Springs, MI: Andrews University Press.

Kaufman, S. A. (1974). *The Akkadian influences on Aramaic.* Assyriological Studies 19. Chicago: University of Chicago Press.

Kaufman, S. A. (1984). On vowel reduction in Aramaic. *Journal of the American Oriental Society, 104*(1), 87–95.

Kautzsch, E. (1884). *Grammatik des Biblisch-Aramäischen. Mit einer kritischen Erörterung der aramäischen Wörter im Neuen Testament.* Leipzig: F. C. W. Vogel.

Kautzsch, E. (1902). *Die Aramaismen im Alten Testament.* Halle: Max Niemeyer.

Kelley, P. H., Mynatt, D. S., & Crawford, T. G. (1998). *The masorah of Biblia Hebraica Stuttgartensia: Introduction and annotated glossary.* Grand Rapids: Eerdmans.

Khan, G. (2020). *The Tiberian pronunciation tradition of Biblical Hebrew. Vol. 1.* Cambridge: Open Book Publishers.

Klein, M. L. (1979). The preposition קְדָם ("before"): A pseudo-anti-anthropomorphism in the targums. *Journal of Theological Studies, 30*(2), 502–507.

Köhler, L., Baumgartner, W., Richardson, M. E. J., & Stamm, J. J. (2000). *The Hebrew and Aramaic lexicon of the Old Testament.* Leiden: Brill.

Koller, A. (2017). Aramaic. *Oxford Bibliographies Online.* www.oxfordbibliographies.com/view/document/obo-9780199840731/obo-9780199840731-0149.xml

Kottsieper, I. (1990). *Die Sprache der Ahiqarsprüche.* Beihefte zur Zeitschrift für die alttestamentliche Wissenschaft 194. Berlin: de Gruyter.

Kottsieper, I. (2007). "And they did not care to speak Yehudit": On linguistic change in Judah during the late Persian era. In *Judah and the Judaeans in the fourth century BCE* (ed. O. Lipschitz, G. Knoppers, R. Albertz; Winona Lake: Eisenbrauns), 95–124.

Kraeling, E. (1953). *The Brooklyn Museum Aramaic papyri.* New Haven: Yale University Press.

Li, T. (2009). *The verbal system of the Aramaic of Daniel: An explanation in the context of grammaticalization.* Studies in the Aramaic Interpretation of Scripture 8. Leiden: Brill.

Lindenberger, J. M. (1983). *The Aramaic proverbs of Ahiqar.* Baltimore: Johns Hopkins University Press.

Lindenberger, J. M. (2003). *Ancient Aramaic and Hebrew letters* (2nd ed.). Atlanta: Writings from the Ancient World 14. Atlanta: Society of Biblical Literature.

Machiela, D. A. (2009). *The Dead Sea Genesis Apocryphon: A new text and translation with introduction and special treatment of columns 13–17.* Studies on the Texts of the Desert of Judah 70. Leiden: Brill.

Machiela, D. A. (2018). *The Dead Sea Scrolls: Hebrew, Aramaic, and Greek texts with English translations. Vol. 8A: Genesis Apocryphon and related documents* (ed. J. Charlesworth). Tübingen: Mohr Siebeck.

Mandelkern, S. (1896). *Veteris testamenti concordantiae hebraicae atque chaldaicae.* Leipzig: Veit.

Marti, K. (1896). *Kurzgefasste grammatik der Biblisch-aramäischen sprache.* Porta linguarum orientalium. Berlin: Reuther u. Reichard.

Milroy, J. (2007). The ideology of the standard language. In *The Routledge companion to sociolinguistics* (ed. C. Llamas, L. Mullany, & P. Stockwell; London: Routledge), 133–139.

Moscati, S. (1980). *An introduction to comparative grammar of the Semitic languages: Phonology and morphology.* Wiesbaden: Harrassowitz.

Muchiki, Y. (1994). Spirantization in fifth-century BC North-West Semitic. *Journal of Near Eastern Studies,* 53(2), 125–130.

Muraoka, T. (1976). Segolate nouns in Biblical and other Aramaic dialects. *Journal of the American Oriental Society,* 96(2), 226–235.

Muraoka, T. (2011). *A grammar of Qumran Aramaic.* Leuven: Peeters.

Muraoka, T. (2012). *An introduction to Egyptian Aramaic.* Lehrbücher orientalischer Sprachen 3 (1). Münster: Ugarit Verlag.

Muraoka, T. (2015). *A Biblical Aramaic reader: With an outline grammar.* Leuven: Peeters.

Muraoka, T., & Porten, B. (2003). *A grammar of Egyptian Aramaic* (2nd rev. ed.). Atlanta: SBL Press.

Naveh, J., & Shaked, S. (2012). *Aramaic documents from ancient Bactria (fourth century BCE.) from the Khalili collections.* London: The Khalili Family Trust.

Noonan, B. (2020). *Advances in the study of Biblical Hebrew and Aramaic: New insights for reading the Old Testament.* Grand Rapids: Zondervan.

Parry, D. & E. Tov. (2004). *The Dead Sea Scrolls reader.* 6 vols. Leiden: Brill.

Porten, B. (1996). *The Elephantine Papyri in English: Three millennia of cross-cultural continuity and change.* Leiden: Brill.

Porten, B. (2003). Request for letter of recommendation (first draft) (3.51). In *The context of scripture. Vol. 3: Archival documents from the Biblical world* (ed. W. Hallo; Leiden: Brill), 125–130.

Porten, B., & Lund, J. A. (2002). *Aramaic documents from Egypt: A key-word-in-context concordance.* Winona Lake: Eisenbrauns.

Porten, B., & Yardeni, A. (1986). *Textbook of Aramaic documents from ancient Egypt. Vol. 1: Letters.* Jerusalem: Hebrew University.

Porten, B., & Yardeni, A. (1989). *Textbook of Aramaic documents from ancient Egypt. Vol. 2: Contracts.* Jerusalem: Hebrew University.

Porten, B., & Yardeni, A. (1993). *Textbook of Aramaic documents from ancient Egypt. Vol. 3: Literature, Accounts, Lists.* Jerusalem: Hebrew University.

Porten, B., & Yardeni, A. (1999). *Textbook of Aramaic documents from ancient Egypt. Vol. 4: Ostraca and assorted inscriptions.* Jerusalem: Hebrew University.

Qimron, E. (1986). *The Hebrew of the Dead Sea Scrolls.* Harvard Semitic Studies 29. Atlanta: Scholars Press.

Qimron, E. (1993). ארמית מקראית [Biblical Aramaic]. Biblical Encyclopedia Library. Jerusalem: Bialik.

Rosenthal, F., ed. (1967). *An Aramaic handbook.* Porta linguarum orientalium. Wiesbaden: Harrassowitz.

Rosenthal, F. (2006). *A grammar of Biblical Aramaic* (7th rev. ed.). Porta linguarum orientalium. Wiesbaden: Harrassowitz.

Sachau, E. (1911). *Aramäische papyrus und ostraka aus einer jüdischen militär-kolonie zu Elephantine.* Leipzig: J.C. Hinrichs.

Saeed, J. I. (2003). *Semantics* (2nd ed.). Oxford: Blackwell.

Sayce, A. H., & Cowley, A. E. (1906). *Aramaic papyri discovered at Assuan.* London: Moring.

Schattner-Rieser, U. (2004). *L'araméen des manuscrits de la mer Morte I: Grammaire.* Éditions du Zèbre.

Schwiderski, D. (2008). *Die alt- und reichsaramäischen Inschriften / The Old and Imperial Aramaic inscriptions. Vol. 1: Konkordanz.* Berlin: de Gruyter.

Schwiderski, D. (2004). *Die alt- und reichsaramäischen Inschriften / The Old and Imperial Aramaic Inscriptions. Vol. 2: Texte und Bibliographie.* Berlin: de Gruyter.

Schuele, A. (2012). *An introduction to Biblical Aramaic.* Westminster John Knox.

Segert, S. (1975). *Altaramäische Grammatik: mit Bibliographie, Chrestomathie u. Glossar.* Leipzig: Verlag Enzyklopädie, VEB.

Sokoloff, M. (1976). *ʿămar nĕqēʾ,* "Lambs Wool" (Dan 7:9). *Journal of Biblical Literature, 95*(2), 277–279.

Stadel, C. (2008). *Hebraismen in den aramäischen Texten vom Toten Meer.* Heidelberg: Universitätsverlag Winter.

Steiner, R. C. (1997). The Aramaic text in Demotic script. In *The context of scripture. Vol. 1: Canonical compositions from the Biblical world* (ed. W. Hallo; Leiden: Brill), 309–327.

Steiner, R. C. (2005). On the dating of Hebrew sound changes (*$ḥ > ḥ$ and $ġ > ʕ$) and Greek translations (2 Esdras and Judith). *Journal of Biblical Literature, 124*(2), 229–267.

Steiner, R. C. (2007). Variation, simplifying assumptions and the history of spirantization in Aramaic and Hebrew. In *Shaʿarei Lashon: Studies in Hebrew, Aramaic and Jewish languages presented to Moshe Bar-Asher* (ed. A. Maman, S. Fassberg, & Y. Breuer; Jerusalem: Bialik), 52–65.

Strack, H. L. (1901). *Grammatik des biblisch-aramäischen, mit den nach handschriften berichtigten texten und einem Wörterbuch* (3rd ed.). Leipzig: J. C. Hinrichs.

Sukenik, E. L. (1931). Funerary tablet of Uzziah, King of Judah. *Palestine Exploration Quarterly*, *63*(4), 217–221.

Testen, D. (1985). The significance of Aramaic *r* < **n*. *Journal of Near Eastern Studies*, *44*(2), 143–146.

Tropper, J. (1997). Lexikographische Untersuchungen zum Biblisch-Aramäischen. *Journal of Northwest Semitic Languages*, *23*(2), 105–128.

Tuten, D. N. (2007). Koineization. In *The Routledge companion to sociolinguistics* (ed. C. Llamas, L. Mullany, & P. Stockwell; Oxford: Routledge), 185–191.

Van Pelt, M. (2011). *Basics of Biblical Aramaic: Complete grammar, lexicon, and annotated text.* Grand Rapids: Zondervan.

Van der Toorn, K. (2018). *Papyrus Amherst 63.* Alter Orient und Altes Testament 448. Münster: Ugarit-Verlag.

VanderKam, J. C. (2010). *The Dead Sea scrolls today* (2nd ed.). Grand Rapids: Eerdmans.

Vogt, E. (1971). *Lexicon linguae Aramaicae Veteris Testamenti documentis antiquis illustratum.* Rome: Pontificium Institutum Biblicum.

Vogt, E., & Fitzmyer, J. A. (2011). *A lexicon of Biblical Aramaic: Clarified by ancient documents.* Rome: Gregorian and Biblical Press.

von Soden, W. (1966). Aramäische Wörter in neuassyrischen und neu-und spätbabylonischen Texten. Ein Vorbericht. I (agâ-* mūš). *Orientalia*, *35*(1), 1–20.

von Soden, W. (1968). Aramäische Wörter in neuassyrischen und neu-und spätbabylonischen Texten. Ein Vorbericht. II (n-z und Nachträge). *Orientalia*, *37*(3), 261–271.

von Soden, W. (1977). Aramäische Wörter in neuassyrischen und neu-und spätbabylonischen Texten. Ein Vorbericht. III. Orientalia, *46*(2), 183–197.

Wagner, M. (1966). *Die lexikalischen und grammatikalischen Aramaismen im alttestamentlichen Hebräisch.* Beihefte zur Zeitschrift für die alttestamentliche Wissenschaft 96. Berlin: de Gruyter.

Wardhaugh, R. (2011). *An introduction to sociolinguistics* (6th ed.). Oxford: Wiley-Blackwell.

Weninger, S., ed. (2011). *The Semitic languages: An international handbook* Berlin: de Gruyter.

Whitehead, J. D. (1978). Some distinctive features of the language of the Aramaic Arsames correspondence. *Journal of Near Eastern Studies*, *37*(2), 119–140.

Williamson, H. G. M. (2008). The Aramaic documents in Ezra revisited. *Journal of Theological Studies*, *59*(1), 41–62.

Yeivin, I. (1980). *Introduction to the Tiberian masorah.* Tr. E. Revell. Masoretic Studies 5. Missoula: Scholars Press.

Zadok, R. (2007). Two terms in Ezra. *Aramaic Studies*, *5*(2), 255–261.

INDEX OF CITATIONS

Numbers refer to pages in the text. This index does not include citations in Ch. 18 (Reading Guide).

BIBLICAL ARAMAIC

Jeremiah

10:11 1, 7, 30, 34, 36, 40, 43, 84, 91, 118, 124, 125, 145, 158

Daniel

2:4 24, 26, 40, 41, 45, 53, 78, 120, 164, 166, 196, 213, 217

2:5 33, 36, 47, 58, 69, 156, 165, 172, 232

2:6 66, 71, 137, 150, 167, 170, 256, 262

2:7 36, 55, 63, 158, 167, 182, 195, 213, 217, 243

2:8 41, 44, 45, 53, 67, 164, 188, 211, 251

2:9 32, 44, 157, 158, 168, 170, 211, 230

2:10 41, 58, 59, 68, 97, 144, 160, 182, 251, 259

2:11 53, 71, 137, 170, 258

2:12 35, 45, 97, 136

2:13 40, 68, 156, 157, 260

2:14 35, 151, 173, 247

2:15 67, 102, 118, 154, 160, 209, 225, 242

2:16 31, 161, 174, 210

2:17–18 248

2:17 45, 89, 116, 118, 159, 181

2:18 97, 159, 165

2:19 43, 47, 55, 165

2:20 41, 43, 53, 63, 101, 103, 169, 193, 211, 251

2:21 41, 47, 61, 63, 71, 167, 173, 209, 233

2:22 44, 47, 65, 66, 114, 151, 187, 194

2:23 25, 36, 39, 60, 94, 95, 145, 164, 178, 181, 251

2:24 136, 145, 159, 166, 195, 196, 204, 239

2:25 43, 53, 69, 122, 137, 153, 156, 160, 209

2:26 45, 93, 164

2:28 47, 53, 69, 73, 90, 233

2:29 36, 69, 95, 132, 145

2:30 25, 47, 126, 160, 221, 246, 249

2:31 26, 61, 62, 135, 172, 214

2:32 33, 62, 85, 90, 91, 103, 229

2:33 61, 125

2:34 41, 45, 155, 175, 239, 255

2:35 34, 45, 61, 63, 66, 68, 92, 109, 110, 119, 163, 164, 174, 204, 218, 235

2:36 158

2:37 62, 63, 66, 144

2:38 61, 64, 103, 121, 172

2:39 59, 132, 146, 183, 203, 211, 213

2:40 33, 48, 53, 107, 174, 175, 176, 187, 214, 253

2:41 36, 67, 92, 123, 148, 151, 210, 227, 253

2:42 34, 76, 97

2:43 61, 97, 113, 123, 131, 148, 157, 164, 169, 192, 206, 244, 253

2:44 85, 91, 104, 156, 157, 173, 203, 217

2:45 24, 57, 90, 124, 132, 155–156, 179, 204, 253

2:46 44, 67, 129, 144

2:47 47, 97, 145, 202

2:48 32, 53, 71, 109, 117, 118, 202

2:49 66, 102

3:1 63, 89, 103, 108, 145, 208, 224

3:2 47, 56, 70, 73, 87, 92, 144, 149, 173, 176

3:3–4 190

3:3 44, 47, 157, 203, 206, 233

3:4 25, 34, 49, 64, 67, 87, 122, 221

3:5 31, 53, 66, 71, 73, 103, 146

3:6 23, 31, 41, 66, 117, 146, 148, 161, 168, 184

3:7 31, 48, 110, 136, 190, 233

BIBLICAL ARAMAIC (cont.)

3:8 40, 41, 53, 58, 59, 116, 136, 145, 243

3:9 182

3:10 24, 31, 119, 171

3:11 168

3:12 45, 91, 93, 97, 126, 166, 173, 181, 222, 235, 243

3:13 116, 177

3:14 39, 41, 45, 173, 193

3:15 25, 31, 40, 66, 124, 145, 161, 168, 179, 230

3:16 182, 238, 260

3:17 36, 76, 100, 179, 235

3:18 45, 62, 78, 146, 185 n.1, 193, 238

3:19 67, 87, 100, 107, 130, 165, 168, 177, 212, 218, 219

3:20 63, 67, 99, 151, 260

3:21 44, 100

3:22 31, 47, 87, 92, 136, 150, 154, 177, 178, 194, 213, 215, 226, 252

3:23 100, 121, 145, 151

3:24 67, 122, 171, 182, 197, 209, 240, 262

3:25 41, 47, 107, 121, 165, 188, 190, 236

3:26–27 190

3:26 59, 63, 93, 98, 144, 162, 164, 176, 204

3:27 48, 61, 76, 97, 144, 157, 165, 206, 233, 245

3:28 34, 110, 146, 148, 156, 166, 179, 194, 206, 248, 251

3:29 69, 109, 124, 156, 159, 162, 217–218, 251

3:30 153

3:31 76

3:32 131

3:33 64, 71, 99, 113, 131, 215, 229

4:1 44, 45, 47, 65, 72, 121, 245

4:2 63, 71, 72, 87, 150, 186, 244

4:3 176, 248, 260

4:4 58, 148, 160, 175, 190, 232

4:5 39, 48, 60, 61, 67, 70, 145

4:6 182

4:7 237

4:8 44, 61, 65, 67, 164, 186, 202

4:9 62, 67, 138, 153, 171, 172, 175, 186, 229

4:10 25, 61, 90, 102, 160

4:11 34, 42, 138, 150, 162, 175

4:12 36, 41, 43, 47, 67, 78, 157

4:13 44, 45, 47, 63, 65, 66, 125, 156, 166

4:14 36, 41, 45, 61, 66, 99, 114, 123, 185 n.1, 249

4:15 91, 159, 251

4:16 33, 41, 42, 44, 60, 61, 66, 108, 155, 195, 205, 220, 231

4:18 146, 171

4:19 145, 164, 169

4:20–21 95

4:20 97, 150, 175, 190, 246, 255

4:21 231

4:22 44, 66, 150, 169, 188, 220, 221

4:23 43, 67, 104, 149, 255

4:24 40, 41, 44, 63, 66, 122, 129, 147, 175, 195, 197, 245, 257

4:25 24, 111

4:26 65, 102, 120, 150, 191

4:27 45, 63, 90, 93, 99, 119, 170, 220, 240

4:28 61, 124, 216

4:29 95, 108, 221

4:30 61, 68, 122, 149, 171, 186, 208

4:31 40, 45, 46, 55, 69, 94, 145, 150, 171, 244, 251

4:32 37, 48, 63, 145, 148, 165, 234, 239, 241, 254

4:33 34, 48, 69, 117, 154, 161, 186, 225

4:34 41, 42, 44, 47, 62, 71, 95, 150, 154, 173, 233, 251

5:1 62, 119

5:2 44, 98, 122, 153, 162, 164, 249

5:3–4 33

5:3 122, 162

5:4 164

5:5 36, 60, 62, 63, 94, 102, 145, 148, 189

5:6 148, 170, 189

5:7 45, 58, 68, 86, 146, 170, 176, 259

5:8 41, 83, 160, 175, 190, 259

5:9 48, 129, 157, 190, 214

5:10 48, 63, 78, 135, 145, 168, 174, 182, 195

5:11 43, 69, 71, 122, 156, 233, 235

5:12 35, 44, 48, 53, 71, 98, 164, 195, 197, 210, 235, 251, 261

5:13 48, 60, 177, 240

5:14 130, 145, 235

5:15 42, 83, 169, 248

5:16 146, 149, 160, 165, 184, 223

5:17 160, 169

5:18 69

5:19 25, 95, 125, 148, 154, 172, 173, 178, 192

5:20 47, 144, 154, 167, 171, 173, 182, 202

5:21 44, 71, 131, 173, 221

5:22 60, 153, 251

5:23 41, 65, 94, 118, 150, 173, 177, 188, 189, 205

5:25 34

5:26 209

5:27 33, 36, 39, 149, 156

5:30 31

6:1 33, 59, 107, 123, 150

6:2 41, 137, 144, 244

6:3 36, 66, 124, 213, 216

6:4 164, 173, 194, 205, 250

6:5 47, 119, 154, 179, 229, 236, 251

6:6 153, 183, 257

6:7 178

6:8 44, 47, 48, 58, 69, 88, 103, 127, 164, 168, 172, 202, 203, 204, 223, 258

6:9 47, 98, 146, 164, 167, 173, 198, 247

6:10 136

6:11 45, 61, 64, 69, 129, 136, 148, 166, 178, 191, 217, 218, 253, 254

6:12 190, 205, 210

6:13 32, 43, 44, 145, 168

6:14 69, 145, 182

6:15 71, 127, 129, 154, 205, 214, 222, 260

6:16 160, 185 n.1

6:17 26, 64, 71, 103, 222

6:18 72, 123, 128, 172, 177

6:19 60, 118, 129, 174, 175, 213

6:20 72, 122, 186

6:21 62, 179, 240, 254

6:22 132, 175

6:23 43, 47, 69, 71, 145, 150, 235, 251, 262

6:24 31, 129, 178, 179, 214, 222, 225, 251

6:25 47, 69, 123, 145, 164, 175, 255

6:26 40

6:27 61, 104, 229, 251

6:28 53, 61, 179, 221, 251

6:29 46, 89

7:1 60, 224, 245

7:2 63, 64, 131, 173

7:3 108, 113, 165, 202

7:4 24, 42, 43, 45, 47, 59, 107, 174, 230

7:5 36, 64, 69, 108, 118, 133, 159, 171, 174

7:6 65, 102, 132, 231, 237

7:7 45, 47, 71, 132, 136, 151, 166, 215

7:8 45, 47, 59, 63, 68, 78, 107, 125, 150, 156, 211

7:9 41, 47, 58, 65, 66, 67, 71, 99, 123, 148, 165

7:10 63, 80, 136, 149, 171

7:11 41, 64, 90, 149, 150, 159

7:12 53, 127, 217

7:13 58, 60, 92, 127, 131, 176

7:14 69, 185 n.1

7:15 45, 168

7:16 109, 129, 172, 249

7:17 62, 91

7:18 44, 150, 153, 225

BIBLICAL ARAMAIC (cont.)

7:19 24, 164, 165, 176, 193, 202

7:20 65, 115, 121, 145

7:21 228

7:22 47, 153, 176

7:23 80, 124, 158, 217, 227, 231

7:24 59, 117, 132, 153, 164

7:25 121, 156, 166, 175

7:26 154, 159, 167, 221

7:27 70, 98, 138, 157, 206

7:28 64, 168, 214

Ezra

4:8 62, 108, 145, 213

4:10–11 261

4:10 91, 167, 203, 261

4:11 129, 261

4:12 26, 33, 43, 45, 48, 67, 78, 91, 134, 148, 176, 179, 188, 221

4:13 55, 153, 162, 168, 179, 256

4:14–15 248

4:14 145, 251

4:15 45, 64, 69, 98, 102, 121, 150, 153, 154, 162, 188, 220, 229

4:16 135, 168, 179, 234

4:17 94, 225, 261

4:18 45, 78, 145

4:19 41, 157, 188, 205

4:20 43, 53, 191

4:21 44, 168, 171, 172

4:22 47, 149, 250

4:23 33, 69, 93, 150, 240 n.2

4:24 41, 44, 100, 127, 144

5:1 88, 168

5:2 48, 89, 131, 150, 165, 171, 189, 260

5:3 34, 56, 165, 176, 179, 225, 241

5:4 60, 69, 91, 94, 145, 229

5:5 63, 173, 184, 231, 255

5:6 227

5:7 66, 110, 181

5:8 38, 43, 63, 71, 76, 154, 168, 172, 213, 218

5:9 41, 118, 145, 165, 179, 217

5:10 78, 122, 145, 146, 210, 247

5:11 41, 44, 104, 158, 165, 169, 193, 197, 217, 232

5:12 31, 181, 224, 252, 263

5:13 122, 165

5:14 89, 124

5:15 84, 91, 159, 162, 169, 196

5:16 126, 127, 188, 216

5:17 5, 69, 78, 130, 157, 235, 261

6:1 154, 252

6:2 70, 71, 156

6:3 92, 96, 155, 221

6:5 160, 162, 173, 184, 221

6:7 120, 164, 224

6:8 98, 131, 156, 192, 194, 198

6:9 44, 61, 68, 113, 123, 238

6:10 44, 154, 166

6:11 109, 167, 210, 222

6:12 25, 33, 150, 171, 195, 218

6:13 135, 253

6:14 125, 154, 179

6:15 100, 179

6:16 63, 122

6:17 47, 69, 97, 105, 120, 166

6:18 71, 72, 123, 173

7:12–13 261

7:12 41, 73, 102, 261

7:13 157, 171, 172, 205

7:14 48, 88, 99, 120, 221, 251

7:15 71, 84, 157, 160, 205 n.1, 230

7:16 157, 205 n.1

7:17 71, 136, 150

7:18 76, 95, 160

7:19 120, 156

7:20 41, 69, 98, 161

7:21 80, 228

7:22 68, 128

7:23 25, 218, 250

7:24 67, 250

7:25 47, 67, 72, 95, 166

7:26 69, 257

IMPERIAL ARAMAIC (BY *TAD* NUMBERS)

A2 (Hermopolis papyri)

A2 1:1 88, 97

A2 1:2 248

A2 1:3 88

A2 1:6 177

A2 1:7 177

A2 1:10 86, 177

A2 2:2 170

A2 2:3 159

A2 2:7 160

A2 2:11 119

A2 2:13 160

A2 2:14–15 222

A2 2:14 164, 250

A2 2:15 171

A2 3:4–5 259

A2 3:4 195

A2 3:5 237

A2 3:7 253

A2 3:8 232, 237, 240

A2 3:10 147

A2 3:11–12 192

A2 4:3 159

A2 4:4 169

A2 4:11 177

A2 5:3 162

A2 5:4 177

A2 5:5 177

A2 5:6 176

A2 7:2 206

A2 7:3 165

A2 7:4 77

A3 (Private Letters)

A3 3:5 176

A3 3:6 194, 242

A3 3:7 176

A3 3:10 177, 212

A3 3:13 149

A3 4:4 160, 233

A3 6:2 220

A3 6:3 169

A3 8:11 147

A3 8:12 175

A3 8:13 218

A3 9:1 110

A3 9:3 177

A3 10:3 160

A3 10:4 160

A4 (Jedoniah archive)

A4 1:6 164

A4 2:8 258

A4 3:3 130

A4 3:4 148

A4 3:5 134, 176, 236

A4 3:6 113

A4 3:7 255

A4 3:8 95

A4 3:9 238

A4 3:11 125

A4 4:6 33, 159, 236

A4 4:8 173

A4 4:9 164

A4 5:7 169, 212

A4 5:8 225

A4 7:1 89, 126, 225

A4 7:3 107, 164, 217

A4 7:5 73

A4 7:6–7 263

A4 7:6 167, 195, 198

A4 7:7 197

A4 7:8 70, 147, 161

IMPERIAL ARAMAIC (BY *TAD* NUMBERS)
(cont.)

A4 7:9 127, 227

A4 7:10 172

A4 7:11 32

A4 7:12 103, 111

A4 7:14 86

A4 7:15 131, 166, 191, 233

A4 7:16 93, 170, 204

A4 7:17–18 96

A4 7:17 91, 149, 217

A4 7:19–20 127, 188

A4 7:19 126

A4 7:20 101, 123, 194

A4 7:21–22 221

A4 7:21 165

A4 7:22 261

A4 7:23 129, 130, 206, 221, 252, 260

A4 7:25 253

A4 7:26 109, 128

A4 7:27 217, 255

A4 7:29 110

A4 8:19 91

A4 8:22 110

A4 9:2 33, 158

A4 9:4–5 216

A4 9:8 216, 253

A5 (Official/Semi-official Letters)

A5 1:3 164

A6 (Arshama letters)

A6 2:13 177

A6 2:14 98, 107

A6 2:15 107, 112

A6 2:16 107

A6 2:18 160

A6 5:3 176

A6 6:1 171

A6 7:7 175

A6 7:8 172

A6 8:2 227

A6 8:4 208

A6 9:4 111, 135, 204

A6 9:6 147

A6 10:4 157, 205

A6 10:6 162, 214

A6 10:7 175

A6 10:8 70

A6 11:1 235

A6 11:3 217

A6 11:4 231, 254

A6 11:5 101, 167

A6 11:6 191

A6 12:1 177

A6 12:2 131

A6 12:3 245

A6 13:3 162

A6 13:4 218

A6 13:5 176, 224

A6 15:4 177

A6 15:7 174

B1 (Bauer-Meissner papyrus)

B1 1:13 161

B2 (Mibtahiah archive)

B2 1–11 6

B2 1:2 102, 104, 238

B2 1:4 231

B2 1:6 88, 136

B2 1:7 256

B2 1:12 158

B2 1:15 224

B2 2:4 177

B2 2:6 177, 223

B2 2:7 237

B2 2:11–12 130

B2 2:12 259

B2 2:13 104

B2 2:14 170

B2 3:17 238, 244

B2 3:9 217

B2 3:10 70

B2 3:12 170

B2 3:14 239

B2 3:18 162, 218

B2 3:19 196

B2 3:20 158

B2 3:24 177

B2 3:26 88

B2 3:27 135, 162

B2 4:3 218

B2 4:6 263

B2 4:10 134

B2 6:3 151

B2 6:6 108, 175

B2 6:19 234

B2 6:23 183, 208

B2 6:25 207, 215

B2 6:31 159

B2 6:32 234

B2 6:33 159

B2 7:7 101

B2 7:8 95, 182

B2 7:16 164

B2 8:4–5 189

B2 8:5 177

B2 9:7 154, 235

B2 9:8 149

B2 9:12 70

B2 9:14 101

B2 11:2 112

B2 11:3 228

B2 11:6 218

B2 11:13 254

B2 11:14 112

B3 (Anani archive)

B3 1:9 102

B3 1:5 112

B3 1:14 39

B3 1:15 220

B3 1:17 169

B3 2:8 170

B3 3:3 176

B3 3:12–13 133

B3 3:14 258

B3 4:9 202

B3 4:12 159

B3 4:18 161

B3 4:21 102

B3 4:22 33, 176

B3 5:8 59

B3 6:3 39

B3 6:9 148

B3 7:1 100

B3 7:10 178

B3 8:10 82

B3 8:26 33

B3 8:33 133

B3 9:7 210

B3 9:8–9 246

B3 10:1 262

B3 10:4 71

B3 10:15 178

B3 11:3 161

B3 11:12 73

B3 12:21 119

B3 13:10 158

B3 13:11 88

B4 (Deeds of Obligation)

B4 1:3 178

IMPERIAL ARAMAIC (BY *TAD* NUMBERS)
(cont.)

B4 2:4–5 93
B4 2:7 192
B4 2:9 128
B4 2:10 96
B4 4:17 158
B4 6:5 147

B7 (Judicial Oaths)
B7 1:6 177

B8 (Court Records)
B8 2:5 149
B8 9:3 177

C1 1 (Ahiqar)
C1 1:1 89, 227
C1 1:13 182, 198
C1 1:17 185, 259
C1 1:33 125
C1 1:38 108
C1 1:41 160
C1 1:44 173
C1 1:45 182
C1 1:46 179, 232
C1 1:47 104
C1 1:49 120, 125
C1 1:50 137
C1 1:51 178, 214
C1 1:52 160, 217, 253
C1 1:54 178
C1 1:55 111
C1 1:56 92, 263
C1 1:63 226
C1 1:79 172
C1 1:80 255
C1 1:81 164
C1 1:82 126, 162, 232, 239
C1 1:84 164, 230
C1 1:85 32, 138

C1 1:87 222
C1 1:88 132, 184, 241, 245
C1 1:89 115
C1 1:90 168, 207, 239
C1 1:91 241
C1 1:92 98
C1 1:93 182, 216, 244
C1 1:109 174
C1 1:114 99
C1 1:126 122, 173, 250
C1 1:127 158
C1 1:129 160, 248
C1 1:130 159, 171
C1 1:131 151
C1 1:132 179
C1 1:133 58 n.1
C1 1:138 173, 252
C1 1:139 59, 175
C1 1:140 99
C1 1:146 167
C1 1:147 214
C1 1:157 195
C1 1:158 32
C1 1:159 169, 181, 234
C1 1:161 185
C1 1:162 216
C1 1:163 114
C1 1:164 72, 225
C1 1:165 169, 185
C1 1:166 176, 230
C1 1:167–168 258
C1 1:168 160
C1 1:170 197
C1 1:171–172 256
C1 1:171 161, 231
C1 1:173 93, 94, 165
C1 1:174 241
C1 1:175 172

C1 1:177 128, 147, 169, 256

C1 1:178 262

C1 1:186 118

C1 1:188 237

C1 1:190 109

C1 1:191 260

C1 1:200 168

C1 2 (Bar Punesh narrative)

C1 2:23 130

C1 2:25 158

C2.1 (Bisitun historical text)

C2.1:V.15 135, 247

C3 (Accounts)

C3.7A 2:4 236

C3 11:8, 10 161

C3 15:1 112, 120

C3 15:123 85

D2 (Papyrus fragments)

D2 10:2 59

D2 29:6 173

D7 (Ostraca)

D7 1:9–10 237

D7 6:8–9 242

D7 6:8 176

D7 8:1–3 237, 260

D7 8:2–3 101

D7 8:6 176

D7 8:14 158

D7 14:3 162

D7 16:12 158

D7 20:4 176

D7 20:10 176

D7 57:4 79

D20 (Carpentras stele)

D20 5:2 86

D20 5:2 32

D20 5:3 137

D24 (fragment of dubious authenticity)

D24 1:4 101

QUMRAN ARAMAIC

1QapGen (Genesis Apocryphon)

0:5 172

1:13 33

2:7 42, 238

2:13 187

2:14 114

2:20 160

2:21 111

2:22 160

2:25 176, 215

3:13 62

5:8 62

6:1 120

6:2 218

10:13 111

11:12 77, 111, 212

11:14 98

11:15 23, 124

11:17 110, 184, 246

12:9 163

12:9t 133

12:10 149, 218

12:11 108

12:12 23

12:16 157, 206

13:9 163, 175

13:13 205

13:14 173

13:17 162

14:9 44

14:17 175

15:11 176

15:18 169

16:14 160

QUMRAN ARAMAIC (cont.)

17:10 98
19:8 216
19:9 33
19:10 53
19:12 99, 216
19:14 223
19:15 134
19:16 100, 134, 167, 175, 195
19:17 206
19:18 249
19:20 133, 134, 231
19:23 170, 215
19:25 50
19:27 32
20:2, 3 79
20:4 241
20:5 215
20:6 23, 110, 182, 185
20:7 59, 216, 230
20:9–10 259
20:9 130, 169–170, 181, 205, 218
20:10, 11 149
20:12 157, 175, 182, 189, 197, 205
20:13 44, 111, 229
20:14 167, 183
20:16 247
20:17 204
20:18–19 245
20:19 50, 159, 257
20:20 166, 172, 252
20:21 128, 176, 184, 262
20:22 128, 166
20:23 77, 129, 178, 249
20:25 133
20:26 220, 241
20:27–28 207
20:28 91, 166, 249
20:33 121, 215

20:34 224
21:1 23, 213, 217
21:2 88, 99
21:3 42, 131, 137, 178
21:5 125, 134
21:6 101, 130
21:7 191, 203
21:8 178, 207
21:9 96, 164
21:10 55, 91
21:11 127
21:12 183, 209, 218
21:13 93, 165, 196
21:14 132
21:15 121
21:16 92, 255
21:17 118
21:20 178
21:21 33, 58, 88, 245
21:23 138
21:25 32, 206, 218
21:26 23, 105
21:27–28 224
21:27 105
21:28 204
21:31 135
22:2–3 216
22:3 170
22:4 175, 233
22:5 130
22:6 107
22:7 132, 255
22:9 137
22:10 162, 163, 172, 194
22:11 262
22:12 211
22:13–14 244
22:14 162

22:17 125	17 ii 3 178
22:19–20 194	18 12 171
22:21–22 257	18 14 178
22:21 128	18 15 178
22:22 192, 250	**4Q197 (Tobit)**
22:23 23, 133, 216	3 5 160
22:24–25 222	4 i 3 147, 159
22:25 165	4 i 13 55, 88, 136, 148
22:27 132	4 i 17 234
22:28 96	4 i 18 258
22:29 255	4 ii 2 79
22:30 197, 239, 261	4 ii 3 249
22:31 115	4 ii 4 252
22:32–33 242	4 ii 8 175
22:33 72, 109, 238, 254	4 ii 17 148
	4 ii 18 166
22:34 161	4 iii 1 215
1Q21 (Testament of Levi)	4 iii 3 190, 216
3 217	4 iii 4 175, 176
1Q72 (Daniel)	4 iii 5 202, 242
1+2 12 179	4 iii 7 240
2Q24 (New Jerusalem)	4 iii 11 102
4 5 161	4 iii 12 158, 165
4 13 105	5 10 176
4 18 113	**4Q198 (Tobit)**
4Q112 (Daniel)	1:1 160, 260
3 i +17:16 34	**4Q201 (Enoch)**
9 17 253	1 i 5 161
4Q113 (Daniel)	1 ii 2 164
7 ii +8:12 160	1 ii 5 172, 205
4Q196 (Tobit)	1 ii 6–7 207
2 1 167	1 ii 12 220
2 2 86	1 ii 14 234
2 6 73	1 ii 15 31
2 10 174	1 iii 1 177
2 11 137	1 iii 5 177
2 13 23	1 iii 11 107
6 8 154	

QUMRAN ARAMAIC (cont.)

1 iii 16 163, 192

1 iii 19 118

4Q202 (Enoch)

1 ii 26 103

1 iii 5 166

1 iv 10 44, 158

4Q203 (Book of Giants)

4 4 136

4Q204 (Enoch)

1 i 20 164

1 i 28 111

1 v 2 44

1 v 4 23

1 vi 1 113

1 vi 13 48

1 vi 17 48

1 vi 23 23, 154

1 xii 25 216

1 xii 27 167

1 xiii 25 161

5 ii 18 175

5 ii 25 169

5 ii 26 170

5 ii 29 196

4Q206 (Enoch)

1 xxvi 18 161

1 xxvi 20 214

1 xxvii 21 167

4 i 16 236

4 i 18 212

4 i 19 172

4 ii 2 31, 149

4 iii 15 212

4Q209 (Enoch, Astronomical Book)

1 i 7 100

2 ii 7 218

6 9 109

7 iii 2 161, 172, 176

23 3 221

23 7 252

4Q210 (Enoch, Astronomical Book)

1 ii 2 178

1 ii 15 209

1 ii 18 168

4Q211 (Enoch)

1 i 2 162

4Q212 (Enoch)

1 ii 18 99

1 ii 19 160

1 iv 15 133

1 v 16 259

4Q213 (Testament of Levi)

1 i 8 95, 176

1 i 13 147, 226

1 ii+2:1 204

1 ii+2:4 136

1 ii-2:9 159

4Q213a (Testament of Levi)

3:18 23

4Q213b (Testament of Levi)

1 1 126

1 2 172

4Q214 (Testament of Levi)

3:2 158

4Q214b (Testament of Levi)

2–6 i 3 32, 178

4Q242 (Prayer of Nabonidus)

1+2 5 167

1+3:3 148, 193

1+3 8 252

4Q243 (Pseudo-Daniel)

1 1 197

1 2 77

24 2 157

4Q246 (Apocalypse)

1 i 2 176

1 i 4 176

1 i 9 168

1 ii 1 104, 170, 183, 220

1 ii 1+2 217

4Q318 (Divination text)

7:2 44

8:8 175

8:9 256 n.1

4Q529 (Words of Michael)

1 1 227

1 5 170

1 9 168

4Q530 (Book of Giants)

2 ii 7 167

2 ii 12 127

2 ii 24 177

7 ii 8 161

4Q531 (Book of Giants)

5 4 79

22 5 206

22 7 115

4Q534 (Book of Noah)

1 i 4–5 96

4Q537 (Testament of Jacob?)

1+2+3 2 236

1+2+3 3 162

12 2 178

12 3 169

4Q540 (Testament of Levi?)

1 1 212

4Q541 (Testament of Levi?)

2 ii 3 161

4 ii 4 77

9 i 3 123

9 i 4 159, 177

22 ii 2 206

24 ii 3 166

24 ii 4 83

24 ii 5 79, 147

4Q542 (Testament of Kohath)

1 i 2 249

1 i 4 32, 154

1 i 7 211, 162

1 i 8–9 192

1 i 8 100

1 i 10 91, 133

1 i 12 161

1 ii 1 62

1 ii 3 23, 50

1 ii 5 172

1 ii 13 161

1 ii 16 166

4Q543 (Vision of Amram)

1a-c 1 227

4Q544 (Vision of Amram)

1 1 151

4Q545 (Vision of Amram)

1a i:5 90

1a i:7 179

1a-b ii 13 151

4Q547 (Vision of Amram)

4 ii 1 160

9 6 172

4Q550 (Persian Court Tale)

5+5a 5 172

5+5a 6 95, 150

5+5a 7 175

7+7a 2 158

7+7a 6 172

4Q551

1:4 158, 187

4Q552

1 ii 5 210, 229

4Q553

1 i 4 168

2 i 6 178

3+2 ii+4:3 173

QUMRAN ARAMAIC (cont.)

4Q554 (New Jerusalem)

1 ii 14–15 113

1 ii 14 218

1 ii 16 126

1 ii 20 112

1 iii 18 135

1 iii 19 208

1 iii 20 218

4Q554a (New Jerusalem)

1 5 108

4Q558

33 ii 4 175

4Q559 (Biblical Chronology)

3 3 126

4Q560 (Incantation)

1 ii 5 178

1 ii 6 178

4Q561 (Horoscope)

3 5 169

4Q569

1–2 9 150

4Q580

4 4 166

4Q583

1 1 165, 176

1 4 133

5Q15 (New Jerusalem)

1 ii 5 94, 227

1 ii 6 170, 175

1 ii 11 148

11Q18 (New Jerusalem)

13:3 177

13:4 178

15:2 179

15:3 134, 175

18:3 107

19:1 135

11QtgJob (Targum of Job)

4:4 31, 171

11:10 159

14:4 32

14:8 72

15:4 115

16:2 176

21:1 262

21:3 237

21:4 250

21:5 172, 238

22:6 252

23:1 170

23:6 157

23:9 174

25:7 134

26:2 241

27:2 148

27:3 173

28:4 238

29:1 162

29:3–4 257

29:6 23, 96

30:2 242, 254, 256

30:3 241

30:4–5 254

30:7 98

31:4 86, 93

31:5 162, 234, 240

31:7 205

32:2 159

32:3 23

32:5 210

32:8 177

33:3–4 185

33:8 205

34:2–3 123

34:3 174

34:4 172, 249

34:5 240, 246

34:6 167

35:3 161

35:6 205

36:2–3 113

37:2 129

37:4 185

37:6 196

37:8 119, 157

38:4–5 134

38:4–6 189

38:4 107, 176

38:7 112, 177

38:9 222

HEBREW BIBLE

Genesis

14:23 257

19:4–5 187

Judges

19:22 187

Job

32:10 262

32:12 237

33:12 252

37:22 176

39:22 185

40:9 246

Psalms

139:8 31

Nehemiah

2:5 5

TARGUMS

Targum Onqelos

Gen 3:6 160

Gen 7:9 174

Gen 12:12 58

Gen 27:23 163

Exod 2:22 59

Exod 21:3 174

Deut 15:6 160

Targum Jonathan

2 Kings 15:12 59

Isa 62:9 170

Targum Neofiti

Exod 35:29 177

OTHER TEXTS

KAI

233 2

264 214

Uzziah burial plaque

198

SUBJECT INDEX (NUMBERS REFER TO § SECTION)

adjective
    attributive 145
    final -*āy* 97
adverbial noun phrases 352
adverbs
    degree 347
    location 349
    manner 351
    time 350
agreement 153d, 158b, 166b, 355
Aktionsart 328
ʾaleph
    elision 47–48
    insertion 26, 49
anaptyxis 60c
appositives 153
Aramaic
    Daniel 13
    Imperial 3–5
    Jewish Literary 18
    Middle 11
    Old 1, 4
    Qumran 14, 15
    uniformity of 16
Arshama letters 7
aspect 290
assimilation
    consonants 42–44
    vowels 76b
asyndeton 395

borrowed words
    nouns 122
    verbs 288

C stem
    general 232
    finite verbs, strong root 233
    participles and infinitives, strong root 234
cantillation marks 31
cardinal numbers *see* number
causativity 324
cluster, consonant 60, 101
cognate object 361
compensatory lengthening 77c
construct phrase as genitive 153
construct phrase, with numbers 157
copular clause
    classification 375
    identification 378
    prepositional predicate 377
    participial predicate 379
Cp stem, strong root 235

D stem
    general 226–230
    semantics 231
dagesh 28
declension
    first 89
    second 90
    and gender 91
    mixed 93
defective spelling 27
definiteness 85
demonstratives
    independent pronoun as 137
    modifying noun 146

413

diphthongs 72

dissimilation 45–46

doubly weak verbs 282–286

dropped word
  object 360
  subject 356–358

dual number *see* number

Elephantine papyri 6

Enoch 14

ethical dative 336

existential, with verb השתכח 381

extraposition 368–372

Ezra, Book of 10

final letters 22

final weak roots
  C/Cp stem 265
  D stem 263–264
  G stem 256–262
  pronominal suffixes on 270
  tD stem 267
  tG stem 266
  III-ʾ*aleph* 269
  III-y 255

fricativization 55

G stem
  infinitive, strong root 225
  jussive and imperative, strong root 222
  participle, strong root 223
  passive, strong root 224
  prefix conjugation, strong root 220–221
  strong roots 214–225
  suffix conjugation, strong root 216–219

gapping 394

geminate verbs 278–281

gemination 54

genitive
  attributive 156
  construct phrase as 153
  of material 161
  periphrastic 160, 163
  with די 160

gutturals 75

habitual action 312

ḥaṭeph vowels 24

Hebrew
  cognates 38
  Late Biblical 9

heh, elision of 50

Hermopolis papyri 7

hollow verbs 272–275, 277

imperatives, usage 318

impersonal constructions 357

inalienable possession 162

infinitive
  as complements 428
  as *nomen actionis* 320
  modal use 322
  of אמר 321
  object preceding 366

initial ʾ*aleph* roots 245–248

initial *nun* roots 252–254

initial *yod/waw* roots 249–251

interdentals 36

irregular nouns 94

jussive, usage 317

Ketiv-Qere 33

koine 3

L/tL stem 236

lateral fricative

   emphatic 37

   voiceless 40

left-dislocation 369

long vowels, survey 66–71

m > *n*, word final 51

mappiq 29

maqqeph 30

Masoretic text, vowel points 17, 20, 23

matres lectionis 25

mergers, phonemic 36

metathesis 53

modality 291, 301

mood 291

nasalization 54, 77d

Nehemiah 5

noun formation

   biliteral bases 99–100

   consonantal afformatives 113–119

   final -*ē* 96

   reduplication 120

   triliteral bases 101–112

noun phrase, compound 142

number

   cardinal 166

   dual 65

   general 84

   ordinal 165

object, direct 359

ordinal numbers *see* number

Papyrus Amherst 63 7

parenthesis 372

participles

   with איתי 315

   without subject 358

past progressive 310–311

pataḥ furtivum 76c

pause 32

periphrastic construction 313–314

plene spelling 27

prepositional phrase, as noun modifier 147

prepositions

   biconsonantal 185–189

   derived 190–205

   proclitic 176–184

present (tense)

   actual 307

   general 296, 302, 306

   imminent 308

questions

   information-seeking 391

   polar 390

R stem 276

reflex 35

relative clause

   headless 150

   independent 150

   non-restrictive 149

   restrictive 149

   with absolute noun 152

   with noun 148

   light-headed 151

resumptive pronoun 148b, 168b, 369

rules, list of phonological 78

secondary opening 76a

shewa 74

short vowels
  loss of final 59
  reduction 57d, 61c
  survey 61–65
spirantization 55
state
  absolute 86
  construct 87
  determined 85
stem names 208
stress 56
subject, grammatical 354–356
suffixed nouns as genitives 158
suffixes, pronominal, with verbs 130–133
syllables 57

T stems 237
tantum plurale 92
tC stem 243
tD stem, strong root 241–242
tense
  future 299, 300
  past 292–295, 303–304
  present 296–298, 302, 306–308
Testament of Levi 14
tG stem, strong root 238–240

theme vowel 210
Tobit 14
topicalization 370–371
triphthong, simplification 58

unpointed text, vocalization 79
Uruk incantation 7

velar fricatives 39
verbs, types of
  motion or change of location 331
  stative-inchoative 330a
  transfer 339
  transformation 340
virtual doubling 77b
voice
  active and passive 326
  general 327
  middle 332
  reciprocal 335
  reflexive 334

$w > y$, word initial 41
w, y, changes involving 52
word order 362–366